PRAISE FOR ROBERT D. KEPPEL
AND *THE RIVERMAN*

"[Keppel] knows more about identifying, tracking, and finally arresting and convicting serial killers than anyone else in the field."

—Ann Rule, *New York Times* bestselling
author of *Heart Full of Lies*

"[A] page turner. The obvious excitement Bundy felt at the chance to recount his murderous career to Keppel sends chills down the spine. Keppel took Bundy's intricate tale of homicidal insanity and turned it into a cogent and useful primer for law enforcement agencies trying to catch serial killers. It will be the standard for such investigations for years to come."

—*The Detroit News*

"One of the classic studies of criminology . . . *The Silence of the Lambs* owes tons to the investigation of the mind and modus operandi of the serial killer conducted by Robert Keppel."

—*Time Out* (U.K.)

"Superb on many levels. Not only is Keppel a superlative detective, he is an excellent writer."

—*Daily Mail* (U.K.)

THE
RIVERMAN

TED BUNDY AND I HUNT FOR THE GREEN RIVER KILLER

ROBERT D. KEPPEL, PH.D.,
with WILLIAM J. BIRNES
Foreword by ANN RULE
Revised and Updated
with Details of the Confession
of Gary Leon Ridgway

POCKET BOOKS
New York   London   Toronto   Sydney

Certain names have been changed to protect the identity of various people involved in the cases covered in this book.

POCKET BOOKS, a division of Simon & Schuster, Inc.
1230 Avenue of the Americas, New York, NY 10020

Copyright © 1995, 2005 by Bob Keppel and William J. Birnes

Foreword copyright © 1995 by Ann Rule

All rights reserved, including the right to reproduce this book or portions thereof in any form whatsoever. For information address Pocket Books, 1230 Avenue of the Americas, New York, NY 10020

ISBN: 0-7434-6395-1

First Pocket Books printing of this revised edition February 2004

10 9 8 7 6 5 4 3 2

POCKET and colophon are registered trademarks of Simon & Schuster, Inc.

Manufactured in the United States of America

Front cover photo courtesy of AP/Wide World

For information regarding special discounts for bulk purchases, please contact Simon & Schuster Special Sales at 1-800-456-6798 or business@simonandschuster.com

To David,
may he never forget his last name

Acknowledgments

In the twenty years I have worked on serial murder investigations, I have been fortunate to have experienced the dedicated work ethic of the most effective homicide detectives in the world. All—each in their own way—are special, all passed on their wisdom and encouraged me to write about my experiences. In no particular order, I am forever grateful to:

Detectives Roger Dunn, Kathleen McChesney, Kevin O'Shaughnessey, Jack Kidd, George Leaf, and Dave Reasor; Major Nick Mackie and Sgt. Bob Schmitz, King County Police; Investigator Mike Fisher, Pitkin County District Attorney's Office; Detective Jerry Thompson and Sergeant Ben Forbes, Salt Lake County Sheriff's Office; for their work in the Ted Bundy cases.

Sheriff Dave Reichert; Detectives Fabian Brooks, Tom Jensen, and Jim Doyon; Sergeants Bob Andrews, Rupe Lettich, and Frank Atchley; Lieutenants Jackson Beard and Daniel Nolan; and Captain Frank Adamson, whose work on the Green River Murders Task Force was unprecedented in murder investigation history. And Jeff Beard, King County Prosecutor's office.

Captain Robbie Robertson, Michigan State Police (Michigan Child Murders); Sergeant Frank Salerno, Los Angeles Sheriff's Department (Hillside Strangler and Nightstalker cases); Sergeant Ray

Acknowledgments

Biondi, Sacramento Sheriff's Department (the Gallegos Family and Richard Trenton Chase cases and author of the books *All His Father's Sins* and *The Vampire Killer); Chief Joe Kozenczak, Des Plaines Police (John Wayne Gacy cases and co-author of the book *A Passing Acquaintance); Captain Robbie Hamerick, Georgia State Bureau of Investigation (Atlanta Child Killer cases); Detectives Marv Skeen and Dale Foote, Bellevue Police, and Larry Petersen, King County Police (George Russell murder cases); Detectives Billy Baughman and Duane Homan, Seattle Police (Morris Frampton murder cases); Sergeant Jim Sidebottom, Orange County Sheriff's Office, and Captain Lee Erickson, Oregon State Police (Randy Kraft murder cases), and Detective Bob Gebo, Seattle Police.

The efforts of the members of the FBI's National Center for the Analysis of Violent Crime have been significant in the area of serial murder investigation. From VICAP were Terry Green, Ken Hanfland, Jim Howlett, Jim Bell, Eric Witzig, Winn Norman, Mike Cryan, and Greg Cooper. From the Behavioral Sciences Unit were John Douglas, Robert Ressler, Roy Hazelwood, and Bill Hagmaier.

Without the members of the Homicide Investigation and Tracking System (HITS), murder investigation would not be as effective in Washington State. The hard work and dedication of Bob LaMoria, Tamera Matheny, Tom Jones, Sally Coates, Joan Martin, Vicky Woods, Dick Steiner, Bo Bollinger, Frank Tennison, Gary Trent, Ken Hanfland, and Marv Skeen have set the guiding course for homicide investigation, and made my futuristic ideas a reality.

Three prominent authors are worthy of note for their inspiration: Steve Michaud, co-author with Hugh Aynesworth of *The Only Living Witness* and *Ted Bundy: Conversations with a Killer,* has given valuable consultation about his experiences with interviewing Ted Bundy in the months before Bundy's execution and has encouraged me on numerous occasions to write this book.

Ann Rule, author of *The Stranger Beside Me* and true friend of law enforcement, has written numerous articles about my cases for

Acknowledgments

detective magazines early in her career. I am thankful for her skillful technique in describing those investigations and her encouragement for this book.

The consummate homicide detective and author of the textbook *Practical Homicide Investigation* is Vernon Geberth. Vernon has taken his experiences with the New York City Police Department and converted them into the finest homicide investigation training sessions in the nation. For his devotion to "telling it like it is" and his motto, "We work for God," I am forever grateful.

Thanks to Bob Evans of the King County Police, my first detective sergeant and one of the commanders of the Green River Murders Task Force, I realized that detective work could be fun. He encouraged me to document Ted's conversations so other law enforcement officers could learn from my experiences.

A special place in my experiences is saved for Pierce Brooks (retired Captain, Los Angeles Police Department, and founder of VICAP), my mentor and good friend. His dedication to improving homicide investigation goes unmatched, and I will always be indebted to him for his insightful guidance and gracious encouragement.

With the expert assistance of Dr. John Berberich, clinical psychologist, and Dr. John Liebert, forensic psychiatrist, I was able to construct the Bundy interview strategies in such a way as to preserve my own mental well-being.

My course of study on murder solvability factors was made possible by the academic staff at the University of Washington: Ezra Stotland (society and justice), Charles Z. Smith (law), Joseph Weis (criminology), Herb Costner (sociology), Elizabeth Loftus (psychology), Daris Swindler (anthropology), Donald Reay (pathology), and Tom Morton (dentistry), all experts in their field.

Special appreciation goes to my family—Sande, David, Allie, and John—for their loving support of my search for the truth.

Acknowledgments

This book wouldn't be a book without Bill Birnes. He found my name in a NEXIS search and convinced me I had a multitude of valuable experiences to write about. Bill guided me through what began as the drudgery of writing and the pain of long-buried memories. His skills at thoughtfully weaving together my sometimes-fragmented writing were invaluable.

A joyless, dismal, black and sorrowful issue:
Here is the babe, as loathsome as a toad
Amongst the fairest beings of our time
—Shakespeare

1995
Foreword
by
Ann Rule

As anyone who reads this remarkable book will quickly conclude, Bob Keppel is a superlative detective. He is one of perhaps a half dozen of the most gifted and intelligent investigators I have met in the 26 years I have been writing about true crime. I have known him for two decades. When we met, I was a young writer and he was the "new kid" in the King County, Washington, Police Department's Homicide Unit. In those days, I wrote under the pen name "Andy Stack," and I covered murder cases for *True Detective, Master Detective,* and three or four other fact-detective magazines. In fact, I wrote an article on the first homicide Bob Keppel ever worked as a detective.

It was called "Washington's Strange Case of Murder Without Rhyme or Reason."

I have always believed that there is a cyclical pattern in life. Everyone who excels in his or her profession can usually look back and see how one learning experience weaves itself into another—and another and another—until that person is so prepared to deal with complicated problems that his response is almost instinctive. Never have I realized that more than when I dug through a stack of yellowing detective magazines to reread "Murder Without Rhyme or Reason," which was published in *Master Detective* in July 1975. The picture of Bob Keppel looks as though he's about 25—which he was.

The crime had occurred a full year earlier, in July 1974. July 1974 was a watershed point not only in Bob Keppel's career, but in the lives of so many people who lived in the Northwest—including my own. Bob Keppel would go from his first, relatively uncomplicated murder probe into the investigation of a killing swath that may never be equaled.

Bob Keppel and Roger Dunn were called out in the wee hours of July 11 to investigate the senseless murder of Chris Stergion, 68, a popular businessman in Enumclaw, Washington. Stergion's wife said Chris had gotten out of bed to investigate suspicious sounds. She had heard a struggle, and when she'd gone to see what had happened she found her husband lying bleeding, in their bathroom.

Enumclaw *is* in King County, but it is about as far removed in ambiance from Seattle as a windmill is from the Space Needle. The newest detectives usually got the homicides in the little towns on the edges of the county, and Keppel and Dunn drew the Stergion case.

As I write this, the O. J. Simpson trial is in full flower, and so much of the prosecution's case—and the defense's—hinges on a pair of black leather gloves.

And so did the successful solution to Chris Stergion's murder twenty-one years ago.

The biggest case of Bob Keppel's life would break three days after the Stergion homicide: the "Ted" murders that rocked the Northwest in 1974 and for years afterward. The answers that were so long in coming in the serial murders "Ted" committed were elicited, finally, because of Bob Keppel's extraordinary—and, yes, innate—skill at interrogation.

And so did the successful solution to Chris Stergion's murder twenty-one years ago.

On July 10, 1974, a hugely tall teenage drifter wandered into Enumclaw, Washington. He was broke and hungry, and a number of people had taken pity on him. Some sawmill workers gave him money for food, and Chris Stergion, who owned Stergion Concrete, had let him sleep in an old truck he owned.

Late that night, Stergion woke to hear the sound of the cash register drawer being opened in the office adjoining his living quarters. Minutes later, Chris Stergion lay dead in his own bathtub.

The King County detectives learned that Stergion had been beaten, and stabbed more than twenty times.

Identifying the most likely suspect wasn't difficult. The 6-foot-6-inch-tall teenager who had rolled into Enumclaw the day before had frequently been seen around local businesses. Patrol units quickly spotted James Lee Slade walking along a road heading out of town.

Bob Keppel would interrogate Slade. Twenty years later, when I reread that interview, I can see that Keppel's inherent skill at verbal jousting was already in place. That didn't surprise me; he was good then and he's only gotten better over the years. What did surprise me was how jarringly familiar the details of the conversation were.

Jim Slade first told Keppel that he hadn't even *been* in Enumclaw that night—he'd hitched a ride to another town, and he'd left his blanket roll in the victim's truck.

Keppel had learned that the suspect had been wearing black leather gloves ever since he got to town and was quick to notice that he wasn't wearing them anymore. Keppel also noticed that Slade had a cut on his right index finger and another on his little finger.

Bob Keppel quietly asked him where his gloves were now.

"They made my hands hot and sweaty, so I took them off and left them in a truck. When I went back for them, they were gone."

"It seems a little strange," Keppel said, "for someone who likes his gloves as much as you seemed to, to put them in a parked truck. Why didn't you just put them in your pocket?"

"They wouldn't fit."

Slade's body language showed that he was becoming more and more nervous. His Adam's apple jumped wildly as he gulped frequently, and he drank cups of black coffee.

But he didn't want to talk.

James Slade first demanded an attorney, but when he was alone with Bob Keppel, he suddenly asked, "Is the old man dead?"

"Yes."

"All right. I want to tell you about it."

And Keppel wanted to hear. But first Keppel warned Slade not once but twice that whatever he said could be used against him in court, repeating the familiar phrases of the Miranda Warning.

"I still want to tell you."

It would be the first of scores of confessions Bob Keppel would hear. It was a tragically simple story. Slade, wanting money, had broken into Chris Stergion's office. When Stergion caught him at the cash register, Slade told Keppel that he had stabbed him with some calipers he'd picked up.

"I don't know what came over me. I saw a light flash. He had asked me who I was, saying, 'The cops are coming.' I just kept hitting and hitting him with the calipers."

When detectives found James Slade's black leather gloves in a warehouse where he had tossed them in his flight from the crime scene, they had their own story to tell. The right glove had a jagged cut on the right index finger and the lining was soaked with blood.

Three days later, Bob Keppel was plunged into the "Ted Murders," a real baptism of fire into the world of an entirely different kind of killer. And in the ensuing years, he has probably investigated or advised investigators in more serial murder cases than almost any detective in America.

Bob Keppel and I share a common hero, a common mentor: Pierce Brooks. Pierce Brooks was the Captain of the Homicide Unit of the Los Angeles Police Department for a dozen years, and Chief of Police in cities in both Colorado and Oregon after his retirement from the LAPD. It was Brooks who first recognized the very existence of the phenomenon we have come to know as "a serial killer." He was also the first to insist that the only way to track and trap this kind of elusive criminal was through the establishment of a central information system on victims and suspects that could be contributed to and shared by law enforcement agencies nationwide.

Pierce Brooks began building his own files by poring over out-of-town newspapers and looking for cases similar to those he was investigating—way back in the late 1950s. Bob Keppel, as you will read in the pages ahead, conceived the efficacy of using computers—still a newfangled gimmick in the mid-seventies—to track criminals long before most investigators had thought of such a possibility.

Today, the HITS program that Bob Keppel oversees in the Washington State Attorney General's Office is one of the best tools we have in the Northwest to solve homicides.

I didn't have to be asked twice to read the manuscript of *The Riverman*. One of the things that makes Bob Keppel a superior detective is that he is inscrutable; he never tells *anyone* what is not ready to be told. It is also one of his most maddening traits. For years, he had known things about Ted Bundy that no one else knew. My natural curiosity about those "things" has been difficult to live with, but I have always known better than to ask Bob Keppel for information before he was ready to give it. Now all my questions have been answered.

The Riverman will fill a long-vacant spot on the bookshelves of both professionals and laypeople who have searched for a definitive study of serial murder. There are hundreds of pages of heretofore unpublished information—not only on the Ted Bundy cases but on the Atlanta Child Killer, the Michigan Child Murders, the Son of Sam, and Washington's Green River Murders.

Bob Keppel never claimed to be a diplomat, and he is bound to ruffle some feathers as he points out the sometimes-catastrophic errors made in the investigation of serial murders. Many mistakes were made out of inexperience, some were the result of inefficiency, and more were probably made because of turf wars and scrambling for political advantage.

Bob Keppel pulls no punches. What will make *The Riverman* a bible for working investigators *is* this searing dissection of what went wrong, *coupled* with brilliant insights into successful investigations of crimes that were almost impossible to untangle.

I don't think Bob Keppel ever set out to become an expert on serial murder. There are less frustrating and more pleasant roads to follow. In the early 1980s, we talked for hours on our way to a VICAP Task Force conference in Huntsville, Texas—extra hours because our plane was grounded in Denver in a blizzard. The thing I remember most is hearing Bob Keppel say, "I *know* this for sure.

Foreword

I never want to get involved in the boiler-room pressure of working another serial murder task force. Once is enough."

He was talking, of course, about the Ted Bundy investigation . . . an investigation that he would never really be finished with.

Even now.

I had to smile when I read *The Riverman*. I don't think it was a year after our flight through the blizzard before Bob Keppel was up to his elbows in work with the Green River Task Force. So much for no more boiler-room pressure. But as his career unfolded, it became obvious that there was no way Bob could *not* go back.

And back. And back again.

Reading *The Riverman* brought back many memories to me—some good, some horrendous. The toe-dancing and the conflicts that marked some of our VICAP conferences are all here, as they should be. The interpersonal conflicts in various police agencies and the turf wars that slowed—or stopped—forward progress are noted. I am gratified to see Pierce Brooks receive the credit that he so richly deserves. If I'm to be completely honest, I'm probably just as gratified to see that some of the popinjays have been deflated.

I lived through the Bundy years in a different dimension than Bob Keppel did. I knew the man who wore the mask, and it was a very long time before I saw the monster exposed. It hasn't been easy for me to read the explicit confessions that Ted made to Bob Keppel. It will not be easy for any reader, no matter how hardened he—or she—may be to the psychopathology of the sadistic sociopath. But the details are necessary for us to understand what made Ted Bundy tick. Outside of police files and psychiatric reports—which are usually classified—I have never read the actual words and thoughts of a brilliantly twisted killer as they appear in *The Riverman*. We may not *like* what Ted Bundy had to say to Bob Keppel, but we will learn a great deal from it.

In January of 1989, when Bob Keppel journeyed to Starke, Florida, to spend some of Ted Bundy's last hours on earth with him, he was like a finely trained athlete (which he, in fact, *is*). He knew all the facts; he knew when to speak, when to keep

Foreword

quiet, when to show approval, when to show disdain, and he was ready.

Bob Keppel heard, at last, the answers to horrific questions.

I am honored to write this foreword. There have been many Bundy books—including my own—but the whole story has never been told until now.

Introduction to the 2004 Edition

It's the year 2003, and since Ted Bundy's execution in 1989 and the reduction of the Green River murders investigation to a single detective, Tom Jenson, new information about both sets of cases has since come to light.

Regarding Ted Bundy, his confession to the warden of the Florida State Penitentiary about the one last murder is now a matter of public record, as are his confessions to Vail Police Department detective Matt Lindvall about the murder of Julie Cunningham. Regarding some of the homicides grouped under the Green River investigation, in November 2001 King County homicide detectives arrested Gary Leon Ridgway, who was subsequently charged with the murders of Carol Christensen, Opal Mills, Cynthia Hinds, and Marcia Chapman. Ridgway subsequently pled guilty to 48 homicides, in October 2003, new names were added to the Green River list of victims, and Ridgway will spend the rest of his life in prison.

As for myself, after I retired from the Washington State Attorney General's office in 1999, I continued to teach at the University of Washington. In 2003, I became an Assistant Professor of Criminal Justice at Sam Houston State University in Huntsville, Texas. Also under a grant from the Bureau of Justice Administration, developed the ideas for a homicide investigation database—ideas that first began germinating in my mind back in 1975 during the Ted Missing and Murdered Women investigation—into a full-blown computer database program.

My old Green River Murders Task Force colleague, Dave Reichert, also took his own path during the twenty years since two boys riding their bikes over the Peck Bridge discovered the first bodies floating in the Green River. Dave, even after the investigation shrank to a single investigator, never gave up, believing as I believed that a piece of evidence the task force gathered back in 1987 would eventually lead to a suspect in some of the homicides. Dave's beliefs kept him inside the King County Sheriff's Department, moving up through the ranks from detective to captain to major—and eventually into politics when he ran for sheriff of King County. He never gave up on the search and was on the job when Tom Jenson told him that there was a DNA match in the Green River case.

What Bundy never knew during Dave's and my interviews with him over the years, when he attempted to provide us with a model of what the Green River Killer's behavior might be, was that an individual had been under police scrutiny (as the publicly released affidavits from King County investigators show) ever since 1983. Bundy could not know that because it was not information that was made public at the time.

Even as the task force interviewed witnesses and sexual companions of the person who was ultimately arrested for the Christensen, Mills, Hinds, and Chapman murders—as well as the suspect himself—the police proceeded so as to compromise neither the suspect's constitutional rights nor the investigation itself. And it was only when forensic biological evidence, developed because of advances in DNA amplification and testing technology, indicated that there was a match between crime-scene DNA and the suspect's DNA that an arrest was made. The story of that investigation and the arrest is also contained in the affidavit sworn by Detective Sue Peters and subsequently made public by the King County District Attorney, along with the prosecutor's summary of evidence and Gary Ridgway's written confessions and admissions.

For the present, the confessions Bundy made to Mike Fisher and Matt Lindvall about his Colorado murders in the previous chapter and to the warden at Florida State Penitentiary are his final words as he faced his ultimate punishment. They are revealing, particularly his confession to Lindvall, in that they show Bundy trying to hang on to his last bit of dignity, which itself was only his delusion about himself. Bundy confesses that he lived in hell as he trolled for his victims across the four states that we know about and that what was consuming his victims was also consuming him. How much of those statements are self-serving and how much of those are true can only be judged by those who read them.

CONTENTS

1

Too Many Bodies

Not invisible but unnoticed, Watson. You did not know where to look, and so you missed all that was important. I can never bring you to realize the importance of sleeves, the suggestiveness of thumb-nails or the great issues that may hang from a boot-lace.
> —Sherlock Holmes

One can only surmise what the great detective Sherlock Holmes would have gleaned from private conversations with Ted Bundy or the hunt through the dense, wet underbrush of rural King County and brassy strip joints along Seattle's red-light Sea-Tac district for the Green River Killer, whom Ted Bundy called the Riverman. But Holmes and his amanuensis, Dr. Watson, were fictional, and anyone who works in the day-to-day world of law enforcement knows that cases do not resolve themselves neatly as they do at the end of a story. The Green River murders investigation, which began in 1982, continued until 2003, when Gary Leon Ridgway, who was arrested for four of the murders in the series, confessed to forty-eight of the murders. The clues to the killer's identity lay for years in the cyberspace of lists of names, contact reports, and tip sheets. We know that somewhere among the hundreds of thousands of leads, along the hundreds of miles of Mylar tape, the name of the Green River killer and all the evidence that would incriminate him awaited us. I had a few guesses as to who the killer was, although I let the computer assemble the information for my probable cause—a hasty accusation can invalidate years and years of investigative work. Ted Bundy and his guys on death row in Starke, Florida, taught me how serial killers think and what will encourage them to give up their secrets. It's all a waiting game, unless you catch them with their hands dripping red with the blood of their victims. I learned that to bring the suspect in, you must advance your investigation in orderly phases, corner the suspect, and carefully conduct the interrogation in order to gain his confidence. But first you must break down the barriers within your own department, among your own colleagues, and within a command structure that will usually deny the existence of a serial killer at large and all the trouble it brings.

Ted Bundy was speaking to me.

"I just said that the Hawkins girl's head was severed and taken up the road about twenty-five to fifty yards and buried in a location about ten yards west of the road on a rocky hillside. Did you hear that?"

Hear it? I was stunned!

The squeaky, chipped metal folding chair that I was sitting on suddenly shrank; I felt oversized upon it. The prison walls closed in around me and became covered with dancing, bloodstained apparitions of murdered college coeds and young girls ripped away from life in the first blossom of their beauty. I had slipped into a light hallucination in reaction to the horrifying confession I had just heard. The infamous Ted Bundy, my personal nemesis, was confessing to murder, confessing in his own name for the very first time. As the words tumbled out of his mouth, my mind was sucked into the past, swirling through a deep, dark funnel of time. Details, follow-up facts, the material from the 15-year investigation of Ted and my pursuit of him, which had been fixed rigidly in my memory, began falling away like little chunks of calcium sediment from the walls of a cave. It was almost too much to comprehend. After my 15 years of searching for the missing pieces of the Ted Bundy puzzle, it was January 1989 and Ted himself was almost casually confessing to the murders our baling-wire computer program had assigned to him. And now, in this small prison interrogation room, I was gripping the edge of my chair, waiting for him to divulge the specific facts about the murders, mutilations, decapitations, necrophilia, and burials he had carried out at the Issaquah body dump site, all of which we had uncovered years before anyone even knew there was a Ted Bundy. Now Bundy and I were face-to-face and he was in Florida's maximum-security penitentiary. All those memories came back to me as I began probing Ted for details.

Too Many Bodies

I remember the day the name Ted first came into my life—little did I know the number of years I would spend tracking the man with that name or the number of deaths to which that name would eventually be linked. But here that day was, coming back to me amid the claustrophobic atmosphere of death row.

The Lake

Lake Sammamish is the nearest thing to an outdoor shrine for many of the college-age men and women who live in and around Seattle. It was particularly crowded on the Sunday afternoon of July 14, 1974, because several large companies, including Rainier Beer and Lockheed Shipyards, were having their employee picnics. Over 50,000 people had come to spend a day at the state park. Throughout the elaborate mating dance that took place in the 90-degree sunshine that afternoon, who would have noticed the appearance of another Volkswagen bug with a light-haired pretty-boy smiling from behind the wheel? Who would have been afraid of such a person?

Certainly not Janice Ott, who had ridden to the lake on her yellow Tiger 10-speed bike for a day of sunning. Janice was a pretty young lady—dainty and slight, about 5 feet tall—who had long blond hair that hung straight down to the middle of her back. She was dressed for a perfect day in the sun: short denim cutoffs and a midriff shirt. She peeled these off to reveal her black bikini as soon as she reached the sandy beach, and lay down on her towel, which she'd had stashed in her blue nylon knapsack.

Janice sunned herself, unaware of the fate that awaited her and the danger working its way toward her in the guise of a seemingly average guy. At that moment in another part of the park, a blond 25-year-old man about 5 feet 10 inches tall, of medium build and wearing a beige sling on his left arm, approached Mary Osmer on the grassy area near the bandstand where Rainier Brewery was sponsoring races. He was described, by people who saw him later that afternoon, as a good-looking all-American type wearing blue jeans and a white T-shirt. The young stranger asked Mary, who was clad in a very short backless, halter-type dress, if she would help him load his sailboat onto his car. She agreed with a perky "sure." He asked her what she was doing and she replied that she was waiting for her husband and parents. He quickly changed the conversation by saying, "This is out of sight; there are so many people." As they walked toward the parking lot, he stopped three times to clasp his left arm as if he were in pain, explaining that he had hurt it playing racquetball. He tried to engage Mary in conversation by asking if she had ever played the game.

When she didn't respond, the young man changed the topic, asking, "Do you live around here?"

She said, "Bellevue, and I work at Boeing."

The man led Mary to a metallic brown VW bug. Mary didn't see a sailboat and asked where it was. The man said, "It's at my folks' house; it's just up the hill." He motioned to the side door as if to open it for her. Mary told him she couldn't go because she had to meet her folks. She asked him what time it was, and he replied, "It is 12:20." She said she was already late because she was to meet them at 12:15. Almost apologetically, he said, "Oh, that's okay, I should have told you it wasn't in the parking lot. Thanks for bothering to come up to the car." He walked Osmer about halfway back and repeated himself: "Thanks for coming with me. I should have told you it was not in the parking lot."

When Mary Osmer later told us her story, her eyes glistened with guilt. To her, the stranger seemed friendly, sincere, very polite, and easy to talk to. He had a nice smile and didn't get upset when she told him she wouldn't go with him. She was pretty, 22 years old, newly married, and almost overwhelmed by the dangerous excitement of the mere thought of infidelity that she had had when she was approached by this attractive stranger. She wasn't your average vague eyewitness, but gave us a detailed physical description of him when questioned. She had paid attention to every move he made because she was sizing him up for the thrill of it—the thrill of flirting with him and maybe even the thought of doing more than that. She remembered him perfectly, it turned out, and we were able to assemble the stranger's physical description, his gait, the car he drove, his leisure activities, and the way he talked. Mary had listened to him so well, we even had a handle on his conversational style. But Mary was one of the lucky ones. This predatory stranger had had a harmless brush with her, but quickly moved on to find his next victim, leaving Mary unaware of the danger she had escaped.

When he and Mary parted, the stranger wandered away from his car again and approached the beach, where several people were sunning, among them Janice Ott. Several other sunbathers had seen Janice arrive. One of them was Jim Stanton, a Drug Enforcement Administration agent who was always happy to take in the pleasurable sight of a good-looking young woman willing to take off most of her clothing in front of him. Stanton watched as Janice applied cocoa butter to her skin and positioned herself on her towel, facing the sun. Cynthia Baker also watched the newcomer arrive. She and two of her girlfriends were lying two feet away from Ott. Another witness, Gloria Samuelson, was 10 feet away from where Janice Ott was sunning.

Ott had been lying on the beach for about half an hour when a white male, this time described by witnesses as dressed in white tennis shorts, white T-shirt, and white tennis shoes, approached her and asked, "Excuse me, could you help me put my sailboat onto my car? I can't do it by myself because I broke my arm." Stanton, who had been watching Ott, heard the stranger's line and thought to himself what a shame it was that he had just been aced out by this guy with his left arm in a sling.

Cynthia Baker, the witness sitting closest to Janice's towel, also heard the stranger's opening line and Ott's response: "Sit down, let's talk about it." Stanton, however, having lost his shot with this woman, quickly lost interest, and tuned out.

The stranger said, "It's up at my parents' house in Issaquah." When we compared witnesses' comments, we noted that the good-looking injured man had apparently learned his lesson quickly and changed his strategy to address the concerns of the first person he tried to pick up. His experience with Mary Osmer had taught him that he must relay to his unsuspecting prey that they would have to leave the park. This man was a very quick study.

Janice Ott established common ground with the stranger quickly by saying, "Oh really? I live in Issaquah. Well, okay." Then, as Janice put on her cutoffs and shirt, she said, "Under one condition, that I get a ride in the sailboat."

Gloria Samuelson heard Ott say, "I don't know how to sail."

Then she heard the eager stranger answer, "It will be easy for me to teach you."

Janice asked, "Is there room in the car for my bike?"

The man quickly assured her by saying, "It will fit in my trunk, and my car is in the parking lot."

"I'm Jan," Ott said.

The stranger said, "I'm Ted."

As the couple set out, walking toward the parking lot, Cynthia Baker heard Ott say aimlessly, "Well, I get to meet your parents, then."

As Ted and Janice walked out of earshot, the last words Baker heard Ted say to Janice Ott were "Who do you know in Issaquah?"

Mary Osmer recalled that it was about 12:30 when she saw her handsome stranger walking with an attractive woman toward the parking lot. She didn't know Janice Ott, but thought to herself about the stranger's pretty companion, *Boy, it didn't take him long to find someone else.* Mary Osmer remembered Ott's 10-speed bike with curved handlebars and wondered where he was going to put the bike.

Janice Ott would never be seen or heard from again, and her disappearance would haunt me forever.

Around one o'clock that same afternoon, Denise Naslund, her boyfriend, and two other friends pulled up to the beach at Lake Sammamish in Denise's Chevrolet. They joined the other sunbathers about 220 yards in front of the east restroom. Denise was a beautiful young woman, strikingly similar in appearance to Janice Ott. The main difference was that while Janice had long golden hair, Denise's was long and black. She, like Janice, was also dressed in the uniform of the day: blue denim cutoffs and a dark blue halter top.

At about three o'clock, Diane Watson was close to the concession stand, where she saw Denise simply waiting there alone. As Watson approached the stand, she noticed a man nearby just staring at her with an intense expression. It made her nervous. He was tracking her with his eyes. She walked faster and became extra cautious as he followed her, never pulling his gaze away from her. He caught up with her, in spite of her increased pace, and asked, "I need to ask a really big favor. Will you help me load my sailboat? I normally wouldn't ask this favor, but my brother is busy and unable to help." She remembered that he sounded embarrassed and a little out of breath. He pointed in the direction of the parking lot with the elbow of his sling as he explained his situation.

"I'm sorry, but I'm in a hurry to go," she told him.

He said apologetically, "That's okay."

Watson could feel his eyes bore into her back as she walked

away. She was sure his gaze was still following her as she disappeared into the crowd of sunbathers. Her description of the man who stared at her was strikingly similar to the one that other witnesses had given of the good-looking stranger who kept approaching women in the park that sunny day.

At four o'clock that same afternoon, Laurie Adams was walking back from the restroom when the man with sandy brown hair and his arm in a sling struck again. He reached out to her as she walked by and almost belligerently demanded, "Excuse me, young lady, could you help me launch my sailboat?" He tugged on her arm—she pulled away and said, "Sorry." Laurie Adams, Mary Osmer, Diane Watson, and Janice Ott were so similar in appearance—with their long hair, bright Pepsodent smiles, and cheerleader features—that they all might well have been sisters. This was a type of physical appearance that all of Ted's victims shared, but we wouldn't understand that until much later.

The stranger persisted. If he had been simply a lonely guy trying to find just the right line to pick up a girl, he would have been pitiable except for his one score. But he was a predator stalking victims, and on that Sunday at Lake Sammamish, he popped into view just long enough to become a blip on our police records. The clues he left on that day would remain, waiting for us over the months and years it took to track him down and put them together.

When we questioned witnesses, it became obvious that the stranger had approached one woman after another all afternoon. Denise Naslund was the last. At 5 feet 4 inches tall with a slender build, the 18-year-old was more than pretty. She was the girl in the yearbook upon whose face your eyes lingered. On this day, she was last seen wearing a pair of cut-off jeans, a dark blue halter top, and brown Mexican-style sandals. Shortly before 4:30, Denise Naslund and her boyfriend got into an argument with each other. Denise got up off the blanket, left her boyfriend sitting there, and went off in a huff to the east restroom, where a Seattle Police Department employee saw her. The stranger calling himself Ted crossed her path as she left the bathroom and led her away. She vanished, leaving her friends, purse, keys, and car behind.

The stranger known only as Ted had taken two victims from Lake Sammamish that day. Five had escaped. Each woman who

7

walked away from Ted and certain death got away for different reasons, but three escaped because they noticed something vaguely dangerous about the man who suddenly appeared out of nowhere, asking for help. Mary's reluctance to go to a stranger's house, Diane's wariness at being followed and approached by a stranger, and Laurie's suspiciousness about the nervous young man who spoke rapidly and seemed very intent on getting her to his car kept each of them from being abducted. These three women picked up subtle signals that Bundy was sending off. When questioned, they said that he seemed too intent on what he was after and was uncomfortably nervous. Furthermore, they said he had spoken rapidly as if he were reading a script and he acted as if he had had a hidden agenda. Of the five different women who were approached by the stranger that day but didn't go with him, two would later become severely psychologically traumatized when the truth about "Ted" came out, at the thought that they could have become a murder victim.

Issaquah

It had been hot all day in Seattle on September 7, 1974. Roger Dunn, my partner in the homicide unit of the King County Police Department, and I were talking about the upcoming operation on my knee, which I had blown out playing recreation-league basketball. We were bouncing around, thanks to the worn shocks of Dunn's pickup, tooling north on Interstate 5 toward Seattle. We were returning from Tacoma after loading over 20 railroad ties for the landscaping we both needed around our homes. The loose cartilage in my knee was burning because I'd been lifting the ties—it felt like the joint was actually on fire. Dunn's radio was scratchy and the reception almost indecipherable. Voices of news announcers were drifting in and out amid the static and crackle. Despite the fuzzy reception, we caught the edge of a familiar name and we tried to tune the station in a little clearer. Just barely audible over the rasping of Roger's ancient tuner we heard, "King County police are investigating the discovery of skeletal remains, just east of Issaquah."

We looked at each other without saying a word and knew we were thinking the same thing—could this be it, the end of an intense investigation into the disappearances of Janice Ott and Denise Naslund from Lake Sammamish State Park on July 14, 1974? Lake Sam was one mile from where the bones had been discovered. We spotted a phone booth near the interstate and pulled off to call the squad room. If dispatch wanted us to respond to the scene, it would be over an hour before I could get there and two hours before Roger could, since he lived 25 miles farther from the site than me. It was four o'clock in the afternoon and Len Randall, our sergeant, relayed via radio for just me to respond to the call. My partner would be off the hook, at least for that afternoon. But we had to shake a leg—we still had to get the ties off the pickup bed before I could report to the newly found bone yard.

We pulled the truck up to my place and unloaded 10 ties. By the end of that chore, I was reeking of creosote and slimy with sweat. But I had to get to where the bones had been discovered as soon as possible. This was the first break in a missing-women case that had been tearing up the Seattle and King County area and making the police look like fools for months. With this thought burning in my mind, I didn't even think about niceties. Without saying good-bye to anyone, I jumped into my unmarked car, slammed it into gear, and backed out, stopping only for a loud snapping sound that came from under the rear wheel. I opened the door and looked out. In my haste I hadn't noticed anything in the driveway—but I had just demolished my son David's plastic Hot Wheels car and, as if in instant retribution, my left rear tire blew out. I felt terrible. This all-important call-out wasn't going right from the get-go, but I couldn't be held up. I changed the tire and was on my way.

By the time I neared the crime scene I was smelling like a ripe hobo and looked slovenly and dissolute. I made a left-hand turn across two westbound lanes onto an unused road that intersected with Interstate 90 to the north. The road was blocked by a prowl car and a flock of reporters. The officer overseeing the entrance to the site did a double take when he saw me because I probably didn't look like any cop he'd ever seen. As I walked by, I could hear a "who's he?" from a crowd of reporters complaining about the officer refusing to let them up to the scene while permitting someone who looked like a bum to pass the barricade.

As I walked up the dirt road and across the railroad tracks, the pain in my knee opened up again and shot through my entire leg. I

9

was in agony, but I kept walking. I was sure this was the break all of us had been waiting for. However, my high hopes were quickly dashed. I was stunned when I saw Sergeant Len Randall, who told me straight out that the skeleton they'd found was not the remains of victims Janice Ott or Denise Naslund, the missing women from Lake Sammamish who seemed simply to have vanished into thin air along with the mysterious Ted. I was more than a bit annoyed; I started wondering why I had been called to the crime scene. Then I found out that Lieutenant Dick Kraske had just told the press and Naslund's mother, Eleanor Rose, that Denise's remains had not been found. I wondered how Kraske was able to come to his conclusion so quickly. He wasn't an expert in dental identification, nor had he studied the dental charts as I had. No clothing, wallets, or jewelry—items commonly used for preliminary identification—had been found on the site. I quickly surmised that he really didn't know anything for sure, and I was suddenly depressed and wearied by the realization that he had released a statement to the press that hadn't been confirmed by a forensic report. On top of it all, my knee was exploding with pain, and every step over this terrain only made it worse. My earlier premonition that this call just wasn't going to turn out to be a good one was proving correct. The next words out of the commanding officer's mouth assured me that my luck wasn't going to change anytime soon.

Sergeant Randall ordered me to return the next day with Explorer Search and Rescue (ESAR) personnel to scour the area for any additional bones. It was pickup work. The more senior investigators had obviously thought it was a shit detail for the rookie homicide detective. Even my colleague, Detective Rolf Grunden, chuckled and commented—with a snobbishly superior attitude—that I probably wouldn't find anything. He said they had already searched the hillside and had found nothing but bones.

Randall showed me the location where two grouse hunters had stumbled over the remains that morning. The hunters were walking along the hillside, following what seemed to be animal trails. About 50 feet west of the dirt road that ran over the hillside was the site of their first discovery, a skull. The entire hillside was engulfed in nettles and blackberry bushes intertwined with thick grass and ferns. About 30 feet downhill from the skull, the hunters had found a backbone with some ribs that had been gnawed on by animals but were still intact. By looking at where the footpaths were and where the dense overgrowth of vegetation obscured the ground completely, it wasn't hard to figure out that the search Detective Grunden had led was through only those areas where a human could walk. He had conducted a traditional walk-through that could not replace a thorough search of the area. In that hunt, the only thing these investigating officers found was a matted mass of black hair that had been hidden under leaves about 15 feet midway between the locations of the skull and the rib cage. The officers had removed the remains from the scene and taken them to the medical examiner's office before I had had a chance to see what they looked like. I had never seen a human bone before, and if the bones were not those of the missing women, why did I have to search the next day? That task should have been one for the assigned detective. My assignment didn't make much sense, but it would soon prove to be a defining moment in my career as a homicide detective.

I returned to the Issaquah hillside discovery site the following morning before dawn, when the air hung wet and still with the fragrance of late summer. I scanned the ground I was to search—it was a wooded area of about 130,000 square feet of fir and cedar trees. The terrain was inhospitable and wild, divided only by narrow, interwoven animal paths that twisted and turned. To the east of the hillside was a narrow dirt road that climbed up and over the hill's crest. The road was covered with off-white round rocks that contrasted strikingly with the deep-green foliage that bordered it. The surrounding tree cover was so dense that even in daylight the forest floor was very dark, like the mysterious landscape in a fairy tale, and only occasional sunbursts escaped through small openings in the thick canopy of leaves. The pebble-covered road was the only route near the crime scene that was traveled by people, usually on horses or dirt bikes. The multitude of smaller trails through the nettles and bushes were carved by scavengers such as coyotes, wild dogs, porcupines, bears, and rodents, the types of animals that, in a final irony, had left their teeth marks on the human bones. An owl hooted through the darkness.

I was first at the scene at five A.M., not expecting the rest of the searchers until eight. I wanted the solitude and the privacy to look around by myself before I had to manage a teenaged crew of ESAR personnel. I also wanted to half mourn, half ruminate over the remains of these victims amid the desolate atmosphere of the place where they had been buried. The young patrol officer who had been ordered to secure the crime scene overnight seemed to have been truly frightened during his lonely vigil and was relieved to see another human being. His thoughts having gone in and out of dreams, rendering him barely able to distinguish reality from nightmare, he described his sentry duty as something out of Edgar Allan Poe. He'd lurched at every sound, he said, and the hours had been full of them as animals scrabbled across the hard ground, following the scent of dead things. I didn't ask him whether he'd fired his revolver—the acrid odor of burned powder hanging heavy in the forest dew made it clear.

It was just before dawn, and the silence on the hillside was ominous. No birds were chirping, no animal paws were crunching the underbrush, and no insects were buzzing. It was desolate and lonely, as if all living things had abandoned the hillside, leaving nothing but the physical signs of death and decomposition.

Miles away at King County police headquarters, someone keyed a mike, and the sudden burst of static over my police radio interrupted my thoughts. Dispatch ordered me to go to landline—the nearest telephone—for important information. I was making plans for the search my COs (commanding officers) had ordered me to run, and now I felt they were jerking me around again at the last minute.

"How ya doin', Slick?" Sergeant Randall began. I knew this tone of voice. It was the way he always delivered news you didn't want to hear. Then, he paused. He had my attention. He began, cautious as he always was when on the phone, explaining that despite yesterday's press release, the skull they'd found had positively been identified by dental comparisons as Denise Naslund, the woman abducted from Lake Sammamish. My first thoughts were of Eleanor Rose, Denise's mother. What must she think now of the King County Police Department announcement the previous day? The news release was just one example of how poorly we were prepared to handle a case of this magnitude and to deal with the feelings of grieving parents and living victims that accompanied it.

I could have complained about this yesterday, but now there could be no complaints. This was my case. In spite of the missteps the day before, I was eager and in excellent spirits at the thought of finally closing this missing-persons case. I didn't know then how my mood of optimism would soon alternate with gut-wrenching disgust, revulsion, and horror at each new discovery I was about to make. This missing-persons case that I was expecting to close was really a case of multiple murders so savage that it would shake each of us who worked on it to the core of our psyches and would not release me from its grip for another 15 years.

Soon after the sergeant's phone call, the ESAR team members who were to help me search the bone site arrived. ESAR is a voluntary rescue organization whose members are trained in search techniques for locating lost hikers and downed aircraft. ESAR's 50 or so teenagers, who were supervised by a small cadre of adults, had never participated in a police evidence search before. However, we believed that the techniques they used to find missing persons in the woods would be extremely successful in searching for bones on the Issaquah hillside.

ESAR began the search by establishing x and y coordinates, using string lines to form quadrants. The string lines were formed from a fixed point and a quarter-sectional marker. The area each quadrant covered was based on compass directions and preestablished distances. Within each quadrant, a hands-and-knees search was conducted. This method is similar to one archaeologists use in an archeological dig. Bones and other items of evidence that we discovered in our hunt were recorded with similar identifiers—the date, the time, the location, and the finder—and would be assigned an identification number. For example, a found item would be labeled:

> 09-11-74, 1010 hours, Det. Keppel found a turquoise
> comb near body decomposition site #1 which was 10
> feet west of search base, photographed by Det. Dunn
> and marked by Det. Keppel as Evidence Item #5 and
> Search Find #305.

The 305 referred to its respective number on the search find diagram.

The number of discoveries these 15- and 16-year-old kids made was alarming and gruesome:

0850 hours:	Search teams began searching.
0908 hours:	Found hair near where two bodies were dumped.
0920 hours:	Found leather sheath, two feet long.

0923 hours: Found screwdriver.
0924 hours: Found blond hair near original dump area.
0950 hours: Found rib bone.
1012 hours: Found jawbone directly uphill from dump lo-
               cation.
1050 hours: Found blond hair along animal trail.
1110 hours: Found bird's nest with blond hair inter-
               twined.
1115 hours: Found fecal material with small hand bone.

On and on it went, one discovery after another, day after day, for seven days. We hadn't only uncovered a cache of human remains, we'd literally unearthed a graveyard, a killer's lair, where he'd taken and secreted the bodies of victims.

Typically, homicide investigators process a crime scene for evidence, not human body parts. I wondered what these teenagers were thinking and feeling with each new discovery. What would they be like after a few days of finding hundreds of animal-ravaged skeletal parts? Did they wonder how bones wind up in coyote fecal material? Or how birds know to use human hair to weave their nests? Did they think about what kind of monster would leave a once-living, vibrant human being in such a humiliating state of desiccation? Was this why primitive tribes learned to bury their dead? Whatever their thoughts were, their willingness to kneel shoulder to shoulder, meticulously inspecting every inch of hillside, fighting stinging nettles, and lifting every twig and leaf with the care of a surgeon, was unbelievable. Not one word of complaint was uttered. No police officer that I knew would have searched with such dedication from dawn till dusk for seven days straight. I would always be thankful for their help on this tedious but all-important level of the investigation.

They were as methodical as they were dedicated. The bones and items of evidence were plotted on a diagram using the "baseline" method of sketching crime scenes. In the end, we recovered many bones, clumps of hair, fingernails, and hairs from within animal dung and fecal soil from three separate and distinct body decomposition sites. In addition to the human remains, we found a crowbar, shovel, screwdriver, female clothing (unrelated to the three victims), and many animal bones.

What we didn't recover was the skull of Lake Sam victim Janice

Ott—we had recovered the rest of her remains on the site—and a skull and jawbone that would have been useful in identifying a third person whose name we did not know but the rest of whose remains we found as well. We believed, at first, that these missing parts were not found because animals had taken them somewhere outside our search perimeters. Unfortunately, we didn't even consider that they could have been buried. We had found so many bones on top of the ground we didn't even think the killer's modus operandi involved burial. Our inexperience was telling, and it favored the killer.

I was the photographer most of the time and packaged all the evidence for processing. I used a Mamiya 110 camera, a clunky, boxy device resembling an old press camera from the 1950s, which I had never operated before. It was cumbersome and heavy and required a battery pack that was 12 inches high and 4 inches thick. A thick leather strap wrapped around my shoulder to help steady the camera while I focused the lens. Here was a machine definitely not made for dragging around a wooded hillside where I needed both hands for balance as I tried to step over ground cover that twisted around my ankles every time I moved. The whole point of a clumsy camera like this was its huge 110-mm negative that produced an image so fine that every minute detail of the evidence came out in perfect resolution. The camera produced prints so perfect that even when enlarged to almost poster size, they could be used in court before the most critical judge and jury.

Before touching or moving the evidence, I took two rolls of film and had an officer run it over to the photo lab for immediate processing. I didn't want to interfere with the evidence and later find the photos I had taken hadn't developed well. It was fortunate that the first two rolls were tested. I had not locked the lens in the open position, and as a result, all the prints were blurred. Subsequently, Roger Dunn was sent to the scene to be my assistant photographer. He constantly reminded me of the proper camera settings prior to each photograph, and from then on, the prints turned out fine.

So what began as a search for a few more bones belonging to a single skeleton had turned into a major bone find in which over 400 items of evidence and bones from the remains of three women were recovered. This was a first. The ESAR search techniques proved invaluable for us since we had never been faced with processing this type of outdoor crime scene before. We learned the importance of thoroughness and of animal behavior, the latter of which helped us find remains along their travel paths. This search really was revolutionary and would be a model for crime scene processing forever.

As I went up and down the hillside, photographing, measuring, and packaging evidence and bones, I was obsessed with what the killer had left behind. What signs of him were left for us to find? Was there anything here that could be linked to this murderer? Locard's Exchange Principle—Edmund Locard's theory—states that when a murderer comes in contact with things at the crime scene, a cross-transfer of evidence occurs. This meant that we should find something of the killer at the crime scene and, conversely, that when we found the killer, we should find something from the crime scene on him.

The "fresh" physical and circumstantial evidence, such as eyewitnesses, lead bullets, bullet casings, and weapons, were noticeably absent from this scene. The area had been stripped of all these usual forensic clues. It was a scene of great mystery. In the history of King County homicide investigation, no murder case had a crime scene with so little evidence as this one.

What would the evidence that we did find tell us about the psychology of the killer? What might be detected from this scene? At this stage, it was all guesswork, since no one had ever had to solve such a series of crimes. First of all, even though the crime scene was only one mile from a populated area, I was impressed by how secluded this location really was and how much advantage the location gave to anyone lying in wait. It was the perfect terrain for staging an ambush or scouting for enemies. If you parked a car just off the dirt road, you could see or hear anyone coming from any direction. I got the feeling that this was no accident—the killer chose this site so he could cover his tracks well before anyone's arrival.

The implication that the killer chose this location prior to committing the murders was also a frightening thought. We understood from this carefully selected multiple-body crime scene that each of his kills was premeditated and would share the same final scene. The killer had been there many times—if not to leave a body, definitely to scout out the area. The more we thought about the dump site, the more it seemed that these were no random catch-as-catch-can murders, but were premeditated, with escape routes and victim disposal already planned out. For example, the distance from where the victims were last seen to the dump site indicated that the offender was not overly concerned about traveling some distance with a victim in his car. He was confident that he could elude the police and dispose of the body between the time when the victim was reported missing and when the official search began. The fact that we found no clothing remnants on the remains was evidence that the killer did not want his victims found with their own clothing, which might contain trace evidence that could be linked to him. He must therefore know how police collected evidence and developed theories of the crime from the remains at the crime scene. The killer probably saw for himself the results of predators scavenging human remains, since one body was there for over a month before the other two were discarded. How many times had he visited the dump site to note the progress of the corpse's decay and the way wild animals scattered the remains? He must have stepped over his first victim to leave the other two.

It was my own rookie detective theory—crude both in empirical substantiation and manner of induction, and nothing more—that the killer was more than simply an opportunistic preplanner. I had concluded that he was rehearsing all of his options. The killer's modus operandi, I felt, was dynamic and he was willing to change it out of convenience and necessity, leaving his clear signature as only a fantasy in my mind. The conditions of the crime scene were indicative not only of extensive pre-event planning but also post-event planning and superb execution, leading to the conclusion that the offender previously had been successful at committing murder. This killer was more experienced at cold-blooded murder than any of us were at watching people like him. Somehow I sensed he knew this and he knew he could get away with it. He was so elusive and so aware of his ability to strike and disappear that he was especially dangerous. His methods would make him almost as invisible as a shadow in the darkness. He was a community's worst nightmare, a stalker of their daughters who was able to strike with impunity and invincibility. I had come up with this theory after a week's investigation of the Issaquah bone yard. These ideas that were jelling within my head were no more than quivering bits of probability waiting to be confirmed by more substantial evidence. As it turned out, the killer's own confession would prove me correct.

However, my theory was not even mildly supported by most police personnel at the time. Most of the homicide behavioral theorists on the case, especially the hot dogs from the Federal Bureau of Investigation, expected that any day a crazy psycho would be found running down the street with a bloody knife in his mouth and screaming "Mother." They did not go for the subtlety of the murderer's methods that I had envisioned.

As for tangible evidence, we identified the remains of Janice Ott and Denise Naslund, the missing persons from Lake Sammamish State Park, as the result of the search at Issaquah. In the less than two months since the women had been murdered and dumped there, their bodies had thoroughly decomposed and their remains had been scavenged and scattered over the hillside by animals. There were also other bones, extra pieces of vertebrae and leg bone belonging to a third victim whom we were unable to identify.

Those extra bones rattled in my mind for the next decade. It would not be until Ted Bundy's chilling and detailed confession to me in his final days before his walk to the electric chair that we would know the identity of that third set of remains. Ted would tell us that they were those of missing coed Georgann Hawkins, a victim we had included in the Ted cases but could not positively identify until Ted told us where he brought her body.

Georgann Hawkins

She was a strikingly beautiful coed, 5 feet 2 inches tall, with a slender build and long dark-blond hair. Near midnight on June 11, 1974, students at the University of Washington, 15 miles away from Issaquah, were returning to their dorm rooms after studying for final exams. Georgann was one of those students. The alley behind her sorority house was dimly lit, and the sound of footsteps could be heard echoing as people entered the small buildings on either side. It was the perfect setting for a handsome stranger named Ted to blend seemlessly into the campus setting and strike his next victim. What had Georgann Hawkins to fear from this man, who could have belonged to any one of the houses on the University of Washington's fraternity row?

The University of Washington was not one of the country's most sedate campuses. Students and faculty ranged from the ultra-left to the ultra-right, with a broad middle band of moderate middle-class students. It had an active fraternity and sorority life in the mid-'70s. The off-campus Greek-letter society houses were the site of many parties and were regularly patrolled by the Seattle Police Department. There were arrests for drunken and disorderly conduct, vandalism, a petty theft once in a while, and, of course, marijuana possession. Perhaps the most violent reported crime was date rape. There were few transients roaming through the area. Most of the crimes were committed by locals and nearby residents. So Georgann, walking across campus late at night, would probably not be concerned about the kind of danger Ted presented.

Georgann was last seen by a friend who leaned out of a window of a fraternity house to talk to her. She was wearing a white backless T-shirt, a flowered-print long-sleeved shirt that was tied in the front, white open-toed clogs, and navy blue cotton bell-bottom pants that were too big around her waist and therefore held together with a safety pin. Only the police knew this last salient fact; they withheld it from public disclosure after her disappearance. Years later, Ted would mention that little-known fact. Georgann also had on a black onyx ring and a cultured-pearl ring in a Tiffany setting with a gold band.

Behind Greek Row, where Georgann was talking to her friend, was an alley that led to an unlit parking lot in which was parked a solitary VW Beetle. A franseria shrub blocked the view of the VW to passersby crossing the alley. Under the cover of darkness the VW's driver, Ted Bundy, silently placed a crowbar and handcuffs on the ground near the rear of the car. This was to be the performance for which Ted had rehearsed two weeks earlier. Then, he had approached another pretty woman in front of the same sorority house where Georgann now stood. Upon his request, the first young woman walked Ted all the way to his car in the same parking lot, where he said "thanks," turned, and left for his house only five blocks away. His furtive movements that night were the dress rehearsal for the murder of Georgann Hawkins.

As Georgann was saying good night to her friend in the window, Ted was moving north up the alley, carrying a briefcase full of books, navigating his way through the darkness on crutches and feigning difficulty. Ted saw the young woman round the north end of the block, pause for a moment, and then walk toward him. Georgann was only 60 feet from the rear door of her sorority house when Ted approached her out of the shadows. Georgann Hawkins smiled at the young man hobbling toward her—she always smiled when she had the chance to help others in need, her friends reported when questioned after her disappearance. At precisely the right distance, the well-practiced Ted dropped the briefcase as he limped closer and asked her if she would pitch in and carry it for him since he was having so much trouble managing it alone. She obliged, almost without thinking, and said, "They call me George." They walked up the alley, across the street and toward the dark parking lot where the Volkswagen was waiting.

They were at the car when Georgann, unsuspecting, turned her back to Ted. He quickly picked up the crowbar he had hidden and—in a single motion—delivered one perfectly placed blow to the back of her head. Georgann's knees buckled and she dropped to the dirt, unconscious. As she lay there perfectly still beside the wheel of his car, Ted grabbed his handcuffs and secured them around her limp wrists. The harsh clicking noises of the locking manacles echoed in the darkness. Then Ted scooped up the petite Georgann, loaded her in the passenger side of his car, swung into the driver's seat beside her body, and drove away. Knowing he would be committing murder that night, Ted had already removed the passenger seat before he had left home. He did it so that the body of his captive prey would lie unseen and motionless on the floorboard next to him. No one looking at him stopped at a traffic light would have known that the handsome young man behind the wheel was actually transporting a helpless victim who would soon die.

Noticing every light and car around him, Ted put-putted the car out of the university district to southbound I-5 in his little VW. Traveling via the I-90 cutoff, he drove onto the old floating bridge, proceeded across Mercer Island, and past the city of Issaquah about one mile. Making sure there were no police about, Ted made an illegal left-hand turn across the two westbound lanes of I-90 onto a dirt road that crossed some railroad tracks and twisted up into the security of the woods. His entire trip from the parking lot at the university to this secluded site covered about 20 miles and took around 30 minutes. That quickly he was out of the thousand eyes of the U-district and into a private wooded area known only to experienced hikers and hunters in the Northwest. As he was driving,

Georgann, lying next to him, was slowly beginning to stir. Suddenly, her eyes opened up like headlights and she spoke. He was frightened by her sudden torrent of babbling. As if she were awakening from a dream, Georgann began talking about her Spanish test the next day. She asked Ted questions, believing he had come to tutor her for her exam. *This is unreal,* Ted thought to himself. He was on the edge of panic. She had awakened while he was in his most predatory and private state. He was almost sick at the thought of exposure, especially to his victim. He could not let this go on, but he could not stop the car. He had to keep on driving to reach his killing site. Ted steered his VW about a hundred yards north of I-90 toward a grassy clearing adjacent to the dirt road, where he parked.

Ted turned off the engine, carried the wiggling body of Georgann Hawkins out of the car, and laid her down on the hard ground. She was still talking as if in a half-delirium. He raised the crowbar over his head and knocked her out again. The babbling stopped.

Ted didn't pause for a moment; he immediately reached inside his black bag—the murder kit he carried in his car—and pulled out a small piece of rope. He wound it around Georgann's neck and twisted it tighter and tighter until her slow breathing stopped. Then Ted dragged the body about 10 yards from the car into a small grove of trees, where he carefully undressed her, undoing the pin holding the top of her slacks together. There, behind the trees on the hard dirt ground, amid the brambles and shrubs, he stayed with Georgann Hawkins's naked body until dawn. Finally, when the first rays of sun filtered through the branches above and illuminated the cyanotic lips of the dead girl in his arms, Ted pulled back in panic. The shock and horror of what he had done came upon him as if he were taken with a seizure, and he broke out in a wild sweat. He left the body where it was and threw everything else into the car. Then he drove down the road, tossing everything—the briefcase, the crutches, the rope, the clothing, and the tools—right out the window. He was in a complete state of psychotic flight as he drove east on I-90 and then south on Highway 18. It was there that he pulled over to the side of the road again and threw more articles of clothing out the window. He rid himself of every item that might possibly remind him of the incident. He didn't want to take anything home.

Later that afternoon, Ted's paranoia about discovery took over his personality in waves. Like a robot mechanically acting out its program, Bundy returned to check out the dump site to make sure nothing of his or hers had been left there. Strangely, he had the feeling—and half expected—that it had all been a dream, that Georgann Hawkins herself might not even be there.

Retracing his route, Ted recovered most of the items he had thrown away except for one of her shoes. Might it still be in the parking lot where he clubbed Georgann and stuffed her into his car? He had to return to the crime scene to check and retrieve anything that might be found to connect him to the crime. Knowing, however, that police would be looking for someone in a car, Ted got on his bicycle and rode back to that parking lot in the U-district. Ted felt he was completely camouflaged now as he pedaled onto the lot, and that gave him the boost of confidence he needed to conduct his search in broad daylight. Nobody would know him. Nobody would recognize him. But he was in for a surprise, because there were Seattle police cars all over the campus by the time he got there. Just the sight of police in uniform walking around made him nervous, even though no one seemed to notice his presence and there were no police in the parking lot. He blended right into the group of people watching the police and surreptitiously scanned the site for any evidence. Amazingly enough he had become almost invisible, because the police were too busy looking over the layout of campus streets to pay attention to casual passersby, especially an all-American type on a bike. Now Ted had the advantage. He knew almost exactly where he had abducted his victim. The police didn't even know there had been a violent abduction at the site. Ted was able to walk right to the spot where he'd parked, locate Georgann's pierced earrings and the shoe on the ground, gather them up while no one was looking, and ride off. By securing for himself all the remaining evidence of the abduction, Ted had guaranteed that no one would connect him forensically to the scene. It was a feat so brazen that it astonishes police even today.

But the incident still wasn't over for Ted. Needing to satisfy his aching fascination with death, to feed his need for necrophilia that surged over him in chemical tidal waves like a craving for a narcotic, Ted returned to the Issaquah hillside three days later. This time he brought more tools for use when he had finished having sex with the corpse of Georgann Hawkins. Because he was still unconvinced that he was totally in the clear, he took the hacksaw he had brought and methodically sawed through the corpse's neck just below the base of the skull. When he had severed the dried and bloodless skull completely from the victim's torso, he carried it 50 feet up the roadway, where he buried it in the dirt and hoped that he had concealed forever her most identifiable characteristics—her teeth.

As he had done with the arm-in-a-sling routine at Lake Sam, Bundy had again succeeded by feigning an injury, asking for help, killing his victim, and burying her body where no one would find it until he was long gone. Georgann Hawkins had been the ideal victim for Ted. She was in a perfectly secure setting only steps from her sorority house on a campus. Ted's presentation was flawless. There were no witnesses. He had complete control of the crime scene. Nobody even knew a homicide had taken place until almost a year later. Ted had left Seattle by then and was in Utah, and there was no way to connect him to the crime, or so he thought. He had killed efficiently and thoroughly in the throes of his feral savagery and he had gotten away with it. Had that been his only crime, it might have been the "perfect" homicide.

Taylor Mountain

The rotary-dial telephone on my desk had an obnoxious ring, as if every incoming call were trumpeting its singular importance. This call happened to warrant its jarring alarm. It was the radio-room operator and he was very explicit. "You have a found skull off Highway 18. Two citizens will meet you where the power lines cross, four miles south of I-90." What Roger and I had predicted about the Ted investigation was coming true: there was another significant skeletal remains discovery in a different location. We had a strong premonition that that would be the case, but we couldn't prove why. We just had a feeling that the Issaquah site was only the beginning. There were missing girls and women from all over the Pacific Northwest who should have been discovered—dead or alive—by now. Our team's major fear was that the expected body recovery site would be in another jurisdiction, leaving us no control over the crime scene processing and keeping key clues to the investigation out of our hands. We knew from prior experience that another agency's investigators would pick up the surface remains and leave. Our team had developed a unique approach to this investigation, and unless our methods were followed, we were afraid we'd never catch this killer. It was becoming more clear that this killer couldn't stop. He kept on killing and had to leave the bodies somewhere. The question was where. It turned out that some of them were on the slopes of Taylor Mountain.

No ordinary police officer would understand the detail and on-scene planning that had been necessary for the recovery of evidence and body parts at the Issaquah scene. It had been King County's first experience with such a site and our handling of it was somewhat flawed. Were we to have another body dump site to cover, we would be far better prepared to gather evidence. We had learned from Issaquah that there was a pattern established by small animals when they carry remains along animal trails away from the original dump site where the major decomposition takes place. Animals that tugged away a decomposing skull pulled at the remains as the skull was being dragged along the ground. At Issaquah, some teeth and a mandible, as well as the mass of hair, were dislodged and fell off along the trail. We learned that if we searched in logical directions along known animal trails after the discovery of the skull, we would discover the dislodged parts. We also had discovered that it was important to sift through the dirt along the animal trails for teeth, bullets, fingernails, and jewelry that had been dislodged from body parts. Human beings are more than stray bits of fingernail, matted hair, and gnawed-upon bones, and no one took pleasure in this search to reassemble the victims of the mysterious Ted. However, it had to be done if we were going to find the culprit, and this time we were prepared for Ted's next site.

It was March 2, 1975, a typical foggy and rainy Seattle day, and Roger Dunn and I were eastbound on I-90 past the Issaquah site. Eleven miles east of the city of Issaquah was the Highway 18 cutoff to the south, a major Seattle bypass to Tacoma. Because we were rising in elevation toward the gray, dismal clouds, the rain was pounding down hard on the hood of our car. Going south on Highway 18, it is desolate, bordered by woods on both sides; there are no houses, gas stations, or any other buildings, for that matter.

Too Many Bodies

The forestry students from Green River Community College who had found the bones while marking trees for a class project greeted us at the power line road in a fever of anticipation. They led us through a web of wet, slippery branches of vine maple. With every footfall, my still-degenerating knee burned with pain as the branches cracked beneath my steps and snapped back into the soles of my shoes. The foresters had tied red fluorescent tape to tree branches to mark our path. My first thought was that no person would carry a dead body in this far—the remains were over a thousand feet from the road. After what seemed like a never-ending trek through brush, we reached the area where the skull was resting. It was definitely human; no animal teeth had ever had the gleam of shiny dental work that this skull did. The skull lay on its left side, exposing a massive fracture to the right side of the cranium. At least an eight- by four-inch piece of skull bone was missing. As I looked at it, I thought the crack could have been caused by the teeth of gnawing, hungry animals. Soon I was to learn that no animal could have done this kind of damage to a human skull. Aside from this skull, we found no other bones in the immediate area.

I could tell that the foresters had not touched the skull. The previous autumn's fall of maple leaves filled the cranium and a spider's web stretched over the jagged hole. It was lying quietly in a depression in the leafy surface of the ground. No body tissue seemed to be left. I didn't need a forensic anthropologist to tell me that the skull had been there over five months.

The dentition of the skull contained a pattern of silver fillings that were familiar to me. Since September 7, we had gathered all the missing-person reports of females throughout Washington, Oregon, and British Columbia. With those records we had requested the dental charts of each victim. I had memorized the dental work detailed on over 15 of these charts and easily recognized the jawless expression of Brenda Carol Ball. My crude on-site identification was to be confirmed by a forensic odontologist three days later.

We photographed the cranium from all angles and measured its position to two temporary triangulation stakes, which we set into the ground to mark the skull's precise location as it would appear on a land survey. We carefully picked up the skull and preserved it in the position in which it was resting. Roger Dunn and I also collected the leaves and dirt that had been in the depression under-neath the skull, hoping that if the skull had decomposed there, crime laboratory technicians would discover trace evidence, such as foreign hairs and fibers, that might belong to the killer. Since dusk was setting in, we decided to wait until the next day to resume our search for the remainder of the skeleton.

With the identification of Brenda Ball's skull, we did not imme-diately believe that we had made the first major skeletal discovery we had been hoping to find. Brenda's disappearance was thought to be an isolated event that did not fit the mold of abductions such as those of Janice Ott and Denise Naslund or the other five coeds who had disappeared from the University of Washington and Oregon State University. Ball, white, 22 years old, 5 feet 3 inches tall, with long brown hair parted in the middle, was last seen on May 31, 1974, at the Flame Tavern, five miles south of Seattle. She was wearing blue jeans, a turtleneck top with long sleeves, a shirt-style jacket, and brown cloglike wedge-heeled shoes. The Flame Tavern was a topless bar, known for the crowd of outlaw bikers it drew. Brenda, a hitchhiker and occasional drug user, was known to have dated male customers from the Flame on previous occasions.

Everyone thought that Brenda had just taken off for a few days. Her mother would dispel that idea 16 days after her disappearance by claiming that she had never been absent for so long without call-ing home collect. Even so, no one believed that Brenda's disap-pearance was connected to the deaths of Ott and Naslund or to the other missing coeds from the area. Months later, a subsequent in-vestigation revealed that on the night of her disappearance Brenda had been dancing at the Flame Tavern and had left with a Ted look-alike who matched our description of him from Lake Sam, right down to the sling on his arm.

The day after the initial discovery of Ball's cranium, six German shepherd search dogs, their handlers, and I combed the Taylor Mountain site, hoping to find more bones. We met at the intersec-tion of the power line road and Highway 18. Our first mission was to find the marked location of Ball's skull and spread out from there, searching for the rest of her skeleton. I thought I'd be able to walk directly to the site. Unfortunately, a day earlier, I hadn't paid much attention to the markers placed on trees by the foresters. Their red tags were too far apart, and the density of the forest made it difficult to determine where the next one would be. Suddenly, I was lost. The forest was a blizzard of vine maple branches dripping water from a recent rainfall, and we quickly became soaked to the skin. The dog handlers and I decided to split up. We all headed out in different directions, and whoever found the path first was to call out to the others.

I had just walked down into a narrow hollow between two hillsides when I heard a handler yell that he had found the marked location about 25 yards away. The darkened forest was so thick that I couldn't see him from where I was standing. As I began to stumble toward the sound of his voice, an unforgiving maple branch smacked my legs out from under me and down I went, face to the ground. With my hands firmly pushing against the wet, slimy leaves, I pushed myself up as far as my knees. By this time, I was reeling at the pain in my knee again and wishing I had never played basketball. My contact lenses were a blur. As fate would have it, 4 feet from my squinting eyes sat another cranium, obviously sunbleached and clean from exposure to the elements. It had been there a long time—a branch had grown through the opening in the facial bones of the skull. A 6-inch radial fracture extended up the center of the skull from its base. Without hesitation, I recognized the brilliant-white bridgework of Susan Elaine Rancourt, a coed missing since April 17, 1974, from Central Washington State College, which was over 150 miles away to the east.

With embarrassing glee, I yelled to the others that I had found a cranium. I was sickened at the thought of how joyful I was. However, the evidence of another major skeletal discovery was unfolding, and I felt the weight of the world settle on my shoulders at the thought of finding more clues that would help me track this killer. The extent of this killer's crimes was growing as more of the pieces of the puzzle came together.

As the handlers rushed toward me with their eager search dogs sniffing the ground ahead of them, it suddenly dawned on me that I didn't want them anywhere near this cranium. Dogs don't care where they put their paws. Crucial evidence could be destroyed or altered if the dogs ran through this site. A basic tenet of Criminal Investigation 101 was racing through my head: protect the scene. But it was too late. Almost on cue, and certainly by accident, a dog's paw struck the ground and a human jawbone erupted through the leafy surface. I yelled for everyone to stay back, but within a few seconds another dog walked across the leaves and dislodged another human jawbone. Then another dog stepped on another mandible. In stunned amazement, we all realized that a detailed search of the mountainside was required. At the very least, we had just discovered the remains of two people.

While I drove to a telephone to break the news to Captain Nick Mackie, an ESAR dog handler specifically marked the area by running a string line due north of the quarter-sectional marker at the intersection of the power line road and Highway 18. Eleven hundred feet from the corner, the string line bisected the area of the bone find. Measuring at 90-degree angles off the string line, the remains were easily positioned on a diagram:

1. Bone find #1, cranium (Ball's), 1,010 feet in, 90 degrees west off string line number one, 65 feet
2. Bone find #2, cranium (Rancourt's), 1,105 feet in, 90 degrees east off string line number one, 22 feet
3. Bone find #3, mandible, 1,098 feet in, 90 degrees off string line number one, 20 feet, and so on

We had begun to lay out the master search diagram of bones and other pieces of evidence.

I informed Captain Mackie of the find. Naturally, he was surprised and not a little irritated that his lieutenant and sergeant had informed him that the initial discovery of bones was just an isolated incident and that nothing else would be found.

Since it was late afternoon, Roger Dunn and I planned to meet ESAR personnel at the intersection the next morning to begin excavating Taylor Mountain for further evidence. On the following day, this once-quiet and obscure forest was alive with the sounds of ESAR commands and the growl of chain saws our search teams used to prune the ultra-dense forest. We had to get beneath the surface of the last leaf fall because that was where valuable evidence would be located. ESAR personnel raked through each ounce of soil for even the most minute traces of physical evidence. Each branch was evaluated for its forensic value. A meticulous shoulder-to-shoulder, hands-and-knees search of the mountainside, similar to that conducted at Issaquah, was under way. The searchers would sift through over 2,000 ounces of soil per day for five days. Since the Issaquah crime scene search techniques were a model for other searchers to follow, we had prearranged that ESAR supervisors would inform their other teams statewide of them, so that all ESAR personnel would become experienced at these evidence search techniques. By now, the local ESAR kids were more dedicated to and proficient at carefully brushing an area for evidence than a group of excited archaeologists.

Detective Ted Forester was assigned to assist in evidence collection. Several weeks before, he had been investigating the double murder of an elderly couple. When he arrived at their home, he found the house in flames and, with the assistance of a firefighter, pushed the victims' pickup to safety. Unfortunately, the processing of that arson scene ended after a long day and Forester had forgotten about the pickup truck and didn't search it for evidence. Several days later, a newspaper reporter covering the story discovered the considerable amount of blood inside the pickup that Forester had overlooked. Detective Forester was sentenced to five days on the mountain with me not only as punishment but as a harsh lesson in what it takes to unearth evidence. Forester was a welcome addition to our team, since he was an accomplished woodsman and an expert with a chain saw.

After the discovery of the skulls and mandibles our search finds were few and far between. The only human remains we discovered were on the only animal trail that ran along a small creek that meandered down the gentle slopes of Taylor Mountain. About 50 feet from the nearest vehicle access, we found the shattered mandible of Susan Rancourt, over 800 feet from her skull. We surmised that some animal must have dragged her skull into the dense forest, since the terrain was virtually impassable by any human being. About 10 feet from her mandible, ESAR kids found a small clump of blond hair. It was a miracle that this portion of the full hair mass was discovered at all, since the area was full of densely intertwined vine maples and blackberry bushes.

At two P.M. on the third day, searchers who had begun walking slowly at three-foot intervals on a hillside adjacent to the one where we were finding most of the remains froze in their tracks. They had come upon a live explosive charge. As I approached the explosive, I could see another group of unexploded large ammunition rounds and rockets. The ESAR team had uncovered a dumping field created by a nearby explosives plant at the end of the dirt power line road that extended to the east from Highway 18. Employees at the plant had used the forest for their testing grounds. They had been informed we were conducting a ground search in hazardous territory but had failed to offer one word of warning. I was so infuriated that I closed access to the plant until the bomb squad cleared their pyrotechnic litter and our search was completed several days later. The dud rounds were very dangerous and been strewn over thousands of feet of hillside. The last thing I needed was for an ESAR kid to blow off a foot while searching. As if our job wasn't difficult enough, now it was highly dangerous, too.

As the search for "Ted victims" progressed over the week, an ominous scenario began to unfold. No bones other than skull parts were being discovered. Twenty yards up the hillside from Rancourt's skull, we found what was left of a battered cranium. I was shocked that the maxilla, the bone that had once contained the upper teeth, was completely gone. We never found it, despite our intense search. We located her lower jawbone, which neatly fit into the narrow skull. The fracture lines were evidence that this victim was probably beaten beyond recognition. After eight days of searching, we could account for only three skulls, three human jawbones, and a small hair mass. We found numerous individual bones, but they were all confirmed to be animal bones by Dr. Daris Swindler, a physical anthropologist from the University of Washington. So what did all of this mean?

Theories of intentional decapitation were quickly dismissed by our supervisors because we didn't find the neck vertebrae that would have confirmed it. Typically, when a person is intentionally decapitated, the cut is made below the base of the skull because it is relatively easy to sever the vertebrae with the appropriate cutting tool. Thus, neck vertebrae at a site where a skull is found usually indicate that the person was decapitated. For our supervisors, therefore, a lack of neck vertebrae meant no intentional decapitation. Although this logic was not infallible, it was often seized upon by police commanders, presumably to avoid undue fear in the community and increased pressure on themselves to find a "monster." On the other hand, we were confident that if those vertebrae were once on Taylor Mountain, we would have found them.

The most popular theory circulating among the police department supervisors was that the rest of the skeletons were obviously outside our search perimeter. If this were true, however, based on crime scene retrieval experience at Issaquah, we should have found other skeletal parts within close proximity of the crania. But what we learned from Issaquah was summarily downplayed.

My own theory—considered outrageous—was that, for a period of time, the killer had parked the skulls at another location, where they decayed individually, and then dumped his entire load just inside the edge of the forest. The physical evidence, which consisted of leaves in skulls from one previous leaf fall, the growth of the maple branches through and around the skulls, and the lack of any tissue on the crania left me with the feeling that they were exposed to outdoor elements, in one place, where they decayed at the same rate. In other words, they were put someplace else for a period of time and then brought to Taylor Mountain; the killer was moving around the body parts of his victims. It seemed as though nobody in the department wanted to consider my theory seriously—maybe because it gave too much credit to the ability of the killer to manipulate evidence and escape detection. They also probably didn't want to consider what it would take to catch a killer so remorseless that he could handle the body parts of his dead victims long after he had murdered them.

Due to the growing intensity of the news coverage of the dump site discovery, I was forced to set up a line across the power line road beyond which no reporter could pass. Most of the press were familiar faces by now: John Sandifer, Ward Lucas, Lou Corseletti, Dick Larsen, and Julie Blacklow. Over the next year, all would become veteran, self-appointed Ted Bundy experts. I was accustomed to coming out of the woods about every two hours to give them a report. Usually, I really couldn't say much, but I learned 20 different ways to say that we had found more remains. What I didn't want to reveal was that only skull parts were found. The reporters sensed something was awry because we didn't bring many large packages out. I felt so uneasy about this that I started bringing small bones out in large packages so no one would be the wiser. We also had to use different radio codes every day because the media had radio scanners tuned into the ESAR walkie-talkie frequency. It was like a game of spy versus spy. After several days, the search process was beginning to wear on me and I got testy with the media. A new television reporter arrived and abruptly demanded that she brief her on everything that had taken place the preceding week, I blew up—which was very uncharacteristic of me—and I told her to get the hell out and go review the news clips. Then I turned around and walked away.

By the sixth day, I was getting worried about the political aspect of this search. Over 250 volunteer searchers were working the site, a gaggle of 30 reporters was dogging our heels, and Ted Forester and I were the only officers on the scene. No brass! Sergeant Randall, Lieutenant Kraske, and Captain Mackie were conspicuous by their absence. They were career police officers, supervisors in the detective division, and not one of them ever came to the scene. Their absence made me insecure; I began to second-guess myself, wondering whether I was handling the case correctly. The brass were the ones with all the experience. My seven months on this case wasn't enough time to get off probation, the initial period of time during which the performance of a new homicide detective is carefully scrutinized and evaluated. Surely the brass should have some input on the conduct of this huge case.

At about three P.M. that same day my fears were assuaged, if only momentarily. Chief Donald Actor arrived at the scene. *Finally, someone with authority to talk to the press and give me some relief,* I thought. But I would have no such luck. Actor drove right past the press barrier and motioned for me to come over. I asked him if he'd like a tour of the hillside. He said no, he didn't want to contaminate the scene. Once again, I was stunned. I asked him why no other brass had come to the scene to inspect it. He said that he had told them to stay away so they wouldn't screw up the crime scene. I felt honored and scared at the same time. What bombshell would he lay on me? He said kindly, "It's all yours. I'm very impressed by your professionalism and the way you handled the press." Gee thanks, Chief. I was beginning to feel more inadequate, fearing that if anything went wrong, I'd have a walking beat on Mud Mountain Dam. My fear would return many more times, even in the minutes before my last interview with Ted Bundy. I was on my own.

The final tally of remains for Taylor Mountain paled in comparison to Issaquah: three crania, three mandibles, two small pieces of a skull, one tooth, and a small blond hair mass. Not one other remnant of a human skeleton was discovered.

The remains of four women were identified from the sparse skeletal remains we had recovered: Susan Rancourt, who disappeared April 17, 1974, from the library at Central Washington State

College; Kathy Parks, last seen May 5, 1974, at Oregon State University, over 260 miles from Taylor Mountain; Brenda Ball, who was last seen May 31, 1974, at the Flame Tavern in Seattle; and Lynda Healy, who was reported missing from her basement bedroom at the University of Washington on January 31, 1974.

Lynda Healy

The Lynda Healy disappearance was one of the most intriguing and sinister aspects of Ted's career as a serial killer. Lynda Healy was probably Ted's first victim. Had that case been investigated more carefully in the beginning, we might have picked up the cousin of one of Lynda's old roommates by the name of Theodore Robert Bundy. Lynda, an aspiring psychology student, 5 feet 7 inches tall, slender, with long, dark brown hair, was a truly beautiful young woman. She worked at Northwest Ski Productions, where she broadcast the daily ski report for Crystal Mountain, Snoqualamie Pass, and Mt. Baker. She was expected early at work on that morning of February 1, 1974, to give the report. She was a no-show, unusual for Lynda, who had been well known as a very reliable person. When she didn't show, someone from Northwest Ski called her house and her housemate checked Lynda's room only to find the bed neatly made and Lynda nowhere to be seen. The bicycle Lynda sometimes rode the 10-block route to work was still at the house. Because this disappearance just wasn't like Lynda, the police were called immediately and a missing-person report was filed. Later that day, Lynda's friends and family checked her room. When covers to her bed were pulled back, a large amount of blood was found near where her head would have rested on her pillow. Further searching revealed that her nightgown was neatly hung behind the strings of beads that were the door to her closet. The nightgown was bloody also. The clothing she was wearing the day she was last seen, as well as her red nylon backpack, was missing. The clothing and jewelry missing were a pair of blue jeans, a white smock blouse with blue trim, a pair of brown waffle-stomper boots, a brown belt, and a number of turquoise rings. Also, the top sheet of her bedding was gone.

When the evidence was discovered, the police were called back to the green three-story residence. The house was a typical multi-person dwelling in the university district. It had several rooms on each floor, a common bathroom on each floor, a front door, a rear door, and a side door. It was, in fact, identical in layout to Ted Bundy's residence eight blocks away and similar to Bundy's girlfriend's house three blocks away. By car, the house was accessible from 17th Northeast and from an alley that parallels 17th Northeast near the rear of the house. Lynda's room was located on the basement floor, just a small flight of cement stairs down from the side door to the house.

Police officers photographed the front and side exterior of the house, the stairs to the basement, and Lynda's room. They quickly collected the sheet, pillow, and nightgown, and restricted access to the room so that they could look for additional evidence. After that, no further processing of the crime scene took place.

No sign of Lynda would ever be found until her lower jawbone was discovered by the search dogs on Taylor Mountain. I put the very highest personal priority on solving this case and when we finally solved it, we understood that Ted had behaved just like a stalker. Had we investigated Lynda's death more thoroughly, we might have had Ted in our sights a full six months or more before he showed up that fateful day at Lake Sammamish.

Donna Manson

About 60 miles to the south of Seattle is Olympia, the capital of Washington. Nestled in the woods about five miles west of downtown is the campus of Evergreen State College, a nontraditional school where the students could immediately enroll in classes with a focus on what interested them. This was an alternative college where the rigid core course requirements of the other state institutions did not apply.

It was early evening on March 12, 1974, when Donna Gail Manson was last seen walking across the campus to attend a jazz concert. Like Lynda Healy, she was an attractive coed with long brown hair; she was 5 feet tall and 19 years of age. She was a part of the counterculture population at the college, an individual. If she had disappeared for a couple days, that would not have been unusual.

Too Many Bodies

She had done it before. But this time when she left, she would never be seen alive again. Her body would never be recovered. Donna was thought to have been wearing a multicolored red-, orange-, and green-striped shirt; green slacks; a black maxicoat; a Bulova wristwatch; and an oval-shaped black agate ring. Her dental charts would be compared to those of at least 100 female homicide victims over a 10-year period. Ted Bundy would take her body's location to his grave. All he would say was, "She is somewhere in the mountains, the Cascade Mountains."

Susan Elaine Rancourt

The town of Ellensburg is 150 miles east of Seattle on I-90. Ellensburg is the home of the famous Ellensburg Rodeo and of Central Washington State College, often noted as a teacher's college. On April 17, 1974, Susan Elaine Rancourt was attending a meeting at the main library with about 100 other people. The meeting ended at ten P.M., and that was the last time Susan was ever seen. She was another pretty coed, 18 years old, 5 feet 2 inches tall, with long blond hair. She was believed to last have been wearing a yellow coat, a yellow short-sleeved sweater, gray corduroy pants, and brown Hush Puppy shoes.

By May 1974, the precinct squad room clipboards contained bulletins outlining known details about the disappearance of Healy, Manson, and Rancourt, and their physical descriptions, all in the hope that someone would come across them.

Kathy Parks

Two hundred sixty miles south of Seattle, along the I-5 corridor, is Corvallis, Oregon, the home of Oregon State University. In the evening hours of May 6, 1974, Roberta Kathleen Parks, a 5-foot 7-inch 21-year-old attractive coed with long, dark brown hair, was last seen in her dormitory. It was thought that she left to go for a walk because she was depressed over her father's failing health. She was last seen wearing a cream-colored jacket, a navy blue sweater, navy blue corduroy slacks, platform sandals, and silver rings, and carry-

35

ing a brown purse with a shoulder strap. She was never to be heard from again. We found her remains on Taylor Mountain years later.

As of June 1974, four coeds were missing from universities that were over 200 miles apart. The individual missing-person circulars listing the few facts known about their disappearances were only reminders of their shattered lives. No one made any connection among these women's disappearances beyond observing that they were all missing. No one even suspected that the last person they ever saw was the same man. There were no news reporters making even the most casual links among the cases. In addition, there were other missing women, such as Brenda Ball, and not even the investigating officers tied her to the Ted cases.

By July 1974, the whereabouts of six missing women—Healy, Manson, Rancourt, Ball, Parks, and Hawkins—were mysteries. Their last known locations—the cities of Seattle, Corvallis, Ellensburg, and Olympia—were spread apart by hundreds of miles. No trace of the clothing or jewelry they were wearing would ever be found. It would not be until the investigation began into the disappearances of Janice Ott and Denise Naslund from Lake Sammamish on July 14, 1974, that the real investigation into the "Missing and Murdered Girls Cases," more popularly known as the "Ted Murders," would begin in earnest. The similar characteristics of their disappearances were to take shape only after their connections were substantiated by common body recovery sites.

These were the memories flooding my mind as Ted Bundy described to me how he buried Georgann Hawkins's severed head.

2

Grisly Business Unit: In Pursuit of a Killer

A Different Kind of Killer

Seven months of committing murder after murder, each of them invisible, each of them leaving not even a ripple of turbulence on the surface of the water, each of them carried out seemingly without a trace of evidence left behind. This series of events showed that the Ted killer was equipped to survive undetected for the long term. His method of operation seemed flawless, almost scholarly, leaving his hapless pursuers on the police task force very little in the way of clues. Unbeknownst to us, Bundy was practicing his routines for approaching victims almost daily during this period. He was returning to crime scenes and retrieving evidence that would have connected him to the victim. Furthermore, he was reading voraciously from detective magazines and books, gaining valuable information about how police investigators perform their duties. In addition, he knew exactly how the King County Police Department conducted its investigations, because in the early 1970s he researched the crime of rape for the King County Crime Commission, which enabled him to review the actual case files of rape investigations conducted by county detectives. He pored over this information and took steps to cover his homicidal instincts and vicious temper from those around him.

We didn't know who our Ted killer was, where he lived, or what motivated his attacks on women. There was very little, therefore, that we could do about him other than follow what few possible leads there were, even if we were led right down blind alleys or into dead ends. Whatever scant information existed had become our case, and it carried the gravest responsibility that had ever fallen upon the shoulders of King County detectives. The locations where each victim had last been seen and the two multiple-body recovery sites were all that was left of this elusive murderer's trail. A very faint path of possible evidence lay to the east. No visible traces of the killer were left at the crime scenes themselves. But witnesses at the Lake Sam and Ellensburg areas gave some valuable clues that provided an outline of the young man calling himself Ted.

As a result of our searches at Issaquah and Taylor Mountain and our ongoing investigation of the Ted abductions at Lake Sam, Roger Dunn and I were to oversee the Ott and Naslund missing-person cases. We willingly took on those investigations, even though there wasn't much we *could* investigate. We kept these cases on active status in the hope that somewhere, somehow, we would find the facts that linked Janice Ott, Denise Naslund, the mysterious Ted, and the horrible death lairs where their remains were discovered. The whole case ultimately took on the aura of a legend. But the real truth is much more exciting than it has ever been portrayed.

The newspapers said that Ted Bundy first came into our lives on that bright summer Sunday in Seattle on July 14, 1974, when Janice Ott and Denise Naslund disappeared from Lake Sammamish State Park. However, for Roger and me, the Ted case officially started on the following Tuesday, July 16. It began when the Issaquah City Police chief and his detective, both of whom were wearing long, confused faces, walked into the offices of our Homicide/Robbery Unit of the King County Police Department. They told us about these two young women who had disappeared from the same park on the same sunny Sunday, and asked for our assistance. They wanted us to take over the case—their own detective would help us in any way possible—because they didn't have the human or physical resources to investigate the mountains of leads that had begun to pile up surrounding the two disappearances. The case was simply too big for a small municipal department.

There was, in the beginning, an aura of imminent success in the air simply because of Issaquah's handing the cases over to us, the big boys from the "county." It was very much like the feeling we got when we called in the FBI for assistance in a major case. You believe, at first, that you've called in the experts, the "closers," but then you discover that the promises, the handshakes, the transfer of files to a department with lots of detectives signing on and off watch, or intently poring through cases in the squad room, don't catch serial killers at all. The detectives from Issaquah City held on to a lingering hope that Ott and Naslund would be found happily frolicking in some nearby playground with a good-looking guy with his arm in a sling. If this investigation was to be handled without undue confusion and blundering, a more organized and experienced force of investigators was required.

Unfortunately, there was a very faulty notion held by the local police that the King County authorities could put its force of 400 officers behind the search and quickly resolve the two disappearances. There was a basic mistake in all of our thinking. We all reacted as though the investigation was to cover the missing and murdered women cases that began on July 14, 1974. It didn't. In reality, the killer was already at least seven months ahead of us, having snatched coeds from major area universities and colleges as far back as January. Investigations into those disappearances had begun at the police departments in their respective jurisdictions, and case files were already being assembled. Our case files on our missing women would soon begin to duplicate some of the information already being collected in other locations. Together, our material and that from the other missing-women cases were a detailed composite portrait of a serial killer at work, the ruses he used to entrap victims, the profile both of his victims and situations in which they were abducted, a road map of his travels and the ways he disposed of his victims. All of this constituted a valuable resource, but we couldn't use it because we didn't know how many missing and murdered women cases existed in other jurisdictions. The Ted cases had actually begun seven months earlier, but because we were only looking at our own jurisdiction, we had no idea that a specific pattern of abductions of young women with strikingly similar descriptions was under way. This is the problem of 90 percent of all serial killer cases.

The typical assumption among homicide investigators that the first body discovered within the jurisdictional boundaries of one agency is truly the first homicide in a particular series is an incorrect one in 9 out of 10 instances. However, police departments continue to make that assumption, so it remains a constant obstacle in solving most serial murder investigations. When we realized the wide web that Ted had cast, as we expanded our Ott and Naslund investigations, it became important for us to look for similar missing-persons cases in other jurisdictions. In 1974, this was a difficult task because prior to that time, neighboring police agencies rarely exchanged this type of information. Prior to the Ott and Naslund cases, we never spoke to the Seattle police about their missing-persons investigations of Hawkins and Healy. No one made any direct connections to those cases until after multiple body recovery sites were discovered.

A few days after we'd uncovered the second dump site and circulated the suspect's description and his apparent modus operandi, hundreds of police officers in Washington State were hunting for a man who matched the Ted suspect's description. In the beginning, our strategy for investigation was prescribed by how investigations had been handled previously. Cases were traditionally assigned with a parochial outlook and the entire investigation was the responsibility of a single detective. The investigation of Janice Ott was assigned to Roger Dunn, and Naslund to me. As far as the department supervisors were concerned, as goes Naslund, so goes Keppel. Theoretically, anything that came in regarding each victim was given to their respective detectives to pursue and information was not automatically shared.

While we sorted out different methods of investigation, the mystery of an invisible kidnapper of young women caught the imagination of Washington State's population. All of Seattle was stirred and horrified at the thought of what had happened to Ott and Naslund. With media coverage intensifying from July 15 and continuing for the next two months, our investigation collapsed under the volume of unsolicited tips and Ted sightings because we had no way to manage the information that was suddenly pouring in. We were receiving as many as 200 calls a day about men matching the description of the Lake Sam Ted, far too many for one detective to handle, especially the rookie who had been in the unit for only a week. Each day the stack on my desk would get higher. The backlog of calls was so huge that Denise Naslund herself could have called in and told us she was fine and we wouldn't have found the message for a week. We didn't know where to begin chasing leads. Moreover, because of the volume, we couldn't separate the truly valuable phone tips from phantom leads that were impossible to verify. One message would say that Naslund was seen on a train in Sacramento, California, and at the very same time, another would report she was waiting for a bus in downtown Seattle. Which one should we have chosen to investigate? Knowing what we knew by the September discovery of their remains, probably neither one, because all of the reported sightings were nothing more than the work of vivid imaginations of the media's overenthusiastic audience.

Even while feeling overwhelmed, Roger and I came up with some innovative follow-up activities. For example, we knew that several television stations had recorded the picnic activities at Lake Sam that Sunday. We asked to view their film footage. Of course, it wasn't easy. When station managers found out about our request, they had to make it into a major production. We could only review their tapes if they were permitted to videotape our looking at it. Naturally, they had reviewed the footage before we arrived and told us that they didn't see anything of value. Well, their view of an investigation was different from ours. When we saw the footage we realized that the park really was a draw for young women with long hair parted in the middle. We didn't see Ted Bundy, the victims, or women who were approached, but we did pick up an extremely valuable lead in the news footage: other people taking photographs.

Bingo—we had just uncovered multiple possibilities of evidence that was gathered firsthand on July 14—private citizens who took photographs that day at the park. We opened Roger and Bob's Photomat. The news media had kindly asked parkgoers to send us their negatives or film that they had taken at the park that day. We agreed to process and return any film sent in. After sifting through several hundred photos the strategy paid off. One person had photographed a potentially volatile incident in which police were called in to throw some rowdy bikers out of the park. One particular black-and-white photo was taken of the area around the very tree under which Mary Osmer saw the metallic brown VW bug parked. The picture was of several parked police cars with officers in the background confronting a group of outlaw bikers from the motorcycle gang called the Jackals. By parking in the only open lane, the police vehicles prevented any parked cars from leaving. Wedged in by the police vehicles was a light-colored VW bug with its driver behind the wheel. The license plate was obscured from view by a police car, but the ski rack on the rear of the car was clearly visible. Had we ever attempted to introduce it as evidence, a court would probably have thrown the photo right out because we couldn't make out who was behind the wheel. But in our minds there wasn't much doubt. It was Ted. We tried every process known to science in order to enhance that photographic treasure, but were unsuccessful at making it any clearer.

However, widening the circle of the investigation continued to pay off. The most significant breakthrough, thanks to our connection of the Naslund, Ott, and Rancourt missing-person cases, occurred on July 25, 1974. Carol Maher, a recent graduate of Central Washington State College, called me to report a confrontation that she had had with a Ted look-alike in front of the same library from which Susan Rancourt disappeared and on the very same day of her disappearance. Maher, who now lived south of Seattle, had received her copy of *The Crier*, the college newspaper. A composite drawing of the Ted suspect was featured on the front page, supplemented by a story of the stranger's approaches to females and a description of the Ted suspect last seen walking toward the Lake Sammamish parking lot with Janice Ott. The article asked anyone with information to call the local police. So she called our office directly and I happened to pick up the telephone.

This is what she told me. At about ten P.M., Maher was walking from Boullion Library when she heard the sound of packages hitting the ground behind her. She turned around to see a man dropping a few boxes and a backpack full of books. She asked if she could assist him. She thought for a minute that the guy was going to the library, but he continued to walk right on by. She asked where he was going and he said he was returning to his car, which he had parked a little ways away. She said okay, she'd walk there. Cautious, Maher never let the man walk behind her. For some reason, which she could not explain, her guard was up. She noticed that his right arm was in a cloth sling and a metal brace was on one of the fingers of the man's right hand. Also, on his left hand he wore a metal plate that braced his fingers on the palm side, with bandages holding the brace on. He claimed that the injuries were the result of a ski accident. The man had dark brown hair that hung below his ears. She estimated the man's height between 5 foot 8 inches and 5 foot 11 inches, with a medium build.

The man led her across the Grupe Conference Bridge, under a trestle, and right into a dark alley where his VW bug—she couldn't recall the color, but thought it was a newer model and shiny—was parked near a log. He walked to the passenger side and started to unlock the car, when, almost as if he'd rehearsed it, she thought, he dropped his key in the dirt. Maher had already set down the books. Making motions as if to feel for the key with his metal brace, the man asked if she would find it for him. Sensing danger, Maher did not bend over in front of him, but suggested that they stand back to see if the key's reflection in the light would reveal it. Luckily, the key did shine through the dirt, and Maher quickly scooped it up, handed it to him, and left in one fluid movement before he could react. What was it about the eerie disabled stranger that signaled Maher to stay back? And if he did have intentions of assaulting her, what made him resist the urge to attack? Maher's extreme caution saved her life, for that very same evening Susan Rancourt was not so lucky and caught the crash of a tire iron that caused the fracture I observed on the back of her skull. The details of Maher's statement were kept extremely confidential to enable us to use them when we questioned potential suspects and, of course, to protect her lest the Ted suspect return to silence a potential witness against him.

Maher's report was shocking and very revealing to us. We quite possibly had a killer whose method of approach to his victims had any number of variations depending on the environment in which he was operating. It was almost as if he were a shapeshifter who cloaked his intentions according to his victims' situations, the setting of his attack, and the time of day or night. If this was so, King County had never been faced with the threat of such an insightful, premeditated killer who understood not only his victims' habits but the movements and strategies of the police investigators as well. This was a true predator; police departments are not set up to catch these types of killers. As a consequence, most police departments don't want to believe they have a serial killer in their jurisdiction even when the evidence points to it. In the Ted cases, this type of skepticism is what Roger Dunn and I encountered from the moment it became apparent to us that the killer was not only tracking series of victims in different jurisdictions, but tracking the movements of police in those areas as well.

The Homicide Bureaucracy

In spite of Maher's report, many of our colleagues—from other jurisdictions and our own—were still very dubious and continued to believe that the Maher/Rancourt and the Ott/Naslund incidents were not connected. The rigid thinking among some career detectives forced every bit of new evidence of the connection among cases to be proven beyond a reasonable doubt. Since we had no bodies and little tangible evidence, they wouldn't even consider that we had a series of murders committed by the same person. Free thought that included consideration of all the possibilities was not part of their crime-solving methodology. Their work was slow and unproductive. Their lack of motivation to do anything on these cases and their reluctance to believe that we even had a murderer on our hands stymied Roger's and my progress. Nothing we could say or do would change their minds, not even the discovery of the women's remains.

By July 28, 1974, the *Seattle Post-Intelligencer* offered a $5,000 reward for information on the disappearances of the missing women in the Pacific Northwest, but to no avail. No helpful information regarding their whereabouts was reported. Their list included every one of the coeds whose disappearances we were investigating except Brenda Ball. She just didn't fit their profile. For Roger and me, this further solidified our view that these women were never to be found.

While we had a number of leads, our follow-up was producing few results. Until September we were chasing every broken taillight on any VW Beetle we saw, groping for any reason to pull it over to see who was driving. It was not a great time to be a VW owner in Seattle. We pulled vehicles over more than once, prompting owners to carry the business card of the officer who had previously interrupted their day. We also checked out every Ted suspect by showing a photograph of each one to a select few of the Lake Sam witnesses. This turned out to be unproductive. Because we wanted to create a control group to test the reliability of other people and witnesses we questioned, we intentionally saved three witnesses until we positively knew who the killer was. On the other hand, just to test the reliability of one witness, we planted a photograph of her brother among those of the suspects. She treated it like one of the 200 photos she had viewed to that point, not even mentioning it was her brother. In addition, in October of 1974, several witnesses were shown the four different photos of Ted Bundy that we had, and no one identified him. Our questioning of various suspects didn't help us out either. Our inability to question every one of the vast number of suspects would be something we would grow to regret.

Once the remains of Denise Naslund and Janice Ott were identified in the dumping area discovered on September 7, their missing-person cases were officially closed and the homicide investigations opened. The media coverage intensified immediately and the public responded by inundating the department with thousands of tips. By November 1974, my desk was covered with a dense layer of call-back slips, all of which looked exactly alike. There were too many Ted suspects and too many leads to prioritize.

We finally minimized this organizational nightmare with our invention of the tip sheet. The design of the tip sheet was simple. It contained blocks to check which phase of the investigation the particular tip was about—Lake Sammamish, Ott, Naslund, Ted suspects, VW bugs, Ott's bicycle, additional bone finds, and a miscellaneous category. There was also a space for the full name, address, and telephone number of the caller. There was even a free text area so the message-taker could summarize the nature of the information provided by the caller. Now we had a way to prioritize the significance of the call and better relate it to the different cases. This tip sheet was the prototype of clue or lead sheets that would come to be used nationwide in future serial murder investigations.

In December 1974, Roger Dunn followed up a lead involving Mary Denton, another young woman, like Maher and Susan Rancourt, who was approached in front of the main library on the campus of Central Washington State College. To the best of her memory she recalled that sometime in April 1974 she observed a man with a sling on his arm drop his books on the sidewalk. She asked if she could assist him and he said yes. He asked her to carry the books to his car. The man's yellow-colored Volkswagen bug was parked on a dark street several blocks away from the library. Like Maher, Denton was nervous about the stranger. As she reached the car, he opened the passenger door, and when he did, she noticed that the seat was missing. Acting upon her instinctive fear, she immediately dropped the books and ran. She never saw the man again.

The Ted Missing and Murdered Women Task Force

On March 10, 1975, after having spent nearly one week on Taylor Mountain, I returned to the office to learn that the investigation had taken on a new urgency. I was greeted by my new sergeant, Bob Schmitz, who confirmed rumors from the previous week that the Seattle and King County Police homicide units formed a combined investigation of the Ted murders. The now-legendary Ted Task Force had been officially created and tucked away on floor 1A of the King County Courthouse, away from the department-store atmosphere of the police department. The office was a 10-foot by 25-foot windowless rectangular room at the end of an Escheresque stairway that was too large for a jail cell, but certainly as dank. Roger and I would be sentenced to that back office for over a year.

The newly assembled task forced looked far better on paper than it actually was because, despite the best intentions of everyone, its development was flawed from the start. Sergeant Schmitz himself was an organizational genius. However, he defined his role on the task force too narrowly to be of much help. Claiming to have been assigned only to organize information previously compiled and not to supervise us in the tracking down of new information, he was a filing clerk rather than a manager and was quick to tell Roger and me that we were still in charge of the investigation proper. No doubt the case files needed to be organized, but we were disappointed that he resisted taking the role of investigative team leader. Try as we might to convince him to coordinate the operation, Schmitz was very strong-willed and assumed only those duties that he felt he should. He would not go beyond organizing the existing files.

Grisly Business Unit: In Pursuit of a Killer

While it seemed practical at the time, assembling a team of one sergeant and two detectives from the Seattle Police Homicide/Robbery Unit and the contingent from King County was very counterproductive and short-lived. No one was ever clearly in charge and there were constantly conflicting opinions concerning the order of daily business. The task force eventually broke itself into two different groups—the Seattle police, who followed up the Healy and Hawkins investigative leads, and Roger and I, who covered the rest. That might have worked, except that none of us could get away from the incoming telephone calls long enough to investigate anything.

With the discovery of the remains on Taylor Mountain, information about the Ted investigation was the news media's main focus. In response to this increased coverage, over 500 private citizens called each day of the first weeks of the task force's existence to provide information about possible Ted suspects and suspicious circumstances. We were accomplishing less work that would lead to finding the killer because 99 percent of the telephone calls we received had nothing to do with Ted Bundy—unbeknownst to us, all the calls referring to Ted Bundy had been received by October 1974 and had long since been submerged under an ocean of paperwork. In retrospect, we would discover later in the investigation that there was nothing we were doing at that time that would get us closer to Ted Bundy.

By April 1, 1975, less than one month after the beginning of the task force, the Seattle police contingent was reassigned to their old duties, leaving the investigation of the Healy case in our hands. King County reassigned 2 more detectives to bring the total to 10 officers on the task force. This reorganization would ultimately help the task force do the job it had been formed to do.

However, when the reorganization took place, we were still floundering. Our archives of files had expanded, spilling out of our filing cabinets and across the desks. The mounting tip sheets and other police reports had become too clumsy to be useful and were indicative of a creeping crisis that would soon overwhelm the task force detectives. Given the thousands of pages of files and the confused memories of detectives from which most of the meaningful details had long since evaporated, it became impossible to find anything quickly. Sergeant Schmitz continued to organize our files as if he were driven by inner voices, but he was constantly in danger of falling behind. Many investigators had contributed all kinds

47

of paperwork, none of which was indexed for easy retrieval. It was nearly impossible to find out if someone else was working on a particular suspect without leafing through piles of investigative files.

Eventually, Schmitz provided priceless assistance by devising a master indexing system that enabled investigators to find certain types of information quickly. He took all the tip sheets and information about suspects and filed it, alphabetically, by the person's name who provided the information. He created a file for tips that were turned in anonymously and were indexed by the suspect's name. Additionally, he made out 3- x 5-inch index cards and filed them by the name of a suspect, cross-referencing the card with the name of the caller on the bottom.

Now, for the first time, if a detective wanted further information about a suspect, he looked at the caller's name on the bottom of the card and checked that name in the tip sheet file. Schmitz's filing system immediately uncovered a critical time and paper management problem that would continue to bedevil most subsequent serial murder investigations—too many people calling in and providing useless information. One such person called in over 600 times. If we had employed Schmitz's system from the beginning, we would have caught this joker by the second call, preventing him from interrupting our investigation further.

Even though we finally felt organized, we still had volumes of paperwork to analyze. However, the dilemma of how to deal with thousands of names collected during the investigation fired Schmitz's imagination. By mid-April 1975, he had sat in his airless corner monotonously filling out over 3,000 filing cards when an idea struck him. He created what became known as the computer name-matching program. His idea arose out of a gnawing resentment of the futility of the investigative procedures employed to date. We were collecting names, but we had no meaningful way to analyze the weight and significance of the names we had. Thus, Schmitz became fascinated by the prospect of categorizing the numerous lists of suspect names into various aspects that were important to the investigation.

This system gained supporters soon after Schmitz checked it with the county's computer experts and got their approval on it. The computer guys welcomed the challenge of developing an untried application for the computer in the field of criminal investigation. Schmitz then convinced Captain Mackie to assign Sergeant Bill Murphy to the task force to act as our liaison with System Services.

Unfortunately, Sergeant Schmitz had not yet reckoned with the stolidly unresponsive nature of the King County police's administrative bureaucracy. He soon discovered that at least in Mackie's view, organizing the files was not the only duty he had been given. Even though he was doing useful things for our investigation, his perception of his role on the task force conflicted with Captain Mackie's. The captain said he originally assigned Schmitz to supervise the investigation, not just organize the files. Clerks organize, sergeants supervise, and captains rule. So, by May 29, Schmitz had to content himself with an administrative transfer to the Communications Center. He would not be around to see the results of this project to which he had contributed so much. Schmitz would always remain one of my favorite associates since the nature of his contribution to the investigation far surpassed what police sergeants are normally expected to do. Even today, only a few people realize exactly what Sergeant Schmitz accomplished.

The Northwest Missing and Murdered Women Conference

By May 1975, there was a sense among task force members that our Ted killer had moved on to a new location, because we had not had any similar disappearances in the King County area since July 1974, 10 months earlier. We also believed, based on our premise that Ted was a traveler, that our murder cases were probably related to similar murders in other jurisdictions. So we decided to examine the murder cases in other jurisdictions, hoping to glean suspect information from them that might have a bearing upon our investigations. Maybe one of the locations we investigated would hold Ted's signature multiple-body dump site.

With this aim in mind, Roger Dunn attended a conference in May 1975 in Boise, Idaho, that highlighted missing and murdered females from seven western states and British Columbia. All the investigators were faced with a number of extraordinary and still-unsolved cases of murdered females. Fortunately for us, there were attendees from Colorado and Utah who were investigating single, not multiple, murder cases that had occurred in October 1974—the cases of Laura Aime and Melissa Smith—and, from January 1975, the Caryn Campbell case. Those murders would eventually be tied to Ted Bundy, even though a firm connection had not been made at that time owing to the extreme difficulty of comparing the aged and significantly decomposed skeletal remains in Washington to the fresh discoveries in Utah and Colorado. Time and nature are great levelers and make most forensic comparisons like the ones that confronted us close to impossible.

What was most interesting and troubling about all of the cases described at the conference was that there was only one instance in which a signature multiple-body recovery site was located, like those at Taylor Mountain and Issaquah. It was 700 miles away from King County in rural Sonoma County, California. From December 1971 through March 1972, Sonoma County authorities recovered the bodies of four nude females, ages 12 to 19, at this one site located beside a steep precipice that bordered a country road that wound into the woods of rural Sonoma far away from any towns or villages. Two were skeletal remains from which the cause of death had been wiped away by time, and two were recent kills who had been strangled. It seemed all of the bodies were dumped from a vehicle onto the same hillside from the side of the remote county road. Then another nude female victim was found at the same location in July 1973. This surprised the investigators, because the killer had returned to a previously discovered dump site. On the strength of modus operandi alone, the Sonoma series appeared strikingly similar to the Ted cases, but we could not find any common suspect whom we could link to Seattle and Sonoma County. So, frustrating as it was, we had to be content simply with monitoring each other's cases and nothing more.

Lieutenant Bill Baldridge and Detective Mike Fisher, who were investigating the murder of Caryn Campbell in Aspen, Colorado, stayed in close contact with our task force. Their gut feeling, which would ultimately prove true, was that their murder was connected to the Ted cases. Therefore, anytime they discovered a suspect who had ties to Seattle they called us. When we started using our computer tracking system in the investigation, we included in the lists of names all those people who were registered guests at the Snowmass Inn in Aspen, where Campbell was last seen. While we were communicating and sharing valuable information with Colorado at the detective level, there was never a movement at the administrative level to begin a multistate investigation team prior to Bundy's arrest in Utah. This made it difficult for us, because at the investigator level everything was required to stay informal—and nothing was funded. Had we begun a formal multistate investigation, the money would have been there to allow us to travel and to set up joint facilities to pursue the case.

Meanwhile, through June 1975 Roger looked into the many murders in the Northwest, trying to uncover those with any similarity to the Ted cases. He collected 94 homicide reports on unsolved murders of females between January 1969 and May 1975. Entry after entry on his follow-up report read the same—a gruesome account of carnage like what befell Beverly Jenkins: age 16, 5'6", 125 pounds, brown hair, blue eyes, last seen 5-25-72 at 0300 hours in Springfield, Oregon, found 6-5-72 alongside roadway in Douglas County, Oregon, asphyxiated, throat slit, nude, with branches over the body. The body count of murdered females during this time was incomprehensible by rational standards. What was out there killing these young women? The police reports offered little help. Each investigation was as shallow as it was inconclusive—there was no common suspect among them. There was no suspect, period.

Too Many Teds

While Roger was busy collecting cases involving murdered females at outdoor locations, I was assisting other detectives in the investigations of a steady stream of white males who wanted nothing more than to be eliminated from the suspect list for the Ted killer. It was difficult then for any male in his early twenties, 5 feet 10 inches tall, medium build, with dark blond or light brown hair, who drove a VW bug, and whose first name was Ted to have any social life whatsoever. Those same men were getting dubious looks while at work and anywhere else they chose to go. There were hundreds of Teds out there, too many to count. Every Ted suspect we contacted cooperated and opened up their lives to us. Some even called us first because they wanted to be officially eliminated from the active Ted list. They gladly handed over checking account records, credit card receipts, employment records, medical records, vacation travel vouchers, and anything else that accounted for their time. One by one, suspected Teds from the master list accounted for their whereabouts on the critical days when the victims were abducted and were eliminated as the possible murderer. There was only one Ted we were after, and he still remained at large and invisible to our investigators.

While the true Ted hid, Ted serial killer impersonators popped right out of the woodwork. I will never forget the morning I arrived at the office to find five strange men sitting on the benches in the reception area of the Detective Division. There was nothing outstanding about them. All had varying shades of hair color, one was 6 feet 6 inches, and another was 5 feet 1. As I passed by the receptionist, she released the electronic door lock and motioned for me to come around so she could talk to me. She informed me that all five were waiting to see me. Unbelievably, they had each confessed to the receptionist that they were the famous Ted killer.

I invited them all in to a large interview room together and had each one introduce himself to the others. I told them when they decided among themselves which one was really the Ted suspect to knock on the door and I would return to book him in jail. The five Teds each replied that they would return to their therapists for treatment. Their respective psychotherapists, for whatever reasons, had told each of them to confess to the police as part of their treatment programs. This was really great, I thought; not only were we trying to identify the real Ted, we were assisting in the therapy of the entire Seattle psychiatric-patient community. As I looked on the calendar, I noticed that it was five days before the full moon, the monthly astronomical marker that indeed signals psychics, psychos, and those self-ordained with extrasensory perception to contribute clutter and unusable information in the case files. The unusual occurrence was the talk of the task force. I probably just should have booked them all and been done with the whole case.

As months dragged by, the investigation into the Ted cases was pared down. It was simply costing too much for the county to fund the task force, so it was cut back even at the risk of slowing down efficiency of the investigation. The Grisly Business Unit, as we were referred to by the department, was reduced to only a fraction of its former size and was disbanded by June 1, 1975. This left the county's sustained commitment to the case at less than one year. Shortly thereafter, even its former members stopped talking about it.

Roger and I were left alone to carry the flag; even so, we were determined to make progress in the investigation. Captain Mackie assigned us two additional police officers who had been ordered to light duty—one had a broken leg and the other had a cast on his little finger. They were to man our telephones. I was designated the case coordinator or supervisor, but my official rank, for pay purposes, was only detective. Captain Mackie had become so disappointed with the lack of progress by every supervisor he had assigned to the case, he chose not to put a certified sergeant or lieutenant in charge. Relatively little administrative control was needed in the resulting scale-down to a small investigative team, he believed. We reported directly to Captain Mackie anyway, putting him in the ultimate role of supervisor, which was what he probably wanted.

At first, we conducted a weeklong examination of the circumstances within each Ted murder case, as tradition dictated. But that served only to complicate the entire investigation. Realizing this, we changed our methods and began to approach the overall investigation as a united process. Instead of eight separate cases, we had one case that consisted of eight crimes. Now, we asked, what could be done for the investigation as a whole? This, it turned out, would be the only way we would ever get to the bottom of the Ted murders.

Our strategy was threefold and it was roughly based on what two full-time detectives could be expected to accomplish in one year. First, the Lynda Healy murder case was the apparent beginning of our series, and after looking through the case file again, we realized that the initial investigation into her disappearance had been inadequate. In light of this, we decided to start with day one of her case and exhaust every possible lead, just as if we were starting from scratch on a case that had never been investigated. There was the possibility that the Healy case was the murderer's first and that he may have made some mistakes not previously uncovered, like killing an acquaintance and thus making himself traceable.

Second, 3,500 persons were snitched off or investigated as suspects during the course of 11 months. Some subjects had apparently merited packets containing extensive follow-up investigations, while others had seemingly warranted only minor criminal records checks. We examined every file for each suspect to determine if he had been thoroughly investigated. In addition, we decided that those who had been eliminated as suspects would be reinspected to assure ourselves that conclusive elimination procedures were used. It was our gut feeling that the killer was already in our files hiding beneath all of the paperwork. We would later find out that this instinct was right.

Finally, our third strategy, albeit nontraditional, was to continue the effort started by Sergeant Bob Schmitz to use King County's computer to cross-check names from one list of suspects against another. During the investigation, many lists of potential suspects were gathered from various sources. We had over 30 lists, with one list containing over 41,000 names and many others with well over 1,000. Manually cross-checking the lists was now virtually impossible because of the amount of information we had.

This action plan impressed Captain Mackie because never before had anyone offered him a logical, absolutely reasonable course of action for these cases. Until this time, we had conducted the investigation somewhat haphazardly. Owing to the volumes of leads on the multiple cases, we had meandered, wandering aimlessly from case to suspect with no overall direction. What we had now was a method he could understand and for which he could expect weekly progress reports. He was so enamored of our proposal that he authorized us to select a detective willing to join us in our search for the phantom we had nicknamed the "angel of decay." We soon found our prospects limited by our own requirements for the person who would hold the post. We wanted someone interested in the case, but most of the detectives in the department had been turned off by the nit-picking aspects of following up on a killer who had already left the area. Only one person really showed any interest in the job—Detective Kathleen McChesney.

McChesney had been frustrated at being assigned only jobs that the male police executives in the department felt a woman could handle. They had assigned her to the check unit, a paper-shuffling experience at best, and she wanted out in the worst way. Luckily for us, Kathy was no average detective by any means. Her zest for detective work was unending, and she eventually earned a Ph.D.

and went on to get a job as the FBI's top female agent. Her ability to handle the small details and enthusiasm for a difficult investigation helped us solve the Bundy cases.

The Healy Investigation

Roger, Kathy, and I began by turning over every stone in the Healy investigation, starting from day one of the original case. We treated this as if we were the primary detectives on a call that had just come in. The first solid clue we found was the arrest of Gary Addison Taylor for murder in Houston, Texas. He had lived across the street from Vonnie Stuth, who disappeared while apparently cooking dinner in November of 1974 and was thought to have been one of our Ted victims. Vonnie lingered on the newspaper's list of Ted victims until Taylor told police where to find her body on a property that he owned in Enumclaw, Washington, 45 miles southeast of Seattle. Taylor had shot Stuth in the head with a 9-mm automatic pistol. The cause of death was markedly different than in the Ted cases and thus set Vonnie apart from the rest of the victims.

In spite of the differences of this murder from the other suspected Ted killings, Taylor interested us as a suspect since he had killed more than one female. At the time of his arrest, he had many keys in his pocket. He didn't explain where they were from. We immediately contacted Lynda's parents and the owner of the U-district house from which she had disappeared. His name was also Taylor. Was Gary Taylor related? Just one of the many coincidences of this case that was just that, only a coincidence. We retrieved the house keys, car keys, and keys to other locks belonging to Lynda. They did not match the keys in Taylor's possession. Roger eventually eliminated Taylor as a suspect by placing him out of state at the time of our murders. But the investigation into Gary Taylor still held some value.

The matching of a victim's keys to keys found on a possible suspect was an angle into the case that had not previously been considered, and it opened up a new path in the investigation. It gave us the idea to collect duplicates of all the keys that each of the victims would have had in their possession at the time of their disappearances.

Kathy McChesney's first job was to interview Karen Sparks, a woman who had been almost fatally bludgeoned and was in a coma for six months. On January 6, 1974, she was asleep in her bed when the attack occurred. Her memory had been impaired by the blows and she could remember only what happened on the previous day. She didn't recall seeing her attacker. Her address at the time was 4325 8th Avenue NE in the U-district, a stone's throw from 4143 12th Avenue NE, Ted Bundy's residence at the time of the assault. We visited Sparks's residence and noted the floor plan of the house. After seeing it and comparing it to Lynda Healy's residence at 5517 12th Avenue NE, we felt that Sparks was a living victim of the neighborhood killer.

While Kathy and Roger began contacting the former roommates and friends of Lynda Healy, I contacted the Seattle police evidence room to look at the items in evidence that were collected at the time of Healy's disappearance. I signed a temporary evidence removal form for 74-5953, Healy's missing-person case number. Much to my disbelief, I was informed by a stuttering evidence clerk that all of the material taken from the Healy residence had been destroyed. He said that if an owner could not be found and a case was not labeled HOMICIDE INVESTIGATION or marked for court, the evidence was routinely destroyed after six months. Big mistake! I was pissed! I asked if anyone had tried to contact the owner. If so, who? Who authorized the destruction? But I was getting no answers. The file tracking on that evidence was marked DESTRUCTION APPROVED. The authorization signature was indecipherable. Good thing I couldn't find him. This time *I* was ready to kill. Maybe the clerk felt the need to look for a new job because I threatened to go directly to the chief of police unless I learned who had approved the destruction of evidence for an active, open homicide investigation.

As I cooled off, I understood totally how such a thing could happen. The police officers who oversaw investigations were people after all and were bound to make mistakes. I turned and walked away from the counter, extremely disconsolate. Crime laboratory technicians would not get the opportunity to examine the only case with possible physical evidence that could be linked to the killer. Would any of the fibers, hairs, and other trace evidence on Healy's bedding have similar characteristics to anything we found at Issaquah and Taylor Mountain? We would never know.

As I reached the outer door, I saw a pile of plastic and paper ev-

idence bags heaped next to it with a sign above them that read
ITEMS FOR DESTRUCTION. I thought to myself that this was probably
where Healy's former belongings sat before they left the department for good. To this day, I don't know what prompted me, but I
walked over to the pile. Case number 74-5953 flashed at me like a
neon sign. I reached down and pulled out bags containing Healy's
nightgown, sheet, and pillow. As soon as the evidence clerk realized that I had discovered the treasure, he rushed over and laid
claim to it. He said he would have to get an authorization slip
signed by Homicide for me to take the goods. Give me a break!
Five minutes before, the evidence had been destroyed, as far as he
was concerned. Now he had to get approval for me to take out the
trash?

Eventually, after checking out the items in evidence according to
department procedure, I delivered Healy's belongings and the photographs of her room to Kay Sweeney, our crime lab expert. Sweeney
suggested that we retrieve as many items that were in Healy's room at
the time of her murder as we could. Maybe someone had packed up
all her stuff and hadn't touched it since the crime. We noticed in the
crime scene photographs that her photos had been pinned on the wall
above the headboard of her bed. It appeared as though some were
askew and, from the empty spaces, that some were missing from their
place on the wall. We figured they might have been dislodged and
fallen down between the wall and the bed during the assault. If so, we
wanted to process those for latent fingerprints. The crime scene photos didn't show the floor, so we didn't know if there was a rug, which
is often a magnet for the kind of physical evidence—hair or fibers—
we were in search of. As it turned out, there *was* a rug.

Healy's friends and relatives were now the focus of intense investigation. We hoped they'd provide information about suspects
as well as some physical evidence from the crime scene. Under-
standably, the family members were suspicious of our queries,
since no one had been that interested during the initial investigation. They thought we had something since we were asking probing questions. We didn't. We were fishing for that all-important tip,
the one that would lead us to the solution to the case.

Healy's housemates were an untapped gold mine of information.
One roommate who had let Lynda borrow the rug had retrieved it
from Healy's apartment after the crime and had given it to her fa-

ther. He had rolled it up and placed it in a storage closet. Lucky for us, he had never bothered to clean it. So when we asked him for it, he simply turned it over in the same condition it was right after the crime, and Kay Sweeney quickly figured out which part had been underneath Healy's bed. We found several light brown human hairs in the rug that did not belong to Lynda or her friends. We couldn't wait to compare them to control samples from the likely suspect. We felt empowered at finally having the possibility of placing a live offender in Lynda's room.

A different roommate told us that Lynda was not having her period at the time of the assault. This was a key point of information since the investigators handling the initial interview over a year before led her to think that they believed the blood found on Lynda's bed was menstrual blood. If so, it might have explained the apparent police disinterest in Lynda's possible abduction. Because they assumed Lynda Healy was possibly having her period at the time of her disappearance, they couldn't figure out why anyone would kidnap her—they assumed no kidnapper would want to have sex with her. This, as it turned out, was a false assumption and no excuse at all for their failure to pursue the matter.

This same former roommate eventually provided very enlightening testimony after Bundy was publicized as the Ted killer. She had been a roommate of Bundy's cousin, who was friendly with Lynda Healy. Thus, there was a connection between Bundy and Healy that meant that her murder might not have been a "stranger murder" but a murder committed by someone actually stalking a victim he knew. The possibility of a close association between Bundy and Healy was so strong that it could well have provided the means to catch Bundy even if he had not been identified in Utah or a suspect in the Colorado murder cases.

The friends of Lynda Healy whom we were able to contact were also very cooperative. They had not been pressed for details about Lynda by the Seattle homicide cops and had a lot of helpful information they were willing to pass on to us. But it was a struggle at this late date to locate transient students who had been friends and neighbors, because many had long since left the university. Even though these students were difficult to locate, they were easy to eliminate as suspects since they accounted for their time and cooperated fully with our investigation.

Grisly Business Unit: In Pursuit of a Killer

We also interviewed Healy's professors. We found that she was in classes with as many as 400 students. We subpoenaed university records for her transcripts and ultimately obtained the rosters of students from each one of her classes. We followed this same procedure for the investigations of all of the missing college coeds. Those lists of students became part of the lists of names we entered into the county's computer and used to narrow down our list of suspects.

Healy's class rosters became instrumental in connecting her to Ted Bundy because his name appeared with hers on three separate class rosters, two of which were independent study classes with the same advisor. So close and yet so far. At the time we obtained these we didn't notice the coincidence. Bundy was only one of thousands of names in our files.

Next, I arranged for an appointment to meet Lynda's parents at their home. The Healys were extremely cooperative, yet cautious. They were wondering why there should be all the fuss now about Lynda's disappearance and they were suspicious just as Lynda's friends had been. Once we explained that the Seattle police had turned the Healy investigation over to us since Lynda's remains were found in King County, they were more than willing to answer our questions. We explained to them that we were starting all over again as if the crime had just been committed.

The Healys let me go through Lynda's belongings from her university basement room. I checked the photographs that were in the police photograph of the wall in Lynda's room. I placed them in their exact position, replicating the mosaic pattern on the wall as they appeared in the crime scene photos. Finding the photos the police had retrieved from the floor after the crime, I processed them for latent fingerprints and found none. We examined each of Lynda's written records, noting dates and times she was in certain places. For instance, her checking-account records revealed that on the day she was last seen she had cashed a check for groceries at the U-district Safeway store. Much later, after our investigation focused on Bundy, we found that he also had cashed a check at the same store on the very day Lynda disappeared. This raised many questions in my mind. Could he have followed her home from the store? Might he have been silently stalking her for months on the campus as their paths crisscrossed? Might she have become an object of deadly passion for him from the time that his cousin was

59

her roommate? How many parties had they attended together? How many times had he looked across at her during a large lecture or seen her coming and going from their independent study classes? How much and for how long was the image of the beautiful Lynda Healy burning into Bundy's brain? Had they been at all friendly? Had he tried to date her? Had he been rebuffed? Our Healy investigation had helped us out immensely just by raising these new questions about our killer. Undoubtedly, when we received the call that Bundy was a suspect in murders of females in Utah, the investigation of Healy's case would pay even greater dividends and make part one of our investigative strategy a success.

The 100 Best Ted Suspects

Our second strategy for the overall Ted investigation was to review the investigative files of about 3,500 suspects and prioritize the top 100 for further inquiry. We felt that within a one-year time frame three detectives could investigate and eliminate 100 suspects. The first criterion used as a basis to determine who qualified for the top 100 was the physical description of the suspect and VW Beetle at Lake Sam and Ellensburg. If a particular suspect and the cars available to him didn't match, he was deprioritized. The next criterion used was a psychological profile of the offender assembled by a team of two psychologists and a psychiatrist. Their profile suggested that our suspect was most likely a white male who was not psychotic. So if someone snitched off a someone who was psychotic, that person was also placed on the back burner. The last criterion was for us to inspect the specific reasons why a particular person was eliminated. If the elimination procedures were conclusive, such as if the person was in prison during the murders, the person would not be investigated again. However, if the elimination of a name was weak, then the name was brought back for further examination. This was a catchall category that allowed us to sift through the list one more time to make sure that we included all the names of possible suspects.

The inadequate organization of our case files made the review of all our suspects next to impossible. Traditional detective follow-up reports were written in chronological narratives. If this method was followed it would mean that in a 50-page report, any investigation of one person could be scattered throughout the document. One detective might have investigated 40 different suspects, intermingling separate entries about all of them in the same report. We defeated this problem by cutting and pasting all activities associated with one suspect into its very own case jacket. Our offices soon looked like a first-grade classroom, with paper clippings everywhere. But after a week of reorganization, we were able to reconstruct the logic of the suspect entries and assess each suspect's file.

Alphabetically, the file marked THEODORE ROBERT BUNDY was seventh, and when we opened it for the first time since assembling it, the contents were a real surprise to all of us. No one had ever heard of any of the other investigators or the media talking about him. He was initially investigated by Detective Randy Hergesheimer, who had reported that Bundy had first come to the police's attention when his Seattle girlfriend called the police in October of 1974 after she read in her hometown newspaper that female murders were occurring in the state of Utah. She reported that her boyfriend, Ted, had left Seattle to attend the University of Utah School of Law and that she had noticed several other similarities between her Ted and the suspect killer's profile. Ted had a tan VW bug, and she specifically remembered that on July 14 he returned to her house in a bad mood, angrily switching her ski rack from his VW to hers. She recalled this day specifically because they were supposed to go out for a nice dinner and he begged off. He finally relented and took her and her daughter for a hamburger. To convince the police that her story was credible, she claimed to have found a sack containing female underwear in his apartment. She said he was mad when she confronted him with it. Trying to further interest investigators, she said that Ted left Seattle at the same time the murders stopped there. She finally came to the office and turned over three pictures of Ted, which demonstrated the chameleon that he really was. None of the witnesses could pick him out of a photo display of suspects. However, Hergy appeased Ted's girlfriend by calling the Salt Lake County Sheriff's Department and providing Ted Bundy's name to them as a suspect. It would be 10 months before Detective Ben Forbes's record of Hergy's call would prove crucial in identifying Ted Bundy as the Ted killer.

Within Ted Bundy's case jacket was a record of his former psychology professor reporting him as a Ted suspect look-alike in September 1974. Another significant hit! This same professor was Lynda Healy's mentor. Also, an anonymous caller provided Bundy's license number to his VW as a possible suspect vehicle. Judging from the age of the anonymous caller's record, the call came in sometime in July 1974, along with several thousand other calls. Thus, three separate individuals thought it important to call in a report of Ted Bundy for some reason. The information contained in our Bundy file qualified him as one of our top 100 candidates for further investigation.

When the call came in from Utah, Ted Bundy's packet was second in the basket, ready to be pursued. To have painstakingly sorted through every paper in over 3,500 files, prioritized the top 100 suspects, and have Ted Bundy in the group told us our second strategy for investigation had worked.

Computer-Assisted Investigation

To some degree, the third strategy, sorting our lists of suspects with the help of a computer, was totally experimental. Numerous lists of names had been gathered at various stages of the investigation. The reasons for obtaining a particular list evolved from one aspect or another of the investigation. For example, a police administrator once believed that the killer must have been incarcerated in a mental institution and had just recently been released. This particular administrator surmised from the horrible crimes that only someone who was crazy would commit them. Therefore, he ordered a detective to retrieve names of all the persons who had been released from Washington State mental wards over the last 10 years. The detective returned with a computer printout of over 5,000 names. We didn't believe in this theory at all; therefore, we used the list to eliminate someone who was reported as a suspect. Anyone who was on the list was not immediately investigated because we didn't believe that our killer had a recorded history of mental problems. To have supported such a theory would have undermined our fundamental premise that a card-carrying psycho could not have smooth-talked Ott and Naslund out of their lives. In the amount of time that the psycho' would have spent with them, both would have noticed his unusual demeanor and would have picked up that he was not functioning with both oars in the water. In any event, the mental patient list was one of many false lists.

By June 1975, we had gathered over 30 credible lists for investigative purposes, including each university's class rosters that included the victims, the victims' address books, people who were vendors around the locations where the women disappeared, individuals who had received traffic tickets near the body recovery sites and the sites where victims had been reported missing, and many others. At this point, we became curious about who appeared on the greatest number of lists. Determining this information was not an easy task. It was much different than investigating a certain individual, in which case we'd merely look up his name on each list alphabetically.

The police view of murder investigation asserts that it is primarily a reactive process, and that the only efficacious strategy is to proceed along the lines that the investigation dictates. Certainly, this view worked in domestic violence murders, ones in which the outcome was predetermined long before the investigators arrived. But in the words of a prophetic sergeant of mine, "this ain't no fuckin' chicken larceny." We had to employ innovative and risky tactics that were often called for in unsolved murder cases.

Up to 1975, there had been virtually no independent use of the computer in criminal investigations and there had certainly not been any programs designed specifically to catch a killer. We consulted King County System Services computer personnel, who thought a suitable application could be written for their mainframe computer, which was then used only for maintaining payroll records and other noncriminal records. The decision to use a computer to help crack the Ted cases in the Pacific Northwest was indeed a pioneering effort in murder investigation, and, quite frankly, a stroke of genius. The traditionalists of our department looked at us like others probably looked at Thomas Edison or the Wright brothers, questioning our sanity in addition to the validity of our new idea. Our effort was mocked by some police supervisors: has the computer caught Ted yet? But our pioneering efforts soon disproved this naysaying and led us to great success.

From an investigative standpoint, the computer task we wanted to accomplish was simple—give each list an alphabetical letter, A, B, C, and so on; enter every name on that list under "A" in the computer, and run a cross-check to come up with the list of names that appeared on the greatest number of independent lists. This was the "weighted" list of the likeliest candidates for further investigation. Thus, the manifest of lists was born:

A: 3,500 suspect names gathered through June 1975
B: 5,000 mental patients released, 1964–74
C: 41,000 registered owners of Volkswagens
D: 300 campus vendors at the University of Washington
E: 2,162 guests at the Mar Si Motel in Issaquah
F: 4,000 classmates of Lynda Healy
G: 1,500 transfer students among all the universities
H: 600 participants in the Rainier Brewery picnic

When the alphabet had been exhausted, the coding format continued with AA, AB, AC . . . BA, BB, BC, until we came to the end of our groupings. This scheme provided for the addition of an infinite number of lists. In the course of one month, our categories for names expanded enormously, identifying over 30 separate lists, containing more than 300,000 names.

Those lists of names related directly to the activities and surroundings where victims had disappeared and where their bodies were recovered. An examination of those sites proved to be quite useful in discovering possible sources that would help us obtain the names of people who were associated with those locations. We also analyzed the routes to and from both the murder and dumping sites. For example, Susan Elaine Rancourt disappeared after a meeting at the main library at Central Washington State College on April 17, 1974. After analyzing her disappearance site, we identified several sources of names—her address book, fellow students and instructors, people who attended the meeting on the night she disappeared, those people registered for library privileges, traffic citations issued in the Ellensburg area one week prior and up to her disappearance, campus vendors, registered owners of VW Beetles who lived in the Ellensburg area, and transfer students from Central to the University of Washington, University of Washington to Central, Evergreen State to Central, Central to Evergreen, Oregon

State to Central, and Central to Oregon State. We compiled similar lists for all the other victims.

Then—it seemed almost too easy—we simply asked the computer programmers to print out each suspect with the most alphabetical letters behind his name. For example, the computer readout should have produced "John Q. Citizen: A, C, and F," who was on the suspect, Volkswagen owners, and Healy classmates lists.

Apart from the normal costs of doing county business, such as those incurred by holding meetings between departments, this project would also, under the conditions at the time, have to be allowed unlimited funding. No one really knew how much the project would cost.

The creation of the computer's manifest of murder, on such a scale, was received by our critics as nothing more than dubious make-believe. To them the information we had gathered and organized appeared to be beyond the powers of county resources and truly a folly.

The realistic problems for System Services personnel were enormous: programming the computer to meet our needs and, worst of all, keypunching into the computer over 300,000 names on their individual punch cards. Unlike computer technology of the '80s and '90s, the county's hardware consisted of conveyer belts of rolling ball-bearings carrying punch cards to be sorted into their properly located bins. The entire process took over a month to complete, periodically delaying county employees' paychecks for a few hours.

The process was awkward, but the results were stunning. The first command completed by the computer experts was "identify the names with two or more alphabetical letters by their name." Simple request but with a very slow response time of one week. The results were 1,807 names with two letters by each name. The total number of suspects was too many for the three of us to investigate. After the first question, the computer people had already anticipated the subsequent questions and had the answers. How many names had three or more letters with their names? The unruly number of 622 was a smaller number than 1,807, but still far too many for us to pursue on a person-by-person basis. And the last question—how many names had four or more letters associated with their name? The number of names identified was 25, a more workable number of persons whom we would try to investigate within the next year.

Incredibly, and almost with the mathematical probability of two people having the same fingerprint, the computer program identified "Theodore Robert Bundy: A, C, F, and Q." He was one of 25 persons who appeared on at least four or more lists. He was an A,A,A because he was in the suspect file three times, a C because he was a registered owner of a Volkswagen bug, an F,F,F because he was in three of Lynda Healy's psychology classes at the University of Washington, and, finally, a Q because he was observed by an anonymous citizen driving a Volkswagen bug near where two women disappeared.

The total cost of the project was $10,000, a small price to pay for such enormous success. Even today such a project can undoubtedly be counted on to produce high results, notwithstanding the inhibitions of long-standing rigidity toward an enlightened investigation that employs all of the latest technology. The programming time is at most two days and, with a high-quality database, the retrieval time is negligible, only seconds. The real cost today is paying for the legwork involved in gathering all of the names.

The computer run was completed one week prior to August 19, 1975, the date of the call from Detective Ben Forbes from Salt Lake City, Utah. The computer results, which we did not actually see until after the phone call from Salt Lake, caused a shudder of excitement the likes of which I had never before experienced. The entire task force squad room froze stone cold as the name Theodore Robert Bundy came up on the computer record.

3

Ted #7

Until the weekend when Ted was pulled over by the Utah state trooper, the course our small Ted task force in King County was following was steady, productive, and continued to bolster our collective mood. The paperwork was tedious and daunting, but we believed we would eventually find our Ted. Therefore, instead of fatigue setting in as a result of our following too many dead-end leads, our strategy was energizing us. Detectives Dunn, McChesney, and I were chasing down good Ted suspects like retrievers after shot ducks. Every time we left the office we returned with one suspect after another in tow. The parade turned heads in the bullpen with each walk-through. Other people in the building knew something had changed on floor 1A as the tiny Ted task force churned on like a machine. Those detectives who had grown tired of peeking in to check on us suddenly popped in with renewed interest. Even the veterans could sense the growing intensity as our search progressed.

With the elimination of one possible Ted after another, the pile of 100 good suspects was slowly dwindling. The expectation was that eventually we would unmask the real Ted lurking somewhere in the stack. Maybe he was at the bottom. Maybe he was hiding there in the middle. Or maybe he was right on top waiting to be turned over. Wherever his case jacket was sitting, we knew he was there. Our confidence was high because we believed our killer had to have left a trail. He was no phantom. Our gut instinct would be correct.

The Phone Call

August 19, 1975 began as did every other day, with Officer Kevin O'Shaughnessy manning the phone lines. Kevin had been reassigned to the task force because his injuries required him to be placed on light duty. But to us his duty was far from light—he was the first in line for all incoming information on the investigation. His responsibility encompassed answering the phones and obtaining as much information from the caller as possible so we could assess the importance of the new data. In addition to taking the calls, Kevin filled out 3- x 5-inch index cards that cross-referenced names of suspects, names of callers, and license numbers of all vehicles. This system quickly became the backbone of our investigation because it was the quick-reference index to calls and tips. Fortunately for us, Kevin's mind for detail was as exceptional as it was reliable. It was Kevin O'Shaughnessy who took the routine call on August 19 that refocused our entire investigation and brought us squarely to the suspect whose case jacket was sitting right on top of our file: Theodore Bundy.

It was three days earlier, Saturday, August 16, 1975, at two A.M., when an off-duty Utah state trooper on his way home in his patrol car spotted the shadow of a car streak by him. The car had no headlights on. It was late and he was tired, but the trooper couldn't let this one go by. The state police officer pulled a U-turn in his quiet subdivision and followed the mysterious VW as it snaked its way through the dark streets. Then the trooper pulled up to the VW's tail and flooded the inside of the VW with his colored lights. But the driver didn't pull over. Instead, the VW kept on going and the trooper thought he saw the driver dumping marijuana out the window in a frenzy.

Then, the driver simply pulled over to the curb, stopped the car, and waited. The trooper, not knowing what he was going to find, approached the car cautiously. The driver had tried to evade him and had ignored his instructions to stop. Now the trooper had probable cause that a crime had been committed and was going to detain the driver and make a search of the vehicle. First, poking his head inside the window to get a look at the driver, the trooper asked for the driver's consent to search. When the driver agreed, the trooper made a cursory eyeball search. He looked around and noticed that the driver had an overnight bag of tools alongside the front seat and that the passenger seat had been removed. Trooper Hayward searched the bag and found a large ice pick, pieces of rope, a pry bar, insulated electric wire, pantyhose with two eye holes and a nose hole cut in them, a full-face knit ski mask, and a pair of made-in-Spain handcuffs. These, thought the trooper, were burglary tools, and based on that assessment, he arrested the driver, who identified himself as Ted Bundy. Ted was brought to the Salt Lake County jail, charged, booked, and released on bail the following day. The next Tuesday, Detective Ben Forbes of the Salt Lake County Sheriff's Department made the call to the King County Ted Task Force that changed the nature of our investigation and started a media firestorm in Seattle. It was the morning of August 19, 1975.

Kevin O'Shaughnessy answered Ben Forbes's call, following the same routine he did for every other call. He methodically entered the important data on the tip sheet: Forbes's name, telephone number, agency name, Bundy's full name, date of birth, vehicle type, and license number. He thanked Forbes for his promise to send him Bundy's booking photo. Underlying his dispassionate telephone demeanor on this call, O'Shaughnessy was crazy with curiosity. Why did Ben Forbes from Salt Lake County call us about Bundy?

"You asked for it," Forbes told him.

O'Shaughnessy was stunned into speechlessness. He had no idea what Forbes was talking about.

The Salt Lake sheriff had received a telephone call back in October 1974 from Detective Randy Hergesheimer of the King County Department of Public Safety, Forbes explained. This was long before O'Shaughnessy had joined the task force and explained why he was unaware of it. At that time, Randy Hergesheimer had taken a call from Ted Bundy's girlfriend, Liz Kendall, who reported that Ted had moved from Seattle to Salt Lake City, where he was going to law school. She'd read the stories of the missing and murdered young women in Salt Lake—a pattern similar, if not identical, to the pattern in King County—and wanted to alert the police in Utah. She had previously reported her suspicions about Ted to our task force, as had other people, including one of his college professors. From these leads we compiled a case jacket on Ted Bundy, who then was just another one of the 3,500 suspects. Randy Hergesheimer had forwarded Kendall's tip to Ben Forbes, an information pack rat who fixed the notes he took onto a spindle sitting on top of his desk. There they sat for almost an entire year.

On August 19, 1975, Forbes reviewed a case assigned to him via the Utah state troopers concerning the arrest of Theodore Robert Bundy for evading police and the investigation into the burglary tools found in his VW during the ensuing search after he was stopped. Theodore Robert Bundy! A light went on somewhere deep in Forbes's brain. He fingered through the slips of paper on the spindle and found the note he had written 10 months before still sitting right where he had left it. It was no accident that he found it. Like most great detectives, Forbes retained every bit of information he ever received.

After Ben Forbes hung up the phone, Kevin O'Shaughnessey scrambled for the file cabinet to pull the Bundy folder. It wasn't there. He looked around quickly, but couldn't locate the folder. Coincidentally, Kathy McChesney had the file in her wire basket. It was the next up, the seventh of 100 alphabetically organized folders from our cross-referenced list, to be investigated fully. Kathy McChesney was ready to begin the systematic evaluation of suspect Ted Bundy because our plan was to subject each of the top 100 suspects to a thorough investigation of their lives, their whereabouts during the period when the King County–area victims were first reported missing, their relationships with any of the victims, and their whereabouts since bodies had stopped turning up in King County. Ted Bundy might have been just another name that had been buried in our files for almost a year, but our computer picked him out from all of our lists and all of the logged tip sheets, and placed him among the top candidates. Only we didn't know it until Ben Forbes called Kevin O'Shaughnessy to report Bundy's arrest.

When I got to the office later that day, I noticed a tangible difference in the atmosphere. The dogged monotony of the daily routine was gone. It had been replaced with something closer to a buzz of excitement. There were smiles on their faces, mischievous smiles, that signaled that Kathy McChesney and Kevin O'Shaughnessey had something they were dying to brag about. They were onto something. Since the first of June, we had been working on some good, credible leads, but none of them had the substance to make us think we had our suspect. We were still digging, hoping for the piece of evidence that would turn the investigation into a real hunt for a live killer. Kevin told me about the call from Forbes. Kathy handed me Bundy's case file as if she were a kid giving a Christmas present to a parent. I looked at the case file, then at Kathy. The excitement was contagious.

The Bundy Case Builds

Two days later, on August 21, 1975, Ted Bundy was formally arrested again in Salt Lake City, Utah, for possession of the burglary tools found during the search of his car on the night of the sixteenth. At seven in the evening on the twenty-first, while Bundy was still in jail, a team of police officers in Salt Lake searched his apartment. They found a brochure from the Wildwood Inn ski resort near Aspen, Colorado, where several women, including Caryn Campbell, had been reported missing. Police also found a program from a high-school play in Bountiful, Utah. Debra Kent was last seen on the night of that play in Bountiful, and she was one of the missing young women whose story had made the Seattle papers. The Utah missing-persons cases had been part of our conference on related cases in the Northwest, and the publicity about them had prompted Bundy's girlfriend Liz Kendall to call Detective Randy Hergesheimer to warn him about Ted. That was one of the reasons Ted had made it to our top-100 list. The circle of evidence was closing around Theodore Bundy.

* From here on out, the evidence against Bundy began to mount in a terrifying manner. Now police called Carol DaRonch, a young woman Ted had attempted to kidnap from a Salt Lake City–area shopping center, to identify Bundy's car. Ted had posed as a police officer, lured her into his car, handcuffed her, and attempted to attack her when she started to struggle. She escaped, flagged down a passing car, and Ted fled the area. The missing key to the handcuffs was found in Utah in the Bountiful High School parking lot where Debra Kent had disappeared. On September 8, 1975, DaRonch identified Ted's VW. Less than a month later, on October 3, at nine in the morning, Bundy was standing in a police line-up. He had cut his long hair and parted it on a different side, but Carol DaRonch identified him anyway. At eleven that same day, he was arrested for aggravated kidnapping and attempted criminal murder. That's when the story hit the newspapers.

We had just begun our own independent investigation into Ted Bundy's background when the Seattle newspapers ran a front-page story implicitly linking the Utah Ted with the King County Ted. Whereas the Seattle police denied, for the record, that they were investigating Ted Bundy as a suspect in the King County abductions, Captain Mackie of the King County Sheriff's Department refused to eliminate Bundy from consideration. Actually, we had been much further along in our piecing together the Ted puzzle than either Captain Mackie or anyone on the task force was willing to reveal. In fact, we were so interested in the connections among the Utah, Colorado, and Washington cases that Kathy McChesney, Roger Dunn, and I immediately began separate inquiries into tips and information from these different locations that were in Bundy's file.

Liz Kendall

Within a week after the call from Ben Forbes, Kathy McChesney had made contact with Liz Kendall. Kendall called after Kathy had spoken with Bundy's former landlady. By 10:15 that same morning, Kendall sat across from Kathy in the task force office and began to unfold her story. She explained her general misgivings about Bundy and then went into detail. As Kendall described Bundy's movements from Seattle to Utah and between Seattle and Colorado, it became obvious to McChesney why Kendall had first reported her fiancé to Randy Hergesheimer. It was also obvious why Hergesheimer had followed up the lead with Ben Forbes in Utah.

Liz Kendall told Detective McChesney that she and Ted had met at the Sandpiper Tavern in the U-district during a damp September six years ago, in 1969. Since then, they had broken up once for a couple of weeks while he was dating another girl he had met at a mental health center where he was working at the time, but they had gotten back together.

Kendall went on to say that Ted had held a number of jobs, including one at a medical supply firm called Pedline. Liz remembered that she'd been concerned about some plaster of Paris that she saw in his room during July of the previous year when the papers reported a guy in a cast who had been seen at Lake Sammamish at about the time two women were abducted. Liz Kendall told Kathy that she knew Ted had been to Lake Sammamish at that time. He had shown up at her house dressed in a T-shirt on Sunday, July 14, while she was getting ready to go to church. They had gotten into a fight and Ted went home. When Ted returned to her house that evening, he was wearing a gray turtleneck and long pants and complained to her that he wasn't feeling well. In spite of that fact, however, Ted took the ski rack off his VW and put it back on her VW before taking her out to dinner.

Liz said she also remembered seeing a stolen television in Bundy's apartment and stolen stereo equipment around that time as well. She also saw a pair of crutches, Ace bandages, and medical plaster. All of these things aroused her suspicions about Ted, especially after the series of abductions and murders had been reported in the Salt Lake City area shortly after he went to Utah to attend law school.

For the next few weeks Liz Kendall's conversation with Kathy McChesney continued and the task force investigation into Bundy's movements became more intense. He was our number-one suspect. We were in contact not only with Salt Lake City on an almost daily basis as they pursued their leads into the missing women's cases in Utah, but also with Colorado authorities who were investigating the homicide in Aspen. In addition, we were following up leads that showed that one of Bundy's acquaintances in the Ellenburg, Washington, area had been registered in a jogging class with the missing Susan Rancourt. It was all circumstantial, but, for the first time in over a year, the leads were there for us to follow.

Three months into our investigation of Ted Bundy, we had encountered nothing in Ted's history or the pattern of his whereabouts that would have derailed our efforts, so the case was still on track. We were working 16-hour days, following every lead and tip that had been compiled. The web of circumstances identifying Ted case file #7 as the prime suspect closed tighter and tighter around Bundy. At every juncture and with each new piece of information, he became a stronger suspect. There was nothing we turned up that eliminated him from consideration, and the only negatives— people who failed to identify him—eventually turned out to be positives. For every one of his friends who had only laudatory things to say about Ted, we found three acquaintances who questioned his every move. As we inched forward in the shadows of the Utah and Colorado cases, an outsider would have thought we would have been exuberant. Yet we were still frustrated and our patience was wearing thin because even with mounting evidence, we had not made contact with Bundy. Both the extensive news media coverage of Bundy—they had linked Ted to the Seattle cases in their stories—and Bundy's lawyer in Utah kept us away from Bundy himself even though contact with a prime suspect is routine protocol for homicide investigators. Then the Utah case broke open.

On October 15, 1975, after he had been arrested in the Carol DaRonch kidnapping, the Utah police searched Ted's VW and found a piece of hair. This discovery became for us another ironic twist of luck that we couldn't have planned for. Ted had expected the search, of course, because he knew what the police procedure would be if he was caught. Therefore, he had carefully cleaned the inside of his car as thoroughly as any car had ever been cleaned. His shock can only be imagined when he learned four months later that the one area of the car that he'd forgotten about—the long, spindly stick-shift lever of his VW—had wrapped around it a pubic hair from Utah murder victim Melissa Smith, Police Chief Smith's daughter. And in the trunk of the VW, police located and forensics identified a hair from the head of Colorado murder victim Caryn Campbell. How many other clues had been scoured away by the meticulous Ted Bundy? We'll never know, but the presence of Campbell's hair formed the basis for the eventual murder charges in Colorado.

We were still very wary of contacting Ted and his attorney, John O'Connell, because of their aggressiveness in defending the Utah kidnapping charge that had been filed. We didn't make formal contact with Ted right away when he was in Seattle after his release on bail because of the presence of the news media. As soon as Ted showed his face in public, camera-laden journalists were right there to record it. There were actually two primary reasons for our not pursuing Bundy publicly with this kind of press attention. First, there was precious little we could do to get Ted to focus on our questions while defending himself against reporters' questions about the Utah case. Second, Captain Mackie had already gone on record dismissing Bundy as a suspect in the King County Ted cases.

Encounter with Ted

The Seattle Police Department's quick October 1975 denial of the task force's interest in Ted was a clear, although technically accurate, example of public disinformation, but it had a good purpose. On the one hand, Captain Nick Mackie didn't want to give the media a suspect to pursue until that suspect was the prime one. As far as Captain Mackie was concerned, Ted wasn't the prime suspect until the task force named him. We weren't about to name him too soon and blow our whole investigation. Thus, Bundy simply remained Ted #7 until we had all the loose ends tied up. Furthermore, had Mackie mentioned Ted's name as a possibility, Ted might have been far more defensive about his dealings in Seattle than he actually had been. We needed an overconfident Ted, not a defensive Ted, because overconfidence breeds mistakes, and that's just what we needed our Ted to make in order catch him.

As it turned out, disinformation is probably the best way to lure a serial killer out into the open, because serial killers carefully read the newspaper accounts of their crimes. Going public with our suspicions about Bundy would have focused media attention on us. We would have had to have fed the media constantly to keep their hunger for news satisfied, and that would have tipped Bundy to what leads we had and where we were getting them from. Even more important, I was to find out years later, was that in our reluctance to pursue Ted aggressively in the first weeks after he was picked out of a Salt Lake City line-up, we had inadvertently established a level of trust with Bundy that would remain until his execution took place years later in Florida. Because of Utah Detective Ben Forbes's aggressive pursuit of Bundy and the perseverance of Colorado's Mike Fisher, Bundy was determined to give neither man the satisfaction of full face-to-face "deathbed" confessions to all the crimes he was suspected of having committed. He felt these men hounded him and that he was superior to them because he had escaped their custody. However, he did confess to the Caryn Campbell murder in Aspen and to the Julie Cunningham disappearance from Vail, Colorado, to Mike Fisher and Vail Detective Matt Lindvall. He confessed to Detective Dennis Couch the eight murders he committed in Utah.

But our relationship with Bundy was different. We were laid-back, because we always assumed that after Utah and Colorado our time with Bundy would come. We had more background information on Bundy than the Colorado and Utah police did and our investigation actually held the key answers to the entire Bundy case. In fact, even by mid-November 1975 we were confident that we had our man. But whereas we were convinced, proving his guilt in court and convincing a skeptical press would be a different matter. In successive news stories, Ted Bundy was portrayed as the good-looking, aspiring law student and friend to Republican politicos around Washington State. Every time I read that another of his acquaintances couldn't believe he was a brutal killer and that the police definitely had the wrong guy, my stomach turned. If only they knew what I knew.

Finally, the time came when I telephoned Bundy's attorney, John O'Connell. We had to talk. I asked to speak with Bundy so he could help us eliminate him as a suspect in our cases and thus end the media mob still pursuing him and asking about his activities in Seattle. This would be more like housekeeping, I told him, just get this mess cleaned up so he and his client could concentrate on their Utah case. I told him that it would help us, too, by getting the media off our backs. Mr. O'Connell was courteous, cautious, and interested. I wanted to know, I said, whether Ted had an alibi for any of the times when our young victims were missing. O'Connell, a skillful attorney, said he understood and requested that I write a letter with the important dates listed. Then, maybe, he suggested, Ted could "intelligently" reply. Impatient as I was, I thought his request for a letter to Ted from me was just a stall tactic and that Ted would never answer it. By law, he didn't have to provide answers to anything that he thought might incriminate him. Therefore, I kept my hand facedown as well. Fortunately, O'Connell had no knowledge of the mountains of circumstantial evidence that we had accumulated against Bundy.

After a month of waiting for a return letter to my request, I called O'Connell. "Did you receive my letter?" I asked him. He said yes. "Did Ted have an alibi for any of the dates?"

He answered by saying, "Ted can't."

I was stunned by his answer. "You mean he didn't do anything or he can't give an answer for any of those dates?" I asked. I didn't quite believe what I was hearing.

"He just can't answer your questions about those days," the cautious attorney said, leaving any interpretations regarding the nature of our conversation entirely up to me.

I could tell by the tenseness of O'Connell's voice on the phone and by listening to his interviews on television that he, too, risked becoming one of Ted's many psychological victims—people who wanted to believe what Ted was saying even though they had doubts about his story. But even he couldn't get Ted off the hook with us because Ted never had an alibi. Ted Bundy was the only suspect of the entire list of 3,500 that we could not eliminate. Every other one was alibied.

In December we found out that the judge in Utah was permitting Ted Bundy to travel to Seattle while he was out on bail. We made immediate plans to put Bundy under 24-hour surveillance. By now we were certain that Bundy was our Ted, and there was no way we would allow him to snatch a female while in our county again. At first, our stakeouts were covert, but that didn't last long. Ted easily recognized the people following him and stopped to make conversation. After a while there was no point in continuing the charade. Many of our crews either transported Bundy wherever he wanted to go or followed closely behind him. Bundy knew that we were looking for some indication that he was guilty, some behavior that would have tipped us off to his fear that we were getting too close, but he played the game well and gave us nothing.

On one particular occasion, Roger and I were in different cars. We were following Ted while he was driving a green VW Beetle that belonged to one of his attorney friends. Ted led us back to his apartment. Roger had been thinking that the time was right for us to confront Ted to see if he would talk to us. It was close to Christmas and the time of his Utah trial was drawing near. Maybe he would confess or give us a clue that would lead us somewhere. I had agreed with Roger and we took the opportunity on this particular day to confront Ted in the apartment where he was staying. Ted was already inside when Roger and I pulled up in our separate cars. Roger went in first. I was just coming up the stairs when Roger knocked and I heard the front door open. I reached the floor just in time to hear Bundy say sheepishly, "I can't talk to you guys right now."

"We do want to talk to you someday about our cases," Roger said. "Yes, but now is not the time," Ted answered.

At that, Roger gave him his business card and we turned and left the apartment. Roger and I thought later that it was odd for Ted not to have proclaimed his innocence like the other defendants we had spoken to. He was trying to tell us something. He would want to talk someday to his pursuers, but we just didn't realize how long we'd have to wait or under what circumstances that discussion would take place. Unfortunately, his answers to my questions came many, many years after that encounter in the hallway of the apartment building just before Bundy went back to Utah, where he would be tried, convicted, and sentenced to jail.

The Ted #7 Scenario

In the history of the Ted Bundy investigation, the phone call from Ben Forbes has always been thought of as the keystone to the entire case. It was fate, many of the newspapers said, that Bundy was driving along without his lights, was flagged down by a trooper whom he tried to evade, was stopped, searched, and arrested. It was fate that the call to our task force from Utah intersected with our routine follow-up of case files at a time when Bundy could be flagged. Had Bundy not crossed paths with the trooper, he would never have been picked up and the Utah and Colorado murders would have possibly gone unsolved. But for that fate, Bundy would have slipped through our net and our missing and murdered women's cases would never have been solved. Bundy would never have escaped from the Colorado courthouse where he was being tried and he never would have fled to Florida. But for fate, Bundy might still be alive today, invisible and menacing. It was fate, they say, that caught up with Bundy on that night in a Salt Lake City suburb.

It's true that although the phone call from Ben Forbes was indeed vital to our case, the big question actually was: would we have identified Ted Bundy as the Ted killer without the phone call? I've often speculated about that, and here's what would have happened, inasmuch as the Bundy file was next on our "to be investigated" list, had there been no phone call from Salt Lake City. Call it the *Twilight Zone* scenario.

We were struggling with an investigation with many murder suspects and without much firm evidence on any of them. Each investigation of a suspect followed its own unique course with each individual. Each of the suspects' willingness to cooperate with the task force provided us with the specific details or alibis that put them in the precise places where the killer could not have been at the critical times when crimes were being committed. However, while we were eliminating suspects one by one through our investigation, the same process also told us that the real killer had to have a trail that we would eventually cross. If every other suspect had left a path, the real killer could not possibly have been a phantom. At the same time, with the closure of each new file, the intensity of the investigation also diminished. We had gotten to the point where we were accumulating just enough information to take another suspect off the list. One suspect would look good for a while, then, as Roger Dunn liked to put it, "he'd look just like shit in a handbasket."

The routine of following up 100 suspects, one after the other, over the long term was almost like a mind-numbing disease. If you weren't careful, the monotony was debilitating; you could easily miss a key element to the entire investigation. It was also tempting to take the easy way out: minimal work, tell yourself you'd done enough to close the folder, and move on to the next file. There was no inspector's manual for dealing with these things. You just had to navigate into the fog by dead reckoning and hope that you found the right markers before they slipped by you in the night.

Ted Bundy's case file was #7. It was sitting in Kathy McChesney's to-do basket when I walked into the task force office on August 19. On the Saturday night before, unbeknownst to any of us, Ted Bundy drove by a Utah state trooper who, by the time he made his U-turn, lost the VW after it turned onto one of the side streets of the subdivision. The trooper was tired, and after a fruitless search down three or four streets, decided his quarry had disappeared and headed home. Bundy drove back to his apartment and went to bed. There was no phone call from Ben Forbes by the time I walked into the office and noticed the file marked BUNDY and picked it up.

I looked down at the legal-size case file in the wire basket and opened it. The contents of Ted's manila folder had the appearance of severe disorder: several tattered tip sheets, handwritten notes on small pieces of torn paper, and photographs in small envelopes stashed inside. Initially Hergy had been tipped off by this Ted's girlfriend, Liz Kendall, and a few other callers. I now had to follow up on Hergy's investigation, to trace the steps he took, to see whether those steps could eliminate Ted #7, Theodore Robert Bundy.

I found the file full of unworked leads as if Hergesheimer had taken the information and simply not followed it up. The information from each caller had been recorded, but the nature of the call itself seemed not to have piqued the interest of the officers who had taken the call. What had gone wrong? Had Hergesheimer simply misjudged the importance of the calls, which was not typically his wont, or was there something else at work? As I looked more closely at the file, I realized that if this case file had not made it onto our top-100-Teds-of-all-time list, I might well have passed it by myself, because at first glance the callers' information didn't seem that vital. One thing was certain: had Hergy been made aware of the connections between Taylor Mountain and Issaquah, he would have jumped all over the information he'd received. But by the time he'd gotten the information in October 1974, no one had even thought to connect the seven cases.

Four photos of Ted Bundy were in the file. The only way I knew they *were* Ted Bundy was because the captions *read* TED BUNDY. At first glance, the photos could have been of four different people. He was a real chameleon, this guy, whoever he was. We had no current photos of Bundy, so I couldn't immediately rely on showing his picture to the witnesses at Lake Sammamish. Two of the snapshots were taken by his girlfriend in 1972, and he was wearing a beard in a 1973 shot. His driver's license photo depicted a much older-looking man.

The information in Ted Bundy's file came from three primary sources. The first, probably only because it was already in the file before his fiancée's lead, was from an anonymous person who reported Ted's license tag, Ida-Boy-Henry-Six-Twenty-One. I could see that someone had worked this tip after the initial call came in. He ran the tags through the Department of Motor Vehicles (DMV) to get the name Ted Bundy, the make on his car, and his address at the time. Then he ran the name Ted Bundy through the Department of Licensing to get a date of birth. Hergy had gotten the driver's license photo himself even though the handwriting on the tip sheet belonged to someone else. The unknown officer who worked this information soon broke off his follow-up because that tip, by itself, didn't merit a high priority. There were hundreds of registered owners of VW Beetles who were named Ted.

The second Ted Bundy tip source came from one of Bundy's psychology teaching assistants, Joel Kast, whose call proved to be a critical lead. Kast called initially to report spotting a police composite sketch Ted look-alike. A Ted Bundy, one of his former students, looked remarkably like the police sketch that had appeared in the papers. Kast said that his Ted was a good student, personable, had a possible accent, and had taken a class in abnormal psychology. Although Kast had no way of predicting Ted Bundy's violent tendencies, his tip put one immediate fact in the file that struck a resonant chord in my memory. One of the living witnesses to the Lake Sammamish abductions reported that the Ted who had chatted her up spoke with what seemed like a British accent. And it was from the Lake Sammamish descriptions that we developed the police composite sketch. This would have been an important lead to follow in our investigation of Ted #7.

Following just that lead, I would have checked with the university registrar for a printout of all of Ted #7's classes. I would have routinely cross-checked this list with the lists of classes that the coed victims at the University of Washington had taken and, to my amazement, I would have found that Bundy, our Ted #7, and Lynda Healy had shared several psychology classes together. A Ted victim and a top 100 Ted in a class at the same time—that's where their paths surely would have crossed initially. Thus, from that information alone, Bundy would have become my prime suspect. We would have found Bundy's name and Healy's name on other class lists, and suddenly one of the basic theories of homicide would come into play—that people are usually murdered by someone they knew.

Other pieces would fall into place immediately, too. For example, Lynda Healy was the "first" victim, according to our investigative model. We were already following up her homicide as if it were a routine murder case on its own. Thus, the fact that she was in the same class with someone whose description matched a police composite of a suspect in other murders would have brought us to Ted via her case and not just through the case file folders sitting in the task force office. Also, as we pursued her list of acquaintances, we would have found other items that brought her into Bundy's circle of acquaintances. We would have considered the crossing of their paths much more than mere coincidence as we pursued our leads.

The third source in Bundy's file was his girlfriend Liz Kendall. Her call and subsequent persistence led Randy Hergesheimer to notify Utah authorities because Liz knew Ted had moved to Salt Lake City to go to law school at the same time that surrounding jurisdictions were reporting a string of female murder cases. She believed that these cases shared aspects of the King County cases. What Liz didn't know was that we had already exchanged information with Utah and Colorado detectives and knew about all the female murders, especially the murder of Caryn Campbell in Aspen on January 12, 1975. But Liz provided us help with a valuable lead in this homicide investigation as well.

We had already used store credit card and gasoline credit card purchases as a method of eliminating other suspects, so it would have been logical to assume that we would have used Bundy's credit purchase records in the same way. Liz Kendall would tell us about Ted's Chevron and Nordstrom's credit cards and we would have retrieved his records. From Chevron security, we would learn quickly that Ted made prolific use of his credit card because he was forever buying gas. We would note that Ted seemed extremely paranoid about running out of gas. In fact, his record showed that he had always been topping off his tank with purchases as small as $1.88 on the very days surrounding the murders in Washington State. I would have noticed that there were numerous instances when Ted charged his gasoline on many of the days the women were killed, the days before they were abducted, and the days immediately after the murders. One conspicuous purchase, I would have noticed, took place at a gas station only minutes from Aspen in Glenwood Springs, Colorado, on January 12, 1975—the exact day and precise location of the Campbell murder. Bundy's credit records also placed him right near the ski resort at Vail on March 15, 1975, when Julie Cunningham disappeared. During a lifetime of police investigations you learn that these coincidences just don't happen. Our Ted #7 had been all of these places for a reason.

The search through Bundy's credit records would have been quick and invisible. Ted would never have known that we had pulled copies of his credit transactions because we would not have been required to notify him. Liz Kendall certainly would not have told her boyfriend that she had snitched him off to the King County task force and the Utah authorities. Utah investigators would have regarded him as a viable suspect because not only did his credit records not eliminate him from any of the Washington murders, they actually placed him near the scenes of the Utah and Colorado murders on or near the days they were committed. However, because Ted was already in their jurisdiction and would have been unaware of all the police activity surrounding him, he probably would not have acted defensively and might have actually done something to incriminate himself—like trying to abduct someone like Carol DaRonch. Therefore, believing that any aggressive move on their part might have spooked someone against whom a homicide case was being constructed in three states, the Utah police would not have wanted to move too quickly against Ted and would have probably put him under surveillance.

We would have checked Ted's bank records and would have found even more surprises. Bundy's checking account records showed that he had cashed checks at the Safeway food store at 47th and Brooklyn in the heart of the U-district only eight blocks from Lynda Healy's residence on the date that she disappeared. We were also checking Healy's bank records because we were pursuing her murder as if it were a separate crime. In so doing, we found that she had cashed a check at the very same Safeway store on the very same day and at the very same time as did Ted. We contacted the clerk whose initials were on the check and asked her to tell us how long she worked that day. Only four hours, she told us, so the window of opportunity for Ted was very small. If they were both in the same store at the same time, could Ted Bundy have actually been stalking Lynda Healy that very day, keeping her in sight from food aisle to food aisle or standing behind her in a checkout line, dogging her footsteps from a safe distance along streets crowded with students and waiting for the right opportunity to abduct her?

What exactly was the connection between Bundy and Healy? We knew they were in the same classes. We knew that they were in the same store cashing checks at the same time on the day she disappeared. How long had Bundy been interested in Lynda Healy? Our search through the Bundy file would have continued, especially as it related to his connection to Healy. We would have discovered from the list of Bundy's acquaintances that his cousin had been a roommate of Lynda Healy's housemate, part of an extended tribe of friends and housemates that are typical of relationships in a large college town like Seattle. We would have realized that, of course, Ted knew Lynda Healy. They'd attended the same classes, sat in the same independent study sections, and had probably been at parties together. They would have encountered each other time and again as their paths kept on crossing. Unfortunately, Lynda didn't know that the Ted who might or might not have said hello to her as they met outside a classroom or in the Safeway wasn't really a casual acquaintance but a stalker—she was his intended victim. We don't even know now how long Ted thought about Lynda before he decided to break into her basement apartment, knock her unconscious as they struggled against the wall of her bed, carefully undress her as she lay there in a pool of blood, and hang her nightgown neatly in her closet, wash her hair, dress her in her ski jacket and pants, and then take her with him into the night. No matter what we discovered about the other missing-and-murdered-coed cases, it would have been clear that in the Lynda Healy case, Ted was by far the most viable suspect we had. We would have pursued the investigation aggressively while letting the Utah and Colorado authorities continue their observation of Bundy. The net would have begun to close.

The leads Liz Kendall gave us in the folder would have required another interview with her for background information. She would describe Ted's behavior on July 14, 1974, the Sunday when Janice Ott and Denise Naslund disappeared from Lake Sammamish. Liz and Ted had fought that morning and Ted had gone home. But when Ted had returned to her place at six in the evening, the first thing he had done was to move a ski rack that was on his VW Beetle to her VW Beetle. This detail would have interested us because Ted had originally moved the ski rack from her car to his so that he could carry his bike with him on a trip to Eastern Washington weeks earlier. How convenient! This meant that Ted already knew how to strap a bike to the ski rack with little trouble. If we had had any lingering questions about what happened to Janice Ott's 10-

speed bike on the day of her abduction from the park, this detail would have gone a long way to resolve them.

Liz would have told us about Ted's mood on the night of the fourteenth. He was a moody person, she said, despite his personable demeanor. Liz would have said that they had planned to go out for dinner, but when Ted showed up, he was bristling with hostility. He announced that he wasn't taking Liz and her daughter out to dinner. Then he had relented and driven them out for burgers. He had been angry about something, but he had been trying to get over it. It was part of his typical behavior, which ran hot and cold. It was as mysterious as the crutches Liz would have told us that she found in his room in May or June, 1974. She had also seen the plaster of Paris and would have told us about his ability to get medical supplies from the company he worked for. He delivered prosthetic devices to their clients. It was circumstantial, at best, but these medical devices were also the implements our killer used for camouflage and were key in the ruses he used to lure his victims.

And then there was the bag of women's underwear that Liz discovered in Ted's room in 1973. We had not been called in yet and the Ted task force was a year away from its inception. The Seattle police weren't even investigating missing or murdered women at that time. So whose clothing was in that bag? Were these the souvenirs from nameless women whom Ted had taken from places other than Seattle? Were there still scores of unsolved missing-persons cases from jurisdictions that we didn't even know about? If Ted was already a serial killer in 1973, was this his bag of totems that he pulled from the bodies of his dead victims? Liz hadn't known what she'd discovered, but by the time she reported it to the task force, it would have been enough for us to build a real case against Ted Bundy.

Liz provided another vital piece of the Ted Bundy puzzle for us when she linked Ted's travels to Central Washington State College and the disappearance of Susan Rancourt. She told us that Ted had a friend who attended Central. We very quickly made contact with that friend, who told us that about a week before Rancourt was reported missing, Ted was in Ellensburg visiting him. At that same time, the first woman was approached in front of the school's library and ran away when the Ted she was helping dropped his keys in the dirt beside his VW.

Within days of the Kendall interview and our follow-up on her leads, we would have been very encouraged by the Ted Bundy file. Not only could Ted be placed at Ellensburg, but he was clearly cross-ing paths with Lynda Healy to the point where he could have been stalking her. In this way, all of our separate investigations into the Washington State activities of Ted Bundy would have intersected. Moreover, he was in Utah and Colorado at just the right times, and nothing in his gasoline credit card records put him in a spot where he would not have been able to commit any of our homicides. In a cir-cumstantial case such as this, suspects who were purely coincidental would have been eliminated by this point, as the previous six had been. For *all* paths to have led to a suspect, even if they were circum-stantial, that suspect had to have a very high probability as the prime suspect. We knew that Ted was our man; we just had to make the case.

Since Ted was attending the University of Utah School of Law, our next strategy was to contact those agencies that had open cases of murders of females in both Utah and Colorado. It would have taken very little convincing to get Salt Lake to assemble an informal multistate task force on their dime and to have covertly staked out Bundy. Ideally, they would have wanted to gather firsthand infor-mation about his movements, and observe him as he rehearsed his crime or stalked his prospective victim. Maybe they'd even catch him with the evidence, as police had caught the Freeway Killer—Randy Kraft—in Southern California with a body in his car. In any event, his predatory travels could have been monitored—speculat-ing on the basis of Ted's propensity to drive and return to his crime scenes—and he might have actually led police to the body of a mur-dered female decomposing at one of his burial sites.

Even if the surreptitious surveillance would have failed to catch him in the act of a crime, the mounting circumstantial evidence al-ready available would have provided the probable cause for a judge to issue a search warrant for his apartment and VW Beetle. They would have served the search warrant without any prior warning. Ted Bundy would have had no chance to prepare by removing evi-dence from his apartment or by scouring out the inside of his car. Searchers would have most certainly found an abundance of foren-sic evidence in the car that had been used to transport over 25 vic-tims from pick-up locations to dump sites for at least two years.

Using the same circumstantial evidence that provided them with the probable cause for a search of Bundy's car, investigators would have searched Bundy's apartment, where they would have found more than a map of Colorado and the ski brochure with the circled name of the Wildwood Inn. They would probably have found much more. Because Ted sometimes took a whole corpse home with him, instead of just the heads as he did in Washington, the police might have discovered an entire body in his apartment. In a Jeffrey Dahmer–like police seizure of human remains, the evidence would have sealed Bundy's fate right on the spot. Not even the bravado-driven Bundy would have been able to bluff his way out of that kind of discovery.

At the point of the search of his apartment, Bundy would have been interviewed by the Utah police. At first, Bundy would exert complete control with as much boldness as he could muster. Bundy was a blowhard and, as he always did when challenged, he would try to bully his way out of any confrontation. By the time of the interview, Bundy would have been well aware that he was a suspect in some sort of investigation, and he would assume that the police had connected him to the murders in Utah. However, the police would have the advantage of surprise with respect to the Colorado murders, especially in light of the discovery of Caryn Campbell's hair in the trunk of Ted's VW. But Bundy had great self-confidence as a killer and he would have resisted all attempts to get him to confess.

The police would have confronted him with their strongest circumstantial evidence. He would have provided them with alibis. They would have confronted him with the handcuff key they discovered in the Bountiful parking lot. He would have denied any knowledge of the handcuff key even though they fit the handcuffs in his car. Standard handcuffs and standard locks, Bundy would have said, don't automatically make a matched set. This would have gone back and forth until the police brought Bundy in for a line-up. Carol DaRonch would have identified him and Bundy would have been arrested. At the same time I would have presented my evidence against Bundy to the prosecutor and would have gotten a charge for murder in the first degree in the case of Lynda Healy. I would have sought additional indictments in the cases of Susan Rancourt, Janice Ott, and Denise Naslund even though I would have had weaker cases. But nonetheless, my indictments and the indictments in Utah and Colorado as a result of a multistate task force investigation on kidnap and murder charges would have been enough to have kept Bundy behind bars the entire time.

Whether Bundy would have been able to escape from the Colorado courthouse and flee across the country, as he did in reality, is a matter of pure conjecture. But with the information on Ted's movements I had gathered from the Lynda Healy investigation, I believe we could have mounted a stronger case against him in the other jurisdictions as well. Therefore, who can say what might have happened had Bundy not been caught by the Utah state trooper? Can it be argued that, arrested unaware and caught off guard, he most likely would have never escaped custody in Colorado? Can the case actually be made that, had Ted Bundy managed to escape the trooper that night, no phone calls would have been made between Utah and Seattle and, perhaps with Ted sitting in a Seattle jail instead of a lockup near Aspen, his escape to Florida would never have happened and Lisa Levy, Margaret Bowman, and Kimberly Leach might still be alive today? It is all pure speculation.

History Plays Out

As it turned out, Ted Bundy was tried and convicted in Utah in 1976 for the aggravated kidnapping of Carol DaRonch and in July was sent to a Utah state prison. That should have taken care of him for a long time, but his troubles with other agencies weren't over yet. In October of 1976, he was charged with the murder of Caryn Campbell at the Wildwood Inn in Aspen, Colorado. In January 1977, Bundy was taken into custody by Mike Fisher from Colorado and transported to the Glenwood Springs jail, where he would be held during his trial in Aspen. Ted escaped from the Pitkin County Courthouse in Aspen in June, was recaptured within the week, and escaped again six months later on New Year's Eve. This time, Bundy made his break through a hole that he had sawed in the ceiling of his cell. He made it out of the jailhouse, stole an old MG, which broke down, got a ride to Vail, took a bus from Vail to Denver, and then caught an early flight from Denver to Chicago. Bundy had propped up clothing under a blanket to make it seem as if he were still on his cot and thus managed to fool his guards until noon on January 1, 1978. Then the news of his escape was flashed to major cities. Ted saw the television bulletin of his escape while he was staying at the Ann Arbor, Michigan, YMCA. He was running out of money and was getting desperate, so he stole a car and headed south for warm weather.

Bundy wound up in Atlanta, where he discarded the car and caught a bus for Tallahassee, Florida. He rented a room at a rooming house called The Oaks near the Chi Omega sorority house at Florida State University. On January 15, at about two in the morning, just two weeks after his escape from Colorado, Bundy snuck into the Chi Omega house and bludgeoned Lisa Levy and Margaret Bowman to death and injured Karen Chandler and Kathy Kleiner. Ted was spotted by sorority member Nita Neary as he was coming down the stairs, club in hand. Two and a half hours later and five blocks away, Bundy attacked again. He broke into Cheryl Thomas's house but fled before he could kill her. For the next two or so weeks, he went on a rampage of stealing credit cards, cash, and cars, and driving around Florida in a desperate attempt to elude the police.

Then, on the morning of February 9, 1978, he spotted a 12-year-old girl walking behind a building at her junior high school in Lake City, Florida. At about five minutes to nine, paramedics passing by spotted a man leading a young girl away by the arm. Later, they would identify the man as Bundy and the girl as Kimberly Leach. It was the last time anyone would see Kimberly alive. She would be discovered in April 1978 at a dump site Bundy used 32 miles out of Lake City.

Between February 9 and February 13, when he was arrested in Pensacola, Florida, a desperate and disoriented Ted Bundy was on the run. He was out of money; people had reported the credit cards he had stolen and police had been alerted to the vehicles he had stolen as well.

Finally, police arrested Bundy in Pensacola wearing the same torn shirt he had worn when he killed Kimberly Leach. Fibers from his shirt were later matched to fibers at the crime scene. For the next three days, Bundy was held in jail while the Florida authorities were unaware of Bundy's identity as well as his role in the Chi Omega murders in Tallahassee. At eight P.M. EST, the evening of February 16, 1978, the day he was identified as Ted Bundy, he placed a call to his former girlfriend Liz Kendall.

When I interviewed Liz about that phone call five days later, she described how Ted almost, but not quite, admitted to having something to do with the disappearances of the young women at Lake Sammamish, the event that had brought me into this case. This was the closest he would come to anything even resembling an admission to murder in the state of Washington until he and I began communicating.

I would have to wait another six years to reopen the cases while Bundy was tried, convicted, and sentenced to the electric chair in Florida for the deaths of Lisa Levy, Margaret Bowman, and Kimberly Leach. At the point of his conviction and sentencing, I had assumed that the story of Ted Bundy would end in Florida. Fate, however, had charted a very different course.

4

The Splash Heard 'Round the World

The excitement of being part of the task force and chasing Bundy had all but died away by early 1981. I had returned to the daily routine of homicide investigations. My Bundy cases were as silent now as the hillsides of Taylor and Issaquah mountains in the dead of winter and Ted was neatly tucked away on death row at the Florida State Penitentiary. We were busy investigating several intriguing murders in a row that were difficult, yet solvable. They weren't smoking guns, so we weren't required to charge off through a crowded shopping mall in hot pursuit of a homicidal maniac who was frothing at the mouth. These were cases that challenged our methods of deduction and required us to be imaginative if we were to be successful. I relished working those types of cases and when we broke them, the excitement we generated spread to all of the many police officers involved. Those cases enhanced my belief that practical experience was the main way to develop a detective's nose for choosing the right lead to pursue.

The Bundy investigation had taught me important lessons in patience and provided me with the ability to develop leads from what looked like less than nothing. Moreover, having investigated a long-term unsolved case at the beginning of my career, I didn't have the expectation of the "24-hour solution" that many homicide detectives have. My attitude was that the job should be done right—investigators should proceed deliberately, intelligently, and thoroughly. Long-term investigations gave me the opportunity to deduce in a logical manner and in relative quiet what step to take next. The rush-rush attention of police supervisors for a quick resolution in the pressure cooker of public scrutiny had usually subsided by the time the case got to me because I was one of the detectives who usually handled the long-term cases. Thus, additional pressure from the media for a quick solution wasn't usually something I had to deal with. But all that was about to change.

The Atlanta Child Murders

Between July 1, 1979, and May 1, 1981, a frightful series of crimes against young boys terrorized Atlanta, Georgia. Police authorities had connected 28 unsolved murder cases and one missing person, most of whom were children. These were soon known by the nationwide press as the "Atlanta child murders." The victims were black, school-age children who were kidnapped, assaulted, killed, and dumped within an average radius of 10 miles away from their homes. The pattern of assaults and body discovery sites suggested to detectives that a serial murderer using a vehicle was operating in the greater metropolitan Atlanta area. Because most victims had died from some type of asphyxiation, the cluster of murders was thought to be discrete, that is, a part of one series, and related. Because the crime locations were spread over a number of jurisdictions, a multiagency task force involving local, state, and federal officers had been established to investigate the series of murders. The task force had determined that they were looking for a serial killer.

Ted Bundy had demonstrated to the world the horror of a serial killer. His Florida trial had been a showcase of his pseudograndiosity, bravado, and overinflated ego. The press coverage of that trial and the persona Ted presented to the public revealed one aspect of a serial killer. Ted was not, as he had been previously called, a mass murderer. He was not a crazed fanatic on a wild-eyed rampage taking out whomever was unlucky enough to be in his line of fire. He was personifying himself as the embodiment of the ultimate methodical superkiller, trying to demonstrate his control over the criminal justice system, over the press, and over anyone who came into his purview. Thus, by 1981, the term *serial killer* had come to represent killers who operated like Ted Bundy, and when the task force uttered it, the world's press corps descended upon Atlanta.

There is a great truth about press coverage few people ever understand. I saw it take place in Atlanta, experienced it firsthand a few years later in Seattle during the Green River investigation, and saw it graphically demonstrated on television during the Los Angeles riots of 1992. The press creates its own magnified version of an event. The more intense the feeding frenzy for exclusives, the more the story changes from reporter to reporter until what the public gets is a distorted version of the truth. It's as if the Heisenberg Uncertainty Principle were at work every time a large story unfolds in the media, so that the presence of the media itself creates, changes, and redefines the story. You always have to be wary of what the media reports because the media itself has created parts of the story. For example, in Atlanta, every move the police investigators made was carefully tracked by each reporter seeking to scoop the competition in discovering the identity of the Atlanta Child Killer. Members of the press were relentless in their pursuit, jealously guarding their own tips and leads while criticizing the task force's follow-up activities in the cases. Much of the confusion that took place among members of the multiagency task force was the result of rumors that came out of the press coverage. At times it was as though the police were reacting to the press more than they were to the case.

Among the press and investigators as well, theories about the nature of the killer abounded as each expert column in the newspapers seized upon new interpretations of the evidence. Meanwhile, the killer kept on striking, abducting black children from local neighborhoods and dumping their bodies in the woods outside Atlanta and along the banks of the Chattahoochee River. The most politically sensitive theory about the killer that the press picked up characterized the murders as hate crimes carried out by members of a white racist group. If one were to think about the crimes seriously, it'd soon be obvious that an ongoing series of murders of black children in black neighborhoods during a full police mobilization required the killer to have been virtually invisible. It would have been impossible for a group of white men to have carried out these crimes. A gang of whites roaming through black neighborhoods would have been noticed—more than noticed, they would have set off a full alarm. Furthermore, white men wouldn't necessarily have been able to gain the confidence of young black children. The organized racial conspiracy theory just didn't add up when you took a serious look at the evidence. However, because the police were cautious not to expound upon their own theories in public, the press chose to emphasize the racial conspiracy in their coverage. Suddenly, the police found themselves having to play political correctness games as they pursued the case before the eyes of the country.

Never in the history of federal intervention had any one case commanded so much attention as the Atlanta child murders. The federal government contributed millions of dollars in a grant to the city of Atlanta to help fund the investigation as well as to bolster the preventive aspects of the cases. There was also an unfortunate political side to the grant that, while well-meaning at its inception, created a great deal of confusion among the agencies trying to catch the killer. Grant money was earmarked for victims' families even though police weren't really always sure which child was a victim of the Atlanta Child Killer and which child wasn't. In order to be a victim and be entitled to money, it became important for a family of a dead child who might fit the victim profile to have that child's name placed on the list. Once officially on the list, the family would be entitled to receive as much as $100,000 on behalf of their murdered child. That policy actually prolonged the investigation because it meant that police had to check out leads that took them far away from the real investigation. After all, if a child's name had been added to the list, it meant he was officially a victim. If he was listed as a victim, it had to be checked out whether he was truly a victim. That took police on a number of wild-goose chases after phantom leads. Meanwhile, the killer kept on killing and the police kept on tripping over themselves in the race to find the next body before the "other cops" did.

I followed this case with great interest on the national television news, which, because of the number of leaks at the competing police agencies, was privy to far too much sensitive information and was providing updates to the cases from inside the police investigation.

Profile Consultant

There was no exchange of information among police departments in the Northwest and Atlanta until I was called by Dr. John Liebert. Dr. Liebert was the Bellevue psychiatrist who, along with Dr. John Berberich, provided the only criminal profile in the Ted cases. Dr. Liebert was invited to Atlanta to consult with Commissioner Lee Brown on the cases. Before he flew down, he spoke extensively with me about my opinion of the characteristics of the Atlanta Child Killer. I was pleased to make any contribution I could to Dr. Liebert's work and flattered that he'd consulted me. Because the Atlanta Child Killer had become something of a national publicly acknowledged synonym for *terror*, there was extreme political pressure to highlight a white extremist political motive for the murders.

This, however, was definitely not the profile Dr. Liebert and I felt comfortable with. Our discussions covered and then dissected every possible motive for the killings. After we looked at the crimes from every angle, we kept returning to a diagnosis of the borderline personality disorder for the killer. This was Dr. Liebert's term. My more practical assessment was that the Atlanta Child Killer was a very intense long-term, control-type lust-murderer. We both agreed that these types of murderers could sustain apparently normal, socially acceptable behavior for long periods of time. That part of the killer's public appearance was higher in profile than his periodic regression to violence, much like the behavior pattern of Ted Bundy. The killer would seem like a well-adjusted person who might be a role model for other people. Therefore, he could be the neighbor next door, and the untrained observer wouldn't be aware of his murderous dark side. Someone like a girlfriend or wife would be aware only in retrospect, long after he was arrested and confirmed as the murderer, that he wasn't normal. They, like Ted's fiancée Liz Kendall, would see through cracks in the veneer, but wouldn't be able to arrange a pattern out of what they saw until afterward. The mask was too difficult to penetrate.

In our discussions, Liebert and I considered the impact of suggesting that the killer was a black man who could wield authority over the children. That was really the only feasible choice. With the limited knowledge of the case, we had to rely on statistics and common sense. Blacks historically kill blacks more often than blacks are killed by people of other races, especially when the victims are children. And, as mentioned before, a white man leading a black child out of a black neighborhood would have been noticed after the very first crime.

After Dr. Liebert returned from Atlanta, he informed me that I would probably receive a call from the authorities down there. He wouldn't tell me what he discussed with them, and I didn't ask. It wasn't protocol. Because he was a consummate professional, he wasn't about to relate any information outside of the standard channels. He merely said that he would be submitting his profile of the killer to Commissioner Lee Brown. Because he obviously related the substance of our joint discussions about the nature of the killer in his profile, I realized that I was going to be asked to consult in some capacity on the Atlanta child murders. This would be a high-profile, reputation-building consulting job. I had to be aware of the political impact of this case and my public role as one of the consultants on it. It was as if I were being put on some sort of standby.

Sure enough, one day some weeks later, I recognized the particular sound of a familiar knock on Lieutenant Frank Chase's one-way glass office wall. His office overlooked the detectives' bullpen. Each of us had a peculiar knock that was supposed to summon us to his office. This knock was my summons and I didn't wait around for Chase to repeat it.

Much to my surprise, Sheriff Barney Wyncowski was sitting there waiting for me when I entered the lieutenant's office. I could tell this was important. The sheriff was kind of an elder statesman in state law enforcement and the former head of Department of Justice programs in the Seattle area. He was unhurried and gracious, as he usually was when speaking to one of the deputies. He appeared truly honored by what he was about to announce. Commissioner Lee Brown called him, he said, and requested that I go to Atlanta to consult with him about the Atlanta child murders and the organization of the task force. Several other investigators from high-profile cases had also been invited as part of the consultation group. I had to sit down—nervous and surprised at the same time—even though I had suspected something like this from what Dr. Liebert had said. What could they possibly want from me in person, though? Under the best of circumstances, I could only tell them what *not* to do. The air in the office was filled with anticipation. Lieutenant Chase, who was not part of the Ted investigation, jokingly said he would accompany me to Atlanta to carry my bags. It was his way of saying that he didn't want to miss an opportunity like this.

Supercops II

I was still somewhat apprehensive about going to Atlanta, however. Several months before, Lee Brown had assembled a group of highly touted "supercops" as consultants. They were investigators who had handled some of the most notorious high-profile murder cases in the nation. As was expected, their image was overhyped by the media, who represented them as the "seven samurai" aiming to solve the case for the Atlanta police. It was hard to imagine what more we could add. Weren't the Atlanta police satisfied with the supercops' advice or were they consulting them about something entirely different? That's the first question I would ask when I got to Atlanta.

We arrived at the Atlanta Hilton on May 20, 1981. It was a magnificent hotel by my standards, giving every appearance of a place far beyond my means. Our rooms and meals were direct bills and required no money out of pocket. As we checked in we were given a packet containing a welcoming memorandum, a list of conference attendees, a meeting agenda, and a background summary of the investigation and murder prevention efforts. The registration clerk treated us differently from the other people in the lobby who had registered before us. It wasn't just that we were treated like VIPs, it was as if we were there on a secret mission. I felt caution in the voice of the employee who greeted us at the desk, and his hush-hush attitude hinted that he would not divulge our presence and identities. Obviously, no one was to know we were there. The previous media display over the "supercops" left the Atlanta administrators with a bad taste in their mouths. Secretly, I wondered how long this honeymoon from the media would last.

My eyes quickly scanned Commissioner Brown's memorandum and landed squarely on the list of attending detectives. At the time, the list carried no special impact. The names of detectives and the cities where they were from were listed without any mention of each person's importance to the consultation. I was in for a shock the following day when this information was disclosed.

Our consultation took place in the secure surroundings of the Milan Room, guarded by Atlanta police officers in civilian clothes who were there to keep out the press and other curious onlookers. The entire atmosphere was very formal and shrouded in secrecy. Lee Brown presided over the gathering. Brown sat at the head of the table, surrounded by Morris Redding, commander of the Atlanta task force and future city police chief; Inspector Robbie Hamrick, Georgia Bureau of Investigation; and Major Fred Taylor of the Atlanta police. Members of the consultation group sat at a U-shaped set of three tables. The strain of keeping the press away could be seen everywhere. It almost appeared as though most of the Atlanta officials were more consumed with what the press was doing than with catching the killer. There were the minority, however, who concerned only with the case. Most of the players were concerned about their image.

Goose pimples came across my body as Lee Brown introduced each of us as if we were medieval sorcerers with just the right remedies to break the spell of evil over Atlanta. Now, for the first time in my career, I saw others who had endured the same hardships of multiple-murder investigations that I had struggled with. I could tell this was going to be a privilege as well as a challenge.

The group of consultants who were called to Atlanta with me had handled two basic kinds of cases: those in which investigators had not known that a series of murders had taken place before the offender was caught and those who were already pursuing serial cases but who did not know who the killer was. In the first contingent were Captain Sidney Smith and Detective David Millican, the investigators who had handled the brutal and sexually sadistic murders committed by Dean Coryll and Elmer Wayne Henley, who buried 17 bodies in a boat storage building in Pasadena, Texas. With them was Lieutenant Frank Braun, one of the investigators in the notorious John Wayne Gacy murders. Gacy buried 27 males in the crawl space underneath his home in Des Plaines near Chicago.

The second group consisted of Inspector Joseph Borelli from the New York Police Department task force that investigated the famous Son of Sam—David Berkowitz— who kept the city at bay while he assassinated couples parked in their cars; as well as Lieutenant Ed Henderson and Detective Philip Sartuche of the Los Angeles Police Department, who investigated the Hillside Strangler cases in Los Angeles and in Bellingham, Washington. Also in this latter group was Inspector Jeff Brosch, who investigated the Zebra killings in San Francisco, which were committed by black religious extremists and were viewed by most of the consultants in attendance as those most similar to the Atlanta child murders cases. Lieutenant Frank Chase and I, from the Ted investigations, rounded out this group.

I felt honored to be included in this group of detectives. We had never been gathered together before, but we'd followed one another's investigations closely over the years. A group such as this with many years of accumulated serial murder investigative experience shared basic assumptions about the cases we pursued. We knew what questions to ask and understood certain axioms about the behavior of a serial murderer. Because of the cases we had solved, we knew how to cut through the administrative protocols between agencies that often got in the way of crime solving. That didn't make any of us popular—quite the contrary. We knew we were going to butt heads with the establishment of the Atlanta Police Department, the Georgia Bureau of Investigation, and the FBI. We also knew that even if we found the killer, we'd wind up on the wrong side of the political fence. But we weren't there to win friends—we were there to help solve a series of brutal murders.

According to Lee Brown, our consultation had two objectives. The first was to provide a profile of the killer by identifying characteristics of his behavior and the way they related to the signature of his crimes. After profiling the offender, we were asked to develop strategies for catching him. Inasmuch as the FBI had been running around the bushes for years before we were called in, our profile wasn't likely to fit their profile. Moreover, because they hadn't caught the guy, our strategies for apprehending him, we thought, might be likely to raise a few official eyebrows.

The discussions began with Inspector Hamrick and Major Taylor sharing the podium and giving a chronological description of the murders, the most significant events in the investigation, and the preventive efforts. Their presentation was mainly a slide show of body discovery sites, missing-person locations, maps reflecting the distances between the disappearance and burial sites, and the death-scene photos of one murdered child after another, many of them left in sexually degrading positions. We all squirmed in our chairs at the gruesome sights. There was nothing more stressful than knowing that a sex-crazed killer of children was still on the loose.

Atlanta Victims

Hamrick and Taylor's brief history of the homicide cases started with the murder of Edward Hope Smith, a fourteen-year-old black male, last seen July 20, 1979, leaving a skating rink, and found eight days later in the 1700 block of Niskey Lake Drive. Smith's death was caused by a firearm. Remarkably, on that same day, at the Niskey Lake Drive location, police investigators found the remains of Alfred James Evans, a 13-year-old black male who had been missing since July 25. He was last seen headed for a theater on Peachtree Drive, a major street running through Atlanta. The cause of Evans's death was listed as undetermined. Unfortunately, for purposes of an appropriate follow-up in the case, Evans's body was not identified until October 13, 1980, almost 14 months after his body was discovered. Atlanta investigators realized that the appreciable delay in the identification of that homicide victim left the trail of the killer very cold.

Through March 1980, four more children disappeared. Those four victims further complicated the Atlanta investigation. The first was Milton Harvey, 14, found November 5, 1979, in a wooded area of the neighboring city of East Point. Harvey had been dead approximately one month. The decomposition made it difficult to determine his cause of death. Like Alfred Evans, Harvey's death was classified undetermined, a classification that was frequently used when the medical examiner or pathologist could not assign the exact cause of death. Detectives had not immediately connected the Harvey case to the first two cases because his body was found outside of the area where the first two bodies were found.

Second was Yusef Bell, age 9, whose strangulation murder was dissimilar in certain characteristics traditionally used to link one case to another in the growing number of child murders. He was last seen October 21, 1979, on his way to a grocery store and was found November 8, 1979, in the basement crawl space of an elementary school near his home. Because his body was found in a building close to his home and not outdoors in a remote part of the woods like the others, investigators had a difficult time relating his case to those of the other victims. He was, in spite of these issues, included on the list.

Third was Angel Lanier, a 12-year-old black female, the first girl to be added to the list. Lanier had disappeared on March 4, 1980, and was found stabbed to death on March 10, 1980, in a wooded area off Campbellton Road and Willowbrook Road Southwest. Campbellton Road was an important location to the case because the body of Jeffrey Lemar Mathis, a 10-year-old black male, would be found on February 13, 1981. Mathis's body was found near where Angel Lanier was discovered almost one year after he disappeared on March 11, 1980, which was seven days after the disappearance of Lanier.

Mathis's body had deteriorated badly and his cause of death was also listed as undetermined. The length of time between the Lanier and Mathis disappearances was important to the investigation because it showed a pattern killer using the same dump site for victims abducted within a week of each other.

The presentations of the cases were interrupted occasionally by the two speakers including significant events in the investigation. For instance, in March 1980, after the discovery of the first five victims, police authorities reviewed the records of missing and murdered children over the previous five years in an effort to determine any patterns, trends, or similarities related to the cases. They proclaimed the result of their analysis: "no common denominator was determined."

With that announcement, I saw the other investigators moving in their chairs and trying not to let their rolling eyes be seen by the speaker at the podium. No questions had been asked up to that point, and no one seemed ready to throw any out just yet. But I couldn't resist. Weren't the Edward Smith and Alfred Evans murders evidence enough that they were causally connected because they were found at the same location at the same time? Just because the causes of death were different in both cases, they ruled out the possibility the victims were killed by the same person. Smith was shot and the cause of Evans's death was undetermined. Even a novice investigator would have concluded that, at the very least, the cases might be somewhat connected, so I wanted to know more about the details of the police analysis. Did they really review all murders in depth? Did they read the entire case files or merely scan lists of victims that contained limited data? Was the proliferation of unsolved child murders from July 1979 through March

1980 markedly different from those in the previous years? In other words, were those first five murders indicative of the normal murder rate in other years for the same time period? As presented to us, their analysis suffered from a defective premise, namely that the characteristics between murders had to be exact in nature before similar methods of operation were determined between two or more cases. The police were being exclusive rather than inclusive in their grouping of the individual cases. As a result, they were excluding cases that might have contained valuable clues that would help solve the other cases. This is still a typical problem in serial murder investigations, but nowhere have I seen it more pronounced than in the Atlanta child murders case.

Furthermore, what was the depth of the investigations into the deaths of Yusef Bell and Angel Lanier? Was there any evidence of previous injury to Yusef Bell that was indicative of child abuse? Had the family or friends of either been positively eliminated as suspects? I asked all of these questions, but no one in the room had the answers.

Now the mood in the room had changed as the other Atlanta investigators braced themselves for a barrage of what would turn out to be hostile questioning from the consultants. Also in March 1980, according to the official chronology of the case provided by our hosts, "the Bureau of Police Services personnel requested and received the assistance of the FBI's Behavioral Sciences Unit (BSU) in Quantico, Virginia, in the analysis of all pertinent data related to the cases." We couldn't wait to hear what gems of wisdom would come from the BSU's agents, most of whom were only self-proclaimed experts in murder investigations and had never investigated one lead in an actual murder case. The FBI were the kings of follow-up but couldn't solve a crime in progress. Most local homicide detectives knew this. It was no surprise, therefore, that there were few friends of the FBI in this room. The profile of the probable killer provided by the BSU mirrored the wishes of the community, that is, the killer was white. Almost to a person, the frowns came across our faces. Had they told the BSU something that they hadn't told us yet?

We were even more incredulous when the Atlanta staff admitted to us that there was a task force of over 150 FBI agents working the case in a separate facility and not one of them had been invited to this consultation. The FBI didn't even know we were in town because no one had told them. Each one of us was aware of the problems created when the necessary personnel are not informed of what was important in the cases. But an FBI task force with separate headquarters in the same city investigating the same case was unprecedented. This fact caused us to believe that little or no sharing of investigative information was taking place.

The Eric Middlebrooks murder, the seventh case on their list, was an example of the difficulty the command staff had answering many of consultants' questions about the facts of the investigations. Middlebrooks, a 14-year-old black male, was last seen at midnight on May 19, 1980, at his home. He was not officially reported as missing. His fully clothed body was found on May 20, 1980, off Flat Shoals Road Southeast. He died of a head injury.

Again, the consultants inquired about any previous indications of a history of child abuse. The Atlanta police officials did not know the details of the autopsy report or family history of the victim. I noticed that Middlebrooks was lying at the base of a tree. I asked whether he had suffered a coup-contracoup injury, an indicator that the victim's head was in motion at the time the blow was struck. If Middlebrooks had fallen out of a tree, his head would have been in motion, causing a blow to the exterior of one side of his head and subdural hematoma on the opposite side on the interior of the skull from where the blow was struck. Unbelievably, the presenters couldn't answer. Their lack of knowledge about information that was crucial to forming the characteristics of a profile would prevent intelligent decision making. It would be months later before I learned that Middlebrooks also sustained two stab wounds, confirming that his death was no accident.

While the Atlanta area had seen the disappearances of five black males, ages 9 through 13, and one 7-year-old black female during the four months from May through September 1980, the Atlanta authorities increased the resources dedicated to the investigative effort. Several innovative investigative strategies were tried. The combined assistance of Dr. Lloyd Baccus, a psychiatrist from Emory University, and Dr. Nicholas Groth of Connecticut State Prison was enlisted to develop offender profiles.

Several experts in the area of homicide investigation were individually consulted. Captain Robbie Robertson, commander of the Michigan Child Murders Investigative Task Force, whose opinions I would grow to respect, advised the task force on follow-up techniques. Investigators interviewed all previous runaway children in the same age group as those who were missing or slain. Someone may have escaped from or developed a friendship with the killer. Quite possibly, one of these children could have been recruited to lure in victims for the killer. FBI Special Agent Roy Hazelwood, an expert in developing sex offender profiles, provided analysis of taped and printed evidence. Other experts gave assistance to police management personnel on how to conduct investigations of this sort and to develop computer programs for sorting data. By the end of September, the task force was expanded to 25 full-time investigators, who included detectives from areas where the Atlanta Child Killer had dumped bodies—Atlanta, Fulton County, East Point, and Dekalb—and the Georgia Bureau of Investigation.

Only three bodies of the six missing children were found before the discovery of the remains of Charles Stephens on October 10, 1980, the day after he disappeared. He was a 12-year-old black male whose cause of death was listed as probable asphyxiation. Stephens's body, missing its T-shirt, belt, and socks, was dumped off Normandary Drive in East Point, five miles from his home. Unlike the other bodies dumped by the killer to this point, Stephens's body was openly displayed and laid out next to the road. It was intentionally placed to ensure discovery.

There were only two more victims found before January 1981, according to the task force list of victims. It seemed like there should have been more, based on the frequency of previous discoveries. Had the investigators' search of missing and runaway children, focusing as it had on exact matches to the killer's modus operandi, been too quick to dismiss other possible victims? Those missing and runaway children complaints filed with the Atlanta area police jurisdictions should have been aggressively pursued in light of the ongoing murder cases. Checking on the circumstances leading to the disappearances of any children may have developed suspect information in the form of someone who was last seen with a child.

The Murders Continue

By mid-February 1981, three more young black males had been found murdered. Lubie Geter, 14 years old, had last been seen in the vicinity of Stewart Lakewood Shopping Center in southwest Atlanta on January 3, 1981. His remains were found on February 5 in a wooded area 70 feet off Vandiver Road in Fulton County. That road runs off Campbellton Road, where the bodies of Angel Lanier and Jeffrey Mathis had previously been recovered. The cause of Geter's death was asphyxiation, probably by a chokehold.

Terry Pue, 15 years old, was missing from the Krystal Restaurant on January 22, 1981. Pue, like many of the others, had no car and hung out at the Omni, a place that Geter was also known to frequent. The next day at 7:30 A.M., Pue's body was discovered in yet another police jurisdiction near Atlanta, Rockdale County. It was almost like the killer was dumping victims in as many different police jurisdictions in and around Atlanta as possible. Pue's fully clothed body was located near Interstate 20 on Sigman Road, laid out as if the killer had wanted it to be discovered. Pue had apparently suffered manual strangulation.

Another juvenile known to hang out near the Omni was Patrick Baltazar, 11 years old. Baltazar was last seen on Courtland Street in the early evening hours of February 6. His body was found on Friday, February 13, 1981. It was behind the Corporate Square Office Park, off Buford Highway, three blocks from Interstate 85 in Dekalb County. He was fully clothed, but his clothing was unbuttoned. Probable asphyxiation due to ligature strangulation was the cause of his death.

Through the end of March 1981, five more young black males went missing and were found either in the South or Chattahoochee rivers. They ranged in age from 13 to 23 years old and all of them had died of some form of asphyxiation. In February 1981, an Atlanta newspaper carried a story that revealed that several different types of fibers were found on two of the murder victims. It seemed no coincidence that following the publication of the fiber story, five bodies, clad only in undershorts or nude, were subsequently deposited in rivers in the Atlanta area instead of being dumped on land. It appeared to police investigators that the victims were being disposed of in rivers without clothing so that the water would wash away any fibers that might otherwise be left on their bodies.

The next body found in the series, that of Larry Rogers, was dumped in a vacant apartment on Temple Street, less than a mile from Bankhead Highway, on April 9, 1981. He, too, was clad only in undershorts but was wearing his tennis shoes. Asphyxiation due to strangulation, possibly by chokehold, was determined to be the cause of death. Rogers was last seen on March 30, 10 days prior to his discovery date, at his residence in northwest Atlanta. Less than a month later, at 3:30 P.M. on April 27, 1981, the body of 21-year-old Jimmy Ray Payne was found snagged on a tree limb in the Chattahoochee River, one quarter of a mile downstream from the Interstate 285 bridge and between it and the Bankhead Highway bridge in the city of Atlanta. He was clad only in shorts and died from asphyxiation by unknown means.

The last murder victim on the task force list was William Barrett, age 16. Barrett was last seen by his court services officer on May 11, 1981, in the Kirkwood area of Dekalb County. His body was found dumped on the road at one A.M. the next day in the vicinity of Winthrop Drive, just off I-20 in Dekalb County. Even though his cause of death was determined to be asphyxiation due to strangulation, the medical examiner discovered five knife pricks in his body but only two holes in his shirt. His clothing was unbuttoned and his pants were loose. Also, Barrett's body had two horizontal post-mortem stab wounds.

Profile of the Atlanta Child Killer

On the day following the first meeting, our consultation group gave its first response to the Atlanta task force senior commanders. We believed that at least 23 of the 27 murder victims on the task force list were connected and committed by the same person. The cases of Jimmy Payne, William Barrett, Larry Rogers, Patrick Baltazar, Lubie Geter, Terry Pue, Charles Stephens, Eric Middlebrooks, and Alfred Evans were linked to each other. The same fibers and animal hairs were present consistently from one case to another. Because other young black female and male victims were discovered, probably strangled, in the same rivers or along the same roads in close proximity to the main nine victims, they could not be excluded from the investigation. We didn't have any direct evidence that tied their deaths to the nine primary victims, but it was too soon in the process to throw them out on that fact alone. We conceded that with very few or no similar fibers and animal hairs identified, an absolute connection from the other victims to the nine linked victims could not be made. However, there was still a very high probability that 23, if not all 27, murdered children were killed by the same person. Moreover, we reported, we were unable to develop a strong rationale for connecting all 27 murders into one series because of either an incomplete investigation into the murders of the early victims or insufficient data given to us by the Atlanta task force. The more information available for analysis, the more effective we would be in attempting to link these crimes. Some assurance that friends and family members were not responsible for some of the murders was necessary before connections to other cases could be made.

The style of killings, with victims missing from areas popular with young blacks and asphyxiation being the most predominant cause of death, didn't fit logically with the most publicized theory that a white racist person or group was eliminating the black children of Atlanta to create fear in the community. These were not terrorist murders in the political sense of the word. The Atlanta child murders were more than likely committed by a black male whose method of operation reflected a personality with a need for hands-on activity with each victim before and after death. This would be a killer who could move about freely, who had relationships within the community, and whose presence in the area on any day he chose would not be considered out of the ordinary. This would be a killer who was trusted by his victims. Thus, we concluded, the killer was part of the community and, like a Ted Bundy, was taking victims who had no idea they would ever be in danger.

Probable asphyxiation was the cause of death in a number of cases. A lack of telling marks of death or signs of a struggle were indicative that the killer more than likely got the victims into a sleepy stupor by using drugs or alcohol. Then he quietly strangled or suffocated the children. Getting the victims to the point of drowsiness took patience and a plan. That meant that the killer spent considerable time with each victim from the point of initial contact until the induction of the state of drowsiness and subsequent murder. To accomplish all that meant that the killer was deceptively cunning in his approach and the victims had complete trust in him.

Some of the boys who had been murdered hung out in the fringe areas of Atlanta, neighborhoods populated principally by the unemployed drug users and hustlers. This was the killer's primary trolling ground, and we figured that he had something these young victims wanted. This was how he lured them into his trap. The killer's line of approach was most likely the offer of a short-term job to make quick money. This was the ploy that John Wayne Gacy used to entrap his young male victims and that Jeffrey Dahmer would use 15 years later. This is a typical serial killer lure. The job offer might have been for prostitution, posing for photos, or running drugs. To the younger victims, the killer may have looked like a role model or big-brother figure, and the victims probably hoped that their association with him would eventually develop into something long term. To the older victims, the killer was nothing more than a very short-lived employment opportunity for the evening, such as a "john" or a drug dealer in need of an on-the-spot carrier. The killer, we believed, was able to change his approach according to the victim. He might have been able to lure his younger victims with money and his older victims with money and a job offer. Whatever the case, the killer was able to get those male victims from 9 to 28 years old under his complete control.

What added to his ability to attract those boys was that each one of them was a clone of the murderer's own self-image. Even though his choice of victims was purely random, they were a ready pool of handsome boys just like him. He looked, thought, and talked just like his victims, and that is what appealed to them the most—he was someone with common threads. He identified with them so well, the victims probably were never afraid of him, nor was he frightened by them. But his common ground was seductive because he probably presented himself as educated, well-integrated into the community, and always having a good job. The major obstacle for each victim—primarily because they were young—was that they were unable to see through his mask of superficiality.

Based on the killer's ability to mingle across a spectrum of elementary school boys, older teenage victims, and adults, you would expect to find the killer comfortable in each of those atmospheres. He could have been or still was a volunteer or employee of a boys' service group, such as Boy Scouts, the YMCA, or other types of boys clubs or community groups. He might have been a frequent volunteer, substitute teacher, or vendor around the elementary-school scene. He might have frequented boy prostitutes and, at the same time, been part of the gay disco scene. He was not likely to have been an out-of-the-closet homosexual. In fact, he might have been known to hate gays in some circles and be superficially heterosexual with his own family of origin.

On the other side of the child-killer's mask was evidence of his need for total possession of his victims by engaging in postmortem activities with them. He had a sex drive that embraced necrophilic tendencies and a willingness to spend considerable time with victims after death. Even though direct evidence of sexual assault was not confirmed for most victims, it was expressed through the killer's signature: leaving the nude or partially clad males in a sexually degrading manner. He also partially redressed previously nude victims and disposed of their bodies in obviously posed positions at preselected locations, as if he'd rehearsed this before the killing.

The killer's arranging of various victims in contorted or sexually degrading positions or leaving them in open places so they would certainly be discovered was a form of death ritual as well as a message. He revealed that he was treating the police as enemies and demonstrated with his victims' bodies that he not only exercised absolute control over the corpses, but over the police as well. The police were completely unable to catch him even though he was leaving the bodies in plain view and in posed positions that said to investigators, "I am a murder victim." The police looked more and more inept to the public as the search intensified, reinforcing the killer's mentality with feelings of extreme superiority even as the hunted fugitive that he knew he was. He wanted the police to feel, psychologically, as he really did, helpless and controlled.

We also knew the killer was very aware of his environment, sensitive to the nature of the police pursuit, and clever enough to modify his patterns the moment he knew people were on to him. His changing of victim dump sites from mainly land surfaces to rivers, for example, was a response to the publicity his crimes had received. In so changing these styles, he revealed his media awareness and his ability to monitor the progress of the investigation through public sources. How the police tracked him, mainly with the remains examined for similar fibers and hairs, was very important to him. Leaving partially nude or nude bodies in a river diminished the chances for finding that crucial microscopic trace of physical evidence that could be linked back to him. There was no question that the Atlanta Child Killer was well-versed in police procedures. Having police-science knowledge was part of his survival technique of acting only when there was least possibility of detection. He didn't want to get caught—ever.

The killer's predilection for postmortem engagement with his victims should have led investigators to check out those individuals who had been employed at—no matter how briefly—or were applicants for positions at funeral homes or medical examiners' offices. Previously convicted multiple murderers had expressed their interest in morbidity by applying for jobs in police departments and in the death services area. Killers like Ted Bundy and Kenneth Bianchi worked at crisis clinics and applied for sheriff's officer positions, respectively. Bundy, at one point in our interviews, reflected on his fascination with decomposing bodies.

The distance from where victims were last seen to the location of their body recovery ranged from a few blocks to over 15 miles. That feature could mean only that the killer had access to reliable private transportation. Each of the respective multiple murderers whom we had investigated had had several vehicles that were available to transport their victims to secluded areas. Also, each had driven hundreds of miles pursuing potential victims and checking out prospective dump sites.

The profile of the killer as a black male in his mid-twenties, with a record of intermittent employment around elementary schools, interest in medical examiner functions, obsession with necrophilia, traffic with boy prostitutes, a role model for young boys, and constantly driving around Atlanta in pursuit of potential victims was a characterization that the task force brass must have wanted to believe. The pressure was so intense to link the murders to some white racist conspiracy or to the occult that the black lust-killer theory was not emphasized publicly.

The white racist conspiracy and occult responsibility were poor theories to promote. For one thing, there were none of the typical indicators or paraphernalia, such written messages claiming responsibility or symbolic references such as "666" or "KKK" carved in a tree or discovered at any crime scene. In addition, only one of the victims had been shot, but more gunshot-type murders, which were characteristic of previous murders by members of extremist groups, would have been expected.

How to Catch the Killer

It was proposed by the Atlanta task force command that supporting the white racist theory through the media would make the killer think that the police were far from his tracks. We didn't think that was a good idea because the killer already knew that they had linked cases through fiber identification. Besides that, previous attempts made by law enforcement to play games with a serial killer through the news media had failed miserably. The main reason that those strategies were not effective was that the killer was the only person who knew all the facts of the murders. Any attempt to deceive the killer by portraying distorted facts or attempting to lure the killer to a particular location through a remorseful appeal served only to alert the killer to how close the investigation really was to catching him—about as close as the planet Pluto is to Earth.

The second strategy suggested by the Atlanta staff was already in place, and they were hoping that this effort would be endorsed by the consultants and would ultimately be productive. Several days prior to our consultation, they had set out to conduct surveillance of bridges that crossed the South and Chattahoochee rivers. This rationale was sound because at least six of the last seven victims had been dumped in one of the two rivers and there was no reason to believe that the next or a subsequent murder victim would not be dumped into one of those two rivers. For the last two days, nagging doubts surfaced among our group of consultants about whether the task force had given us any meaningful criteria upon which to base our suggestions for apprehending the killer. At the very least, I doubted the Atlanta staff's ability to relate the features of their series of murders that were important for our assessment. But their idea to stake out bridges was outstanding and a stroke of brilliance. We wholeheartedly endorsed their proactive effort to catch the killer, even though it meant using manpower in an area that took away from other parts of the investigation, such as following up leads, checking sources, and interviewing potential witnesses.

The task force had planned to watch 11 bridges that crossed the two rivers. It was a very labor-intensive proposition, taking at least five officers to watch one bridge—two on each end and one near the water where he could hear the splash. That meant the equivalent of at least 55 full-time officers had to be on duty 24 hours a day. At the rate of relieving them every eight hours, it required 165 surveillance officers, a crew larger than 95 percent of the police departments in Washington State. What an expensive proposition to continue through the summer months while there were still routine traffic patrols and anticrime details that had to be staffed. But we all thought it would be worth it.

Some of the bridges were very long, so it was necessary to station someone underneath, near the water, to detect the splash of a body. If a vehicle stopped in the middle of a bridge, the surveillance crews on either side might not see it, so they had to be alerted by the splash detectors below. There was an elaborate notification procedure set up so that when a splash was heard, responding officers would quickly place large nets across the river in an effort to snag the body that would presumably come floating by. The officer under the bridge would notify the crews on top and the bridge would be barricaded and catch the Atlanta "riverman" in the act. The Atlanta task force staff members really appreciated our assistance and advice. We were confident the bridge stakeout would work.

At about 10:30 A.M. on our last day in Atlanta, May 22, 1981, we were putting the finishing touches on our Child Killer profile when a messenger entered the room. It was a time that the entire city of Atlanta would never forget. Lee Brown and the others politely excused themselves for about an hour. When they returned, nothing was said about their abbreviated absence. Looks of frustration, nervousness, and stress lined their faces. Brown was especially apprehensive and remarked only that something critical to the murder series had occurred and he would inform each one of us, personally, what it was at a later date. He never did. He presented us with Atlanta City Police Department commemorative coins and paperweights, and thanked us by saying that the serial murder consultation process was the most valuable part of their investigations. With that we left Atlanta.

My pen was flying across my yellow legal-size pad on the airplane flight home. Our one-hour presentation of the Atlanta Child Killer's profile and discussion about staking out the bridges left me with a very shallow feeling; I felt as though the consultation process was very superficial. I was concerned about what I saw and heard during the presentations and felt that I had to make written recommendations to the task force, so I composed a letter to Commissioner Lee Brown. First of all, I didn't get the impression that there were any homicide detectives in the room from the Atlanta task force, except for Sergeant Bolton, who was very quiet the entire session. I knew that police administrators were highly effective at summative evaluation—Monday-morning quarterbacking—and less effective at formative evaluation. I just felt that experienced investigators needed to be involved in the planning process of in-progress investigations. Murder cases cannot be run from above.

Another concern of mine was the reclassification of deaths that were originally declared accidents or suicides to homicides after the series became known. I didn't get the feeling that investigators drained all the information about those deaths from the various medical examiners on the cases. One reason this might have happened was that some of the investigators had perhaps not been properly schooled in all aspects of death recognition and investigation. I felt strange recommending homicide investigation training for investigators in the middle of an intense investigation, but the probability that more bodies would be discovered was high. And the correct interpretation of each death scene was crucial. For those deaths that were incorrectly classified during their series, valuable evidence that might have been directly linked to the killer was not gathered.

I believe that death scenes tell stories. It's the only way victims can relate to the investigator what happened to them, and, more important, who assaulted them. It somewhat disturbed me to hear Chief Redding comment about finding only dump sites and no crime scenes, therefore leaving the impression that crime scene processing was not as thorough as if they had discovered the real murder scene. I believe the dump site is a crime scene. It must be processed with equal thoroughness. I was concerned that his apparent attitude could quickly spread to the evidence searchers: it's only a dump site; therefore, you're not going to find anything—so why look?

There were two children, Eric Middlebrooks and Patrick Rogers, who died from head injuries. There was no mention of other trauma or defense wounds on them, wounds they might have received while trying to defend themselves against blows with blunt instruments or knives. The greatest chance to find other wounds existed in the Middlebrooks case because the Rogers corpse was discovered in a more advanced stage of decomposition. The presenters didn't give any information about the existence of other wounds. Had the medical examiner found any wounds or, in fact, even looked for them? Had the homicide investigator asked about them? I was worried about eliminating the possibility of child abuse in the Middlebrooks case because he was fresh when found and his body bore fibers similar to the ones found in other cases. I would hope those fibers were not generic to everyone's surroundings. A complete investigation into the Middlebrooks murder was necessary to rule out fibers from his home.

The strangulation cases were intriguing me. Most of the quickly discovered victims had an evenly defined, unobstructed line of strangulation around their necks. Clearly, there were no interruptions of fingernail-type bruising on the neck from someone struggling to prevent the strangulation. The strangulation mark was a straight line and not in the pattern of the inverted V mark that would be indicative of a hanging motion.

The victims must have been taken totally by surprise or in a state in which they were almost ignorant that their murder was about to occur. The presenters offered no information about a blood scan for drugs or alcohol in each victim's system that might have affected their alertness. I would reinquire about the presence of drugs in their systems.

In addition, the presenters did not tell us whether the strangulation caused a fracture of the hyoid cartilage. The presence of the fracture would indicate a more forceful application of pressure than if the assailant only cut off the blood flow to the brain. The clean appearance of the line of strangulation meant that the killer used a cord or rope. Therefore, the width of the line needed to be compared from one case to another. There was a good chance that the killer might still have the strangulation device in his possession. When the killer was finally apprehended, this might be the single piece of evidence the police would need to begin the long process of getting him to confess.

My report to Commissioner Brown ended with a recommendation that, when all else failed, they use their computer in much the same way that we did in the Ted Bundy cases. They could create lists of names from the investigations of each victim by dividing the names of persons mentioned in their files into categories such as family members, persons interviewed, suspects investigated, employees of businesses frequented by victims, vendors, volunteers and teachers at schools, suspects with driver's licenses, those people who were field-interviewed at crime scenes and disappearance sites, and so forth. Then they could see if one name appeared on more than one list.

Stakeout and Arrest

On May 22, 1981, the day we left Atlanta, a four-man surveillance team, stationed at the James Jackson Parkway Bridge, reported an encounter with a suspect. The stakeout team consisted of an FBI agent and an Atlanta police officer, both plainclothes, at each end of the bridge in unmarked cars. Two Atlanta police recruits were positioned at the foot of the west bank of the river. The team members, from where they stood on the bridge, could see headlights from cars approaching the bridge. Also, cars driving at over 10 miles an hour across that bridge always tended to make a loud noise when they passed over an expansion joint in the roadway toward the middle of the span.

Early in the predawn darkness, at about three A.M., a loud splash was heard directly beneath the bridge where two recruits were on surveillance duty along the bank. One officer thought the splash sounded like a human body hitting the water below the bridge. Up to that time, no lights had been observed on the bridge and the characteristic sound of a car moving over the expansion joint had not been heard. There was light traffic at that time, and at least 10 minutes transpired between the time the last car was seen on the bridge and when the splash was heard. Shortly after the splash, a car's lights appeared directly above where the splash had occurred. The officers observed a white Chevrolet station wagon close to the edge of the bridge traveling at an estimated speed of three to four miles per hour. The car exited the bridge at one end and turned around in a parking lot. It proceeded back across the bridge at a speed of about 35 to 40 miles per hour. No other vehicles passed over the bridge during that time. The police pursued the station wagon back to the highway.

A short time later, on I-285, the driver of the station wagon, Wayne B. Williams, was stopped by the bridge officers and detained for 90 minutes while they interviewed him and, with his permission, searched the station wagon. The officers found dog hairs inside the car and discovered a nylon cord and a paper bag containing men's clothes. They subsequently released Williams at the scene of the stop.

Weeks later, I learned that the reason for the apprehension and frustration in the faces of the Atlanta brass on our last day of consultation was that they were not informed until eight hours later of the incident. Their plan to mobilize the officers with the river nets was appreciably delayed. They couldn't catch the body they had heard fall, which would have brought to an end the riverman's reign of terror. Their notification plan had failed.

On May 21, 1981, Nathaniel Cater, a 28-year-old black male, was last seen holding hands with Wayne Williams outside a theater in the city of Atlanta at about 9:15 P.M. Three days later, on May 24, 1981, his nude body was found in the Chattahoochee River, 200 yards downstream from the I-285 overpass and near the Jackson Parkway Bridge. He had died of asphyxiation, probably by a chokehold. A crime laboratory expert found five fibers on Cater's body that were consistent with the environment of Wayne Williams. Animal hairs from Williams's dog were also identified on Cater's body. Two witnesses had spotted Cater in the company of Williams the week before and had noted a German shepherd dog sitting in Williams's white station wagon. At the very least, the bridge officers had gotten Williams's name and a description and had put him at the scene of a body disposal. Now, at last, they could pursue a solid lead in their case.

The investigation of the Atlanta Child Killer, Wayne Williams, began to unfold. Williams was charged with two counts of first-degree murder in the deaths of Cater and Jimmy Ray Payne. Further investigation revealed that Payne disappeared on April 21, 1981, and had been seen with Wayne Williams on April 22, 1981, on Highway 78, approximately one mile from the Chattahoochee River near a parked white station wagon. Even though Williams dumped Payne's body in the river to prevent fibers from being found, six fibers associated with Williams's environment and animal hairs from his dog were located on Payne's remains. The river had not been as thorough as Williams might have wished.

The evidence of 10 other murders, extrinsic offenses, were used against Williams to prove a common scheme or plan that was part of the crimes. The earliest victim in the series used against

Williams was Alfred Evans, who was found on Niskey Lake Drive. His body was clad only in slacks, but three fibers consistent with Williams's environment and animal hairs from his dog were found on Evans. The bodies of Eric Middlebrooks, Charles Stephens, and Patrick Baltazar contained fiber associations consistent with Williams's surroundings and animal hairs from his dog. There were no sightings of Williams with these boys prior to their murders, however.

The Terry Pue murder case revealed the narcissistic characteristics of Williams's personality. In addition to fibers and animal hairs similar to those from Williams's home and dog being found on Pue's body, a witness saw Williams with Pue about a week before the witness learned that Pue's body had been discovered. With a sense of bravado, Williams arrived at the crime scene where Pue's body was recovered and offered to shoot crime scene photos. The officer did not suspect the photographer might be the killer at that time, although now we know that serial killers sometimes do return to the crime scenes, especially in the presence of the police. It gives them a high and boosts their bravado to know that they are standing next to a person they have killed and are still invisible to the police. Additionally, and in keeping with the theory of serial-killer bravado, witnesses observed Williams driving his white station wagon at Pue's funeral. Those bold appearances were evidence that Williams did not fear getting caught. The closer he got to the police, the more superior he felt. He was acting as though his armor could not be penetrated.

In the case of Lubie Geter, Williams was seen with him on the very day he disappeared. The witness recognized Williams from a previous contact of his own with Williams. The same man who was driving the car that Geter got into picked up the 15-year-old witness in the same area the previous August and offered him a job. Williams fondled him as they drove around. The teenager escaped when Williams stopped and got out, saying he needed something from the trunk. That same juvenile witness saw Williams at Geter's funeral, but at the time, he didn't report Williams to the police.

A female witness in the Larry Rogers case actually saw Rogers in Williams's green station wagon—which Williams owned in addition to the white station wagon. Rogers was seen with Williams three times in one day. The female spoke to Rogers, who was slumped over and didn't reply. Incredibly, no report was made to the police. Williams also attended Rogers's funeral.

The case of John Porter, a 28-year-old black male, was never presented to us by the Atlanta task force command. Porter was last seen getting into Williams's station wagon. Another witness got a ride from Williams when Porter was in the car. Porter's body was found on April 12, 1981, near Capitol Avenue, one mile from I-20 and three miles from I-85. Porter was fully clothed; he died from some type of neck manipulation. Fibers from Williams's environment were located on Porter, but no animal hairs were discovered.

After Williams was convicted on two counts of first-degree murder, I spoke with Chief Morris Redding. He very candidly admitted that Williams had been right in front of their noses and they hadn't seen him. While officers were walking up to elementary schools to give safety and crime prevention talks to children, Williams was walking out after having just photographed them for their school pictures. Williams was highly integrated into community affairs. The Williams cases were classic. Our profile was right on point in an uncanny way. Not only were we correct in our prediction that the killer hung around or was a vendor at elementary schools, but also Williams had applied for work as a photographer at the local medical examiner's office. His willingness to volunteer to take crime scene photos proved his lack of fear of getting caught. On one occasion, he was even a volunteer searcher who assisted the police in the hunt for another victim of the Atlanta Child Killer. Williams was uncommonly familiar with the places where victims were last seen, the dump sites, and the routes to and from the body recovery sites. The theory of a white supremacist responsible for the murders was soundly eliminated. Our profile was correct and the strategy for surveillance of the bridges was extremely successful. The experience of being a consultant for the Atlanta task force helped me focus my career. From then on I was committed to finding out as much as I could about the investigation of serial murders. I wanted to be prepared to assist others with those very difficult investigations.

5

The Violent Criminal Apprehension Program and the Story of the Michigan Child Murders

By midsummer 1982, there were still only a few homicide investigators around the country who had had encounters with serial killers in their jurisdictions, but serial murders were on the increase. Typically, the serial killers struck and then moved on. Their extreme mobility and compulsive driving habits permitted them to reach a wide pool of victims, often breaking over county lines into different jurisdictions. But the strategies and tactics common to murder investigations were almost always very traditional and restricted most detectives' abilities to keep pace with the increasing incidence of "traveling murderers." These killers routinely desecrated the remains of their many victims, eluded the police, and were popularized in lurid news headlines with such monikers as the Hillside Strangler, the Freeway Killer, the Trailside Killer, the Trash Bag Killer, and the Zodiac Killer. For a variety of reasons, not the least of which was that it was the largest growing part of the country and still had vast rural areas, the Pacific Northwest attracted more than its fair share of those slugs.

Despite a growing awareness among metropolitan-area homicide investigators of the serial killer–type crimes popping up in different jurisdictions across the nation, there was still a basic flaw in our approach. We were mainly reactive in our responses, and the cases were usually resolved by some serendipitous occurrence even though we had a sense of the killer's identity. For example, the foul odor rising from John Wayne Gacy's basement gave him away; Atlanta police belatedly discovered a witness who put Wayne Williams with a victim at a crime scene; and a Florida police officer noticed the stolen plates on Ted Bundy's van. All of these killers were caught long after they had begun their skein of murders. However, in each case, the traditional methods of investigation were ineffective for apprehending the upstart serial killer. Even in the Ted investigation, where traditional methods actually did identify the Ted suspect himself, it would have done us no good without our computer-generated "top 100" list of suspects.

As a case first unfolded, those killers were pursued much like the suspects in a routine murder in which someone killed an acquaintance and the police eventually eliminated, one by one, the victim's circle of friends and relatives. But once the investigations of the circle of acquaintances were exhausted, the cases stalled. That dead-end trail, coupled with the reluctance of investigators to pursue leads outside their own jurisdictional boundaries, characterized serial-murder cases as all but impossible to solve. The lack of new, creative, and useful investigative avenues contributed to the practical reality that the police were far from knowing the killer's identity or even understanding his criminal intent. By the time the police started tracking them, the killer's tracks were so faint that catching the killer was, at best, a very remote possibility. It wasn't that police were reluctant to expend time and resources to follow a very cold trail; they were, in fact, stumbling along in the dark with no trail at all.

Maps with red pins marking the locations of the murder scenes and yellow pins highlighting where each victim was last seen dotted the squad-room walls of detective units in those areas where a serial killer was on the prowl. In some cases, maps of one state were connected to its neighboring state's map to indicate that the killer had crossed state lines. The dilemma facing each investigation was that there was no easy way to locate similar murders in other jurisdictions, and the need for a way to do that was growing stronger by the day. While one investigator's case might lack any viable suspect information, perhaps a similar case in another unknown jurisdiction would help provide some missing pieces. Likewise, maybe the killer one department was tracking was arrested in a subsequent case somewhere else. But without any formal method of sharing information between departments, the lack of that knowledge caused a lot of wheel-spinning and wasted hours of investigative time. The communication process among police agencies was not systematic, causing each investigator to do the same labor-intensive search for cases as we did in the Ted murders. Because there were no clear limits as to how far killers traveled around a specific locus to search for victims, the task of finding them was often next to impossible. What was needed was a kind of national coordinating committee to gather data on homicide cases and cross-match suspect profiles in different jurisdictions. But no one local or state agency could undertake that task on its own. Ultimately, I would be a factor in bringing into being a system that would help remedy this problem.

The Formation of VICAP

It was December 1982. The jet stream had whipped around from the north and drenching winter storms were hitting Seattle early, rolling in from the Pacific into Puget Sound day after day behind a swirling wall of fog. The world was gray and wet, and the personnel at the attorney general's office were already thinking about Christmas when my own winter doldrums were interrupted by a call from a living legend. The scratchy, high-pitched voice on the other end of the telephone was Pierce Brooks, the retired detective captain from the LAPD's Homicide Unit, the detective who worked on the notorious Black Dahlia case, the detective of the Onion Field murders, and my future mentor. Pierce was one of the "supercops" whom Lee Brown brought to Atlanta to review the child murders investigation. I was shocked and honored that Pierce called. We certainly had never before communicated on a first-name basis.

Brooks had called to ask for my support for a national serial-murder tracking program, later called the Violent Criminal Apprehension Program (VICAP), and currently housed within the Behavioral Sciences Unit (BSU) of the FBI Academy at Quantico, Virginia. Brooks described his early attempts to find murders that might have been committed by a murderer he was investigating. He told of his painstaking effort to leaf through the archives of newspaper morgues to read reports of murder cases in other jurisdictions, desperately trying to identify a similar case. In lieu of the newspaper-search method and our haphazard hunt for similar murders in the Bundy cases, Brooks proposed a nationwide centralized repository of homicide information where investigators could request a search for cases with similar characteristics with the help of a computer. That was the inception of the VICAP project.

Brooks defined VICAP as a centralized information and crime analysis system designed to collect, collate, and relate all aspects of the investigations of similar-pattern multiple murders throughout the nation regardless of location or the number of police agencies involved. He reasoned that if a detective was investigating a murder, one with or without an apparent motive, the officer could request that analysts at a national center query their computer for murders in other jurisdictions that contained similar characteristics. Then, if a match or matches were found, the national center would alert the agencies that they were probably pursuing the same traveling killer, thereby helping the police investigators communicate more effectively, solve cases sooner, and prevent further murders. He planned to have the unit housed at a central location, such as Colorado Springs, Colorado. This location was his favorite because the police chief there offered free office space. The unit would be staffed with experienced civilian homicide investigators and crime analysts.

The entire concept sounded great to me and I told him so. But I could feel what he really wanted was the name of Ted Bundy, an internationally notorious, headline-grabbing serial killer, associated with his endeavor, and I would be his Bundy link. I was more than willing to help. A project associated with Ted Bundy's name would assist in convincing the politicians in charge of the purse strings that the program was indispensable. I figured Brooks would want to pitch the VICAP idea as an investigative aid as well as a preventive tool against future violence. Brooks asked, "If VICAP were operational ten years ago, would it have helped in the Bundy cases?" I leaped at the chance to explain.

I told Brooks that Roger Dunn and I had searched in vain for similar murders in other places because we felt the Ted suspect had not limited himself to the boundaries of King County or Washington State. We had Kathy Parks, who was last seen 265 miles from Seattle in Corvallis, Oregon, and dumped on Taylor Mountain in rural King County. There was no reason why Ted couldn't have abducted a girl from another state and dumped that same victim's body someplace else. At that time, there was no central homicide information center to contact with questions regarding similar murders. Our efforts in this vein were restricted to use of the teletype, telephone, and letters written to police and sheriff's departments. Even though over time, some of those murderers were eventually located and identified, traditional tracking techniques were far from adequate and not systematically effective. If VICAP had existed as Brooks described it to me, we would have discovered that Utah and Colorado authorities were the only states that reported the bludgeoning and strangulation murders of college-age females after our murders had apparently stopped. A quick scan of our records would have revealed that there was only one suspect in our files who had left Washington and traveled to Utah—Theodore Robert Bundy. An analysis by experts from a national serial-murder tracking program that provided the necessary links to Salt Lake City cases would have enabled us to focus on Bundy much sooner, probably as early as October 1974, instead of August 1975. How many murders would have been prevented? Brooks's voice crackled. Such fervent support of his proposal was unexpected. Noting my gold mine of supportive examples of VICAP's potential value, he invited me to become a consultant to the national planning group, which was established to examine the feasibility of tracking the victims of traveling killers.

A little more than six months later, in July 1983, I attended my first VICAP planning meeting, the Sexual Abuse and Exploitation of Children and National Missing/Abducted Children and Serial Murder Tracking and Prevention Program. It was held at the Criminal Justice Center at Sam Houston State University in Huntsville, Texas. Red brick by red brick, the center's huge structure had been built with the sweat of prisoners from nearby Huntsville State Penitentiary. It was at this meeting that I would learn about the Michigan child murders and share with the story's narrator my own frustration at how serial killers could elude police.

The long title for the VICAP planning workshop encompassed the broad spectrum of experiences of the people in attendance. Even though we were exploring the feasibility of tracking all ages of murder victims, the group focused heavily on missing, abducted, and murdered children because the Office of Juvenile Justice and Delinquency Prevention initially funded the planning committee meetings. I was extremely impressed by the dedication of those around me. Represented at the meeting were homicide investigators, crime analysts, computer experts, investigators of child pornography, child abuse, and missing children, members of the BSU of the FBI, personnel from the Office of Juvenile Justice, and university criminal justice faculty. Much to my surprise, the meetings were not led by Pierce Brooks, but by Robert Heck, an administrator at the Office of Juvenile Justice and Delinquency Prevention, and Dr. Doug Moore, a professor with the Criminal Justice Program at Sam Houston State University. The VICAP concept was Pierce Brooks's idea, and the others jumped on his bandwagon when they saw an extremely innovative and useful method of homicide investigation. Years later, there are still some people who try to lay claim to Brooks's original idea.

At one particular session we discussed the contents of the VICAP form, a vehicle to collect homicide information. Based on their vast experience, the attending homicide investigators were to determine what information was necessary to link cases. The notion was for local homicide investigators to fill out forms on their unsolveds and submit them to VICAP crime analysts. Then the analysts would query the computer and identify those cases that had similar characteristics. The entire process of question selection and interpretation was quite intriguing because I was able to see, firsthand, what experienced homicide investigators focused on to make associations between cases. What struck me initially was how those detectives confirmed that investigators must look for progressive changes in a killer's method of operation from one murder to the next, instead of looking for only those characteristics that were exactly the same. For instance, perhaps a traveling killer strangled his first victim and then stabbed the next one in his series because his strangulation method didn't work. The Son of Sam Killer in New York stabbed his first murder victim, resulting in a bloody mess, and he didn't like it. So he changed his modus operandi, and his subsequent victims were shot from a distance. Murderers change their modus operandi out of necessity and convenience. A repetitive killer's method of operation changes, as he develops experience over time, from one crime to the next. Predictably, the modus operandi changes in dynamic fashion from one murder to the next because the killer learns from previous mistakes and resorts to actions that are comfortable and convenient for him.

In the old days, cases were cleared only by exact modus operandi matches, such as a number of house burglaries attributed to one burglar who used a pipe wrench on all the front door knobs. Short of a confession, would another burglary in the same area be connected if the burglar forgot his pipe wrench and kicked in the front door? Probably not, because the modus operandi was not exactly the same.

With different modus operandi characteristics noted from one murder to another, what doesn't change is the killer's signature or calling card. It consists of acts performed that reach beyond what is necessary to commit the murder. They must be acted out each time in the same manner. Does the killer re-dress the victim after the murder? Is an increasing length of time spent with each victim after death because the killer performs his basic necrophilic ritual? For instance, one such killer posed his first female victim in a sexually degrading position with her legs spread and braced up against a wall, and openly displayed her in order to shock the finder. His subsequent victims were also found posed spread-eagled in various ways and openly displayed. Therefore, the questions on the VICAP form needed to capture information in a way that demonstrated changes in modus operandi as well as a killer's signature in the form of additional postmortem behavior from one case to the next.

During the first session on VICAP forms, I met Captain Robbie Robertson of the Michigan State Police, a seasoned homicide investigator and supervisor. He had the presence of a university provost and commanded more respect in the discussions than anyone else, even more than Pierce Brooks. He was definitely outspoken and his own man. I hovered around him like a drone near a queen. His superior homicide investigation intelligence was unchallenged throughout the workshop. He became a wonderful mentor for me during the formation of VICAP.

Even though we came from different regions of the country and had never met, I felt an extreme professional closeness to Robertson. When he and I talked, I didn't want the conversations to end. I was absorbing everything he said. Unsolved murder cases wore heavily on his pride. One particular series was very special to him. It was the Michigan child murders, a series of murders in the Oakland Corridor that continued from October 1975 through March

1977, when they appeared to stop. They remain unsolved to this day and were his lifelong obsession.

The Michigan Child Murders

One night, after a long day of discussing the brutal elements of murder, Robertson and I sat in the quiet of the Criminal Justice Center's cocktail lounge. Captain Robertson told me, in detail, about the Michigan child murders. His description of the child murders and what they meant to him had a lasting effect on me. During this discussion, Robertson illustrated that he possessed a mental toughness and that he would never quit the fight to catch killers. Notwithstanding the Ted Bundy cases, the thought of investigating a long-term series of unsolved murders of small children was gut-wrenching. Based on my knowledge of problems associated with previous serial-murder investigations, after what Captain Robertson told me, I was even more determined to discover as much about the serial-murder phenomenon as possible so that others could learn from our successful investigations as well as from our mistakes.

In the quiet, dimly lit surroundings of the lounge, as Captain Robertson described his investigation of the Michigan child murders, my memories of our inadequate pursuit of the Ted killer immediately came to mind. Even though each series was different in nature and unprecedented for our respective departments, they started in the same reactive way. Each case began as investigators responded to a dead-body call, identified the victim, interviewed the parents—a most unenviable task—and waited for the next dead-body call.

Mark Stebbins

Like most long-haul homicide detectives who assemble the bits and pieces surrounding the deaths of innocent children, Robertson was soft-spoken and almost melancholy. It was almost as though he were telling a story about his own dead children. The first victim he talked about was Mark Stebbins, a 12-year-old boy. Stebbins was noted as missing on the afternoon of February 15, 1976, after leaving the American Legion Hall in Ferndale, Michigan. He supposedly was headed to his home, also in Ferndale, to watch a movie on television. Just prior to leaving the Legion hall, his mother spoke to him. When he didn't return home by eleven P.M., she called police, informing a police dispatcher that she was concerned because he had never done anything like this before. How many times do police officers hear that same story and the child turns up alive and well, much to everyone's relief? Unfortunately, that is not what happened this time. Stebbins's mother provided a detailed description of her son: he was 4 feet 8 inches tall, 100 pounds, with reddish blond hair and blue eyes. He was wearing a blue hooded parka, blue jeans, a red sweatshirt, and black rubber boots. A stranger would later describe the same clothing to police *four* days later when he discovered a dead body.

At 11:45 A.M., on February 19, Stebbins's body was found by a businessman who had left his office in Southfield, Michigan, to walk over to a drugstore at a nearby shopping mall. In a corner of the parking lot that the man crossed on his way to the mall, he discovered what he thought was a mannequin or dummy dressed in a blue jacket and jeans. As he went closer, he saw that it was the body of a small boy. Stebbins, the forensic team later reported, had died from asphyxia due to smothering. He had sustained two crusted lacerations of the scalp on the left rear of his head. Discolorations of his wrists and ankles indicated that he was possibly tied up with rope or a similarly shaped binding device. Obvious evidence of sexual assault was discovered in the form of superficial lacerations in his widely distended anus.

A witness who worked in the same business complex as the person who found Stebbins's body provided investigators with evidence that Stebbins's body was placed at the scene after 9:30 A.M. on the day it was discovered. The witness stated that he had walked his dog in the same area at about 9:30 that morning, and the body had not been there. That information led investigators to believe that Stebbins's body was held at another location for a period of days and was not immediately dumped in the parking lot after his disappearance. A major question was, why would the killer not conceal the body to prevent it from being found? The Stebbins murder was the first of four related killings of children in the Woodward Corridor.

Ten months after the murder of Mark Stebbins, the bloody shotgun slaying of Jill Robinson was discovered. There was such a disparity from the Stebbins murder in murder weapon used and victim profile that no one related the Stebbins and the Robinson cases to each other. At that time, male and female victims were not linked routinely in the same series of murders unless there was a preexisting relationship between the victims.

Jill Robinson

It was late in the afternoon of December 22, 1976, when 12-year-old Jill Robinson had an argument with her mother over household chores she had not done. In the heat of the dispute, Jill's mother ordered her out of the house. Jill packed some clothes and a blue-and-green plaid blanket into her denim backpack. She walked out the door of her home in Royal Oak, Michigan, wearing blue jeans, a shirt, snow boots, a bright orange winter jacket, and a blue knit cap with a yellow design on its border. Jill was not seen alive again.

The day after Christmas her body was found dumped alongside Interstate 75, just north of Sixteen Mile Road in Troy, Michigan. Astonishingly, her killer had placed her on her back on the snowy shoulder of the road in plain sight of anyone driving by. Bloodstain evidence revealed that the top of her head was blown off by a blast from a 12-gauge shotgun while she was lying supine in the very position in which she was found. The following day, a neighborhood boy found Jill's bicycle behind an office building in Royal Oak. It was a mystery whether Jill rode the bicycle there on December 22 or it was placed there sometime later.

Captain Robertson freely admitted that the Stebbins and Robinson murders were not immediately connected by police authorities because the gender and cause of death for each victim were different. The police did not consider the fact that they were both held as living captives for a period of time and then dumped in plain sight where they would be discovered enough cause to attribute both deaths to the same killer. A disturbing similarity between the cases was that police investigators had no viable suspects in either murder.

Kristine Mihelich

However, within one month another child was found dead and detectives in Oakland County realized that they were dealing with a serial killer. On January 2, 1977, 10-year-old Kristine Mihelich left her home at three P.M. to go to a nearby 7-Eleven store. Her mother reported her missing at six P.M. that same day. By noon the following day, all police departments in the area were alerted to her disappearance and were given photographs of Kristine to distribute. Investigators believed that she was seen at the 7-Eleven store because the clerk remembered that a girl who tentatively matched the description of Kristine had purchased a teenage movie magazine. The Detroit-area radio and television stations broadcasted information about Kristine's disappearance. Over the next two weeks, police investigators chased many tips from the public, all to no avail. A temporary red herring in the investigation was calls from a 14-year-old girl pretending to be Kristine Mihelich. Fortunately, the impostor was quickly exposed.

Blatantly challenging the investigators as if to say "catch me if you can," the killer discarded the body of Kristine Mihelich in plain view in the snow-filled ditch alongside a dead-end road in Franklin Village on January 20. At about 11:45 A.M. on January 21, a mail carrier discovered her half-frozen body. The police investigators determined from body temperature that she had been there less than 24 hours. Forensics also concluded that she had been smothered, just like Mark Stebbins. According to Robertson, the autopsy physician did not find any evidence of sexual molestation, but claimed to have found sperm in her vagina and rectum. However, state police laboratory technicians had examined the doctor's tissue slides and were unable to detect any sperm. The doctor tried to account for his finding by a theory based on the forcefulness of ejaculation. The police lab technicians concluded that the doctor's determination was incorrect and that, like Jill Robinson, Kristine had not been penetrated.

Also, upon inspection of Kristine's body, investigators decided that Kristine's killer had re-dressed her. She was found with her blouse tied in front and not in back, the way her parents said she usually tied it. Her pants were tucked into her boots, something her parents said she never did, but something her killer might have frequently done with his other victims, police believed. This might have been part of a signature, as if the killer were wrapping up his victims for discovery. Even though Kristine had been away from home for over 19 days, her clothes were neat and clean, which meant that she had been physically cared for by her captor.

The police response to the three child murders was to organize a meeting of officers among the local and state police agencies to consider setting up a task force. This was an unprecedented move by the Oakland County Homicide Department, but was necessary since the frightened community was up in arms. At this meeting, the problem of handling duplicate leads was discussed and resolved by a then-revolutionary plan to track those leads by computer. It was only 1977 and the use of personal computers had not yet become a common practice.

Timothy King

By now, as he was telling me his story, Captain Robertson's voice was quivering with emotion. His frustration at not catching the child killer really affected him, drawing him closer to the line that divides the stone-cold resolution of a professional from the burning desire for personal revenge. Captain Robertson continued his story. He told me next of the disappearance of the fourth victim in the series, Timothy King, a slender and attractive 11-year-old boy who lived in Birmingham, Michigan, who was last seen on March 16, 1977. It was almost as though the killer *wanted* to tangle directly with the investigators, Robertson said, because the child was abducted in the face of the police dragnet for the killer of Kristine Mihelich. Most killers would have laid low until the intensity of the police search subsided. But this killer wanted to show the police that even while they were fully mobilized, he could snatch a child right off the street. King was last seen by his older sister at 7:40 P.M. when she gave him 30 cents to spend on candy at a nearby store. When he went out, Tim asked his sister to leave the front door ajar so he could get back in, since she was leaving to see a show with her friends. When his parents returned home at nine P.M., they found the door ajar and the house empty.

The family's search for Tim was fruitless. His parents canvassed the neighborhood, telephoned friends, and then reported Tim's disappearance to the Birmingham Police Department. By 9:15 the next morning, the small task force working the three previous murders knew that Tim King was missing—the Birmingham police chief requested their help in pursuing many incoming leads. They obliged and had set up their headquarters in Birmingham by the afternoon of March 17.

The Violent Criminal Apprehension Program . . .

A saleswoman at the drugstore where Tim was supposed to buy candy described to the detectives a boy who resembled Tim. She had seen him the night he disappeared. However, the most important break for Michigan police was the account of a witness who had seen Tim at about 8:30 P.M. on the night he disappeared. A woman who had been loading her groceries into her car in the parking lot also used by patrons of the drugstore observed a small boy talking to a man standing by a car about two car lengths away from her car. The boy was wearing a red jacket with emblems on it, which resembled Tim's red nylon Birmingham Hockey Association jacket. The woman was able to provide enough details about the man's face so that a police artist could produce a composite sketch of him. She described his car as well. It was a dark blue Gremlin with a white, sweeping stripe, called a "hockey stick" stripe, along its side. This woman's description of the man and his car was a valuable set of leads for the police. It became their central focus. For the first time, the police had a possible suspect, and they immediately covered the neighborhood, trying to locate someone who could recognize the description and name the man.

Again, however, in a move of sick bravado, the killer openly displayed Timothy King's body in a ditch in Livonia, Michigan, six days after his disappearance. A person passing by saw the body and reported it to the police. At the time of his discovery, Timothy was wearing his red nylon jacket with a Birmingham Hockey Association crest, a denim shirt, green trousers, and white tennis shoes with blue and red stripes. This was the same clothing he had been wearing when he left for the store. Timothy's orange skateboard was found about 10 feet from his body. Police concluded that Timothy King had been smothered to death about six to eight hours before his body was found, and investigators determined that the boy was placed in the ditch about three hours before discovery. This would mean, as with the other children, that the killer had kept King's body at another location for several hours before dumping it. The autopsy revealed that King had eaten a meal that included fowl about an hour before death. His body was very clean, including his usually dirty fingernails and toenails. Although the bindings were not present, Timothy's wrists were marked as if he had been bound for a period of time. There was evidence of sexual assault in the form of a distended and penetrated anus.

131

THE RIVERMAN

The four murders were similar in nature, which suggested to Robertson that they might have been committed by a single killer or small group of killers who operated like a predatory wolf pack. The reasons for his belief were clear and simple. First of all, the victims were all alone when abducted from or near parking lots adjacent to business areas where they were last seen. Two victims were abducted on a Sunday afternoon and two on Wednesday evening. These were clean, almost seamless abductions with none of the signals of turbulence or violence that might alert anyone passing by that a child was being taken against his or her will. Each child was held captive for from 3 to 19 days before death. They were well nourished, well cared for, and kept clean during the days preceding their deaths. Their bodies were not subjected to extreme weather or exposure before or after death. Authorities concluded that the children had adequate toilet facilities because there was no evidence that they had fouled themselves with urine or excrement. The children seemed to have been cleansed after their death, and Tim King's body appeared to be clinically sterile. The killer's ritual included neatly dressing the children just before or after death. All of their remains were found alongside roadways, openly displayed to ensure discovery. There was no evidence of sexual assault on either one of the girls, but both boys showed obvious anal assault.

However, there were some clear differences in the murders that disturbed the investigators and made them doubt they were firmly connected. For example, a shotgun was used to kill Jill Robinson. The killer risked attracting attention with a noisy shotgun blast. The shotgun was not used on the other three, who were smothered, possibly by holding something over their mouths and noses. Therefore, one widely promoted theory was that the Robinson murder was not related to the other three murders. I took this to be a premature assumption because it relied on a belief in "the exact modus operandi" theory that police often use to connect cases. This is a wrongheaded theory because, as Ted Bundy and Wayne Williams so clearly demonstrated, serial killers often change their modi operandi during a skein of killings for a variety of reasons, one of which is to throw investigators off the track. When the most obvious elements of a signature are present—similar victim profile, similar handling of the bodies before and after death, similar or identical patterns of body discovery—police should assume that they are looking at the signature of the same killer. In other words, police have to be inclusive when they look for evidence of a serial killer, not exclusive.

Many investigators believed that the timing was inconsistent and that there were too many unexplainable gaps between murders for the children to have been killed by one person. The Stebbins boy was killed in February 1976, the next suspected victim was murdered 10 months later at the end of December 1976, and another child was found dead 3 months later, in March 1977. Also, the time the killer kept the children in captivity exhibited a lack of consistency, ranging from 3½ to 4 to 6 and then to 19 days. But Robertson reasoned that maybe the killer's inconsistency was a premeditated effort to not form a definite pattern that could be detected by authorities. The clever killer didn't want the police waiting for him when he dumped his next victim. But there could have been other reasons that had more to do with what the killer used the children for than with the killer's plan to outsmart authorities. What if the children were used to pose for pornographic photos or films? What if the killer took them out of the area and then returned to kill them? What if these murders were part of a national pattern that was so broad, no one noticed it back in the 1970s? If these were some of the killer's ploys, they were successful, because the murderer was never caught and whatever larger conspiracies might have existed are still unknown.

Other Michigan Child Murders:
The Same Killer?

As Michigan investigators tried to crack these crimes, they were faced with two major questions. Was the Stebbins murder the beginning of the series? And had the murderer struck in other locations, either inside or outside the Oakland Corridor? There were three additional murders of juveniles along the Oakland Corridor during the same time period. Was the same killer responsible for these, too?

Cynthia Cadieux

In the early morning hours of January 16, 1976, the nude body of 16-year-old Cynthia Cadieux was found by the side of the road in Bloomfield Township. She suffered from a fractured skull caused by impact from a blunt object. Cynthia had been sexually assaulted and sodomized. Cadieux was last seen on January 15 at about 8:30 P.M. in Roseville, Michigan, her hometown. Informants heavily influenced the police investigation, since the only information police developed was speculation from those sources that she had been abducted, raped, and murdered by four hoodlums. Supposedly, third- and fourth-hand information revealed that her clothing was once in the possession of one of the slayer's girlfriends. Her clothing has never been located, and none of the information originally given to police about the four hoodlums could be confirmed by the original source when investigators looked into the case again later.

Sheila Srock

The murder of Sheila Srock, a heavyset 14-year-old, was also never officially linked to the Michigan child murders. Srock was babysitting at a house in an affluent community in the north end of the Oakland Corridor on the night of January 19, 1976. Much to the horror of a neighbor who was shoveling snow and watching from a nearby roof, an assailant sadistically raped and sodomized Srock. With brutal finality, he executed her with a rapid-fire barrage of gunshots from his small-caliber semiautomatic pistol. The neighbor described the killer as a thin, white male, 18 to 25 years old, 5 feet 10 inches to 6 feet tall, with a sparse beard, prominent nose, and pointed chin. This was a slightly different description than the police had received for the abductor of Timothy King.

After murdering Srock, the killer stole a .38 revolver, some jewelry, and some other loot. Following his burglary-murder, the intruder mingled with the crowd that assembled after hearing the shots. Like a curious observer, the slayer calmly asked several people what was happening, listened to their responses, and then got into his 1967 Cadillac parked nearby, and drove away. Though investigators had a clear description of the assailant and his car, they were never able to solve Srock's murder.

Jane Allan

Not wanting to rule out any possibilities, Robertson cautiously included the murder of Jane Allan on the list of those deaths loosely linked to the four child murders he was investigating. To other homicide investigators, the linkage of Allan by members of the news media to the series of crimes was erroneous. Allan, a 14-year-old frequent hitchhiker, was last seen on August 7, 1976. That afternoon, she hitchhiked from her Royal Oak home to see her boyfriend in Auburn Heights, Michigan. He scolded her for hitchhiking, after which she left his home. Four days later, her decomposed body was found floating in the Miami River. The coroner believed that she was dead before she was dumped in the river near Miamisburg, Ohio. Owing to her state of decomposition, it was impossible to tell if she had been assaulted, but it was noted that she died possibly from carbon monoxide poisoning. A river disposal was thought by police to be too different a modus operandi for this killing to be included in the series of murders of young children. Another difference between this and the other cases was that the victim's hands had been bound behind her back with pieces of a white T-shirt.

Police informants linked Allan with the Dayton Outlaws motorcycle gang. However, the police had no evidence that connected her killing to the outlaw gang. Even though there was proof of Allan's association with the gang, police still openly theorized that she was picked up hitchhiking.

The murders of Cadieux, Srock, and Allan remained unsolved and were not conclusively linked by investigators to the series of child murders. The existence of those three murders in the midst of the child murders series exemplified the problems that investigators will always have when trying to determine which murders to include in a series. These three deaths were reasonably close in proximity and time and possessed somewhat similar characteristics in modus operandi to the other child murders, yet they were different. Robertson knew the question of whether they should have been included in the series would be second-guessed until the murders were solved. The fact that Robertson didn't arbitrarily rule out any murder was just another reason for me to admire him as an investigator.

The police authorities reacted to and investigated the Michigan child murders in a very predictable manner. Not unlike the Ted investigation, a small task force was formed initially to investigate the first two murders that officially were linked as a series. They were totally unaware of the enormity of the investigations to come. But unlike the Ted cases, over 200 detectives eventually worked on the four murders as more and more leads piled up. The Timothy King case brought forth the first potential suspect information from a witness who observed King talking with the suspected killer. The description of the man and his car was widely publicized and resulted in the accumulation of over 11,000 tips. Just like the Ted Murders Task Force, the Michigan Child Murders Task Force members were forced to create a tip sheet of their own. To handle all the incoming information, they stored the tips in a computer. Computer database programs enabled investigators to improve handling procedures, prevent duplication of effort, and provide for clear and organized recordkeeping. Strangely enough, most serial killer investigations that I have reviewed had adopted, out of necessity and without the knowledge of what was done in any other similar investigation, some form of lead, tip, or clue sheet to handle the mountains of incoming leads. By using the tip sheet, investigative supervisors could better evaluate and prioritize what was crucial to investigate immediately.

In keeping with their trailblazing nature, Michigan's police authorities were the first serial murder force to apply for federal assistance in the form of a $600,000 grant from the now-defunct Law Enforcement Assistance Administration. The grant money was needed to cover a steadily increasing heavy burden on the budgets of many police departments. The only string attached to the grant was that the police force that received it would have to continue funding the task force so they could continue to search for the killer. Altruistically, the grantor and Robert Heck, program manager and VICAP committee chairman, performed a retrospective analysis into the investigative activities of the Michigan experience that he hoped would serve as a guide and be a benefit to future serial-murder investigative efforts. That formal evaluation process remains unique to the Michigan child murders case. Unfortunately, previous serial-murder investigations were buried like their victims, because they were too frustrating, stressful, and embarrassingly inept for investigators and members of their departments to participate in a meaningful critique of their work. Most supervisors of those cases would just as soon have forgotten what went on in the past, even though clues from those investigations could help solve future serial-murder cases.

Similar to the beliefs of investigators on the Atlanta Child Murders Task Force, Captain Robertson was convinced that the Michigan Child Killer was right in front of their noses all along, that they had probably even talked to him. In his sadder moments during our conversation that night, Captain Robertson said that he fantasized that the killer probably laughed to himself in the shadows as the Michigan Child Murders Task Force's own life expired.

As our conversation came to an end, the darkened lounge emptied out, leaving us alone with our mutual frustrations, brought on by unresolved serial-murder investigations. We were thankful that at times, the roaring laughter from police officers across the room responding to one war story after another had interrupted us during the evening. But what happiness there was around us disappeared when those people left the lounge. The preceding hours of discussion had left their mark on Robertson. I sensed his seriousness, stress, and intensity in his constantly changing body movements and his carefully chosen words. At least I knew who committed the Ted murders, even though Ted was still beyond my reach. Robertson hadn't had the same kind of closure; the unsolved child murders wore heavily on him. Even with all his frustrations and the embarrassment of never catching the killer, he was clear in his resolve to air the problems confronted by the Michigan child murders investigation so that other dedicated investigators would not suffer similar experiences. In any serial-killer workshops, Robertson was the most vocal and strong-willed of any of the participants. When it appeared that the wheels of the federal bureaucracy were not moving fast enough toward establishing a serial-murder tracking program for him, he started one of his own in Michigan, independent of VICAP. He—and I, too—felt that those slow wheels meant more of our children murdered at the hands of serial killers.

VICAP Is Born

By the end of our working groups, two FBI agents, Robert Ressler and Roger Depue, were noticeably quiet. There were the meetings for the workers, namely us, and then there were meetings for the "administrators," who included Ressler and Depue. Keppel and Robertson were not invited. Something secret, which always accompanied any FBI involvement, was going on behind closed doors, not meant for the entire group's ears.

My next and last VICAP workshop was in November 1983. We had returned with over 30 murder cases that had been entered on the draft VICAP crime report. The data was entered into a Xerox computer. The Xerox folks were courting the VICAP administrative staff in hopes of landing a megabucks deal with the federal government. The crime analysts, Ken Hanfland, Jim Howlett, and Charlie Hill, were to experiment by analyzing the 30 cases and demonstrating their similarities to the workshop participants. The attempt at computer analysis was a failure since the database program was ill suited for crime analysis, so they compared the cases manually. The rudimentary analysis worked partially, because some cases were very similar to each other, but the sample was far too small to claim a resounding success, even though it was portrayed so in the media.

At this workshop, I met Sergeant Frank Salerno of the Los Angeles County Sheriff's Department for the first time. He was the primary investigator in the Hillside Strangler cases and pursued Kenneth Bianchi to Washington State. No doubt about it, he was one of best serial-murder detectives I have ever met. He and his partner, Gil Carillo, were to gain notoriety later as principal investigators in the Nightstalker cases, which frightened the citizens of Los Angeles and the surrounding communities for several months until Richard Ramirez was caught. Salerno, like Robertson, was not afraid to air the problems he experienced in order to help other investigators avoid them. Salerno, Robertson, and I hung fairly close together during the meetings.

The mood of the workshop was ominous because there was a basic division in philosophy about where to house the VICAP unit. Also, the agenda at this workshop seemed to be staged. It included a presentation by Bob Ressler and Roger Depue on criminal personality profiling, later referred to as crime scene assessment. It was always interesting to hear a presentation on profiling murderers because it contained graphic slides of the most bizarre and sexually sadistic murders, but I didn't see the point for its inclusion at this meeting. We weren't at a training seminar. We were there to figure out how to make VICAP work. Toward the end of their presentation, Roger Depue revealed the apparent ulterior motive behind their presence. The FBI was making a strong bid to have VICAP as part of the FBI's Behavioral Sciences Unit. He was quite convincing since they intended to hire civilian homicide investigative experts as personnel in the unit in hopes of satisfying local law enforcement officials. They hoped even to entice investigators by proposing to appoint Pierce Brooks as the first VICAP manager. Their thinking was that having the FBI's manpower and budget behind the VICAP effort would enhance its chances of success.

Salerno, Robertson, and I knew that housing the VICAP unit within the FBI meant a certain death of the program. First of all, promises of financial backing are just that, promises. After all the hoopla about VICAP died down, would the FBI's commitment and resources dry up? Furthermore, civilian police investigators would not systematically submit murder cases to an FBI VICAP unit because distrust of the FBI had been long institutionalized. In some quarters, there was flat-out refusal from local police departments to cooperate in any fashion with the FBI. Information sharing between the FBI and local police agencies has long been perceived as a one-way street; the locals shared their information with the FBI, but the FBI never reciprocated. Why should we expect anything different from the VICAP unit if it was housed in the FBI? What would the FBI do if no one sent any cases to them? We were shocked at the idea and objected to the FBI's plan, but, unbeknownst to us, the decision had already been made behind the scenes. Apparently, the administrators of the VICAP planning group had already bought the idea of placing VICAP within the FBI. They didn't offer a proposal for us to ratify, but still wanted our support for the Department of Justice fait accompli.

Far away from Washington, California, and Michigan, and within the secure confines of the FBI Academy, a one-day VICAP workshop was held in November 1984. Most of the participants at previous workshops were present, except for three homicide investigators—Salerno, Robertson, and Keppel, persona non grata. We weren't invited. During the last two hours of that workshop Robert Ressler and Roger Depue introduced the National Center for the Analysis of Violent Crime (NCAVC). The three components of

NCAVC were the Criminal Personality Profiling Unit, the Violent Crime Research Unit, and VICAP, all to be housed at the FBI Academy in Quantico, Virginia. They announced that VICAP would officially open its doors in June 1985. I felt slightly exploited, but because to me the program was so important no matter where it was housed, I told Pierce Brooks that I would do everything I could to help him succeed.

In the 20 years since the formation of VICAP, the unit has been involved in more than its share of major serial killer investigations. It can claim some successes for itself, just as others outside the FBI can point to some of the unit's spectacular failures, but the basic philosophy that brought us all together in 1983 is as sound now as it was then, particularly in light of regional and municipal homicide tracking and investigation systems that have broadened the retrieval capabilities of offender database programs. All investigators of major homicides believe that information about serial crimes should be shared so killers can't hide behind the administrative walls that separate agency from agency. I can claim that VICAP was something of a success for me, too, because it brought me together with investigators like Pierce Brooks, Captain Robertson, Frank Salerno, and others. What I didn't know in December 1982, when Pierce first called to talk to me about VICAP, was that in a few short months, I would be in the thick of another serial-murder investigation. This one was to become the nation's most notorious case and the event that would bring me face-to-face once again with my old nemesis—Ted Bundy.

6

The Green River Murders

When my friend Gregory P. Canova, a highly respected senior deputy with the King County Prosecutor's Office, was hired to become the chief prosecutor for the attorney general, he asked me to move over from my desk at the King County police and join him at the AG's office. It was an offer I couldn't refuse. The chance to supervise statewide investigations, especially the tough cases that found their way up to the state level from local agencies, was very attractive to me. Nine months earlier I had looked into a similar position in another state as a criminal investigator, but rumors of corruption within the police force there kept me home. I'm glad I stayed, because the attorney general's job offer was just what I wanted. So, in March 1982, I left the King County Police Major Crimes Unit to take the newly formed position of chief criminal investigator with the Washington State Attorney General's Office.

The First Body Discovery

I was in my new position for only a few months and just acclimating myself to the job when, during the summer of 1982, a short newspaper article describing the discovery of a female body spinning in the shallow eddies just beneath the Peck Bridge over the Green River caught my eye. At the time, there was nothing special about the article, other than the location of the find. It was not uncommon for people to drown in the Green River, but usually they were found many miles farther upstream in the gorge area, not within the city limits of Kent, Washington.

The Green River runs south of Seattle, bisecting the towns of Auburn and Kent and emptying into the Puget Sound. It meanders through Seattle's suburbs, produce farms, and the county's wooded areas. From the air, the Boeing Airplane Company's buildings and other industrial complexes appear to hug its edges like mussels that have clamped themselves onto dock pilings. Along its banks are some of the finest steelhead fishing spots in western Washington. At its closest bend, Issaquah and Taylor Mountain are about 15 miles away to the north.

Two young boys riding their bicycles across the Peck Bridge on July 15, 1982, spotted a body hung up on snags in the middle of the Green River. The Peck Bridge, about 150 feet long and painted that ugly state-government green, intersected the Frager and Kent–Des Moines roads. Kent police officers knew right away that the river victim had probably been murdered because she was nude except for a pair of blue jeans tightly knotted around her neck. Obviously, this was not the typical garb of an accidental drowning victim. The body was later identified as Wendy Lee Coffield, a 16-year-old white female prostitute who was last seen July 7, 1982, 15 miles to the south in the Tacoma area. The King County medical examiner officially listed her cause of death as ligature strangulation. Ever since my days tracking Ted Bundy, any discovery of a murdered female was like an alarm that made me want to mobilize an investigation. My first thoughts were that there was another Theodore Robert Bundy lurking in the wilderness and using the river as a dump site the way Wayne Williams did in Atlanta. At the time,

142

some investigators openly criticized me for always making the assumption that a murdered female found in a river was possibly the work of a serial killer like Ted. The memories of the Ted murders were unpleasant for all the agencies in the area, so many detectives shied away from making any connections among murder victims. Furthermore, they regarded any theories about serial killings as bad ways to start a case. It seemed as though some of the detectives from police departments in the area were prejudiced against conducting serial-murder investigations. I think this attitude was one factor that prevented authorities from solving Washington's longest open murder case.

Less than one month after the discovery of Coffield, an employee of P. D. & J. Meats, a meat company located on Frager Road just south of the Peck Bridge, was taking his afternoon break. On August 12, 1982, the startled employee saw what appeared to be a nude female body exposed by a low tide and lodged on a sandbar. Because her body lay just outside the Kent city limits, Detective Dave Reichert of the King County police was called to the discovery site to process the scene for evidence and retrieve the remains. Dave Reichert recovered the body of Deborah Lynn Bonner, a 23-year-old white prostitute. She had been missing since July 25, 1982, from the strip area of 216th and Pacific Highway South, a red-light district frequented by men looking for an easy pickup.

Despite what the media reported about the lack of contact between the Kent police detectives and King County detectives, the two agencies did exchange information about the Coffield and Bonner murders soon after the bodies were discovered. Their intent was to establish some connection between the two strangulations, but they made a big mistake when the they drew the flawed conclusion that the only similarity between the murders was the location of the bodies in the Green River near the Peck Bridge. Their conclusion that the killers were different was partly based on a hot suspect King County detectives thought they had in the Bonner murder. Police leapt to this conclusion when they were told that an acquaintance of Bonner's had been overheard threatening her life in a Tacoma tavern just days before her murder. That was all the detectives needed to convince them that they had a traditional murder, and they got confident that an arrest was imminent. Inasmuch as their suspect was completely alibied for the Coffield murder, King County assumed the Bonner and Coffield murders were not part of a series. They were wrong.

It was late that summer, just as King County homicide thought it was closing in on its primary suspect in the Bonner case, when their traditional murder theory was blown apart with the discovery of three more bodies. All Seattle was stunned by the story that broke on the evening news about three more prostitutes who were found dead in or near the Green River. The detectives in King County homicide were in shock. They had good reason to be.

On August 15, 1982, a man, rafting down the Green River looking for bottles—a common practice for area residents—saw what he believed to be a mannequin, submerged in about two feet of water. As he poled his way closer he realized that this was no mannequin, it was a corpse. Petrified by his discovery, the man shrieked for help and people in the area called the police.

On that hot sunny summer day in the serene Kent Valley, the surface of the Green River was remarkably clear, rippled only by the presence of police divers. The crystalline water reflected the sunlight with a dappled sparkle, forcing Detective Dave Reichert to make frequent f-stop lens adjustments on his unwieldy Mamiya camera. He photographed every aspect of the crime scene as divers discovered not one, but two bodies beneath the surface of the water. Both corpses were held down with 40-pound angular basalt rocks common to the riverbed. This was a first—never before in the records of King County murders had any bodies been found secured and hidden in such a way.

Body Find

Detective Reichert kept snapping away at the crime scene, getting as many angles as possible on film for forensic teams to analyze. But if he thought he could wrap up his work early, he was wrong. The banks of the Green River held a surprise for him that day. It had been a lush spring and summer, and the grass growing on the slope of land bordering the river was over five feet high, tall enough to obscure the line where the land ended and the river began. Reichert wasn't mindful of this as he backed up along the gentle slope of the south bank in order to get a wider angle and clearer focus on the crime scene. Stepping carefully backward into the high grass, Reichert suddenly disappeared from sight. He had tripped and fallen over another horrifying discovery—the nude body of a third female victim. This was a day that conjured up memories of the same terrifying discoveries of the bodies of murdered females along the Green River that police authorities had stumbled through in the foothills of the Cascades eight years earlier during the Ted case.

The first of the women discovered underwater was Marcia Faye Chapman, black and 31 years old, who had been last seen leaving her home near South 188th and Pacific Highway South on August 1, 1982. A mother of three children, Chapman was described by beat officers as a novice at prostitution. The other submerged victim, Cynthia Jean Hinds, 17 years old and also black, had been last seen hooking johns on August 11, 1982, just 12 blocks south from where Chapman disappeared. The third victim, over whom Reichert had stumbled on the riverbank, was 16-year-old Opal Charmaine Mills, also black. Mills was last seen on August 12, 1982, at a telephone booth at South 194th and Pacific Highway South, where she had made a collect call to her home.

The three victims died from probable asphyxiation, but their bodies were lacking the obvious indicators of ligature strangulation. They were nude, but unlike the previous victims, Coffield and Bonner—who had been found with clothing tightly knotted around their necks—Chapman, Hinds, and Mills had nothing to show how or even whether they were strangled. Now, suddenly, the investigation was fixed on the possibility that a serial killer was operating once again in Ted Bundy's old stalking grounds of King County. But not everyone within the ranks of the investigators agreed with this theory. Even though the sheriff of King County assigned 25 detectives to investigate all the Green River cases, some officers felt that Coffield and Bonner were not linked to the other three. After all, there was no evidence that these two women were ever held down with rocks. Besides, some argued, Coffield and Bonner were white, and Chapman, Hinds, and Mills were black. Those investigators who wanted the cases separated were making the same mistake investigators had made in Atlanta. Weighted bodies versus nonweighted bodies, black versus white, clothing versus nudity— these were insufficient grounds for separating the cases. The larger profile was still intact: all of these women were prostitutes and easily accessible; they all died from asphyxiation; and they were all found in the Green River. Find out who picked up any one of the victims from the strip or who dumped any one of the bodies in the river and in all likelihood that person would be the serial killer.

While Kent and King County detectives gradually cleared prime suspects in the murders of Coffield and Bonner, others were working feverishly to I.D. the last three women in the river. But it took eight days before the three latest victims were positively identified, because two of the women had not been reported missing. This was a major stumbling block for the Green River investigators because missing-persons reports are usually one of the first clues detectives look for when they stumble over an unidentified corpse. So it took eight days of showing photos around the Sea-Tac strip and scraping together whatever forensic evidence was available. And during those eight days, the killer's trail became cold. But considering what was lying in store for investigators—numerous victims of the Green River Killer who would not be identified for more than a year after the discovery of their skeletal remains—eight days wasn't bad at all.

Investigators knew that serial killers returned to crime scenes for any one of several reasons. They returned either to dump more bodies, to discover what the police found or didn't find, or to perform necrophilic acts with undiscovered victims the way Bundy did. Killers feel comfortable at sites with which they are most familiar. The Green River Killer continued his work, dumping three successive quarries in the river within close proximity of one another, even though the recoveries by police of the first two had been highly publicized. We knew that the killer would probably be monitoring police activities by reading the newspaper and watching television newscasts, because that's what other serial killers had done. But the first two recoveries by police didn't scare the killer away; they only forced him to change his tactics. It was almost as though the killer learned he must do something to prevent future discoveries of his work at his watery disposal site. So instead of choosing a more remote site to avoid detection, he weighted his subsequent victims' bodies down with rocks in the same river.

The Surveillance Strategy and the Media

A general Green River surveillance was not conducted after the Bonner or Coffield discoveries because police were not sure where they were dumped into the river or whether a repetitive killer was at work. However, finding three relatively fresh murder victims at a single location was enough incentive for the King County police to then set up surveillance. Reichert and the rest of the detectives were very familiar with the success of bridge surveillance in Atlanta, the strategy that ultimately brought in the Atlanta Child Killer.

Whether it was watching 7-Eleven stores after a couple of commercial robberies, or areas of prostitution as in the Yorkshire Ripper cases in England, surveillance was a proven method of finding killers. King County police set up surveillance vehicles in several locations along the Green River. They were well hidden, yet within the range that powerful scopes could record the license numbers of passing vehicles. But the vehicles were not concealed from the hovering helicopter of one of the television channels in Seattle, which quickly became the Green River Killer's eye in the sky. The five-o'clock news and every subsequent news broadcast revealed the police surveillance to everyone, including the previously uninformed killer. I and many police experts believed the Green River surveillance would have developed firsthand information leading to the identity of the killer had it not been for the television news teams covering the story. While it is true that the police had set up the surveillance much too quickly for an off-the-record news briefing to obtain the cooperation of the traffic helicopter units, I think that the news teams should have checked in with police sources about the units the helicopter cameras picked up before going on the air. The exposure of the surveillance vehicles has been the central focus of homicide investigation seminars for police officers nationwide.

Unfortunately for police, the killer seemed to have seen the afternoon news pictures of his pursuers waiting for him, for he never returned to his river spot to dispose of victims. In the year following the first of the Green River murders, the killer would go undetected, while abducting and murdering over 20 women. He discarded their remains in remote wooded areas where our surveillance couldn't pick him up and where the bodies would be scavenged of any meaningful evidence by wild animals.

The Green River series continued with the discovery on September 25, 1982, of a white 16-year-old named Giselle Lovvorn. Her partially decomposed nude body was found in a wooded area a quarter mile away from the Sea-Tac airport's southern runway, about seven miles from the Green River dump sites. Because she was not found in the river, some investigators felt she was not part of the Green River murder series. But like four other murdered women in the series, she was last seen heading to hook in the same area along Pacific Highway South, on July 17. Lovvorn also died of ligature strangulation.

The year 1982 ended with King County law enforcement officials feeling that the killer had left town because no new bodies had been discovered since Lovvorn and little or no information was incoming about potential missing prostitutes. The force of detectives working on the cases had dwindled to five. The case, though active, had been relegated to the administrative back burner. That was when I got involved.

The Green River Murders Report

At the time, in February 1983, my office on the thirteenth floor of the Dexter-Horton Building in downtown Seattle was a mess, with the investigative files from a San Juan County murder case piled elbow-deep and covering just about everything on my desk, including the telephone. That didn't stop it from ringing loudly, however, especially one day in late February. It was Dave Reichert on the other end, asking if he could come to my office for a talk. His request surprised me—we usually met in his office—and there was an unusually sorrowful tone to his voice. My head was swirling with what might be happening. What was his terrible news?

Reichert's five-minute trek to my office seemed to me like an hour. It was common that my secretary, Shirley Lindberg, would escort visitors down the long hallway leading to my office. But on this occasion, Dave had negotiated on his own the maze of open file cabinets lining the walls.

The Green River Murders

I had my very first sight of Dave when Sergeant Sam Hicks, my homicide sergeant at the time I left the King County police, was murdered while pursuing a murderer. Dave and Sam were close friends and deeply religious and he was terribly grieved by the murder of his friend and colleague. I remembered how sloped his shoulders were at the time, as he if were carrying the grief of all of us around on his own back. On this February day, as I saw him walking down the hall to see me, he was slumping again. I wondered what had happened.

As he tried to explain what was going on, Dave seemed frightened and confused. His face and demeanor reflected the frustration and despair his ongoing serial-murder investigation had caused him. He had been thrown into a brand-new territory that had no road map, an investigation where the rules seemed to change every time you thought you had a solid lead. He looked like he was experiencing what Roger Dunn and I felt during July 1974, when the Ted investigation appeared hopeless. With his eyes welling up with tears of frustration, he said he needed help. He had worked countless hours trying to catch the killer. The more his frustrations built, the more he became possessed, and the longer he worked. If it can be said that serial killers, through the control they exert and the terror they spread, make victims of the entire communities—families and loved ones, the police who track them, and the general public who must live in fear—then in his own way, Dave was a victim of the Green River killer, just as I became one of Ted Bundy's victims.

No one who has not been there knows what it's like to be on the trail of a human killing machine who will not stop. Every day, you second-guess yourself about clues that might have been missed, hot leads that turn cold, and prospective witnesses who've stared right into the face of the killer but remember nothing because they didn't know what they were looking at. Families call you for information and you wish you could say something positive, but you can't. Newspaper and television reporters dog your steps, hoping to find the one clue you've missed just in time for the news at eleven so they can hand it over to the killer, who's also dogging your path. Each morning you wake up dreading the thought that someone will find another body, and by the time you get to the site, there are satellite TV trucks already spreading information, most of it pure conjecture, about the victim. You're making the police department look bad because the killer is still at large, so police brass give you withering stares in the halls of the administrative building as you pass them, and your fellow detectives don't even want you around because they don't want to be associated with failure. Neither your friends nor your family can offer any consolation because no matter where you turn or what you do, the killer's hiding in the shadows, always looking for victims and always watching you. The truth is out there, and you haven't found it. I suspect this is what Dave Reichert was feeling as he walked down the hall to my office that day.

King County PD administrators were at the point of transferring away what few detectives were left on the Green River Murders Task Force and leaving the entire investigation to Dave Reichert to pursue. In effect, that would have imprisoned him for life along a Mobius strip of an unsolvable case and intertwining blind alleys. Up to that point, the respective worlds of six dead women and their families had consumed his life and dominated his every waking moment at the expense of his own family relationships. And during this period, he had slowly withdrawn into an intellectual and emotional corner. Reichert was totally immersed in thoughts of how to catch the killer and feeling guilty that he wasn't out there trying at that moment he was talking to me in my office.

I was thinking that maybe if he just stayed on the street long enough, trolling from tavern to tavern along the Sea-Tac strip, he might just stumble into the encounter between the phantom killer and his victim, the killer making himself visible just long enough to lure his victim into a trap before he disappeared into the woods. Maybe something, just something in the way a car or a van pulled over to the curb and a hooker disappeared inside, would trigger Reichert's street instincts and he would follow them and catch his killer. It could happen any day or night. That's what Roger and I thought when we were looking for clues in the Ted cases. I could understand Reichert's emotions completely. I also sympathized with him because I knew he wanted to tell someone his story, much like Robbie Robertson told me his story about the Michigan child murders.

Like Captain Robertson's, Reichert's story was not about a cop who couldn't solve a case, it was a tale of personal devastation brought on by what he believed to be overwhelming failures. Cops are supposed to be tough—at least that's what they tell themselves. But nobody tells them how to react when they're faced with failure every day on the job, which was what was happening to Reichert. All he felt was his own inadequacies. Nothing he did brought him any closer to success. He was taking this case personally, and each new body find was like a left hook to his gut. Had he lost his abilities as an investigator? Had the Green River Killer defeated him in a classic contest of good guy versus bad guy? These were his private fears. He told me that his demons had taken him over, and, now, though he masked it very well around others, he realized that his personality and reality had been taken over by the search for the Green River Killer.

Dave had come to me not just for counseling purposes and the release of pressure from a psyche about to explode; his visit had to produce something tangible for him as well. Since I was no longer with the department, I could not become officially involved with the investigation in any way, and thus was now an outsider. By coming to me privately as he did, Dave had violated the strict procedures of his department. Under the unwritten code of investigators, as archaic as it might seem, Reichert had admitted personal defeat. If the story got around, he would be totally ostracized by the other members of his department. Thus, he suggested, my discretion was as well known as my abilities, and I was the one person in the world who could help him get through the process of an impossibly difficult investigation that had no end in sight.

I thought for a moment; then an idea stuck. What if Dave suggested to his superiors that I review the Green River murder investigations with an eye to discovering something they had overlooked? What if my report recommended a direction that the investigation might take? Dave's eyes widened with pleasure. For the past couple of months, he was having extreme difficulty convincing his superiors to increase and not diminish the investigative effort. Dave felt that the Green River Killer hadn't stopped in September and wanted the task force inquiry to continue. However, the King County police hierarchy decided to fold the murdered-prostitute cases back into the regular homicide department workload. The cases would be relegated to the back burner, and as long as no new serial murders were uncovered in the area, the Green River murders would be a painful but forgotten piece of history buried forever in the King County homicide files.

Dave Reichert and I had hatched our plans, and he returned to his office. In less than an hour Major Richard Kraske from King County police was on the line. Dick was my lieutenant when I was first assigned to homicide at the beginning of the Ted murders. He had consulted with me on previous occasions in the Green River investigation. He, too, was looking for some way to approach the investigation. Kraske was torn between reducing departmental expenditures, for which he was directly responsible, and avoiding neglect of open investigations into the murders of six individuals. Unaware that Reichert had been my emissary, he asked if I would be willing to review the Green River investigations, come up with an objective analysis of the way the case had been handled, and make whatever recommendations I could. Reichert had carried out our plan very well, and had set the wheels into motion. I requested that Kraske, out of formality, write a letter of request to my boss.

My Green River murders review officially began on March 7, 1983, just after Dave Reichert had delivered all the case files and photographs. I started my analysis, logically enough, with a look at Wendy Coffield's file, since hers was the first known homicide in the series. I was amazed at the small amount of paperwork regarding her case. In serial-murder cases, usually the first and the last cases are most revealing about the suspect. A cursory examination of the files served only to make the cases more complex. In the first place, there seemed to be numerous leads in the Coffield case that had not been followed up on by our Green River Task Force after the Kent police investigation. There was the real possibility that the name of the murderer was in the Coffield file, and it appeared that the King County authorities had not pursued several clues to her murder. The absence of information from the Green River files about the Coffield case was disturbing.

I was also dismayed after I realized that any evaluation of the cases was next to impossible without first making major changes in the existing Green River files. Information about each victim and suspect was scattered throughout all the case books. Thus, it was difficult to decipher what work was actually completed with respect to each suspect and victim. At my request, the investigators reorganized the notebooks. The variety of information in many of the detectives' follow-up reports, officers' reports, statements, and lab reports pertaining to a particular suspect and victim were placed chronologically in individual files for each suspect and victim. The examination of those newly organized files made sense of exactly what was accomplished in each separate investigation and how that information could be related.

Finally, after I had a set of files I could work with, I noted two physical locations in the area that I felt were crucial to the Green River investigations. They were the first point of contact between the victims and the killer, which in most instances was probably the strip area along Pacific Highway South, and the body discovery sites along the Green River and several blocks off Pacific Highway South.

The active prostitution strip along Pacific Highway South, or Highway 99, ran from South 216th Street north to South 140th Street toward Seattle. Parallel to Pacific Highway South and within one block is Sea-Tac Airport, the major airport serving the greater Seattle-Tacoma area. A carbon copy of any strip area in a large city, Pacific Highway South is a checkerboard of cheap, "no-tell" motels, topless dancing spots, card room taverns, rent-a-dent rental car agencies, massage parlors, and "stop-and-rob" grocery stores sprinkled amid expensive hotels and glamorous business buildings housing companies affiliated with the airline industry.

Prostitutes could be found walking along Pacific Highway South and congregating at bus stops and in parking lots of hotels and small grocery stores. The finer hotels always had off-duty police officers working as security, trying to rid the premises of the hookers, but the cheaper motels were their magnets.

It quickly became apparent that any person looking to abduct those women had to blend into the surroundings. Prostitutes, pimps, drug dealers, and street people populated the three-mile strip section of Pacific Highway South. But a major problem for investigators was that the common john didn't look out of place, whether he was driving up in a rented BMW or an old beat-up four-door sedan. Red-light districts such as the Sea-Tac strip can attract a cross section of people, so no one looks obviously out of place.

Four of the murder victims had confirmed arrests for prostitution, and the other two were only suspected of engaging in prostitution. Experience had told us that prostitutes and street people were hustlers, most of whom had mastered the art of the quick trick, but that even they could be fooled by a highly motivated killer. The transient lifestyles of the Green River victims and their willingness to associate with pimps, drug dealers, and men who seek prostitutes made them very high risk victims of violent crimes. They were victims of opportunity for a phantom prostitute-killer masquerading as a customer, cabdriver, pimp, or even an undercover police officer. Why the killer was drawn to prostitutes was a matter of conjecture. Most important for our purposes, at the time of the separate investigations there were no statements taken from witnesses to the actual approach to each victim by the suspected killer. Therefore, how they were really enticed and abducted was known only to the killer himself.

As I analyzed the investigation of the circumstances surrounding the disappearance of each victim, beginning with Deborah Bonner and proceeding chronologically and longitudinally through the last victim, Giselle Lovvorn, I uncovered an unfortunate trend: as the number of murders investigated increased, the quality of the investigation appeared to suffer. In other words, there was extensive investigation of the Bonner case, but the results seemed to drop off a bit in each of the subsequent cases. I was appalled when I examined the Mills case file: I found virtually no useful statements from any source and no active follow-up reports from any detective, despite the existence of what seemed to be real leads.

Frankly, the quality and thoroughness of any investigation depends, quite directly, on the quality of interviewing done with witnesses. It looked as though the interviewing techniques in many of the Green River cases were not structured properly from the beginning of the investigation. The interviews may have been affected by the lack of experience of some detectives and by indifference, impatience, or a negative attitude toward some of the prostitutes and pimps who were close to each victim. In order for a witness interview to be successful, the interviewer has to be focused on the information he or she is trying to elicit. The officer has to put all personal feelings aside in order to make the witness feel as comfortable as possible about talking. In the Green River case, detectives were interviewing prostitutes, runaways, and possible drug users. These were individuals already at risk and afraid that they would be picked up on vice or some other charges. Therefore, officers had to work harder at interviewing those types of witnesses. But some of the officers seemed to have lost their intensity during the interview process itself. At any rate, the outcome was that the amount and quality of information obtained during some of the interviews was minimal.

Experience in serial-murder cases has shown that highest investigative priority must be given to isolating, as accurately as possible, the dates and times victims were last seen and to delineating their activity patterns up to the time of their disappearances. Proper questioning of suspects about their whereabouts at the time of the murder required focusing on those important areas. It appeared, from the file, that while patrol officers, likely inexperienced in follow-up investigations in homicide cases, were doing those high-priority interviews, many statements gained were vague and incomplete. For example, "When was the last time you saw the victim?" was rarely asked or, if it was, the crucial information about exact time and date was not recorded. When pimps and prostitutes recalled dates and times, they were seldom asked to corroborate their recollection. Thus, the resulting information was questionable. Unfortunately, the only solution to this mess was to recontact the witnesses, which would add even more work to an investigation already bogged down with an enormous amount of follow-up.

During the first month of review, I turned the facts over in my mind, trying to develop some theory that would reconcile the cases. With each file line I reviewed, I could see more and more faults evident in the interview process. I discovered, for example, that statements taken from more than one witness on the same case regarding disappearance times and potential acquaintances were often confusing and conflicting. Therefore, there was more than one set of "facts" per victim. It often appeared that statements taken by one officer were not reviewed before other statements were taken. That created even more conflicting information. In fact, I could hit upon nothing that would bring together all the disparate elements.

There was a considerable effort in the initial months of the Green River case on gathering information, and it was clear that all officers were directed to obtain specific statements from certain people. However, it wasn't clear from the files *who* was responsible for examining and synthesizing the content of those statements into potential lead follow-up. That job, which is a major part of any homicide case, still needed to be done. Thus, the task still ahead was huge. A major part of my synthesizing process was to reduce the discrepancies in the witness statements in the case files.

The number of leads collected on tip sheets and developed through detective work was enormous, and, as in most cases, leads were assigned for follow-up. Unfortunately, the investigation into the Green River murders had followed the traditional course of most serial-murder investigations: when there is massive input, investigators become so overwhelmed with the data that they are unable to complete their assigned tasks. As a result, the case quickly dissolved into chaos and the clues that might have led to the identity of the murderer were buried under increasing amounts of paperwork. The only solution was for someone to step forward and assume a role in organizing an overview.

I followed the course of the investigation through the paperwork by randomly checking about 10 of the over 200 suspect packets that had been filled with information. I observed that the entire investigation's ebb and flow depended on the intensity of the investigation of any one suspect at a given time. The major portion of the investigation activities slowed down to a crawl when a hot suspect was being pursued. In other words, a number of investigators were working on a top suspect, and the other arms of the investigation didn't seem to be moving. Acquaintances of some victims were recontacted and shown photographic montages of some suspects; this wasn't done for other victims. There was no clear, discernible priority system that was set up for the active pursuit of quality suspects. Accordingly, only a quarter of the suspects had been eliminated by police investigators.

After viewing the course of the task force's work from the perspective of the victim pick-up sites, I turned to the dump sites, the places where the killer chose to dispose of his victims. What was there about them that was important to the evasive killer? Viewing photographs and reading police reports describing the scenes weren't sufficient. I had Dave Reichert take me out to the body recovery sites.

The day we chose to go was dull, foggy, and drizzly. The ground was saturated not only with rain, but with spring-melted snow from the Cascades. The nearby foothills and treetops were banked in with rolling clouds, which rose now and then to show the dreary curves of the desolate forest. The Green River was unusually high that season, churning mightily with the winter runoff of melting snow.

The first thing I noticed about Frager Road at the point where the three remains were found was how isolated the location really was. Even though it was less than 10 minutes from the honking airport traffic along Pacific Highway South, the killer could quickly be in solitude with his victim. Right above the recovery site was a small pull-off, conveniently concealed by high grass, offering the killer all the camouflage he needed to do whatever he wanted with his victims. In the summertime, a driver would not be aware of the pull-off until he was right on top of it, nor could he see any vehicle parked there from any distance away. Conversely, a cautious murderer could easily be alerted by the sound of any approaching vehicle or, at night, by the headlight beams filtering through the leaves. But despite the ideal site nearby—mostly because the local television coverage had handed the killer our game plan for the investigation—the Green River had exhausted its usefulness as a dumping spot for him. The area was now too well known, a tourist spot even for a curious outsider. But the Green River Killer was still lurking out there somewhere, and both Dave and I felt that he would retreat to even more remote areas. The big question was where. The bigger question was what was the relationship of the Green River to the other possible dump sites.

The River

For any serious homicide investigator, the historical understanding of the significance of the Green River as a dump site for bodies should have been essential to his pursuit of the case. It was not clear from the reports if any other deaths in the area had ever been investigated prior to the discovery of the Green River victims, or if they had been, whether the deaths had been classified as natural, homicide, suicide, accidental, or undetermined. This was a step that should have been taken at the outset. For example, when the Atlanta task force looked into their child killings, they found previous possible victims of the Atlanta killer in the Chattahoochee River, but those deaths were initially classified as accidental or undetermined. Reclassifying those deaths as homicides connected with the Atlanta Child Killer might have provided more possible leads for investigators to follow.

If there were possible victims from previous cases around the Green River, as there had been in Atlanta, anyone involved in those cases could have been a suspect in the Green River murders. Additionally, field interview reports, suspicious circumstance reports, police case reports, officers' notebook entries, Department of Fisheries officers' reports or notes, and any other creative resources relating to activities along the Green River should have been investigated for potential suspect behavior. Questioning of suspects and witnesses should have focused on their access to, knowledge of, and visitations to the Green River area in a specific time frame when the deaths occurred.

The Lovvorn case was initially investigated by detectives who had not been involved in the Green River investigation. Many felt there was no connection. But Lovvorn's dump site was as handy to the killer as the Green River. That wooded area had long since been abandoned by residents who moved away because of the noise of low-flying jetliners on their approach to the Sea-Tac Airport. Houses had been demolished and carted away and only empty, overgrown cul-de-sacs remained, perfect for the consummation of tricks and quick returns to the highway, only seconds away. A john driving his "date" to the cul-de-sac area would not have alarmed any prostitute since they themselves frequently directed their out-of-town johns to those areas and considered them safe streets.

On the night Dave Reichert and I explored the body dump site, the atmosphere was melancholy outside and in. Through narrow spaces between trees to the northwest, I could see the eerie silvery luminescence of the airport runway lights. To the east, I could see the alternating glow of neon lights of the topless bars along the Sea-Tac strip. The wooded area around the Lovvorn recovery site was a vast thicket with many intertwining roads that, just as often as not, twisted off into dead ends. It was a perfect location for quiet but quick sexual interludes in a vehicle. Little did Dave and I realize that a quarter of a mile away, several other prostitutes would be discovered dead—more victims of the Green River killer.

Suspect Profiles

With the body disposal sites permanently etched in my memory, I returned to the case files. Very prominently mentioned throughout each one was the name of one prime suspect. Of all the potential suspects in the case, he definitely was *the* prime suspect at one time based on all the follow-up work that was documented in police reports. He was an unemployed cabdriver and definitely part of the Seattle area "street" scene. When first contacted by police, he admitted that he knew several of the victims and had difficulty accounting for his whereabouts during the time the murders took place.

There were two decisive factors affecting a continuing police investigation of him. First of all, detectives located a female associate and street person who claimed to have talked with him prior to any public announcement about the identities of the last three victims. She told police that he told her the names of Chapman, Hinds, and Mills before their identities appeared in the newspapers or on television. The bad part was that she was interviewed after the victims were identified, so her recollection of the time the suspect told her their names might have been mistaken.

Second, the prime suspect's lifestyle and personal characteristics fit the psychological profile of the Green River killer done by the FBI's Behavioral Sciences Unit. It was in that suspect's packet that I found the actual report documenting the psychological profile of the Green River Killer. Its characteristics of the killer, along with the street person's version of her contact with the prime suspect, were used as the basis for a search warrant affidavit for his person, home, and vehicles. I also noted that the prime suspect was overly cooperative with police investigators. They probably didn't need the warrant, because he consented to everything, including polygraph examinations. Unfortunately for those investigators, he drew an inordinate amount of attention to himself by conducting numerous interviews with members of the news media about what the detectives had told him or were doing with him. That behavior to me was inconsistent with my impressions of what the Green River Killer was like. I felt the last thing the Green River Killer would want was any public attention. It was obvious from a lack of eyewitness information that he had diligently avoided apprehension by intentionally concealing his approach to and disposal of his victims.

The profile was a real piece of work. On the one hand, it attempted to give investigators some idea of what a prostitute killer might be like, but it also described most of the male population engaging in illicit activity along the Sea-Tac strip. I believed the profile to be a major distraction for the investigators because, since it was too general, it forced police to focus on tweaking the profile to the killer instead of investigating the known facts of the case. The profile, like too many serial-killer profiles, winds up becoming the be-all and end-all for investigators instead of the means of solving the crime. Quite frequently, administrators have used it to fend off press inquiries about the status of the investigation, saying, "We're waiting for the profile."

In some cases, profiles can be valuable if the offender is an arsonist or a completely disorganized and mentally disturbed killer. More is known about the personalities and crime scenes of those types of offenders than is known about the repetitive, evasive, and experienced serial killer. The proactive tactics recommended by the FBI behavioral scientists for capturing arsonists and disorganized killers have frequently worked, but recommendations about detecting the identity of an unnamed serial killer have yet to be proven.

The disclaimer at the beginning of that profile report, and of every profile report I have seen since, should have been the first hint of its utility in the Green River investigation: "The final analysis is based upon probabilities, noting, however, that no two criminal acts or criminal personalities are exactly alike and therefore the offender at times may not always fit the profile in every category." But with the Green River profile, the characteristics of the offender were *not* exclusive to the point where most males along Pacific Highway South could be eliminated. In fact, the profile was more inclusive than exclusive and fuzzed the investigation to the point where it almost became useless. In fact, as we eventually learned, even Ted Bundy corrected the profile, pointing out that one of the murders of a 36-year-old female should *not* have been on the Green River list. In 2003 the killer himself confirmed Bundy's observation. The killer also revealed how flawed the FBI profile was. In addition, and probably more crucial to the value of the profile, the very nature of a prostitute killer may be the reason for the more general profile, along with insufficient crime scene information left by the killer. But a flexible and astute homicide investigator, willing to consider input from all sources, must be wary of the sometimes overconfident attitude of an FBI profile, for it is not necessarily reliable.

Years later, what surprised me was that much of the same terminology and descriptions used in the report, which I believed to have been unique to the Green River Killer, appeared as the routine characteristics of sexual homicide offenders in the book *Sexual Homicide,* written by John Douglas and Robert Ressler of the FBI's BSU and Ann Burgess. My concern today is, has the profiling effort in serial-murder cases by the FBI been only a superficial guess about the background of killers in any series of cases? They have consistently avoided any academic scrutiny of their research into serial killers while exploiting those of us who have so faithfully given cases to them for examination over the years.

Carefully examining the FBI's profile in the Green River files and desperately looking for those unique features that would assist investigators, I found a paragraph in which profilers interpreted the phraseology of the medical examiner who performed the post-mortem examination on Marcia Chapman's body. It read: "ulceration consistent with anthropophagy was located over the right nipple. With these findings, we can now categorize this subject as a lust-murderer." I was shocked and excited by that discovery, so I immediately called Dave Reichert. I inquired, "How come you never told me that the killer had left his bite marks on Chapman?"

"It's news to me, too," he said, surprisingly interested in the prospect. What that meant to the case was that it was the only known physical evidence in any of the murders that could be linked directly to the killer, should he be identified.

I told Dave, "If there truly was a bite mark, I didn't see any evidence forms in the file that reflected the collection of bite mark evidence." Routinely, the King County medical examiner, Dr. Don Reay, ran an efficient office. If there was bite mark evidence present on any homicide victim, he would have called in a forensic odontologist to take the necessary photographs, measurements, and casts of the teeth marks.

I checked the autopsy report on Chapman, and, sure enough, the sentence was there. I was quick to find out from Dr. Reay that *anthropophagy* was used to refer, in general, to bite marks of any species from the animal kingdom, not specifically human bite marks. So, in the case of Chapman, the wound was nothing more than a fish bite. End of excitement! Perhaps the FBI should use a dictionary—or at the very least, verify questionable statements. By this time, my curiosity had been piqued. Would the FBI dramatically change their profile with that amended information? I called John Douglas with the correct information. He said the absence of a human bite mark didn't change his views about the Green River killer being a lust-murderer. I didn't see anything else in the profile report that was usable. In fact, I was hopeful that the prime suspect was not the Green River Killer, because if anything was found that would have linked him to the murders, a search warrant affidavit based on the FBI's nonspecific profile would never have survived the probable-cause test of an evidence-suppression hearing.

I continued to fight the urge to investigate the cases myself. It was highly likely that the prime suspect was more than just a casual acquaintance of some of the victims. Interestingly, if he was the murderer, it would have been an unusual instance wherein, like Ted Bundy, a repetitive lust-killer had already acquainted himself with his victims. It would have shot down the FBI's premise that the killer was a stranger to his victims, but then the FBI hadn't really been aware of Bundy's stalking Lynda Healy until well after the fact.

I was also surprised to find a critical deficiency in the investigation of the prime suspect: not one friend, family member, or acquaintance of any Green River victim was contacted regarding their knowledge of the prime suspect. The timing of the discovery of that omission was unfortunate. I realized that, owing to the publicity that followed the suspect, care had to be taken in the approach to those potential witnesses to assure that they neither claimed knowledge just for the sake of convenience nor sought to embellish their statements.

There was also insufficient information in the files about physical evidence and the results of its examination in the Green River murders. Because of that, I could not do a meaningful assessment of the evidence. I suggested that the construction of a chart listing physical evidence by victim, cross-referenced by trace evidence found and the likely comparison against suspect trace evidence, was essential. Investigators could not search for evidence in a suspect's house or car without knowing what they were to look for and what had already been discovered by laboratory personnel. I found several references to laboratory examinations that stated "nothing matches." What was the "nothing" that they were referring to? The items checked were not listed in a specific lab report contained in the Green River files. Investigators needed that information to know what to search for. It wasn't the fault of laboratory personnel that the reports were not in the files. It was up to the detectives to get them and examine them for usefulness to their ongoing investigation.

The Green River Report

Up to this point, I had focused on general investigative problems with the investigation. Fifteen pages of my 33-page report on the Green River investigation covered a detailed description of questions to ask various witnesses in each murder investigation. The specific details were necessary because there were so many unanswered questions about the murders. I supposed that the most obvious reason for the seeming lack of follow-up was that any inquiry about a particular prime suspect almost always set the investigation back and took valuable time away from interviewing others who might have had important information to supply. Given the limited manpower available and the tremendous scope of the investigation, it was in some ways remarkable that the investigators had made the progress they had.

Up to that point in my preliminary analysis, I had been able to review from reports that had been forwarded to me. Now, however, I was at a point in my review where I was compelled to abandon that method and to trust my gut instincts once more and provide my recommendations on what should be done with the Green River investigations.

First of all, I wanted to give my own disclaimer. My review was not all-inclusive. I felt an investigator or administrator familiar with the cases could have undoubtedly discovered more potential leads to follow up and assure the thoroughness of the investigation. What was eerie was that my assumptions about the Green River killer eventually came true.

The killer demonstrated his zeal to conceal the bodies of his victims even though he was unsuccessful. Wendy Coffield, the initial victim, was found floating on the surface of the river. Subsequent victims were found in the river even though they had been weighted or anchored to the bottom, but Lovvorn, the second in the series, was not in a river. That change indicated the killer's ability to be flexible and to use those disposal areas that were convenient to him. The delay in finding Lovvorn's body might have suggested to the suspect that he utilize similarly remote areas away from the river for disposal of bodies in the future, I suggested in my report. I also said that the Green River dump site had become too well known an area to dump a body in, and thus it was likely that the killer's flexibility would lead him to more remote areas, where he would feel comfortable.

Information we had gathered up to that point from FBI profilers, psychologists, and psychiatrists formed a consensus that the killer wouldn't stop as long as he felt he was successful. Every clean abduction and murder, every getaway, every body disposal that went unnoticed by the police until after the victim was discovered was a boost to the Green River Killer's ego and an encouragement for him to go on. He was demonstrating his control—sexual control—over his victims, over the tribe of hookers on the Sea-Tac strip, over the police, and over the press. Killers such as Ted Bundy, Wayne Williams, John Wayne Gacy, and Gerald Stano didn't stop until they were caught. They would not give up their power as long as they walked free. I predicted in my report that the five or six victims we had linked to the Green River killer was just a good start, or merely the continuation of a long chain of murders. I surmised that the organizational complexities of the continuing investigation would only mount.

My overall recommendations were just the opposite of what King County administrators probably wanted to hear. Instead of suggesting that they pare down the force of detectives, I recommended that they beef up the task force and pursue the investigation as aggressively as possible. I based these recommendations on the fact that no serial-murder case, to my knowledge, had ever been solved using the time and abilities of just one or two investigators. To give this case even the slightest chance of being solved, an immediate formation of a full-time Green River team of detectives was necessary. How many detectives? I left that up to the administration.

Eliminating duplication of effort was a priority. In my report, I went on to point out that check-and-balance procedures in the follow-up investigation among cases must be implemented to share information among different detectives, in order to prevent the duplication of interviews and the overaccumulation of information. I suggested that those detectives familiar with the cases should synthesize the information gained and assure that each member of the task force be assigned so that all leads were followed up on and reported back to a central processing desk.

Because so much information would be generated by a full-time investigative team, it would be necessary to designate one person on the team through whom all information would initially flow. That person could not be assigned field duties because his or her assignment would primarily involve case organization and assignment. What was characteristic of previous serial-murder investigations was that large amounts of information and leads flowed through many hands, resulting not only in duplication, but in an almost total lack of coordination and direction.

The Green River Murders

Someone needed to establish a priority in the investigation of suspects and their elimination. Previous investigations had shown that a lack of a clear priority for the processing of information on suspects resulted in some suspects being partially investigated, their elimination postponed by investigations of a "better" suspect, which in turn resulted in the team's having to play catch-up, trying futilely to avoid being overwhelmed by masses of work. The current suspects needed to be rated on a reliable scale of probable guilt. Spurious suspects needed to be eliminated from the case so that the remaining suspects could be investigated aggressively.

In an effort to identify cases with similarities that might contain viable suspect information important to the Green River cases, I suggested that task force detectives also research all homicides of prostitutes and strangled females in western states during the previous five years. My bet was that the Green River Killer did not begin with the murder of Wendy Coffield, just like the Ted Bundy cases didn't begin with the murder of Lynda Healy. There was a high probability that other cases would be discovered that had occurred before the one the police now thought of as the first in the series.

I advised that task force detectives keep uniformed patrol officers up-to-date on the case. I encouraged weekly briefings to promote information sharing and to update patrol officers on which pieces of information had been followed up on. Much has been written about how serial killers really catch themselves. But what usually occurred was that some patrol officer on routine duty came across the killer doing something—like chatting up a hooker or trolling back and forth in his car or leaving the scene with a potential victim too quickly for a casual encounter—that caught his attention. It then took alert and intelligent investigators to turn that clue into final resolution of the case.

Police officials from jurisdictions neighboring King County also needed to be kept informed of the status of the investigation, I recommended, in order to ensure maximum cooperation and coordination of leads. Serial murderers are random, mobile killers and touch many jurisdictions. Because they are often compulsive about traveling to pick up victims, crossing jurisdictional boundaries is a play—either conscious or unconscious—on their part to confound the investigation. Historically, murders by the same serial killer have been committed in different jurisdictions, and the King County Police needed to be prepared for this eventual event. When police cooperate, leads that would usually be lost are retrieved and the killer's position is fixed. I will always remember that it was Hergesheimer's coordination with Ben Forbes of Salt Lake City that reminded Forbes to contact the Ted task force after Bundy was picked up by the Utah state trooper.

The streetwalkers in the district where the serial killer was picking up victims were probably some of the most reliable witnesses, even though they might not believe it. It was more than likely that they'd seen the killer, knew the killer, or had driven around with the killer without realizing it. Since prostitutes frequently get arrested, I advised police officers to interview them as they were booked into the King County Jail because that's when they were most talkative and most eager to trade information in order to be released. That would save untold hours trying to contact them for information about suspicious events they might have seen. I believed that some of the local hookers might have been approached by the Green River Killer without knowing it at the time. Maybe someone at a booking or even an arraignment might remember some fact that hadn't been uncovered. My report ended with the recommendation that King County officials develop an interview strategy for all suspects and potential witnesses. They all needed to be interviewed by investigators who were working from the same frame of reference and possessed the knowledge of what others have said.

The New Task Force

In May 1983, I turned over my report to the new sheriff of King County, Vern Thomas, to Major Richard Kraske, and to Detective Dave Reichert. Dave appreciated the report, but Kraske initially seemed depressed by it. Kraske's immediate reaction was for Dave to write a report either verifying or refuting my observations. Dave Reichert's detailed point-by-point follow-up of my Green River murders investigative evaluation mimicked my every word. He was unable to locate one of my criticisms that was unfounded. At first, Kraske chose to number the existing reports and seal them forever. Luckily, his fellow administrators gave him wise counsel that his choice to have the case reviewed by an outside authority was an excellent management strategy. He should be commended for his foresight. It took a while before he forgave my harshness or would speak to me again, but the sting of my report gradually wore off.

Throughout the fall of 1983, Seattle newspapers reported the sporadic discovery of skeletal remains that they connected to the Green River Killer. A sense of urgency to fend off impending doom filled their stories. Members of the news media documented questions about the quality of the King County police investigation. In November, *Seattle Times* and *Post-Intelligencer* editorial headlines read COUNTY KILLINGS DEMAND REVIEW and TIME TO INTENSIFY THE INVESTIGATION. The articles were direct. Their intent was exemplified by the closing paragraph in the *Post-Intelligencer* editorial, which urged that County Executive Randy Revelle and members of the county council order an urgent review of the police investigation in the Green River murders to determine its effectiveness and to see whether a greater effort should be made to "eradicate this continuing succession of obviously premeditated killings, and to bring their perpetrators to justice." Unbeknownst to the media, a review had already been completed by me the previous May, and county administrators were already gearing up for that sought-after increase in the intensity of the investigation.

By December 1983, the police had linked 13 murdered prostitutes and several missing persons to the Green River investigation even though no additional victims were found in or near the river. Five more skeletons of prostitutes were recovered by King County police in remote wooded areas. The killer had officially changed his method of operation just as I had predicted.

Rumors ran amok through the courthouse that an enhanced task force was being formed. They came true when, in January 1984, the Green River Murders Task Force was formed under the able command of Captain Frank Adamson. I was glad that my report had not fallen on deaf ears. Dave Reichert was both pleased and disturbed at the news he received about the task force. He had gotten what he wanted, 50 additional personnel to help him look into the Green River murders. But he was not commissioned the commander. He was one of 25 detectives assigned to the task force. For all his hard work, Dave felt he should have had more authority in making decisions, in selecting the personnel for the task force, and in overseeing its subsequent investigative activities. He desperately wanted the lead detective role.

Task Force Consultant

Sheriff Vern Thomas, one of the few very seasoned Seattle-area police administrators whom I really admired, called me early that December when the task force was being formed. If anyone could pull off getting a separate appropriation from a usually fiscally conservative county council to fund a task force without losing existing positions, he could. And he did.

He asked me to be part of the task force full-time as a consultant, a right-hand man off whom Captain Adamson could bounce ideas. I was surprised at the sheriff's request because I'd never heard of a full-time consultant to a law-enforcement operation before, but I was pleased to work with Captain Adamson. Sheriff Thomas had surveyed my report from beginning to end, concluding that the Green River investigation was unprecedented and required a non-traditional approach. Wary that his task force would fall victim to the bad habits of former task forces, he wanted me to assist Adamson in helping minimize problems, such as internal bickering and jealousies, improper press relations, tunnel vision, inadequate cooperation among police agencies, and general disorganization. I was so honored by Sheriff Thomas's request that I accepted immediately. He had to contact the attorney general for permission to have me on loan, but I knew that was only a formality.

Sheriff Thomas's telephone call was followed within minutes by a visit from Frank Adamson. Captain Adamson had never been a detective, per se, but he had supervised internal investigations for some time and had a squeaky-clean reputation. His greatest asset was his big heart. He was a very stable and respected leader. He had never commanded a task force like the Green River Murders Task Force before, but neither had anyone else, and he was a fine pick for the job.

Adamson was very clear in his perception of my role. I would be "of counsel," which meant I would be an advisor, an idea man, a sounding board, an objective conscience, and I would be available to Captain Adamson on an informal basis. He invited me to work in the same office with him and to share the decision-making process. Also, he would give me the freedom to consult at every level within the task force. I could advise detectives how to work leads they were unsure of and help sergeants and lieutenants with their work as well. This was going to be an attempt to create an operation with a policy—unlike that of other investigations that I was aware of—that was totally open. Any officer, regardless of rank, was welcome in Adamson's office.

Additionally, Adamson wanted me close by to advise members of the news media on the general problems of investigating serial-murder cases. It wouldn't take long before Adamson was an expert on the same topic. My main job, which was closely related to that of media liaison, was to advise him about the use of the multitude of consultants who volunteered their expertise to the task force effort. With the Green River Murders Task Force in the national news every day, forensic consultants crawled out from every rock, some very legitimate and useful, others very crazy and capable of taking up a lot of my time before I caught on to their act. Prior to the Green River task force, I'd never heard of forensic philosophers and foren- sic theologians, who were self-appointed experts in their fields. This could have easily become a carnival if we were not careful.

I assumed my role as consultant and for the first two months of the task force's existence, detectives were busy setting priorities, investi- gating suspects, considering the most appropriate computer hard- ware and software, reviewing all the case files, and handling a deluge of inquiries of reporters from around the world. I was interviewed by hundreds of reporters so often that I rarely could do my work. Within a month, I was exhausted by all the attention and ready to slim down my glorified media liaison role.

The Green River Killer's Dump Sites

Several months after the formation of the new task force, inves- tigators had identified several body dump sites where the killer had left the remains of the 13 victims. Of course, the first site was the Green River. A second was at the south end of the airport along South 191st and 25th Avenue South. There, the remains of Con- stance Naon, a white 21-year-old, were found in October 1983. Naon's remains were found just several blocks from the site where Giselle Lovvorn's body was discovered. While searching the same area for evidence in the Naon murder, investigators found the skeletal remains of Kelly Ware within 100 feet of Naon. Naon was last seen June 8, 1983, in the area of South 188th and Pacific Highway South, just two blocks from where her body was found. Kelly Ware, also a white female, 22 years old, was last seen July 18, 1983, in downtown Seattle at 22nd and Madison, a red-light district. Unfortunately, her disappearance would not be reported until December 1984, so her remains weren't identified until that time. This unfortunate and difficult-to-follow pattern of finding skeletal remains of unreported missing persons continued throughout the life of the task force. This phenomenon left investigators far behind the footsteps of the killer. Ultimately, the Green River investigations had become nothing more than archeological digs, in which investigators recovered remains of long-dead and unidentified victims, and then historical surveys that tested the never-reliable recollections of pimps and fellow prostitutes. You can imagine how all of this made it nearly impossible to assemble a factual account of the circumstances behind each victim's last moments of life.

A most unusual discovery was found within one block of Naon and Ware, but on the south side of South 191st. The buried body of Mary Bridgett Meehan, a white 19-year-old, was disinterred on November 13, 1983, over one year after her disappearance on September 15, 1982. The remains were found 30 blocks from South 165th and Pacific Highway South, Meehan's last seen location. Meehan was the first and only person who was discovered fully buried. Since Meehan was over eight months pregnant, novice speculators reasoned that the killer wanted to give her and her baby a "righteous burial." Most people held out hope that killers like the Green River Killer had remorse for some victims. I didn't agree with that. The more logical reason for Meehan's burial was that the killer was experimenting with another method of disposing of a corpse. He probably had a shovel along with him that day and decided to try burying a victim. It was apparent that leaving victims on top of the ground in wooded and secluded areas to be scavenged by the local animals was his primary choice of disposal. We now know that burial worked for him in concealing evidence for long periods as well as had disposal in remote areas and transporting victim remains to Oregon.

Lost in the body count of the Green River Killer was Meehan's unborn baby. Even though killed by the same hands that squeezed the breath out of its mother, the baby has never appeared on any publicized list of victims attributed to the Green River Killer or Killers. Even the ever-relentless members of the news media forgot about the unborn baby.

The north end of the airport and the noisy flight path of approaching jetliners was where the skeletal remains of Shawnda Leea Summers, a black 17-year-old female, were found by fruit pickers on August 11, 1983. Summers disappeared in October 1982 from South 144th and Pacific Highway South, just 20 blocks from her dump site. Most believed that the vast area north of the airport—once a teeming single-family residential area but long since abandoned and left overgrown with weeds, blackberry bushes, and empty cement foundations—would be the site of future discoveries.

We discovered another one of the killer's dump sites farther away from the airport on Star Lake Road. The remains were found near where Star Lake Road nearly intersects Pacific Highway South and about four miles south of the main Sea-Tac strip. There is a one-mile stretch of that road where tall fir trees closely border the narrow winding road, which is marked by frequent pull-outs for cars to dump garbage. It was an obvious comfort zone for the killer, who knew the area well. The remains of the first of six victims that were found along Star Lake Road belonged to Gail Lynn Mathews, an American Indian female, 23 years old; her body was discovered on September 18, 1983. She would remain unidentified for nearly two years. A member of her family reported that she was last seen on April 8, 1983, at South 216th and Pacific Highway South, even though it was her pimp who actually saw her last. Another family member claimed to have seen her after that date and reported it to police, so she was taken off the missing-persons list. Then the King County Medical Examiner's Office had forensic anthropologist Clyde Snow from Oklahoma examine all the unidentified skeletons for identifiable characteristics not previously recognized. Dr. Snow discovered that one set of remains had, at one time in the recent past, probably suffered an accident, because her pelvic bone had healed from a previous fracture. Once this information was publicized, a family member came forward with Mathews's name again. This time, the identification was confirmed through medical and dental records.

On December 18, 1983, another dump site was discovered along the Mountview Cemetery Road, located about three miles from Star Lake Road. It, too, was a narrow winding road bordered by a steeply rising wooded area. It was at a desolate spot along the side of that road where we found the skull of Kimi-Kai Pitsor, a 16-year-old white female, sitting upright right near the sign that read AUBURN CITY LIMITS. No other remains were found in a several-hundred-yard ground search of the area. Some speculated that the killer intentionally left the skull in that location so it would be found. Others felt the local predators had dragged it to that point from an original dump location of Pitsor's body outside the perimeter of the search.

Each of those five dumping grounds would be the future resting place for at least three sets of remains. They would be the most influential evidence that led us to believe that a serial killer was in operation, for they were all classified as multiple-body recovery sites.

As we uncovered more and more dump sites in the forested areas surrounding the Green River, it was only natural that we would expect to keep finding more and more of the killer's victims. But the discoveries of bodies came at random and were agonizingly slow. Even though investigators located several other victims, it was only a small portion of the total count yet to be found. From the years 1982 to 1984 inclusive, the Green River Killer was a very busy man, preying like a demon on the prostitute population around the Seattle area. And we were still playing catch-up with history because the missing-persons reports had been filed months or even years before we found the remains. We knew there were more bodies out there, but couldn't account for the gaps between victims. We thought at first that the killer had left the area for long periods or had been arrested for another offense. But we were wrong. We just hadn't yet recovered those prostitutes who were decomposing in deeply concealed wooded areas of King County. We also didn't know, until he confessed in 2003, that the Green River Killer hadn't stopped killing until just before his arrest in November 2001. But that was to change on March 13, 1984, with the start of a series of discoveries of a multitude of murder victims. That day marked the beginning of a new notoriety for the Green River Murders Task Force. It would eventually become famous in the media for processing outdoor crime scenes for body parts and evidence.

A wandering moss hunter stumbled upon the first body as he was searching a wooded area just off I-90, about 38 miles east of

Seattle. Hidden within the confines of fallen and rotten trees were the skeletal remains of Lisa Lorraine Yates, white, who was just 19 years old when she was killed. Yates was last seen leaving a friend's residence to work the johns in the area of Rainier Avenue and South Graham Street on December 23, 1983. Less than one month earlier, she had been arrested by Seattle police for offering and agreeing to an act of prostitution.

Naturally, the finding of Yates's body during the initial work of the task force caused some excitement and unfounded expectations that the killer would have left his signature. Within the four months that it had lain in the wooded area, her body was totally skeletonized, leaving her cause of death a mystery. Not a scent of the killer was found at Exit 38—only another murdered prostitute to fill December's gap in the task force's calendar of horrors.

Through May 1984, a succession of 10 more female murder victims of the Green River Killer were discovered. That pressure-packed three-month period left task force members literally running from one skeleton to another. It was very obvious to all that everyone had seriously underestimated the extent of the murders. The task force of 50 people was formed on the basis that there were 13 murder victims in all. But, in reality, by January 1984, the prolific slayer was suspected of killing at least 47 females, making the total task force contingent itself only the minimum crew of personnel that would have been necessary to handle the investigations. Ultimately Gary Leon Ridgway would confess to the murders of 48 women in a plea bargain that let him escape the death penalty.

Suspects

While some detectives were busy trying to identify the 10 new victims and retrace their last steps, others were corroborating information previously gathered on the first 13 victims. Having drawn every other cover and picked up no scent of the killer, I tried my luck with tips that had been gathered in each case to that point. Much to my surprise, no one had done any type of review of the old Green River cases. After I thought about this for a moment, I realized that was probably because seven more victims were found in 1983 and leads in those cases were worked by our short-staffed team instead.

The first thing I noticed when I began my follow-up was that the investigation of suspects was an incredibly difficult process. By June 1984, over 100 potential suspects had been intensively investigated and only a few were absolutely eliminated. The rest of the investigations went just so far before there was simply nothing more to do in many of them. Many of the suspects' whereabouts were essentially untraceable because there weren't enough people around them to keep track of their travels. Most Green River suspects never left a paper trail by writing checks and using credit cards for purchases. The only certainty was that most of them had been arrested previously, and that was the only reliable indicator of their whereabouts at certain times—when they were behind bars. Corroborating their alibis was next to impossible. Compounding the inquiries even more, many suspects were uncooperative with police, unlike suspects in the Ted murders. Only one person didn't cooperate in the Lake Sammamish murders, and that was none other than Theodore Robert Bundy himself. Regrettably, only a handful of suspects were totally cooperative with detectives in the Green River cases.

After six months as commander of the task force, Captain Adamson was concerned that what we were doing wasn't working. After half a year and the accrual of a lot more evidence, we were still no closer to the killer. Adamson was starved for ideas about what to do. So he assigned me the task of contacting the commanders of successful serial murder investigations to ask them what worked best at catching a killer. And, in retrospect, was there anything they would have done differently to catch the killer sooner. Of course there was. What we did not know back in 1985 was that three years earlier, in 1982, Gary Ridgway, the individual who would be identified as the Green River Killer, had been arrested for soliciting a prostitute by an undercover police officer. And in 1983, Ridgway had been interviewed by two local Des Moines police in connection with the disappearanc of Green River victim Marie Malvar (whose remains were recovered in 2003 after Ridgway led Task Force detectives to her burial site as part of his plea agreement Confession). In 1987, Task Force detectives interviewed Ridgway, who would become, for the next 11 years, one of the five major suspects in the Green River murders.

The first person I contacted was Morris Redding, the former commander of the Atlanta Child Murders Task Force and the chief of police of Atlanta. I was already aware of how Wayne Williams was apprehended, so I was more interested in what Chief Redding would have done differently. Almost without being asked, he said, "He was right in front of our noses the whole time." As the Atlanta police were going into elementary schools warning children about the possibility of impending danger to them and how to avoid it, Wayne Williams was coming out of the same schools after having taken photographs of those same children for their class pictures. Also on several telephone poles around where children were missing, a sign was posted that read:

Can you?
Sing or Play
An
Instrument
★
If You Are Between "11–21" (male or female)
And Would Like To Become A
Professional Entertainer.

"YOU" Can Apply for POSITIONS with
Professional Recording Acts
No Experience Is Necessary, Training Is Provided
All Interviews Private & Free
★
For More Information Call
3PM–7PM
404/794-8980

The telephone number was for Wayne Williams.

7

Ted Versus the Riverman

One day in October 1984, I was buried in a pile of paperwork at my desk. I looked up to see Detective Ed Striedinger of the Seattle Police Department. He had retrieved a letter from a judge in Pierce County who wanted it delivered to task force staff. It was a letter from a "wannabe" consultant and the most unlikely person I ever expected to be of assistance in the Green River murders. The letter came from a cell on death row in Florida; the sender was Theodore Robert Bundy. I was stunned.

The Offer

Ted wrote that he had some information that he thought could prove useful in apprehending the Green River Killer or Killers. But his offer of assistance was conditional. He wanted our assurance that his correspondence and subsequent communications would be kept confidential. He did not want anyone outside our task force, especially members of the news media, to become aware of his offer. Even though I felt Ted's offer was sincere and honest, I was wary because Ted Bundy always seemed to have a hidden agenda.

At the moment that I opened his letter, I couldn't begin to determine what that was.

Did Ted believe that we would take his advice, whatever that was, and catch the killer, and somehow news of his assistance would help his appeals? Other killers had tried to trade their help or information with law enforcement as a means of convincing reluctant courts that they were worth more to society alive than dead. Was Ted going to use the Green River cases as a forum to tell us about his murders? Or did he want to become involved just for his own perverse satisfaction? After all, Ted had been locked up for a long time—his pent-up fantasies might well be ready to explode. Or was he up to some trick? Was he planning a way to get us in a position of confidence, thereby catching correction officers with their guard down and escaping? Whatever Ted was up to, I was sure his motives weren't at all altruistic.

Breaking the ice with us slowly, Ted first claimed to have occasionally read about the Green River murders and complained that the coverage in Florida was sensational, superficial, and sporadic. He did not have any special or exceptional reaction to the news of the Green River cases beyond what most other people in that part of the country had, except that by being from the Seattle/Tacoma area, his interest was, perhaps, keener than most. Ted wrote that his daily access to media coverage increased when he began receiving a subscription to the *Tacoma News Tribune*. It was at that point that he developed what he believed were valuable insights into the Green River murders. His interest was piqued by the discovery of the body of a woman in a remote area of Pierce County, his home territory. He explained that the descriptions of the scene in a *News Tribune* article, general though they must have been, were far more detailed and evocative than any he had read before. Apparently, CNN's accounts of the latest possible Green River murder site aroused in Ted some vivid impressions about the behavior of the person or persons responsible for the series of murders. Did Ted see the Riverman, which is what he called the Green River Killer, as a mirror image of himself? Or did Ted so envy the Riverman, who could fulfill his violent sexual fantasies and go undetected, that he had to experience the Riverman's crimes vicariously and then take part in the hunt for him?

Setting his hook slowly, Ted claimed that it was presumptuous of him to believe that we would be interested in anything he could provide. We may have already developed impressions, observations, and hunches similar to the ones he had. Justifying the inadequacy of his own theories, Ted was quick to point out that we had access to an enormous amount of information on the case that he didn't. However, in spite of this, Ted suggested that an investigator be sent to talk to him only about the Green River matter. Any investigator we sent would have his hands full with the task of interviewing this "expert."

Before the dust had settled on Ted's first letter, another came rolling in, this time through John Henry Brown, a Seattle attorney whom Ted trusted. It was similar to the first in content, but in this one, Ted was more humble. Not claiming some noble, civic-minded motivation for offering his help, he simply stated that the Green River cases really intrigued him. He went on to say that he was sure the series of killings probably interested a lot of people, but the difference was that he had knowledge and a point of view that no one else did. Quite candidly, he admitted that he had something productive to offer. Imagine, a brutal killer like Ted Bundy desiring to be a helpful citizen.

Ted's offer of assistance in the Green River murders rekindled the hope I had held since investigating his case of speaking to him someday about the murders he had committed. Captain Adamson felt Ted couldn't help the Green River investigation much, but agreed that it couldn't hurt to talk with him. Maybe Ted wouldn't help with this case, but he could confess to murders that we hadn't nailed him for yet.

Before we contacted Ted, I wanted to get in touch with Dr. John Berberich, a clinical psychologist, and Dr. John Liebert, a psychiatrist. Both of them were vital in producing a profile of the Ted killer in 1974. We had spoken extensively in the past of Ted Bundy's rare personality type. Now it was time to devise a strategy to deal with the real Ted Bundy, with the ultimate goal of obtaining a confession to his murders.

The Confession Strategy

First of all, we decided that any written correspondence back to Ted must be short and contain phrases similar to the ones he used in his letters so he wouldn't misconstrue our intent. We had to agree with everything he said. If anything, our words must mirror his; otherwise, he might become suspicious of our motives for speaking to him. On the other hand, we had to play somewhat hard to get. After all, we just couldn't run down there at his first request. If we did, he'd have the upper hand psychologically—he'd know he had us hooked from the beginning. The strategy of the day was to make him squirm a little, make him really want us.

I wrote to him:

Dear Ted:

This is to acknowledge receipt of your letter to the Green River Task Force dated October 1, 1984. Your request that any communications we may have be kept in "strictest of confidence" is absolutely honored. I, too, am concerned that any comments made by you could be detrimental to the Green River Investigation.

I am interested in what information you have that could prove useful in apprehending the person(s) responsible for the Green River murders. In order to assess the immediacy of your assistance, could you provide just some facts about the nature of your help? I could, tentatively, visit Florida in the middle of November in conjunction with other investigative duties. I have made inquiry to your local FBI to arrange a possible visit. You may hear from them. The sensitivity of this matter was emphasized.

I respect your statement of "playing no games," and, frankly, playing games with you is presumptuous on my part and a waste of my time. I am interested in what is useful in resolving the Green River killings and what your contribution is. We will communicate at your request only about the Green River murders and "nothing else."

Bundy's Initial Analysis

In less than two weeks, Ted responded with a 22-page letter. I didn't expect him to write so soon, and certainly not at length as he did. By being so informative, Ted gave me the chance to analyze his effort at assistance and plan questions for our future meeting.

Ted was starved for our questions and wanted to be sure we knew that he would answer them fully. Ted immediately clarified that he had no desire to play detective. It was not a role he felt capable of playing, he said. I guess he thought we might characterize his help in that way, but he was wrong. We saw him as someone with a different and highly practical point of view.

With the seriousness of a counselor, Ted sensed he had strong insights into and feeling for what was going on in the mind of the man responsible for placing the bodies in the locations the "Riverman" had. Ted was convinced that those sites offered the best opportunity for apprehending the man. For purposes of brevity, Ted used the name Riverman to refer to the Green River Killer.

There was much more that the Riverman was doing at these dump sites than disposing of his victims' bodies and Ted knew it. How, where, and when the Riverman hunted for, approached, made contact with, lured, and eventually abducted his victims were clues to his frame of mind and his personal motives for killing the women he did. All of this intrigued Ted. As a killer who meticulously practiced each of those things, Ted intimately knew the importance of them to our killer. However, Ted believed that this psychological aspect of the investigation, the police guesswork about the killer's mind, was a puzzling, time-consuming, complex, and highly speculative exercise that would be less likely to lead us to our man than the kind of hard-core evidence that police dig up from good investigative work.

Ted made the disconcerting point that even if we had some firm answers to how, when, and where the Riverman abducted his victims, those answers could easily have left us a long way from finding our suspect. So what if we found out what turned the killer on? Ted suggested that we still wouldn't know who the killer was. Unfortunately, that kind of speculation was the part of the investigation that was heavily dwelt upon, resulting in endless lines of inquiry that focused on countless leads that needed to be checked out regardless of the outcome. Ted thought if we got lucky and actually found the killer in this way, it would be called good police work. If not, it was just another wild-goose chase.

Ted revealed that his preferred strategy for catching the Riverman would be to put a newly discovered dump site under surveillance. But before getting into detail about his strategy, Ted asked a lot of his questions about the Green River cases and approached each one of them with the acumen of a skilled researcher. Initially, Ted wanted to know what kind of "scene" the victims were into. He had heard the Green River victims characterized as teenage prostitutes. Ted asked if we thought there were exceptions. He felt that some might have been called prostitutes because they had "reputations," were party girls, runaways, school dropouts, or delinquents. Perceptively, Ted had drawn the same conclusion about the victim class that we had—it was broader than just prostitutes.

Acknowledging the Riverman's study of his victims, Ted emphasized that the Riverman had a sensitivity to and knowledge of the "scene": the lifestyle, habits, movements, hangouts, and likes and dislikes of the women he was hunting from the time he started pursuing his victims. Ted didn't know how the Riverman obtained such knowledge and understanding, but there was a good possibility that he was very much a part of that "scene" or at least on the fringes of it. Ted was sure that the Riverman's understanding of this set could only have increased over the past couple of years.

Ted went on to say that the "scene" was more accurately described as a subcultural milieu that included prostitutes, delinquents, runaways, party girls, and their friends and peers who hung out at arcades, malls, and taverns, and who were also into drugs and partying and, generally, whose members were free-spirited and mobile. His point was that somehow the Riverman came to know his class of victims and their lifestyles in an intimate way that allowed him to manipulate and lure them to him. Ted felt that the better we understood the whole scene where the murderer was preying, the better we would understand how the Riverman works and who he is. Frequently, Ted found himself speaking from the Riverman's frame of reference. From the Riverman's point of view, that class of victim he chose could not be better; from law enforcement's vantage point, it could not be worse.

Appreciating the difficulty of our investigation, Ted reiterated the litany of reasons why the Green River murders were hard to follow up on. First, the disappearances were usually not reported until days or weeks after the victims were last seen. Second, their movements were hard to trace. Third, a comprehensive list of their friends and associates was difficult to compile. And fourth, in the beginning, neither the news media nor the police paid the disappearances much attention. All these conditions were ideal for the

Riverman, who probably wanted attention as much as he wanted to get caught.

What made the police investigation almost impossible was one of the primary reasons the Riverman continued to operate in the very face of an intense police presence and publicity: his victim pool continued to provide him with ample candidates. Ted described the group of victims as extremely vulnerable because it seemed to be comprised of young women who are, in some respects, bolder, harder to intimidate and control, and more mobile than most people, as well as being inclined to adopt the it-can't-happen-to-me attitude. Ted's conclusion was that the Riverman continued to work his territory in part because he was confident of his abilities. He knew the police weren't close— he might not have had the time or money to go elsewhere, but more important, he still had ready access to his potential victims.

Next, Ted spoke about the different ways the Riverman was approaching and abducting his victims. Ted emphasized the simplicity of his technique. Ted speculated that he could have played the role of a cop, like Bianchi and his cousin had, stalked, and physically carried off his victims. Hadn't Bundy himself posed as a cop in Utah when he tried to abduct Carol DaRonch in his VW? It's easy to purchase a police badge, stick it in your wallet, and demand that a streetwalker come along with you for questioning. Once she's in your car, you can take her to an isolated place where you can talk. By then, it's too late for her to escape. This process was so simple, we would probably have said, "Why didn't we think of that?"

However, Ted's initial sense was that the victims, like the public, were looking for the stereotypical murderer, the Henry Lee Lucas/Ottis Toole type straight out of a B horror movie: the grizzled, older drifter type with sunken eyeballs, salivating lips, and a lewd demeanor. Overall, the Green River victims took steps to avoid such people and any other males they considered strange. And for a matter of weeks or months, they were confident they had been successful in coming up with defenses adequate to the threat of the Riverman, until they met the Riverman, who fit none of their preconceptions.

Ted described the characteristics of the Riverman, and in doing so he could have been describing himself. For the victims, the Riverman didn't fit their image of a killer and he was able to place them at ease. In spite of what people thought, he was one of the crowd, maybe a peer, maybe a pimp, maybe a john, which was why he was so effective and hard to find. He didn't do anything out of the ordinary that would help people remember him. His best qualities were that he didn't stand out or come on strong in a heavy, intense, or threatening manner. Quite possibly, lots of girls he never abducted were approached by him, and he drifted alongside, scoped them out, engaged them in a conversation, dangled a lure or two in front of them, and when they didn't bite, he casually faded out. Ted's self-concept was that he and the Riverman were nice guys—easygoing—and looked like many of the men they hung out safely with every day. There was nothing memorable, threatening, or unusual about them; they were just other faces in the crowd. While we thought that Ted was probably right on the money, his comments didn't really get us that much closer to our man.

Noting that the Riverman was working a relatively small geographic area, Ted was interested in whether any of the victims knew each other. Ted's next few comments really were indicative of how much Ted thought about how to abduct easy victims. He wondered if any of the victims carried address books. Ted knew that the telephone was the perfect way to anonymously and facelessly set up a safe rendezvous. In an even more frightening portrait of a predator exploiting his victims' abilities to find new prey for him, Ted suggested that the Riverman was asking those he abducted for names of friends and for places where they might hang out in order to supplement his existing knowledge of the scene, which he was always looking to expand.

The lapse of time between a person's disappearance and the time the body was dumped or buried was very important to Ted because it revealed insight into the Riverman's living situation. Simply stated, if several days elapsed, then a strong inference could be made that the Riverman lived alone in an apartment or house that afforded some privacy, especially for entering and exiting, just like Ted's apartment near the University of Washington. We had a hard time following up on this possible lead because in 100 percent of the Green River cases, that crucial period of time was unknown.

Next, Ted wondered if any of the girls the Riverman had killed didn't fit the model of his typical victim. If there were those types of victims, Ted hypothesized that maybe the killer changed his tastes occasionally or made a mistake, thinking one of those exceptional victims was something she wasn't. Ted also cautioned us not to limit the description of the victims to prostitutes, since the Riverman might have been looking for a general type, rather than someone who was actually a prostitute. Ted believed that the Riverman was hunting for young women who exhibited a certain range of characteristics, possibly a display of sexual promiscuity, which prostitutes as well as hitchhikers, runaways, and barflies demonstrated. More important, Ted pointed out that the Riverman focused on a kind of place or situation, as well as specific victim types. Occasionally, a hapless victim strayed into a situation or place and she was close enough to the Riverman's profile for him to move on her. Ted emphatically explained that should the Riverman abduct more than prostitutes, then obviously his approaches, lures, and modus operandi were flexible and not tailored specifically to prostitutes. Ted predicted that the Riverman would expand the pool of women he was interested in, but for now he would continue with his present selection pattern.

The space of time between each of the Riverman's murders was vital to Ted's understanding of the factors that influenced the killer's behavior. Ted surmised that when and how often the Riverman abducted his victim depended on what he called internal and external factors. The killer's need to abduct, the time spans between which might vary and be separated by long periods of time, was an internal factor. External factors, such as the demands of family, job, or school, also came into play. Therefore, the pattern of victim's disappearances—in the daytime or nighttime, during weekdays or on weekends—would probably reveal work schedules and family responsibilities the killer had. Ted believed that a close analysis of when the Riverman abducted his victims would give insight into his mind and lifestyle. As it turned out Bundy was dead right on this call.

Ted called the whole business about when, where, and how the Riverman abducted his victims the "front end" process. Ted admitted that all the various questions, hypotheses, speculation, lines of investigation, and possible clues were mind-boggling. But the investigation of the body recovery sites, or what Ted called the "back end" process, was just the opposite. Ted believed that the where, when, how, and why of the sites were much less of a mystery and, not coincidentally, offered us the best clues and trap to catch our man red-handed.

Ted most strongly advised that we stake out a newly discovered victim dump site to catch the Riverman. Ted could not think of any objection to his tactic, emphasizing that if the site had a fresh victim, the Riverman was sure to return. Ted was so certain of this because that's exactly what he had done—he had returned to old dumping sites, over and over again.

Ted divided his plan for surveillance of the fresh dump site into two parts. The first involved those actions of approaching and determining if a fresh find was indeed a Green River victim, and the second was the full-scale surveillance of that site.

Part one of Ted's plan required that the newly discovered body be kept secret; that would be achieved by sequestering those who found the body. Ted recommended using land-based telephone lines instead of police radio frequencies for communication among task force members to avoid alerting the news media at all costs. Reporters and helicopter news units were all equipped with police band scanners and would phone in any body discovery message to their stations for broadcast. If the Riverman was anything like Ted, he'd surely be watching the five-o'clock news.

The next step of Ted's plan was to rapidly deploy surveillance teams and equipment to the area and debrief those who had found the body. A review of detailed maps of the area with witnesses would also be required, with initial surveillance posts identified. Teams would take up positions to monitor traffic in the area by recording license plate numbers and types of vehicles traveling key roadways near the site. Team members would be dressed as civilians, and would drive to posts in old, beat-up four-wheelers, pickups, and station wagons. Ted advised that officers should never survey the area from a vehicle and that no officer should have to seek camouflaged cover. And, he stressed, officers should leave no vehicles in the area, nor should people be taxied in and out by police in uniform.

The last phase of part one of Ted's plan called for a survey team to view the site and determine if it was a Green River site. If it was determined as such, then part two, a full-scale stakeout, would be enacted. As Ted explained part two to us, he warned us about what we should expect from the Riverman. Ted believed the Riverman would first drive by the general area of the site a few times. He might park some distance from the site and hike in. Undoubtedly, the Riverman would closely examine all activity and vehicles in the area before moving in, Ted said. If the Riverman returned to the site with another body, he would drive as close to the site as he could at a time when there was the least amount of activity in the area. And finally, he could be expected to turn up at the site at any time, probably on foot. Ted's surveillance theory was wonderful except for the fact that we hadn't found a fresh body at the 20 or so sites we had discovered up to that time. And the way the cases seemed to have petered out, it didn't look like we would find any new victims there.

Ted closed the second letter by taunting us with what he thought we would be interested in, and he was right. He said that his other ideas included a method of getting the Riverman to come to us, ways of hunting for his dump sites, and his own profile of the Riverman.

Ted Bundy as the Living Witness

Ted's communication revealed a great deal about his own behavior, in addition to his thoughts about what the Riverman was like. We felt Ted couldn't talk about the Riverman's behavior without detailing some of his own experiences. It was almost as though Ted wanted to use the first person rather than the third person to describe the Riverman because he felt he knew the Riverman so well. He crept inside the killer's mind. These were Ted's experiences, we believed, lusts and predatory strategies that control-type serial killers shared, not with each other directly, but from a pool common to all of them. From what Ted said, we discerned that each serial killer recognized an "other" on sight, either by description or through perception, and could relay through "others" the things that he couldn't say at first about himself. It seemed like Ted was able to animate the Riverman as a presence, bring him to life in a way that we couldn't, see through his eyes, and walk in his footsteps. That was why it was as if Ted were talking to us at first in a language we couldn't translate. And that was why it became clear to me that I had to lay the groundwork for confronting him face-to-face—not only to get Ted's help in finding the Riverman, but also to get the confessions we so desperately wanted from Ted himself.

8

Innocent Victims

The city of Starke, Florida, was the home of the Florida State Penitentiary, a kind of Serial-Killer Central where some of the South's most notorious multiple murderers were waiting on death row to have a seat in Florida's equally infamous electric chair—"Old Sparky." Dave Reichert and I had the privilege of visiting the town and the prison to make face-to-face contact with Ted Bundy. We had booked a room at the Econoline Lodge, which was about two steps lower than a Motel 6 and our home for two days. We didn't want our presence to become general knowledge, so we registered under Dave Reichert's name—the lower our profile the better. If anyone caught wind that we were interviewing Bundy, members of the news media would have flocked to the prison like ants on a bird's carcass, and that was the last thing we wanted.

But Dave Reichert was an iron-pumping fanatic whose bodybuilder's physique was something to envy. He had carted his dumbbell weights, boom box, and aerobic tapes all the way from Seattle to Starke. While we waited through the hours early in the day before seeing Ted, an upbeat Reichert set up his weights on the motel's lawn to work out in the Florida sunshine. With his well-developed body rocking on the lawn to an aerobic tape that boomed through the oversized speakers and his weight-lifting technique

that made him look more like machine than man, Reichert capti-
vated the attention of the housekeepers, who were peeking out of
windows or standing outside instead of cleaning rooms, asking,
"Who is this hunk?" Word spread fast among the motel employees
about the bodybuilder who'd just checked in. It didn't take them
long to get his name from the front desk and show him their appreciation for the show he'd put on that day. When we left to have dinner and returned later that afternoon, I noticed that the front
marquee brightly displayed WELCOME, DAVE REICHERT. So much for
incognito. I asked Dave to request that the greeting be removed.

First Meeting with Ted

That day, Dave and I made our first visit to the prison. As we
pulled up, the lime-green state penitentiary was an impressive sight,
rising austerely and dramatically above the surrounding landscape.
The guard tower stood next to the main gate, and the fence that bordered the penitentiary and grounds was constructed of three separate coils of razor-sharp, 10-foot-high concertina wire. The grass
between the wire rolls was neatly manicured. The sally port entry to
the prison, like a hatchway on a naval vessel guarded by sentries,
blocked our entry. After undergoing a search of our possessions, we
were taken to Assistant Warden Pete Turner's office. He had approved our visit before we arrived. With the savvy of a man who had
dealt with hardened cons, he warned us of Bundy's constant game-
playing. "Try not to get used by him; he always has an agenda," he
warned. It was basic advice we wouldn't forget. Turner led us to a
small, drab, cream-colored interview room. A creaky wooden table
and three metal chairs filled the room, and one wall had a barred
window that was a constant reminder of restricted freedom.

Ted, adorned in interwoven chains around his waist, wrists, and
arms, looking much like Houdini being led to the water tank, was
escorted by a burly prison guard. His figure was hunched as he said
sheepishly, "Hello, I'm Ted." His reach for my hand was slow,
weighted as it was by the chains of death row. The touch of his
hand was sticky wet. Was the great Ted Bundy nervous? As I
looked directly into his eyes, they quickly turned away. Ted's face
was pale, his cheeks hollowed, his eyes lusterless, and his voice

feeble. He was almost feral in our presence, like an animal just out of his cave.

Apologetic about his appearance, Ted expressed reservations about our interview, claiming that he was presumptuous to think he could be of assistance. Ted was setting the hook convincingly, in a way, we would come to discover, that only he could. What were we supposed to do, get up and leave? He had a captive audience and all of us knew it. His phony self-effacing attitude and feigned weakness were part of a preconceived act, a method to sucker us in. Sure, he was partly debilitated, caged together with other murderers on Florida's death row, but he was also acting out a weakened state of health as a crutch, just like the arm-in-a-sling ruse he had used so cleverly in the past. Bundy was working on our sympathy, getting us to drop our guard in order to accept his view of reality. That was how he had lured his victims years earlier, and that was going to be his approach to us now.

But Ted also desperately wanted some form of validation from us. I was to realize years later that we were part of his grand scheme not only to extend his life, but to restart it by giving him an investiture as a homicide consultant. As bizarre as this sounds, it was almost as though he had found new meaning to life right there in the interrogation room on death row. Every body gesture, every aspect of his speech and phraseology, was keyed to convincing us of his expertise in the field of serial murder. Yet he was also dependent upon our approval that he was not the hapless person, the outcast of society, that we all knew him to be. Reichert looked at me while Ted settled into his persona for this first interview. I looked back at him. None of this was going to be easy.

Victim Types

From my point of view, we started with something simple—how the killer approached his victims. Serial killers have been known to approach their victims at the most opportune moment, when there was the least possibility of detection. People who became victims of a serial killer were involved in activities that were either high or low risk. Some victims were looking for dates in a bar, were hitching rides from strangers, or hooking in bars or along the strips of red-light districts—all high-risk activities. Those activities made the women easily accessible, not requiring the sophisticated approach of a predatory and seasoned killer. However, other murder victims were doing things that did not take them out of the sphere of normal everyday life. They were sleeping in their beds, working at convenience stores, shopping at a mall, or just walking home. Those low-risk activities were common for most people and required the killer to use premeditated abduction routines in order to attack his victims. In either case, the killer chose victims who were vulnerable and easy to control. Frequently, victims were small-framed males and females, the elderly, or children.

Ted believed that the Riverman picked the ideal victim class: the car-date prostitute. These prostitutes had a vested interest in getting into a car quickly and surreptitiously with any nonthreatening person who appeared to have the necessary cash. But Ted was very cautious about classifying all the Riverman's victims as prostitutes. He wanted confirmation that all of the Green River victims were prostitutes at the time they disappeared. "Were they?" he asked. "All of them?"

"We're pretty safe in saying that they were all prostitutes," Reichert told Ted. "If there's no arrest record filed, we have associates who say that the victim was known to do a trick here and there. But it doesn't necessarily mean that each one of these victims had an arrest record," Dave went on.

The fact that some of the victims were not prostitutes was significant to Ted because, in Ted's experience, those were times when mistakes occurred. Since Ted had deviated from his own victim class by picking up Brenda Ball at a topless dance tavern frequented by bikers, we felt that Ted knew the Riverman also approached victims with different lifestyles. Therefore, we knew that Ted was trying to substantiate in his own mind the reason why the Riverman would pick up women who were not prostitutes. But Ted also warned that those victims not fitting the mold could have been killed by someone other than the Riverman.

Whether Amina Agisheff, the first victim on the Green River list, was a prostitute was questionable, we explained to Ted. She was known to hang out at First Avenue and Pike Street, a vice area in downtown Seattle, but she had no record of prostitution arrests. She could have been mistaken for a street person. On the night she disappeared, she was last seen going to a bus stop and was expected home by her three children.

Innocent Victims

Ted explained that for a lot of reasons Agisheff didn't seem to fit the Riverman's prototypical victim personality. And "that's something you guys have to deal with, the ones that don't fit. The ones that aren't prostitutes would be the ones that I would say 'why?' How were they approached? If they're just sort of hanging out, it's one thing for a guy to focus on prostitutes. He has a certain M.O., a way of approaching his women. If it's just a matter of driving up somewhat carefully and picking a girl standing on the street corner, well, that doesn't speak to a very sophisticated method of approach."

Whereas on the one hand, Ted was intrigued with the Riverman and his apparent elusiveness, Ted also criticized the killer's lack of a calculating and more distinguished approach to his victims. Dave and I knew, and Ted knew also, that the Riverman's repertoire of victim lures was limited. His victims were in high-risk environments and were therefore low-risk victims who needed to go with strange men in order to make money. Technically, a client could "abduct" a prostitute for a couple of hours for the right amount of money. Anyone, even Ted, could abduct prostitutes, but Ted believed that the Riverman did not rise to his own level of sophistication because the Riverman didn't venture out into victim communities where a killer had to use more elaborate techniques to lure the victims away from their safety zones. To serial killers, this was all part of the cunning and bravado. Ted perceived himself to be the master and, therefore, able to critique others.

But, Ted said, if the Riverman had a "method that's more generalized to pick up anybody he selects—if he's just selecting prostitutes, now, that's one thing—but maybe later he's going to start selecting runaways or juvenile delinquents or girls that hang out in bars. They are the kinds of people who you don't identify as directly falling into your profile. Let's say he chose those who were not car-date prostitutes, but who are delinquents and runaways—he just shifted his approach to victims a notch to the right. He's not going for prostitutes but prostitute-types, who dress or act or look to him like prostitutes. If you haven't found them yet, he's just disposing of them very well or it would be my guess he may have moved and [is] no longer operating in the King County area."

The prospect that the Riverman approached and killed victims other than prostitutes was just one of several fascinations Ted had with the Green River cases. Probably the largest attraction for Ted was his belief that the Green River list of victims was incomplete and should have included more victims from Pierce County, Ted's childhood home. Ted would emphasize throughout our interviews that long-term serial killers, like the Riverman, often have more bodies hidden elsewhere that police haven't discovered. We suspected, of course, that Ted was also alluding to himself, holding out the possibility that if interviewers were smart enough and willing to follow Ted down the psychological trail he blazed, we would find the location of his most private dump sites, which still remained undisturbed. Ted was already, even in that first interview, inhabiting the mind of the Green River Killer.

Where Was the Riverman From?

"There are people who don't appear on your list," Ted pointed out, "and your statement about possible victims in Pierce County fascinates me. I don't know why. And I just offer it for pure speculation. I think the man's out of Pierce County. I don't know why. I just get a strong feeling he's out somewhere between the cities of Auburn and Tacoma. I don't know why. That's why I was so fascinated; I just had a strong feeling the guy's out of Pierce County and that intrigued me. I said, 'Whoa. I'd like to find out more about him.' "

Ted had good reasons why he thought the Riverman was a fellow Tacoman. "I feel that way because all the victims are moving south from where they were last seen to where their bodies were discovered. And that could be a deliberate attempt by him to set you off. All the victims, except for the ones moving west, have moved south from the point where they were last seen, some distance south; it was significant that he went north of Tacoma. Except for the Tacoma victim, Wendy Coffield, that you put on your list, they're all moving south, and my guess is it's not a mistake. I think he's going south—home.

"And he knows the mountains—he's just saying, 'Well, I'm going to try this, this time.' But you notice the ones east of Enumclaw; Enumclaw is really northeast Pierce County, southeast King County. And probably in terms of access to his homing area, one of the nearest mountain-pass areas to Tacoma, Puyallup, and Auburn area, in terms of getting up to the mountains. And I know that Enumclaw, the area east of Enumclaw, like the back of my hand, and that is an area—probably what this guy's looking for. There

192

should be a number of the victims' bodies up there, considering you have already found three bodies. When I saw two, I said, 'There's more up there.' I said, 'There's at least five more up there.' Looking at your list, there's surely more than three. The river, like you say, isn't the only thing that matters to him, something like, you know, a needle in a haystack. If you look at your turn-arounds, places to pull off the road, and look at your sites on dirt roads, you might get lucky and find more bodies, it seems to me.

"What I'm saying is that you guys saw some trends, like the trend to take Seattle victims west and up toward the mountains or way south, or the trend to get better as time went along, or the trend to go east of Enumclaw after September and October of eighty-three. You know, that interested me. And I felt from the beginning, though, from what little I knew, selecting these sites with some care, that he's going back probably a number of times to bring bodies in the area or to come back and check on a body or check out the area."

Ted picked up on what seemed to be the Green River Killer's pattern of lining up his abduction sites with his body dump sites. Ted hypothesized that the killer wanted to spend as little time on the road with the victim as possible, probably because he was afraid, and therefore had come up with specific sites for victim pick-up locations before he struck. In 1984, before we interviewed Ted in Florida, his idea would have made a workable theory because we still hadn't uncovered the extent of the killer's movements. However, by 1985, we had realized that the Green River Killer was traveling over 50 miles between pick-up and dump sites. Nevertheless, even in 1984, the Riverman's trolling patterns were intriguing to investigators pursuing a long, cold trail. We used what Ted gave us, however, and tried to get him to help us build something of a miniprofile.

Ted's Profile of the Green River Killer

With all the traveling that the Riverman appeared to be doing between Seattle and the remote areas of King and Pierce counties, Dave Reichert asked Ted, "Has his selection of sites given you any impression at all as to what type of work this guy does? Or what his interests are?"

Ted answered, "If this guy works, he works at odd hours because he's Monday through Friday on the victims." Ted plotted on a map those victims who were missing and those who were found, and had an almost even distribution Sunday through Saturday with a slight emphasis on Sunday, if the dates were right. "That's a big *if.* Of the found victims, the emphasis is clearly on Sunday, Monday, Tuesday, Wednesday, Thursday. Only one disappeared on Friday and one on Saturday, interestingly enough. But all of them together, it looks like it's fairly even," Ted continued, looking at his modus operandi chart. "Those who were missing and *not* found and those who were missing *and* found. It's hard to say in terms of day of the week. He doesn't have any particular preference. That's kind of odd. I mean, I think it is the lack of a pattern that strikes me here. If you see something different, tell me. But I looked at the days of the week and that's what I saw." In other words, we understood Ted to say, the pattern was that there was no real pattern that police could use to set up surveillance.

As he spoke to us, I could see that Ted was projecting himself into each Green River murder as if he were the killer making decisions on the spot. Whom to lure? How to lure? Where to drive? This made sense because Ted had the actual experience of scouting victims and making his getaway to a preselected dump site. Therefore, in any description of the Riverman, there should have been a personal description of Ted. And inasmuch as the Ted cases in Seattle were open just like the Riverman's, I was after Ted at the same time I was after the Riverman. I hoped to catch one by catching the other.

In Ted's description of the Riverman I was listening for any clue I could find about Ted's behavior. Could Ted's disbelief about the lack of a pattern have revealed something about himself? Either Ted had a discernible pattern to his crimes, known only to himself (we never detected one), or he was amazed that another killer would have the foresight to assure that a pattern was not detectable. Whatever the reason for Bundy's fascination with the Riverman's pattern, it revealed something about Ted's thinking.

Traditionally, investigators have looked for patterns in a series of crimes because it offers the possibility of catching the perpetrator in the act by staking out the next predictable location at the time he is expected to strike. This procedure is most effective for apprehending suspects who rob fast-food stores or burglarize homes. And, because it is an effective method for catching some criminals, it is a frequently used procedure in multiple-murder investigations, probably for the lack of anything better to try. But in all fairness, using pattern identification to predict the time to stakeout certain locations has been successful in a few serial-murder investigations. The most famous and successful stakeout of a serial killer was for the Atlanta child murders investigation. Our investigation had borne out what Ted said.

At several points in our conversation, Ted justified his answers by stating, "Let me say, first of all, I have a lot of preconceptions based on nothing, just based upon feeling, intuition. And then I got your list of victims' bodies and their locations, and it reshaped a lot of my feelings about looking at what you actually had here—in terms of when your victims disappeared, when and where they were found. It's kind of fascinating watching some of this unfold, assuming they're all related, and I'd say there's a good chance that they are. I mean, obviously, they're closely related. And so I sat down and I started taking notes. And I don't know where to start. I guess what confounds me is the fact that even though—as you correctly pointed out—you're dealing with a class of victims who are hard to trace and are hard to investigate, who disappear without being reported, whose movements are hard to trace, whose friends are difficult to run down."

The Green River Murders Task Force had two detectives who were exclusively devoted to following up missing-persons investigations. It was an endless task since Washington's police agencies did not prioritize missing-persons investigations unless there was an obvious indication of foul play. Even more neglected were the runaway-juvenile reports. So the task force detectives ended up with mountains of names on many lists that they had to verify with missing-persons lists. In many cases, nobody had cleared the missing person's name from the police computer when he or she returned, which further complicated the task. Ted was very aware of this problem. Ted's surmised that the Riverman had figured out this police shortcoming by now as well.

Ted went on to say, "Still, quite significant to me is that after October 1983, it dropped off like it did. Nobody has turned up yet. And I'm not saying he's stopped. Like you said, that's no guarantee he stopped. But he's gotten a lot smarter, somehow. Something has changed around October of eighty-three, because he may not have moved. He may not have been struck by lightning."

Up to this point, we had found no victims or had any reports of missing persons that would indicate that the killer operated after late 1983. So, displaying just normal curiosity, Reichert asked Ted if he thought it was possible for the killer to stop.

The gleaming smirk on Ted's face was his answer. "No! Not unless he was born again and got filled with the Holy Spirit in a very real way." And, indeed, Ridgway had become a Pentacostal Christian for a time. "He's either moved, he's dead, or he's doing something very different." The prospect that the Riverman was murdering in a different way was frightening. *What would he be doing differently?* I thought.

After pausing for a while as if he were meditating, Bundy announced, "My feelings are this! There's no question in my mind, if he's straightened up, he's changed his victim class just a little, dealing with runaways, generally, rather than prostitutes specifically. He broadened out a little bit more just to deal with runaways and delinquents, was more careful in the way that he disposed of their bodies, and there's no question that this explains the apparent drop-off." As it turned out, Bundy was correct on this assumption as well. Gary Ridgway was targeting younger victims, runaways, and delinquents, many of whom were cocaine addicts desperate for money for their score.

"And I've thought of it every way that I could—days of the week, frequency by month, any intense periods, more intense than others—things like this. And you were still finding people when he was still killing. For instance, he appears, and there's no guarantee of course, to have begun in July of eighty-two, and you've gone over this a thousand times, but forgive me if I'm boring you!"

Early Victims

Ted was on a roll of redundancy. A casual look in another direction and a well-placed yawn caught Ted's eye. He needed, frantically, to continue his message as Dr. Berberich had said he would. I showed Ted, through deliberate body language, that what he was saying was unimportant to me, and he tried even harder to please by providing even more information. Ted now had to impart that the first victim in a series known to the police was generally not the first victim killed by a serial killer. As Ted had killed many before the police had located his "first" victim, the Riverman probably started killing long before our file on him had come into existence.

He continued aggressively, "It's a good chance Agisheff or Coffield is not his number-one victim. Coffield is fascinating. And not only in terms of the geographic area." Coffield disappeared from Ted's home territory and Ted continually stressed that any references to the Tacoma or Pierce County area were important. It was as if the Riverman had been created in Ted's mirror image, in that he began his homicide career in Tacoma, Washington, Ted's home.

Reichert pressed on. "Why is she fascinating?"

"Well," Ted answered, " 'cause she disappeared from Tacoma. At least, it appears that she was last seen in Tacoma. Now, she may have migrated up to Pacific Highway South. Who knows? And you may know something about that, that I don't.

"But it's a little bit odd, for instance, if you consider Agisheff your number one on this particular Green River list, if in fact—and that's a big if—she disappeared on the seventh of July, and then Coffield—and back on the seventh to downtown Seattle. Agisheff's body was found up by North Bend near I-ninety. Less than twenty-four hours later, this guy has dumped a body and he's gone to all this trouble late on the seventh. He runs up to North Bend and drops off Agisheff and then goes down the next day to Tacoma and drops Coffield off in a river—there's something here.

"And there are age differences that kind of startle me, too," Ted went on. "Agisheff is thirty-six; Coffield is sixteen. That's a little bit weird. All the running around within one day, a twenty-four-hour period, more or less. I don't know how much we want to check on these places and dates, probably not a great deal, but they're all you got to work with."

I suggested, "Well, actually, the times might be screwed up, but the dates—"

And Ted interrupted, "The dates are more reliable than the time."

Ted seemed fascinated by our mentions of the dates and times of the crimes on the reference list of victims we sent to him. He questioned the reliability of dates and times because he knew from experience that the dates police assigned to events sometimes bore little relation to when the events actually took place. Therefore, the issue of the reliability of dates and times was important to Ted. Unfortunately, in some cases, the time was more reliable than the date because some of the victim's pimps recalled the time better than what day of the week it was, mainly because they knew what time they usually sent their ladies out to hook. Their memories were affected not only by their reluctance to talk with the police but also by the passage of time from when they last saw their prostitutes to when investigators interviewed them. We also surmised that because of the extensive use of drugs on the Sea-Tac strip, many recollections of potential witnesses were clouded by their drug use as well as by alcohol use or by the aberrant behavior that governed their daily routines.

Reichert flattered Ted and deliberately bolstered his feelings of self-importance by asking, "You said something that interested me. You said that it was weird, the difference in age, thirty-six to sixteen. Why is that weird?" Bundy was always in search of what was going on in the Riverman's head. I suspected that Ted thought it might give him a clue to what was driving him as well.

Ted thought for a second and answered, "Oh, what does this guy got going on in his head? What's he looking for? And it's hard to say. You have some variation here, with one of the black victims being thirty-one, but most of them are sixteen to twenty. Agisheff may have looked younger. I don't know. It's just the age and then the geographic differences and the closeness in the time and the difference in where he dumped her. Why would he dump one up in the mountains and another one in the Green River the next day? Why? I mean, you can ask that question if you get him, if you ever find him. But it seems to me those circumstances, but not necessarily, eliminate Agisheff as a victim of the Riverman. You know that Coffield is a part of it because of all these other people found in the Green River. But Agisheff is up in North Bend. You notice that all of the victims along I-ninety, near North Bend, were last seen or hooking in Seattle. Where did Yates disappear? Downtown Seattle, right?"

Dump Site Patterns

Ted believed that he had plotted the abduction locations and body discovery sites correctly and made a prediction about the killer. "You notice all the North Bend victims are from Seattle. And opposed to those in the Green River area, in fact, all of those in there, are Pacific Highway South victims—except Delores Williams." He became even more emphatic. "In fact, he took all the Seattle victims either east or south, where his Pacific Highway South victims are right near Sea-Tac Airport, Star Lake Road, and the Green River."

Ted went on, "Delores Williams, a black girl out of downtown Seattle, very well could have hopped a bus and been on the street down on Pacific Highway South. I don't know. But if she disappeared from Seattle, she is an anomaly because her body is the only body at these four major dump sites that did not disappear from Pacific Highway South or that general area. All the other Seattle victims went east, south, or southeast—way away. That's what I notice.

"I'll bet you your bones twenty-five and fifteen that were found east of Seattle—still unidentified—will probably turn out to have disappeared from Seattle," Ted firmly predicted. "For some reason, he's running off, abducting and dumping the Seattle victims in a much different way than he was the Pacific Highway South victims."

Dave and I learned quickly that questions framed with particular words allowed Ted to expound more openly without the immediate fear that he was revealing information about himself. Words like "would you speculate" or "why do you think" were intentionally part of our interview strategy because they enabled him to believe that he was distancing himself from self-incriminating statements. Because Dave and I knew that Bundy's basis for speculation and hypothesis came from his own feelings and his similar crimes in the exact same areas, we knew that in reality Ted was talking about his own behavior. Reichert pointedly asked, "Do you have any speculation as to why he may be doing that?"

Now behaving as if he had become our mentor, Ted said, "Well, first of all, he's trying to dispose of the bodies where they won't be found. This guy doesn't want to get caught. Neither does he want any of his bodies found. I think it's clear that, over time, you can see him trying to improve his dump sites. He's trying to get better at disposing of those bodies."

We were watching a classic performance of a serial killer's bravado. Ted had eluded us for years in King County and he believed he would have gotten away with the Colorado and Utah murders had he not been stopped by the trooper. He had beaten us at our own game and now we had come to his cell to learn from him. Thus, he could be almost professorial in his explanation of why not only the Riverman was eluding us, but how he did it as well, albeit without confessing to a single incident. Ted would change back and forth from first person to third person continuously throughout our conversations to emphasize his point. With his ego swelling almost to a point of explosion, Ted was obliging, but critical, in his assessment of the Riverman's ability to learn from one murder to the next.

"Generally speaking, looking at them all, I'd say, 'Well, he's really clumsy. I would not have done it that way.' But who knows. With his mental apparatus—you're given what he thinks is effective and what isn't. But I think as far as the downtown Seattle victims went, there was obviously no close-by place to dump them. Along Pacific Highway South, he's got all this stuff within, you know, short driving distance. It appears to me that they're killed shortly after he picks them up because he's not going far with them. That's just a real right-off-the-cuff guess." Ted smiled coyly as if the word *guess* was a modest expression of fact from the mouth of the only authority. Cocksure, he felt that he had opened the Riverman's mind for us. But what Ted did not know, nor did we, was that the Green River Killer was taking a large number of his victims back to his very own house.

Easy Victims

While Ted was on a roll, I wanted to continue with the idea that the Riverman picked on easy victims, knowing that Ted thought that, too. And, once again, I knew I was feeding his ego even more when I suggested that, unlike Ted's ruses and lures with coeds on campuses and ski resorts, the Riverman's picking up streetwalkers by car didn't take much skill. "Almost all of them," I said, setting up Ted, "were exclusively car-date prostitutes. They're not the type that have a motel room they take somebody back to. So they're all eligible for the car."

Not wanting simply to agree with me, Ted responded, "That's what I was going to ask. Were they plying their trade on the streets or inside establishments? Were they standing on the street?"

"Standing," I said.

Ted answered, "He's not taking their car." Thus, Ted reinforced his own ego and our own belief that the Riverman's pickups couldn't have been any easier. He took the most vulnerable, most available victims—people who wouldn't be missed until days or weeks after their disappearance. Furthermore, he took them to the nearest dump site he could find after spending as little time with them as possible.

Now that Dave and I had stroked Ted's ego and had him speaking very comfortably about the Riverman, it was time to get him psychologically closer to his own murders. We began with caution by asking, "Why do you think that he'd picked up two in one day?" I reminded him, "He had a couple of them at the same time."

Ted didn't appear to suspect my motive. He gave my question some thought and listed the possibilities of the Riverman's thinking processes. "I thought about that for a long time," he said. "He got Agisheff and Coffield, who were close in time. He got Hinds and Mills on the eleventh and twelfth of August. And then you had Pitsor and Gabbert snatched on April 17. And Bush and Summers. This guy gets hot, he gets hot—I guess. It's possible he picked them up both at the same time, and all you have is a discrepancy in date."

Then he conjectured about the racial makeup of the victim list. "You know, you have a black victim and a white victim here, then another black victim, I believe. Lee is white, but they're one day apart from each other. And Bush and Summers are both black, I believe. So they may have been together. You know, I don't know how they take care of business, but maybe he just put himself in a position of picking up two at the same time. It might not be because he wanted to, but because he just got locked into a situation where he was so driven he had to. He saw one, and to get one he had to get two, and took two."

Ted was putting himself right into the mind of the killer on the street, and there was a validity to what he was saying. Maybe the killer couldn't isolate a single victim from time to time. He was cruising, saw a particularly vulnerable-looking streetwalker, but she was not alone. He would have rather had the one, but had to take the other just to make the pickup. It made sense once you put yourself—like Ted, who had obviously been there—into the mind of the Riverman driving along the strip.

Ted continued. "But it does seem to confound the general pattern where he goes for one, you know. One person is easier to control than two, unless he has a very good technique. And no one has escaped from this guy, and, obviously, he has a very good technique once he makes the move. But it's clear he gets very intense. And, it could be that he did come back one day and then another. But when you get in with two blacks together here and two blacks together, maybe he just had to take two to get one. Or maybe, he was so 'hot,' he was so driven, that he had to go one day and come back the next, although it doesn't fit the general pattern. My guess would be he had to pick up two to get one."

Living Victims

Bundy and other serial killers, such as John Wayne Gacy and Wayne Williams, had living victims or witnesses who eventually came forward to testify against them. Thus, we assumed, there were living victims of the Green River Killer. And we were right, as it turned out. We wanted to pursue with Ted this very possibility to see how he would react, especially in light of Carol DaRonch's escape from him and her subsequent testimony.

Dave Reichert sneaked up on this question, asking, "Would there be anything unusual that he might do that maybe our officers have not asked living prostitutes about? Because we interviewed prostitutes out there, of course, in the areas where prostitution occurs. Is there anything that you can think of that our officers might be asking these girls that this person displayed in his contact?"

Ted knew exactly what Reichert was referring to—living victims—and he offered his own opinion eagerly. "I think there's an excellent chance that he has picked up a number of prostitutes who he's later released, for any number of reasons. Perhaps he just felt an unusual wave of compassion. Maybe he was surprised at some point and felt it's too risky to kill that particular individual. Maybe somebody saw him at some point in time after he had made contact with her, or maybe it's just entirely too risky to go through with it. But I think he's doing it fairly quickly—he's probably killing them fairly quickly. At least most of them, maybe not all of them."

Trying to make Bundy think and work in order to give us something to use that we hadn't already thought of, Reichert clarified the question by asking, "I guess what I'm getting at—is there anything this guy would say to the ones that he let go? Is there anything that he would do to maybe tip them off? 'I think I left a killer'? He released them, but they don't call us, and we end up interviewing them later. Maybe we're not asking the right questions to get the information that we need."

Patiently, like a mentor to his attentive students, Ted continued with, "Well, what I've outlined before is nobody has gotten away from him, once he's made his move, that I know of." Ted momentarily avoided this issue by asking his own question. "Is this true? I mean, he's not tried to, you don't have anybody who's pulled a gun on somebody or tried to tie them up or whatever, do you?"

"No," said Reichert reluctantly as if not wanting to admit it. Dave had searched high and low for anyone who had escaped the Riverman and could have revealed what was behind his mask. In November 1984, however, Rebecca Gande Guay would tell the Task Force that she was a living victim of the Green River Killer, but Ridgway would be able to explain her complaint away by saying that she bit him and he reacted in self-defense when he choked her.

Noticing that Dave was beginning to wear his feelings of frustration with the Green River cases, I interrupted with, "We've had all kinds of kinky incidents happen with prostitutes out there."

Ted reassured us. "Sure. That's the problem."

I continued. "So we more than likely have identified those type of people. We've followed up on those incidents and discovered that they were not associated with the Green River Killer, but that's different. We don't have anybody—we feel anyway—that's escaped from him."

After a minute of reflection, Ted sat up in his chair and his eyes positively gleamed with the light of revelation. "Sure," he said. "I see what you mean. Whatever he's doing, he's doing it very effectively. I mean, he's done three dozen at least and nobody's gotten away from him. That's very impressive. Sometimes, it looks like he might have two at a time. It's hard to tell. What I'm saying is, my guess is he's driving to a location he feels very safe in, where he can make a move. Okay? And if there's trouble, nobody will hear or see any kind of struggle or whatever he ends up doing effectively to take control of his victims. And so I don't know how these prostitutes conduct their business once they get in the car, but I guess it is fairly standard procedure to go somewhere where they won't be observed. But this guy is going to go somewhere, at least initially. My guess would be that he makes a move and there's no question in his mind. If there is trouble or some kind of problem, they won't be seen or witnessed by anybody passing by."

Ted knew he was on the right track. "One of the questions I would ask, that comes just off the top of my head, is 'Have any of your clients taken you to locations that were particularly remote or secluded?' See what I'm saying? As far as him saying something—'You got away from me this time'—something obvious. You know, like you say, you're going to have men, clients of these women, who are fairly bizarre in their relationships with women for one reason or another. And if they say something out of the ordinary, I don't know that it would be significant. My guess is that he's making his move really quickly, and he's doing it in locations he's very confident in making a move in.

"Unless he has a unique kind of vehicle—you know, a van, for instance, gives him a lot more control, as opposed to an automobile, where you can see any kind of struggle inside the windows. So, that's just the first thing that comes to mind, but let me think about it, and that's one of the things I'll write back to you on."

Victim Pick-up Locations

It was time to turn up the heat a little by confronting Ted about what he had delicately avoided up to that point. We at times wanted to see how Ted handled slightly antagonistic questions. I pressed by inquiring about the pick-up point. Ted had strayed away from talking about that in detail. Of course, he had a reason. He wanted us to show him photographs of dead bodies. We had predicted that crime scene photos would refuel him, but we weren't yet ready to launch into that stage of the questioning. We wanted Ted to go through all the elements of the initial contact sites with us first.

I asked, "You seem to concentrate on how important the dump sites are, but the pick-up points are too. The killer is there, he created activity, and he felt comfortable. And the pick-up points, quite frankly, are heavily patrolled. I mean, police contact at those locations routinely, not only with john patrols, where we're trying to catch the johns, but there are police officers out there busting prostitutes all the time. And generally there's a lot of police around there. How does he feel so good in there?" We wanted to know how the predatory killer knew how to act only when there was the least possibility of detection.

Ted's explanation involved how comfortable a long-term serial killer really was in his familiar surroundings. He was presumably also talking about his own high comfort levels on college campuses, ski resorts, beach parties, and anywhere coeds gathered. He, therefore, was more than confident in his answer. "The same way that Wayne Williams felt so good in Atlanta. He knew that scene inside and out and operated in spite of all the heat that was coming down in Atlanta. There was more heat in Atlanta than there was in any case, you know, maybe except for yours now. Because there were young black children disappearing, there was an incredible amount of pressure, as I'm sure you're aware, and, yet, he was just doing his thing. Even after all that publicity and all that heat. Why? Because he knew that scene inside and out. He was a fish in water. And that's why—in that last letter I wrote to you—even though I was sort of speculating, you know, rashly at times, my feeling was, even with what little I knew, that your man was a part of the subculture that these women found themselves in."

"A fish in water." That was Ted in Seattle's U-district and that was the Green River Killer on the Sea-Tac strip. Bundy continued along this same line. "Now, I don't know if you can say there is a particular set of factors which characterize the subculture of prostitution, but I try to perceive it as a subculture that involves, you know, drugs and runaways and certain individuals just comfortable in dealing with that kind of scene, whether it be the bar scene or the drug scene and the prostitute and runaway scene. The person who's doing it knows it very well. He knows these individuals. He knows how to manipulate them. He might not even be coming up to them as a john, even though that appears to be the most reasonable explanation."

The Approach

It was as if a bell had gone off. Ted identified an approach to the prostitute-type victim that, up to this point, our investigators had not been able to pursue. Maybe a prospective john was not the abductor. Maybe it was someone coming in under completely different camouflage and was slipping right through our net. It was a disturbing realization since the proactive methods we were using to detect the killer were heavily focused on his being a frequent customer of prostitutes. Stubbornly, Dave said, "Well, he sure doesn't stick out like a sore thumb, that's for sure."

With the assurance of an expert, Ted proudly explained, "No!

Sure, and he's not your typical client. And my feeling about the guy is he's very low-key and inoffensive. My guess is he's got more than one approach to these girls."

Feeding Ted's ego with his tone of voice while at the same time probing for some angle the killer may be using, Dave asked, "Have you thought about the approach at all?"

Ted immediately responded, "I have. You know, what the hooker might be."

"What do you think he's accomplishing then?" Dave asked.

"If he were just some john driving in and snatching prostitutes," Ted said, "I think you would have caught him by now. But, like I say, I think he knows what these girls are like and what they need. Whether he's coming on as a john or, in fact, maybe offering them employment, money, or drugs, I've thought out the various ways he might approach them, even calling them on the phone. Let's say somehow he was able to contact them by phone—some of them, not all of them. I'm not saying he has one technique. In fact, he may not be a wizard, but he's bright enough to understand that he can't be approaching the same way every time. He knows that those areas are under heavy surveillance, even under the best of times. But he was going back there after the heat was on. I continually was amazed by this guy's balls. I mean, after all the victims he'd snatched from Pacific Highway South, it seems that they continued to disappear from there. My guess is that he just blends into that environment—he may be a familiar-type character to that area. He may feel so comfortable with these type of women and understand them so well, he knows how to manipulate them."

Ted was on a roll and needed to be brought back to our line of questioning, so, I asked, "How stable do you think he is in his occupation? Probably our number-one ruse is to pose as a cop, because that happens all the time. They show badges, flash badges. The city of Portland is going crazy right now. Cops can't even go up and interview the prostitutes because there's so many johns out there flashing badges at them. And just getting it for nothing."

Ted admitted, somewhat embarrassed because I'd mentioned the cop lure that he himself had used in Salt Lake City before he mentioned it, "Yeah, you're right. I left out parts of my number-one ruse or lure. Well, I don't think it'd be my number one, necessarily. Maybe number two would be the police badge. You know that commands a lot of power. At least initially, until the cover is blown. I mean, Bianchi and his cousin, the Hillside Stranglers, stretched that to the limits down in Los Angeles. That's a good one, except, like you say, these girls, after a period of time, the prostitutes that are working Pacific Highway South, must have been very wary of something, even a cop flashing a badge. I don't know what their reaction would be. But after a while, I think even that would scare them."

He continued along the same line, explaining the way the Green River Killer tentatively approached his victims, bouncing off the ones that seemed resistant, and luring the ones who went along with his ruse. "I'm sure you've interviewed them and asked if they've had people approach them flashing badges, and that's probably another question you should ask. Again, I'm sure you've asked it. To all the prostitutes out there, have they been approached by anybody flashing badges, because my guess is if the guy is using that technique, sooner or later he's going to run into somebody, flashes a badge on her, and something happens. She either backs away or somebody, some other event, intervenes, because he's not getting everybody he approaches."

Undoubtedly, Ted was thinking of his attempted abduction of Carol DaRonch and how his use of a badge was not that convincing. Unlike other killers who had been successful in their ruses as cops, Ted was not only singularly unsuccessful in luring his victim, that victim turned out to be the lone living witness whose testimony landed Ted in jail in Utah and began, at least in his mind, the unraveling of his criminal career. Accordingly, in the same way that Ted didn't get DaRonch, he predicted that the Green River Killer "[is] not getting everybody he approaches, whether he's successful or not. Some of them he'd only make contact with. Using all his mental powers to assess the situation, and he's in the progress of trying to convince her to go with him, something doesn't feel right. She doesn't appeal to him for some reason. And you know that too. If he fails as Bono and Bianchi did—at least once that I know of—that's going to be something to follow up on. And I don't know if you have any reports like that or not in the Green River case. You say it's happening in Portland. Because these prostitutes are so wary, I think the guy is coming on really low-key, [in a] nonthreatening manner. And he knows them so well and I don't think he's coming on as a cop. Because if he did, I think you'd know about it. You'd have a pretty good feeling about it.

That's not to say he's never done it or hasn't thought about doing it, or wouldn't try it, you know."

Even more disturbing for proactive strategies, Ted gave us a picture of how serial killers invent new ways of approaching their victims and why they are so able to slip through defenses. "But if he's always reading—I'll bet you, like I say—some people—hundreds—read *Field and Stream,* this guy's reading *True Detective.* So he's always thinking of new ways. My guess is he's so nonthreatening, so low-key, he knows them so well, that either he's coming on sometimes with a job or sometimes with something else. And what that something else might be is anybody's guess."

Ted was intuitive about our interest in what he was saying. Our curiosity was probably written across our faces. Next, Ted wanted to know whether the victims were clothed. I pressed him for what significance that had to him. He eagerly responded, as if he were putting himself at the actual dump sites, by saying, "Well, let's assume you had victims who were not prostitutes, and obviously he's coming on to them—and this is what I feel—he has a method of approach. He has a lure or a ruse which applies to more than just prostitutes. He's not walking up to them and saying, 'Okay, hey, baby, you want to go for a ride?' You know, 'Pay you fifty bucks or whatever to go.' If you have victims who are not prostitutes, it says he has a ruse that's more generalized. That he's in fact not coming on all the time as a john. That he's coming on as something else. Or offering them something else. See what I'm getting at?"

We nodded. We were getting somewhere. He continued to draw us a picture of the Green River Killer at work as if he had teleported himself directly into the guy's brain and was looking at victims through his eyes. "If he picked up a hitchhiker or somebody who's in a bar who may have dressed like, acted like, or looked like a prostitute, but in fact was not, who may have appealed to this man for one reason or another—she would not have responded to an approach that a john would make to a prostitute. Then I would say you have a guy who's obviously capable of using ruses that are not applicable only to prostitutes."

There were times when Ted would lose his focus or when he would seem to be ill at ease while talking to us. These lapses, our psychological research into Ted's case told us, resulted from Ted's very severe ego issues. We were prepared for this, of course, and had a variety of techniques to focus the interview back on Ted's thought process, while at the same time getting to focus on our concerns. One of these was to repeat a phrase that Ted was using to bring him back to a point in the conversation that we wanted him to elaborate on. Specifically, our using Ted's own words to frame a question made him feel comfortable and, in a way, obligated to answer. Words like *this guy, his thing, get what I'm getting at,* and *you know* were frequently part of Ted's phraseology. So I asked, "What is this guy's thing? Is he all wrapped up in the approach, wrapped up in the event, or wrapped up in postevent behavior? There's three questions there. What is he like after each of these, you know, like he might be somebody's neighbor or live-in boyfriend for a while. Is there something here that we could key on about his before or after behavior that somebody else might see? We have a lot of people that call in, and they give us indications there's something wrong with this potential suspect, and I don't know what it is. Something happened before, something happened after. Understand what I'm getting at?"

Of course, Ted realized what I was getting at, and it was the last thing he wanted to talk about. We knew from the postmortem medical reports from Utah and from Florida that Ted had committed acts on his victims after death. In other words, he was a necrophiliac, and he knew we knew it. It was the one part of his criminal behavior that truly embarrassed him because it satisfied him sexually by going right to the center of his dysfunctional need for control. Bundy was so severe a sexual deviant that he was probably unable to reach an orgasm unless his victim was dead or unconscious. Women threatened him. He was petrified of his victims, which was why he had to take control of them and incapacitate them. Everything—his ruses, lures, traps, murders, and dump sites—was secondary to his sexual satisfaction at having a dump site where his victims would wait for him in silent decay. Sitting there in that visitor's death row reception room in the Florida State Penitentiary, Bundy knew that we knew his deepest and most intimate sexual desires, even though he pretended to be aloof and on a throne of superiority.

He was not about to talk about postevent sexual gratification. "Yeah," he said. "I see what you're getting at. When I don't know something, I'll tell you. When I don't have a feeling for something,

I'll tell you. And I don't have a feeling for that. I don't know what condition the bodies were in or anything and, you know, if you have any evidence if they were sexually assaulted or have been somewhat physically traumatized. And I think, quite frankly, in most of your cases there's no evidence at all, that would help you on that. And I just don't know. I can answer part of your question, or try to answer part of your question."

The Thrill of the Hunt

Ted quickly turned to what he wanted to talk about. "I think that the hunt, the searching out, is always a big thing for him. He's probably invested a lot of time and effort into it. And you asked another question earlier. Well, how would this affect his job? Well, I think, you know, especially in that period from July eighty-two until October of eighty-three, he was doing two and three a month, and some months he was doing four and five. And that takes an enormous amount of effort and concentration. And to be able to hold down any kind of serious job under those circumstances can be extremely difficult. And this is why I think his employment history might be somewhat uneven. And I would expect also that he's not earning a lot of money. Or he would range further away, or that might be one of the reasons why he's stuck around so long."

At the same time as Ted was describing the practical difficulties of being a serial killer and holding down a full-time job, he was also blowing his own horn. Ted was a superannuated perpetual graduate student whose lifestyle was campus-oriented. In order to live among his victim pool, Ted had worked out the logistics of attending classes, holding down jobs that would earn him a living, and killing full-time. Thus, he was well prepared to discuss the Riverman's predicament. "Quite frankly, he might not have been able to afford to go further or take more time off from work. There are other explanations, but that one appeals to me. But as to what he might do to them once he gets them, that's a big blank spot in my mind. I don't know. I mean, I can't even begin to guess. Boy. Although I think he probably is a good deal more interested in, or caught up in the hunt than the actual doing of the deed. But that's only a guess."

Ted focused on the hunt because he was so intense about the

hunt himself, which was part of the thrill of anticipating his exercising complete control of a victim's body. Feeding off our previous discussion about the Riverman's picking on less-sophisticated victims and wanting to pursue the profile of the killer that Ted had held out for us, I asked, "In the hunt, he's initially picked on an easily approachable victim. If he is wrapped up in the hunt, comparatively speaking, to going into a bar and picking up somebody or stopping by a bus stop and seeing if somebody wants a ride, he doesn't seem to be that skilled. And he's picking on a very vulnerable population that's right there."

Ted said, "That's a good observation." Even Reichert was amazed at Bundy's bravado in complimenting me on simply repeating what Bundy himself had said just moments earlier. But I wanted to make Ted feel superior. That was part of our strategy. I indirectly complimented Bundy in return by saying that the Riverman, unlike Bundy, "doesn't have to work that hard, in my opinion. He's a lazy son of a bitch. You know."

Ted jumped at the compliment. "That's right!" he almost shouted. "That's right! Although I think, again my guess is, he's a little bit more skilled than we might think if, in fact, he's picking on people who are not prostitutes, who are close to being prostitutes, who are vulnerable. Maybe 'cause they're runaways, maybe 'cause they're lonely, and on the run or need some drugs, or something. But you're right. He is lazy, and I say not lazy. He's pretty sharp in one respect. None of them have gotten away from him. He's definitely thought a lot of this stuff out. He may not be very sophisticated in his approach, but given time, he's working on it." He truly believed that the Riverman picked up more than just prostitutes.

"And if," Bundy continued, "he ever feels like he has to change a class of victims, comes up with a more sophisticated approach, then you will find him. And you're going to see that start to show up. But right now, he is picking on somebody that's vulnerable. And it's good for him in the sense he doesn't have to work that hard. He also knows that it's not just vulnerable victims, but police have a devil of a time investigating the disappearances precisely because of the kind of women they are. So it may not be easy because they're vulnerable, but also because their murders and disappearances are difficult to investigate. But what really intrigues me is—and once again the fact that you don't really have anybody other than prostitute types—

you don't have any other apparent nonprostitute cases in eighty-four that you discovered. And if you had a number of prostitutes who disappeared in eighty-four, they'd be on your list, I would suspect."

In fact, some of the victims on the Riverman's list were not confirmed prostitutes. I reminded him of that. "Well, we've got one that's on the list that probably is not a prostitute, but because of the time, we'd have to put them on the list. We have some missing prostitutes that cannot be accounted for; their bodies have not been discovered yet. Some are prolific travelers from city to city."

Dave pressed on about the hunt by saying, "Let's go back to the hunt for a minute. You might have covered this already a little bit. How would you think he conducts the hunt?"

"Well," Ted said, now hypothesizing *ex cathedram electricus,* as it were, and going back to my earlier assumption that he already had an insight into this, "the kind of subculture out there is a part of what he understands. Or he has observed them in the past, or he's been in the same kind of environment where they lived and worked. He understands their movements. So his hunt is somewhat simplified by the fact that he understands, more or less, he knows where they are, generally, and how they behave and where he can find them."

Dave asked, "Do you think that he parks his vehicle?"

"Oh, sure," Ted answered, even before Reichert had a chance to complete his question. "And just watches."

Dave continued. "Does he drive up and down and make notes of certain people walking on the highways? Maybe he stops and talks and visits with this person who later turns out to be his victim. Do you think that there is some kind of a need for him to get to know that person?"

Ted never felt the need to know any woman he killed, except maybe Lynda Healy, but he wasn't about to admit that. Killing, for Ted, was probably the gateway to the act of knowing, to the only real intimacy he would ever experience with another human being. Even Liz Kendall, although she was his fiancée and lived with him, would never be as much an object of intimate bonding the way Georgeann Hawkins would become on the night of her abduction and murder. His victims were his relationships, and it was through that dysfunction that he was able to talk about the comings and goings of the Green River Killer.

Innocent Victims

Ted grudgingly answered Dave's question. "I don't know about that," he said. "But your earlier question, is he closely observing the scene? And I have to say this guy is in and out and closely observing his victims, if not all the time in the area, at least a particular victim some period of time. He's going to a great deal of trouble to check out the area, and everything that goes on in that area. It's not just the prostitutes or the police. He's very conscious of the police. I bet you he can feel them, undercover or whatever, because he's very conscious of not wanting to have anybody observe him approach one of those girls, but also because, you know, he's lived in that scene long enough; he knows what they look like. He can sense when they're coming. And so he's very conscious of all kinds of activity. And my guess is, generally speaking—and I'm sure there are exceptions—when he's just driving along and sees something he likes, it feels right, he looks around, parks the car and, you know, starts looking. I don't know how many suspect vehicles you may have on your list, but I'm pretty sure he's very careful about where he puts his car. I just don't think he's the type that's going to drive up to the curb and have them get in. That might be another question you've probably already asked your ladies out there—if they have to walk any distance to his car. And is his car parked in kind of an unusual place. Have you asked that question?"

We hadn't.

9
─

Hunting the Killer

In my experience, the hunt for the killer is as exhilarating for the detective as the hunt for victims seems to be for the killer, especially when you feel that you're making headway on a case. Unfortunately, too many times during a long-term investigation much of what is done feels useless and nonproductive. Investigators find themselves following leads on many different theories promoted during the case. One of those time-consuming theories that required a lot of follow-up regarding the Riverman was that he would deliberately draw attention to himself by contacting members of the news media and using them to communicate with police authorities.

There was bloodthirsty competition for Green River news among the hundreds of reporters who came to Seattle from around the world during the height of the investigation. At this time, media types became relentless in their pursuit of information, especially that from task force members, that would satisfy their daily, sometimes hourly, need for a story. When someone was identified as a potential suspect, the media suddenly had a story to market and took advantage of this situation each time it arose. Between the tabloid newspapers, the tabloid television programs, and the talk shows, suspects became marketable commodities and some defense lawyers became nothing more than publicity agents. One suspect in particular had excessive contact with the news media after it became known that he was a "person of interest" in our case. Dave Reichert and I asked Bundy about this type of personality and how it related to the Green River Killer.

Publicity-Seeking Suspects

Ted asked, "You mean after he's come in contact with you?"

"Yeah, make it a game," Dave said with the exasperation of one who had to live through one suspect appearing on the nightly television news and proclaiming how inept police investigators were.

"Make it tough, not a game," I clarified.

Ted was dismayed that any detective would suggest that a sophisticated killer, like the Riverman or himself, would want to draw that much attention to himself. With his voice pitched high, Ted sarcastically replied, "Well, and still be active? And still do his thing?"

"Yeah."

Laughing, Ted gave us a hypothetical situation to work from without referring to any one suspect by name. "Let's say that this guy came to your attention in the first part of eighty-three when this thing started. Somehow, you talked with him. Then he went to the news media, and subsequent to his press interviews, you had all these other victims in eighty-three. I don't think, quite frankly, that anything like that can happen. I don't pretend to be a clairvoyant, but this guy doesn't want to get caught. If he comes to your attention, he's going to stop dead in his tracks and not do anything. I doubt that he's going to draw attention to himself, but who knows?"

Another popular theory in the Green River cases was that the killer left town or stopped when the enhanced task force was formed. Why else would the killing appear to stop in March 1984? Up until August of 1983, there were, at various times, as many as 15 investigators working on the cases on a regular basis. On a couple of occasions, the investigation involved the efforts of over 20 personnel while investigating a "hot" suspect. Just prior to January 1984, only three detectives were assigned to catch the Riverman. Throughout the course of the investigation, the police force was inundated and therefore only nominally effective. A bare-bones team was trying to maintain the course of the investigation when, boom, 43 people were added and the official Green River Murders Task Force was formed. I asked Ted, "Is that enough to scare him off, for him to get out of town, or would he consider that another challenge?"

Confidently, Ted responded, "I don't think it'd be enough to get him out of town. I don't think it is enough. On first glance, when I first saw this lucent, it appeared things just seemed to stop around October of eighty-three. I mean, on paper. He hasn't stopped. Okay. He's obviously somewhere else or doing this thing in a different way in Pierce County, King County, or western Washington. Aw, no! That's not enough to scare him."

Ted provided an interesting but weird analogy. "Because he knows, he's like your boyfriend. He knows he still has an edge. And he reads the newspapers like everybody else, probably has one in his pocket. Recently, I read an article—I got all my back issues of the *Tacoma News Tribune* after being released from disciplinary confinement—well, here's what happened. I read an article about the Kapowsin find. [A murdered female was found near Lake Kapowsin in rural Pierce County.] Just the initial find. At the time, I'd say the Kapowsin victim is not a Green River victim. I say, shit, you know, there he goes again. Like an asshole, I say, hey, I figured something out here. I see that this is the Green River task force. It doesn't want to have any more publicity than necessary. No more details in the papers, wants to keep the amount of stuff that goes in the papers to a minimum. And that's kind of fascinating because it cuts both ways, as you know. You need the public to help you, but I think this guy does not like—he does not like the task force."

Grinning with pride, Dave stated, "Obviously."

Unaware of what Reichert was thinking and not skipping a beat, Ted continued. "He doesn't want to get caught. So he's going to make changes in his behavior to stay ahead of you and avoid publicity. Because the best thing he has going for you and himself is a lack of publicity. The less the public is looking for him, has their eye out for him, I know that means a lot to him. It creates problems having a lot of people out there giving leads, but the less publicity, the better for him. And I quite frankly think the task force simply made him reevaluate what he's doing and changed in some ways to improve his chances of avoiding detection. He may not be a sophisticated type to sit down and analyze this, but he knows it, like a fox knows stuff. He knows it like any predator seems to know his victim, not in an analytical way but in a sensory, an intuitive way. And he knows that the kind of victims he's looking for are difficult to trace and not reported right away. Except for a couple cases, they were investigated way down the line and hard to investigate. So he's just taking advantage of that in a different way, in my opinion."

Anxiously, Dave was concerned about the content of certain news reports spurring the Riverman to kill. He asked, "Do you think that certain news articles and TV reports could set him off to kill?"

That question appeared to puzzle Ted, but he wanted to warn us about emotional broadcasts. With his head cocked down and a coy smirk on his face, Ted said, "I don't know. That's a good question, one I can't answer. I'm sure if you analyzed, for example, last weekend, when the TV stations in Seattle had a half-hour special on the task force. I was interviewed, and some other people were interviewed. One of the comments I heard was 'We're not giving up.' And you will catch him, or somebody will catch him. In time. Aw, but you can't tell him that. He's not the type, to me, he's not a show-off in that respect. I mean, he's not like the Hillside Strangler. He's not dumping his bodies on the hillsides. He's not doing it in a spectacular way. I think he's still very concerned about hiding people. He's hiding his people, his victims."

Dave informed Ted that the day after the broadcast about the task force, we got a telephone call, and somebody said, "You're never going to catch me." It was the only phone call like that we got. Would the Green River Killer have called?

Ted believed that the Riverman at all costs did not want to draw attention to himself, especially by calling the police. Therefore, he assumed that the caller was probably some crank. Ted warned, "Well, it's not inconceivable. It's entirely possible he's getting an ego charge out of beating you people, staying ahead of you. I mean, that cannot be dismissed all the time. But that's not what's motivating him."

Killer's Motivation

Ted had opened a door to a place we wanted desperately to explore. What motivates a serial killer? Dave and I sounded like we were singing the same song when we asked simultaneously, "What do you think is motivating him?"

Ted prepared himself for his long answer by clearing his throat and placing his finger alongside his head as if he were winding up for a long lecture. This was something he wanted to talk about, at least in the third person. "He's an active killer," he said, almost as if it were a proclamation. "In his own way, he knows, in the detail recesses of his mind, how this particular behavior pattern evolved. He obviously did not start on July the seventh, nineteen eighty-two, and he was feeling like he wants to kill. I could speculate more—and some speculation might be useful in terms of your investigation, but some of it is purely academic."

Ted hesitated because he knew that we knew he would be talking about himself and his motivations for murder. But Dave encouraged Ted to continue about the Green River Killer. "Go ahead. I'm interested in what you have to say."

Ted shrugged. "Oh well, sure. I mean this would be purely speculating. Just looking at his victims. There are an infinite number of ways to explain how a man can come to the point where he destroys human life as this person has. And I suppose the only way to really know, someday, is to have the man studied. Even then, who knows. You get some verification from the killer. He's killing because there's some link, obviously, between sex and violence. Look at the number of prostitutes that were found nude more often than not; the fatal link between sex and violence has been made. I don't know whether it's anything anybody can rationally describe or explain, except the fact that sometimes our society promotes that link between sex and violence unknowingly through the media and whatnot."

Ted volunteered that he had a couple of ideas about developing suspects by exploiting the possible sources of motivation if we really want to stretch it, but didn't want to talk about it at that time. He continued, "I think for whatever reason, however, he got to the point of killing prostitutes because he made a deliberate determination that those were prey. It may be that he has something specifically against prostitutes. What really confounds me in this case is the number of black prostitutes. I mean, this guy is an equal opportunity killer. And that fascinates me. He doesn't seem to have a preference racially. That's kind of odd. I don't know if it's odd in the whole scheme of things, but it certainly did puzzle me. Obviously, he did not shy away from black prostitutes. And I don't know if, looking at the data on teenage prostitutes, he might not be seeking out a greater share of blacks or not. I don't know. There certainly are a number at the moment. Whatever inner drives are motivating him now, it's sort of like it's sort of obvious that it's either a preoccupation or an obsession. He is influenced by a number of factors, both internal and external. Internally, I'm sure his desire to kill ebbs and flows, as you can see, generally, by your list of victims. Externally, there may be any number of things influencing him: publicity, the formation of the task force, car trouble, job trouble, illness, you know, a whole host of things, everyday stuff that everybody goes through.

"There are some interesting gaps in the series. For instance, he skips November eighty-two, if your list is complete. He skips January and February of eighty-three, again, assuming your list is complete. Sometimes these gaps are significant. He might have been sick or had car trouble. The gaps may have been just an anomaly, or maybe an accident. Perhaps he did get somebody you don't know about. Or maybe, in fact, when he did Colleen Brockman, somebody saw him or did something that scared the shit out of him. Because he really put himself out on the line and was at risk. Therefore, he pulled back to see if anything would come of it. Also, your gaps can be explained by the fact that he left some loose ends and he's going to sit back and see if anything materializes. And once he gains confidence . . ."

Once in a while, Ted needed to be interrupted because he sounded as though he was just rambling. Realizing he was loading up to babble on, I quickly asked, "What do you say about his pattern?"

"Ummm, what?" Ted muttered as if he were just awakened from a sort of trance.

I was more than impatient. "What do you say about a pattern? Do we have an erroneous assumption that there even is a pattern?"

Shaking his head to clear his mind, Ted emphasized, "Oh, sure. You shouldn't lock yourself into a pattern. I'd hate to restrict my own analysis of any problem by saying, 'That is the pattern.' "

I decided it was now appropriate to verbally acknowledge Ted's statements more frequently. He needed affirmative confirmation, so I occasionally said yes.

Ted continued. "Because that limits your options, and you don't want to limit your options. Anybody could be doing this. Whoever the Riverman is, he is fairly well composed and, generally speaking, a normal guy."

I silently choked on Ted's reference to the Riverman as a "normal guy" even though I knew that Ted meant he was normal-looking to the outside world and did not look like a wild-eyed, chain saw–wielding mass murderer. Still, it was shocking to hear anyone call a serial murderer normal.

Unable to detect my feelings and wanting to assert some of his own ideas on killing, Ted said, "So, yeah. There are patterns, but that may be imposing my own hit stuff on what's already there. That might not be what is actually going on. And so there's some interesting things I think we're talking about: location of the bodies, how he progressed from area to area, and how he seems to jump around from dump site to dump site and so forth. But as far as his pattern goes, I'm just looking here at frequency—how often he does it—and just trying to get a feel for his own inner intensity. What is driving this guy, you know, from the inside out? And how often does he have to satisfy that, notwithstanding his desire to be cautious and avoid detection? And this guy, again relying on these lists as pretty accurate, he does one a week in July, does five in August, settles down to two and three a month until next May, when he gets four. That's pretty damn active. He's going Sunday through Saturday, generally speaking, not showing a preference for weekends. He's going all days of the week, spreading them out. Two and three a month is pretty intense, even after some of the bodies have been discovered. But like you say, the task force wasn't formed until January, and the bulk of the bodies weren't found until early eighty-four and I think that's probably what's motivating him."

With Ted's suggestion that the publicity and the formation of the task force motivated the Riverman to move out of the area, Dave got the nod from me that it was time to change the subject. Ted would only say so much about a killer's motivation before he realized he was talking too much about himself. So Dave changed the subject by asking, "Do you think this might be the type of person who would have to tell someone? Say he's married; I'm not sure he'll tell his wife. But let's say he's got a friend, a close friend; would he talk about it to somebody? Would he have a partner in this or do you think there's just one person?"

Does the Killer Share His Confidence?

Ted appreciated the new question and turned to answer it with the confidence of complete understanding. "Good question. My best guess is that I don't think he has to talk to anybody about it. Again, I would not want to assume that if he had, nobody would come forward, but quite frankly, it's not too probable that he'll ever want to talk to anybody about it. He's well composed. This guy has gone for over a year and a half."

"He's keeping it all inside," Dave offered.

"You can't use labels," Ted admonished. "He's got himself under control, a certain amount of control."

"How long can he keep that up, do you think?" retorted Dave.

"Until you catch him," Ted stated, sarcastically.

Trying to maintain order in the interview and not play word games with Ted, Dave came back with, "Do you think that he's going to be able to control himself indefinitely? Will he ever lose control or make a mistake somewhere?"

Apologetically, Ted recognized his flip attitude and simply commented, "Oh, I see what you mean. Good question. Sure, he can make mistakes. And—he has made mistakes."

"Severe enough to get caught?" Dave asked.

"Oh, well. You know what law enforcement is. It's oftentimes luck." Ted was instructing us. He'd been there, he was there, a convicted killer who was highly experienced in the subject. "There's no question in my mind that you have eyewitnesses all over, people who saw this guy and just don't know what they've seen. The place is covered with eyewitnesses, people who saw him walk up to them, and it went right in through their eyes and right out the back of their heads. He is not a phantom. He is good. He is well composed, and he knows how to approach those people. He knows how to limit the risks, but there's not a way to *eliminate* the risks. And, he's able to do it. The main reason he's been so successful, apart from his own canniness and wariness, is the fact of the kind of victims he's dealing with. If he were snatching high-school girls, he would not have gotten as far as he's gotten because of the nature of the victim. He's successful because of the kind of victim he's choosing. Again, if he decides to change his victim class, he's going to have a lot more trouble. And the reason you don't have a lot of eyewitnesses, I assume, you may have something along those lines. But the reason you don't have anything really reliable is, because any time you have a space of days or weeks before the victim is reported missing and no publicity about the disappearance, there ain't nobody coming forward. No, I don't think he would have to tell anyone, and he will continue to do it. He will make mistakes, but he's obviously covered his tracks."

Since Ted was on a roll, I felt that it was time for him to tell us how to catch the Riverman. Seizing the moment, I cautiously asked, "Do you think there's something that we can do to draw him to us, draw him out of the woodwork?"

Strategies to Catch the Riverman

As if he were just waiting for the chance to discuss this, Ted said, "Yes. Yes." Then he explained, "I think there are a couple of things that may sound a little bit strange. But I'll offer them to you for what they are worth. And my opinion about my ideas has changed radically and significantly. That is, I feel that if you find a fresh body—the likelihood of that happening is somewhat small—and if it looks like it's a Green River victim, I'd put that site under surveillance. I wouldn't move in. I think that that sounds a little bit odd to you. I got a twenty-page outline on why I think surveillance should be done and how it would be done. And, let me see if I can back up a little bit and try to make this sound a little bit more reasonable. First of all, I thought the guy was active as hell in eighty-four because there was all this stuff in the media about bodies being found. Well, now I understand that the bodies [showed that] the victims actually disappeared in eighty-three and eighty-two. So, on the surface, at least, he's not as active in the same way as he was in eighty-two and eighty-three. That's a fair statement.

"But let's say, assuming sometime down the line you start to find more fresh bodies, you find a fresh body, somewhat fresh anyway. I would move in, secure the area, try to keep everything off the radio, and set up. I know it's a lot more complicated than this, but set up a surveillance network on that area. Now you might want to move the body under cover of darkness, because, let's face it, by the time your man comes back to that site, by the time he gets on top of that body, he's already to the point where the body was and you've already got his number. You're already going to be in on him. So the body doesn't have to be there. If it has to be removed, I'd remove it. And I know the instincts that the police system moves in. Everybody is called in and scours the site. The explorer scouts crawl on their hands and knees, and this always fascinated me and appalled me, because I said, 'Jesus Christ, if they'd only waited, they'd [have] found somebody. The guy would have come right up to them.' In my opinion, the best chance you have of catching this guy red-handed is to get a site with a fresh body and stake it out. And I realize that you fight a lot of people who have conventional ideas, and they would object to that."

Amazingly, while Ted was on a roll, talking profusely on a subject, a totally abstract question didn't faze him. "How about computers?" I asked.

Dave was so enthralled with Ted and his steady flow of advice that he was oblivious to my question. Dave inquired, hypothetically, "How about this? You said there were probably several victims still out there on Highway 410 east of Enumclaw, and they're going to be skeletal. Do you think he's going back to the site of those three or to another site?"

"He's not going back up on 410," Ted reassured us.

"At all?" Dave questioned.

"No. I don't think so," Ted said. "Please don't rely on me. But I think this guy is not going back up there, not for a while, not for a year or two."

Knowing that Ted was ready for a question to reaffirm his beliefs, I posed, "You don't think he has some curiosity as to what the police did to the area where he dumped those bodies?"

"Sure he does, but he's a very wary character. I don't mean to tell you that, but I don't think he'd go back up there, not for a while. He'd balance out the risks first versus his curiosity," Ted explained.

"In some cases, we found just a skull. We haven't found the whole skeletal remains. Maybe he wants to find out if we actually found where he placed the body. Would he have that kind of interest?" Dave inquired.

"You got a point there. I would tend to say no because there are lots of other sites where there are remains which haven't been found," Ted explained. "If he wants to get his rocks off, he'll go to those sites. He's not a thrill-seeker in terms—I don't think—of trying to tell the police. You may have information to the contrary. This guy doesn't want to be caught. He doesn't want to play around. He's not Son of Sam and he's not even the L.A. Hillside Strangler. He doesn't want notoriety. That's why he's going to all these lengths to dispose of these people in the way that he has. Some people might read him entirely differently, and I'm just saying what I feel."

Trying to give Ted the lead, I suggested, "I'm sure you understand what his instincts are."

"I understand every single one," Ted replied. "I believe one hundred percent, if this guy was still active and you were still finding fresh bodies in eighty-four, why, there's no question in my mind if you staked out that site, you would snare this guy. There's no doubt in my mind. Now he's not as active. My opinion is slightly different, because you don't know. All you're finding is remains, and I doubt that he's going back just to see bones. I have been referring to finding a fresh site, one that he's actually using."

Ted was hesitant to talk about what the Riverman might be doing at the site where a body was dumped. I wanted to press him, so I asked, "What do you mean when you say 'using'? What's he doing there? Is he just coming there to lay the body out and leave? Or is he there for a period of time?"

Temporarily, Ted avoided answering the questions completely but responded to them partially by saying, "It's hard to say. My guess is that he is not there for a period of time. He's coming back from time to time. I don't say that he's doing any elaborate ritual or anything, you know. I'm not suggesting that. But I am suggesting he's coming back to check out the scene. You asked the question, 'Would he come back after the police found the scene?' And you cited some reasons why he might come back. Well, for the similar reasons, he would come back before the body was found. Perhaps, even if there were just remains, he would want to check to see what the conditions of the site were." In keeping with his own necrophilic fantasies, Ted obligingly said, "Because again, he might be seeing if the body has been completely destroyed."

"You think he talks to them when he leaves?" Dave pressed him with more things he might be doing at the scene.

Ted pushed his point aggressively as if he really were speaking from firsthand experience. "Oh, I'm not sure. But as far as coming back, generally speaking, especially for the recently disappeared victim, that he's going to be coming back, one, either to look at the scene for whatever reason, like is that body still intact, or has it been disposed of by the predators in the area? Or two, for some other reason such as personal gratification or to dump another body. And some of these sites, of course, are single sites like Pitsor and Brockman. And the two east of Enumclaw are apparently single sites. But even so, I think he's come and gone. It may be just nothing more than a drive-by, but I'll tell you what. I know that a surveillance of a site can be accomplished. This guy is not Superman. He can't see through the trees. He's good, but he is not infallible. And I think you have the skill and the equipment to stake out a site for a period of time. You can sit on it and collect all kinds of information. If it's just nothing more than just getting license plate numbers and makes and models of cars that drive by there that look kind of funny. But my guess is that if it's a good site with a fresh body, you're going to get more than a drive-by. You're going to get the guy coming up to the site, on foot or in his car. I realize the stakeout is an enormous moral and logistical problem."

At this point, Ted was focusing on bodies that were dumped in wooded areas, but the first five victims of the Riverman were found in or near the Green River. I wanted to determine if water sites were as significant to Ted as land sites. So I explained to him: "Coffield was the first victim found in the Green River in Kent police jurisdiction. The second one is Bonner, and she's a King County police investigation. At the time we're finding Bonner on August 12, Chapman, Hinds, and Mills are probably upstream in or near the river already. When we discovered Chapman, Hinds, and Mills on August 15, we set up a surveillance of the Frazier Road area, an asphalt road that borders the Green River. There was no surveillance for Bonner or Coffield on that road. What I'm wondering about, considering your theory, were these fresh enough?"

"Oh yeah. No question there," Ted responded.

"It was immediate publicity that we found the bodies," I reported. "We obtained over a hundred license plates of people that used that road. Channel Four Television's helicopter crew filmed the surveillance crews and were shown on the five-o'clock news. What do you think the odds are that the Riverman's license number was in that group?"

Ted commented that those in the river were a "little bit different than our terrestrial scene—a land dump site. Nevertheless, it's a good possibility he's coming by just to check things out to see if there's any unusual activity. All right. Now, how much publicity was there about Bonner?"

"Well, there was a little more than usual because the news media had tried to make a connection between Bonner and Coffield since they were found so close together," I answered.

"I mean, was it a big splashy thing? This guy is prone to attention," volunteered Ted.

"It wasn't headlines. It was probably in the Northwest section of the *Times,* at the most," I replied.

Ted was almost patronizing in the way he brought us back to how to conduct surveillance. "About surveillance of that area. I think that I would go back and look at all your license plates and try to figure out where these cars are registered. You know, and I don't need to tell you basic police stuff, but you know all this anyway. If there's anything that's really out of that area, you might want to ask yourself, 'Well, what's that car doing here on that road?'

"If I was the guy and was reading the newspapers and I knew on the twelfth that Bonner had been found and I had been there on the twelfth, I wouldn't go back. But let's say he misses that article—unlikely, but possible—if I were in your shoes, I would look at those hundred license plates. I think there's an outside chance. If I was in your position, that's what I would look at. And I might eliminate those that are the residents of that vicinity. But somebody that's out of Pierce County or Snohomish County that's driving along that road in that three-day period, then I would take a look at that person."

I asked, "When we're out at these sites processing the scenes, do you think when it's finally released to the news media and there are broadcasts on radio and TV, he'd have the balls to get in his car to drive out there and drive by us?"

"That's a good point," Ted replied. "If he's as sure as I think he is, I don't think he would. But, you know, there are the arsonists types that like to light the fire and stand back and watch the people putting out the fire. You know, in terms of creating a situation where you might be able to draw the guy to you, that's a good idea. But my guess is he wouldn't come there. But I wouldn't overlook it as one of the things he'd do."

Ted was speaking now as if he himself had played the game he was telling us to play with the Riverman. Perhaps Ted had crossed paths with police units going to and from the dump sites and I still didn't know it. But I believed he knew exactly what he was talking about as he described the Riverman's private game of tag with the police and his dead victims. "Let me tell you where I'm coming from," Ted said. "My emphasis is maybe too narrow, and I was saying surveillance of an undiscovered site that nobody knows about except for you and him. And that to me would be just an ideal situation, perhaps beyond anybody's capacity to do. I don't know. Beyond that, if that can't be carried out, then an idea like you have might be next best step. Who knows, maybe he is a type that gets a kick out of driving a lot. The Riverman is not going to want to get near you, unless he is a little bit off and a thrill-seeker. But he doesn't look like a thrill-seeker in terms of talking to his victims. Do you follow me?"

Of course I said yes.

Green River Killer's Fantasies

Given only limited information, Ted tried desperately to analyze the Green River cases prospectively and retrospectively. Not only were we his only source of personal approval and validation at this point in his life, we were bringing hot information about a subject that absolutely thrilled him: murder accompanied by sexual deviance. Therefore, because he wanted to please us as much as possible to keep this relationship going, he volunteered his wildest notion. "I mentioned earlier that I looked at the Green River situation and tried to imagine what's going through the Riverman's head. There's obviously the link between sex and violence. It was not a sexual act or a violent act, per se, although there is a relationship here. And who knows what factors combine to cause a person to reach this point, where he acts out the way he does. But I think it's safe to say that the guy fantasizes a lot. That is, he finds ways of vicariously experiencing the thing that gets him off, which is killing young women in this case. One reason for doing it vicariously is, it's safer. It's a lot safer sometimes to read a book or go to a movie and maybe a lot more convenient than to run out and actually do it. Let me give you an analogy. You have hobbies, and you're a skier or a fisherman. I used to be a skier. My hobby is skiing, so when I read magazines, I read something about skiing. I subscribed to *Skiing* magazine. I always watched the Warren Miller film that came out every fall. And so, that was one way of me vicariously enjoying something that I enjoyed doing. But being able to watch or read about other people is part of the hobby, a fantasy satisfaction. So I think it's safe to say, in my opinion, if you follow what I'm saying here, the guy who's killing his women, it's like a hobby to him.

"Well, it may be more than that. It may be an obsession. But just like anybody else who has an obsession, whether it be fishing, bowling, or skiing, he has ways he can vicariously satisfy it. Maybe he is going to peep shows and reading detective magazines. I think there's an excellent chance that one way he gets off is by going to look at what they call the slasher films. And I know it sounds weird. Years ago I read about a psychiatrist who said, 'If you could only photograph everybody who came out of the *Texas Chainsaw Massacre,* you would have a mug book of all the active violent offenders against women in that particular area.' And I would have to say that he was right on the mark, generally speaking. And, if I ran up against a dead end in this case and I was really looking for and developing some new exciting leads, first I [would say], 'Well, how will I take this idea that, in fact, people who want to act out violently also get a thrill out of indulging their fantasies through vicarious means, through media, through books and magazines and films and TV? How could it be done to turn this into an actual technique for developing possible suspects, in this case even?' And [then] I [say], you know, 'Have a slasher film festival.' "

Bang! The loud sound that startled us was Dave's tape recorder hitting the floor. Dave had not noticed where the recorder was sitting and, in astonishment at what Ted had very seriously proposed, had swung his arm around and swept the thing right off the table. Breaking up the serious atmosphere of the room, Dave said, "We're still alive."

The Slasher Film Festival Strategy

Ted laughed, but continued in all seriousness, "I'm trying to tell you something here that you might think is a little bit odd, but I really can tell you I don't think it is. Let's say that there's a film in a can somewhere that hasn't been distributed or released in the Pacific Northwest, and it's a particularly violent film that appeals to *Friday the 13th* or *Halloween* followers, that deals with death and young women, a violent murderer and young women.

"There have even been a few out recently that dealt with the death of young prostitutes. I don't know if you have kept up with that kind of stuff. Hopefully going to all the trouble and not being too obvious about having five or ten of these movies playing all at once somewhere, I thought, 'What would I do if I was trying to narrow down and bring this guy to me?' I would try and get the bloodiest, coolest slasher movie that's out there in a can which has never been broadcast or shown in the Pacific Northwest. I would pick two theaters, one in Seattle and one in the Tacoma area, outside of the general vicinity where these girls have been disappearing. I'd find a certain theater that was out and away from other activities so that people who came to the theater would have to park right in front of it. You know what I mean? As opposed to a downtown theater, where they'd park away. I'd get the cooperation of the theater owner and the film distributor. I would see if I could find a really vivid, lurid sex murder kind of flick. There are some pretty good choices out there, if you looked around for them.

"For a couple of weeks or so, I would assure that the film was well publicized in the Seattle/Tacoma newspapers, with the most lurid photos in the film section depicting the girls being held with a knife to their throat and the whole thing. Kind of the glitzy, guaranteed to arouse those kinds of passions, which, quite frankly, are unfortunately very unhealthy to arouse in people. I mean in the kind of sex and violence tendencies.

"Then for a period of a couple of weeks, I would photograph everybody that came in and out of those theaters. Now, I know this sounds weird, but believe me, it isn't. I'd photograph every male that came in there, and I'd try to correlate the guy's photograph with the license plate number of his car. Once he got out of the car, you'd have people in the lot. That's a lot of work, but just follow me and do what you want.

"You have people in the lot, and they would be writing down makes and models of cars as they arrive. Basically, as they were coming in, they'd be filmed, maybe even videotaped, coming in singly. Have them come through a turnstile or something. And later on, go back and correlate the photographs with the car evidence. I think you could correlate the photographs with the automobile, because that would be the only way you could link a face with something concrete which you could follow up on later, see? And that way you would have some way to follow up. And, quite frankly, I really believe if you have the resources to do this, and any eyewitnesses at all, or if you in the future have any eyewitnesses, you would have them look at photographs that you took of these people coming in. You would put them in a mug book of the males that were coming in the theater. After a couple weeks of film showing in Seattle and Tacoma, you would have a collection of individuals that I would think would truly amaze your Crimes Against Persons detectives. Not just you as a task force, but I think you could take that book of photographs and show it to victims in unsolved cases of assaults against women, and you would have people coming out of the woodwork.

"Men who, generally speaking, are as normal as the day is long, who really are highly controlled individuals, but who indulge their violent fantasies, not only in acting out but vicariously through the media. Their names are on no computer, their fingerprints are in no files, and the only time you ever see them come out in public is to view some of these movies, a way for them to get off. There's no other way you can reach them. There's no other way you could find them. It'd be like, you know, bees to honey."

Ted repeated himself to emphasize his point. "And what you would have after a couple of weeks is a pile of photographs, and hopefully you could correlate the photographs with the particular car or vehicles. You would have also a whole pile of suspect vehicles or you could go through and see if you have any suspect vehicles you're interested in. Are any of these showing up in the lots? If you have any potential eyewitnesses, are any of these showing up?

"Have a way of sorting the license plates of the vehicles showing up and see if any come from particularly a long distance away. If a guy drives from Auburn to Bellevue to see this kind of a movie, what does it say about him? It says he's really into sex and violence. And, hey, there's no better indicator of whether a man is capable of this kind of act, of killing all these women, than if he has that interest and goes out of his way to indulge that interest. That is, if there's any hook out there that predicts whether a person is capable or is disposed toward killing in the way the Green River man kills, it's whether or not he is interested in sitting down and viewing all of these gruesome movies. I know that's a generalization. But I can't think of a better way to tap into a whole reservoir of potential suspects who are interested, obviously, in sex and in violent sex and murder when it comes to young women than that."

"He may even have a VCR at home and rent those kinds of movies," I added.

"That's quite possible," Ted said. "I mean that's another excellent idea, if he's that well off. One of my feelings was this guy is staying, was active so long in the same area, and perhaps one of the reasons was because he didn't have enough money to go further. Maybe he was stuck to a low-paying job and didn't have the bucks to range further. I don't know. But he might be well off enough to have a VCR, and he might, in fact, indulge his fantasy in that way. I know if I was in a Crimes Against Persons unit in any law enforcement agency, I'd love to be able to know the name and I.D. of every male that would creep into this building. You know, the porn bookstores and peep shows. I would love to have their photographs in my mug book. Because I know that the first persons I would show that mug book to would be the cases where I had an eyewitness of some sort, but I didn't have any suspects."

"You don't think he'd go to any type of pornographic film? You want graphic sex murder, right?" I asked to clarify.

All the while Ted was talking about his strategy, he was becoming intensely excited, so we let him go on and didn't suggest that what he was proposing was entirely illegal. Even if we did learn who the killer might be, we'd lose our ability to deal with him because we'd have no probable cause to pursue the investigation based on the killer's attendance at a slasher film festival.

Ted spoke faster and became more articulate. Emphatically, he replied, "Sure. Get right down to his basic instincts. It doesn't have to be prostitutes. This guy is not going to go to the *Deep Throat* type of thing. He may or may not vacillate, but the clear link in this case is that he's going to be on whatever kinky sexual thing he has; if he has anything peculiar, [it] has gone way beyond just sex. There's that fatal link between sex and violence. The key is here. And so, the kind of stuff he's interested in is not just a skin flick, but he's more into vicariously experiencing what he loves to do, whatever he can do, and that's go out and kill young women. And, quite frankly, the closer the movie, the book, or whatever it is comes to that, the more interested he's going to be in it."

Sexual Totems

Following up on Ted's theory that a serial killer would attend his sex-slasher film festival, I asked Ted about some of the unusual items we'd found in the secluded and wooded areas of King County. "We have found clothing all the time where some sex freak has gone out in the woods and used specially cut pantyhose or wears female clothes and discards them. It's all over. You can pick out any turnaround and it's there. There's also, at periodic points, pornographic literature. In fact, there's a possibility that there's been someone with literature in close proximity of a couple of our finds. And it's not your sex murder–type pornography. It's just regular scenes of people fucking or whatever, you know, people doing their thing. Is this something that would interest this guy?"

"It could be," he said, and once again I suspected that Ted was talking more about himself than about the Green River Killer. "I mean, I'm not saying that this guy is one-dimensional. Sexually speaking, there are probably many levels on which this man relates to women. We hope several, anyway. And, quite frankly, it's possible that he has normal relationships or at least has had something that approaches normal relationships with women. You can't rule anything out. In fact, he may be a loner and hates women or he may not be. He may be single, he may be married. And I wouldn't rule anything out for sure.

"Therefore, he may get off on regular, say, mainstream pornography, whether it's *Playboy* or whatever. But I think obviously he's gone beyond that. He's gone beyond that here. It's obvious to me that it's an ingredient of violent death. It's indispensable now to his fantasy, to his acting out. And so while you may have found clothing, pornography, or soft pornography in the area where some of these bodies were found, I don't think it means that he was drawn to those areas because he found that stuff there, necessarily. You know that you find lots of stuff dumped, because people dump stuff. You know, go around in those locations, the turnarounds and back roads. I guess there's some people that think that is a good place to dump. It's just garbage. No, I don't think that finding that kind of material would necessarily mean anything to me, unless I found it right on top of the victims. Then it would have been important, certainly."

Important? Why? Was Ted revealing something about his own private necrophilic fantasies? Trying to get Ted to focus on this, I asked, "What is significant about finding things on top of victims?"

Avoiding that question entirely, Ted replied, "I don't know. It depends on what they are. If they were left there by the guy who killed the women, then you'd have to determine what it was he left there."

Necrophilic Fantasies

I proposed to Ted a slightly different approach to the same question. "Say you had a lot of bodies where you don't find or can't tell that anything is left, but you have one where there is obviously something left behind intentionally. And it's meant to be there such as—'look what I left for you'–type attitude."

As if he were turning that image over in his mind, Ted slowly began thinking aloud. "Ummm. May have not left it for you, but left it for himself. If it's something that you think is significant, he may have left it there because he got off on that and came back to find it there."

"Do you see any religious aspect in this whole thing?" Dave Reichert asked. Maybe Ted had some false altruism that drove him or maybe he could fathom something in the Riverman's fascination with prostitutes, street hustlers, and runaways.

Ted suggested that he once wondered if the Riverman was the "Charles Bronson type, getting rid of prostitutes for the good of the community. I don't think so, quite frankly. I don't think that he might be doing the Lord's work. Is this one possibility?"

"That's one thing that I'm trying to get at, yes," muttered Dave.

Ted tended to lecture, but in so doing revealed that he was a seasoned sexual thrill–killer who understood the motivations behind the mutilated victims he had left for us. He seemed to understand that we realized he had sexually manipulated his victims after he had killed them. It was chilling just how much he did comprehend and accept without any apparent remorse. The Riverman seemed to be Ted's objective correlative for describing his own fascination with his kills.

"In examining some of those bodies," he said, "if you find that they have been sexually mutilated in any way, he was not doing the Lord's work. If he was altruistic, he'd just go out there and knock them off and dump their bodies somewhere. But those murders are more than that. It's part of getting away with it, not limiting him [from] having fulfilled his fantasies at the scene."

"What would you say about mutilation?" Dave inquired, unaware, because he had not investigated him, that Ted was the supreme mutilator. I knew, more than anyone else except Ted, about the level of sexual perversion that Bundy wallowed in, and thus I sat there transfixed by the scenario that Ted unfolded.

"Well, if he's in fact sexually assaulting the victims and mutilating them in some way, I doubt that he has any religious motives," Ted said, repeating himself to make sure that we understood what he was explaining to us. "Motivations here, they're seriously complicated with some sexual and violent motivations, and you wouldn't see him as one primarily motivated by religious drive. My guess is if he's not picked these victims because he knows they're accessible, easily picked up, and difficult to investigate as far as law enforcement is concerned, he's picking them because he has some particular grudge against them and a real hang-up, you know, beyond viewing them as young women. And I sense in this [that] it's not a venting of religious anger or moral outrage, but a desire to kill and to harm these people. He will be doing that and probably continue to do it. I can't imagine him stopping."

Dave seemed to take the questioning deep into a speculative vein when he suggested, "It's been mentioned as a theory that the victims are put in the river for some form of baptism." But in reality he was probing Bundy from a different angle.

Ted seemed to have taken the bait when he shook his head in comic disbelief and replied, "No. Well, okay. My opinion is that this guy is a straightforward individual who gets off on graphically killing and sexually assaulting his victims, involving himself completely. For whatever reason, who knows? Perhaps. I mean, anything is possible. My opinion [is] he was dumping the bodies in the Green River because he thought that they wouldn't turn up, and they did, so he changed. It's as simple as that."

Serial Killer Diaries

Some killers were known to have kept a diary of their misdeeds. Dave asked Ted if he thought the Riverman kept a log of who he killed and where.

Reflecting for a while, Ted answered, "I see what you're saying. Yeah. Over the years I've had an opportunity [that] I'm sure you've had, to read about cases where a man accused of mass murders had his belongings examined. Some of them had the effort, you know, newspaper articles on the wall and everything. The Riverman is not flamboyant in the way that the Son of Sam types are. I mean, he's not trying to be sensational. He's low-key, not only in the kind of victim he's going after—and this is my own opinion—but not disposing of them in a way to arouse sensation. He's not going about looking for victims that would be a particular sensation. He seems to be going to great lengths to avoid detection, and, quite frankly, even may have some mementos or photographs of his victims. I'm sure he's keeping that to a minimum, if he's keeping anything at all. I wouldn't. But my guess is the time between when he picks up the girl and the time he kills her is fairly short. Relatively speaking, there may be exceptions.

"He doesn't have an opportunity to collect a lot of stuff. He gets their clothing. I think he may or may not have the ability to photograph them or get some other kind of information, which is another idea I have. Looking at some of the victims on your sheet there, I began to wonder if he might be interrogating some of them before he disposes them, to find names of other prostitutes. That may be why, for instance, I'm moving away from that question."

Knowing Ted was now embarking on a subject we had previously discussed among task force members, Dave encouraged Ted to proceed.

So Ted continued. "That may be why you have a situation where you have a Cynthia Hinds taken on one day and Opal Mills the next. He may have interrogated Hinds before he killed her and found out the names of several other girls in the area. That may account for his success in hunting down prostitutes aside from just taking whoever was available. But anyway, getting back to your question, I would tend to doubt that he would keep much in the way of elaborate things around, because he might get caught. So much of this is pure supposition. And it's interesting to speculate. My strong feeling is, from your point of view, you want to catch him, and there are all sorts of speculation that doesn't get you any closer.

"What I tried to think about were the possibilities you had with those sites, perhaps ones you've already located. Maybe he will be drawn back to those. But any you locate in the future, you know, I can't urge you more strongly to devise a technique of securing those sites and keeping them under surveillance some way. I know it's tough. But boy, I'm just absolutely certain that if you have an opportunity, in terms of a good site, that the man will turn up."

Categorizing Serial Killers

Picking up a previous reference Ted had made, I decided to confront him and press him about what he meant. I said, "You mentioned a while ago a typical serial murderer. What are you talking about when you say that?"

Ted really wanted to answer the question, but to do so would have violated his canon of not categorizing serial killers and, in so doing, becoming one of the profilers. Ted's attitude was that profilers put the emphasis on psychological categories rather than solving the homicides. Now, however, he had fallen into the trap of categorizing the killer types himself. He said humbly, "I don't know. I shouldn't have used that, should I? I don't know that there is a typical type. In fact, I should be critical of myself for saying that because I think there is no typical type, from what I've studied over the years. I mean, you have your type of mother-hitting homosexual to the apparently normal marriage heterosexual, and all different versions in between—the other guy who is mad—that is, insane—and then you have those who are apparently normal. You have those who hate women, those who love women, generally speaking. So you have a lot of the gamut. You have drifters, regular guys, upper-middle class, lower class, so I don't know that that's a fair statement. I know that that's not a correct statement to say typical serial murderer."

Ted's feeble attempt at classifying his "guys" struck me as being a remarkable mixture of denial and absurdity. On the one hand, Ted refused to define them and on the other, his deductions were uninformed and general. He knew very well that his "type" differed from others, but he declined to face the difference. So I reminded him of the serial-murder research done by the FBI's Behavioral Sciences Unit, which Bundy had followed closely. "Have you read some of the articles the FBI has published on their serial murderer theories?"

Sheepishly, Ted said, "I've read one in *Psychology Today* several years ago. It wasn't much, but I felt they were right on track." Trying to avoid the discussion, which undoubtedly would have included his crimes, Ted answered abstractly, "I can't remember what it was about that article that made me feel anything about what they were up against. It was some statement someone made that they would kind of base their understanding of this kind of behavior on the facts. And I know that's a cliché, but I think sometimes when you get too much into profiles and try to understand why and speculate why people do this, why people do that, what kind of person is he, and you get away from the hard-core facts, then you really lose something. From what I've seen, they start to limit their options. They start to believe profiles. Then if somebody doesn't fit a profile, they may dangerously eliminate the real suspect. Obviously, a lot of these girls here knew that there was somebody out there who was looking for people like them. Those prostitutes along Pacific Highway South were disappearing for a year and a half, and they continue to disappear, because the guy who finally approached them did not fit their profile or anybody's profile.

"When I read that article about the FBI, I said the only thing they can go on is what people actually do. And maybe later on, a psychologist can try to get into his head. If I was in your shoes, I would try not to put too much weight on the profile and all the psychological mumbo jumbo, because all you got is the hard-core facts, and that's the only thing that's going to catch him, sooner or later. Or he's going to catch himself."

Profiling

It was time to lure Ted into a more detailed discussion of the value of profiling because we wanted Ted, the only true, seasoned expert we had in serial murder on this case, to give us his profile of the Riverman. I sensed that Ted did not appreciate the so-called behaviorists who placed other killers in his class. So it was to our benefit to vilify efforts to profile killers. I reported, "We have the FBI profile, a psychological profile, an active profile, and profiles that we could read for days and still not get through them."

"Yeah," muttered Ted.

"I'm kind of [of] the same opinion that we're working at the wrong end. What can police do to actually attack this problem? We always look to the experts, who have been historically like psychiatrists and anthropologists. We ask them questions about 'What is the guy like that does this?' And they lend absolutely nothing toward telling us how to catch him," I commented, looking for Ted's approval.

"Exactly," Ted asserted, pounding his fist on the table.

"The experts tell us a bunch of bullshit about the killer and what his background might be like," I continued, "but for cops trying to catch him, there's no contribution. Now, what is the give and take? If the FBI is really serious about profiling, what should they be looking for?" I stopped talking because I could see that Ted was in a hurry for me to stop so he could begin.

Appreciating the opportunity to offer some significant insight, Ted started by saying, "Well, there are a lot of questions there. It's a good question. And I think if the experts can give you some kind of background from which you can take concrete steps in your investigation, to locate someone, to help you understand a man in such a way that helps you focus your investigation, that's one thing. But some of the profiles I've seen were wrong, and if they're wrong, they're taking you down the wrong path. Let me put it this way: the only thing that's not wrong is the names you have on this list, general dates when the bodies were found, where they were found, and where you are working with hard-core facts. That's what you got. Who knows what the guy's like? And I know that's approaching it from a backwards point of view that says, 'Well, we want to know what's going through this guy's head because that'll help us understand him better.' That's true. But on the other hand, that tends to lead you down the wrong road. It could lead you away from your man. You may have him right under your nose, and the profile says, 'Well, this is the kind of guy he is.' And there's some people in law enforcement who don't even know of somebody who's right there in front of them. And this guy is normal as the day is long. At least normal generally speaking. And what are you going to do? Arrest everybody? Every man who has been sexually assaulted or abused when he was a young person or hates his mother or whatever? Or everybody who walks out of a porno shop? You can't do that."

Ted was now on a roll, making his points, supported by what I believed to be his core beliefs. The mentor had transformed from one who was feigning knowledge of profiling to the clever psychopath who had intensely studied every aspect of profiles, especially those that pertained to him. "These profiles," he continued, "I've seen them over the years. I've seen how they work, and I think, quite frankly—my understanding is they tend to mislead. They can help, but they can only help if they give you a direct focus on your investigation, just like my idea about using that movie." Disingenuously, Ted admitted, "You know, I'm not an expert. I mean, I don't have a degree. I do have a degree in psychology, but that doesn't make me an expert in human behavior, certainly."

But before Ted could talk himself into being the expert he already said he wasn't, I interrupted. "In that article you read, there were several proactive strategies. Do you know what I mean by proactive? They are the things that the police can do to catch the killer in the act."

"Affirmative steps," Ted said to clarify.

"Right. There were several proactive things that they suggested have been done in the past." Ted didn't remember them because when he first read the article, he probably focused on the antecedent behaviors of the murderers whom he was so desperately trying to understand, not how they were caught. He was always more interested in the killers themselves. Therefore, I suggested, "Okay, one of them that they mentioned was that some killers have a tendency to come back to the gravesite." Ted muttered as though he understood. I clarified the strategy by explaining that the victim was now buried and the police could make a public display, appealing to his emotion.

"And hope to draw him out," Ted offered. Ted pushed his previous discussion of staking out fresh crime scenes as a preferred proactive method, rather than struggling with one he had not considered. "I don't remember that proactive technique that you mentioned. I wouldn't want to say that wouldn't work. I don't know. That's an interesting idea. I do know that I can say that the other thing would work. And that a person is just as likely to come back to the site that hasn't been discovered, especially a fresh one, as he is to one that has been found. In fact, if you have somebody who's clever and as vigorous as the Riverman is at attempting to avoid detection and apprehension, it makes sense to me that he's going to do what he can to avoid coming in contact with law enforcement. And, yes, the dump sites where the bodies were left are significant. There's no underestimating that. In fact, that's really all you have right now. All you have are the burial sites. You don't have anything else. The only places you know of for sure that the Riverman and the victims were at were those sites. There may be some other evidence, but these are certainties, no question that the victim and the guy were there. That's a tremendous advantage. That's where I would focus. Someone sitting where I'm sitting, that's where I would focus my investigation. Not all of it, but certainly a significant portion of it. Perhaps there would be some curiosity on a murderer's part once it's been discovered. But what if it isn't? What if he doesn't come back to a fresh site because it's under surveillance? Well, it's a risky take. But I think they're good risks, considering what you're up against."

Supercop

Another proactive measure recommended by the FBI was creating a supercop image, somebody coming into the investigation who's going to crack the case. And then, it was hoped, the suspect would communicate in some way with him. "What do you think of that?" I asked.

"Ummm, well," muttered Ted, as though the supercop technique was absurd. "What dummy would fall for it? In terms of a good understanding of what's going on, this is what I would start with. And what I see here is when you formed your task force and most of the bodies had been found. I'm not saying he stopped, but it would be fair to say that he's not as obvious as he was in eighty-two and eighty-three. You're not finding them the way you were, anyway. That's not to say he's not putting them out there, but it doesn't look like it to me, unless there's something going on beyond the scenes and you are in fact in contact with somebody who sounds like he's taunting you or getting off on something."

"Boy, we can tell you about the cabdriver who was a suspect. Have you read any of the articles about him? This guy has been in the news. He calls Channel Seven all the time, and they interview him," I said.

Ted said he heard something about a cabdriver. He said, "You don't have any fibers? No. It's no question to ask, but you must not have much because I'm sure you've done what you can to pin him down. It sounds like he's a little weird."

Polygraph Tests

Sooner or later we were bound to get to the subject of the polygraph. It seemed like a good time, since the Green River investigators had used it on several suspects. I asked, "What do you think about the polygraph? Do you think that a guy like the Riverman could pass a polygraph? Could a guy flunk a polygraph that wasn't the killer or, conversely, could a guy who was a suspect pass?"

Ted's polygraph experience was limited. For his responses to those questions, one could surmise that he had been given a polygraph about his murders at one point and flunked. He said, "I used to watch the F. Lee Bailey program. It's on late at night. And I know a little bit about polygraphs. You can have experts coming out of the woodwork, but I can tell you, if it's properly administered, I don't think they can be beaten. But they tell me innocent people can flunk. But Bailey's theory is if you have a good person, they should be able to figure that out. And that's probably the bottom line. If your man is good enough, I don't think that the person who's killed all these people will pass."

Riverman's Hiatus

Ted mentioned on more than one occasion that the Riverman might have stopped, moved, was hiding bodies better, got sick, died, or got himself locked up for something else. I asked him, "If he's locked up, what's he locked up for?"

Surprisingly, Ted said, "Unrelated or something that only went so far but didn't end. I mean, like burglary. Or car theft. That's just a wild guess. He could be locked up for something else."

Additionally, I inquired, "Is there another reason he could stop, such as [being] born again?"

Emphatically, Ted replied, "No. As far as the radical personality change, whether it be a religious experience or a moral reformation or whatever you want to call it, it's not out of the question, but highly unlikely, to the point of being impossible that he stopped of his own accord."

While Ted was making notes, I saw that he wrote down to check out the triangle of Bellingham, Spokane, and Portland, cities over 300 miles apart. I asked him if he saw some special significance in that.

Ted explained, "If I was in that position, compelled to range further because I felt that things had just gotten too hot close to home, then I would go to areas further away like Portland, Spokane, Bellingham, Everett, or the nearest metropolitan areas of any size. He's still focusing on the same types of victims, so that was the only reason I mentioned those three. Going all the way to Spokane might be a little bit out of the question. That's a several-hundred-mile drive. And this guy might not have the time or the money to be doing that very much. Spokane's out of his territory. And I think he's successful in Seattle and Pacific Highway South because he just knows it. He's been up there enough that he knows it and has a feel for it. When he starts to range far afield, he's more likely to make mistakes because he doesn't have that sensitivity to what's going on, to the scene, to the presence of police, and who's supposed to be where. And so if he goes to Portland, he hasn't the experience of being in the area."

Hunting the Killer

I told Ted, "If you want to compare prostitute areas, Spokane is nothing like Portland. Portland is rivaling Seattle as does Ponders Corner in Tacoma or the downtown area in Tacoma of Pierce County."

With a high degree of certainty, Ted made a prediction. "Well, I think the Pierce County people are missing a bet. I just get the feeling the guy is working out of Pierce County. Don't ask me why. It's the pattern of where the bodies are. South King County is like north Pierce County. Somebody should look over their shoulder, because this guy could very well be working out of Tacoma and just coming up to an area which is so notorious as Pacific Highway South. Even though he's trying to stay out of his own backyard, I'll bet you from time to time he can't help himself. Just a matter of circumstances might prevent him from some period of time getting up to Seattle or up to Sea-Tac. He might see a situation in his own area that he can't ignore, that he can't overlook, something too good to refuse. What perplexed me about the Green River list is, there's only one from Pierce County, Wendy Coffield. I had the feeling that there should be more."

Surveilling Pick-up Points

Ted focused heavily on the body recovery sites, so I asked him what creative things we might do at the pick-up points. He said, "I think Pacific Highway South is pretty well played out. Sometime in the near future he's going to move, like you say, to Ponders Corner, maybe even Portland, if he feels like he's played out the Seattle area. So you might want to look into cooperation with other agencies. You might want to do the obvious things. There are decoys. I don't know what else you could do. And I doubt that simple surveillance, writing down the license plate numbers of every weirdo which stops and pulls out a pair of binoculars would be an effective proactive technique.

"If he's coming into an area, he's coming in there often, even though he may not be taking anybody out. He is conditioning himself to be very familiar with the place. He's working with what he's up against, and he's looking for surveillance. He's looking for cops. He's looking for plainclothes. He's looking for anybody who seems to be out of place or is hanging around. He doesn't want anybody watching him."

Offering Reward Money

Rewards for any information leading to the capture of a killer are one way for the public to participate in the investigation. I wondered what Ted thought about rewards. So I asked, "How about the significance of a reward fund? How do you feel about something like that?"

Almost too obligingly, Ted said, "Well, it gets you a lot of information. I don't think this guy's talked to anybody. It's unhealthy, if he's talked to anybody. So you would get a lot more of what you got already, a lot of people whose boyfriends or guys they picked up in bars did something weird to them, talked weird to them, looked strange. They call in about *Hustler* centerfolds hung up in the bathroom. I'm sure you cannot underrate the value of having citizens calling in and expressing their fears to you about different individuals, because, of the five, ten, or twenty thousand reports you get, one of them might be your man. But how do you know that? Well, what I'm saying is the reward fund by itself wouldn't give you what you want. I think you're going to get the same stuff you're getting already. If somebody's going to talk to you, they're going to talk to you. This is not a situation where anybody knows something and is holding it back for money or waiting to come forward. The reason no one has come forward is because nobody knows. And, sure, it will get you more stuff, but it gets you so much more stuff, would you really be ahead of the game? It gets you more people calling. You don't need that. You might get lucky, and maybe it's the politically wise thing to do. I wouldn't overlook it, though. My opinion is it's not going to give you a better quality of information than what you're getting already. Just like anything else, it wouldn't hurt."

In the case of Canadian serial killer Clifford Olson, Olson's own family was paid $10,000 for every victim that Olson confessed to killing. This prompted Dave to ask, "Do you think if the reward was high enough, this kind of person might come forward and say, " 'Okay, I'll take the money as long as my family gets it.' "

Ted eagerly clarified what he'd just said. "That's a horse of a different color. You said 'reward'; I thought you would have meant rewards for somebody other than the man to come forward. That might be a proactive technique of a different kind. It might not get him to come forward, but it might get him thinking. It would put the pressure on him of a different kind. It would get him wondering that you think he might be weak enough or disposed towards doing something like that. I think that would be answered."

Troubled, Dave inquired, "Would that make him mad?"

"I think it might insult his intelligence or his own opinion of himself for someone who goes out of his way to not get caught. And if the police are saying, 'Call and turn yourself in, we'll give you some money.' "

Pressuring the Killer to Kill

Then Ted moved into a new area of proactive strategies. "I think the more you can disturb this guy—well, I have two opinions of it. On the one hand, it sounds kind of callous, but maybe the best thing that could be done is to get this guy to start killing again, at least openly. And you start finding something. I know that's hard, but if he goes underground, you're really up a creek. So, it depends on the kind of guy he is. Now, if he's the kind of guy who loves for things to be quiet, he doesn't like any publicity. He wants things to quiet down. Then the lack of publicity over a period of time would quiet his nerves and bolden him to the point where he would start killing again. I think the publicity and the activity of the task force does intimidate him. On the other hand, he may be just unstable enough where if you fuck with his mind, either with proactive techniques you mentioned about the supercop or some other things, or something like a reward, you could make him more disordered, make him less capable of covering his tracks, and make him more nervous. Because a nervous man is going to make mistakes, a complacent man is going to make mistakes."

Dave was interested in how Ted would put pressure on the Riverman to make a mistake that would lead to his capture. He asked, "Do you have any suggestions on how to make him more nervous?"

Ted thought before answering. "Well, publicity makes him nervous, but perhaps in a way that you don't like. It makes him inactive. Or he may change. I was thinking last night—I had a note to myself, trying to think of some way to manipulate him. I guess you guys got to be honest with him. But what could you put in the paper, if you're going to put anything, that would make this guy react in some way that you could exploit or detect?

"I haven't given that a lot of thought yet. And I'm going to put a note down on my list of notes to think about that some. Because I know publicity has a powerful effect on somebody in that situation. He wants to know what you know. But, on the other hand, he may assume that if there's no publicity, it means you don't know anything, things are cooling down, and people are forgetting about the cases. Everything is cool."

I reminded Ted, "One of the things that we talked about before was the fact that the bodies in the river didn't work. He went on to land. But they had worked before in other cases. Do you think that probably he has dumped in the river before someplace?"

Confidently, Ted said, "My answer to that is yes. I think there's a good chance he has. It's not a novel way of disposing of a body, but, like I'd say, anybody who follows the search-and-rescue news over the summers in the Pacific Northwest, when people are searching for hunters, fishermen, and rafters and such who've been swept away in a river, knows that there are times when they don't find those bodies. And he dumped them in there for a reason. He dumped Coffield and company in there because he didn't think they'd be found. He must have had some reason for believing that. Maybe if he dumped them up north of Enumclaw, in that stretch of water, there was a better chance they wouldn't have turned up. I'd only be guessing there. But I think it's either something he either heard of somebody else doing, or he did it himself and was successful. My impression was since he did it five times, and did it four times even after one had been discovered, he was evidencing some kind of belief that that kind of disposal technique worked. And that indicates to me that he'd done it before and it worked. Sometimes, the rivers will swallow people up."

Frequently, Ted mentioned that the Riverman was from a city south of Seattle. I said, "You keep mentioning south. Do you think he could have started farther south, like Olympia? Does it look like he's heading in a direction?"

"He could have started anywhere in the Pacific Northwest," Ted claimed, "anywhere between Olympia and Bellingham, or even Portland. It's hard to say. But because he shows a preference to range in such a restricted area, and because it's quite possible he didn't just start with Wendy Coffield, then, sure, any kind of related disappearances of young women prior to Coffield. If the guy had school or work, Olympia is an easy drive. Bellingham is even an easy drive. Portland's a little far."

Serial Killers in the Pacific Northwest

I saw that Ted made a note that serial murderers are active in the Pacific Northwest, even without the Riverman. "Which ones do you know of?" I asked.

At first, Ted rambled on, but then he became very informative by saying, "That's an unsupported supposition on my part, based mainly on the fact that over the years when I receive newspapers or clippings from the Pacific Northwest, I read of the bodies of young women turning up with relative frequency. And I don't know what it is. I don't know if it's just because I'm paying so much attention to the Pacific Northwest or if there's something about the Pacific Northwest that seems to encourage this kind of activity, because I know it doesn't seem to be as frequent down in this part of Florida as it is up in Seattle/Tacoma. The mountains of Washington offer some excellent terrain for hiding bodies. So you're not finding a large number of the bodies. That statement of mine about there being other serial murders is just something intuitive. I just sense it. I know about how difficult it is sometimes to detect a serial murder. And how some serial murderers tend to be very aware of how to cover their tracks, change their M.O. They're studying things all the time. So you might find one victim in one place and another victim in another kind and another way in another place.

"By varying an M.O., a highly controlled, intelligent, and alert serial murderer can go on for years and years. And he might only get two or three a year. Or there are others, like the Riverman, who just go hog wild. You cannot go for long doing four or five murders a month without drawing attention. It's just a sense of the whole problem of serial murders or multiple murders. There are a whole mess of serial murderers out there who are undetected because the way they go about it is so low-key, and they're not frequently exposed. And as in your case, a number of anomalies, a number of exceptions, people who were clearly killed by other individuals. Some of them you know and some of them you don't know who the perpetrator was. I just made that statement from my own judgment, just off the top, because I feel like you've got more up there than just the Riverman."

How to Profile a Killer

Bundy had studied all of the information available to him on this serial-killer case and had thought a lot about what the Riverman was like. He said he believed that an understanding of what type of personality the Riverman has may lead to avenues that would reveal his identity. In addition, Ted had read all of the literature produced by the FBI's Behavioral Sciences Unit and their methods of profiling an offender based on crime scene dynamics. Because he had a special perspective to bring to a profiling effort, namely that of an experienced killer, Ted fashioned himself as the only expert profiler of murderers. Realizing that Ted relished just such a spotlight, I asked, "What do you think that the profile of a serial killer should include? What are profilable items? What are the real categories—tangible things—about the killer that are not just general subjects or psychological bullshit, but things that are going to tell us who he is?"

It was obvious from his detailed answer that Ted had prepared himself for this question in advance, even though he started his response by complaining about his lack of information. Completely understanding the question, he confidently said, "Oh, yeah. Of course, I'm working with so little, but even, like you say, you might have a room full of information, but a lot of it is reduced right down to this: when they were last seen, where they were last seen, where their bodies were found, and some of the characteristics of the victims themselves.

"My opinion about the Riverman hasn't changed a lot. Some of my impressions of this case have changed quite dramatically since I got this little bit of information that you sent me. My initial impression was this guy is young. He is more or less in the same socioeconomic strata that these young women are associated with—lower-middle class, let's say. He's between twenty and thirty, probably closer to twenty. He's young. He probably has a low-paying job that restricts his movement. He doesn't have a lot of money. He can't move around."

"What race is he?" Dave inquired.

Without pausing to contemplate Dave's question, Ted said, "White. These are just impressions. Just impressions, just impressions."

"How young is young?" I asked, trying to pin Ted down to a more specific age.

Ted provided a fairly good account of why he thought the Riverman was "Twenty, twenty-five. That's only because he is not much older than the girls. My gut reaction is these girls are being approached by somebody who really puts them at ease. And they don't trust anybody over thirty.

"Have you ever sat down and asked these girls, 'What kind of person do you think the Green River guy is? What does he look like? How old is he?' Have them give you their profile. I'll bet you the guy would turn out to be old, maybe wearing a business suit or with an unshaven face, staring out of tunnels, you know, the Henry Lee Lucas type. But I bet you the last person they would expect to be the killer would be one of their own peers."

"What do you think some of his habits are?" Dave grilled.

With seasoned assurance, Ted resumed. "I think he's into, you know, pornography. He's into violence. That is, I don't think he may have beaten his ex-wife or his girlfriend or assaulted his teachers or anything, but I think he's into violence media. You probably would find that from time to time, like I say, in the pornographic bookshops, some of the more violent flicks."

"What about smoking, drinking, drugs?" Dave asked.

"That's something I don't know. I don't get any feeling for it. You know, drugs might be one of his hooks. Drugs might be one of his things he uses with these women. That fascinates me that once he gets ahold of them, he doesn't let go. He doesn't lose them. You're talking about young women who are streetwise. We've even talked about some young black women who must know the streets and who probably beat the crap out of a lot of white guys who try to do anything to them. So he's throwing down on them real good. And it could be he's using drugs to sort of take the edge off of some of that retaliation. I'm sure you've looked at their autopsies to determine that. But even that's not conclusive, I'm sure. Agh, you know, he lives alone. Not married," Ted predicted.

"Does he have girlfriends?" Dave asked.

"Possibly. But when he's as active as he is, it's certainly going to put a strain on any relationship he's trying to maintain. And there are probably times when he doesn't have a girlfriend."

Dave asked, "Do you think that his girlfriend might be able to detect the strain and wonder what's bothering this person? Or is he so well controlled that he's utilized that?"

Clearly lamenting his own plight in his relationship with Liz Kendall, whose report to our Ted task force ultimately led to the exchange of phone calls between Salt Lake's Ben Forbes and Kathy McChesney, Ted said, "Well, it's possible that he's been hiding it all his life. It's just become part of his nature to conceal what he can from the people around him, as much of that as he can. Certainly, someone around him might notice that he's not showing up for work, or he's tired or restless. He doesn't make appointments that he tells people he's going to make. He doesn't seem to have any money. He's always working on his car 'cause he's using it so much. As far as bizarre behavior is concerned, if he's acting out toward his girlfriend in any aggressive way, well, I'm sure you have a whole pile of reports from suspicious people who say that their boyfriend or somebody has mistreated them."

"Do you think he's athletic?" Dave asked cautiously, aware that Ted might think we were talking about him because he was such a skiing enthusiast.

Ted responded as though he didn't notice that Dave asked a question that was intended for him. "Well, that could explain his ability to overpower or otherwise subdue these girls. I'd imagine that he has to have something more than just physical strength, because somebody might think they're fighting for their lives. They will produce a kind of strength that he might not be able to handle. I almost think he has to have some kind of weapon to throw down on them with. Let's talk about girls like Williams, Antosh, Naon, and McGuinness, who disappeared in mid-eighty-three. Now, they should have known that there was somebody out there hunting them. And at some point in time, they knew he was right there. They were in the hot seat. They were going to fight for their lives, and yet they didn't get away.

So even though he may not be killing them with a weapon, he's got to use something to intimidate them pretty effectively. Or has some kind of vehicle that they can't get out of, you know. It might be interesting to check that out someday. Any guy whose passenger door does not unlock at any time, you might want to check that."

Dave and I wanted to move the conversation in a new direction from here, and discuss the kind of control certain serial killers wielded over investigators. One way for them to do that was to insert themselves directly into the investigation. Ted knew very well that some guys like him sustained control of their need for continuing the excitement of the murder by taunting the police or trying to throw them off the track. By pursuing that concept, we would get some idea whether Ted ever actively involved himself in the investigation of his murders. So I asked Ted if he thought there was any chance that people like the Riverman would offer information on their own case.

Without hesitation, Ted answered, "Yes. Sure there is. It's hard to figure, unless he felt like somebody was getting close. That's the only thing I can imagine. If this man has been active in the area since 1973, and then all of a sudden he takes off with Coffield and company, doing three, four, five a month, that shows such an intense drive. To control it over that period of time and then just unleash it and then control it again, it would be an extraordinary individual you're dealing with. It's unbelievable to be so controlled and avoid detection for ten or twelve years at least and as intense as the person who did the Green River case was and then shut it down again. It certainly would be very, very unusual."

Since Ted had examined the possibility that a suspect like the cabdriver would have been around since 1973, nine years prior to the beginning of the Green River cases, Dave followed up by asking, "Do you think that this guy could have started as early as seventy-two, seventy-three, seventy-four, by placing the bodies of his victims on land and then gone to water and then back to land again? I noticed in your notes last night when Bob and I were going over them, you indicated that you were pretty sure he used the river once before. It worked for him or at least somebody had told him about it, and he thought it'd be a good idea, it'd probably work. But do you think as early as seventy-three or seventy-four he could have used the land?"

Clarifying his notes, Ted explained, "Oh, sure. For some reason he started with the river because he'd heard about it or tried it as a variation of something he read about. Yeah. All through the years, he'd have to be pretty good to survive that long and be very well controlled. But the guy in the Green River case just explodes sometimes. That's not to say that people with that kind of acting-out behavior don't go through changes over time—periods where they're more intense than others—because they do. But, you know, we're talking over several years.

"Well, if the cabdriver is the Riverman, he's been doing it for a number of years, and so it's quite clear that he's pretty good at it it if he's been doing it for that length of time. But what I see with the Green River man is somebody who's experimenting. I mean, you'd think that the cabdriver would have it down after ten years or so. Who knows. But by trial and error, if he survived that long he's got to have a good technique, and he's got to have a good way of disposing of the bodies. And after ten years he should have had a favorite technique or two."

Ted just eliminated the cabdriver as a suspect by emphasizing that the cabdriver should have been a more efficient killer after so long. Showing his frustration at not being able to conclusively eliminate the cabdriver, Dave was eager to suspend the investigation of the cabdriver, and supported Bundy's statements by saying, "He should have known with Coffield, Bonner, Mills, and Hinds to go out in the woods and dump them, rather than throw them in the river right there in the middle of Kent."

Ted agreed, "Right in the middle of Kent, where, you know, I'm sure that over the years, it may have occurred to him to dispose of a body in the river. And maybe it worked. But he should have known, being so close to civilization, that it was a good chance the bodies would be found in the river."

Killer's Souvenirs

Another personality quirk found in some killers was to collect some item of the victim's clothing and keep it as a souvenir. Some killers used an item as a way to engage their fantasies. They seemed to transfer the sexual thrill of the hunt, the kill, and the activity with the corpse into the item itself as if it were a totem. To others, these items were trophies representing the ultimate possession of their victim. Ted knew that his girlfriend told us she found a paper bag that contained women's underwear that was not hers. Therefore, we had to be careful how we asked about the subject. Instead of asking about underwear, I inquired, "Is he a collector, like a shoe fetish guy? There was Jerry Brutos in Oregon, who collected not only many shoes but also his victim's feet. Does the Riverman knock them over, take their shoes, murder and rape them, and then weight them down in the river? Is that a necessary part of his framework?"

Clearing his throat as though he was shocked by the nature of a question that seemed to be so close to the core of his own fantasies, Ted cautioned, "I would say it's not necessary. Certainly, that's not to say that people don't have their fetishes, don't collect things, and maybe clean house every once in a while. But I don't think it's necessary. Every guy is different. And when you finally run up on your man, and if you found a houseful of stuff, then you've really got it. If you don't find it, that doesn't mean he's not your suspect. Just 'cause he doesn't have anything may, in fact, mean that as it appears here, he's somewhat fastidious. At least as fastidious as he can be. But he could easily have a fetish with underwear or stockings or shoes. I mean, that's something of a true wild guess.

"We're dealing with such a unique individual, who knows what it is that sets him off, specifically? Generally, what sets him off are the young teenage prostitutes. But beyond that, whether he likes to keep a photograph of them or collect newspaper clippings, whether he gets off by going back to the sites and molesting corpses or whatever, any number of different things that it might be part of the pattern, I'd say it's a ritual. I only mean that in the most general sense, nothing religious necessarily, but part of his syndrome that he's caught up in, which is evolving over time, too. I mean, changing as he changes. Everybody changes. But it may be a fetish, it may be necrophilia or any number of peculiar things. More importantly, is there any indication that the man is, has been back to the sites we've found whole bodies to see if the bodies have been disturbed postmortem?"

Control Fetish

"The reason I ask is this guy is responsible for twenty or thirty or more deaths at least, and there's a certain aspect of possessiveness in that. I think that's one way of describing it in rather bland terms, a possessiveness where the corpse could easily be as important as the live victim, in some respects. I mean, it's that physical possession and ownership, a taking, if you will, that is just part of the syndrome. I think that sense of power and ownership is one of the reasons why I think in certain cases—not all, certainly—is why I think he might be individually intending to return to the scene to either view his victim or, in fact, even interact with the body in some way."

Stunned that Ted would suggest that a killer would want to physically possess and "interact" with a dead body, Dave stammered when he asked, "And you're saying that this would occur before we find them?"

Ted continued by slightly changing the subject. He stated, "Generally speaking, yeah. But I thought about it last night and you definitely have a good point. There are the arsonists who just burn down buildings and run off, and then there are the arsonists who like to watch the fire department put out the fire. And, who knows, there might be a side to the Riverman's character where he gets off seeing you guys' cars parked beside the road, and, you know, crawling on your hands and knees in the bushes or something." Then, clearly tracking my expressions, Ted asked pointedly, "You seem troubled. Am I boring you?"

Ted fell for my staged body language just as I had hoped he would. Dr. Berberich was proved right once again. He had advised that when Ted got off the track, yawn and look in another direction. Try to make him think, without saying it, that you were bored. Most psychopaths constantly try to keep your attention by involving you in their fantasies. One way to get them back on track is to look bored and, with that, they will be more specific as they try to draw you back into their world. At this point, Ted was treading on thin ice. He wanted desperately to talk about necrophilia, but was afraid that in doing so we would discover too much about him.

254

Sensing he had no choice, I pressed him, saying, "I was just thinking about postmortem activities. You seemed absolutely sure that he's not going to come back once we've found the body. Our capability of monitoring a dump site long afterwards is really possible."

Eagerly, trying to please, Ted said, "Yes."

Previously, Ted had elaborated on his favorite method to catch the killer, staking out the body recovery site. I felt we probably had more capability to stake out a site long after the body was recovered. So I asked, "And I just wonder how fruitful you thought that would be?"

"Let me understand what you just said. Monitor it afterwards?" Ted asked, trying to define my question.

Monitoring Dump Sites

I gave him an example of what I meant. "We discovered a site along a roadside. We have been there, processing the area, and then we leave. That's a different concept than staking the body out and him driving by while we're there. What are the odds of his coming back in this area, several months later, thinking we're not there?"

Ted reminded us, "And, of course, there's a good chance in some of these areas that you haven't found everyone. I mean, it's obvious you haven't found everyone. And there's a good chance that where you've found only one that there are probably more than one. And you said yesterday that you found one buried where the others were aboveground. It may be very well that the reason you haven't found some of the others is because they, in fact, are buried. And it's more difficult, obviously, to find them, but if the animals haven't dug them up, it'll be more difficult to find. He might want to come back to an area. So I would look at your list and see where the most likely sites are that might have somebody there you haven't discovered. For instance, it occurred to me, and I don't know why, I was just looking at the maps and I saw what would have been the site where Naon and Meehan and an unidentified individual were found. They were all pretty close together. But there's a good chance there are some more down by Star Lake and maybe, even better, down by Auburn, where you only found one. So it would be a matter of just picking a site that you felt had some potential, where you just didn't want to spend days on your hands and knees trying to find something else, and monitoring it. I think there's a fairly good chance that if there's somebody left, he would be back. If there's somebody left and you're long gone, as opposed to actually trying to get in your face while you're at the site, there are some people who get off on doing that, but I don't think this guy would."

Pursuing the thought, I asked, "How about if we hadn't found them all up along 410?"

Anxiously, as if he were actually in the Riverman's mind as he tried to play Battleship with people looking for the guy's kills, Ted continued, "Oh, yeah. Right now, it appears he's spread them out up there. They're not all in one place. For instance, it's not that he won't return to an area once it's been discovered. You found Lovvorn in September of eighty-two, and yet he came back just about ten blocks away to dump three more. No telling he won't come back to an area, but the exact same spot—that might be something else again. You got ski season coming up, so you're going to have a lot of traffic along Highway 410 in the not-too-distant future. It's going to be hard to separate the wheat from the chaff, let alone those folks going up there skiing.

"But your fellow might not be so smooth as to put the skis on top of the car. The thing is if he puts his skis on top of the car and drives by at seven in the morning and comes back down at nine, he's not going to hang around up at Green River or wherever for the next ten hours just to come down and see what you are doing. He's going to get cold. He's not a skier, and he wants to get back to business. Your people might see him pass at seven or eight and come back at nine or ten that same morning. Even with the skis on his car, that would look a little bit weird. And if you start to see that same car do that over a period of a couple of months, then you might have something. But it'll take a little bit of work."

Flaunting his knowledge of the area, Ted explained, "I think the sites east of Enumclaw have the most potential for that kind of proactive technique because there are more bodies out there. They may be all between Enumclaw and Greenwater. There's a lot of space up there, but not so much you can't handle, because the roadway is between the river and the mountains on the left (as you're going up). And there's not a lot of room to move around except off the side roads. Some of them have gates across them, don't they? And some of them don't. Like up past the town of Greenwater, there used to be a section where there were summer homes. And the mountainsides are honeycombed with second-growth timber when I was last up there. It may be ready to harvest by now, I don't know. But there are lots of side roads up north of Greenwater."

Ted was aware that one of the main problems in serial-murder investigations was how to link bodies found as murders committed by the same person. How far back in time or far away in distance did one go to find cases that might be related? Could a woman found raped and stabbed in a county 60 miles away over nine years previous be a case related to the Green River murders? Better, could a case that might have been one of Bundy's own crimes bring him closer to the Green River Killer and get him talking about his own cases?

I had previously spoken to Drs. Berberich and Liebert about showing Bundy a crime scene photo as a method of attraction to keep him talking whenever I believed his enthusiasm or attention was flagging. Both predicted Bundy would be invigorated by the photo and think, by explaining to us precisely what's in it, that we were participating in his fantasies. It was hard to believe seeing one photograph could fuel his long-interrupted lust for dead females. But, at this point in our interview, I believed it was worth a try.

The Case of Kathy Devine

Rather than pick just any case as an example to discuss with Ted, we purposely chose the case of Kathy Devine, who was murdered in December 1973. Her murder was never solved, but the case was one in which Ted himself was a great suspect. Devine was last seen getting into a green pickup truck driven by a white male with a beard near 90th and Aurora avenues in north Seattle. At that time Ted owned a green pickup in addition to his Volkswagen bug, and was sporting a full beard. Devine's body was found near a campground in southern Thurston County about 15 miles south of Olympia, the capital of Washington, where Bundy worked. I obtained permission from Lieutenant Mark Curtis of the Thurston County Sheriff's Department to use photos from the Devine case since it had not been under active investigation for years. Certainly, Bundy's facial expressions and psychological reaction to evidence from this case would help us assess whether our hunch that Ted was a good suspect in her murder was correct.

I had to approach this phase of our talks in a way that didn't alert Ted to the fact that we were carefully observing his body language and the manner in which he was answering our questions. Even though the temptation was there, I couldn't immediately plop down Devine's crime scene photo and ask him if it could have been committed by the Riverman. This might have signaled to Bundy that I had just violated his request not to discuss crimes for which he was under investigation. So I started out talking about a different subject and drew Ted into a position of wanting to see the photograph.

A curious aspect of serial-murder investigations was whether the killer had come into any type of contact with the police before his arrest. Many experienced detectives believe that information about the killer they are seeking is somewhere in their files, but they just don't see it. It was a topic I knew Bundy would talk about. It was close to Ted's heart because he had said on previous occasions that some police officers had mistreated him. I carefully chose my next words to conceal my real intent. I commented, "Seems inconceivable to me that the Riverman, who was very familiar with the strip area, wouldn't have been hassled, rousted, or something by the local uniformed patrol officers."

"Field-carded?" Bundy asked. This was Ted's phrase for field interrogation or interview report. Patrol officers completed those reports when suspicious behavior that did not lead to an arrest was recorded in police files for future reference. "Sure. Check the field cards for what kind of behavior? Lurking behavior? Which is exactly what he'd be doing if you'd be field-carding in the area. Maybe he'd look out of place. I'm not saying he'd be peeking in windows or anything. He's more than likely gone far beyond that stage.

"We're talking about a patrolman, out in the field and is a hot dog, and he doesn't like anybody hanging around his area that he doesn't know. He'll field-card them just for spitting on the sidewalk. And sometimes those contacts by police officers are the most valuable. Someone will catch this guy entirely by surprise," Bundy explained like a man of vast experience.

"But if he's just lurking around and trying to observe the behavior of these women, it's not like him to be doing anything illegal unless he's hiding in the shadows. The Riverman certainly uses shadows, you know, from time to time. So check your field cards for single males with suspicious behavior, suspected prowler, burglar, or whatever. A young man, twenty to thirty, hanging around Pacific Highway South and field-carded. And that is a little bit far out. I'm sure you checked all your arrests for indecent exposure or prowling or window peeping and all that kind of stuff, right?"

Bundy had just given a list of what a serial killer would have been stopped for when searching for victims. Ted continued by asking, "Do you have names? You have your computer running, right? It's possible your man is going to appear on more than one list. There's an excellent chance your guy has already been reported, too. But where do you start? You know how I feel. So, if you can start developing alternative lists and matching them and working through a computer to find him, then you start to have something: field card here, arrested there, reported over here, car license plate number shows up over here. You know, the kind of stuff like you're talking about, things that contain people's names—maybe a little bit more sophisticated."

It was ironic how Ted went right to the very way the task force had identified him from the thousands of names in our computer. I don't think he ever realized how close we were to him even before the Utah arrest, even though he knew what the typical methods of police investigation were. But now, no matter how fruitful this line of questioning was, it was time to redirect Ted. As I placed a black-and-white photograph upside down in front of Ted, I said, "Whenever we've gone through our records, we found cases similar in nature to the Riverman's." Ted obviously understood that the photo was turned so he couldn't see it, and he didn't hesitate to grasp and rotate it until he was looking at the photo correctly.

Immediately, the contortions of Ted's face told us that he was morbidly transfixed by the Devine scene. His jaw protruded, and his pupils were hideously dilated. His pulse bulged and radiated through his carotid artery like a huge water bump in a garden hose. I felt suddenly as if he were alone with his thoughts, replaying an internal video of his murder, even with us there.

In a droning voice, Dave reported the facts of the case while Ted stared down. My guess from his reaction was that Ted didn't need the explanation. He patiently waited while Dave explained what he already knew. "She was actually found in Camp Margaret McKinney. Later in nineteen seventy-four another girl, Brenda Baker, was found nearby in Millersylvania State Park. And you're kind of aware what our M.O. is. We've got prostitutes, some in the river and some on land. And I just picked out a few photographs that were taken back there in seventy-three of this young lady. And that's one of the reasons I asked you the question about whether or not he could have started putting these bodies on land, then the river, as far back as nineteen seventy-three."

"Ummm," Ted said, licking his lips while searching for the relevance of that particular photograph to the Riverman and not himself. Groping for some quick relationship to the Green River cases, I said, "We're interested in her case because Ninetieth and Aurora is an area frequented by prostitutes."

Coyly, Ted reminisced with himself and kept the photo in front of him. He asked, "Now, where was this body located?"

"She's about ten miles southwest of Olympia. Five miles west of I-Five," Dave answered.

Ted interrupted as if he wanted to take over the description of the locale for us and came tantalizingly close to a confession of a detail only the killer could have known. "Off a dirt road," he said in a voice that seemed to indicate that a deep memory had been evoked. But he caught himself and desperately tried to revert to a third-person narrative. He asked, "How far off the road?"

"Found near the parking area at the park," Dave quickly responded. "He didn't have to carry her too far. She was within about ten feet of the parking lot."

Ted regressed quickly back to his first-person version, "But there's no attempt to conceal the body. And there are clues, there's clothing here. Pretty strong individual to be able to rip those—or cut, possibly cut—those jeans like that."

I was astonished by Ted's observations since I could hardly decipher from the photo what condition the clothing was in, let alone how the jeans were cut. He had to have been there. He *was* there, right then, in his memory.

Reading my mind, Ted denied any connection to the photo. "Ummm, I don't think I've even been there—that is, to the park.

When I was a kid my parents used to go there all the time. Found a picture of that area once, Millersylvania State Park."

"Well, Devine was found in Camp Margaret McKinney, southwest of Olympia, not Millersylvania Park," Dave reminded him. "She was picked up in Seattle. That's where she was last seen."

"That would have—that was seventy-three?" Ted responded, like he knew nothing about the case and was avoiding any reference that he might have murdered Brenda Baker, too. Ted mixed up the facts of his murders.

"Yeah, Ninetieth and Aurora on December seventh," Dave volunteered when he didn't need to. I would have pulled his plug if I could have to keep him from giving Ted any information.

Glancing at the photo of the Devine body, Ted reverted to his mode of speaking hypothetically, like he usually did when we got too close to his cases. "Well, the obvious presence of clothing. 'Course, this was ten, eleven years ago, and they're apt to change and will change as he discovers what works and what doesn't, and studies—but the way the jeans are cut, that's kind of unique."

Cautiously, Dave continued by asking, "What are your impressions of the kind of guy that would have done something like this as compared to what we're looking at?"

Ted was about to reveal an important concept, yet to be written up in any homicide literature at the time. This concept would upset modus operandi purists, those who believed that the characteristics of one murder must be replicated in another in order for both to have been committed by the same person. Ted said, "If he's capable of it, he's had ten years to change his M.O. and his—whatever you call them—fetishes or his rituals or his fantasies will change every time, too. So he might be taking the girls' clothes over one period of time or not. He might be subjecting them to a certain type of abuse at one period and changing the next time. There's no question about that."

Dave sustained the hypothetical tone by stating, "But let's say that our Green River person did this one, but, as you said, his M.O. is different. What was going through his mind back then, you know, just from your impressions of the photographs you looked at? I know it's kind of difficult when you're looking at black-and-white photographs, but what do you think his mind is doing then?"

"Well, that's not much to work with," Ted pleaded.

"You got the torn or cut pants," Dave added.

"Oh, yeah. The whys of the cut pants are bizarre. And I don't know what the autopsy revealed in terms of the presence of semen or any other marks on the body. The cut pants are really odd, boy. You know. Why? Why they're cut? I don't think they're ripped. I think they are cut, unless he performed some sort of sex act right before or right after he left her there and came back and ripped her pants in order to do that. But that's a little hard to figure. I mean, he didn't have to hurry. He obviously had control of the situation. So, that's a little bit bizarre."

Up to this point, cutting pants and mutilating bodies were classified by Ted as bizarre. But what was most bizarre was the sight of a serial killer in captivity looking at a photograph of what might well have been one of his own kills. From somewhere deep in the recesses of his memory and driven by the still-living sexual lust within him, Ted seemed to be projecting his own motive and patterns onto a phantom killer who was lurking, even then, in the shadows of the Northwestern forests over 3,000 miles away.

10

"The River Was His Friend"

Ted Bundy was downright exhilarated as he described how the Green River Killer might have dumped his victims. When Ted talked about dump sites, he had a fire of excitement charging through his body that was not there when he was talking about abduction sites. His lightninglike hand gestures and his shifting body movements made to emphasize his points reflected his intense preoccupation with the dump sites. It was almost as if he were there and enjoying every minute of it. These moments illustrated that Bundy and the Riverman shared a common fascination with the corpses of their respective victims. It was from sharing a similar experience that Bundy was able to sense how the Riverman had preselected his body recovery sites as a function of his own common sense, choosing them only after extensive trial and error in sampling many sites.

Theories of Dump Sites

Ted began the conversation about dump sites by coyly explaining that he did not want to talk about what we had already considered. "Generally speaking, it's hard to say. It's all speculation. I'm sure you've gone over this a thousand times. But for prostitutes missing from downtown Seattle, there isn't an obviously good, close site where he can just drop them off. He's got to go somewhere. Therefore, he has driven to Interstate Five, more than likely heading south. Then he easily dropped off victims on the roads that intersected I-Five as he did with Delores Williams along Star Lake Road."

It seemed that the killer's direction of travel was an important point in the case for Ted, especially since heading south fit Ted's pet theory that the killer lived in the Tacoma area, south of Seattle. Ted supported his point by arguing, "He dropped off Pitsor on the Mount View Cemetery Road and Colleen Brockman on Jovita Road, both locations on the way from Seattle to Tacoma. Also, he had traveled east on Interstate Ninety and dropped off Agisheff on Highway 18 and Yates along I-Ninety near exit 38. Other victims were deposited in that same general vicinity. And, of course, Snoqualmie Pass along Interstate Ninety has gotten a reputation for that kind of activity, and perhaps that's what attracted him there." Ted had often said that killers learned from previous experiences, and based upon this fact, the Green River Killer would know to dump his victims along I-90 just as Ted had.

Ted had analyzed the dates when each victim was dumped in a specific location. He particularly noted that Abernathy's and Bello's remains were found "way out along Highway 410, over thirty-five miles from where they were last seen in downtown Seattle. They were missing toward the tail end of nineteen eighty-three, one in September and one in October. That was about the time that task force members found several bodies that autumn in locations where the Riverman had previously dumped victims, such as along the Star Lake Road and from around the airport strip." So Ted surmised that the killer would naturally change locations, because he never returned to dump a victim in a location that had previously been found by the police. It was too risky.

With the keen perception of one who had evaded police for years, Ted said, "And I bet he was getting nervous. He said, 'God damn, they're starting to find my bodies again.' " Ted seemed to love speaking as if he were the Green River Killer. It was eerie, particularly after the years we spent on his trail, to hear him speak in the killer's voice. Ted didn't want to confuse us with his eagerness to explain and he hastened to add, "It's kind of fascinating to see how this unfolds, and I'm probably running ahead of myself. If I'm confusing you, please ask me questions, but just looking at how this unfolded—I see here by the dates that you found the first five real quick—Coffield, Bonner, Chapman, Hinds, and Mills." Ted was desperate to answer our questions at this point and responded to them rapidly, without a moment's hesitation.

Ted tried to prove his point that as the Green River Killer progressed, he became a more efficient killer. "You can see, he changes. Due to the five discoveries, he's obviously not going to use the Green River anymore, at least not for a while. It was his friend for a period of time. He's looking for something that's more effective, so he goes back to dry land with his sixth victim."

After August 15, 1982, the date Opal Mills was found on the bank of the Green River directly above two other victims who were in the river, the Riverman dumped Giselle Lovvorn, his next victim, on dry land. Ted said, "And Lovvorn is found in September, but still he sticks to these dry land sites with his subsequent victims." By continuing to dump victims on dry land, the Riverman, Ted believed, had learned that the victim's remains were not immediately discovered, like those found in the river. Also, when the victims were found, they were nothing more than skeletons and the killer surely took note that this type of dumping provided less physical evidence that could link him to his kills.

Ted was somewhat patronizing when he spoke of his analysis of the cases, saying, "I was able to more deliberately analyze it in my notes here. What I'm saying is, between September of eighty-two and May of eighty-three, you didn't find any bodies. So, in his mind, he was effective, and he killed how many between those months? You got a whole mess of them that were not found until much later.

"He started back to dry land, knew you couldn't find any bodies for seven or eight months, anywhere. And this guy is starting to get bold again. 'Yeah. I finally found the ticket, you know, when they're not finding my bodies.' And we didn't find the next one until May. He went from September to May. And the Riverman had changed, changed his path."

Ted enjoyed the hypothetical question because it gave him a chance to make us think that he was guessing, so I asked him, "Let's say he's still in the Seattle area and is continuing to kill. Okay? And we found Abernathy and Bello out there, great distances from where they were last seen. What do you think the Riverman's next step will be?"

Without hesitation, Ted responded, "Well, go with what was working. And, you know, he moved up east of Enumclaw, thirty-five miles from Seattle, to dispose of victims. He's going deeper into the mountains. He's trying something new. He's trying something different. You found three up east of Enumclaw. He probably won't be going up there anymore, assuming he has been going up there. Obviously, he was up there for a time, and I'll bet you'll find another or more up there. At least, in my opinion, four or five more."

Ted never gave us the credit for finding *all* the victims dumped in a particular location. According to him, there were always more. Eerily, Ted's predictions were correct for the dump sites near the Intersection of I-90 and Highway 18 and at the south airport area. More bodies—presumably those of additional Riverman victims—were found in those areas long after our conversations with Ted had ended.

Dave Reichert was concerned about where the Riverman would dump future victims. He asked, "You think he'll go further east on I-90?"

Ted's response was somewhat of a surprise since the Riverman had murdered at least 40 women. "Who knows? This guy is learning! He's trying to find the best way to dispose of those bodies he can think of. He's just been dumping them in one way or another. He's burying some, but God forbid someday he finds a secluded well somewhere that no one can stumble across and starts dumping them all down the well, or finding some other effective way, such as burying them in a basement like the gentleman Gacy." Ted referred to his fellow serial killers as gentlemen, apparently holding them in high esteem. "Because, quite frankly, I think we get a chance to catch him if we can start finding fresh bodies again without him getting the wiser." Ted sometimes talked as though he was now one of us.

"Let's see now, you found three bodies in October of eighty-three. And that bothered the hell out of him, I'm sure. 'Cause you found Antosh, Naon, and an unidentified set of bones, all in different locations. So, you know, I'm sure he was starting to get a little bit edgy about leaving any more bodies around in similar locations. I think that's obvious enough. And it's no accident that your next bodies, in terms of chronological disappearances, start to turn up near Enumclaw, a location far from your most recent discoveries.

No doubt you have more remains in the recent area you haven't discovered, but they're your early victims you haven't found."

As it turned out, Ted's predictions on this matter were way off base. He had just told us who we would find east of Enumclaw. But the Riverman's early victims were not found there, but were later discovered near the Sea-Tac Airport strip.

Choosing Dump Sites

Feeling that Ted probably revisited the Issaquah and Taylor Mountain dump sites with bodies long after his first dump, I asked, "How familiar is he with his dump sites? Do you think they're accidental finds?"

Emphatically, Ted proclaimed, "Oh, no, no, no, no. I think he's pretty sure. The Riverman may not select his dump sites with the precision of a geographer or surveyor, but it's clear that he's searched down and looked them over in daytime and nighttime. They are places he's been back to many times after, obviously— places he's been back to many times." At this point, I felt Ted was telling us that he, himself, returned many times to his own disposal sites. The excitement in Ted's voice was a clue, perhaps, that body disposal sites were the location of his violent exhibitions. They were places where he believed he could commit whatever sexual acts he wanted on the bodies of his victims and not be discovered. No wonder he was so excited at the thought of secure dump sites. They held for him the thrill of a honeymoon cabin.

After we took time to flip the tape, Ted tried to systematize his thoughts. He was striving to express himself clearly. "This is just sort of a spontaneous dialogue we're having here. I'm not approaching it in any organized fashion, and I'll go over my notes later to see if I miss anything that I'd like to talk to you about," he said.

I wanted Ted to refocus on the dump sites and tell us what the Riverman would be doing when he returned to them. Ted repeated my question by saying, "He does. He is returning to the dump sites, not just to bring bodies back, but probably in the interim. I think it's a high probability that he's returning, if only to drive by. He's returning to check those dump sites out after he's dumped a body there."

Dave wanted to know if he would return after we found a victim. Resoundingly, Ted declared, "Oh no. He wouldn't touch it with a ten-mile pole. You see, that's the problem. Again, that's a whole new subject on surveillance, and we'll have to get back to that later. But the interesting thing about his dump sites is he uses more than one. He doesn't put subsequent victims at one site all together and then move to another. Like, I have it in my notes somewhere, not all the girls who were found at one site disappeared sequentially, I don't believe. They disappeared at different times. So he might dump one here and one there. He didn't use some, you know, one, two, three, and then go over here one, two, three. He jumped back and forth. Why he did that, I don't know. It seems a little bit inefficient, but that's what he was doing. But he's still coming back to them, obviously. And I think he's coming back to look at the possibility for returning with more bodies. He's also coming back to check out and see, you know, the condition of the body. He may be going back for whatever kick he gets out of it. You know, obviously, what he is doing is not normal, so you cannot apply normal standards to it. But my guess is he's coming back, if just nothing more than just check the site out and drive by or see if it's been discovered or see if it's been disturbed. Okay?"

The Bodies Are Clean

Many of the dump site crime scenes offered no more tangible clues than anthropological digs by the time we got to them. Bones were the only remains found of most victims. Some bodies were stripped clean, either by animals or by the Riverman. There was no clothing, no jewelry.

Ted asked his own question. "Why is he doing that? He's keeping it to a minimum amount of items found, I'd say. No fibers, no hairs. He may have a thing for clothes, but more than likely this guy doesn't want to be caught. Leaving a victim nude is the best way to leave the least amount of evidence."

Dave asked, "Do you think he's saving any of that?"

Ted responded, "Who knows? That's too hard to say. If he's being that careful, probably unlikely, unless he really has some sort of thing. But he doesn't seem like a mentally disturbed individual, somebody who's just really bizarre. And he's going about it in a very businesslike, very efficient, way. And I don't think his type is going to keep anything, if he's being so meticulous as to leave bodies without any clothing and to try to dispose of bodies as best he can, and he's learning all the time how to do it better. The Riverman is not the kind of person who's going to leave stuff around the house, I don't think. I mean, that's just my guess. He doesn't want to get caught. He's learning more and more. And I'd be fascinated to read a collection of news clippings over this time to see when the publicity, the intensity of publicity built up and receded, or when it intensified, and try to plot his activity, his intensity, his activity level with the publicity. Because the Riverman understands the difficulty of trying to do something when the public is aroused. And maybe that's the one reason why in the past eight months or so you just really haven't heard a lot from him."

The last known Green River victim was Cindy Smith, missing in March 1984, nine months before we met with Ted. I was curious if the formation of the Green River Murders Task Force two months earlier had any affect on the Riverman's intensity.

"Oh, sure," Ted answered. "And you found all those bodies in March and April. And that is the thing he does not like. And it caused him to reevaluate his entire strategy. If it didn't make him move, it certainly made him rethink what he's doing. It doesn't make him stop. It just makes a difference." Ted felt strongly about this, voicing throughout our conversations that the Riverman would never stop, no matter how many officers were trying to catch him.

Looking for Dump Sites

With that, Dave continued, "To find these sites that are really way out, how does he search for them? Do you think he's got a reason to be out there? Do you think he's found these sites before he picks his victim? Or do you think he's picked up a victim in Seattle and then he's driven off trying to find a spot?"

"Oh, I think the chances are in favor of him having been there at least before, probably looking for them deliberately," Ted answered. "Well, I did some analyzing of the mass gravesites that you have on some maps I was sent. Looks like he certainly has returned to one site over and over again and that would lead me to believe that he's looking for good places. And once he's found one, he will keep going back to it. Generally, in fact, you see him changing all the time, like east of Enumclaw. He's starting to spread them out rather than going back to one place again and again. But my guess is he has a type of area in mind. If he hasn't picked it out beforehand and has a body in the trunk, then he knows what he's looking for. If it's not a specific area, like the Star Lake site that he already was leaving bodies at, and if he's just completely at a loss as to where to drop the next one off, he may just start hunting on his own. But he has an idea of what he's looking for. Like you say, the turnaround, the deserted areas, the dirt road, or whatever. I'd say that he certainly has in mind what he thinks will be an effective place to leave his victims' bodies."

Ted's idea of the Riverman looking for a particular *type* of site, rather than one he had been to many times, was an intriguing concept. We knew that serial killers were very familiar with their body disposal sites. But if a killer found a site that resembled his favorite type of site, that might satisfy him, even if he had never been there before. For example, a serial killer who is a long-haul truck driver may be very familiar with his hometown area. He is also familiar with freeways and off-ramps along his route of travel. Commonly, off-ramps resemble each other no matter where they are. If the truck driver picked up a prostitute at a truck stop and drove for over 100 miles, he would be just as acquainted with the off-ramp area 100 miles down the road as he would be with the one 300 miles farther ahead. So any off-ramp, any secluded guardrail, is a type of site that the trucker feels comfortable dumping a body over. In other words, the killer does not have the pressing need to be in a preselected location where he is totally familiar with the entire surroundings—just the type of site in general.

Pretexts for Scouting Dump Sites

We next wanted Bundy to talk to us about the likelihood that someone might have interrupted the Riverman at any of his dump sites. Bundy had a lot of experience ferrying his victims to secluded areas and spending time with them there. We wondered if Bundy had any experiences with uninvited guests. And along those same lines, we were curious as to what someone might have seen who spotted the Riverman and either didn't know what he was seeing or who simply chose not to come forward unless he was asked. If this had happened we might actually have had an informed witness without ever realizing it.

"Do you think that he's thought far enough ahead to come up with an excuse for himself in case he gets stopped searching for his body disposal site?" Dave asked Ted. "What I'm getting at is, does he have a reason? Let's say you're an officer up there, and you see this guy in a wilderness hunting or fishing area. There's no fishing pole. No rifle. Do you think that he might be a fisherman or a hunter or do you think he might try to pose as somebody else?"

Ted's answer indicated that he had surely thought about what he would do if he ever was caught at the scene. He answered, "It's not unlikely he might try to pose as a hiker; that's a good cover." We knew Ted was a hiker, and hiked in areas where he dumped bodies. "A hiker or a fisherman. Or I would think that a mushroom hunter might be a good one. Then you don't have to worry about being out of season or by a lake. You're just out enjoying nature. Who knows? I don't imagine that has escaped his imagination because I may have underestimated the amount of thought he has devoted to this. Again, he makes mistakes. He's not perfect and probably does a lot of things on impulse. But I think there are a lot of things he does do to try to cover his ass. And one of them is having a reason to be up there. Now, it's not going to be the best reason in the world. I mean, he might have a knapsack over his back or something like that, saying, 'I'm just hiking around.' But, Jesus Christ, if officers are out there, and you find anybody in the area of those dump sites, then they're at the top of your list, no matter what excuse they give you. I mean, if you found anybody on foot within a couple miles of those bodies, you know they'd be right at the very top of your list."

Burial Versus Disposal

Ted once said that a preferred method of disposal was burial. One of the Green River Killer's victims found at the south end of the airport was completely buried. It was a mystery why one victim was left on top of the ground, another covered with twigs, and an-

271

other buried. I asked Ted why the Riverman might have chosen to bury only one victim at that location.

It seemed that the variance in techniques also confused Ted, because he said, "Depends on whether they were close. I mean, if one was buried at the south end, I would expect that to be the last one. Assume that maybe he thought it would be an improvement over dumping them in plain sight. If it wasn't, I couldn't explain it. I think clearly from his point of view, burying is more effective than just dumping on top of the ground."

Dave pressed Ted, knowing that Ted didn't feel any emotion toward any woman, by asking, "Could that mean that maybe she had some special relationship with the Riverman?"

Ted's belief in the lack of remorse a killer feels for his victims was about to surface. Ted answered, "That he felt anything and that burial had some ritualistic or personal significance apart from disposing of the body itself? I'd say no! And I ask you this, how many of those twenty-seven victims you found were buried or partially buried?"

"Less than five."

"That's interesting. That's a cover-up, isn't it?" Ted argued.

I injected, "Well, let's define what burial is. You said buried or partially buried, okay? There's one here in the dirt, all right? Then there are probably three others who are covered with twig-type branches and maybe a little bit of dirt. And then there is something unusual about the two victims in the river, who were held down by large rocks. The Riverman did not want them discovered, either. They're not the normally dumped victim. You know, he's not Wayne Williams. He's not throwing them into a river from a bridge. Right? Something else special he's done to the girls."

"But not all."

"Not all. No," I agreed.

Ted went on to say, "You know, look at yourself, nobody's consistent. They don't do everything the same every time. Why he would do something to one victim as opposed to another— sometimes it may be baffling, maybe even to him. If it's a him."

The way Ted ended this response led to a broader question— who was the Riverman? Was he one man? Were there two people acting in concert? Ted covered all his bases by saying, "You know, when you say something like that, it raises the possibility of maybe two people. Like one guy buries them; the other guy just drops them off. You asked me earlier if I thought it was one or two and I—or even women or anybody—I mean, I certainly wouldn't want to limit my own possibilities there. I mean, my guess is it's one, but when you start finding variations like one buried, one not, or some of the bodies mutilated in ways that others aren't, then you have to start thinking about more than one, I guess. But I'd say that if he's just raking stuff over some of them and burying others, that may be just the fact that he just happened to have a shovel in the car this time. And the other times he forgot it. I mean, you might say, 'Well, this guy is more competent than that.' Perhaps. But perhaps not. I think that the last thing that he's thinking when he leaves the house is, 'Is a shovel in the trunk?' Maybe he doesn't like carrying the shovel in the trunk because it looks dirty, or only puts the shovel and the pick in the trunk when, you know, he really got his head together when he was leaving the house."

Ted had read the material published by the FBI's Behavioral Sciences Unit about buried victims having some emotional attachment to the killer. So I pressed him. "How about any compassion and emotion for the particular victim that was buried?"

Ted replied, "I see what you mean. I don't know. I'm not saying that a person is devoid of compassion or might have more compassion for one victim or the other. But I think, my guess is when it comes to disposing of the victims, he's doing the best he can to dispose of them as unattractively as he can. Given what he knows about, which is rudimentary, he learns by trial and error. And, you know, sure, there may be some ritualistic significance by burying that one body, but my guess is there is no more ritualistic significance than the past. He just happened to decide to bury that one that day as opposed to not burying the others. But in all cases, it's obvious he's trying to hide them. And, you know, I bet you, if he's started burying them all, a lot less of them would have been found. You know, if he had been burying them properly. So, this is just one man's opinion. Right? And I'd say anything is possible, but my guess is it's just an exception to the rule. One of those nagging inconsistencies that I'm sure, you know, keep you awake at night. Right?" Ted chuckled.

"Keeping" the Victims

Knowing that some killers keep their victims for a period of time before disposing of them, I asked Ted, "Is he keeping one? Do you think he's keeping them for any length of time at all?"

Finally, I had struck a real nerve with Ted. Instead of just cooperating with us from the perspective of an expert, things suddenly got personal. Ted himself had kept victims in his possession for different lengths of time after he had killed them, and talking about this subject suddenly invigorated and excited him. He responded, "Good question, and I have asked that throughout my notes. You know, I felt when I got this data you sent me the other day that I might get some handle on or some feeling about how long he is keeping them. And my guess is, considering the fact you see these burial sites all over the place, a concentration of burial sites in the Kent valley between I-5 and Star Lake and that area, he's doing a lot of hunting around. His victims disappear Sunday through Saturday, like I said. My guess is he doesn't have a family, like probably, in many cases, your typical serial killer. He has a lot of time on his hands without worrying about who's asking where he is. And . . . I kind of lost track of where I was. Excuse me. Oh, as far as . . . So, I said there's a good possibility, let's say he lives alone, that he could well take them home. Right?"

When Ted would get excited about what he was talking about, he frequently lost track of what he was saying. It was almost like Ted was talking about himself and then was thrown off his line of thought when he realized he was talking to us.

Ted continued, "And keep them for a while. And perhaps some of your evidence would show that. In fact, the girl disappeared definitely at this particular time and place, and her body was found seven days later, and she'd only been dead for two days. Now, it doesn't look like you have very many fresh bodies that can be analyzed like that. You have a few in the Green River that are close and the Christensen girl was close, between five days. Between the time she disappears and the time her body is found. Right? Well, that gives you something to work with. But when I started looking at where the girls are being found and where they disappeared from, my feeling is generally he's killing them shortly after. You know, he's not taking them a great distance. That is, he's not taking them home."

"You think he's probably doing it in his car, then?" Dave asked.

"I would guess that whole thing is taking place in a car. He's picking up in the car, [then] they're being killed in a few hours in the car, and dumped. You know, the most efficient way he knows of and as quickly as he can. And he's not lugging them all over, either dead or alive, and keeping them for a few days. There may be exceptions. There are always exceptions to the rule. I'd say you can't count on this guy doing it the same way every time. I'd say the pattern that showed itself to me, here, where the bodies are found so close to where they disappeared and even there up along Interstate Ninety, just indicated to me that once he's killed them, that he's getting rid of them. And let's say every once in a while he may just—if he has someplace he can take them, if he lives alone in a house or in a private apartment that he has a private entrance—he may take them home. But it doesn't look like it to me." We don't know if this was indeed what the Riverman did, but we did know that Ted had just explained what he himself did with his victims.

Break-ins

According to Ted's description, the Riverman had used the river and then the woods, farther south and southeast, as disposal grounds for his victims. But I wanted Ted to discuss whether the Riverman had entered a residence to attack victims, as he had done. Would the Riverman have begun his series by breaking into someone's house in the middle of the night and strangling her? There were unsolved murders involving females who were attacked in their own houses, apartments, and condos in the years preceding the first river victim we had located. Would the Riverman enter a building or would he think it was too risky?

Eagerly, Ted asked, "And their bodies were left there?"

I responded, "Yes."

Ted's expression indicated his perplexity as he said, "Were they prostitutes?"

I clarified that the women had questionable morals. "They go to bars and get themselves picked up for a one-night stand."

Speaking as someone as efficient in different modi operandi as the Riverman, Ted said, "Well, he did not start with either Agisheff or Coffield. I feel that very strongly. He didn't just work up to committing four or five murders a month without extensive practice." Ted likened it to "somebody who is looking for the right hole to fish in. And he was fishing here and there and maybe not catching much, but taking too much of a risk in the meantime. And it very well could be that someone like this would break into a house and kill a woman—you can't rule it out—and then subsequently find it so risky, unnerving, and difficult, quite frankly, that he would look for something that was maybe perhaps easier. And then when he smartened up, he just sort of blossomed with all those younger women on the streets, if you will. He became much more active. That's one scenario." That was Ted's own scenario. Having done everything from entering and removing Lynda Healy's body from her rooming house at the University of Washington and bludgeoning the coeds inside the Chi Omega Sorority House at Florida State University, Ted knew that a very active serial killer was capable of performing any type of murder, inside or outside a building. Therefore, not surprisingly, Ted said that if he were us he would definitely consider that murders indoors might also be part of the Green River series.

Trying to raise Ted's dignity and confirm his proclamation that he was "the only person with a Ph.D. in serial murder," I asked a question that was meant to focus on a type of murder that was more exhilarating for a killer: "How about the hunt, though? Is the fact that he would kill someone in a residence more of a thrill for him versus, you know, just picking up a hooker on the street?"

Bundy said, with a throaty voice, "Oh, yeah."

I knew that this line of questioning suited Ted because entering a residence was one of Ted's methods of operation. The more our questions about the Riverman's modus operandi resembled Bundy's own methods, the more likely Bundy was to tell us more about himself.

To keep Ted talking, I fed him information on the Green River killings that he didn't previously have. This was a boost to his ego and made Ted feel privileged and respected. I said, "You know, possibly taking a girl back to her residence or conceivably knocking on the door and when she opens the door, *boom,* a blitz attack occurred— we had that very experience in one of our cases. Is that part of the thrill that you equate with approaching the prostitute?"

At this point in our conversation, Ted was ready to bring out his vast knowledge of the Boston Strangler cases as an example for us to think about. He said, "Well, to be able to track a woman from a bar, let's say, to her home is not a random act, and knocking on doors is. The main question is, did he select this woman beforehand or is he just like Albert deSalvo, choosing his victim by just knocking on doors randomly? It makes a difference. But still, there's hunting involved in either case. A certain amount of expertise is necessary. And sort of feeling out the area, you know, apartment complexes, and looking at names on mailboxes, are things of art. I would imagine if you talked to Albert deSalvo or could talk to his spirit, you would find out that there's something of an art to it. But if in fact he tracked a woman from a bar, that's a little bit more sophisticated."

I didn't want to offend Ted by questioning him on his claim that serial murder was an art form. Actually, it really didn't surprise me that Bundy would consider murder a form of art, as repulsive as that thought was. Bundy thought about murder 24 hours a day and considered himself an accomplished artist. Ted possessed a visible arrogance and an elitist attitude about his main avocation. Every time Ted spoke, his feelings of superiority over the Riverman would show. The Leonardo da Vinci of serial murder was Theodore Robert Bundy's perception of himself. I wondered whether I would ever get the chance to see this ego of Ted's rupture and collapse. I hoped so.

With all of this running through my mind, I managed to maintain a poker face as Ted continued. "You certainly can't rule out anything like that. If you have unsolved murders involving young women in the Pacific Northwest, in terms of violent murder, which occurred prior to Coffield, or for that matter, even recently, you got to think about the Riverman, because he hasn't stopped and didn't just start with Coffield." Now Ted revealed for the first time a subclassification of murder, which he called "violent murder." Ted would elaborate on his perception of murder classification in interviews we would have with him years later. In Ted's mind, there was a kind of morality to murder. Some people, he would tell me shortly before he was executed in 1989, deserved to be sadistically murdered and raped. It was a concept that would be difficult for anyone to grasp, especially me. I had been investigating murders for 10 years, and it never crossed my mind that it was "okay" to murder and mutilate any human being. What kind of detective would have real empathy toward a killer who did believe in such a thing?

The First Green River Murders

As I choked on the implication of Ted's words, Dave continued the questioning. "How soon before Coffield do you think he started? Ten years? Fifteen years?"

Unless a convicted serial killer confesses truthfully to his complete series of murders, the first one he committed is almost impossible to identify as such. Usually by the time the police discover that a serial killer is in operation, he has already had a number of victims. Ted realized, because he understood that serial murderers like himself improved with practice, that the first or last murder of the series contained the most information about a killer. Discovering where the killer was in the series might help police trace his changing modus operandi and what his next step might be.

On this subject, Ted backed off from his previous statement that the Riverman had been killing for a long time. "If he'd been as active as he was between July of eighty-two and October of eighty-three, sooner or later, it's got to catch up with him. And my initial impression is that he'd not been *that* active before Coffield. I said *that* active. Not that he hadn't been trying to work up to it and not that he hadn't killed anyone before, but I just get the impression that's too much of work. He may have moved in from another area, and unless he's extremely shrewd and is just moving around the country, not exactly in Henry Lucas style, but maybe moving in, hanging around for a while, and then moving on. Imagine what it takes to be able to do seven a month or four in July of eighty-two and five in August of eighty-two. That's a lot of work, especially attempting to avoid detection, too. If he'd done all thirty-five by just driving up to the street corner, then I'd think that you'd have a pretty good line on him by now. But he's more careful than that. Obviously, he's very, very wary. You see that not just in how he picks up the victims, but how he disposes of them. He may not be as effective until we say 'Well, he could have hidden them better, but he's doing his best and learning.' And he has learned. But you have a good point, he knows the area. He's looking for a good place to park his car. He's waiting for the right time to approach them. He doesn't want anybody around. He doesn't want anybody to over- hear what he says to the girls. He doesn't want anybody to see him, if that is at all possible. And he certainly doesn't want anybody to see him getting into his car. So all those cautions are one part. That's the actual approach. What he's actually saying, whether it's a straight offer of sex or whether it's something more sophisticated, is another question." In other words, the killer, like Bundy, simply approached on foot and brought his willing victim to his car. He lured them and trapped them one on one rather than in a drive-by. Therefore, if police on surveillance were looking for a guy in a car, they'd miss the killer if he walked right by the front of the police car, chatted up a girl, and walked off with her.

Dave commented, "He's got to be feeling pretty confident and cocky."

Ted gulped with pride as Dave pointed out the Riverman's prowess. Even though Ted thought he was superior to the River- man, the Riverman was one of the gentlemen, a fellow serial killer. And Ted rushed to explain the Riverman's certainty, "Yeah. Yup. He's got to feel very confident in his abilities, and yet he also knows that he's failed, in that you've been finding the victims, and he doesn't want you to. So he knows he's got to get better. Even though he knows he's outdistancing you, he's got a brain in his head and knows there's always a chance and he's doing his damned best to reduce those risks. And, you know, he could feel like he's in competition with the task force, you, Bob, or with somebody, and point totally towards being an individual who gets off on that. Cer- tainly, there's an amount of competition between this individual and the police. It's just got to be. But whether he really gets off on that or whether, in fact, that's just sort of a benefit, I don't want to say that.

"It is a corollary kind of thing, you know. It's not the main course. I mean, he's getting off on killing these women. That's what he's getting off on. I just don't get the feeling that he's really eager to come out and taunt you or play games. Not to say that he might not want to, at one time or another. But to just give it all up in that way is a lot of pressure on him. And not to say that he's not deeply disturbed, because obviously he is. But he's also well controlled. So some time or another, you might have a break. It's not unrealistic to think he might call you or write you. But that doesn't seem to be his basic thing. He's not unstable in the way that he's going to play a game with you right now. He might, at one point, become despondent because, when he's doing all this, he can't be conducting normal relationships with people. His whole life is upset. He might find it hard to hold a job, hard to make relationships with other people. The pressure of threatening detectives, not to mention the fact that there's an entire task force after him. Notwithstanding what anybody says—I'm sure there's got to be a sense of remorse. It may not be very strong. It may be stronger sometimes than others. But all of this is speculative."

Killer's Remorse

Now seemed as good a time as any to focus on the amount of remorse expressed by serial killers. Common beliefs among forensic psychiatrists were that psychopathic killers did not feel any remorse toward their victims. The only remorse Ted ever felt was over being caught, if you can call that remorse in a general sense. If there was any ounce of remorse in a killer, Ted was about to tell us how to exploit those feelings. So I asked, "You don't believe in the theory that serial killers have no remorse?"

Ted said, "Oh no. No. I don't believe that. I don't believe that theory at all. Alcoholics who I've known suffer a great deal of remorse. That doesn't stop them from drinking. Some alcoholics can't hold a job, and their families are falling apart. They know they're being mean and cruel to people, yet they still drink. And they feel very bad about it, but can't stop themselves. And I'm sure there are some people who kill who feel no remorse. But I think it's very accurate to say that just 'cause a man feels remorse doesn't mean he wants to turn himself in and be executed by the state. Because a man feels remorse doesn't mean he can control the deep drive or compulsion that causes him to kill. So I think there very well may be gaps, periods between victims, where the reason he doesn't do anything is because he's just despondent over his inability to control his behavior. Who knows? You can't stereotype this kind of individual. Anything is possible, and unfortunately there's only one individual. There is one person who knows the real person. And he's quite capable of feeling all the ranges of emotion that you do. And don't overlook the fact that he, in many respects, is as normal as anybody else. He may not be, but this guy has lasted long enough that he's not a raving maniac. He's not obviously disturbed, in my opinion, or else I think that he would have come apart. He would have made a more serious mistake. He would have made himself more obvious to you. Do you get—follow—me?"

Obligingly, I said, "Oh yeah."

Foreshadowing his own efforts to save his neck, Ted warned, "Don't underestimate his capacity to plead his remorse. And as a matter of fact, I would say if you ever feel like you have a good suspect, and [he] does not know that he's a suspect, probably the best way to approach him is quickly. I'm serious. If he gets to an attorney—thinking like a cop—the fact of the matter is if you give him any time to collect his thoughts, he's more than likely to be able to compose himself again, 'cause he is a very controlled individual. But if you catch this guy unaware and are able to question him, God forbid that you don't violate the Constitution, I think you'd stand a much better chance of getting him to open up."

The Stano Case

"But you do believe there's a chance that this person might talk about what he's done?" Dave asked.

"Well, sure. If you catch him at it. Sure," Ted confidently answered.

Because Dave knew there was little information left that was known only to the Riverman and police, Dave asked, "Do we show him what we've got against him before he'll open up?"

"You got to make him think you know—it's a tremendous burden he's carrying around with him," Ted said. "And you got to make him think you think he's guilty. That's a terrible thing to say, isn't it? But this is a terrible case. And if he thinks you think he's guilty and he's carrying around this particular burden, he's going to want to just let it off. He's going to be so torn up inside, he'll let it go, if he's the kind of person I think he is. And, which reminds me, let me give you an example of Gerald Stano, who is similar to the Riverman. I don't want to get much into him because Stano is in prison here. Nobody had a line on Gerry that I know of. And he just came out of nowhere and said, 'Hey, I want to talk.' That's my understanding. I don't know if that's what really happened. He was in the Florida state prison before he went to the police and said, 'Hey, I did all this.' You know, whether it was the skill of the detective down at Daytona Beach? It was his skill in bringing Stano along to the point where Stano said, 'Sure, I'll just tell you everything.' But I think it may be a combination of Stano wanting to tell, and somebody knowing how to get it out of him. But Gerry is back on our wing with three to four death sentences and now he won't say anything except hi. He's funny. Finally, he came out of whatever phase he was in, and the state of Florida in its benevolence rewarded him for his honesty by giving him four death sentences. Well, that's the way the game is played. But now I think Gerry is saying, 'Hey, I really didn't mean all that stuff I told you all about. I don't know anything about it.' And that's the position you put somebody in, if you bring the full weight of the state down on them. Start to remind them of that and, hey, you're a goner. But, on the other hand, be nice to us and tell us everything, you are sort of working at cross-purposes. It's not a situation that makes people want to talk, even though they might want to. But Gerry doesn't know anything. I mean, as far as I know, he's one of the nicest, pleasantest individuals I've ever run across, and will not say boo about anything that you say to the police. He's not like Ottis Toole, Lucas's partner. Ottis Toole will sit back there, from what I understand, all afternoon long and tell people about what they did. And Toole is a little bit off center. Agh, he's an entirely different kind of individual than Gerry Stano. Entirely different."

Bundy had followed the publicity charade of Henry Lee Lucas, a self-professed serial killer. Lucas's partner in crime was Ottis Toole, whom Bundy had met on death row at the Florida State Penitentiary. Lucas and Toole were leading law enforcement officers to numerous sites of their murders. At one point, it was estimated that they had murdered, collectively, over 360 people. Their rationale for talking about their murders was of interest to Bundy. He was amazed that they were giving blow-by-blow descriptions on audio-

and videotaped interviews. Since Bundy had previously suggested that the Riverman might have to find a heavenly spirit in order to confess, I offered that Lucas had found the Lord or seen the light.

Unconvinced, Bundy said, "Well, you know, I guess that's good, if in fact he feels he needs to do it."

One of the things that made Lucas different from other serial killers was that he was known to have murdered many people who were acquaintances of one another. He often killed a number of people within a circle of friends. Feeling that Bundy had at least once murdered casual acquaintances of one another, such as the women in the Chi Omega sorority, I pressed him by asking, "You haven't covered too well the fact that the Riverman attacked victims who knew each other, especially those who were apparently abducted on the same day, like Opal Mills and Cynthia Hinds or Bush and Summers."

Using Victims to Get Victims

Bundy's reaction to the idea that one victim lured the other was predictable. Bundy the killer avoided that possibility like it was a disease. We knew not to tread too heavily on this subject because any explanation he gave would venture too close to murders for which he was under the death sentence and was actively appealing. Instead, he cleverly changed the direction of the interview by focusing on why the Riverman would have abducted two women during the same day, even though he had touched on this subject earlier. Bundy temporarily escaped the intended topic, because, in his need for one-upmanship, he prioritized what he thought we needed to cover. He changed the subject, saying, "For some reason, I thought the dates of those victims were close in time. Yeah, I see what you're saying. Like Bush and Summers and Hinds and Mills and—only because of how close they disappeared and how close it appears their disappearances were. In the cases of those two couples, they were both black, which is kind of suspicious to me in that they would disappear so close together. Either he's very intense and does one and has to come back the next day and do the other—or the same day and do a second. Like I said earlier, to get one, he has to do both of them. Or maybe they're both standing there and one walks up while he's talking to the other, and he just really is so intense at that period of time, at that point of time he needs one so bad, that he's willing to take the extra risk of taking two."

Suspecting that Bundy might have kept Janice Ott alive at the Issaquah site while he returned with Denise Naslund, I asked, "Do you think he's keeping one captive and bringing the other one back? If he's picking up two reasonably close together like that, what do you think the chain of events is?" The two closest victims of the Green River Killer in dates of disappearance were Gabbert and Pitsor, but their body recovery sites were miles apart.

Racial Stereotypes

Ted was racially biased in the selection of his own victims. He was never known to cross racial boundaries. Because of that, it was difficult for him to concentrate on our questions regarding the black female victims of the Riverman. Bundy had read the FBI's research studies, which highlighted the fact that white males usually kill white females and black males kill black females unless there is an intervening variable, such as prostitution, in the motivation of the killer. Ted acted as if he and the Riverman were on the same team, colleagues united against the world. Therefore, Ted wanted very much for the Riverman to be like him, so he stubbornly insisted, "Well, I want to take Gabbert and Pitsor separately, not only because they're both white girls, but because they disappeared from different locations and their bodies were found at different places. Also, they were last seen on the same day. Pitsor was last seen in downtown Seattle, but is it possible that she hopped on a bus and was on the streets on Pacific Highway South? Had she ever been known to be down there? Was she ever known to hustle down there?" Of course, the answer was yes.

Ted went on, "The thing that strikes me about Gabbert and Pitsor is that if they disappeared from different locations in the same day, it indicated this guy has, at times, an incredible need, a compulsion. You have to understand that a guy's need to do this ebbs and flows, which probably accounts for the variations and intensity over periods of time. And sometimes it's probably to the point where he has to take unnecessary risks just to do what he wants to do. He's not as rational at times as he is at others."

Ted cautioned, "If you're off by a day, it puts a slightly different complexion on it. But obviously, it looks to me like he did one and just didn't feel like that was enough and went back for seconds."

The surprising thing about Ted's analysis of the Pitsor skull find was that he accurately predicted that "it doesn't appear that she was decapitated or anything. I think the chances are that the animals just drug that skull around and you didn't find the other small bones." That is exactly what we concluded when we discovered the rest of her bones over a year after her skull was discovered. That Ted would even consider decapitation when neither Dave nor I suggested it in any form opened the door to a tempting line of questioning. One widely held theory was that Ted decapitated his Taylor Mountain victims, but we knew talking about that might threaten the longevity of our interview.

Ted continued, "Well, he left Gabbert by the Star Lake area and went back to a familiar location. Gosh, who can say what's going through the man's mind? To him, it's logical. There's a reason why he's doing it. That doesn't make sense to anybody looking at it and saying, 'Well, he's inconsistent or he's not behaving sensibly.' But to him he's making sense. There's some reason why he's doing it. Maybe there's no reason at all. He's just doing it because that's what he feels like doing. It's hard to say. The only thing clear is that he's trying to dispose of the bodies so nobody will find them. That much I can say for sure. It looks like he did them separately, if for no other reason than their bodies were found in separate locations and they disappeared from separate places. But the fascinating thing is he could have done it on the same day, which says something about the intensity of his need to murder at particular times."

Stripping the Victim

The curiosity of what the Riverman did with some of the victims' clothing and jewelry was a burning subject for Dave and he returned to it time and again in these interviews with Ted. It was an important subject, not only because Bundy's opinions shed light on what he did with his victims, but it gave us another line of insight into the Riverman. If he kept the victims' belongings as totems, they would be evidence if we ever picked him up in his car. If he dumped them along the way, they might be a trail from the abduction site to the dump site. Dave asked Ted, "Is he keeping their stuff, throwing it in the garbage can? Or how else was he disposing of their clothing?"

By now Ted knew that we were asking questions about the Riverman's method of operation that resembled Ted's. Ted carefully proceeded by stating the alternatives. "Well, he's keeping the clothing or he's apparently leaving the area pretty well bare and not leaving any clothing on the victims. He could have a variety of motivations driving him, but the one that appears most apparent to me, given his behavior in causing the disappearances of many victims, is he wants to leave a minimum amount of evidence at the scene. He probably read enough about cases in the newspaper or perhaps in detective magazines. He knows about fibers. He knows about hairs and whatnot. And there could also be the element that he gets off on having their clothing. I don't know."

The next phase of our conversations were a harbinger of my final conversation with Ted immediately before his execution. Neither Dave nor I realized at this time that Ted would speak about exactly what he did with clothing and other belongings of victims. Dave inquired, unknowing, "Between here and the Enumclaw sites, we find one of the victim's I.D., in the cloverleaf along Highway 18 near the Mountview Cemetery Road. What causes him to throw things like that out the window? What would cause that to end up there? Would he have been in a struggle with her along? Was she alive at the time or do you think he just disposed of it after he dumped her?"

Ted's response was flattering. He felt the urge to compliment us on our thoroughness so that he could set his hook into us, to get us to continue our conversations. The great Ted Bundy was impressed with our work. He patronized us by saying, "You guys know these cases. I'm impressed. You've been working on these cases long and hard, and I'm still impressed you know them this well. Sure. You said it before I said it. The second thing that he might be doing is simply throwing the shit out the window of the car as he's driving along. That might sound a little bit weird. That's one way to do it. There are any number of ways to dispose of clothing. He could be burying it. He could be burning it at home if he has a fireplace or

Original driver's license photo showing Ted Bundy much older than he really was. (Courtesy of King County Police Department)

Denise Naslund near the time of her death. (Courtesy of King County Police Department)

Janice Ott near the time of her death. (Courtesy of King County Police Department)

Tiger 10-speed girl's model bicycle just like Janice Ott's, which has never been located. (Courtesy of King County Police Department)

CLOTHING —
WHITE GYM BOXER TYPE SHORTS (WHITE
SHIRT - MESH PULLOVER
BEIGE FIELD
(DARK) RED OR RUST STRIPING OR SLEEVES & NECK
LT BROWN TO
MED HAIR - CURLY - MILD FEATURES - UNKEMPT BECAUSE OF WIND CONDITION???
SLENDER THIN BUILD
WELL TANNED???

Composite drawn from witnesses' descriptions of the Ted suspect from Lake Sammamish. (Courtesy of King County Police Department)

Police officers removing members of the Jackals motorcycle club from Lake Sammamish. (Courtesy of King County Police Department)

Light-colored Volkswagen bug, believed to be Bundy's, under the very tree to which one of the potential victims was led. (Courtesy of King County Police Department)

Aerial photo of the Issaquah crime scene with the dirt road crossing railroad tracks leading up to the grassy area described by Bundy. (Courtesy of King County Police Department)

Explorer Search and Rescue personnel searching for bones, shoulder to shoulder and on hands and knees at the Issaquah crime scene. (Courtesy of King County Police Department)

Power line road off Highway 18, leading to Taylor Mountain. (Courtesy of King County Police Department)

Taylor Mountain on March 5, 1975, the time of the discovery of the skull of Brenda Ball. (Courtesy of King County Police Department)

One of the crania found at the Taylor Mountain crime scene. (Courtesy of King County Police Department)

Diagram of Taylor Mountain crime scene. (Courtesy of King County Police Department)

Snowy mountain road near Aspen, Colorado, where the remains of Caryn Campbell were found. (Courtesy of Pitkin County Sheriff's Department)

1975 mug shot of Ted Bundy. (Courtesy of Salt Lake County Sheriff's Department)

October 1975 line-up shown to Carol DaRonch. (Courtesy of Murray Police Department)

Aerial photo of Lake Sammamish State Park. (Courtesy of King County Police Department)

Rear view of Bundy's VW bug showing ski rack. (Courtesy of Salt Lake County Sheriff's Department)

Passenger-side view of Bundy's VW bug. (Courtesy of Salt Lake County Sheriff's Department)

Lynda Healy's residence at the University of Washington. (Courtesy of Seattle Police Department)

Dense vegetation at the Issaquah crime scene in which numerous bones lay hidden from view. (Courtesy of King County Police Department)

Rocky road leading up to the Issaquah crime scene. (Courtesy of King County Police Department)

Bundy's murder implements taken from his car in August 1975. (Courtesy of Salt Lake County Sheriff's Department)

Issaquah crime scene as it appears fifteen years later, in 1989. The terrain had changed so much that we were unable to locate the skull that Bundy said he had buried. (Courtesy of King County Police Department)

Suspect poster in the Ted murders. (Courtesy of King County Police Department)

burning barrel. He might not. If my sense of him is right, he's going for the quick disposal. He doesn't want to have much around at all. He doesn't want to have the body around. He doesn't want to have the body in his car very long. And if he has that kind of mentality, he might be jettisoning the belongings out the window as he drives along. That's not a particularly bad way of getting rid of such things because there's trash along the highway all the time that's collected. In these areas where you found the bodies, have you ever conducted any routine searches along the highways for any distance? Looking for clothing?"

Dave parried, "Oh, yeah, but there's still a lot of distances that we haven't covered yet."

"There are any number of places he could throw it out the window. My guess is you found the I.D. card because he threw it out the window, not because they were struggling. And if he's doing that, it's a very sound indicator that he's employing that method to get rid of the stuff by simply throwing it out the window. Maybe he stops someplace and throws it down an embankment. But he might be of a frame of mind that he wants to get rid of all this stuff as efficiently as possible, but as quickly as possible, too. That means not taking any stuff home. Maybe not always, but most of the time he's getting rid of it quickly. But it might be just stopping and putting it in a Dumpster somewhere or throwing it out," Ted explained.

Dave reminded Ted, "He doesn't know that we've found that stuff; I don't think he considers it to be a mistake."

Ted followed up with "That's a good point. Have your people search up and down the roadways in the Enumclaw area where three bodies have been found. It's not unreasonable to find some things up there because I'm sure that there are a number of more victims up there. I had a feeling last night about that question that you asked. I was thinking about did he keep the stuff or would he keep the stuff or not. And on the one hand I don't know how much difference it makes on one level, because either he's going to have it when you throw down on him or he isn't. If you have a suspect, and just because he doesn't have anything, doesn't mean he isn't a good suspect."

Most of the bodies near Sea-Tac Airport were found in cul-de-sacs where houses had been removed owing to jet noise. "Here's the Naon site south of the airport," I explained as I showed Ted the map.

Ted said, "That's good hiding territory."

"You can see how she was discovered with her foot out of the ground," I said as I showed him a picture.

Ted's curiosity was piqued. He asked, "What kind of soil is that? Does it need a pick?"

"Pretty well packed," Dave explained with authority, since he processed most of the body recovery sites.

"What? So the guy's carrying around a pick and shovel or that kind of thing in the car?" Ted quizzed us.

"Bet he used just a shovel," Dave said.

"But this is the only one he did this with. It's an anomaly event," Ted proclaimed. He had had "anomaly victims," too.

It was clear to Dave and me that Ted and the Riverman shared a great many methods and characteristics as killers. The common ground they occupied mentally was underscored by Ted's tendency to speak in the first person and his obvious excitement when discussing the Riverman's actions and motivations. We learned a great deal about the unknown Green River Killer from Ted, and that information turned out to be extremely prescient when the killer was caught and was questioned. Ridgway, in his note to the task force before he was identified, referred to himself as "the Green Riverman," an eerie confluence with Bundy's monicker. But the final questions we asked Ted in our 1984 interviews were a subtle transition from a focus on the Green River Killer to Ted and his own practices. When these talks with Ted came to an end, I thought he had given us a great deal of information. I didn't know at that point that my relationship with Ted would continue for years to come and result in the kind of confessions I had only dreamed of.

11

"Some Murders Are Okay!"

Someday, Gary Ridgway, the self-described Green Riverman, may write me a letter, just as Ted Bundy did, because he will want to talk about his crimes. He will be in search of someone who "understands," someone he can brag about his crimes to, someone he believes he can control with his stories, someone who will make the commitment to listen to the agony bubbling out of his fragmented personality. He may even be frustrated at the efforts of the police officers who investigated him for his murders but who missed the larger point of his crimes. Even serial killers want to tell some version of the truth as they see it, even if it turns out to be just another lie. So he may call me in because he knows I'll hear him out and help tell his whole story. I expect he'll even know that Ted Bundy taught me how to do that.

Ted Bundy helped me rewrite the book on interrogating killers—this revision would contain a much truer picture of serial killers. In four years of letters, phone calls, and jail-cell conferences under the guise of helping solve the Green River murders, Bundy gave me a look inside the mind of a serial killer. He showed me just how to talk to a person who has eluded the police for years, but who now may be willing to tell his story. This particular function is unlike that of any other interrogation.

Interviewing a Serial Killer

Interviewing a prisoner you suspect of committing a series of murders is much different than interviewing a killer who has just committed a "routine" murder. In fact, few interview techniques work at all. There are no manuals, no police handbooks, and no empirical research whatsoever to help you pick your way through the interrogation over the suspect's psychological land mines that can explode in your face and ruin your chances of getting a confession. I know plenty of detectives who are great interviewers, but rarely have they had the opportunity to sharpen their skills against a serial killer. Unless the incriminating physical evidence was overwhelming or they actually managed to catch the perpetrator in the act, detectives usually need the suspect to confess in order to get resolution to all murders in a series. In most cases the killer is the only living witness and the interrogator may have to gain the killer's cooperation at all costs in order to make a case. Ted Bundy recommended that the most effective approach is to get a suspect's trust by showing him you understand what he's been going through.

We already know from experience that there are two basic types of killers: (1) those who give self-incriminating statements because the evidence at the scene or in their car or from eyewitnesses is so overwhelming that they need you to acknowledge they are being cooperative, and (2) those who refuse to confess even though you might be shoving what you call evidence right into their faces. It is this latter category that can be the most frustrating. These killers know, like Ted Bundy and the Riverman knew that without their help you can't find the bodies they dumped, the weapons they used, the cars they drove, or even the names of many undiscovered victims that they have killed. Without their cooperation, you might have nothing more than suspects who look promising on the basis of circumstantial evidence, but against whom the physical evidence is lacking. You have to get your suspect to work for you.

Bundy showed us ways we could get a serial killer to cooperate by sharing valuable information. Most of the long-term killers have led investigators around for years while the trail turned cold behind them. Like Bundy, they successfully escaped detection by police while sometimes dropping victims right in the middle of heavily guarded dump sites. Like the Riverman, who operated right under our noses, they picked up victims on highly patrolled streets. They probably lived in the communities where they killed and sat just two or three seats down from patrol officers at a local doughnut shop where they listened in on cops talking about the case. Serial killers *know* they're invisible. What would induce people like this to talk with the police and eventually confess?

Bundy demonstrated that most killers of his type, killers like the Riverman, prided themselves on getting victims under their power. Because these killers perceive themselves as power*less,* their ego trips involved spinning a net of power so broad that entire communities and police forces would be entrapped. It's a terror tactic as well as a power trip. Many of them love to follow their crimes in the newspapers and laugh at the experts who psychoanalyze their actions and create elaborate personality profiles. Serial killers know profiles often fall well short of the target and do more to satisfy the profilers than catch the killers. Municipalities spend millions of dollars in an attempt to foil killers' plans with elaborate surveillance techniques. All the killer has to do to avoid being seen is to park his car in a nearby parking lot, walk the streets of his contact sites, find a likely victim, smooth-talk that victim into walking him to his car, knock her unconscious, and scoop her into the car. By the time he closes the passenger door and drives away, the trap's been sprung. The killer has rehearsed this act so many times it's like second nature to him. Techniques like these are so simple and yet they're capable of foiling the most elaborate surveillance procedures, and that is probably how the Riverman has slipped through our net so many times. We were only looking for a driver, but Ridgway parked his truck in a nearby lot and ran counterintelligence to make sure the coast was clear before he approached his teenaged victim.

The killer is also so well rehearsed that he can bounce off a potential victim who resists him and move on to the next without so much as a ripple in the fabric of the moment. Bundy even bragged about his ability to do this and demonstrated his skill at pulling victims right out of a crowd in broad daylight at Lake Sammamish. This type of long-term killer has become an accomplished practitioner at killing and covering it up. Do you think he's going to break down under our accusations? Certainly not!

Ted Bundy explained and demonstrated that someone like the Green River Killer needs to exercise his power over people. He needs to, as Bundy did, have the police under his control. He needs victims. Without victims, serial killers can't survive. If a killer is in custody, his interrogators, the psychiatrists, prison guards, and other visitors close to him will become his victims. A victim, according to Bundy's definition, was anyone the serial killer was able to get into his power.

I even let myself become Bundy's victim by suspending my judgment and playing Bundy's game. I let him teach me how to interview serial killers by interviewing him the way he wanted to be interviewed. Bundy was the teacher; I was the pupil. I put myself in his power by playing his game. But that was the only way I could get any information out of him if I wanted him to help me figure out the mind-set, motives, and movements of the Riverman. It was the only way I could get him to help me catch the Riverman.

Bundy's first lesson was that long-term serial killers are unlike any other types of criminal suspects. They are battle-hardened, reinforced by their own denial, and can stand up in the face of interrogators looking for the quick confession. They also know more about serial murder than almost all detectives do. They have the advantage because they know who the police are and spend all their time eluding them. Detectives don't know who the serial murderers are and, because serial killers are rarely arrested for murder, are often shocked to discover they have one in their custody. Usually, serial killers are picked up for crimes indirectly related to their murder spree. Most investigators, therefore, confront the killer never having interviewed one previously. Most do not know what to expect and have no experience with interview techniques that actually work.

For example, when the authorities in Pensacola, Florida, arrested Ted Bundy, they faced a criminal type they'd never seen before—a fugitive on the FBI's most-wanted list and a suspect in over 25 especially brutal murders. Bundy was captured after being on the run from murder charges in Colorado. He had committed at least three murders in Florida but, at the time of his capture, was not the main suspect in any of those murders. He had even been shot at by the arresting officer while trying to escape apprehension for a multitude of charges, none of which was murder. Now, at last, he was in custody as a fugitive. While steadfastly denying his involvement in any murders for years, after his capture and during the early hours of his detention, Bundy was especially vulnerable, open, and willing to talk. Investigators had a small window of opportunity for an interview that would have elicited incriminating statements.

At first, Bundy refused to identify himself, and investigators didn't realize who they had just arrested. Their prisoner had been drinking while on the run and was physically and emotionally exhausted. He was weak and more capable of making incriminating statements than he had been at any time in his life up to that point. As his bravado failed him, Bundy did things that were very uncharacteristic. During one of the breaks in this interview and before he was identified, Ted called his former girlfriend in Seattle and all but confessed that he was the person that everyone suspected he was. He also came perilously close to giving incriminating statements to the detectives. One officer was trying to get a better understanding of the parameters of what Bundy was stalling about and Bundy muttered, "three figures." In other words, Bundy was alluding to having murdered over 100 women, but the Pensacola police authorities had no idea what he was talking about.

The investigators didn't convince Bundy to confess, but they were close. I asked him about this interview, fascinated because I knew that I could be in the very same situation with a suspect in the Green River murders. Bundy actually complimented the detectives who were holding him for sustaining the interview. Their strategy, if it was one, of platooning the interviewers—rotating in a fresh team every so often to maintain the interview process—was good because Bundy wanted to keep talking. They had a way of keeping him going even though they were getting tired. They didn't give up on getting more information and on encouraging their suspect to cooperate so that he would feel better because he was finally telling the truth about himself to the police. This was working for him. Bundy felt that they were patient over the long haul and probed very carefully. They didn't really know what they were looking for and therefore experienced no obvious frustration.

Would detectives familiar with Bundy's cases have been as effective? Would they have been as laid-back and persistent? I doubt it. Bundy said he would have refused to talk to certain detectives, such as Mike Fisher from Colorado and Ben Forbes from Utah. Those two detectives had dogged him so well that he had built up a resentment for them, so any questions on their part would have been ineffective. But he did say years later that he respected them because they were very thorough investigators. In Florida, it was the last time that any law enforcement officer would have the chance to speak with Bundy at length until Bundy contacted me in October 1984.

The 1988 Interview—Confessing to Murder

Now it was 1988, four years after Ted, Dave Reichert, and I first talked together in Starke, Florida. By the time Ted and I had settled in for the 1988 interviews, the Green River case was six years old and Bundy and I had become something more than pen pals. I was down here at his request because the last of his appeals was running out and his life was being measured in months, if not weeks. I believed that the topic matter of our interview in 1988 was impromptu, but it wasn't. Ted wanted to teach me how to interview serial killers so I could master the techniques to get his own confessions. It was part of a master plan that Ted had to keep face while getting me to learn how to interview him with respect and not disdain. This would be his ultimate attempt at control.

Getting Ted Bundy to talk about interviewing serial killers was a prearranged strategy on my part as well as his. My plan was to talk with him at length about how he would interview serial killers and eventually inquire about the preferred circumstances under which a convicted murderer, like himself, would talk about his crimes. How would he interview the Riverman? But it was also an act. Previous experience dictated that Bundy would talk around the various elements of murder and its investigation, but he would carefully avoid any references to his own murders. This very method was also his way of developing rapport and confidence with the interviewer. Bundy's suggestions about interviewing serial killers were pieces of valuable information for homicide investigators to consider in future cases.

First of all, Bundy emphasized the urgency of immediately interviewing any suspected serial killer upon the arrest. Any delay would allow the killer's denial to harden and ultimately jeopardize any prospect of a meaningful relationship between the killer and the detective. I asked him how he would get the killer to talk if he were the detective who had just had picked up the Riverman.

"Detective" Bundy

Bundy said, "Well, good question! I've thought about this, using my own experiences over the years; I've run across many people who have talked to the police and many who haven't. And I've seen what's happened. And I've seen guys who were handled properly from the standpoint of law enforcement, in my opinion, and those who weren't."

"Legally?" I asked. "According to the Miranda warnings, or in terms of getting information out of them?"

Ted wanted to speak only in terms of getting information out of them, whether the police are giving accurate information or whether they turned the guy off, intimidated him, threatened him, or otherwise caused him not to talk. Ted reminded me that he had lived in the prison environment for over 10 years and that it was sort of an avocation with him to hear guys' stories about what happened to them when they were arrested. Ted was very curious about why some murderers confessed and why some didn't. Ted was even more interested in what they told the police and what they held back. That kind of game fascinated him because he thought it might have been a power issue. Ted felt that he got a version from his fellow killers that was different from what the police could get. Bundy did acknowledge that he might not be hearing the facts, saying, "I may not be getting the straight dope, either."

Not getting the straight story is a real problem for the police, and Bundy appreciated it. The killer has the advantage because only he knows all the facts of the murder. The interviewer is limited by knowing only those facts that have been discovered in the investigation, possibly not having enough information to refute the killer's version. Thus, the savvy serial killer knows when the police are fishing for details and need him to make their case. In this kind of situation, the police can't bullshit the guy into confessing. That's why Bundy approached killers differently than the police could. Bundy had a real interest in knowing about the case. He said, "Not because I want to tell anybody, for just my own personal information." Obviously, it is impossible for police investigators to open an interview with a killer using the same premise.

Ted could express genuine interest owing to his fascination with guys like him. Ted said, "Some guy comes in and he's been convicted of x number of murders; I'm just kind of fascinated by what happened. How and why did he start? I honestly have that kind of an interest. I have approached maybe as many as ten different persons accused of serial murder over the years, just to find out what was going on in their minds and how they did what they did and how they got caught."

Bundy struggled daily with his own inadequacies and compared them to the other inmates'. His fascination with the other prisoners' murders was really genuine. He *had* to know. As eager as a guy was to talk to him about murder, Ted was more than equally interested in listening for his own therapeutic, perverted satisfaction. Talking with other killers about their exploits also relieved the intense stress that Bundy was experiencing, because he was consumed with his compulsion to commit murder. If he couldn't do it with his own hands, he had to hear about it—experience it vicariously through others. It was like a drug. Even in our interviews, it was difficult to make small talk, such as about the University of Washington football team. It wouldn't be long before he would drift right back to the subject at hand—murder. Therefore, when interviewing someone like Bundy, it is important to display an active interest in or a fascination for murder. That can be difficult for someone who's not a killer but who needs to get a confession out of one fast. Accordingly, due to inexperience, interviewers may alert the murderer to the fact that they are concerned only with facts pertinent to the case rather than being sincerely interested in and having compassion for the killer. This difference in approach can blow an investigator's entire interview and only harden the suspect's attitude and resolve to keep his story to himself.

Bundy as Interviewer

Bundy advised me that many killers have been reluctant to talk after they've been caught. He told me to expect this in the Riverman. In order to open up the killers he talked to in jail, Bundy presented a very convincing fascination with what they did. He explained, "This is not because I want to tell anybody, it's because it fascinates me; it honest to God fascinates me, and you probably picked that up perhaps from time to time in my letters." Bundy blew away his fellow killers with his expression of interest and created an air of expertise difficult for the unsuspecting killer to overcome. Bundy told me, "I'm the only Ph.D. in serial murder. Over the years I've read everything I can get my hands on about it. The subject fascinates me. So when I'm confronted personally—not as a law enforcement guy, not as a detective, I'm not playing that role—I'm playing the role of me intrigued about what they did and wanting to know every last detail about it."

Getting guys to open up about their murders was something Ted was proud of. Sometimes, he explained, they're not forthcoming or they don't know how to open up to him, and so "I have to help them tell me the kind of stuff that I want to know." These were the killer's grisly details not softened or adulterated with expressions of remorse. Ted continued, "I suppose the first thing that helps a guy open up that I've used is for him to tell me all the gruesome details of his murders; but he felt absolutely no remorse. He would tell it to me in graphic detail, but there's one [murder] he just couldn't tell; he was holding back on this one situation. But he said his story was that this girl just walked away, and nobody saw her again. And it didn't sound right to me. I knew she didn't walk away, okay? I just knew she didn't walk away, but I couldn't figure out why. I could tell, the way he was telling me, he wasn't opening up to me. He was telling me without hesitation about all these other cases but not this one."

Ted knew how to confront this killer without accusing him. He could say that he knew what really happened to her and just told him "he was bullshitting me." Ted had the authority to say to them, "Well, listen, this is what I think, why I think people don't believe you when you tell them this." Ted's approach on a case like this was "people don't believe you when you tell them this . . ." It was a nonthreatening way Ted used to explain that he didn't believe the killer's story without telling him he was lying. Ted told me that by handling the killer this way, my own judgments and feelings would not be reflecting *my* doubts, that I should instead simply refer to what "other people" didn't believe.

Ted could be convincing in an almost grandfatherly way. He could get to a level of understanding that no one else could. Ted knew firsthand that there were some murders that a killer just could not talk about. He understood what was going through the killer's mind. He told me that he would say to his guy, " 'This is what I think happened. Look at all these other crimes that occurred, and yet you want people to believe this girl walked away, and she never showed up, nobody ever saw her again. Now, I could understand maybe why you're holding back on that one; I mean, there's nothing wrong with that, man, I can understand it.' And he started talking about it, more or less."

The killer wouldn't be under any pressure from Ted, he said, because "I understood why he was holding back: he had a relationship. All these other women were strangers. But this one woman he knew. And he felt justified in killing strangers. He did not feel justified in killing people he knew. He felt these were okay murders; this one was bad. And he could not talk about it." But that's typically the case that can break the killer's back, open the guy up to a confession. Ted said that "that's the one that he still hasn't told anybody about. He's talked to me about it, in the third person." Maybe this killer reminded Ted of himself. Ted said frequently that there are some victims that killers just cannot talk about, because the victim might be someone with whom the killer had a kind of relationship, even if it was only in his own mind or if the victim saw something human or intimate in the killer through their association. Maybe it was someone the killer actually thought he liked. Of course, Ted was not known to have killed *every* woman with whom he had a relationship shorter than 10 minutes' duration, but to hear him talk, it would seem it was almost every woman.

The victim might also be too young; it's not safe to be labeled a confessed child-killer in prison. Not only will the guards hate you, Ted admitted, but other prisoners will too. Finally, the victim might be too close to family or might be one of the killer's own family members. For example, even though Ted knew that he was a prime suspect in the disappearance of an 8-year-old girl who lived near his home in Tacoma when he was 14 years old, he steadfastly did not want to talk about this case, and every denial he made was unconvincing.

Ted continued his discussion on questioning techniques by saying he found it useful to get murderers to talk about themselves. Ted said that while he talked to one killer in particular, "he finally started asking me questions. He said, 'Well, what would happen if they found a body that was like this and like that, what do you think people would think?' He was worried about what people would think of him. And this is a curious thing that you may have run into, that each individual can't be approached like in an FBI profile. He can't be approached as a collection of disorganized characteristics. This guy had unique needs. When I was trying to figure out what happened to this girl, again not as an investigator, just as a curious individual, I had to find out what those needs were.

"And for him, his own view of the world was that certain murders are okay and certain ones aren't. And I had to find out why wouldn't he tell me about this one. Why wouldn't he give me the details on this one? And it took us a while at first, talking generally about, you know, how our minds work, and how I could understand why he might think this was the case. 'But listen,' I said, 'you've already admitted to all these others. Why hold back on that one?' Then he says, 'Yeah, but people would think I'm a really bad person if I told them about that one.' So we had to work through all this guilt he had about this one versus all the others, thinking that people would view him more negatively, believe it or not, for this one murder than for these other twelve or thirteen. And this is something he held, like a secret locked away in his chest. And it was logically a foolish kind of reservation on his part, because no one would think he was any more horrible than they already thought he was. But in his own mind, that was what was holding him back.

"And this is what I found in a lot of guys that I've talked to. There are some things they'll talk about and some things they won't. And they have a particular view of the world that you have to discover. Why are they holding back? Why does this one guy, for example, not want to talk about the twelve- and thirteen-year-olds he killed—and he may have killed a dozen—but he'll talk about all the prostitutes he killed. Because in his own mind, killing all the young girls that he got at roller-skating rinks was bad. The prostitutes off the street corner he'll tell you about in a minute, okay? He had his particular *morality of murder,* if you will; it was such that he could talk about some but not others. He could tell you the truth about some but not others."

The Morality of Murder

I was almost in shock at this point. How could I carry on an interview in an atmosphere that held that "some murders are okay"? Was that what I was supposed to say to the Riverman—"It's okay to kill prostitutes"? How do you get the killer to believe that you are truly sincere? When you confront your suspect for the very first time, should you automatically expect that this guy who's murdered any number of people is going to have guilt or shame about one, two, or several of his victims? And how do you use that information to get more confessions out of a killer?

Bundy referred to these emotional attachments to victims as the killer's soft spots. He said, "Every guy has soft spots. Some of those victims, he wouldn't have a feeling for in the world. And others, he probably feels bad about. It's hard to say. I'm guessing. It'd be easier for him to talk about others and harder to talk about some. It's hard for me to imagine what the particular thought patterns are that he's responding to, what needs he has in terms of just relating to what he's done. But that can become fairly obvious to you over a period of time."

Ted Bundy had the "luxury" of living with these guys. He was in prison with Bobby Joe Long, a killer who was arrested in November 1984 for murdering 11 women—some of them prostitutes—in Tampa, Florida, during a period of less than a year. Ted claimed to be fascinated with the murders committed by Bobby Long. He said, "I wanted to find out all about what Bobby Long did; I wanted to know exactly what he did, even though he'd already told the police. And so if you live with a guy for a few weeks I can figure out what's going on in his head. And he knew where I was coming from, also."

Ted relished being able to get into a guy's head. When he'd talk about it, he would puff up his chest like a big toad, exulting in his superiority. Ted bragged, "a lot of people who come to me have read about Ted Bundy, so they know what—you know, they have an image or an impression of what I'm about. That may help them open up some, too."

Ted criticized the facts gathered in interviews of serial killers by FBI agents. They listened to people like Edmund Kemper give details of his murders that occurred in Santa Cruz, California, in the early 1970s. Ted said, "There's no question in my mind, he's lying, too." He did not tell the whole truth about his own murders. "It's curious that someone would admit to that kind of conduct, and yet over the years, for whatever reason, whatever psychological need they have to fabricate or embellish the story of the account, it happens. I've seen it happen. I've talked to guys who have come to me over the years and, you know, for whatever reason, they'll try to speculate. But they'll say, 'Hey, let me tell you about this.' And they told me some things and I know they're bullshitting me."

I directed my next question squarely at Ted's ego. "Do you challenge them?" He responded on cue. "Oh, yeah," he said. "I know how to—I mean, I can see through a guy very quickly. It's fascinating when somebody comes to me. I know when they're bullshitting me and I know when they're not. I know when what they're telling me is for real and when what they're telling me is a fantasy. And I've had a guy do both with me. It's a curious, curious situation. I had a guy sit down and just tell me stories. I knew he was telling me stories. And yet, I also know that, essentially, he'd done what they said he did, but he had a need to tell it a different way so he looked different, he looked better. In his own mind, okay? He wasn't a savage, lust-filled killer, but he was this guy who just—he just got mad. The bitch made him mad. So it's very curious how guys—some men who committed a series of murders over the years, in their own mind, will rewrite history to satisfy their needs. And they will lie. To themselves, perhaps. I mean, one person in particular. Fascinating." And he knows Bobby Joe Long did a lot more than the police say he did.

Ted claimed that Bobby Joe Long freely admitted a couple dozen murders to the police, many of which he didn't do. "He confessed to murders he didn't do and didn't confess to murders he did do. He was so messed up. And he did it in such a way that his confessions were expressing his inner needs, reflections of his inner self, which were somewhat juvenile. And also there's a need for approval. And he wanted people to say, 'You're doing good; you're a good guy. You're doing a good thing.' But anyway, I don't want to get too lost on this, but it's fascinating to see how people will embellish on their accounts, under the best of conditions. So you don't know what the FBI is getting."

Ted had just rambled on about exposing one of his comrades

when he was lying, while at the same time fearing that I could tell when he was bullshitting. This conversation revealed one of the many flaws in Bundy's personality that he constantly struggled with: his fear of not being believed or, worse yet, of being ignored because I would be able to detect that he was not telling the truth. Lying was a major factor in Bundy's relationships with other people. He lied to everyone: his girlfriends, parents, friends, cellmates, and lawyers. Of course, Ted knew that his murderous friends would lie, because that's all that they—and Ted—did in their relationships with other people. For Ted's upcoming confessions, his real dilemma was providing certain information about his murders that would convince me that he was telling the truth, and at the same time, knowing that his proven credibility, by his own admission, was less than zero.

After having just struggled with his own inadequacies, Ted had to be reeled in and his ego elevated. When we did that, he was hooked. He loved talking about murder, which was nothing more than a glorification of himself. He needed to be told "you're doing well, keep going." So I asked him about all the books that have been written about him. "Have a lot of them read these dime novels that have been written about you?"

With this comment, I successfully stoked Ted's fires. He said, "They all have, as a matter of fact, to one extent or another. And that kind of gives them a sense—at least an impression of—let's face it, of camaraderie, and that may not be the right word, but you know what I'm getting at."

He continued, "This guy will understand. Or sharing, like a kid, like a cat that brings the mouse home, you know. Sharing those experiences which he could probably never share with anybody. And I've had people tell me things. They said, 'Listen, nobody could understand this. I've never run across anybody I felt I could tell this to without feeling like they'd turn me in.' One thing they know about me is they can trust me, because there's nobody the state of Florida wants more than me. So they know I'm not about to turn them in. And of course, in reality, I wouldn't turn them in if they told me about what they did and told me about things that the police didn't know about." But cops knew Ted thought much the same thing would save his neck.

"A second thing: one in particular felt the need to tell me because he—it was a burden. He'd never been able to talk to anybody about it for fear they'd turn him in. Or they wouldn't understand or they would judge him. But when he talked to me, he didn't feel like I would judge him. He was right. I wouldn't. And he felt like I would understand, and he was right. I did."

The art of interviewing a serial killer was clearly interviewing without being judgmental. It was more than just dropping a mask over your face and pretending that nothing he said got to you. Guys like Ted Bundy could pick that right up, and he had told me so. It was more; it was actually believing that this killer had a right to do what he did. But it was a technique that Bundy wanted me to learn from him, and I could only guess at the grand strategy that he had laid out. It would serve a double purpose. I asked, "How does a detective talk to somebody without judging him?" I meant, how should I talk to the Riverman; how should I talk to Ted Bundy?

Now Ted had to perform. He had to explain what no one else could. He struggled. "That's hard. That's very hard. I can't imagine. I mean, it would take an extraordinary individual." I asked him another way: "You talked earlier about the need to get to this person right away and to interview them in any situation, or in most. What does a detective do to get to that same sort of rapport that you have there?"

"It's scary!" Ted said.

"They're [the investigators], not Ted Bundy."

"The scary thing is," he said, "you have to have real empathy. Real, not phony. You don't just call a guy by his first name, shake his hand, give him a cup of coffee, offer him cigarettes, and go through all the standard procedure of putting a guy at ease, which is important. But there has to be a real empathy, which, impossible as it may sound, lacks judgment, lacks—I mean, how do you detach yourself and say, 'This guy did these things which I consider to be horrible and repulsive and I've seen the impact it has on the community and the family,' and how do you detach yourself from all that? And all the personal stuff and just really try to get into the guy's head without these barriers?

"My advantage, in talking to the guys that I've talked to over the years, is that I don't have those barriers. Still, I don't have those barriers that I've erected between myself and the other person. Still, I encounter barriers from time to time that they've erected between everyone—anyone—about knowing the real story.

"And that's something, that's, as I said before, a curious thing.

Even when they do, sometimes a guy does open up to me and tells me about stuff. I can tell sometimes he's lying to me, that he's not telling me the straight story. And I know what that's about too. That's because this guy has lived with this 'terrible' memory, with these urges, and has lived with his behavior for so long and has had to keep it secret, just to be able to survive. Just to be able to survive!

"Let's say a guy has been out there for seven, eight years, periodically doing something, killing people. Now, from the very time that behavior sprang into his brain at some point, for whatever reason, he had to more or less keep that to himself. He couldn't go around telling people, 'Hey, listen, this is what I've been thinking about,' before he ever did anything, okay? 'I've been thinking about going around and killing people. I mean, I've been reading these books and I've been having all these strange urges.' Now, nobody is going to go around announcing that, just for fear of the fact that people will reject them, which they probably would. Right?

"So in order for this guy to be socially acceptable, to be able to just perform his normal life, he's had to erect a security barrier. He's had to keep these thoughts and later be acting out of these thoughts, tight to himself, and share them with no one, because if he did, he knew what would happen. He'd be turned in and arrested." Ted was now describing the basic paradox of serial killers: they want to blow off the sexual urges they have before they kill because they want to be able to navigate among people. Yet they also want some credit after they kill for remaining "socially acceptable." How do they balance the two? They usually don't, but Ted believed that police had to give credit where credit was due if they wanted a serial killer's full confession. And I had to admit there was something perversely logical about his explanation.

"I'm talking in generalities now," he continued. "But I've encountered this in people. I've encountered guys who have held this secret for so long and so tightly, even when it really didn't make any difference anymore that they told anybody; they couldn't let it go. Because the psychological barriers, the mental apparatus that had been in place for years, was so powerful against revealing this to anyone, under any circumstances, that they just couldn't bring themselves to share it. Even though they may have wanted to on some level.

"I mean, the secret, if you can look at it from a layperson's point of view, their secret was so terrible that they couldn't reveal it. Well, that's a judgmental kind of thing. To this guy, it's just something that he was so used to keeping to himself, just for his own self-preservation. And the way that his thought patterns had to be so tightly controlled, that even when the day comes for him to talk about it, it becomes very difficult. Not because, necessarily, that he doesn't want to talk about it 'cause he can, but he really can't open up. It's become—oh, it's—I don't know if I'm explaining this, but I run into it many times and I know how that is."

I asked, "Then you're saying that the detective cannot break that barrier?"

Now Ted was on a roll, knowing that he had just hit the nail on the head. How could he explain having real empathy? How could a murderer who had just taken so many lives in such brutal ways even understand empathy?

He continued. "Well, each person is different, and they have soft spots. And I'm not saying everybody is like this. I mean, there are some guys that are just going to come out and tell you, under the right circumstances. And I think Bobby Long is a good example of that. And the reason why I think Bobby Long was so forthcoming was because he'd only been at it for a few months."

Ted had just explained why one category of serial killers were willing to confess—their murdering careers are short in duration, and they are called short-term serial killers. They had not had the time to strengthen their psychological framework in order to build up those barriers of denial and need for self-preservation, which takes years to accomplish, as in the case of a long-term serial killer, like Ted Bundy or the Riverman.

Gerald Stano Revisited

Ted went on to describe Gerald Stano, who was on Florida's death row and was a suspect in over 40 female murders throughout the southeastern United States. "I knew one person in particular who was out there on the streets for seven years. His very first murder was a double—very first murder he admits to—was a double murder, seven years before he was caught. Now, he was a very busy person over the years. And he only scratched the surface with the police because he was handled so badly. Oh, it was just tragic the way he was mishandled. He had a deep-seated need for approval, which is why he talked to police at all. But they really did exploit him, and they traumatized him to the point where he just stopped talking to them. But he wanted to be accepted. He wanted to be one of the guys. He—to this day, he feels more comfortable with the police than he does with inmates. But the system's gotten ahold of him. 'Course, he won't talk to anybody anymore. But I'm saying he'd been at it for seven years at least before he was caught. So to survive for that long with those kinds of secrets, those very terrible kinds of secrets—at least terrible in terms of most people's perception—he had to have erected this mental barrier within himself about talking about this stuff.

"Whereas someone like Bobby Long, who went through a series of incidents and then, like I said, in June or July started killing people and was apprehended in November, [he] only had really a period of only six months where he'd been involved in this before the police caught him. He just opened right up.

"I think it has a lot to do with how long a person has had to live with this. For instance, the Green River guy, at this point, if he's still alive, and he's still out there somewhere, he's going to be a tough nut to crack. Not because he's intrinsically opposed to talking with police, although he may be, but because he has lived with the knowledge that you want from him for so long and had to guard it so closely. I mean, this is the most precious information in his life. If he would reveal any of it, he'd be a goner and he knows it. So he's had to keep that more secure than any secret he's ever had. Keep it to himself. And he lives with that day in and day out, to the point where it's going to be hard for him, if he ever really was in that position to talk about it. You see what I'm getting at?"

I nodded. I understood.

"Whereas if you'd snatched the Riverman back in August or September of eighty-two, and he'd only been at it for a few months, the likelihood of him opening up and really just telling everything without a lot of strenuous interrogation would be pretty good. So I think that's one dimension of what you face with the Green River guy now is that he's lived with this for so long.

"It's going to be hard for him to talk about it under the best of conditions. But to the extent that you can take the time to talk to him, not just over the course of a few hours, but it took me days sometimes, coming at these guys a little bit at a time. Just one question at a time. I might just ask this one guy, who I told you has had it for seven years, one or two questions one day, and I might wait three or four days before I come back to him. Very gently. And I would catch him with two different stories. And I knew one story was true and one was false. And I'd make him admit to the true version to help us get into what really happened. Or talk about some things that I've experienced that might help, that he might be able to relate to. Just to know."

Ted was explicitly preparing me for how I should act while interviewing the Riverman, but he had a much more important agenda: he was also teaching me how to get his own confessions, which had been bottled up in him for over a decade. "As a detective," he said, "I would come across whenever possible—and I think more often than not—I would try to come across as somebody that would have known a lot of people who had done this. Who's investigated a lot of cases like this, who understood what was going on here. Who understood the kind of thought processes, the kinds of motivations that lay behind, that would compel a person to kill another person like that. And not just one, but one after another.

"What has impressed me about the people I've talked to is they have a need to be understood, to share these burdensome secrets they've kept so long. But they don't want to share them with just anybody. If they're going to talk about them with anybody, they want to talk about them with somebody who is not going to judge them. Who's going to understand this bewildering experience that they've been going through. I mean, I'm not saying I understand it. But it's an awesome thing for a guy to confront. And if they can talk to somebody they feel will be able to say—I'm not saying congratulate them, but say that they understand, that they know they have a good feeling for what's going on in a man's life who does these kinds of things—then you have the best chance, I think, of settling the guy down to the point where he feels free to tell things which he's kept to himself for so long."

Bundy felt that the interviewer of a long-term serial killer should be someone who had established the necessary experience and respected credibility in serial-murder investigation. That was all well and good when you could control who the interviewer was. But I

· wanted Ted to focus on situations when a detective who questions a long-term killer does not have that experience. "He's talked to one killer in his time, and maybe that's it. Then all of a sudden, he gets a case like this, where there could be three or four murders and they have arrested a suspect or they're going to interview somebody as a suspect. They may not have any probable cause to arrest him at all. But just by virtue of the circumstances, the guy's a suspect and could be the killer. That's probably how we would encounter the Green River Killer. How would you approach somebody who could be the killer, but you don't know for sure?"

Ted gulped. "Not knowing for sure? That's a different situation than what I'm talking about because—this guy's already here. They're already in prison. Sure, it's a different perspective entirely and there's no sure answer, but I'll tell you what, in my experience—I guess there's all kinds of theories that detectives have about what works. But—and maybe coming on real strong and real hard and saying, 'I know you did it. You might as well tell us.'—I'm sure it's worked for some people from time to time. But in my experience, nothing will turn me off faster than a detective that comes on too hard. Because implicit in there is a lot of judgmental stuff and that would, generally, tend to put a guy off. 'Cause he knows, again, you have to sense if the detective is inexperienced. He may be an intuitive kind of guy and can sense what's going on in the mind of the man he's trying to question. We'll deny that he's the kind of guy who can be intimidated to the point where he opens up and then once he's opened up then you can gently pull it out of him.

"But I'd say from my own experience that if the detective comes off just willing to talk, someone that's just willing to talk and not come on real strong, that's more likely to be the context where he can use his skills as a questioner and an interrogator to develop certain avenues, certain kinds of information that he wants."

Why Some Killers Confess

Ted had talked at great length about interviewing killers who do not immediately confess. Now he had to talk about some reasons why killers do confess. That, too, would be valuable information for understanding the Riverman. I asked, "When you were talking about how serial killers would talk, is getting caught with the goods an overwhelming thing?" Maybe we'd catch the Riverman with handcuffs in his car, or a police badge in his wallet, or with the underwear from one of his victims. It's not farfetched when you realize that that's partially how Bundy was apprehended.

"That's a good point," he said. "From the standpoint of playing the standard game, playing by the rules of the criminal justice system, where you just proclaim your innocence and let your public defender do the talking, if you're caught with the goods, it's really kind of gone beyond the point of deniability, whether it be in a legal sense or in a psychological sense. And I think certainly, if a guy were caught with the body of a woman in his trunk, even eight years, six years later, I think he might be more vulnerable, you might say—there's no point in denying it anymore. You might just say talk about it. 'Let's talk about it. What happened?' And start with that and I think that certainly, if that were the case, he'd be more likely to tell something about everything, than if he were just arrested in his house and taken downtown.

"Because at that point, based upon everything that's come out, like in the Green River cases, so far, it's clear that the police . . . have next to nothing that's of real value. They've got a lot of stuff— a few profiles and some descriptions of vehicles—but in terms of hard evidence, if I were the perpetrator, I would feel pretty confident.

"Although, still, being arrested, if it's the first time he's ever been arrested, that's another factor. One of the first things I would do, and I'm sure the first thing you or task force people would do, if I had a guy that I wanted and had a warrant issued for to arrest him in this case, find out if he had any kind of criminal background. And I'm not talking just from the standpoint of trying to figure out if he's done anything like that in the past, but try to find out how familiar he is with the system. Has he been hardened? Does he know what his rights are? I mean, not to say that you'd violate his rights, but has he been through the system before, so is he conditioned to how the game is played? Does he know how it is to be interrogated? How it is to go to trial? Does he know what prison is like and what jail is like? Is he familiar with all that? A lot of people, if ever arrested, have gone through the system like that before, gone to jail and gone to prison, even though he's pretty solid in terms of not talking about what he's done, the prospect of jail and prison could still be very frightening to him because he simply has never experienced it before. Anybody who's spent any time in prison, however, would not be as intimidated by the threat of prison or anything. The less experienced he is with the criminal justice system, obviously the better off you'll be—in terms of questioning."

The time from the first murder to the arrest is the main factor that Ted was talking about earlier when he described Bobby Joe Long as a short-term killer. The shorter the series, the more likely the suspect is to talk about it because he hasn't had the time or the inclination to build up his barriers and his bravado that kept him alive on the street.

Ted added, "That's my feeling; I'm very strong, along those lines. Early on, the guy's more vulnerable. And all the experience of going out and abducting and killing someone is obviously a very terrible thing. But in terms of how the perpetrator sees it, it's certainly traumatic; it can be very traumatic, too. If for no other reason that his very life, his freedom, his way of living, his own identity is threatened by possible discovery. So, early on, the guy could be unstable. He hasn't figured it out. Psychologically, he hasn't adapted to it. He hasn't adjusted to it. Doesn't know how to deal with the membranes of the system. And the more chance he has to rationalize it and justify it and work it out in his own mind, and more or less come to terms with it, and carry these very dark secrets, and the longer he carries them, the more he gets used to them, the more difficult it will be to get him to talk."

Ted talked of the inmates who came to him because the media had written so much about him. These killers "got off," he said, on sharing the details of their adventures and their crimes with him. They relived what they did, maybe even experienced again the same thrills of control and domination, but it was all self-serving, as was Ted's interest. He was enjoying the details and hearing the story from them. But Ted didn't tell them anything about his own murders. These he kept private because he knew they were the stuff of media interest as well and could be the keys that got him off death row.

Screened Memories

Ted approached some convicted killers who didn't come to him first, just because he was curious about what they had been accused and/or convicted of. Ted said, "Of course, I would do so very, very discreetly, making sure they understood that I didn't want to know any details. And that may be something, a technique that you could use. I don't want to know the details. I don't want to know names or places. I just want to know what happened. I don't want to know names. That's what I would do. I said, 'Don't tell me. I don't want to know dates, I don't want to know names, I don't want to know specific places.' " Ted believed it was important with some killers not to demand details about names or places. Give the killer a chance to talk around the murder instead of the specific details. This could prove somewhat frustrating for police management personnel, since they want to know specific details right away. They've got cases to clear for prosecutors who need to prepare complaints to go before a grand jury. The detectives have to go for the specifics so the killers can be put away.

Investigators also interview murderers who claim to have blackouts or conveniently do not remember certain details. Ted revealed that the serial killers he talked to did not have real blackouts. If they claimed a blackout, he could take off on another line of questioning in order to identify events within the blackout period that the killer would unsuspectingly reveal. "I suspected that all of them really do remember, but they don't know that they do. Sometimes it appears to them like remembering a dream." The fact that serial killers remembered details of their murders was significant for me to consider in interviewing a Green River Killer who might claim a blackout at critical moments of his story. It was also important to hear from Ted that when a story of a blackout is encountered, it should be pursued with another line of questioning. Ted was also clearly giving me another hint on how to pursue his story as well.

I asked Ted how much they could really remember about their crimes. Ted answered, "That's a good question! The guys I've talked to—my feeling is that they remember. Now, whether or not they are going to tell me exactly what happened, for whatever reason, is another question. But I certainly haven't encountered enough guys, anyone with a split personality, you know, like allegedly Bianchi is. I haven't run across anybody who's got that kind of dual personality or anything. I haven't run across anybody who professes to have had amnesia or blackouts or anything like that. I think I've run across guys whose memories may be justifiably vague for reasons such as they were under the influence of alcohol or drugs or just the fear, the panic, the fright, the causes of that, of the violence that went on there, would somehow cloud their memories. But basically I think the guys I've talked to can remember when they talk to me."

Bundy brought out another important aspect of interviewing a killer—getting as familiar with them as possible. He said, "And again, I've had the luxury of when I talk to any of these men of having lived with them. So I see their normal side, their everyday side. You know, the guys that watch *Let's Make a Deal* and how they root for the guy, I mean, the game shows they watch and the canteen items they buy and what they do in the yard. I see their everyday side and yet I know this other part of them, too. And it's a great advantage in not being law enforcement and not being a psychologist and being viewed as who I am when I talk to them. On occasion, I think my status gives me insight into some of it. Three or four of these guys have been accused of serial murder. And I think they remember. I know they remember."

Without details, like names and places, how could I be a sympathetic interviewer? And on a more practical level, how did Ted verify that what they're telling him was the truth? These were related issues, about which I questioned him. Ted answered, "That's a good question! It's hard to put into words. It's just knowing when they tell you something, when they describe how something happened, whether it's authentic or not. You know, after killing someone, what one experiences is not a common experience. You can read all the murder mysteries you want, and you know that as graphic as some of these detective novels may try to be, you just know they're not for real because you can tell the guy's never been there. He's just making it up. Whether you watch some of these so-called slasher films or whatever—you know that's just Hollywood. It doesn't really happen that way. You just know. And so, if a guy's making it up or if he's read about it, I just have a sense that he's not

being straight with me. You can tell it. Certainly, one way of several
ways is that—it's a tried and true way—he doesn't tell the same
story the same way twice. And I always make them tell it to me two
or three times. And I'll say, 'Hey, how about this? That doesn't
make sense.' "

So he remembered the first version of the story and checked it
against later versions for deviation. Sounded plausible, but the police still want to know times, dates, places, and details that only the
killer would know. This is the only verification that will hold up in
court. I posed this problem to Ted.

Ted said, "Well, this is true. And yet that's a way of opening
somebody up. If a guy has, for whatever reason, insulated himself
from the reality of what he did, but can discuss it in the third person
or better yet, in the first person without getting specific, you're
getting gradually closer to the truth. I mean, the whole truth and
nothing but the truth, including the names, dates, and places—
everything he knows. But maybe the more circuitous route in some
cases may be the better route, because some guys just can't give it
to you right straight. They can't sit down and say, 'Okay, on this
night this is what I did, and this is what happened,' and so on and so
forth. You might be better to work them into it gradually, to the
point where they sort of open themselves up by degrees."

This was the route Ted took during his debriefing in the days before his execution. He chose to reveal facts by slow degree, wanting
to ratchet himself up to the vital statements everyone wanted to hear.

Ted continued our conversation. "Certainly, you want to verify
what they say, ultimately. You want to verify it by making sure they
tell it to you the same way, and making sure what they tell you cor-
responds with the facts and maybe even . . . using sodium pentothal or polygraph, just to make absolutely sure.

"Let's say—in a big case like Green River, you're obviously not
going to believe anybody who comes forward and starts confessing
these crimes, even if they get some of the names, dates, and places
right, because so much of the information has been disseminated to
the public. And I'm sure you've sat down and tried to figure out
how you would identify things you know that have not been made
public. But more than that—this guy's memory might be so bad
after all these years, he might not be able to remember some of
these details that you know about and the public doesn't know

about. That's another problem! Even if he wants to confess, he might not remember enough to satisfy you. Maybe, the only way to do it is . . . through a polygraph or sodium pentothal or something in a very careful debriefing technique.

"One of the things that I've found just really appalling is how they handled Gerald Stano, who was for seven years out there doing this. He started with a double murder, according to his own admission, and confessed, allegedly confessed to some two dozen or so murders over that period of time. What bothered me was that the investigation was so sloppy and haphazard; they did the same thing to this guy that they did to Henry Lucas. You had one detective sergeant [of] this county police or sheriff's department who was, more or less, the head honcho, and he was the guy that all these other agencies in Florida had to go through to get to this fellow. And they would come and plop their files down on the desk; he'd look through them, and they'd talk it over and he confessed to a lot of this stuff. And he was doing it because he likes to be viewed as a good guy. He liked the affirmation. 'You're doing the right thing.' And he liked the special treatment he was getting in jail. He was getting off on all that. But they weren't carefully screening his confessions and verifying them, making sure he was telling them the same thing, you know, day after day. And they didn't bring in any specialists, any psychologists or psychiatrists. They didn't use the behavioral science people of the FBI. And so Gerry Stano is just getting away with all kinds of stuff."

Serial Killer as Witness

Insofar as his own case was concerned, Ted was critical of the quality of investigations and interrogations. But it was clear that Ted wasn't speaking just for himself. The Green River Killer, still out there, perhaps, behind his camouflage and wall of denial had to know as much about the quality of detective work and investigation as Ted knew. They both read the same true-crime stories I read. What would be the point of telling the truth when a poor-quality investigation could affect the outside observer's beliefs about whether a killer's statement is truthful? If the facts aren't known, it might be due to a substandard investigation and the fact that the police just haven't found them when they were there to be found. Therefore, the police look bad and can't begin to convince the killer of their concern for him and for the truth of what he did.

To carry what seems like a ludicrous argument even further, if a killer's impression of the investigators is key to the interview process, how can you make a good impression on him? Remembering, for example, that the serial killer might be the only witness and therefore vital to the case made against him and that his cooperation might be wholly dependent upon how he is interviewed, what, then, did Gerald Stano think of the detective who interviewed him?

Ted was cautious. He really didn't want to embarrass anyone. But he said, "Well, I don't know what he thinks of him right now. I last was with Gerry—we were both on death watch, as a matter of fact, together, and we also lived in the same wing together for some time—and I read a very confidential report, a presentence report prepared by some state agency. It went into great detail about his confessions and his past life. And well, Gerry is a long subject. But Gerry liked the detective. I got the impression at least initially that he liked and trusted him. But my impression was that the authorities, I think down in Daytona—wherever—finally got tired of Gerry confessing and getting life sentences.

"Gerry first confessed when he was arrested in February of 1980 for an assault on a prostitute, and I think Gerry is a case you might want to study from the standpoint of what you might be looking at with the Green River Killer. Because Gerry was out there for seven years, by his own admission, he did prey on a lot of prostitutes, and he was out there for so long, seven years, doing his thing. And so he was arrested for attempted murder when he attempted to stab a prostitute in a motel room. My understanding is that the record shows the day he was arrested, he not only admitted to attacking this prostitute, who lived and could have died, but he confessed to another murder and two other murders that same day. And that was all he admitted to. In fact, they didn't press him any further.

"And so, he came to prison, and he was here for a little over a year, and for reasons which Gerry has never satisfactorily explained to me, he got in touch with the detective. I guess it was said that he wanted to talk some more about this. And he admitted to a few more, maybe half a dozen more. And then he came back a year and a half later in nineteen eighty-three, and confessed to a whole bunch more murders in September and October of eighty-three. And they finally decided to give him the death sentence for some of those confessions.

"And he wasn't finished yet. I mean, it was just as plain as the nose on your face that he was taking a lot of time opening up. And he was doing so a little bit at a time. Perhaps it was maddening that—to the prosecutors involved—that he was dragging this out. Maybe they got impatient with him, but they ended up giving him a death sentence, three death sentences based upon his confession in eighty-three.

"He stopped talking to them after that. And he won't talk to them anymore. They scared him. They managed to set him up. But he was badly mishandled. If he was properly handled back in eighty, when he confessed to those two murders, if they'd known how to follow up on what he'd said and develop and inquire into his activities over the years, they'd have probably gotten more out of him then—instead of waiting for the next two and a half years for him to keep coming back to them."

When the Police Close In

Suddenly I had an idea. I believed we had been close to the Green River Killer once or twice without knowing it. We had identified Bundy while he was still in Utah and would have picked him up ourselves had he not been caught by the trooper. Does the killer ever realize how close the police are to him? And if so, what does that do to his psyche? Does that make him more or less likely to open up when he finally does get caught? How close during the seven- or eight-year span had Stano come to being apprehended, I asked.

Ted answered, "Well, yes, as a matter of fact. He was primarily preying on prostitutes, and again, in many ways Gerry is a classic situation. And it's been a long time since I've reviewed this in my memory of everything he told me, and certainly since I've read his presentence report. But, I think it was in the late 1970s, seventy-seven, seventy-eight. He was arrested by a vice officer who was a woman police officer. Gerry was out looking for a prostitute to kill. This was in seventy-seven, three years before he was caught. He was caught in eighty. And he was arrested for soliciting. What do they call that? Whatever the appropriate charge is. And significantly enough, he was arrested in Daytona, and he was bonded and all that stuff. He was put in jail and he got out, and I think he got some sort of fine or probation. But the next week, instead of going back and looking for somebody else on the east coast of Florida, the record will show—and Gerry's confessions will substantiate the fact—that he drove all the way across to the other side of the state, Tampa. He drove first to Orlando and then to Tampa, in succeeding weeks, after his arrest in Daytona, looking for victims and finding them. So, it's logical, and in fact it did happen, that when Gerry was arrested in Daytona, where he'd been doing most of his hunting—on that prostitution charge—that shortly thereafter, he just drove to another part of the state to do the same thing.

"That's as close as he came to being caught. And, again, only part of the story is known of Gerry. And Gerry—as often as I try to get Gerry to open up to me, he wouldn't. He would always try to bullshit me. And the thing that bothered Gerry to no end was that I had this extremely detailed report that someone else had given me. See, Gerry had allegedly confessed to a murder that somebody else on death row is convicted of committing. And so that person managed to get ahold of this report on Gerry. And so I had this report.

"Gerry is a pathological liar. And one of the sweetest, nicest, most generous guys you'll ever run across. You put him in a three-piece suit, and he'd look like an economist, a frumpy-haired college economist. And one of the most harmless, nice, happy-going, 'good old Uncle Gerry' guys you'd ever want to run across. And so getting to know Gerry was fascinating, 'cause he'd tell me stories about things that happened, and then I'd read that something else had happened in the police report."

I thought to myself as Ted finished, *Can you imagine that type of guy—a college professor type—turning on a prostitute that he had under his control and killing her and then killing others for a seven-year period? Can you imagine this person, who obviously hates women with a vicious fury, being arrested by a* female *vice officer?* That must have been part of his worst nightmare. Yet he knuckled right under to the law, which is what he had to do, took his punishment, and then drove across an entire state to go right back to killing. How many prostitutes paid for what Stano thought that female cop did to him?

I told Ted that I had met that detective who'd interviewed Stano at a seminar in Atlanta. I said to him, "Gee, I don't know why I'm up here talking. You should be up here telling your story." And the detective said, "Look at me!" I didn't know what he meant. It took me a while to figure out what he was talking about and why he was devastated. Evidently, he was considered an outcast by his department for what he'd done in the Stano case. Instead of learning from it and being able to profit from that experience, his department blamed him for not tying it all up in a pretty bow. I know that's impossible to do most of the time when you have a killer you have to get information out of bit by bit, month after month. To make your case, you have to go after what you can get and try for the most cooperation you can. Most police commanders don't realize that and think all murderers are alike.

Ted summed it up even better. "Well, it was a mess. He may have been subjected to all kinds of pressures, I'm sure. But the way Gerry was handled was just a mess. They didn't call anybody who really knew what they were doing. And they were just talking to him haphazardly and piecemeal and running around the state and showing him all kinds of stuff. And so this thoroughly distorted and contaminated everything Gerry said, and it's hard to say what Gerry's responsible for now. And then end up giving—I mean, after being patient with him, while across the course of two and a half years, finally, the prosecuting authorities just got fed up with him. Instead of giving him these life sentences, they gave him three death sentences, and Gerry just stopped talking.

"He wasn't finished talking, believe me. I mean, he wasn't finished giving and telling them all he knew, not by a long shot. They just had not thoroughly been able to sit him down and figure out how do we get this guy to tell us all he knows and make sure he's telling us the truth. I mean, there are still a lot of question marks in my mind. But, I've always felt this.

"If Gerry was telling the truth about the early murders that occurred in seventy-three, and there's a lot more probably that he's involved with, if he was telling the truth when he said he killed those two girls, two hitchhikers in seventy-three, then I know for a fact that he did a lot more than he's talking about. Because there are huge gaps of twelve months where there's nothing there. He's told the police—and I can just look at his patterns and tell, you know, knowing what I know about Gerry and looking at his crime patterns, I mean, sometimes three or four a month, and then there's periods of twelve, eighteen months in that seven-year period where there's just nothing. Big blanks. Nothing he's told the police. Nothing that the police got around to asking him about."

"Is that because he wasn't doing anything out of town?" I asked.

"No, hell no," Ted said. "These were periods of time when, see, Gerry, I'm not trying to psychoanalyze him, but I know Gerry to the extent that he's got a poor self-image. He covers it over with a lot of joviality, but he has a poor self-image that was aggravated by alcohol abuse. He could never finish school. He couldn't hold a job.

"During that whole seven-year period he lived in his parents' home or in homes owned by his parents, or for a short time with his wife in a trailer. He never held anything more than part-time menial jobs, drinking heavily, driving around, getting money from his parents. And in the period following the separation from his wife, where he lost his job with his father-in-law, [he] had to live in his parents' home, was kicked out of his own trailer by this woman he was married to, a period of time when I know damn well he was angry and hostile and probably was feeling as bad about himself as he had ever felt—and had more time on his hands than he'd probably had for years—there's nothing there for twelve months?"

I know from experience, though, that despite concerns raised by police and the media, time delays within a series of murders are fully explainable, sometimes for the most mundane reasons. Even Bundy said that the same things that happen to "normal" people happen to serial killers. Shit happens to serial killers, too. They get sick, hospitalized, fearful of detection, go to jail, or die. Some series have had apparently inexplicable delays, such as the span of over 140 days between murders in the Atlanta child murders in 1979–81, for which Wayne Williams was convicted. But Bundy was emphatic: "If a killer is out there, he's doing stuff. The police have not found them.

"I know damn well that he was out there doing stuff. There's just no question. Some of the other things he's told the police are true about what happened in seventy-three and seventy-four. If that's true, then there's a lot more, and they just didn't know how to get it out of him. And it's a shame now because Gerry's been polarized, and the rare opportunity to really find out what was going on in his mind or what he really knows may have passed. The only disturbing thing about Gerry's revelations to the police is I don't know that he ever turned up any bodies, any remains. And—that doesn't necessarily say he's not telling the truth, but I don't know how much more he has."

Some news reports claimed that Stano had confessed to 41 murders. Ted wanted to set the record straight. "In fact, the presentence report, which is very detailed and goes into great length about his confessions, shows that he confessed to eleven murders where he's been charged and given a sentence of some sort, whether death sentence or life sentence. And ten more murders where they haven't yet got around to charging him for one reason or another. That's twenty-one. Now, there may be others they suspect him of or whatever, but that's—the report's fairly comprehensive and it pinpoints twenty-one specific cases. And I've charted them out, integrated them with what Gerry's told me, with what I know, and what the presentence report says, and there are huge, enormous gaps at very critical times when he was clearly in a state of mind, based upon my knowledge of how these things go, where he would—more likely drink and engage in that kind of behavior.

"Now, I think that's the problem that investigators face even when they get somebody that they think has been involved in a series . . . just finding this out, just how extensive his activities have been. And not just settling for the easy conviction or two and locking the guy away. For whatever reason, the prosecuting attorneys have reached the point or threshold where they weren't willing to wait anymore to find out. It was more important to them to give him a death sentence than it was for them to find out what he really knew. I think they just reached that point where they said, 'We've had enough of this fellow. We can't give him any more life sentences. We've got to—that's it.'"

Ironically enough, the state of Florida felt the same way about Ted. All the information that Ted felt should have been covered with Gerry consisted of the same, seemingly useless pieces of information that Ted tried to use to convince the state of Florida not to execute him. They were some of the same things I would have to dig out of the Green River Killer in order to put his puzzle together. But because both Stano and Ted had been "mishandled," according to Ted, I could not mishandle the Green River Killer. I also could not miss the opportunity to get out of Ted what other investigators had tried to get but failed. Ted was giving me my chance.

Ted wanted to emphasize one final, fatal point. "And despite the fact of these glaring inadequacies in how he was interrogated, and these big gaps, unexplainable gaps in his stories—and I say that not to condemn Gerry, and I certainly wouldn't reveal anything specific that he told me—it's always just appalled me just how badly that specific case was handled, how badly Gerry was handled. It would be a good case study for anyone wanting to know how *not* to approach somebody accused of a series of crimes. 'Cause he was lost. I mean, either they're going to kill him and undoubtedly will—I don't know how that's going to end up there."

Ted's Legal Maneuvers

In talking about Gerald Stano, Ted's face was etched with frustration. Why kill somebody when they have so much to tell? When Ted emphasized Stano's plight, he was also talking about his own dilemma. Should he confess now or wait? Ted was really close to opening up, it seemed. He was moving, fidgeting in his chair like I had never seen him do. Unbeknownst to me, the previous day, Ted's appellate attorney had convinced Ted not to confess to me. It was just not in his best interest during the appeal process, the attorney said. Ted told me later that he had wanted to begin talking at that time. That was why he was so intent on setting the stage with how to get a killer's confession; this was his show. My impression was that there was something wrong with Ted; his appearance was different; it was almost like he was talking about himself all this time—how he wanted to be interviewed. I was flipping back and forth between Ted and the Green River Killer. Now that I had Ted on the line, I wanted to reel him in. I wanted him, after all those years, to talk about himself. But I played for time, even when I knew there was no time. That was the only way I could play it. He had to come to me.

I said, "I'm kind of getting the feeling that whatever the efforts of the police, if a certain time span has gone by and a person has learned to deal with their own thoughts and problems for quite a while, the efforts to somehow understand or reveal the story in somebody during the interview process would almost totally be controlled by the person that's being interviewed. Whatever the police do or say, their presence really doesn't make any difference." I wanted Ted to tell me how to get his confession without really saying it.

He was fidgeting. He said, "Yes. If he wants to tell you, he'll tell you, and if he doesn't, he won't. We're talking, again, about somebody who has been out there for years and years. I mean, he's had this integrated so thoroughly into his consciousness, into his daily life, into his way of being and living and has become so familiar with how to deal with what people commonly refer to as guilt, remorse, or whatever . . . deal with it and/or do away with it. And it's become these thoughts and memories that constitute the crimes. He's adapted so well to them and kept them so close, because he knows the consequences of giving them up. It's not likely that anybody is going to trick him into talking about it or pressure him into talking about it."

It was time for Ted to be specific. I asked him, "How does an investigator visualize what's been integrated into this guy's mind for so long? Time? Patience?"

Maybe I opened the sluice gate for Ted. He said, "Yes. Time and patience. I think those are two good words. You can't hope to drag it out of a guy overnight, okay? And you can't get frustrated if he doesn't give it to you all at once, in one piece. Because you have to be content with slowly learning about what kind of person is this. What demands is he responding to within himself? And they may be very particular, very subtle, and very difficult to find out. Like for instance, this fellow I was telling you about who would tell you at the drop of a hat about all the people he killed, except he just couldn't bring himself to tell anybody how he killed his girlfriend and where he put her body. He just couldn't because his view of the world was, these other killings were good, but killing somebody you know is bad. And he was afraid if he told, people would—he had this vision in his mind that if he admitted to killing his girlfriend and told them where the body was, then people would see him as a bad person. That's pretty bizarre, but that's how he was thinking. And it didn't occur to me until after we talked about it for a while.

"And so I think the more you take time to know somebody, preferably the suspect—if you have a chance to get all of the information you could beforehand, before he was brought in, know as much about him as possible before he was brought in, and then maybe even to talk to friends and relatives about him once he's in. Now of course, once he's in custody, he's in custody. But you get a feeling for the guy as much as you can without talking to the guy.

"And then once you start talking to him you just use your own gut reaction. Just to start, patiently probing without pushing, without being judgmental, taking it a step at a time, the third person, maybe doing it without dates and places and making it an abstract kind of thing. When I'm faced with somebody and I want to learn about the case, certainly what *I* want to learn, my perspective, is different from yours. But still I have to respond to what that guy gives me. And I often know less than you would probably know about someone. My advantage is, we know he's been convicted of some kind of murder, anyway. So, that's certainly the starting point—and he trusts me to one degree or another. Still, if you can—if an investigator can somehow inspire trust and confidence and come off as being nonjudgmental and be patient and probe and get to know how this guy's mind works—I know this is pretty general kinds of things, but—that's how I'd approach somebody who'd been out there, who you suspect for a number of years or is involved in serial murder.

"Somebody who'd only been at it for a short time would be more vulnerable, more unstable, more confused, more guilt-ridden, more susceptible to coercion, you know. Remember that classic case— you've probably run across it—where they bring this guy into an interrogation room and ask if he wants to take a polygraph and tell him to put his hand on this mat or something like this. And every time he gives an answer to a question, the investigator presses a button and a light goes on and said you're lying—and thoroughly convinced this guy that they knew he was lying about these key questions and he finally confessed. Of course, it wasn't hooked up to a polygraph at all. But that kind of ploy, as crude as it was, will work. Once in a while it will probably work on those guys who haven't been at it very long, haven't been through the system, criminal justice system, haven't been imprisoned or jailed. And the whole thing about being in police custody is terrifying for [them]. And everything, their whole identity, everything they know about themselves, is shaping them. And they begin responding to unconscious cues, one of them being that they've always been taught, probably, to cooperate with the police, even when it comes to confessing some pretty horrible things."

Ted on Ted

Up to this point, Ted's interview had been filled with the key qualities that any skilled investigator was supposed to be capable of demonstrating: trust, confidence, understanding, real empathy, and patience. For me, the last one, patience, was running out. I decided to ask him a third-person type of question, one that he knew was for him, "Ted, the convicted serial killer." I carefully asked, "How would you approach a convicted murderer that you know is in prison for murder and is responsible for cases that are technically unsolved? How would you approach an offender like that? I mean, they obviously know the system. They've been tried and convicted, maybe sentenced to death. Then all of a sudden, there are some unresolved matters of the past where this person is a suspect in those matters. How would you approach somebody like that?"

Ted was quiet for a very long time. "Well, I don't—again, each case is going to be different. I think generally you've got to—it depends—it's just an entirely different set of circumstances than you're going to have with somebody who's never been through the system, who's not convicted. And I guess that you'd have to be able to give him something. I don't know. Let's say that you had the Green River guy locked up here—you had somebody locked up you thought was the Green River guy. May have been locked up for assault or something and he's in Walla Walla [penitentiary]. I mean, how would you go to him? I mean, how could you approach such a person who's familiar with the system, who's locked up for ten or twenty years to confess to something which obviously carried some pretty heavy penalties and resulted in being a very notorious guy in prison?"

I said, "I mean, he may be under the death sentence, you know, for crimes he committed now, but what happened in the past there's no death sentence for. I mean, the penalty is not as great for those."

Ted was very pensive.

I let him—and me—off the hook for the moment by saying, "Seems like a pretty impossible situation that where there's still answers to questions that could be resolved—you've talked a lot about how you've approached these people and the development of an appreciation of what was done. And I would expect that a detective in that situation would have to be the same, absolutely with the same criteria to develop some sort of appreciation for what somebody has done and with real understanding. . . . We have several crimes where the circumstantial evidence is pretty well focusing on one person, yet the opportunity to go interview them is not right, and we virtually do not know how to operate that type of interview."

Ted regained his composure and said, "Well, in that kind of circumstance, you see, everything is complicated by the demands of the criminal justice system, of the way everyone is more or less required to play the game. And a guy who's in prison or whether he's on death row or wherever, he has appeals, and he would simply be foolish to talk to the police about anything as long as his appeals are intact. Because the system, as it stands now, is not really geared to getting at the truth so much as it gets at portions of the truth. It gets at approximations of the truth. Whether it be a trial—and as long as a guy goes to trial, all you're getting is what the witnesses say, you know. And that's only part of the story, probably. The same is true on appeal. The guy who's been convicted is bound to try to maintain his position, and he can't say anything, is not in a position to say anything."

At this point, since a killer will not want to speak directly, would that type of person be inclined to speak in the abstract? Is that what Ted was doing all along, especially in the interviews he gave? Were these backhanded, wimped-out confessions? Is this what I would have to look forward to if I ever interviewed the Green River Killer?

Ted began to get defensive. He said, "I don't know what [purpose] that would serve. Remember you told me that didn't totally serve any purpose to the investigators as long as it was so vague that they couldn't really pinpoint anything. Well, I don't know. It depends on how general they are. But I think you know . . . the old Miranda warning: 'anything you say can and will be held against you.' And I—it doesn't necessarily even have to mean in a court of law. But I don't know. It's hard to explain. The way things are set up, I don't see how someone could say that, like you're talking about Walla Walla prison, where they have any incentive to talk to you. I mean, first, on the one hand, he's got his appeals, and so there are disincentives—clearly disincentives—to talking to you. On the other hand, what motivations would there be for someone in that position to talk to you about anything?"

I pressed on. "How about someone like yourself who is obviously astute, by your own admissions several times, that you really like talking to other people about this stuff? You like thinking about crime scenes and seeing pictures. And you like reading everything you can get your hands on about the subject. You obviously like talking to me about it, or otherwise you wouldn't be doing it. Is there something about that atmosphere that is appealing?"

Ted was interested again and said, "Well, with me, I do enjoy it; and yet that interest ebbs and flows. There's some times I'm more interested in talking about it than others. Like right now, I'm sort of ambivalent about it. I mean, it's interesting; I find it interesting. I know a lot about the subject. It's hard to put it in words in the abstract. I mean, to me, it's more interesting to have specific things to deal with—you know, specific cases. I don't like to generalize because, like I say, the guy who's responsible for the Green River Killer is not a profile, he's not a computer program. He's a very unique human being. So I don't want to generalize, but I do like to talk about it, and I like to read about it. And yet I can take it or leave it most of the time. I mean, it's certainly not something that I would rather do than anything else. Like, right now, if I had a choice, I'd rather be outside running around in the sunshine. Sometimes I'm more motivated to talk or read about this stuff than others. But I don't get off on it. I mean, that is, I don't get a thrill out of talking to you about it, in the abstract. I mean, I'm not trying to, I won't try to make myself out to be a good guy, but I do have motivations, and generally would genuinely like to see this questionnaire, for example, of your work." He was referring to our HITS (Homicide Investigation and Tracking System) form.

Ted tried to keep me in his corner by complimenting our HITS program. He wanted to continue our correspondence about serial murder. One last time, he inquired about the crime scene photo I had shown him back in 1984. He asked if I had any more to show him. It was almost as if he needed to be energized. I told him maybe next time.

The stage had been set. Bundy had carefully prepared his student. In an indirect way, by talking about what would and wouldn't work when interviewing the Riverman, he told me what it would take for him to talk about the murders he committed. I "would have to give him something." Ted was talking about his life; he didn't want to die in the electric chair.

Bundy emphasized that he had kept his secret for so long that any statement of admission would be difficult and would have to be made in degrees from the less painful to the most shameful. Ted had nominated me to be his confessor by grooming me from day one under the camouflage of solving the Green River murders. He had warned me about saying "I understand" before he was able to tell me what "understanding" him was all about. My approach to him was that I was always looking for information that contributed to my understanding of the Riverman and, through the Riverman, him. It was an ongoing process that didn't stop even with his execution.

He force-fed me with advice on maintaining a low-key approach and remaining patient at all times. My patience in developing the facts necessary to understand Ted on his terms was constantly being tested by him against the whetstone of his disturbing admissions and pretentious lectures on the Green River Killer. Maybe he had already convinced himself that I would be ready when the time came. Maybe this had always been part of his own exit strategy from the very beginning of our extended dialogue.

I did not know that Ted had made the decision to confess to me in February 1988, about one year prior to his death. If it hadn't been for his attorney's talking him out of it, Bundy would have begun telling all. I was always curious why Bundy kept changing the day of my visit in February at the last minute. Now I know. He was negotiating with his appellate attorneys about the propriety of giving incriminating statements. In 1988 he ultimately chose not to confess.

What controlled Ted's ability to communicate with me was the stage of his appeals. By February 1988, he had received another execution delay. The next stage was less than a year away. His advisors apparently concluded that confessing to new murders might undermine his chances to win an appeal of his conviction for the Florida murders. At the close of our 1988 conversations, I informed him that I would return to visit him anytime he desired.

Unfortunately, Ted waited too long. My next visit was scheduled four days prior to his execution in January 1989. The conditions for his interview were horrible, and it was conducted in a circuslike atmosphere. Representatives from every major television and radio station and newspaper from Washington to Florida were congregating outside the gate of the Florida State Penitentiary to cover the story of his execution. My role was to participate in his "debriefing," which was not exactly the forum that I expected for his voluntary confession. One more time, Ted was going to manipulate me and everyone else around him; this time it was his disorganized and unsuccessful effort to save his own life.

12

The Signature of Murder

Ted Bundy, while he never did catch the Green River Killer as he wanted to do, still played a very, very indirect role in the capture of one of Washington's most outrageously violent serial killers. And he did it from beyond the grave. I wouldn't have believed it possible had I not seen it with my own eyes. It all began with Bundy's advice that police agencies develop a violent-crime tracking system on computer. That eventually became reality with the FBI's VICAP program that was housed in the basement of the organization's headquarters at Quantico. Bundy was indirectly responsible for the development of the program because his cases, spread out as they were across hundreds of miles, were the types of crimes VICAP trackers and profilers were trying to investigate.

However, in the state of Washington, we had other plans. We went on to develop our own computer tracking system that ultimately helped us establish a pattern for and then solve a serial-murder spree that would have slipped right through our fingers if we had used normal investigative methods. The case we solved was that of George Russell, who was caught, in no small measure, because of Ted Bundy's comments years earlier and our subsequent homicide tracking system based partly on our experience with

Bundy. And, like most of my cases, it started with a simple request over the phone.

Inception of HITS

Two months after I left the Green River Murders Task Force, I was surprised by a telephone call from Terry Green at VICAP, who invited me to participate in a meeting at Quantico to discuss changes that would reduce the size of the existing VICAP crime report form. The call amazed me because I thought I was pretty much persona non grata after my friend Pierce Brooks left the unit. My problems with VICAP had more to do with where the system should have been housed—it belonged anywhere but inside the FBI, as far as I was concerned—than the size or content of the form. In spite of my criticisms of the program, I was still one of VICAP's most vocal supporters. For the first six months of the system's existence, one third of VICAP's database contained murder cases from the state of Washington that I had diligently researched for them. Differences aside, I was willing to advise, and my input about what and how information should be collected seemed to be highly regarded by those who ran VICAP.

The initial VICAP form was long—three volumes holding 68 pages of questions. It contained everything you always wanted to know about murder and more. Pierce Brooks had done a stellar job of consulting with experienced homicide detectives to produce the most comprehensive homicide investigation data collection form ever conceived. Unfortunately, its length frightened some officers. Typically, old-timers balked at filling out additional paperwork, especially a 68-page form for only one murder. The fact that the form was created without securing local law enforcement agencies' full commitment created some doubt about their ultimate participation. Concern from police over the size and complexity of the form itself was an obstacle that threatened VICAP's survival. In addition, I believed that certain information that was not collected on the form needed to be added and entered into VICAP's database. Without that information, comparisons could not be made effectively among the different homicides the database system was created to relate. Therefore, the form had to be completely revised—information had to be added *and* deleted.

In order to encourage local police agencies to use the form, VICAP decided to greatly reduce its size. There was a small group that was to decide what stayed on the form and what went—Terry Green, VICAP homicide case specialist; Ken Hanfland and Jim Howlett, VICAP crime analysts; Captain Gary Terry, Hillsborough County Florida Sheriff's Department; Lieutenant Dan Scribner from the New York State Police; and me. Pierce Brooks was invited, but didn't come. He disagreed vehemently with any form reduction.

Pierce called beforehand and warned me that the abbreviated contents of the new form had already been decided. He felt the FBI was only using us for support and would say someday, if the form was a failure, it was our fault. Pierce and I had talked long hours about how to make VICAP a success, and it wasn't necessarily by reducing the content or size of his form. VICAP needed to regionalize its activities.

In the few hours that we discussed the reduction in size of the VICAP form, an idea hit me. The VICAP program was exclusively a serial-murder tracking program. Its only function was to compare an incoming murder case against the database of serial homicides to determine if another murder was committed by the same person. As we discussed which questions on the long form to eliminate, I saw the importance of collecting information about all types of murders, not just those in a series. I asked Terry Green, who would later assume the duties of program manager of VICAP, "If a detective called you and asked if 'so and so' was a murder victim, would you give him the information? Or if he asked, 'Do you have a victim who was shot with a .22-caliber firearm and found in a Dumpster?' " Initially, Green said, "Sure." Then, suddenly, he saw my point. There were specific questions related to nonstranger murders that could be answered by querying the database. If VICAP provided that type of service to local law enforcement officers on a daily basis, their personnel would be overwhelmed with inquiries from thousands of investigators. They could not concern themselves with routine murders; there were too many and, of course, too many questions about them.

The situation was quite different for a statewide system that could monitor fewer murder cases. Therefore, I decided to use the VICAP form as the basis to collect information, and develop a state system in Washington State that could forward serial murder cases to VICAP and at the same time provide information to local investigators about routine murders.

The Signature of Murder

Back at the FBI, the VICAP analysts were eager to deal with a form that was more suited to crime analysis and less of a format for the greater understanding of all murder investigations. They wanted to make some questions on the form more general, such as including broader categories for locations of events rather than specific locations. Also, they wanted to remove the redundancies from one volume of the original form to another. We were obliging and went along with their proposals. Still, I had a lingering bad feeling about the form's contents. I wondered if they would be effective at connecting murder cases committed by the same person with that trimmed-down form.

When I returned to Seattle, I consulted my closest fellow detectives. We discussed the possibilities of a state system, but came up with the same scenario over and over: no funding and nary an agency willing to bear the cost. One day, I was looking through the National Institute of Justice's program announcement. It had a specific section that dealt with the apprehension of violent offenders. I reasoned that it was possible to research the ways murder cases were solved in order to better understand how murderers were apprehended.

For years, the viewing public had watched homicide investigation as portrayed in *Dragnet, Naked City, Kojak,* and *Columbo.* In addition, entire communities have felt the terror of a real-life brutal killer such as Ted Bundy, William Heirens, Ed Gein, Edmund Kemper, or the Boston Strangler in their midst and disrupting their lives. Much to my amazement, with all that fascination with the gruesome details of murder and its investigation, no one had ever studied, empirically and objectively, the methods by which police investigators catch killers. Researching solvability factors in murder cases would entail the establishment of an information system to store and analyze the data on murder. So in September 1987, based on a grant proposal that I and others in the state law enforcement hierarchy put together, the Criminal Division of the Washington State Attorney General's Office was awarded a $228,000 grant to study murder cases in Washington State and set up HITS.

HITS has become a murder and sexual assault investigation system that collects, collates, and analyzes the salient characteristics of all murders and predatory sexual offenses in Washington. HITS relies on the voluntary submission of information by law enforcement agencies in the state of Washington. To date, these agencies have submitted data on murders, attempted murders, missing persons where foul play was suspected, unidentified dead persons believed to be murder victims, and predatory stranger rapists.

We developed the HITS form, in place of the VICAP crime report, to collect information about murders in Washington State. The HITS form was a combination of the shortened version of the VICAP form and Pierce Brooks's long form. In all, there were 250 questions.

HITS Starts Working

HITS, similar to the national FBI-run serial murder tracking system, VICAP, had a different mission. HITS was at first confined to Washington state and was designed to help homicide detectives throughout the state by providing them with a relational database to which they could report homicides and from which they could retrieve the salient data that would help them compare and contrast their cases.

From the start, HITS was an immediate success, helping us bring data together to solve murders committed in different parts of the state by the same person. Our first significant connection involved two murder cases whose victims were found on opposite sides of the state. A Spokane detective filled out the HITS form for a murder of a male hobo found stabbed to death in a railroad yard. The investigation had long since been inactivated. Since HITS contained all murders and not just the potentially sexually sadistic serial murders the VICAP database contained, the Spokane murder was compared to all murders in the state. I found a similar case investigated by Cowlitz County authorities about 150 miles south of Seattle. This time a male transient had been found stabbed to death in a railroad car two years after the Spokane murder. The HITS comparison revealed that a person previously considered as a possible witness in the Spokane case was listed as the suspect in the Cowlitz County case. Spokane detectives were alerted that their "witness" was a possible suspect in the Cowlitz County case and their own. The same person was then identified as a suspect in a similar murder in a Midwestern state. When this same information was disseminated to other law enforcement agencies throughout Washington State another similar case was reported to HITS from Thurston County authorities, 60 miles south of Seattle. Without

HITS, the three police agencies would not have known they were investigating similar murders.

In another example, members of the Green River Murders Task Force were trying to determine the full name and additional information about Diane Merks, who was believed to have been raped and murdered somewhere east of the Cascade Mountains about five years earlier. An anonymous caller had reported that she was killed and found in much the same manner as some of the Green River victims. Task force members were unfamiliar with that death and wanted to look into the circumstances of that case to determine if there was a connection to their series of murders. Prior to HITS, a search for the victim's case would have consumed many hours of an investigator's time. But the HITS computer, with a Soundex program for name searches, identified in a matter of seconds a female homicide victim from Franklin County, Washington. The name of Diane Merckx was provided to Green River investigators, a spelling that would not have been previously found with a name search in any existing criminal justice computer system. Her skeletal remains were discovered in 1978, four years prior to the publicized beginning of the Green River cases.

Since HITS was enhanced to include sexual assaults in July 1990, the program has been successful in providing information on over 300 murder and rape investigations. After an extremely brutal rape and attempted murder, a request was made to the HITS unit for information about rapists who have certain physical characteristics and a previously recorded modus operandi. HITS staff were able to provide the investigating detective with a list of known sexual offenders who had been released from prison in the past five years and the areas to which they had been released. The detective assembled a montage of photographs from those rapists, and the victim immediately identified one of the offenders as her assailant.

The major financial benefit to local law enforcement agencies in Washington is that they incurred no cost for the implementation of HITS; its development and implementation costs were borne by the U.S. Department of Justice and the Washington State Attorney General's Office. The ongoing operational costs are also paid for by the Washington State Attorney General's Office.

The only cost to local agencies is the investigator's time for filling out the HITS form, which is 20 to 30 minutes. This time is negligible when compared to the time previously spent by an investigator trying to obtain by other methods the information that HITS can provide in a matter of minutes.

Local agency participation in the FBI's VICAP program has become systematic in the state of Washington, resulting in added conservation of investigator's time, since the investigator is not required to complete two forms. The VICAP information is collected on the HITS form as well. Therefore, investigators and departments receive the benefits of participating simultaneously in both programs.

HITS Goes Regional

On October 8, 1991, Washington State Attorney General Kenneth O. Eikenberry and Superintendent of Oregon State Police Reginald Madsen signed an agreement to link the two law enforcement agencies in their efforts to fight violent crime. The agreement allows Oregon access to Washington's HITS program. The Oregon State Police (OSP) are able to electronically transfer their violent crime information into the HITS computer. Through remote access, OSP has the capability of coordinating their violent crime information. Data from over 700 murders committed in Oregon during the previous six years have been entered into the HITS computer. As a result, police and sheriff's investigators from Washington and Oregon have ready access to violent-crime information for their investigations.

HITS underscores the importance of open lines of communication and coordination among police agencies, prosecutor's offices, coroner/medical examiner's offices, and crime laboratories in murder investigations of common interest. The HITS unit functions as the central location and repository where Washington's various murder and sexual assault investigators can readily find information about murder and sexual assault cases. The lack of such a process was exploited by serial killers such as Ted Bundy and the Riverman. Its implementation demonstrates that the timely and coordinated sharing of comprehensive information is the key to successful violent crime investigations.

HITS is a model that other states and local agencies have replicated or adapted to their own needs. The creation of the methods and procedures for data collection, the collection instruments, routine analyses, and computer programs are already benefitting other jurisdictions that have discovered the importance of coordinating and sharing violent-crime investigation information.

The George Russell Case

One of the most significant cases in which information gathered by HITS staff put a killer behind bars was that of George Russell, who was convicted of three especially brutal murders. The murders took place in Bellevue, Washington, a suburb east of Seattle, in 1990. HITS personnel contributed two types of assistance. Initially, HITS staff advised Bellevue detectives that the first murder was unique—there was nothing else like it in their database. HITS went on to recognize the second murder in the series by comparing characteristics of it with the first and observing certain similarities between the two. Testimony from HITS staff at the trial revealed that all three murders in the series were definitely committed by the same person.

The series of murders began in the city of Bellevue, a model central business district and shopping mall that is surrounded by middle-income apartments and condominiums. It is a singles paradise with bars, restaurants, and clubs that cater to a young, lively crowd. Many of the men and women who live there have jobs by day and cruise for company at night. Any Friday or Saturday evening, the local mating rituals can be observed in bars at the El Torito, Black Angus, Papagayo's, or Cucina Cucina restaurants. This setting was the perfect location for a gregarious, smooth-talking serial killer to strike successfully.

The Mary Ann Pohlreich Murder

This case began with the startling discovery of a body in an alleyway behind the busy Black Angus. On June 23, 1990, just after 7:30 A.M., an employee of the McDonald's located adjacent to the Black Angus found the murdered female.

The crime scene photographs centered on the single grim, motionless female stretched upon the pavement. Her body was clearly posed; there was no question that whoever committed this terrible atrocity didn't mind spending a considerable amount of time with the victim after death. The body was displayed in a busy area—the killer obviously wanted his work to be discovered quickly—nude and arranged to send an unmistakable message of sexual degradation. The victim was left lying on her back, with her left foot crossed over the instep of her right ankle. Her head was turned to the left and a Frito-Lay dip container lid rested ominously on top of her right occipital orbit. Her arms were bent at the elbow and crossed over her abdomen with her hands gently touching, one inside the other. In one hand, detectives found a startling piece of evidence: a Douglas fir cone. What did this clue represent? Only her dreadful slayer knew.

The victim's gold watch on her left wrist and her gold choker chain with a crescent-shaped white pendant around her neck were the only personal items left on the otherwise nude corpse. Noting that the especially aggressive predator was careful to remove all of the victim's clothing, I figured that he was either too pressed for time to strip her of her jewelry or he didn't see any value in the pieces and deliberately left them as adornments to the body.

The surface of the garbage area, uncommonly clean, was a cement rectangle bordered by the asphalt pavement of the parking lot. A pile of debris was within three feet of the victim's head and two brooms were leaning up against the wooden fence that enclosed the area on three sides. The body was discovered near the unfenced side. In front of the trash compactor, several bloodstains and chips of fingernail polish from the victim were found. It could be assumed from this evidence that the killer had taken the victim deep into the trash area, as if he was going to deposit her in the Dumpster but then decided to display the body prominently back toward the opening, where it could be clearly seen.

The victim had wounds indicative of strangulation; severe blows to the right eye, nose, and mouth; and abrasions—received after death—to the right arm, right breast, both hips, knees, and feet. These postmortem injuries were produced when the killer dragged the body about 20 feet along the parking lot surface inside the fenced garbage area. The injuries Pohlreich had received before death looked like defense wounds, suggesting that she had put up a struggle when attacked.

The medical examiner had determined that death took place between 2:30 and 5:20 A.M. A late-night Black Angus worker who had dumped garbage at 3:15 A.M. said the body was not there at that time. Since the body was discovered within four to five hours after death, we concluded that the woman was probably killed someplace else and brought to the Dumpster.

The autopsy examination revealed blunt impact injuries to the head that produced a fracture to the right base of the skull and similar marks on the abdomen that caused a laceration of the liver. The medical examiner found the victim's stomach empty and her toxicological screen showed a blood alcohol level of .14. The victim had been raped, her anus had been severely lacerated with a foreign object, and sperm was detected in her vagina.

On June 27, 1990, the victim was positively identified through dental records as Mary Ann Pohlreich. Her identity was revealed after a search of local police missing-persons reports. Mary Ann Pohlreich was white, 27 years old, 5 feet 7 inches tall, 150 pounds, with light brown shoulder-length slightly curly hair and blue-gray eyes. She was last seen alive on Friday, June 22, 1990, at about 10 P.M. at Papagayo's Cantina, a popular singles bar and dance spot. Papagayo's is located about one mile northwest of the Black Angus Restaurant. Pohlreich's 1984 Chevrolet Camaro sat undisturbed in Papagayo's parking lot. Her purse, which contained her car keys, was found later in the lost-and-found property at Papagayo's.

Detectives surmised that Pohlreich had met someone at Papagayo's with whom she left after 10 P.M., intending to return and retrieve her purse and car. She was assaulted and murdered at an unknown location nearby and placed behind the Black Angus after 3:15 A.M.

Evidence from the murder suggested that it had been a sexual confrontation gone bad. The circumstances surrounding the victim's disappearance support the theory that Pohlreich left the bar with a date, intending to return. Judging by the number of defense wounds and the blunt-force injuries inflicted by the killer, Pohlreich put up quite a struggle prior to death and left her mark on him. Undoubtedly, the killer had to wash her blood from himself.

The rape-murderer rarely gets any sexual pleasure from the actual killing of the victim. But in this case it seemed the killer derived great satisfaction from his postmortem sexually sadistic activities. He must have spent a considerable amount of time with his dead victim behind the Black Angus. He took the time to carefully arrange her body in its final pose even though the macabre ritual greatly increased the risk that someone might see him with his victim. This after-death victim–offender contact demonstrated the complete possessiveness and ultimate degradation of the female victim by the killer, a modus operandi typical of Ted Bundy. Pohlreich, therefore, was not killed by some common rape-murderer, because the signature of the crime belonged to someone fitting the necrophilic profile of a serial killer.

The Pohlreich homicide was an analyst's ideal case because it contained many distinctive query features that could be fed into the HITS computer for a search for a match of similar features. The Pohlreich murder had three unique, significant characteristics that when taken collectively did not appear in any of the 2,000 murders in the HITS database.

First, posing a murder victim's body was very rare. The analysis of murder victims revealed that there were only six instances—two tenths of one percent of the total cases—of murder in which a victim's body was posed. In one case of posing, a deranged killer repositioned mutilated and amputated body parts back in their correct anatomical positions. Posing is not to be confused with staging, which refers to manipulation of the scene around the body. In 1974, convicted murderer Tony Fernandez killed his wife and staged the death scene. To cover up her murder, Fernandez placed her body behind the steering wheel of their motor home and pushed it over an embankment, hoping to make the murder look like an accident. Both staging and posing require that the killer spend extensive time after his victim's death arranging things in a certain way.

The second unique component of Pohlreich's murder case was the disposal of her body. There are only three notable methods that a killer uses to dispose of a victim's body. With the most common method, employed by murderers 58 percent of the time, the body is left in a position that reflects that the killer is unconcerned about whether the body is found. That usually occurs in domestic violence and argument murders, when the body is left where it fell at the moment of death. A second method of disposal, used 10 percent of the time, is deliberate concealment of the body. Common methods of concealment include burying the body, placing the body in a crawl space of a house, or putting leaves or branches over the body in the woods, much like the Riverman had done. Leaving the body in a specific location where the body is guaranteed to be found, the third method of disposal—also used 10 percent of the time—is commonly referred to as "open and displayed" and is similar to the method used in the Pohlreich case.

The third significant characteristic of murder in the Pohlreich case was sexual insertion of a foreign object into a cavity of the body. HITS analysis revealed that there were 19 cases recorded in their system that involved a foreign object inserted into a body cavity. Examples included cases in which a zucchini was found in the anus of one victim and a dildo was found in the vagina of another. Only 1 percent of 2,000 murders in the HITS database had any evidence of sexual insertion of foreign objects.

Through June 1990, there were no murder victims listed in the HITS system that had all three characteristics of the Pohlreich murder—posing, sexual insertion of a foreign object, and open display of the body—present simultaneously in the same case. To find all three of those crucial factors was indeed a remarkable and horrifying occurrence. Unfortunately, experience led me to believe that Pohlreich's killer would strike again.

The Carol Ann Beethe Murder

On August 9, 1990, 47 days after Pohlreich's body was discovered, a relative found Carol Ann Beethe's dead body in the bedroom of her ranch-style one-story house. Beethe's home was located in a typical middle-class suburban bedroom community and was bordered on each side by neighboring houses. Within the city limits of Bellevue, Beethe's residence was less than two miles from the Black Angus Restaurant where Mary Ann Pohlreich was found murdered. A dime on a Thomas Brothers' street map covered both scenes.

Carol Beethe was the single mother of two daughters, ages 9 and 13, who were asleep in their shared bedroom only 15 feet from the entrance of Carol's bedroom on the night of her murder. Beethe was white, with collar-length light blond hair, 5 feet 2 inches tall, and weighed 108 pounds. She was last seen entering her home alone by a neighbor who was out walking by himself at 2:30 A.M. on August 9, 1990. Beethe had been visiting a bartender friend of hers at Bellevue's Keg Restaurant, another singles hangout. Beethe herself was a bartender at Cucina Cucina Restaurant in Bellevue.

Deliberately arranged by the killer, the crime scene was a ghastly sight. Beethe was carefully positioned in open display on top of her bed. She was naked, lying on her back, with a pair of red high heels on her feet. Her limbs were completely splayed and her exposed groin was facing the doorway of the bedroom. Inserted in her vagina was the barrel of an over-and-under rifle–shotgun combination, with its stock resting across her shoes. The weapon belonged to the victim. Detectives thought for a while that a pillow covering Beethe's face was used to smother her until they carefully lifted it and found that her head was wrapped in a plastic dry-cleaning bag after she died. Was the intruder readying Beethe's body for removal from her house by placing her battered head in a plastic bag before he changed his mind and left her in her own bed? We wondered.

Carol Beethe was savagely beaten—much more than was needed to kill her—with an unidentified blunt object that left forked or Y-shaped impressions all over her head. She had two defense wounds, one on each hand. Police determined that the gun and shoes were placed in and on the victim after death. The bedroom had not been ransacked, although jewelry and cash were taken. The house door to the victim's bedroom was closed and locked; the murderer had come and gone through an open sliding-glass door to her bedroom. The murder weapon was not found.

Beethe's murder, like Pohlreich's, was extremely unusual. To the inexperienced observer, they were quite different. But HITS analysts discovered the three similarities between the Pohlreich and Beethe murders. Based on the extremely rare occurrence of posing, insertion of a foreign object into the body, and openly displayed bodies in two murders within 50 days of each other in Bellevue, investigators should have concluded that both murders were the work of the same person. These were the signature of one killer in particular.

Unfortunately, Bellevue investigators had drawn different conclusions. They focused their investigation on Beethe's boyfriend. The boyfriend had an alibi for the time of Pohlreich's murder, and at least one police investigator was initially reluctant to accept any theory that Beethe was killed by the same person who killed Pohlreich.

The Andrea Levine Murder

The body of Andrea Levine was discovered in her ground-level apartment in Kirkland, Washington, on September 3, 1990, 24 days after the murder of Carol Ann Beethe. Her apartment was within five miles to the north of the Bellevue Black Angus where Pohlreich's body was found.

Andrea Levine was white, with collar-length dark-red hair. She was 24 years old, 5 feet 4 inches tall, and weighed about 120 pounds. She was last seen alive around midnight at the Maple Gardens Restaurant in Kirkland on August 30, 1990. She was at the restaurant with her friends. Like Pohlreich and Beethe, Levine was known to frequent singles nightspots in the Bellevue area.

The display and postmortem mutilation of Levine's body confirmed that a sexually deviant serial killer was on the loose in the Bellevue area. Upon the discovery of this third murder, Beethe's boyfriend was dismissed as a suspect. The real killer would definitely have gone underground after being the central focus of the Beethe investigation. The boyfriend was too closely scrutinized to have continued a killing spree with the murder of Levine. The killer had not yet been under police surveillance and was still exercising his opportunity to kill.

Levine's nude body was left supine on top of her bed. A pillow covered her bloody cranium. Like Pohlreich and Beethe, the killer clearly posed his victim. Her legs were spread, a dildo was inserted in her mouth, and the book *More Joy of Sex* was cradled in her left arm. She had been bludgeoned about the head violently and repeatedly and she had sustained more than 230 small cuts over the entire surface of her body, including the bottom of her feet. The cuts were all made after Levine had been killed. It appeared that a ring Levine was wearing and all the knives in the house had been taken by the killer; the murder weapon was not found. Her pickup truck was parked in its normal spot outside and there were no signs of forced entry into the apartment.

The Killer's Signature

In her prosecution of George Russell, the suspect arrested and tried for the crimes, Rebecca Roe, senior deputy prosecuting attorney for King County, wanted me to consider the following question, independent of any facts connecting George Russell to any of the murders. Was there evidence beyond a reasonable doubt that

Pohlreich, Beethe, and Levine were murdered by the same person(s)? She provided me with all the case materials for an expert opinion. In most cases, I have few clues on which to base my analysis of murder investigations, and therefore it is often very difficult to determine the behavioral characteristics of the killer. But the Pohlreich, Beethe, and Levine cases were so rich in detail, my answer to her question was a clear-cut yes.

First of all, the Bellevue and Kirkland vicinity of King County had averaged only one murder per year for the preceding 10 years. Then, surprisingly, within 67 days, the locale experienced three atypical murders within a five-mile radius of one another. Were these the only crimes in the area? Was there any other activity that should have alerted police to the presence of violence in the community? At the very least, law enforcement officials should have realized that there was a murder problem beyond normal proportions. Crimes of this magnitude just don't take place in a vacuum. Ted Bundy's murders were part of a pattern of missing women, all of them Ted's victims. We knew that something was going on because of all the missing-persons reports. The Green River case involved a macabre circus of bodies popping up in the woods and out of the river. Those murders, too, coincided with a plethora of missing-persons reports, most of which turned out to be about victims of the Green River Killer. Therefore, in Bellevue there should have been some other turbulence that would have been a pointer to the three murdered women. In fact, that's exactly what did happen, but the homicide detectives wouldn't realize it until after the killer was already in jail on other charges.

Instead, the detectives focused their attention directly on the crimes in front of them and tried to see whether the three murders could be related. They began with the modus operandi. For purposes of comparing cases, police investigators traditionally have searched for characteristics that were similar—the modus operandi (method of operation) of the killer. Strictly interpreted, the way a murder is committed is controlled by the actions of the killer, based to some extent on the victim's response to the situation. For example, if the murderer in one case easily controls the victim, the killer will not change the modus operandi in the next case unless he/she has trouble controlling the victim. A killer might use strangulation in the first case, and in a subsequent case, to accommodate resistance by the victim, use a firearm because the strangling method was unsuccessful. Therefore, the killer's modus operandi can change over time as the killer discovers that some things he/she does are more effective than others. Going from the outdoor scene in the Pohlreich murder to the confines of Beethe's bedroom indoors is one example of a modus operandi change in the same series of cases. Also, sneaking into a bedroom while Beethe and Levine quietly slept instead of approaching them in a dating situation, as was done with Pohlreich, was another major change in modus operandi for the adaptable slayer. The killer felt more comfortable indoors.

The modus operandi of a killer is only the combination of those actions that are necessary to commit the murder. Because it can change, simply saying that the homicides can't be related because there are different modi operandi in a number of cases otherwise related by time, place, or area is foolishness. That's what kept the police in the Atlanta child murders and the Arthur Shawcross murders in Rochester, New York, chasing phantoms for so long. However, there are other crime scene indicators that relate murders even when the modus operandi changes. Many sexually sadistic repetitive killers, for example, go beyond the actions necessary to commit a murder. They are not satisfied with just committing the murder, but have a compulsion to demonstrate their own personal expression. The killer's personal expression is commonly referred to as his "signature" or "calling card"; it is an imprint he leaves at the scene, and in Ted Bundy's lingo, is whatever the killer "gets his rocks off on."

The core of a killer's imprint will never change. Unlike the characteristics of an offender's modus operandi, the core remains constant. However, a signature may evolve over time in cases where a sexually sadistic killer performs more postmortem mutilation from one murder to the next. The FBI's behavioral scientists have said that the elements of the original personal expression become more fully developed. Unfortunately, a signature is not always recognized at the crime scene because of decomposition of the body or interruptions in the killer's routine, like the presence of unexpected witnesses.

John Douglas of the FBI's Behavioral Sciences Unit has described the etiology of the signature as the person's violent fantasies, which are progressive in nature and which contribute to thoughts of committing extremely violent acts. As a person dreams and thinks of his fantasies over time, he develops a need to express those violent fantasies. Most serial killers have been living with their fantasies for years before they finally bubble to the surface and are translated into deeds. When the killer finally acts out, some aspect of the murder will demonstrate his unique personal expression, which has been replayed in his fantasies over and over again. It's not enough just to consummate the murder; the killer must act out his fantasies in some manner over and beyond inflicting death-producing injuries. For example, some lust-killers have a need to bludgeon excessively, carve on the body, or leave messages written in blood. They rearrange the position of the victim, performing postmortem activities that suit their own personal desires, and in essence, leave their psychopathological calling card. That's what happened in the case of George Russell.

The Story of George Russell

George Russell, the man who was ultimately convicted for the three murders on the basis of evidence and a pattern-murder profile, was a living example of the changing face of serial murder. He was truly a serial killer of the '90s: a black man from an educated middle-class family who grew up in a white neighborhood and socialized easily in the Seattle yuppie singles community. Russell recognized no racial barriers and therefore was not restricted by them. Like other serial killers who live in the community where they pick up their victims, Russell frequented singles bars and restaurants, dated and lived with young women from different racial backgrounds, and had a practice of robbing his friends. It is likely that his first murder—the imprinting or pattern murder—was a sexual assault/robbery gone awry.

George Russell was born in Florida to an unwed mother. His father probably abandoned his mother before Russell was born. Later, Russell lived in Washington, D.C., and, so people around him have said, his mother left him with family and friends from time to time. While in middle school, he lived with his mother and stepfather on Mercer Island, Washington, an affluent, exclusive upper-middle-class suburban Seattle community. Mercer Island is a five-minute trip across the East Channel Bridge and north up Interstate 405 to downtown Bellevue.

His mother wasn't living on Mercer Island long before she

moved out and left George in his stepfather's care. But George roamed the streets at will. George never finished high school, although he lived through his teenage years on the island, where the beat cops got to know him well. Many times they responded to burglary calls in the community to see George walking away from the scene. He was never carrying any stolen goods or property and was not picked up by the police. After a while, police suspected that he was ditching stolen items before they could arrive. He was always around when something bad was happening. George's rap sheet was littered with entries for criminal trespass, evading the police, and the possession of stolen property. Authorities could never pin a burglary charge on him, so he never spent time in prison; however, he had numerous short jail stays, but none for any sexual offense.

When he was 17, George left Mercer Island for Bellevue, where he lived a transient's lifestyle from the time he first arrived. He boarded with anyone who would take him in, and he could talk himself in anywhere. Most of his acquaintances thought that he always had a job—even though we could never find any records of long-term employment—because he always seemed to have enough money to get by. Police could locate only two employers; he was with each of them for less than two months. Two jobs in 15 years, yet the man always had money. That's why the police thought he must have been one of the best cat burglars in the area. But why did he start murdering?

Russell became a suspect in the three murders in Bellevue after an alert Seattle police detective, Rick Buckland, discovered that the residence burglary about which he was questioning Russell regarding possession of stolen property was close to the murder scene of Andrea Levine. Russell first came to Buckland's attention in May, 1990, after police responded to a call of a fight that had broken out between two men in downtown Seattle. As uniformed officers arrived, a black male who had posed as a police officer to the combatants was in the process of breaking up the fight. The officers were immediately suspicious of him because he seemed to be hiding something. There was a deviousness about him, so they questioned him further and patted him down. That was when they found the pistol he had concealed. He was arrested for impersonating an officer and taken into custody. The pistol was seized as evidence, traced on the computer by its serial number, and found to be stolen property taken in a burglary in the

Totem Lake area north of where Andrea Levine lived. They booked him under the Bellevue name of George Russell.

After Buckland confirmed that the stolen property in Russell's possession came from a Bellevue burglary near a murder site, he contacted Bellevue detectives Marv Skeen and Dale Foote. They, along with King County police Detective Larry Peterson, began winding a tight web of physical evidence around Russell while they hoped they could find another reason to take him into custody and hold him. They were not disappointed because Russell's murder spree was still under way. The start-stop sequence to the three murders had appeared arbitrary, but it was not. The killer wanted to strike again. At the same time, Bellevue police were actively searching for some way to catch Russell in the act. They were on the hunt for the man they believed to be their serial killer. Their only question was whether they would catch Russell in the act or have another murder on their hands first.

On September 7, 1990, two weeks after the murder of Levine, Bellevue police flooded a residential area when a prowler call was sounded. Just as he had done years ago on Mercer Island, George Russell was walking slowly away when police spotted him nearby. Russell identified himself, as if he weren't doing anything wrong and had nothing to hide, but the police arrested him on a misdemeanor commitment warrant.

The police discovered that the complaining party was a female who was an acquaintance of George Russell, just like Andrea Levine had been. There was no doubt about it. Russell was stopped in the act of stalking his next victim's house. His setup was interrupted by an alert potential victim who called the police and became a living witness. Just like Carol DaRonch and Nita Neary had identified Ted Bundy, this woman had identified George Russell and perhaps saved the lives of many other potential victims.

Then the police pushed their investigation full steam ahead. First, they linked Russell to Pohlreich through a DNA analysis of Russell's semen that was found inside Pohlreich's body. Then, when detectives interviewed Russell's friends, they discovered that Russell had borrowed a friend's pickup on the night of the Pohlreich murder. Russell returned the truck with a foul smell inside the next morning. He gave his friend money to have the truck cleaned. Even though the truck had been detailed twice, the detectives found Pohlreich's blood on the inside of the seat cushions of the truck. Detectives also found hair in some underwear discovered on Beethe's bedroom floor. That hair was "microscopically indistinguishable," the lab report said, from the head hair of George Russell.

In the Beethe and Levine cases, the physical evidence was not as conclusive as in the Pohlreich case, which made the signature testimony that much more crucial to the linking of all the cases. It remained to be determined, in linking the murders in the series, why Russell had changed his modus operandi even though his signature had not changed at all.

The Pohlreich murder, we theorized, was more like an experiment at first—a sexual assault or robbery gone awry because the victim fought off Russell too hard. Russell might have been surprised by what happened and by what he did. Thus, the actual murder itself might have even been a mistake because what Russell ended up doing was not what he set out to do. But it gratified him nonetheless. In wanting to control Pohlreich for his own sexual gratification, Russell misjudged her ability to resist his attacks. He hadn't planned on this. After all, he was a quintessential cat burglar, a thief of the night, and confronting someone in an outdoor, nonresidential situation with witnesses who could come around the corner at any moment was way out of his league. But Russell was nothing if not adaptable and quickly learned from his mistake. He also learned that control of the dead body was pleasurable. So he changed his method of operation while reserving for himself the pleasure of posing, fondling, having sex with, and controlling the victim after death. He resumed his old method of breaking into homes in darkness to find his victims.

During the course of the murders, Russell stole rings belonging to Beethe and Levine. The theft of the rings was interesting to me since most serial killers steal items belonging to victims. Frequently, family members or acquaintances of the killers unknowingly end up with those items as the killer circulates them among his group to get rid of potential evidence, while at the same time keeping them in sight. It's a way of reviving the thrill without storing potentially incriminating evidence in your own closet. Detectives Skeen and Foote tracked Beethe's ring to a friend whom Russell had tried to convince to buy it. Larry Peterson recovered Levine's ring, which had passed through several people all the way to Florida.

Russell knew that the police would search his apartment. In a final act of bravado, he called his female roommates and had them present to police, upon their arrival, a 1973 FBI evidence handbook. This was Russell's way of announcing his invincibility by implying, "you're not going to find anything because I know your business, too." Russell was still trying to assert control, to maintain his sense of significance even though he knew the police were hot on his trail. But Russell was wrong. This was 1990, not 1973. His edition of the evidence handbook didn't include DNA analysis, nor did he anticipate the thoroughness of the detectives' search for evidence. At Russell's apartment, a gym bag he always carried was recovered, and inside it was human head hair belonging to Andrea Levine.

In the subsequent murder trial of George Russell, my testimony was simple: the killer's personal expression was permanently etched on the bodies of Pohlreich, Beethe, and Levine. When I analyzed the murders by type and frequency of injuries and other unique characteristics from the first murder to the third, I drew only one conclusion: they were all committed by the same person.

I recognized the distinctive aspects of the killer's imprint. First, all three victims were intentionally left so someone would find them. They were not concealed or hidden but were placed in locations where they would be discovered quickly. The killer left them openly displayed, knowing that whoever found them would be shocked, both physically and psychologically.

Second, they were posed in a sexually degrading positions. The killer got a thrill out of demonstrating their vulnerability after death. Moreover, only implements that the killer found at the scene were used for their portraits. He did this consistently in all three murders. For example, he used a pinecone with Pohlreich, Beethe's red shoes, and Levine's book about sex.

Third, the killer used foreign objects in sexual orifices as part of his protocol. The actual object was absent in the Pohlreich case. The act of sexually inserting foreign objects and leaving them in their cavities evolved from the first murder through the third. It became more of a need for the killer to demonstrate his personal expression by leaving a rifle in Beethe and a dildo in Levine's mouth.

Fourth, the presence of all three of those relatively rare characteristics in each of the three murders was a very extraordinary occurrence. Notwithstanding the fact that the murders were committed in a small geographical area, the chain of those unique characteristics was the fundamental aspect of the killer's signature.

Fifth, the strength of the defense each victim was allowed to put up decreased from the first murder through the third murder. Pohlreich had multiple defense wounds, Beethe had two small defense wounds, and Levine did not have any defense wounds. The state of mind of the killer was influenced by the struggle put up by the first victim, so subsequent victims were not allowed any chance to fight back.

Sixth, the killer spent an increasing amount of time with each victim after death, rearranging their bodies in their final death poses. Remaining for any amount of time behind the Black Angus Restaurant and at the outdoor scene of Pohlreich's killing was very risky, since someone could come upon the scene and interrupt the killer. Therefore, very little time was spent arranging Pohlreich's body. The killer was with Beethe, injuring and arranging her body, for a longer period of time than he was with Pohlreich. With Beethe's bedroom door closed, the presence of her sleeping children in the house posed no immediate threat of discovery to the killer. Levine's apartment was conducive to taking even more time since she lived alone. Assaulting Levine with those fatal strokes, carefully cutting her over 230 times, and dutifully arranging her body probably took a considerable amount of time, at least more than it took to pose Pohlreich and Beethe.

Seventh, the number of injuries sustained by each victim increased from the Pohlreich murder through the Levine murder. Pohlreich sustained just enough injuries to cause her death. Beethe was beaten severely, more than what was necessary to kill her. Levine was also beaten excessively and cut extensively. The increasing number of injuries reflected the killer's need to exercise absolute possession by creatively defiling their bodies.

I summarized that the gradual increases and decreases in certain acts—inflicting an increasing number of injuries in each case, spending more and more time after death with each victim, and reducing the participation on the part of a live victim from the first case to the last—in conjunction with open display, posing, and sexual insertion of foreign objects were the specific factors that identified the signature of the killer in the Pohlreich, Beethe, and Levine murders, leading to the conclusion that they were all killed by the same person.

George Russell was a lot like Ted Bundy. The most obvious similarity was the considerable amount of time he spent with his victims after death. But George's murders were ultimately flawed by his passion, his need to display his hatred, and his need to display his bodies in hopes that they would be found quickly to preserve the element of shock and surprise. George had to be in control, but he misunderstood control and thereby created the conditions for his own capture. Bundy, on the other hand, covered his signature by assuring that not only would his early victims not be found right away, but that when they were discovered, there would be nothing left but bones. His signature was buried along with his victims, and any physical evidence directly linking him to the crimes was buried as well.

The inception and development of HITS helped catch George Russell even though he broke all the rules of serial murder that Ted had laid down during our years of discourse. Russell didn't simply attack prostitutes on the street like the Green River Killer did. He broke into people's homes in the night, killed them in their beds, sexually violated their corpses in the most gruesome ways, and then displayed them like trophies for people to find the next day. He degraded his victims by posing them in their full sexual vulnerability. In death, they displayed the helplessness of the final moments of their lives, when Russell was beating them until the bones in their skulls shattered. But even the beating was part of his need to control. Serial murderers kill out of a need to control people because they can't control anything else in life. In those moments just before and after the death of their victim, their need to control is gratified the most. And very, very few of these killers know how to cover up their signatures completely once they've expended their lust on a lifeless victim. Not even Bundy could cover up all his tracks; neither could the Green River Killer.

13

Suspects

The "My Case" Syndrome

When there are an extraordinary number of murders occurring within a certain geographical area, especially if they are in different jurisdictions, there seems to be a resistance or hesitancy, political or otherwise, to approach those murders as if they were committed by the same person. Why?

It's because police officers have continually investigated one or a pair of killers for just a single murder. Murders committed by the same killer over time are unusual for most agencies. They don't know how to react because they've never investigated related murder cases before. So they end up using traditional single-murder investigative methods just as they have done in every murder case that came before. That reaction is a conditioned response, not the product of Sherlockian deduction. No matter what the type of case, investigators take the wrong approach by starting with the thought, *It's okay, I can do it myself.* It's worked that way before. The illusion has been emphasized over time at the expense of logic by the way cases have been assigned and followed up. The supervisor assigns a detective to a case. That detective has some help with the initial investigation, but when the heat dies down, it's all his. His name is on the folder. So what's developed is a "my case" attitude. Anything that comes in regarding that one case goes to detective so-and-so. Other members of the department relinquish all responsibility for the investigation, thereby placing it solely in the hands of one unwitting detective.

The dangers of this attitude are very real and very large. One detective is left with only what worked in the past—looking for suspects within the closed circle of a victim's acquaintances. How can a lone detective investigate a case that might have multiagency implications? When all the traditional investigative options are exhausted, what does the detective do? Indecision on the part of the investigator, lack of alternatives, and delays in pursuing strangers play right into the hands of the multiple killer. By the time the detective completes a routine investigation, he or she is already many steps behind the killer, and more than likely, the killer has probably murdered again and again. Serial cases call for a traditional investigation of the victim's acquaintances as well as an investigation of suspects who are complete strangers.

Institutionalized Separateness

Another infirmity that cripples serial-murder investigations from the very start is institutionalized separateness. Members of one department just aren't used to working with members of other departments who are pursuing the same killer. The hesitancy agencies have about working together comes from the memory of how previous cases that were shared among different precincts or counties were handled when things were going badly—certainly it was the other guy's fault. And when things were going right, the credit wasn't equally shared. The dynamic is unfortunately horribly infantile, like two high-school girls bickering over the same boyfriend. The cold reality here is that the killer knows that this is exactly what happens. The more cunning killers intentionally abduct victims from one jurisdiction and eventually dump their bodies in another jurisdiction because they know the bickering alone between members of different departments will delay or even prohibit any meaningful investigation.

Whatever the reason for the resistance to recognizing the serial, many investigations have suffered for it. In the beginning of the

Bundy cases, there were those who didn't believe that the victims at the Issaquah crime scene were related to women found at the Taylor Mountain site. Why? Because no one knew how the killer approached any of the Taylor Mountain women until the witnesses came forward in the Susan Rancourt case from central Washington. Even once the information became available, there were still doubters.

The Bobby Joe Long Case

This attitude, apparent in the early stages of the Bundy investigation, was not unique. The early investigation into the victims of Bobby Joe Long, who raped and murdered at least 11 women in Florida, suffered from the same malady. The method of death was so different from one body to another, and the fact that victims came from various backgrounds had police officials publicly saying that there was no serial. Only when conclusive evidence was found—that of an orange trilobal fiber, which was discovered in each case by the FBI laboratory—did investigators link the victims together and conduct a meaningful follow-up investigation.

In spite of their experience with Bundy eight years before, some investigators in the King County Police Department didn't believe the five victims in or near the Green River were killed by the same person who murdered the prostitutes whose bodies were found on land at the north and south ends of Sea-Tac Airport or east of Enumclaw. If that resistance indicated the prevailing attitude, how diligent were those very investigators in pursuing the theory that they were all murdered by the same person? Could their beliefs have been so clouded that their motivation to investigate thoroughly was stifled? Not wanting to admit the presence of a serial-murder case makes it next to impossible to go through any list of suspects with any degree of accuracy. It leads only to a more tense and ugly situation.

My approach to linking cases has been borne out by misinterpretations in the investigations of killers such as Bundy, Russell, Long, and others like New York's Arthur Shawcross and Atlanta's Wayne Williams. All of these killers' victims were found within a reasonably small geographical area and they drove the number of murders in the area above the average. The respective

353

investigations all began in the same way, with the disbelief that the victims were killed by the same person. Even at the earliest stages of the Green River cases, common sense told us that over 90 percent of the victims we discovered during the course of the Green River investigation were murdered by the same person. There are not five or six different killers thrown into the mix. A serial-murder case that has been filtered by reluctance and politics heavily bends the outcome of that investigation in favor of the killer.

For most serial-murder cases, there were no clear guidelines to alert police to the fact that they were dealing with a serial killer. And once the series was identified, there still were no standard operating procedures or textbooks that detailed the proper way to pursue a serial murderer versus a single-victim killer.

Hot Suspects

A nonsystematic investigation of random suspects in a serial-murder case can be a dangerously hypnotic fascination that leads nowhere. Haphazard pursuit of innocent people plagues every serial investigation. Since these cases generate hundreds of suspects, usually in a very short period of time, the investigation gets instantly bogged down because the pursuit of suspects is not systematic. The reason for this problem is inadequate experience among supervisors and investigators in establishing priorities for follow-up. They don't know whom to investigate first.

Every investigation has its hot suspect. The downfall of most investigations is the haste and intensity with which the hot suspect is pursued. Everyone drops everything they're doing to concentrate on one person, and, after a while, the hot suspect fizzles. The time wasted pursuing that suspect puts investigators that much farther away from the real killer. The lack of a clear priority system for suspect investigations results in some suspects being partially investigated, in their elimination being postponed by investigations of a "better" suspect, in having to play catch-up, and in a feeling of being overwhelmed by masses of work.

The Yorkshire Ripper

The hot suspect is usually defined on the whim of the most vocal supervisor. Determining which leads to follow in order to develop a good suspect is as difficult as defining the hot suspect. Some information, coming in the form of tantalizing false leads, called red herrings, takes the investigation in wrong directions. For example, in the Yorkshire Ripper cases in England, a parliamentary review criticized investigators for giving excessive credence to letters thought to have been written by the killer and cassette tapes believed to have been dictated by the killer. Ripper task force investigators expended thousands of hours trying to track the source of both. Finally, when Peter Sutcliffe was apprehended, it was discovered that he was not responsible for either the tape or the letter. It is very difficult to avoid these false leads in the complexity of a serial-murder investigation. Unfortunately, they will probably always be one of the obstacles. The false leads in this case actually took police away from the real leads and needlessly prolonged the investigation.

There is a grim reality to serial-murder investigations. As the body count increases, the elimination of suspects becomes easier because there are more dates, times, and locations to link to any one particular suspect. If a suspect wasn't available for one murder in the series, he's eliminated from consideration and further investigation. As aptly pointed out by members of the Ripper task force, there is a danger in using eliminating factors unless they are conclusive. Therefore, corroboration of information concerning the whereabouts of people is crucial. So many times investigators are fooled by their own records. For instance, a frequent eliminating factor is whether the person was in jail on a certain date. At first blush, the custody status of a person is usually reliable, until the policies of the jail are checked out. A rap sheet may show a person in jail on certain dates, but what the rap sheet doesn't say is that the person was on work-release for several weeks of the custody. So this means the suspect was on the loose for some hours of the day. Undoubtedly, the cautious investigator will go beyond what's listed on a rap sheet to confirm eliminating information.

Confusion of Leads

Another unpleasant and wasteful characteristic of previous serial-murder investigations was that large amounts of information flowed through many hands, resulting in duplication, confusion, untouched leads, numerous individual priorities, tunnel vision, investigations on tangents, and an almost total lack of coordination and direction. In the Atlanta child murders investigation, the task force received as many as 7,500 calls a day; the Ted task force took about 500 calls a day. When vast amounts of information like this are coming in, it is best to designate one person through whom all incoming information must flow first. Leads then can be assigned based on viable investigative priorities that have been set. It is important to note as well that those priorities must be constantly reviewed for their effectiveness.

The best way to monitor incoming leads and sort and organize information is through the use of a computer. As the investigation becomes more complex with additional contacts and companion cases, a system in place will reduce major time-consuming tasks. As much as Bundy and I discussed the utility of lists of names in searching for suspects, he never realized that using the computer to examine lists of potential suspects was the very act that enabled us to discover his name from a large pool of suspects. In spite of my repeated attempts to explain the various lists of suspects we developed in the Ted murders, the light bulb never once went off in his head that I was telling him about a very useful strategy for identifying the killer in series of murders. Instead, he focused on staking out crime scenes or holding sex-slasher film festivals. To placate me, he finally conceded that making lists of potential suspects, based on information collected about the body recovery and abduction sites, and comparing one list against another would be useful. Maybe he did realize how we pinpointed him, but he masked it very well. He wasn't one to throw out a lot of compliments unless it was beneficial to him.

Bundy was very adamant about the importance of collecting additional data around the scenes of murders that seemed similar. Bundy's mind was so tuned into modus operandi, he was convinced that similar murders could be linked to the same killer if the characteristics of those murders could be analyzed in detail. From his standpoint, what he saw from the various crime scenes of murdered prostitutes in the Green River cases was that they were all the work of the Riverman. "Like I said, he got better over time." Bundy believed that the variation among dump sites was a learning experience for the Riverman. At first, the Riverman might have believed that placing bodies in the river was a good method of disposal, but that changed over time. He learned from previous mistakes and changed his modus operandi. If the police don't catch serial killers early, learning from experience will only prolong the killers' apprehension and cause further victimizations.

Bundy believed computers might help. At one point, he confidently asked that I outfit him with a computer and the necessary database program so he could examine the elements of each case more closely. He used computer information as a way to keep our conversations going since he knew that I favored that method.

The intelligence of HITS was based on the killer's methods: collect numerous details on each murder and those murders that are similar will stand out from the others. This very strategy made for a more productive investigation into the George Russell cases. Even though HITS didn't solve Russell's murders, it helped strengthen the prosecution against him. Data had been collected on all murders in Washington State dating back to 1981. By examining the three significant elements in Russell's murders (openly displayed bodies, sexual insertion of foreign objects, and posing bodies), the only murders found in the database belonged exclusively to one killer. Without that data, connecting the murders of George Russell might have been missed by the casual observer.

Serial Killers Do Leave a Trail

Even an elusive serial killer is not invisible. Accomplished murderers appear to be phantoms only because investigators haven't found a way to see someone that has been literally in front of their eyes. Morris Redding, the Atlanta task force commander, once said that Wayne Williams was "right in front of our noses." As officers were going into elementary schools to advise children to stay away from strangers, Wayne Williams was coming out after having taken their class pictures. Also, Williams pinned his recruiting posters to telephone poles near schools, and the police never picked up on it.

A remarkable feature of some serial-murder investigations is that the name of the killer is buried somewhere in the files within the first two weeks of the investigation. We had Bundy's name within a week of the Lake Sammamish disappearances. Los Angeles authorities had Kenneth Bianchi's name on a list of recruits for the sheriff's office. In both cases, Bundy and Bianchi were not immediately a focus for the investigations. With this in mind, a certain logic would tell investigators who are burdened with a long-term, unsolved serial investigation to carefully review the information received in the first two weeks of the inquiry. What information came in early in the investigation? In long-term cases, circumstances within the serial change over time, so examining the early leads based on information collected over time may help to prioritize certain suspects who would not have been originally classified as a top priority because of a lack of information.

In the midst of intense pressure and mountains of leads created in the serial investigation, what do law enforcement officers look for? How do they find that tree in a forest of suspects when every previous lead was useless? Surprisingly, numerous serial killers have been brought down by an unlikely source—the living witness, the one who has gotten way. There is nothing better than firsthand information. Somewhere, in most cases, a living witness has been located.

Both Ted Bundy and Wayne Williams had living witnesses who testified against them. In the Bundy investigation, witnesses surfaced before Bundy became a suspect. Outside the Fashion Place Mall in Murray, Utah, Carol DaRonch escaped from Ted's VW Beetle with one handcuff still locked around her wrist. Nita Neary surprised Ted inside the Chi Omega sorority house and he hightailed it out of there before she realized what had happened and could alert others. In Atlanta, after Wayne Williams was arrested and his name and picture were published by the media, several people came forward to report that they had seen Williams in the company of at least seven victims just prior to their murders. All these living witnesses provided crucial testimony against Bundy and Williams.

Wouldn't it be better if living witnesses could be found more quickly, before more victims fell prey to the killer? In examining the cases of Bundy, Williams, and other brutal creatures, a disturbing truth is evident: there were numerous witnesses who saw the killer and were unable to perceive him as a danger to someone else. But then after the killer's capture was publicized, these people came forward to report what they saw, retrospectively. The women who were approached on that Lake Sammamish beach and didn't help the good-looking Ted load his sailboat saw something less than circumspect. But it wasn't until the disappearances of Janice Ott and Denise Naslund were reported that they came forward. A major problem for all serial-murder investigations is always to sift through mountains of information to find those living witnesses who really saw the actual killer.

Creating Luck

Catching the killer or finding out his identity has been frequently termed serendipitous: some streak of luck suddenly entered the investigations. I believe luck is luck, but creative detective work is still required to turn that luck into a successful resolution of a case. Sometimes the careless killer has assisted police in finding him. For example, California and Oregon had been experiencing the murders of many males from the early 1970s until the mid-1980s. In 1986, Randy Kraft was spotted driving erratically by a California police officer. The unsuspecting officer soon discovered that the inebriated Kraft had the body of a murdered male in the seat next to him. Upon further investigation, detectives found the identification of many of Kraft's victims inside his home. It has been estimated that Kraft killed over 60 males in California, Oregon, and Michigan.

Sometimes officers create their own luck, as the Atlanta task force did with its strategic surveillance of the bridges across the Chattahoochee River when the infamous splash was heard. Then there was the string of prostitute murders I investigated in the late '70s near Seattle. We were looking for a dark green Dodge Charger, driven by a tall white male with bushy hair and wearing glasses. The Charger was linked to the location of a brutal murder of a prostitute; a witness had seen a man put a female in the trunk of his car about five miles from that same murder site. Meanwhile, Seattle police detectives were looking for a beat-up red pickup truck leaving the area where a prostitute's body was dumped in a related case. King

County and Seattle police detectives put out bulletins that described the green Charger and red pickup to all the police precincts within greater King County. On a Sunday, two Seattle Police undercover cops were working the noon to eight o'clock shift in West Seattle. The previous week they had been stopping green Chargers and submitting the field interview reports to detectives. After having made several stops, they were surprised to observe a green Dodge Charger pulling a red pickup with a chain, the two vehicles described in the bulletins. What luck! They carefully waited until the driver committed a traffic violation—failure to yield to oncoming traffic—and was almost struck by the oncoming car while making a left-hand turn. The alert officers noticed bloodstains on the car. An arrest was made, and in one heart-stopping lucky moment, the officers had solved a series of murders.

In spite of the fact that the media portrays serial killers as clever, intelligent, and careful, the glaring truth is that they really do not cover their tracks very well—thank goodness! In almost every instance in which serial killers have been apprehended, their homes and vehicles contained hairs, fibers, bloodstains, and other evidence that connected them to various victims. Proof of this is in the hundreds of exhibits that were introduced in their trials. In the case of Bundy, Utah authorities watched as he cleaned out the inside of his VW bug. But the subsequent search of his bug was conducted in a more thorough manner by detectives. They pulled out his transmission and found the hair of three victims where the gear shaft meets the housing. In the case of the killer who drove the dark green Charger, he cleaned out the inside of his trunk but forgot to look up and see the victim's fingerprint etched in blood on the inside of the trunk lid. And incredibly, a head hair belonging to Andrea Levine was found in George Russell's gym bag.

The Media

The last tip in the taxonomy of logic about serial murder investigations is that law enforcement officers must be careful about what they release to the press. Bundy's words constantly rang in my head as if said yesterday: "The police say far too much to the press." There was a cold reality to his warning. In the throes of a high-profile case, police officials find themselves constantly in a corner, obligated to say something new every day. The feature stories are almost predictable. At first, the columns cover the known facts in the case. As much as media folks think they are covering a story that the public has a right to know, they must realize that the public includes the only person who knows the whole story—the killer. With each new tidbit of information leaked or given to the media, the killer pieces together exactly how close the authorities are to him and changes his habits or works harder to cover his tracks.

When interesting facts dwindle, it's as if someone tosses a match into a volatile mixture. Reporters look for other angles, and they begin to write stories criticizing the investigative effort. If the police stop giving details of the investigation, it's a double-edged sword. The killer won't know what they're doing, which is the good side, but then the public may get the perception from the media that nothing is being done, or that the police are incompetent. Renewed funding concerns for a questionable investigative effort also arise when little information about the investigation is released.

The course of news stories in a serial investigation can almost be predicted. First, the press focuses on life histories of the victims. Then, profiles of leaders of the inquiry or crucial investigators appear regularly to keep the story hot. And, ultimately, editorials criticizing an apparent lack of effort on the part of police authorities cap off the coverage.

My reasons for talking to Bundy were simple. First, I knew there were other "Bundys" out there. His information about their habits and haunts would have a practical application in catching and convicting them in the future. Second, since we had an immediate serial-killer problem in Seattle, I wanted Ted to shed light on the behavior of the Green River Killer, from a killer's perspective. Just maybe we could gain some clue about how to identify the Riverman. And last, someday I wanted Bundy's unbridled confessions.

14

Final Confessions

I never underestimated the strength of Ted Bundy's manipulative powers; he demonstrated them even when he sat on death row. Every so often I read a newspaper article in which a legal analyst covered Ted's options if the U.S. Supreme Court were to refuse his latest appeal. But having seen Ted cleverly avoid the chair for over 10 years, I didn't pay too much attention to these pieces. I always leaned toward the belief that Ted would somehow have the proceedings delayed, no matter how many times the state tried to press forward. Numerous dates of execution passed. Though the signing of death warrant after death warrant was an often-repeated ritual for the governor of Florida, Ted had avoided being marched down the row to the electric chair. It was January 1989, and I was almost positive Ted would succeed in avoiding his sentence yet again.

Phone Call from Ted

It was not unusual for the telephone to ring in my office about once every 15 minutes with a detective on the other end of the line calling about a murder case. But the call I received in the second week of January 1989 was not one of those calls. It was Diana

Weiner, Ted Bundy's civil attorney. Her voice was firm and professional, as always, but underneath her perfunctory manner, I detected an element of doubt when we discussed whether Ted would win his latest appeal. She asked me if I would be willing to participate in a "debriefing" of Ted beginning the Friday before his latest scheduled execution date, should the Supreme Court deny Ted's latest appeal. Debriefing? What in the world did that mean, I wondered. Would Ted be willing to confess if the end were surely near?

I shrugged my shoulders and I grunted something close to a yes as Diana hurriedly tried to explain Ted's latest strategy for survival. My reception was ungracious; being part of a serial killer's scheme to avoid justice made my skin crawl. Bundy's plan was to give detailed information to me regarding the location of the remains of preselected missing women, so that detectives armed with this information would locate remains and "prove" his sincerity. Then other detectives and the family members of victims still missing would speak on Ted's behalf to the governor of Florida, who would delay the execution in order for Ted to confess, in detail, to the rest of the murders he'd committed and provide the locations of the bodies. This seemed to me to be an elegant form of extortion.

Ted's strategy was simple and direct, but there was one big obstacle to its success. There was no way detectives could mount a massive search party through the wilderness in the middle of winter to verify what Bundy had said; any bodies still to be discovered in Washington, Colorado, Utah, and Idaho were currently under three to six feet of snow. And, as we would discover later when we searched the areas for the remains that Bundy had indicated we'd find, there were shifts in the land that had taken place in the 15 years since he'd disposed of the bodies. For example, the road up the hill in Issaquah had moved at least 30 feet, and what used to be a rocky area near the Naslund and Ott bone finds was now covered with over 10 feet of dirt. Whether it was the natural changes in the land or not, the fact remains that no one ever found bodies in any of the areas where Bundy said he'd left them.

After Weiner's phone call I sat silently, thinking, *Leave it to Ted to come up with a wild scheme to once again horrify the family members of his victims by involving them in his vivid fantasy life.* Was this a cruel attempt by Ted to victimize those whom he had already left devastated by his carnage?

The next day Weiner called back and said that Ted's appeal had been denied and that she needed me in Florida on Friday. Still suspicious of being a part of Ted's end-game strategy, I contacted Pete Turner, the assistant warden in the Florida State Penitentiary, to verify with Ted that he wanted me there. Turner gave me the okay. I made the trip and scheduled the behind-bars meeting with my old nemesis.

The conditions for these debriefings were very different from the relaxed, almost casual air of my earlier conversations with Ted. Now the partitions between the cubicles in the debriefing area, instead of being wide enough for two people on one side, as is usual in most prison interview rooms, had barely enough elbow room for one person. The air was also very heavy because of the cramped conditions and the continual presence of the death-row prison guards. As Ted entered the interview area, he recognized FBI Agent Bill Hagmaier standing behind me. Their right hands met each other at the same place on both sides of the glass windows, oddly like lovers greeting each other in visitation areas. I was struck by the friendly gesture between the nation's most notorious serial killer and the FBI agent who represented his pursuers. Ted seated himself on his side of the glass and I on the other, with Bill seated to my right rear and Diana Weiner to my left rear. Because Ted wanted Weiner present, we had to have a noncontact visit—those were the rules when attorneys oversaw their clients' conversations with police. Ted's guards were stationed within shouting distance of where we sat.

I was interviewing Ted as a matter of record, no longer to solve the Green River murders per se. The Green River Killer himself had become history. The Green River task force was doing more archeology and record keeping than crime solving and in fact was about to fade away into history itself. It had been a good idea for Ted to join the Green River task force on an ad hoc basis, but his time was now past and he was looking at the reality of the electric chair. However, the time for Ted's confessions had come. His first-person account of his murders was what everyone anticipated and what I was now prepared to get. Still, there was some doubt about whether Ted would actually go through with this. He had gone for so long and built up such strong resistance against revealing anything self-incriminating that any discussion of his own activities would be incredibly stressful for him. As far as I knew, he had never admitted to any law enforcement officer the details of and personal motives behind his murders. Was he just playing another game? This time the game involved his life. I was the one person he had chosen to speak to and trust to relay to others the credibility he so desperately wanted to establish. He had coached me through our conversations and letters for four years. Now Ted had only three more days to live. The time had come and I was ready.

Ted was a man with an encephalitic head, a clear hairless face, a long thin nose, and a rather confident jutting jaw. The sight of him after all these years was still quite an experience. Ted rearranged his position on the other side of the glass. He left his chair and sat on the shelf so he could talk through the speaker hole for my ears only. Lifting the tape recorder to his mouth while engaging the RECORD switch, he began to speak.

Issaquah

"Okay, all right. Well, let's just do one here. I mean, let's start. Obviously, we have to start somewhere. It's pretty much a long shot, but you might be able to get something out of it, at least some of that so-called tangible evidence that might be of value not only to you but to others. Even if you don't find anything else, it might be of some value to families," Ted said, trying to play on the emotions of his victims' families in order for them to support his one great cause—staying alive through another set of appeals.

"Yes," I said, agreeing with just about anything he said just to keep him going.

"I understand that at the Issaquah site there were remains of three individuals found, two identified and one not, because the kinds of remains that were found were so few and unidentifiable. Okay, what do you want? Description of the site first? How to get there? I mean, you just don't make this up, right?" Ted said confidently.

I said, "I want to know what the site is."

Ted described the Issaquah site like he was replaying a videotape in his mind. With his eyes closed, he continued, "Well, old Highway 90, which is no longer there, not like it used to be, rose up out of Issaquah into the foothills. You rounded a bend about a mile and a half, two miles beyond that bend. This is fifteen-year-old stuff, so be mindful of it. It was not a divided highway at that time, so you could turn left clear across the highway as you are going east, at the risk of getting a ticket. There's a small dirt side road there. You could turn left going east, enter the side road, go over a ravine that was between the side road and the highway, turn sort of, go left again, and go back down toward Issaquah. Traveling on the side road you pass underneath some power transmission lines. There was a creek down in the ravine between I-Ninety and the side road. Maybe a quarter of a mile down this little side road, it would join Ninety again. But if you turned just about the time it reached Ninety again, there's another little dirt road to the right that went up a hill and across some railroad tracks. Just on the other side of the railroad tracks about twenty yards up, there's a little grassy area, some scrub growth and old alders. There is a little path that ran parallel to the railroad tracks and up into the woods, running sort of west. The dirt road went past this grassy area I just mentioned, and went up the hill maybe half a mile. It sort of meandered up the side of the hilly area. Also, in the area, maybe fifty yards to the east, down into another ravine, was an old abandoned cabin. Ring a bell?"

For a moment or two I was breathless and hardly able to believe my ears. This was the voice of the killer playing in my brain, the description, firsthand, of a site that only the killer had known. I was hearing it described through his eyes. My senses and my voice slowly came back to me. Now at last I could confirm that Ted really was the killer we had thought he was. There's nothing like a first-hand account. Ted had been on that hillside so often to relive his fantasies that he could never forget the surroundings.

Still somewhat stunned and momentarily searching my mind for any pertinent question, I asked, "Where should we have found the bodies?"

"Lord knows where and what the little creatures up there did. Well, let me start with one," Ted offered, a little bit unnerved by the presence of the officers who were standing behind him. He didn't want them to overhear that he was confessing. So he decided to whisper and write down any names. "Some of this stuff I don't mind talking about, because they wouldn't know them from Adam. I just don't want the police getting any kind of names at this point. I'll just write the name down for you. All right? Okay, did you see that? The name that I just wrote down was Georgann Hawkins," Ted whispered gently, nervously looking over his shoulder.

"Ummm . . . she's up that dirt road, beyond the grassy area. I'll try to trace it here on a piece of paper. How about that? That might help a little. I'm working from some pretty old memories."

At this point, I gave Ted an aerial photograph of the area as it appeared in March 1974. The photo was taken because there was a property dispute and it was needed for a possible civil suit. Eagerly, Ted said, "Oh, yeah, great. Let me try to orient myself here. Jeeze. Is it still relatively undisturbed? In their construction of the freeway, did they disturb up the hillside much?"

"There's some of that hillside left," I explained.

"This is where I get a little bit antsy, not about you, but it's just the chance of being overheard. There's some of this stuff that gets pretty tough. I can write it down, whisper it. I have no problem with that. I have to draw the line somewhere with being overheard at this point," Ted said.

I suggested, "Why don't you pull the mike closer to your mouth and try that?"

Georgann Hawkins

Ted was trying to write and hold the tape recorder, too. He continued by whispering what he just wrote, "Okay, I just wrote that the Hawkins girl's head was severed and taken up the road about twenty-five to fifty yards and buried in a location about ten yards west of the road on a rocky hillside. Did you hear that?"

How could I not? It was one of those dramatic moments for which Bundy existed. It would be an understatement to say that I was shocked by his amazing announcement. I detected a tinge of cruelty in his singular expression, and undoubtedly, he was callous from such a long period of denial. Yet, even though his emotions were dulled, his clinical account was exceedingly accurate.

Temporarily, my mind went blank. No one had guessed that Ted had decapitated victims and was a perverse mutilator. This news would shock his loyal Washington State friends and supporters. Fumbling for a question, I asked, "Where is the rest of her at?"

"Down where the others were. I gave you that because I felt that it might be worthwhile to start there because that one hadn't been discovered before," he said, unaware he had just unequivocally admitted to the Ott and Naslund murders, something that he had not done up to now. "That was more or less a question mark to a point. We all knew what the suspicions were, but basically the Hawkins family might be able to have information about those separate, unidentified remains. But in any case, I think that was a good place to start."

Little did Ted know that the family didn't want the remains. He wasn't doing Hawkins's relatives any favors. They had already told me that they didn't want them back. They had psychologically buried Georgann's soul long ago.

I was ready to hear the gory details. I inquired, "What was the damage to those remains? What instrument did you use?"

Ted answered as though he did not hear my question. He seemed to ignore me at certain times, perhaps to concentrate on whatever atrocity he was fantasizing about. "But not anything you would have found that I know of. If you'd found it, probably you'd have found damage to the head; the jaw in particular probably broken. But if you'd found that, you'd have known who it was. Is there any reason you asked me that question?"

The fractured crania and mandibles I picked up 15 years ago came to vivid life; their images raised themselves back into my consciousness and were as clear in my mind as if I had just come from the site. I responded, "What I wondered was, were similar things done to Ott and Naslund?"

Obviously, Ted didn't want to get into the Lake Sammamish murders because their remains had already been found. Describing their murders wasn't on his short agenda. He was more interested in talking about the murders that had gone undiscovered over the years. But he said, "We're getting a little bit ahead of ourselves, but I will say this much; no. Well, wait a minute. Now, that's a good question. Not similar things, not exactly. I don't want to beg the question, but they were different. Certainly not as extensive in those two instances as opposed to the Hawkins girl."

Impatiently, I asked, "Okay, what weapons did you use on the Hawkins girl?"

Ted wrote his answer on his pad of paper. He held it up for me to see. "Hacksaw."

Was Ted only going to recount where he buried a skull? Were we going to be left in the dark about how he had kidnapped Hawkins or any other woman?

Ted sensed that I wanted him to talk about how he had abducted Hawkins. The perplexed look on my face gave me away. Was he ready to reveal his long-held secrets? Ted said, "Well, we can go through it, step by step."

"Why don't we take Hawkins and go through it step by step," I suggested. Repeating Ted's own words back to him was a pre-planned interviewing technique I used once again to make Ted comfortable talking about things that he found difficult to discuss. He behaved as I hoped he would.

"Okay. Again, I wasn't specifically prepared to talk about this today," he admitted. "I'm just going to give you whatever comes to mind, and I'm sure that it's not everything."

Making Ted feel that his information was totally authoritative, as only information coming directly from the murderer's mouth can be, I suggested, "The elements of Hawkins, then we can get on to the others. I just want to hear, specifically, the events that happened with the Hawkins girl." Ted smiled as I continued. "The facts I have are basically what's in the newspaper. Tell me about how she was taken. What were the circumstances at the time? How did you get out there? What was the time period between the events of her abduction and murder?"

Ted closed his eyes once again. During his entire explanation, his eyes seemed shut tighter than the trap door that hid his thoughts. He said, "Okay, let me give it a moment's reflection here. Yeah. I'll talk real low to you. You can still hear me? Can you hear me, Bill? You can't?"

"Pull the recorder over a little," I instructed.

"I can't remember what night of the week it was—Thursday night, I believe. I don't know, eleven to twelve. Probably closer to twelve o'clock on a warm, Seattle May night. I think it was clear. The weather had been fairly good. At about midnight that day, I was in the alleyway behind the sorority and fraternity houses that would have been Forty-fifth, Forty-sixth, Forty-seventh Street, somewhere in there. In back of the houses across the alley and across the other side of the block, there was the Congregational Church, I believe, and some parking lots in back of the sorority and fraternity houses. I was moving up the alley, using a briefcase and some crutches, and the young woman walked down. I saw her round the north end of the block into the alley and stop for a moment and then keep on walking down the alley toward me. And about halfway down the block I encountered her and asked her to help me carry the briefcase, which she did, and we walked back up the alley, across the street, turned right on the sidewalk in front of the fraternity house on the corner there, and rounded the corner to the left going north of Forty-seventh.

"Well, midway in the block there used to be one of those parking lots they used to make out of burned-down houses in that area. The university would turn them into instant parking lots. There was a parking lot, dirt surface, no lights, and my car was parked there."

The tape recorder stopped with a loud click—of all the times for the tape to run out!

I felt the break might disturb Ted's concentration, but he changed the side of the tape and continued. It seemed he was going to confess, no matter what. With resolve, he continued, "We were to the car. All right, basically when we reached the car, what happened was, I knocked her unconscious with the crowbar."

I asked, "Where did you have that?"

Ted answered as though I should have anticipated that he had his weapons well stationed and readily accessible. "By the car."

"Outside?" I questioned in disbelief that he had laid the crowbar near the car.

"Outside, in back of the car," Ted verified.

Wondering how he leaned down and got it without alerting Hawkins, I asked, "Did she see it?"

"No, and then there were some handcuffs there, along with the crowbar," Ted whispered. "And I handcuffed her and put her in the passenger's side of the car and drove away."

Now it was becoming clear how Ted could have gotten an apparently intelligent woman into his car when the passenger-side seat was missing. He didn't have to convince them at all; he cold-cocked them from behind. They never knew what hit them and had no chance to resist. There was no verbal interplay here with the victim that Ted could hold over the head of the Green River Killer. Bundy did all his convincing from the business end of a crowbar while his victim's back was turned. He was not the phantom prince that crime writers and reporters had portrayed him to be for over 10 years, but a creep, a spineless, chicken-shit killer.

I asked, "Was she alive or dead then?"

Leaving no question unanswered, Ted said, "Oh no. No, she was unconscious, but she was very much alive."

I probed further. "Okay, what happened next?"

Ted was alerted by the footsteps of an approaching guard. Ted was entitled to a telephone call every hour from his appellate attorneys, and they were on the phone waiting to tell him the status of his appeals.

Ted returned in about five minutes and continued. "We drove down the alley to Fiftieth, I believe, Northeast Fiftieth or, you know, the street going east and west, and turned left. Went to the freeway. Five, is it? It's been a long time. Anyway, and then [we] went south on the freeway to turn off on the old floating bridge, I-Ninety. She was conscious at this time. I mean, she had regained consciousness at this time, basically. Well, there's a lot of incidental things that I'm just not getting into, you know, not talking about, 'cause they are just incidental anyway. We went across the bridge, across Mercer Island, east past Issaquah, up the hill, down the road, and up to the grassy area."

So far, Ted told his story in a way that I couldn't refute. It wasn't that I didn't believe him, but somehow I had to test his mettle. Realizing that I couldn't challenge him too much and risk shutting him up, I used a harmless question, designed not to scare him off. In 1974, the I-90 freeway did not have a barricade separating the westbound lanes from the eastbound lanes. I knew that he turned left across the westbound lanes to get to the dirt road as he had previously stated. But I defied his explanation by saying that it was impossible for him to have turned left because of a cement barricade blocking anyone's turn. "How did you get across I-90? There's a barricade in the middle of that road."

Defiantly, Ted asserted, "Not then there wasn't." Ted's words came much faster, and his voice was rising in pitch.

He continued, "Like I told you, at that time, you could make a left-hand turn, illegal as it may have been because of the double yellow line. Talk about craziness. I mean, if there had been a state patrolman, he'd probably [have] arrested me. Right?"

Without waiting for my nod of approval, he hurriedly and emphatically went on. "Nevertheless, at that time there was no divider running down the middle of that road at that point. I know. I mean, you're right. That would have been pretty damn hard to do if it were there. But all you had to do was just make an illegal left-hand turn all the way across the two westbound lanes of 90 and right into that side road that ran parallel to 90."

Convinced I could now recognize Ted's body language and style of speech when he was defending the truth, I asked, "Okay, what happened after that?"

A sudden defense of the truth was stressful for Ted, who lied his whole life. In fact, the momentary interruption caused Ted to become confused about his facts. He said, "Well, I parked, took her out of the van and took the handcuffs off her and—"

"Took her out of what?" I interrupted, knowing that Ted had a VW bug at the time, not a van. He was thinking about his last murder victim, Kimberly Leach.

"Took her out of the car," he said.

"And you're driving what?"

"A Volkswagen."

"Okay. You said 'van.' "

Apologizing, Ted said, "Well, no I didn't—I'm sorry if I said van; it wasn't a van."

At this point, Ted's attorney accused me of badgering Ted and I explained to her that Ted had said "van," and she thought I was putting words in Ted's mouth.

Ted reclaimed the interview by saying, "Well, okay. Well, it wasn't. It was a Volkswagen, and [I] took her out of the car. I think I said I took the handcuffs off. Maybe that sounded like 'van.' Anyway. And, gee, this is probably the hardest part."

Ted shut off the recorder. He regained his composure for a moment and turned it back on. "I don't know. I don't know, we're talking sort of abstract, not abstractly before, but, well, we're getting right down to it. And I will talk about it. I hope you understand it's not something I find easy to talk about after all this time."

Ted took a big sigh and said, "One of the things that makes it a little bit difficult is that at this point she was quite lucid, talking about things. It's not funny, but it's odd the kinds of things people will say under those circumstances. And she said that she had a Spanish test the next day, and she thought that I had taken her to help tutor her for her Spanish test. It's kind of an odd thing to say. Anyway."

Ted paused for what seemed like minutes but was only about 30 seconds. Another sigh, and then he approached the subject by saying, "The long and short of it, I mean, I'm going to try and get there by degrees. The long and short of it was that I again knocked her unconscious, strangled her, and drug her about ten yards into the small grove of trees that were there."

"What did you strangle her with?"

"Cord."

"Cord?"

Softly, like he was embarrassed, Ted said, "An old piece of rope."

Knowing that the rope was part of Ted's kit, I asked, "Is this something you brought there with you?"

"Yeah. Something that was in the car," Ted verified.

Expecting the gory details to follow, I asked, "Okay, then what happened?"

Ted changed course. His narration left out the time between one A.M. until dawn. He picked up with "Then I packed the car up. By this time, it was almost dawn. The sun was coming up. And I went through my usual routine. On this particular morning, I went through a frequent routine where I was just absolutely shocked, kind of scared to death, and horrified. I went down the road throwing everything that I'd had—the briefcase, the crutches, the rope, the clothes— just tossing them out the window. I was in a sheer state of panic. Just absolute horror, you know. At that point in time, the consciousness of what has really happened is like you break out of a fever or something. I drove east on I-90 at some point, throwing articles out the window as I went, articles of clothing, shoes, et cetera."

Since Ted neglected to describe when he removed her clothing, I asked, "When did you remove those?"

"What?" Ted said.

"The shoes, clothing?" I said.

"Well, after we got out of the car, initially. I skipped over some stuff there, and we'll have to get back to it sometime, but it's just too hard for me to talk about it right now."

For a short time, Ted went into his denial stage. He wasn't going to tell all just yet. He was saving the goriest of details until his execution was formally delayed. Gently, I inquired, "Do you remember what clothes she was wearing that night?"

Ted took time to gasp for air, then said, "Yup. A pair of white patent-leather clogs, blue slacks, some kind of halter top of which she had a shirt tied in a knot." Bingo. Ted just described her clothing without the benefit of any notes. For the first time, he said something that possibly only the real killer would have known. Still, I needed more.

"Okay. And where were these deposited?"

"Along the roadside. I mean, not right along I-90. I went east to the infamous Taylor Mountain Road. What highway is that?"

"Eighteen."

"At 18, turn right. Went south again and at some point, south of Taylor Mountain a lot of that stuff went out of the car. Down the embankments and what have you."

"Embankments?"

"Yeah."

"Did you have to pull over to do it or . . . ?"

"I would stop, pull over to the side of the road. At this time, it was pretty light out, and just tossed it out. There were sometimes I would do that and sometimes I wouldn't. At this point in time I was so frantic, so panicked, so whatever, about what had happened that I just had to get every reminder of that incident out of the car as quickly as possible. I didn't want to take it home, didn't want it to be around," Ted lamented. That part of Ted's modus operandi bordered on the disorganized edge of his personality. By his careless dumping of Hawkins's clothing and the implements of his murder, Ted was providing evidence that might bring him dangerously close to getting caught, and he knew it. The only problem was that no police officer was close by to observe him in action. Suddenly, Ted was not the clever and charming killer—he was showing his weaknesses. During the hours after his murders he was extremely vulnerable to detection. Possibly, other killers like Ted were equally vulnerable to capture during that time period.

"Did you throw away some of your own stuff?" I said in disbelief.

"Oh, sure. I threw away the briefcase and the crutches, all that stuff. And the crowbar, everything. The handcuffs, everything. I'd get mad at myself a few weeks later because I'd have to go out and buy another pair. I mean, it's not comical but that's what would happen," a smiling Ted admitted.

A flashback of the Issaquah crime scene began scrolling across my memory. I remembered one ESAR searcher finding an old rusty tire iron, and several people suggested that we just leave it. Not me—something told me to take it. There was no rational excuse for that tire iron being found in the woods along the Issaquah hillside. Certainly, no one would have been changing a tire out there. But murderous Ted Bundy had a reason to use it at that location.

Under the strain of the moment, Ted was beginning to become weary of talking without some positive support. Even he knew he could talk all day, but who would believe him? He needed to provide details that only the killer and the police would know. With that in mind, I posed a question to him. "Now that you've had a while to think about Georgann Hawkins, is there something you can tell me about her that probably only you know and we know?"

"Well . . ."

"I mean, the Spanish test is pretty darn good, if you ask me," I admitted.

"That's what she said, unless she was hallucinating. She said everybody called her George. Or how about that she used a safety pin to pin her blue slacks because apparently they were a bit too big."

Silently, I relished what he had just said. The safety-pin information was absolute confirmation. I tried not to let on what I knew. *Aha.*

"Or, that's about all I know. I'm sure there are bits and pieces that will come back to me, but there wasn't a lot, obviously, there wasn't a lot of conversation. But that's what comes to mind." Ted sighed as though there were no more convincing details he could supply.

"Okay, how about the other two sets of remains in that area?" I asked, forgetting that Ted refused to talk about the Ott and Naslund murders. There was a long silence. I could see that Ted was pondering whether to continue or deviate from his preplanned strategy. The longer the silence, the more I knew I had to ask him another question about Hawkins, so I could keep him talking. Grasping at anything, I said, "Oh, one other thing."

"Hmmm," Ted said as though it was about time I came up with a meaningful question.

Tapping on my clipboard with my pen and pointing to the word *sever*, I asked, "Oh, one other thing about Georgann Hawkins. When did that happen?"

"When?"

"Yeah."

"Well, May of . . ." Ted stammered.

"I know when she disappeared," I said quickly. "On June twelfth."

"Oh. June?" Ted chuckled. It seemed he was confused. He had murdered Roberta Parks and Brenda Ball in May of 1974, so the facts of another murder in June must have just run together in his mind with the other two. Ted frequently mixed the facts of his murders. After 15 years and so many victims, it was no wonder.

"The severing, when did that happen?" I continued.

"Oh, oh, oh, oh, that. Oh, excuse me. I was thinking of May, see? Ah, my memory. Oh, let's see. I'd say about three days later," Ted stated, opening his eyes and looking at me as if to see if I was believing his bullshit.

"Three days later?" I responded in astonishment. I felt Ted wasn't telling the whole truth. He didn't want to tell me that he removed her head the first day and took it home with him, as I suspected from the skulls without bodies I found on Taylor Mountain. I anticipated that he would come up with some feeble excuse why he removed it "three days later."

"Had you gone back there before that time?" I asked, trying to get him to explain his actions.

"Uh huh. The next day," Ted declared.

"The next day. What did you do the next day?" I asked sarcastically, knowing he wouldn't tell me about his necrophilic activities now.

Unconvincingly, Ted stammered, "Just went back to check out the site, make sure nothing had been left there. See, you know, the feeling is, I reached the point and half expected that she might not even be there. That somehow, I hadn't even killed her, if you will.

"So I went back—oh, yeah. Removed things like the rope. I— no, no, I had already done that. Can't remember if I found anything there or not. But I wanted to make sure. Oh, that's what it was. Talk about details coming back. I couldn't find one of the shoes, so I thought it was there. But it wasn't. So I went back—this was the next day—got on my bicycle, and rode back to that little parking lot. I knew there were police all over the place by that time, but I was kind of nervous—and I'll tell you why in a minute. 'Cause I'd left and my car had been parked there. Somebody may have seen it.

Now, if something was found there, it might connect me. So I went back to that parking lot at about five o'clock in the afternoon and found both pierced earrings and the shoe, laying in the parking lot. So I surreptitiously gathered them up and rode off."

Ted's postoffense behavior was an effort to cover his tracks and evidence of his otherwise organized nature. His disorganized behavior immediately after the murder of Hawkins, shown in his throwing away her clothing and his implements haphazardly, frightened Ted in his lucid moments because he couldn't deal with his own panic. This duality, this bipolarity between the panic at having touched something deep and terrible inside himself during the murder and necrophilic sex and the anal retentiveness of cleaning up every scrap of evidence at the contact and murder sites, might seem like some kind of split personality, but it wasn't. This was almost typical of control-type serial killers who allow themselves gratification with a corpse, only to be repelled by their own behavior in the hours immediately afterward. When the waves of panic subside, they become organized again and return to remove any signs of their presence. It's almost as though his organized self was knowingly protecting his disorganized self.

Ted believed that someone might connect Hawkins's belongings to him if they found them in the parking lot the next day. I found it difficult to understand why Ted was afraid of that, but it was part of his modus operandi, so I pursued it. "After the police had checked that area?" I asked, not to imply that the police had done a poor canvass, but to lead Ted along on his favorite subject, criticizing police investigations.

"Well, you can tell me. I'd seen whole streams of them driving around all over the place, but they were concentrating on places like the nearby parks. I bet you they couldn't have looked in that parking lot and missed the white patent-leather clog and two white pierced earrings—little hoops."

"That was discovered by you the next day?" I asked in amazement.

"Yeah. Around five o'clock, six o'clock," Ted proudly stated.

My curiosity took over. If Ted drove by Taylor Mountain in the early morning hours after he killed Hawkins, why didn't he take her up there initially or take the same power line road off Highway 18, where he had previously dumped Healy, Ball, Rancourt, and Parks, and dispose of Hawkins or her clothing in the same previously successful manner? So I said, "Okay, excuse me. After you left the Issaquah scene that night and went toward Taylor Mountain, did you go back to Taylor Mountain, knowing what was there?"

Before Ted even answered, I experienced a sinking and incredibly horrible sensation. The chills and goose bumps formed on the back of my neck; my stomach turned while I squinted at Ted, readying myself for his answer. A warning bell had just sounded loudly in my head. I had assumed there was a certain order to his murders: abduct, kill, and dump, then abduct, kill, and dump again. And when a previous dump site was not discovered, it could be used successfully again. The theory was that he abducted Healy on January 31, killed her, and dumped her on Taylor Mountain. Then Rancourt was abducted on April 17, killed, and her remains dumped on Taylor Mountain, and so on with the remainder of the women. The site had not been discovered, so he used it again and again. I had been dead wrong. Taylor Mountain was not the original dump site for those four young women, it was only where Ted had left their heads. But you try never to make a mistake with Ted, unless it's part of your plan, because you lose his confidence in your expertise.

Ted casually verified my realization by saying, "No. No, I wasn't going back. I just drove by there. That's all. It was along the highway. I didn't even slow down. Yeah, that was really not on my mind at that time."

Not really on his mind at that time. What a shocking statement. Taylor Mountain wasn't on his mind as a dump site at that time because their heads were someplace else—Taylor Mountain wasn't a dump site until much later. I would eventually learn that Ted had four heads at his rooming house, all stored together. I had realized that I had made a critically wrong assumption that all things happen in a certain predictable order. This is not the case with serial killers.

Other Murder Attempts in the U-District

Ready for something less traumatic, I asked, "Okay, so what happened in the next couple days?"

"Well, again, and this might be something you could plug into, if that's what you want to do. The reason I was so nervous about anything like that being found in that parking lot was that no more than two weeks before, I had been using the same modus operandi in the same neighborhood. In front, now, of the same sorority house that Georgann Hawkins disappeared from, I encountered a girl going out the door and asked her to help me. I walked her all the way to that lot, eleven o'clock on a Friday night. And I was drunk, and I was just babbling on. I told her I worked in Olympia, that I lived in a rooming house. I mean, I was just horrified later on."

"Were you drunk when you got Hawkins?" I asked, again in disbelief, this time because it seemed that his apparently frequent drunken states did not impede his ability to avoid detection.

"Yes, more or less, but yes. That was basically part of the M.O. at that time. Yeah. But I reached all the way to the car—and this would happen sometimes—and just said, 'No, I don't want to do it.' I said, 'Thank you. See you later.' And she walked away. But after the Hawkins thing, I was just paranoid as hell that this girl would say, 'You know, something weird happened to me a couple weeks ago. This guy came along with crutches and asked me to help him. He took me to a Volkswagen and said he worked in Olympia and lived here in the university district.' How many people could that apply to? So, there you are."

It was hard to listen to Ted describe incriminating evidence that would have led us to him if we had seen the case for what it was from the very start. Unfortunately, I knew this woman had not come forward, or at least if she did come forward, the facts as Ted recounted were not in police reports. I now realized in retrospect that all the leads about a guy on crutches in the U-district seeking help for changing a tire, which were received after the Lake Sammamish murders, were probably Ted Bundy practicing his routines. What fools we were! The evidence was there all the time. What had we missed on Green River? The answers were all there, locked up in small memories in Ted's brain, while time was running out on both of us.

"Okay, how about getting back to—going back to that scene?" I asked, wondering if he would actually get into his aberrant sexual perversions.

"Okay. Well, I went back the next day, and I went back about three days later to do that business we talked about earlier and went up the roadway with it." Ted was talking about the removal of

Georgann Hawkins's head, which we had talked about earlier. "It was sort of a crude attempt to disguise the identity—or avoid, I mean—the identification of the remains as such. I don't know. In retrospect, it sounds pretty incoherent, but that's what was motivating it at the time. And then maybe about a week to two weeks later, I went back for a third time. Yeah."

"What for?" I asked. Weren't the other times enough?

"Again, just to see what was going on. You know, there's a lot of psychological stuff going on here that we just don't have time for. I mean, we could spend days explaining it. I mean, there is an aspect here of, you know, the possessiveness I'm sure you're familiar with, the aftereffects. This is why I'm so keen on the staking out crime scenes of this type afterwards, fascination with death, necrophilia, all that. But, of course, you know, in June after a week, what with all the local wildlife, that there's not much left."

Necrophilia

The "big bang" was about to occur. Ted hinted all over the place. I didn't believe for a minute that he went back after a couple days to bury Hawkins's skull. Her head was someplace else. I knew the area he described had been scoured thoroughly by our searchers. We had dug in that area deeper than he could ever get with his entrenching tool. Her head wasn't there, just as Janice Ott's head wasn't there. I didn't know why yet, but I was to get a hint in a couple of days. He was returning to the Issaquah hillside to satisfy his perverted sexual fantasies. He was warped, but he wanted time to explain it. That's why he had conceived his shortsighted plan to save his neck. Give the authorities just enough to get them to speak in his behalf, so the governor of Florida would stay his execution. Play us along with tidbits of information, bread crumbs along the path to the final truth, which would be so tempting that of course the state of Florida would stay his execution to allow him to tell his whole story. But it was also a form of blackmail that would never end because there would always be other jurisdictions that had unsolved cases with which Bundy could draw out his life. Hadn't Henry Lee Lucas strung along the state of Texas and other jurisdictions in much the same way? And in the end it was all just a pack of lies to keep him from going under the executioner's needle. That's why I knew that Bundy's plan wouldn't work. He was fucking with all of us, just like he had done to his victims. I was on the edge. Should I blow his cover now and ruin the chance of my fellow detectives getting information from him, or should I just sit and kiss the little zit's ass and listen to his story? Then I suddenly realized that he needed me to verify that he was somewhat truthful, telling us where we might find remains, while at the same time giving us part of the story. No matter what I asked, I couldn't alienate him. Both he and the other detectives needed me to act civilly.

With the resolve that I had some of what I came for, I bluntly asked, "Were you going back to that scene to commit sex acts?"

Ted, stuttering, muttered, "Well, I don't want to talk about that right now. We will talk about it someday, but I don't have—we don't—not really—have enough to give you the background on that. I want us to work into that."

Now, it was pretty clear what Ted did when he returned to those scenes and what the Riverman might be doing when he returned. We might catch the Riverman, literally, with his pants down, if we staked out a fresh site at Ted's recommendation.

Needing to get onto a different issue to keep him talking about his murders, I quickly said, "Okay, all right. Now, did you always carry the little hacksaw with you?"

Apparently willing to go on, Ted replied, "Oh, it was in the tool kit. I had a metal tool kit in the front trunk, such as it is, in the Volkswagen. It had everything in there. I mean, you know, all the tools you need to repair Volkswagens, just like any tool kit, metric stuff."

"Uh huh?" I said. Somehow Ted's tool kit was much different than the rest of ours. Whose car tool kit contains a hacksaw, a crowbar, a shovel, rope, handcuffs, plastic bags, strips of a bedsheet, a pantyhose mask, and a knit ski mask, such as Ted's did?

"And in there was a hacksaw. And also a little shovel, little army shovel," Ted continued as though everyone carried such items in their cars.

"Did you ever bury anybody?" I asked, knowing what his answer would be.

"Oh, yes. Yeah, in, you might say, my more coherent—not coherent—when I was really going all out and took my time, yeah, I did. I mean, it's quite clear. I mean, there's no question—almost without question, those who have been found were not, and those who haven't been found were buried."

"Uh huh," I said while thinking about all those who were missing, with no trace of their remains.

"It's that simple," he proclaimed.

"How many people do you figure are buried in the state of Washington?" I asked.

"A couple. Just a couple."

"Do you know who?" I prodded.

Avoiding a clear answer, Ted stammered, "Well, I remember the name of—you know, I can't remember names, most of the names I don't remember. A couple, like the one we were just talking about, the name comes back to me. But—let me think. One, two—that's all. Two. Yeah. I don't remember the name on the other one. I included in the two Hawkins, only because it was a partial kind of thing. Plus one other."

Wanting to see how far I could push, I asked, "Who was the other one?"

Other Victims

Ted wasn't prepared to talk during this session about Donna Manson, a woman who had been reported missing from Evergreen State College campus, a murder we had tied to him as well.

"I don't remember the name and I don't want to—I mean, you know, I don't want to guess," Ted lied.

"Is it one during that period of time, from say January through—"

"This would have been in early seventy-four," Ted said eagerly, surprising me with his interruption.

"Early seventy-four? A girl from Olympia? How about the Evergreen College girl?" I suggested.

Ted was smirking. There seemed to be some dark secret about Manson that Ted wanted to save for later.

Laughing surely to himself, Ted said, "Oh, yeah. That's right, yeah."

"Yeah?"

"Yeah."

"Where is she?" I asked, sensing that Ted would deflect any of my advances about Manson.

"Well, she's up in the mountains," he said, generalizing.

"What mountains?" I questioned.

"Up in the Cascades, you know."

No, I didn't know, so I pressed on. "And she's actually buried in the ground?"

Ted approached his response slowly and said, "Well—how did that work? This is something that happened piece by piece, strange as this may sound. I'm trying to remember exactly where it all happened. That's something we're going to have to talk about in the future. I don't know that I was ever more incoherent. And I mean, that night is like some kind of dream, you know, very blurry area, nightmarish, and I have trouble piecing it together. But it's going to take me a while to work on that one."

"Okay."

Ted continued, "As I sometimes had a bottle of wine in the car and was just, among other things, extremely drunk."

After spending about an hour and a half with Ted, I was eager to hear about the extent of his murders in Washington State. If I knew the numbers he was willing to talk about over the next few days, it would be a barometer of what I might get from him. I knew that in the beginning of our conversation he didn't want to talk numbers. So I asked cautiously, "Just so I can get an idea about timing as far as in the next hour, can we get some sort of feeling, if you can't remember names, maybe timing or events or something that will give me an idea of how many people we need to talk about, so I can get an idea of the scope?"

Obligingly, Ted said, "Uh huh. Let's see. Yeah. In Washington?"

"Right."

"Yeah."

"We've got the one from Oregon up there, and that's our case too."

"Well, let's see. I think it's—I think it'll be eleven."

Shocked at Ted's answer, I wanted clarification. "Eleven altogether?"

"Yeah."

"Okay, okay. Which areas? Which jurisdictions or which disappearance sites or—do you remember any names of anybody?" I muttered.

"Well, sure. I remember a lot of it," Ted reassured me.

"Give me an idea of which ones you're talking about."

There was a long silence. Ted had worked himself into a corner and needed desperately to get out. The original number of Ted cases known to law enforcement authorities was 8, not 11 as Ted had just announced. That, just for openers, was a shocker that put Ted on the hook for three more homicides than the ones we knew about. However, since he'd said that the additional three were pre-1974, he held out the possibility that there were more crimes to which he could confess. But I suspected he wanted to save those confessions to pre-1974 homicides until after his execution was delayed, so as to give him more bargaining power. Why play all your cards until you have to? It was the pre-1974 time period he wanted to stay away from at this debriefing. But by announcing that he had 11 cases within the scope of his confessions, he'd just opened the door to the three more cases. Now he started to talk himself out of trouble.

He nervously continued, "Well, I could—give you probably most of the names, or some names and some locations."

"All right." I eagerly awaited the information.

Ted regained his composure and reverted to his mission. He said, "Okay, but this is basically what I want to avoid, putting myself into a position where we more or less run through the standard litany of victims and without the depth of information and the precedent and antecedent stuff, what happened before, during, and after, what was going on in my mind. And that's why I feel that I'd like to clothe these names in some kind of reality, even though it be a distorted reality. And I'm worried that—I won't bullshit you— I'm worried that I—that we just run through it like this, and I can understand your curiosity, believe me, but we run through it like this, and we leave ourselves open to the temptation to leave it at that."

"Right. One of the things that I'm concerned about is time," I said, stroking his ego.

"I know."

"And you haven't finished everything about Georgann Hawkins, either," I reminded him.

"No."

"So we've got ten more to go," I announced.

"That's right," Ted said.

Playing for Time

I realized that from this point on Ted was finished confessing to any more of his murders at our Friday meeting. The cat was partially out of the bag—only partially. In looking over Ted's handwritten itinerary for the next few days, I saw no more time devoted to me, which seemed unreasonable since I had the highest number of murders to cover with him. But technically, it was his show. So, in the time remaining, I decided to put some pressure on him and force him to focus on the scope of his murders. He was trying to handle his last days like some kind of high-level summit negotiation, but he had planned it poorly. I treaded carefully, explaining, "I'm thinking about areas, time, and whether I need to stay with the rest of that Issaquah site. Or whether I need to move on to a different murder I don't even know about. I might be able to corroborate facts in the next couple of days. I know the basic six. Now I know about seven, one that was missing that we didn't know was there. The missing Donna Manson—the girl from Thurston County—we haven't covered where she is. That's all I know about so far from you. Now I need to know what other murders you're talking about. Are there murders in other jurisdictions in Washington? I want to get some perspective because, eventually, I'd like to get as many details on each one that I can. I don't want to go for two hours and say, 'Well, I have no idea what the scope is.' 'Cause if anybody asks me what the scope is," I said, now deliberately fucking with the very thing Ted was most worried about, "somebody of importance—like the governor of Florida—I'd like to know what it is."

Ted said, "Yeah. I don't blame you."

"You and I have talked for two hours already, not counting the other visits I've had [with] you and your letters to me. But what I need to know is if I have to fight for more time. What do I have to fight about? I know the details of things that are here, but maybe some other people don't have as much to talk about as I do. I don't know. It depends on what they have. So I know about those eight. And you're talking about three others. How far back in time? You got January seventy-four through July of seventy-four. Are there more within that time frame that I don't know about in the state of Washington?"

"Yes, there are," Ted proclaimed. "I hear you, Bob. What I'm trying to do, for my own self, is to demonstrate that I am serious about this. You have a legitimate need to know it all. And you want, of course, to start with what is most obvious, that is, the identities, numbers, dates, and that's important. There's a lot more important stuff. And I've never spoken to anybody about this and, for me, it was an important first confession of its kind. I'm not asking for any kind of public-service awards, but the reality is that's what it was for me."

Unsolved Cases

Seeking further clarification on the extent of his murders, I said, "I guess what I need is, rather than me throwing out stuff for you to say, you know, this is what we need to talk about or not, like the August second murders in Clark County. If there's only eleven, then that's fine. I don't want to guess. I'm curious about murdered girls at Washington State University in Pullman, Washington, in 1971 and the two stewardesses on Queen Anne Hill in Seattle."

Ted relented by saying, "Yeah, we can do it that way if you'd like, too. And maybe in some ways that's easier. I can tell you what I'm not involved in, you know, if you have a list of that type in your head."

"There's the gal up in Bellingham in the river, strangled in 1970," I said, without giving her name.

Abruptly, Ted said, "No."

"There's a gal in 1971, Thurston County," I continued.

"No," he blurted out.

Ted was giving a sharp, generic no at the mention of each victim, just to avoid the subject. He was so intent on not cooperating at this point, I could have asked him if he killed Janice Ott and he would have said no. What he didn't realize was that I wasn't interested in whether he would say yes or no. Each question I asked contained a year in it for a reason. It was the year I was looking for, not whether he could tell me the name of the victim. I was observing his body language. What shocked me was that Ted should have asked for a name or asked for clarification of the question, like any normal person would do who was just playing a police interrogation game.

"Not that far back. Nothing that far back?" I carefully asked.

"Nineteen seventy-two," said Ted, unaware of my intent. Falling for my trap, he claimed two years prior to 1974 when he committed a murder.

Quickly, I jumped to the Brenda Baker and Kathy Devine cases, two women I believed he murdered after 1972. I said, "Two girls in Millersylvania State Park in 1973."

"Yeah, I think you once showed me that. No. No, no," he said with a smile, as if he could say no to anything in the next 45 minutes because he had already told me about the only murder he seemed prepared to discuss.

I went immediately to possibly his first murder when I said, "There's a little girl in Tacoma."

"Which one?" he inquired with an astonished look on his face.

"Ann Marie Burr," I stated with a straight face.

It was time for Ted to go into an attitude of total denial. He emphatically said, "No. Absolutely not. It's important for me. It's important for my credibility because there's so much question about my credibility. You know, I would like to be polygraphed, have a polygraph examination if that can be done in these kinds of things. Do something to enhance the credibility. Not just, you know, specifics—I mean, the specifics, of course, but of my overall account of these things. 'Cause I want it to be believable. I don't want to get into a Henry Lee Lucas kind of deal. I have precious little going for me now, but what I do have is I've got to build some credibility."

Ted's argument to convince me that he was not responsible for the Burr murder was weak. He attempted to defend his credibility by suggesting a polygraph he knew he didn't have time to take. He also hinted that his polygraph should not be specific but test his overall account of things. It should be remembered that Ted took a polygraph in the past, and, judging by his previous explanation about the value of the polygraph, he flunked miserably. So he suggested here that he be tested about his overall account, something he thought he could beat.

I changed the subject quickly, since I was interested in what his reaction would be to knowing that I also suspected him in the murder and assault on two stewardesses in the late 1960s. At the time,

Ted was living right across the Fremont Bridge from Queen Anne Hill, one of the five hills that make up the city of Seattle. He was working at a Safeway store near an apartment house where two stewardesses lived. Both were bludgeoned, à la Chi Omega. I had examined that case carefully. Seattle detectives' favorite suspect was the apartment owner's son, since he committed suicide and had a newspaper article about the murder in his belongings. But as I got to know Ted better over time, Ted became a good suspect to me.

Wanting to hear what Ted would say, I said, "Okay, now, up on Queen Anne Hill . . ."

"But, yeah, I must—so, umm . . ." Ted said in a revealing slip, a bewildered look on his face. He wasn't expecting me to ask about this one.

Smiling, I said, "You don't know anything about those?"

Exasperated, Ted exclaimed, "No!"

"Absolutely not," I replied.

Ted was shaking and confused. He had worked himself into a box, knowing all along that I didn't believe him, and so he desperately tried to recover, stammering and doing verbal backflips. "No. No. I have no hesitation about talking about things that I have done, no hesitation about telling you about what I haven't done, okay? So if I tell you something—I may not tell you something—I might not tell you something right now or every single detail right now, but if I tell you something, you can rely on it. And when I say, yes I did it or no I didn't do something, that's the way it is."

Now Ted was expecting me to be satisfied with his one-word answers. One-word answers to this line of questioning were too easy a way out for Ted. It allowed him to say no without an explanation. Good interrogators ask short questions that demand long answers.

"You never lied to me—no reason," I myself lied.

"No. No reason to start now," said the clever psychopath.

Knowing I had less than 45 minutes, I decided to put a little more pressure on Ted, who perceived himself to be in total control. He wouldn't have it any other way. I said, "I have to corroborate a lot of what you say. And you've already given me corroboration on one."

"Sure. I could give you corroboration on— Listen, I know what you're pushing for and I don't blame you." Ted read me perfectly. "You sort through your litany of cases. I don't want to get in a position of telling you, but pick one more case, other than the Issaquah—the other two Issaquah cases—that you want to know about, and we'll talk about it. You want some corroboration and I'll give you one more. I mean, we can talk about one more if that's—if you feel comfortable about doing that. I don't know."

Wedging him into my corner, talking about numbers, I asked, "Have we got the time frame down of when things started in Washington?"

"Yup," he said quickly.

"The time frame is when?" I inquired.

"Seventy-four," he claimed.

"Nineteen seventy-four?" I questioned, smiling and looking sarcastically at him as though he were lying through his teeth.

"Right. Well, yeah, I mean the actual. There were several attempts leading up to that, in seventy-three, seventy-two. But no murders," he lied, trying to avoid that fact that he had just spoken earlier about murders he committed back as far as 1972.

"The public's order of things and your order are obviously something different, because there's some in here that we don't know about that is in your order someplace. And we're talking about one girl that lived—Karen Sparks—just a couple blocks away from where you lived. I don't know if that's the one you want me to talk about," I said, attempting to entice him into talking about any murder himself.

"Well, is that the one you want to talk about?" Ted asked.

"Okay, 'cause the order of things are kind of like Healy, Manson, Rancourt, Ball, Hawkins, Ott, and Naslund. That's eight [counting Sparks]. Plus Parks is nine. Are you counting her as one of your eleven?"

"No. No. She's not in that. See, I didn't—that's not one. No," Ted exclaimed, leaving the living victim out of his count.

"So now you're talking about probably three others that I am not familiar with?" I asked, knowing I had him talking about three more murders he didn't want to get into at that time.

"Yup. Yeah," Ted said with assurance.

"Are they in King County jurisdiction?" I asked, attempting to narrow the scope.

"Well, let's see. Ummm . . . one is and the others aren't. That's the way it is. Yeah," he said, giving the appearance that he was trying to convince himself that what he just said was the whole truth. But with Ted, there was never the whole truth.

The weather in northern Florida wasn't what I expected. The steady rain reminded me of Seattle, but the high winds were like a monsoon in Vietnam, better left avoided. The carpet in my Jacksonville Beach hotel room was soaked from water that had leaked through the sliding-glass door. I was staying in a hotel on the beach and had never felt the sand. Each day, I had come and gone in the dark.

On Saturday, I awoke to the voice of one of Ted's advisors on national television, announcing that Bundy had confessed to Bob Keppel and was totally honest and cooperating with the investigators. I'd never heard anything further from the truth. I felt like I'd been had. Bundy and Weiner had made me promise not to say anything to the media before Bundy's Monday press conference but here was Bundy with an immediate announcement so they wouldn't be upstaged by anyone and could do it in their own way. After that, I felt no obligation to delay speaking to the Seattle press folks, who were anxiously awaiting any news from me. Bundy and Weiner's actions were clear evidence that Bundy and company were not going to be forthright with me.

All day Saturday, I waited inside the prison for a chance to talk once again with Bundy. By now, pressure was being applied by Bill Hagmaier for Ted to give me more time, possibly on Sunday night.

Last Conversation

Sunday, January 22, 1989, would be my last talk with Ted. He had promised to speak with each state's investigators for half an hour each, beginning at nine o'clock at night. This time we got to interview Bundy without Diana Weiner present. The only other person with Bundy was Bill Hagmaier. Dennis Couch of the Salt Lake County Sheriff's Department was first and went over for about five minutes, so I interrupted.

I wasn't in the room one minute before Ted complained that he had heard that the Seattle papers were saying all sorts of outrageous things that he'd been telling me.

"Really?" I asked. "What's that?"

Ted explained that they said that "we went over eight, nine cases and—I don't know. I guess I should ask you flat out. You didn't mention specific cases to anybody in the media, did you?"

Defensively, I said, "Specific ones? No, no."

"I think they're guessing," Ted offered.

I explained, putting more of the blame on his own people, "I told them that you confirmed what our suspicions were, and that was what Diana wanted me to do too."

Preferring not to argue about that, Ted said, "Well, I hear you. I was just curious. I wasn't accusing you."

I explained further, "I told them also that there was one victim we talked in detail about, but I didn't say anything about the details. After that, I contacted each of the victims' relatives and talked to them. I told them how sincere you were, how open you were about talking of your murders, and that it was a difficult process to go through. And, you know, they wished me luck."

Ted realized that the blitz by the news media was his own doing. So he changed the subject and asked, "How about the one in particular, Georgann Hawkins? Is there going to be any attempt to go over that crime scene again?"

Somehow, Ted didn't realize his plan was shortsighted. It had escaped him that there was presently over a foot of snow on the ground at the location where he said he buried Hawkins's head. There was no way a search could take place before his Tuesday date with the executioner. Part of Ted's plan to save his own neck was to give details about where we might find remains, then we would conduct a search of that area, find the bones, and, presto, Ted would have proven that he was credible, telling the truth, and worthy of a stay in his execution. The very places in Utah and Colorado where he buried remains were under six feet of snow. Had his advisors discussed this with him or were they familiar only with Florida's terrain and weather patterns, not the mountains of Washington, Colorado, and Utah?

Wanting to refocus Ted from the Hawkins murder to Donna Manson and keep him from wasting the time remaining, I said, "The only thing that we could possibly cover that may explain some unanswered questions is the location of Donna Manson's body, because she's the one that's missing. We never found any bones that we thought were hers. Plus, we've never found the skeletons that went with the skulls on Taylor Mountain, either. We've found only skull parts. On another subject, we also never found Janice Ott's bicycle. All we found of Janice Ott was her lower jawbone. We didn't find her skull. We found Naslund's skull. We found what we think was Ott's backbone. You know, those animals, they just walk around out there and do their thing."

"They sure do, yeah," Ted said, closing his eyes and leaning his head back against the wall. The effects of his last remaining days were taking a heavy toll. He was physically drained and mentally exhausted by late Sunday night. The realization that his debriefing sessions weren't accomplishing the goals that he set, coupled with the letdown from his grandiose euphoria over the public attention he was getting because of his confessions, was causing extreme fatigue. For the first time, I saw him in a state of absolute vulnerability. He was weak, and if we had the time, the opportunity was at hand to get the greater truth from him. But it still was his show, and no matter how hard I tried, his perception was that there just wasn't enough time to begin the real debriefing.

I woke Ted up with a loud request. "I'd like to know where the Taylor Mountain bodies were placed, because I'm sure if the bodies were dumped there, we would have found at least one other bone. All we found was hair, skull, skull, jawbone, jawbone, and a jawbone. We never found any other bones. Now, are those bodies buried out there someplace? Or are they someplace else where no one's ever found their bones? Are you going to give me a hint where the rest of those bodies are?"

Ted pleaded, "I don't know. To be honest with you, I honestly can't tell you."

"Were they dumped there?" I pressured him while he was half asleep.

Ted explained that the reason we didn't find anything was because the "very poor little creatures out there just take them. I don't know why they leave the skulls the way they do—maybe it's just because they're so hard to break up. If the bodies aren't there, it's because the animals took everything. And where they took them, God only knows. They must have just chewed them up."

In order to keep Ted talking, I agreed with him. "Yeah, that's what I thought. Because, in fact, if they were severed or hacksawed, we would have found some vertebrae, the little piece that fits right in the skull holding the skull together. I found every one of those on all the other cases, except these. And on the Green River cases, we find all those. So we know that the animals don't chew those all the way up, all right? And with thirty-seven skeletons in Green River we know a lot about animal behavior, right?"

"Oh, sure you do. Yeah, I forgot all about that," Ted said. Any mention of the Green River cases brought only a momentary spark to Ted's eye. At this point, Ted was exhausted, and his favorite subject, the Riverman, could not bring him around.

So I asked a few short yet very pointed questions. "Were those heads severed, like Georgann Hawkins?"

"Yeah," Ted said affirmatively, with a smirk on his face.

"They were?" I gasped.

"Uh-huh." Ted reaffirmed with a long silence while he caught a short 45-second nap.

I inquired disbelievingly, "They weren't severed? Are you saying that because we don't have any evidence of severing and you don't want to say it, or are you telling me that's fact?"

"I wasn't going to answer you when you asked," said Ted the smart-ass. He had just played some word games with Dennis Couch and wasn't in the mood for more. Ted loved word games, but admitted, "Well, I just ran out of steam. I just ran out of steam. And I don't have much left."

I could tell there was something so grotesque about the Manson murder that Ted didn't want to discuss it. Also, I realized Ted was stalling because he had told me specifically on Friday, "What you have found is aboveground, and what you haven't found is buried." He must have buried the bodies of Healy, Parks, Rancourt, and Ball, but refused to talk about where they were buried. He blamed the animals for eating them all up. I knew that was bullshit. Bill Hagmaier had told me that Bundy told him some time ago that he had as many as four heads at home with him at one time. Hagmaier didn't have the specific knowledge of the Ted murders to know which ones he was referring to. They must have been the Taylor Mountain women.

Cautiously, I changed the subject to a safer subject that wouldn't embarrass him. I would return to the Manson murder later.

I inquired, "Okay, how about Janice Ott's bicycle?"

Eagerly, as though he was more receptive, Ted asked, "Okay, do you have any maps of Seattle? Show me the Arboretum." Ted explained that he hid Ott's bicycle under some leaves in the Arboretum near the University of Washington. While Ted looked at the map, he joked, "No, that's not it. I think I have a little orientation problem. Shouldn't take me more than a couple days to figure it out. No, let's see. This is kind of mind-boggling. I used to know that place like the back of my hand. Well, it was concealed with leaves and branches."

Donna Manson's Skull

After about five minutes of Ted trying to locate the Arboretum on the map, I pressed Ted again about Donna Manson. "Okay, how about Donna Manson? Gal from Thurston County, Olympia. Where's she?"

Ted reacted quickly. "Where is she? That was different. That was different."

"What was different about it? You told me before that she might be buried," I asked, having Ted's attention.

He smiled like a little boy with a secret. Ted stuttered like he was about to tell a lie, offering that Manson was buried farther up the power line road and slightly inside the tree cover. When I told him that we could probably find her if he was more certain of her location, Ted confessed, "I won't beat around the bush with you anymore, because I'm just tired, and I just want to get back and go to sleep."

"Okay," I said, waiting impatiently for his next words.

"So let me just tell you. I know that part of her is buried up there, but nothing identifiable, probably just literally bones. The head, however, the skull, wouldn't be there," Ted said with some relief.

"Where is it?" I asked.

"It's nowhere," he stated as though it had fallen into a black hole.

"It's nowhere?" I asked in disbelief, sensing that he was about to say something horrible.

"Well, I'm not trying to be flippant. It's just nowhere. It's in a category by itself. Now, I'd just as soon this is something that you just kept. I can see the headlines now. But—"

I reassured him. "Ted, there's not going to be any details. What you told me about Georgann Hawkins isn't going to be known. And I have parents out there that don't even want to know the details." I pointed to Hagmaier and said, "He wants to know, and I want to know for my own good."

"Well, it was incinerated. It was just an exception. A strange exception, but it was incinerated," he announced.

"Where did you incinerate it?" I asked, with shock setting in.

Laughing, Ted said, "Ahh."

I pleaded, "Come on, partner. These are things I don't know about you."

Ted proudly proclaimed, "Yeah, this is probably the disposal method of preference among those who get away with it. It's the most bizarre nature I've ever been associated with, and I've been associated with some bizarre shit."

Incredulous, I said, "Right. It's incinerated."

"It's incinerated," Ted repeated.

"Tell me about it. What the hell happened?" I said anxiously, noticing that Ted's repulsive juices began to flow while talking about it.

"Well, I don't know the address of the place. I never wanted to tell this—I promised myself I'd never tell this, because of all the things I did to this woman, this is probably the one she was least likely to forgive me for. Poor Liz." He was referring to Elizabeth Kendall, his former fiancée. "In her fireplace. That's not really that humorous, but, I mean, the fireplace at that house," Ted said with sinister, satisfied laughter in his voice.

"Burn it all up?" I asked, still in disbelief.

"Down to the last ash, and in a fit of—you know—paranoia and cleanliness, what have you, just vacuumed down all the ashes. That's the twist. It's a twist. And it's a lot of work and certainly very risky, under the circumstances. I mean, the kids come home from school, there's a roaring fire in the fireplace, and it's warm outside," Ted said with finality.

1973 Victims

It was nearing the end of our short interview. Since Ted had broached the subject previously, I wanted him to focus on the three Ted murders I didn't know about, so I said, "Okay, you mentioned the eight before and you gave me three more. And I don't know what three you're talking about. Can you help me a little bit with those?"

"Which three? I was trying to figure that out myself," answered Ted, honestly trying to remember.

"And what did you come up with?" I asked.

"This is what I came up with. It was an earlier one. Nineteen seventy-three," Ted admitted.

"Okay," I said, attempting to hide my glee at the fact that even though he had mentioned earlier that he would only talk about 1974 and nothing more, he had now ventured into 1973, which was a year I expected to be as deadly as 1974.

"Seventy-three. Well, it was earlier than anything. Time confuses me. Time of year: it's—May. I'm not sure," Ted continued, frowning as though he wanted to tell but knew he had said too much already.

"Okay, where was she missing from?" I asked.

"Tumwater area," Ted answered. I knew that Ted refused to admit that he killed Kathy Devine, who was in the photograph I had shown him in 1984. She was depicted in her death pose, a sight that momentarily excited Ted. Ted was talking about 1973 in the Olympia area, a place where he worked and also near the dump sites of Kathy Devine and Brenda Baker, two victims who were killed in 1973. He was the prime suspect in both cases, as far as I was concerned.

"Tumwater area. That's where she was missing from?" I asked, acting interested in what he was about to say. I knew he was stalling so that he wouldn't have to talk about the 1973 murders.

"Well, no, not the area, I mean, Tumwater/Olympia. I'm always bad about where one starts and the other stops. That whole area has always disoriented me. That's the problem. There's a maze. I call it a maze of back roads. It's not a maze, I guess, but there's something about the area that I have a hard time keeping track of the back road system there," said Ted, trying to avoid the question by talking about something other than the actual murder.

I probed further by asking, "Is it a found body? Do you know that?"

"No," Ted replied.

"It's not found," I stated.

"No," Ted said, without his usual long explanation.

"It's a missing girl from the Tumwater area?" I posed.

"Well, I don't know if she was from there." Ted was carefully backtracking.

"Or that's where you picked her up?" I inquired, thinking he was more likely talking about the murder of Brenda Baker.

"She was hitchhiking. Yeah, I never heard anything more about her. But it's hard to explain, Bob. The person I used to be would get into a fit and just drive. And people have trouble relating to that. You sort of lose orientation. You sort of lose track of where you've been. You just get lost. It can be in broad daylight and so panicky, so disoriented. Anyway—I mean, I believe this is where you're going—I can't even remember the road system anymore. The highway goes off and you get to the bottom of Capitol Hill. The highway goes off—one freeway goes off to the left and the other goes off to the right. Used to know what that was. It goes to the ocean. And there's a whole bunch of roads that turn to the right and then just meander. Without really paying as much attention to where you're going, just looking for some place," Ted said while I was nodding my head with approval. Ted had just nailed one of the key attributes of the serial-killer mentality and explained it, first person. Serial killers drive; they troll back and forth to lose themselves in the jumble of their own inability to relate to reality and they start to wander. If a victim crosses a killer's path when he's in this state, the victim's as good as dead.

"I was halfway familiar with those kinds of roads because one of my hobbies, before I started doing this, was I liked places to go where people dumped stuff—literally dumped stuff like clothing, paper, boards, boxes, couches, and things."

"That's where she's off, one of those roads someplace?" I inquired.

Ted was now in his I-can't-tell-you-exactly-where-it-was mode. He was wasting time talking about an area I knew he knew better than the inside of his prison cell. The location he was talking about was a stone's throw from Evergreen State College, where Ted abducted Donna Manson. Could he have mixed up his victims? He tried to explain his mix-up with the number of Washington victims. "Okay, the other two I don't know, Bob. I was thinking about it. You know, you threw out a number and I think what happened is a number lodged in my head, and you said eight. I thought eleven. You know, we didn't sit down and say, okay, one is ———, two is ———, three is ———, four is . . ." Ted complained. Funny, he wouldn't previously talk about numbers, and now that's what he was complaining about. Fine fix he'd gotten me into. "For some reason I'd been thinking—I hadn't really stopped myself and for some reason I was thinking the number in Washington was eleven. I don't know how many individuals," Ted finally said. Even though the transcripts and tape were made available to the FBI and the news media, everyone still says that Ted admitted to murdering 11 in Washington State, but in reality, he withdrew his estimate. He claimed not to remember how many individuals he had killed. He withdrew his estimate of 11 because he and I both knew that he had murdered a lot more women in Washington State than 11.

Finally, I had one last thing to show Ted that he didn't know we had. It was a black-and-white photograph taken on July 14, 1974, at Lake Sammamish State Park. It depicted a Volkswagen bug with someone behind the wheel. It was parked underneath the same tree to which Ted walked with the first woman he approached. She was the only witness to see Ted's Volkswagen Beetle. Also in the picture were numerous police officers escorting some rowdy bikers from the park. If the vehicle license plate had been in the picture and not blocked out by a police car, Ted Bundy would have been a suspect in those murders much sooner.

"I'd like to ask one last question," I said, knowing that Ted was eager to end our session. He was stressed-out.

"Oh, boy," Ted said, mocking me and wanting to get some rest.

I threw down the photograph on the table and asked, "Is that you? It's Lake Sammamish State Park, 1974, the tree. Cops roll in to take care of the bikers."

"Lawbreakers," Ted immediately said with recognition. He knew exactly what was in the picture. It was him, trapped until the police moved their cars—an embarrassing moment for the great Ted Bundy. But would he admit that it was him? Knowing Ted had not assessed the possibility of us actually having real evidence demonstrating that he was Washington's Ted killer, I knew he would not directly comment about it.

"Well, I mean, we're in the ballpark" was as close as Ted would admit. He avoided the issue again, stuttering, "Well, you say there's a person in there. I mean, it appears to be this other person in there, right? I'm not trying to bait the question. I think as you no doubt discovered, there are a lot of light-colored Volkswagens. And I don't mean to burst your bubble. That is an interesting coincidence. But God, I was—you would have never seen me in Lake Sammamish State Park again with all that heat. That's a lot of heat there," Ted answered with guilty, nervous laughter and with the private knowledge that he had never returned to Lake Sammamish State Park again. If it was possible to raise his stress level at that point, I could tell the photograph did. He attacked the evidence like the attorney he had always wanted to be.

Even though Ted was near the point of exhaustion, he was still fighting for his survival on this one issue. He pointed out, "That would have been fairly memorable. No, that . . . that couldn't be me. And besides, at that time, I think you notice, on the back of the car was missing a piece of the ski rack." Thank you, Ted, your attention to detail is astounding.

"A thousand people have asked me to ask you this," I cautiously proceeded.

"Oh God, aspirin, right? Go ahead," Ted said with the kind of sarcasm that only he could display.

"About Ann Marie Burr," I said, knowing what his response would be at this late hour.

"Okay, well, right. That's one that's easy. No. Absolutely not. That's one of the few I wish that people would believe. They believe everything else except my answer, which is no—on that one, you know, and that's very sad. But it's also so ludicrous because I don't know if you ever looked at it in the course of your studies. It's all the way across town, really, from where I—as a kid—hung out and had my paper route. The inference was, for instance, my paper route came close to or included the Burr home. Well, my understanding is it's, you know, for a kid, where the Burrs lived, as it relates to where I lived, it was in a different part of the world. That was a pretty long ways away. Different schools, different high schools. Never went to that area. Never had any occasion to go there. It was just, just another part of the forest. And—agh—I was only like thirteen, fourteen years old, or less," Ted pleaded.

I didn't believe any of his explanation. Ted was a lifelong liar, and he was lying about this. Ted's world was different from the one that normal persons lived in, very different. His explanation didn't hold water, and he knew it. He had told me last year that there were some murders that people like him would never talk about. They were murders committed too close to home, too close to family, and of victims who were very young. Ann Marie Burr fit all three. At this point, Ted still held on to some hope for a stay of his execution, so he didn't want the rap in prison of being a baby-killer. The other prisoners don't like those types.

"When and where was your first murder?" I asked, knowing that my time was up.

"One more question, right?" Ted laughed.

"Oh, I'm sorry." His majesty had just shut me off.

He clicked the tape recorder off and handed it back to me. I put it away and stood up to go. As I left, I shook his hand, knowing I would never see him again. It was time for at least one moment of laser-beam honesty. I told him that he had orchestrated the past few days very poorly. Ted just looked at me.

"You just killed yourself," I said. And that was the last thing I ever said to Ted Bundy.

15

Bundy's 1989 Colorado Confessions

Colorado detectives Mike Fisher and Matt Lindvall fussed with their recording device in the tiny interview room on Florida's death row as a nervous Ted Bundy, in handcuffs in his own tiny chamber, watched them set it up. Bundy knew Mike Fisher from his homicide arrest in Aspen. I met Fisher when he was following up leads in the Caryn Campbell murder in Pitkin County. Campbell had disappeared from the Snowmass Lodge in Colorado ski country.

Fisher, who had tracked Bundy after he broke out of a Colorado jail, reminded me of a dog with a sock, always pursuing, analyzing, and never letting go. So the sound of his voice on my phone when he called to say "The son of a bitch escaped again" is something I still remember.

Bundy had fled from his Colorado jail across the country, up to Michigan, then to Florida, where, after the Chi Omega sorority-house murders and the murder of Kimberly Leach, he was finally arrested driving a stolen van. It was in Florida that Bundy would eventually be put to death in the electric chair. The U.S. Supreme Court had denied Bundy's final appeal and the governor of Florida was steadfastly refusing to grant him a stay. His hour had come.

Bundy still saw an endgame strategy in the final weeks, however. Maybe he could garner enough interest in the confessions he was making, he thought, or maybe he could convince somebody—the governor, perhaps—that he was more valuable alive than dead. Maybe he could convince Mike Fisher, Matt Lindvall, the FBI, or me. Fat chance of that, but Bundy and his attorney scratched out the final hours, dribbling out bits and pieces of confessions to homicides and describing the locations of the bodies of missing women. But in the midst of the fencing back and forth about what information he might or might not give up, and while Bundy was still trying to keep a throne of information from shortly becoming an electric chair, very revealing aspects emerged about what takes place in the mind of a serial killer during, after, and, still later, upon reflection of his crimes.

My jousting with Bundy occurred shortly before Fisher and Lindvall interviewed him. During my interview, it became noticeable that Bundy was stalling so that he could talk to an investigator from the Colorado Attorney General's office, who was on his way down to Stark. Bundy had received a message from his appellate attorneys to the effect that if he was to tell the AG's investigator the truth, the governor and attorney general of Colorado would speak on his behalf to the governor of Florida. I was unimpressed with Bundy's new strategy to wait for that investigator when Fisher and Lindvall were in the corridor waiting their turn with him. So I got in his face a little about the futility of waiting when Fisher and Lindvall were outside thinking they were next.

I told him that with this kind of gamesmanship, the public and the government officials deciding Bundy's fate would only think that this new found strategy was just another one of his insincere ploys. I pushed him on this, and Bundy agreed to speak with Fisher and Lindvall. As I passed Fisher on his way into the interview area, I said to him, "Don't be swayed by any of Ted's tears. They are all fake."

That was what preceded Mike Fisher and Matt Lindvall's setting up of the tape-recording device to pick up what would be Bundy's Colorado confessions.

"It would have been on the east side of town on the eastern end of the main downtown shopping area," Bundy began, explaining where he met Vail, Colorado, victim Julie Cunningham. "There was, I think, there was streets, which are pedestrian streets mainly. And around that core mainly, and around that core is a loop of some sort. And it's on the eastern loop of that by a bridge."

He contacted her using the same ruse he'd used in the Georgann

Hawkins disappearance. "I was again using a pair of crutches and a boot bag, a boot tree, and she offered to help me with it, and we walked from that location to the parking lot, which was maybe a distance of one-half to three-quarters of a mile. It was after dark, early evening. We had to climb, actually, to the location where the car was parked, had to climb a rather steep snowbank and descend down into the parking lot where the car was."

At the car, Bundy also did what he had done countless times before, particularly when he abducted Georgann Hawkins from Fraternity Row at the University of Washington on June 11, 1974.

"We just walked right along," he told Detective Matt Lindvall, until they got to his VW Beetle, at which point, using a metal crowbar, "I knocked her unconscious." He had secreted the crowbar by the rear of the car, alongside and resting against the engine. He snatched it up when Julie reached the car and used a single blow to the back of her head to knock her out. She went down immediately, he told Lindvall. Then he handcuffed her while she was on the ground, lifted her into the VW—alongside him on the floor of his car, from which he'd removed the passenger seat—and drove out of Vail.

"We drove," he said. "I drove, got on the highway, freeway, I don't know if it's a freeway, it was dark, quite frankly, and you know I hadn't traveled that area a lot, so I can't say what the roads were exactly like as everything was pretty much a blur. I was, uh, impaired. The fact is that I think I was intoxicated. I'm pretty sure I was pretty well intoxicated at the time and then under these circumstances, there's a high degree of stress that kind of distorts my memory somewhat."

Bundy was unsure about how much time he spent driving with Julie beside him or exactly how far he drove that night as he fled the scene of his assault. "It's hard to explain at this point in time. Prior to an incident like this for me things can be pretty clear. Once it gets rolling, everything starts becoming kind of a high-pitched kind of blur. You lose track of time, so it's how far, how long, I don't remember. I do remember, all I remember, is how bright the lights were in the rearview mirror, and all of a sudden we were in or near Glenwood Springs."

At some point, also like Georgann Hawkins, Bundy's victim started to come to. But unlike Georgann, who remained disoriented throughout and believed that Bundy was her Spanish tutor,

Julie tried to engage her assailant and captor in conversation. "She began talking," Bundy said. "I remember conversation, but I have a hard time coming up with exact words. . . . She was just asking who I was and all. You know, where I was from. That kind of thing."

On they drove, into the night and toward some spot in the woods where Bundy, unsure of where he was and not knowing the area as well as he did Issaquah and Taylor Mountain, was looking for a spot to dump his still-living victim. "It's dark, but it's not overcast. There's stars in the sky, I think, even at this point. I mean there's not much traffic on the road. It's gotten quite a bit later. I've lost track of time. I'm not thinking clearly, and that's an understatement. I'm looking for a side road of some sort off the main highway. I'm confused about where I am, really."

Disoriented and paying more attention to his victim than to where he was going, Bundy described a level of panic and frenzy that was driving him to unload his victim somewhere, anywhere, and then head out of the area. Again, much like his murder of Georgann Hawkins, Bundy was desperate to get away from his victim. "I was driving and yet my ability to perceive surroundings was somewhat limited. I was paying attention to what was going on inside the car and was still under the influence. It was kind of like I was in a panic, frightened state, not knowing where I was. Now I was looking, after I got through that populated area, I was looking for another turnoff, a side road, a dirt road, or something. And it just didn't seem to be anything, and I was also getting concerned about houses in the area 'cause I knew it was getting late and I didn't want to turn into somebody's driveway."

After a few minutes, however, he found a spot. "It couldn't have been that long, we're talking minutes probably, I found a side road, a dirt road, and turned off onto it and drove maybe a quarter-mile off the road to the right. And I didn't know where I was. I didn't know what was around me. It was pitch-black. It was very disorienting under ordinary circumstances. I mean it was very disorienting for me in particular, so I didn't know where I was and I was somewhere." Then he stopped the car. Julie had completely regained consciousness by now as she lay beside him in his VW.

Asked what happened next after he stopped the car at the spot, Bundy said, struggling to answer because of what he was obviously trying to hide, "See if I can work it this way. At some point, she'd been asking me to loosen the handcuffs. And I did so. I got out of the car and tried to figure out where things were. Walked from the car and apparently she'd slipped out of the handcuffs and began to exit the car. Of course, she didn't know, obviously, she didn't know any more where we were than I did, maybe less so. And I couldn't, even now or then, assess what injuries she had. But I imagine that she wasn't entirely fully physically able, I mean, after being knocked unconscious. But anyway, I noticed her opening the door and getting out of the car. And trying to put it, everything becomes such a blur for not completely . . . I'd mislead you to say I'd blacked out or anything. All I remember is basically, clearly, I can tell you, it's a struggle and knocking her unconscious again."

Bundy explained that he had had the crowbar right inside the door of the car and "probably sometime during the course of the struggle I got ahold of it." He hit her with the crowbar and she fell backward, half in and half out of the car. She survived the blow, Bundy believed, and then he reached back inside the car for the murder weapon.

"I had some links of cord in the car, among other things, obviously. At that time I was thoroughly panicked and in, ah, it's hard to say, it's hard to describe. I won't say. It's just that the sense of urgency, sense of panic, urgency, being in a hurry to get it over with and get away from there. All that happening at once and more, and I used a link of that cord, a length of that cord was used to strangle her."

She was lying on the ground at this point; Bundy was not sure whether she was faceup or facedown. And years after that night, when he was on death row facing his interrogators from Colorado, he was not able to describe fully the sequence of events that followed. "I know some of what took place," he said. "All I can tell you, of course, that's all I can tell you. And I'm having a hard time even articulating what I remember. Well, I, just to be able to find the words, I'm going to want you to note this in your mind or whatever so we can come back to it, 'cause, I think in the context of everything that's happened it's important. And I'm not denying it in the sense that I'm trying to forget it and tell you that nothing happened. I mean I could tell you I dragged her up into the woods and left it there, but that's not what happened. But I'm having a hard time talking about it. Basically, what ended up happening was I carried her up into some wooded area. It's hard to describe again because of the darkness at the time. It was hard to describe what kind of area it was except there were trees of some sort. And I left. Just like that."

Bundy removed all of his victim's clothes, her suede coat, her boots, her jewelry, and all her other possessions and left her on the ground amid the wooded area. He told police that, aside from hitting her twice with the metal bar and strangling her with the cord, she was not injured in any other way while she was still alive.

"How about after she died?" Detective Lindvall asked.

"We didn't get into that" was Bundy's only answer, but he said that he had a better memory of where he left her because he returned to the dump site six to eight weeks later. Bundy said he sped away from the dump site that night with all of her clothing and possessions in his car. He deposited her clothing in a Goodwill container in Salt Lake City and then, weeks later, returned to the body he'd left in the open air.

Because it had been dark when Bundy dropped Julie Cunningham's body out in the open, he didn't easily remember the place when he returned. "Even when I saw it, I didn't recognize it. But I was matter-of-fact. I'd gone to a half a dozen different places before I found that one. So that looks like it. But seeing it in the daytime was just totally different. I was trying to re-create what it looked like at night. But after the better part of a half a day and getting out of my car a half a dozen times, I did locate what seemed to appear to be the spot. And parked my car, left my car down the road off a turnoff area, off a paved roadway, walked across the road and up, it was up the side of this hillside. I mean up the hillside, and this is some scrub trees at the base of a rock, a rocky area, a rocky cliff some fifty, thirty-three to fifty feet high. I wasn't aware of it at the time. And below that little rocky ridge in this little clump of scrub trees was the young woman's body, Julie's body.

"She was on her back, faceup. But the dry weather and all, it sort of, I don't know what the term would be, 'mummified' her remains. Anyway, I'd gone back to bury her, which is why I had a shovel, a small shovel. And which is what I did."

He buried her two to three feet down in the soft soil, on her back, arms extended along her sides to her feet, and covered the burial site with heavy rocks and tree branches that he dragged over. He did it, he said, to prevent any animals from getting to it. And it took him about forty-five minutes to complete the burial.

But Matt Lindvall still wasn't happy with the story of what happened between Bundy and his victim the first night at the burial site. It was difficult to talk about, Bundy said, but Lindvall pressed him until Bundy tried to explain, just as he once tried to explain to me, what it was like to live within a camouflage that you're too afraid to release, even at the point of your own execution when there's nothing more to be gained. What had Bundy done with his victim at the dump site after he had killed her? Now, in front of Lindvall, he struggled for an answer. But he had explained to me years earlier that there are some things a serial killer will do that he will never talk about, even when he believes his interviewer is not being judgmental, like a cop.

"I know you are and you've seen things, I'm sure," Bundy said. "But it's still an experience. I'm not asking for sympathy, but just that you understand that this has been something, this is the kind of memory that I've held so closely for so long that, um, 'course years ago I couldn't have under any circumstances talked about it. Couldn't have psychologically. There are many reasons. I'm not saying that's the only reason, but the kind of identity that I'd created or was created, and I'm not talking about multiple personalities, but identity that was related to what happened to Julie Cunningham more or less thrived on a kind of secrecy that formed the identity and to give us that secrecy was a kind of . . . it felt like a kind of death."

As he floated back to the memories of the night he met his victim, he told Lindvall about the actual conversation he had with her in the moments before he struck her, while they were walking to the car and she thought Bundy was just another guy she'd met up with, not a killer. "She mentioned that she had been on her way to have either dinner or drinks or both with a friend of hers, I believe a woman friend, but I'm not absolutely certain. But she said she wouldn't, it wouldn't matter if she was a little late, something to that effect. Also, I believe, she posted some letters. She stopped and ran over to a post office or a mailbox.

"I know there was some casual conversation," Bundy said. "But that involved some aspects of her life, you know, not intimate, just general kind of conversation. I know it was more of that, but it's, I can't recall specifically right now. It's something I could probably focus on, who knows?"

I remembered, during the visits I made to Florida to interview Bundy, how his moods seemed to change. At one point he was the center of attention, the egomaniacal wannabe lawyer who believed he could defend himself against the most heinous of charges the state had filed against him. Bundy failed at that, and when the sentence of death was pronounced, he seemed to collapse into himself. Then the long process of appeals began as Bundy worked the system to his advantage, hanging on until the end of 1988, when it became apparent that he had run out of time. Even then, when there was no more hope left and it was obvious that his own lawyers had led him astray, he tried to cobble together an ego to confront the police, who were lining up to get their scheduled days with him. But he failed at that, too, and there was nothing left of him at the end.

I always wondered about the different aspects of Bundy's personality and how they probably manifested themselves while he was committing murders and during the periods between homicides. Bundy was never really as smart as he thought he was, or as careful. For example, he told Matt Lindvall, who had asked him about the crowbar and the ropes he kept in his car, about the group of implements discovered by the Salt Lake City cop who had stopped Bundy for driving without lights in Salt Lake City. It was that arrest that proved Bundy's ultimate undoing because it had led to the search of his car, which recovered the telltale strand of hair wound around the stick shift, implicating him in the Utah murder of Melissa Smith.

"The items that were recovered in Salt Lake," Lindvall asked, "or the Utah area from your automobile, were these the items that were involved in the abduction and death in Vail, the crowbar, the ropes?"

"That's a good question," Bundy answered. "It could well have been, but they may have been changed. I went through these fits of despair where I throw everything away. And then I have to get more stuff."

"Did you clean your car between these situations?" Lindvall asked.

"Well, that's an understatement," Bundy answered. "But when the police finally in Salt Lake got hold of the car, it had a new interior in it. I mean and the thing was steam cleaned inside and out, which is why I find it almost humorous why they found so-called hairs in there because, I mean, you couldn't have found one of my hairs in there when I got done with that thing. But anyway, yeah, the inside of that car, the carpets, the seats, the rubber mats. I just went to a junkyard, got the stuff out of Volkswagens, you know, junk Volkswagens, took out everything, replaced the seats, some of the seats, backseats, all the upholstery, that is, all the rugs, all the stuff in there. And I did it myself. Painted it."

Matt Lindvall pressed Bundy to determine how he had managed to connect with Julie Cunningham on the night he killed her. Did Bundy know Vail? Had he been surveilling it, looking for victims? Had he visited it before? Or was Julie Cunningham simply in the wrong place when Ted Bundy drove through?

"Did you plan this in Vail because it was Vail or did it just happen?" Lindvall asked.

"It was just there," Bundy said, reiterating that he did not know Julie Cunningham, had never met her before, and only walked with her straight from the covered bridge, where he had introduced himself and asked for help to the parking lot.

Bundy had spent four hours driving and then wandering around Vail. He said he got stuck in a snowbank behind an apartment complex for a couple of hours and had to dig himself out. Then he left his VW in a parking lot and wandered around on foot until it got dark. After dark, he returned to his car and got his crutches and paraphernalia, then took the crowbar out of the car and propped it up by the engine, thus setting up the trap for the next victim who would cross his path.

Even Bundy himself professed not to understand his own behavior. He'd implied as much to me during our interviews, always talking around the crime and trying to avoid as much as possible the admission that he himself had committed the homicides. You had to pin Bundy down to the facts without being judgmental, get him to open the door a little so that you could peek inside. But although he was not remorseful, he did evidence shame when he refused to talk about what he called the "hardcore" aspects to his crimes. When Matt Lindvall asked him about why he returned to the spot to bury Julie Cunningham and what else might have taken place when Bundy saw her remains still looking fresh, laid out in exactly the same spot where he'd left her, he demurred. What was there about Bundy's returning to the spot?

"Why did you take that risk?" Lindvall asked. "Why did you decide to bury her? You hadn't buried anybody else to that point, had you?"

"Oh, yes, I had," Bundy said. Then he caught himself as if he'd given something away that he hadn't meant to. But he was committed to the answer. "Yes, uh, you know, it was, well, it was. . . ."

"Only you know everything," Lindvall said, and wondered aloud why there had been no discoveries of any of Bundy's buried victims. "I'm trying to think. I don't know of any cases where that has been the situation." But Lindvall had heard the hint of an admission that there were other Colorado victims out there, buried in unknown places that only Bundy knew about.

And Bundy confirmed it by saying, "That's why." He always had to be right. "Because in every case where a woman was buried, there's no body to be found."

"Are there any other people buried in Colorado by you?" Lindvall asked him directly.

"Well, yeah," Bundy answered, but he was suddenly aware that he'd been walked into an admission he might not have been prepared to make. "Well, you know, but it's not a large number. The question, yeah, well, that's something else."

Then, when Lindvall suggested that Bundy's behavior had deviated from what he did normally, Bundy explained, "Well, there is, this is something that I think we can all learn from. I mean, I'm still learning about myself and about this, this, I mean even though these events are remote in time, every time I've had an opportunity to go over this and I've only gone over it in the abstract with people, I've always worked around the edges. I've never told anybody the hardcore stuff before. But I've gone over it in my own mind, trying to understand it. What is ordinary? There is nothing ordinary about any of this."

Lindvall was still perplexed about why Bundy had driven from Utah to Colorado to visit and bury Julie Cunningham's body. It was a very risky thing for him to do, and it seemed that beneath Bundy's explanations there was still something he wasn't revealing. The underlying question was still: Why had Bundy gone back to the body?

In the case of the Washington dump sites, Bundy said, "I went back to that scene a day later, two days later, and I don't know how much, how familiar you are, well, about crime scenes. I mean, after a day or two, the body is relatively fresh, after, depending on the climate, animals, humidity, time of year, you name it. Depends on the decomposition cycle."

In Julie Cunningham's case, however, six to eight weeks after Bundy had left her in the open, "I would describe it as being mummified," he said. "I had never seen somebody who'd been out that long who was not either eaten, I mean consumed by insects in some way. But the body was basically untouched, but, you know, obviously very different looking than someone who is either alive or just freshly killed."

But why had Bundy gone back? He said it wasn't particularly the condition of the body that he wanted to see. "That's not the reason I went back. The reason I went back was twofold. Primarily, for the burial, and secondly, to check the scene to make sure that nothing had been left there."

"Why did you choose to bury her?" Lindvall asked. "You could have just left and reduced the risk greatly."

"My frame of mind at the time," Bundy answered. "It just seemed, well, it just seemed like the thing to do. My motivations were twofold, but primarily to conceal."

Lindvall reminded Bundy that he hadn't concealed his victims' bodies in either the Aspen murder or in Utah, which sent Bundy into an explanation of his modus operandi and how it tended to vary because "I was never an automaton. I would do things differently over time."

Bundy reiterated that on the night of the murder, he hit Julie with the crowbar, an off-the-shelf crowbar you could get in any hardware store or Sears; and when he reached the dump site and hit her again, she was unconscious, half inside and half outside the car. He laid her on the ground, strangled her, removed her clothes, and carried her into the woods, but, "There are details I am not entirely clear about there." He added, first, in answer to a question, that he did nothing whatsoever to the body and, next, asked whether Lindvall meant in the woods or by the car.

"I'm not really clear on that. This is something I would like to reserve until we can talk in more depth about it," Bundy said, arguing instead that they should simply search for the body in the location where he said they'd find it and worry about events at the crime scene later. Obviously, he was concealing something: his behavior, his activity at the crime scene that first night, and the reasons he returned to the crime scene six weeks later. Even though Bundy had told me about his activities with Georgann Hawkins's body, he was holding back with Lindvall about his activities with Julie Cunningham. He even admitted it.

So Lindvall proceeded along a different track. He referred to other cases in Colorado, cases that weren't necessarily Vail PD's, to create a context in which Bundy could talk about why he buried Julie and what he might have done with her body both times he was at the dump site.

"I'm gonna ask you," Lindvall began. "You abducted a girl from Grand Junction. Did you bury her?"

Bundy said he only wanted to focus on Lindvall's case, Julie Cunningham.

"But you know we are focusing on that. But I am verifying, and that's the only way I can verify what you've told me. The only way is by verifying something like that."

Bundy again demurred, saying that he could only verify what he was asked. He wasn't asked to talk about cases other than the Julie Cunningham case from Vail.

"Can you tell me," Lindvall began again, this time referring to the other Colorado cases that Bundy seemed to be alluding to, "if they're buried or not?"

Bundy hesitated again and then finally said, "There are other buried remains in Colorado." And, in a backdoor admission, Ted revealed that there might actually be a dump site with other bodies.

"In Colorado?" Lindvall asked.

"Right," Bundy answered.

"And associated with that Grand Junction situation and then buried in the same place?" Lindvall continued.

"No, no. Okay, okay," Bundy finally said. "Well, we'll get, is there somebody out there we can call to have them stop by the . . . ?"

But no one in Colorado law enforcement would consider it, Lindvall told him, because of the late date and the vagueness of the location. So they had to work on it together, Bundy told him. Bundy would work on it and Lindvall would work on getting maps that Bundy could use to pinpoint the locations of body dump sites for them. And they did this until Lindvall maneuvered Bundy back to Julie's burial site, when he tried, yet again, to get Bundy to talk about his activities at the site.

"How deep was the grave?" the detective asked.

"Two to three feet, at least, maybe three."

"What was the diameter of it?"

"Just enough for the body," Bundy answered.

"How did you place the body?"

"On its back. Yeah, on the back."

"Did you put the body in there whole, or was it folded?"

"No, it was laid out," Bundy said.

"Like normal?"

"Yeah," Bundy continued. "Like fully extended."

"Fully extended, arms at the side? Arms above?"

"No," Bundy corrected. "At the side."

"Ted," Lindvall said. "This is really important to know if the body was placed in whole."

"Okay," Bundy answered. "Fine, well, I'm telling you it's all in one place. It's all there. I mean, it was at one time. At that time."

"And was there any damage to the body other than strangulation?"

"No," Bundy answered. "There was, I think you'll see from, well, when you locate it that it should all be intact." And it would be a skeleton by now, he and Lindvall agreed, and it would have no clothing and no possessions or items from the victim.

Matt Lindvall kept on encouraging Bundy not to hold back about what had happened at Julie's gravesite on the first night Bundy left her there. Bundy, trying to back away from answering the question, kept telling Lindvall to talk to me, presumably about what Bundy did to his victims' corpses, but Lindvall wasn't buying it. "I know it's difficult. Can't imagine too much being more difficult than that," Lindvall said. "I don't want you to hold back. I think you'll feel better about yourself."

"We've both covered a lot of ground today," Bundy replied, still searching for cover as he was pressed to answer about his activities at the crime scene.

"You know," Lindvall said. "I mean you don't tell everything."

"I could have told you, if I had wanted, we're talking about being dishonest. Just, hey, this is all that happened, period."

"But that's not all that happened," Lindvall said.

"And yet I didn't bullshit you," Bundy continued. "And yet I won't bullshit you now. I'm just having a hard time talking about that one segment of this rather prolonged incident."

Lindvall acknowledged what Bundy was telling him.

"And I could just say that I've known guys"—*guys* was Bundy's term for other serial killers, particularly the ones he'd met on Florida's death row—"who've just bullshitted their way through this part of it and said, oh, nothing. I'm not going to bullshit you through it. I'm telling you that's a point we're going to, in my case, we will talk about." He tacitly admitted to Lindvall what Lindvall had suspected about what Bundy might have done with the body, acts performed on the body. "But not today."

"Mike [Fisher] and I want to be able to say at a point in time in the future that you cooperated with us fully," Lindvall said, perhaps trying to get Bundy to think of himself as a part of history, his words still resonating long after he was executed. "And that's what you want us to be able to say. Well, that's why I'm getting the last, should we say, roadblock out of the way and then I'm going to want to excuse myself. I want to thank you, knowing that I know everything about the situation that you know and remember."

He reminded Bundy that there was another burial site in Colorado that he needed to cover with him as well as get as much details as possible in the Cunningham case; it would not only help Bundy, but it would add "validity to the scene of the burial." In other words, what Bundy said about what he did would have to comport with what forensics reported after Julie's remains were recovered from the burial site that Bundy had told Lindvall about.

"I don't like what happened," Bundy said at the close of the interview, referring not only generally to the crimes he had committed, but specifically to the murder of Julie Cunningham. "I mean, notwithstanding any speculation about the kind of personality that I might be. I, it's not gratuitous for me to say that I feel horrible about it. And not that, sadly enough, won't bring her back, but I do. And it's not enough to say it's an atrocity because it was. And not that anybody cares, but if it should ever occur to you to relate this to anybody, you can tell them that I get no secret joy or pleasure out of it. That my own special kind of hell and madness that I lived in ten, twenty years ago was as wrong and as terrible as it could be. And I'm sorry."

Was Bundy being gratuitous in his final interview with the Colorado authorities or was he truly recounting what must have been the cowardly hell he walked through most of his entire life? Not only was he a chickenshit who coldcocked his victims before he carted them away and strangled them, he was a necrophile who sexually aroused himself with their remains as he spent time with them at their resting places, even as they were decomposing into skeletal shadows of what they once were.

But this interview was still not the last the world would hear from Ted Bundy.

16

Peace, ted

Theodore Robert Bundy, like George Russell, John Wayne Gacy, and other serial killers, was a public danger. There are empty bedrooms, lonely people, and broken hearts scattered from Washington to Florida as a result of his murders. Without their families' voices screaming for investigation, some victims are easily forgotten—out of sight, out of mind. But there will be more like them in the future and we must be ready to find their killers. Examining Bundy's carnage and understanding how he thought and acted helps us investigate and deal more effectively with people like him. I had listened to and thought about every one of Ted's words. He never spoke hastily when reflecting upon the Riverman's habits. Even though Ted's analysis of the Riverman was therapeutic for him, enabling him to relive his fantasies, it also revealed to me many of his own previously unknown behaviors, and those of others like him. Ted's reflections about the Riverman were such extraordinary evidence of the quickness of his perceptive faculties that I had no doubt that he could see a great deal that was still hidden from me.

Partly through the luck of the draw and partly because I just happened to be around, I was assigned to the job of investigating the disappearances of Janice Ott and Denise Naslund in 1974 from Lake Sammamish State Park. At that time, I had no idea how to investigate missing-persons cases. I now have a much better idea, and so at the end of over twenty-five years of investigative work and because Ted Bundy is dead, I can supply those missing links in the personality of Ted Bundy, which turned out to be remarkably gruesome. Detective work is of interest itself, but that interest was nothing to me compared to the string of Bundy's murders, which gave me the greatest shock and surprise throughout my long career as a cop. Even now, after the long interval since Bundy's execution, I find myself struggling as I think of the Bundy case, and feeling once more that sudden flood of grief, pressure, and incredulity that utterly overran my mind at times during this investigation. During the years dealing with Ted Bundy, while denying to colleagues and the media that I was doing so, I became something of a Bundy victim and a member of his coterie of investigators. Let me say to fellow police detectives and the public at large, which has shown some interest in this remarkably horrible man, that they are not to blame me for not having shared my knowledge with them before this time. I should have considered it my first duty to do so and would have told what only I knew if I had not been barred by an emphatic prohibition from Ted's own lips.

Even though every murderer is different in nature, Bundy shared certain characteristics with other serial killers. Ted was a loner. Inside, he was extremely insecure. While striving for security, he made life miserable for the rest of us. His relationships with others were very superficial. He was a fellow who could not stick with anyone. His relatives and acquaintances may have tried very hard to have contact with him, thus feeling that they were very close to him. Many of his friends, both old and new, were starved for love and affection. They felt what Ted wanted them to feel because he was able to detect and exploit people's needs. In a way, he made victims of all who knew him.

What added to Ted's convincing nature was that he was intelligent, attractive, and charming—he had traits that were pleasing to most of his admirers. His reputation was that of an aspiring lawyer and a bright young man who was dutiful to family. But when Ted murmured gratitude, his words came from an empty heart. He would cast off friends without a thought, and once alienated, he could reel them back in like bloated trout. There was always something about Ted that they liked and kept coming back to. His efforts to maintain friendships were nothing more than attempts to pre-serve control over those very people he used for his own purposes. Ted Bundy was an almost complete sociopath who made no dis-tinction between what he wanted and what belonged to someone else. Ted had absolutely no sense of boundaries and sought to exer-cise his control over anyone who crossed his path.

Because of Ted's appearance of having a winning, good-guy bravado, his friends thought that he was the last person who would have murdered anyone. Over the years, anytime I saw news stories in which friends of a suspected killer said, "He was such a nice boy, he couldn't have done it," I thought of Ted and said to myself that the police had the right guy.

The Black Hole

Hervey Cleckley's "mask of sanity" was the ultimate description of Ted Bundy as well as of the Riverman and other long-term serial killers. One of my fellow detectives best described Ted as an "empty suit." Ted's mask was more convincing than that of others. What lay beneath the surface was Ted's fatally crippled personality, a dreadfully dark side, a black hole that no one could truly pene-trate but that exercised control over others like a gravitational pull. Ted sucked everyone into that black hole—certainly his murder victims, people who supported him, and even the police interroga-tors who tried to pull information out of him. Ted perceived other killers as black holes also and could talk to them because he under-stood them. Luckily for us, black holes like Ted have unique attrib-utes that make them stand out to police. Ted was attracted to other black holes, and that's why he said he could help find the Riverman by entering what he perceived to be his psyche. Ted understood how black-hole personalities think and react and thus was able to retrace their footsteps or see through their eyes.

Now and then, Ted would gravitate toward normalcy, seeking harmless contact with others. But the rare occasion out with friends was tempered by the realization that when the social hour was over, he would eventually return to his life of despair. Most of the time, Ted was alone, spending his private moments engrossed in murder, rehearsing murder, and fantasizing about murder. I never saw a man with more pain in his face. You had only to get a glimpse of his eyes to see it.

The most obvious of Ted's characteristic behaviors was his high degree of mobility. Ted had a compulsion to travel, usually in a vehicle—prowling, hunting, cruising, and searching for victims. He became, especially when he was acting out the behaviors leading up to an abduction and murder, like the walking dead. There was no emotion except for the compulsion to possess someone else, to inflict upon her a crippling blow that would deliver her into his control. He was chilling in his single-mindedness to kill.

Ted, like other serial killers, who are all rootless creatures, had access to more than one vehicle, which allowed him to always be in transit and throw those who were searching for him off his trail. His tan Volkswagen Beetle was his primary mode of transportation for visiting his dump sites and trolling for victims. Also, he had a green pickup truck and, occasionally, drove his girlfriend's light-blue VW. His use of different vehicles made detection difficult, since we were looking for a metallic brown VW Beetle.

Remarkable also was Ted's ability for long-distance driving. Ted advised us that cities within 300 miles were easily accessible to the Riverman, and we surmised that he said that because that is what he thought himself when he was killing. Ted's abduction and murder of Kathy Parks from Oregon State University over 280 miles from Seattle was the best example. Even worse for Oregon authorities, he dumped her skull on Taylor Mountain near Seattle. This kind of traveling defied the norm for conventional murderers, but fit the model of serial killers, who spread their victims' remains over many different jurisdictions. Ted knew how to cover his tracks.

Ted's Methodology

Ted altered his VW bug to suit his needs by removing the passenger side front seat and borrowing his fiancée's ski rack. That enabled him to have his unconscious victim close to him, while carrying her bicycle on the rack, as he transported her away to the murder and victim dumping site. Other killers have removed inside door handles and locks, installed binding devices and portable "Kojak" lights, and carried radios that monitor police frequencies.

Peace, ted

After his murders, Ted was obsessed with leaving very little in the way of evidence that could be traced to him. Similarly, many long-term serial killers are focused totally on destruction of evidence. Only on the rare occasion would any evidence be left behind at any body recovery site by a serial killer. The risky part was returning to those scenes to clean them up. Someone might see him.

Of course, killers like John Wayne Gacy carried the possession aspect to the extreme by burying many of his victims in the crawl space beneath his home. Bundy experienced ultimate control of his victims at first by taking their severed heads home with him while he was killing in Washington State. He then changed his method of operation, taking the entire body of his victim home with him while he was in Utah.

Ted's tidiness was not the only reason he revisited his body dump sites. His unwritten signature was expressed in terms of his complete control and grisly possession of women. By frequently using the terms *objects* or *things* for *female, lady,* or *woman,* he relegated women to the inanimate in his mind. The young women he attacked were articles to possess as far as he was concerned. His assault and abduction of Lynda Healy while she slept in her basement room was an ultimate high for him at the time. He took total control of her by removing her under cover of darkness. The Chi Omega murders at Florida State University were a different means of control for Bundy. If it were not for one unwitting sorority sister who interrupted Ted's frenzy at a time when he thought he was in total possession of numerous coeds, Bundy would have killed every single woman asleep in that house.

It was almost as though Bundy took complete possession of his victims, in all of their dimensions. As evidence of his morbidity, Ted readily admitted that he was preoccupied with the cyanotic hue of a corpse's fingernails, discoloration of the skin after death, necrophilia, and possession of the female corpse. In psychological terms his behavior can best be described as compulsive necrophilia and extreme perversion. Ted's suggestion of staking out freshly discovered crime scenes was a well-conceived strategy to catch the compulsive necrophiliac in the act. Even though Ted never stated it outright, by suggesting the crime scene surveillances, I think he believed the Riverman was a compulsive necrophiliac.

Ted, like many serial killers, was uncommonly familiar with the

419

routines of police work. This was no accident, because serial killers watch police to find out how they can best avoid detection. Early in his career, Ted had studied rape investigations as part of his role with the King County Crime Council. He convincingly posed as a police detective when he tried to abduct Carol DaRonch at the Fashion Place Mall in Salt Lake City. Many other serial killers were very involved with law enforcement activities. Kenneth Bianchi, one of the Hillside Stranglers, applied for a job with the Los Angeles Sheriff's Department and was working as a security cop when he was arrested. Edmund Kemper of Santa Cruz, California, visited the same tavern that police detectives frequented after work. Arthur Shawcross had his morning doughnuts and coffee at a little shop where he met with local police as the shifts changed and told them how the fish were biting in the nearby Genesee River. John Wayne Gacy had his personal vehicle rigged up like a detective's squad car, blue light and all. He also monitored police frequencies on his portable radios.

Bundy learned a lot more about police procedures by voraciously reading every detective magazine he could get his hands on. Ted's detective magazine interest was twofold. First, he learned about the details of rape-murder investigations and how they were conducted. If bestselling true crime author Ann Rule, then writing under the pen name of Andy Stack, only knew that her research educated the very partner she sat next to at the crisis clinic . . . Second, he took photographs of murder victims, who were graphically displayed, out into the woods to enhance his fantasies about them. During the period when he was living in Seattle and killing, Bundy also took crime photos to isolated places where he could associate their death with his control. This was another way he could anticipate the thrill of control before he ever took a victim to a dump site.

The geographic knowledge Ted possessed of his abduction points and dump sites was formidable. In fact, his familiarity with them is beyond comprehension to the normal person. Ted traced his travels by continuously practicing his routines for abduction. Therefore, he was extremely comfortable in his surroundings, not looking out of place. Often, when police detectives canvass neighborhoods, they typically ask people, "Did you see anything unusual?" Keeping in mind that serial killers are not seen running down the street with a bloody knife in their teeth, which *would* be something unusual, the more appropriate question that police might want to ask when tracking a serial killer is "What did you see that was usual?"

Monitoring the investigation of himself, "the Ted killer," through the news media was a survival technique for Ted. He was able to gauge how close investigators were to his trail by analyzing what they said to the media. Ted told us that police spokespersons say too much to the media and, as a result, often tip off the killer. He realized that police were usually under tremendous pressure to provide details to reporters, but Ted warned that they should not play games with the killer through the media. He admitted that some killers were susceptible, but that the police ran the risk of entering dangerous territory if they tried it with someone like the Riverman. It's not that police would tell the killer something the killer already knew, Ted said; the police were more likely to assume the killer knew something when he really didn't. By tipping the killer off to police strategy when they thought they were feeding him disinformation, the police were likely to impede their own investigation. Ted's main point was that the police would release part of the story, unaware of what the entire story was. Guess who was the only person who knew the whole story: the killer himself.

Throughout his adult life, Ted was a master at juggling his life of feigned normalcy with his life as a killer. While he lived with his fiancée, he killed over a score of other women. He made it a point to be with Liz Kendall at dinner and then would disappear until midnight or later. In those hours, Ted was loose on campus, haunting the paths taken by coeds, practicing his routines, or mysteriously abducting women from their avenues of security. If Liz complained, he would make her feel guilty for not appreciating the time he allotted to her. The rage inside Ted was so intense that he readily blamed others for his problems. The result was that those people were cleverly manipulated by Ted to feel guilty about causing him his problems.

The only physical quirk Bundy displayed, which was noticeable only to an alert observer, was his abnormal use of eye contact. The living witnesses from Lake Sammamish noticed that the Ted who tried to pick them up had a strange stare while he was talking to them. It was as if his eyes were transfixed on his prey, like the eyes of a cat. I remember that the only time he looked at me was when he was manipulating me. At other times Bundy's eyes darted around rapidly in their sockets, following whatever movement was in his area. Then, at a point in our conversation, he would suddenly fix his eyes on me, with that look on his face that said, "Are you believing my bullshit?"

Retrospectively, some of Ted's personality traits can be found in those neat boxes often used in abnormal-psychology texts discussing the characteristics of typical psychopathological behaviors. Unfortunately, he was often able to mask many of those behaviors and go undetected as the dangerous creature he was.

Trust Bandit

Throughout Ted's life, he constantly stole everyone's trust. He conned the best. One such person was Professor Ronald Smith of the University of Washington's Psychology Department. Professor Smith once wrote in Ted's behalf for law school admission: "Mr. Bundy is undoubtedly one of the top undergraduate students in our department. . . . He is exceedingly bright, personable, highly motivated, and conscientious. . . . He has the capacity for hard work and because of his intellectual curiosity is a pleasure to interact with. . . . I recommend him to you without qualification." Ted proved that attending college full-time was not an impediment to his murderous compulsions.

Serial killers are very knowledgeable of the areas they operate in. They literally kill in their own backyards or, as others have written, they live and move about among their prey. Ted was completely at home on a college campus, at sorority houses, or at a ski resort frequented by young adults. The Riverman, we surmised, was very much at home among the bars along the Sea-Tac strip, as Florida's Bobby Joe Long was at home among the topless bars of North Tampa. Arthur Shawcross was so familiar with the hookers in Rochester's red-light district that the women called him by name, confided their problems to him, waited for him to drive them home on cold winter mornings, or sat on the car he was driving because the hood was still warm. If Shawcross himself is to be believed, they literally placed themselves in his trap.

Serial killers are clever and cunning; however, too much has been made of serial killers who have an excessively high IQ. Most people want to believe that all serial killers are highly intelligent, to be able to kill for so long. High intelligence is not a prerequisite. The crude reality is that some are borderline defective or possess a normal IQ, but are clearly literate. What is important is the killer's ability to abduct and kill someone without detection. To operate effectively, a killer must abide by the rules of the neighborhood without drawing attention to himself.

Four Teds

The general public and Ted's acquaintances had the impression that Ted was a clever, good-looking, and intelligent psychopathic killer caught up in the ecstasy of raping and murdering pretty women. What I observed was totally different. In revelations more chilling than Hannibal Lecter's, I saw four Teds behind one mask. He was not a split personality, but there were four different levels on which our relationship worked. They all existed between the two poles of the antisocial narcissistic personality: grandiosity to utter self-devaluation. Let me caution the reader here that in spite of our investigative effort, gaps remain in the understanding of Bundy's personality.

At first, it was as if Ted were the Riverman himself, the cunning psychopath, planning and practicing the lures he used with women, familiarizing himself with appropriate dump sites, checking his routes to and from, and meticulously planning what he would do after the murder to cover his tracks. He projected that personality during our interviews.

The second was an almost hapless version of Ted, the disorganized neurotic, a loser often in a drunken stupor, a frightened, reluctant killer traumatized by his murderous behavior, and afraid of having any remembrance of his most recent murder anywhere near him. It wasn't that he was afraid of getting caught; he was afraid his neurotic personality would completely disintegrate in front of whomever he was with, and he would do anything to get it away from him. His neurotic tendencies also drew unnecessary attention to him. That neurosis allowed Bundy to give too much information about himself to potential victims that he did not abduct.

The third Ted that I observed was the self-serving, swashbuckling, hypergrandiose paranoid, driven by an eerie bravado and dazzled by his own sense of omnipotence, who personally negotiated with governors and attorneys general, and held beleaguered relatives of murder victims and detectives hostage with information. That third Ted behaved like a cruel despot, indifferent to the reality that was taking place around him. Ted's grandiose behavior was exemplified best by his own words, spoken to me after he finished confessing and was ready to negotiate for his life on the Friday prior to his Tuesday execution.

"Do you want to talk about the events leading up to Lynda Healy, the first one on Taylor Mountain, the area that we have on the record?" I asked plainly.

Ted gave a huge sigh, as if he was about to tell all, when he was interrupted by Diana Weiner. She apparently knew Ted was in trouble and intervened to rescue him. I was shocked by her interruption and even more shocked that FBI Agent Bill Hagmaier didn't defend me and tell her to butt out. Ted trusted Bill to some extent, so I anticipated that Ted might have listened to him, but he said nothing. Whatever the substance of their conversation, when we continued Ted would not talk about murders when there wasn't someone missing.

Ted said to them, "I mean, here's what I'd like to do today. No, but I appreciate any advice I can get." Hagmaier was still quiet.

Reaffirming that I might be able to corroborate more from cases I knew more about, I said, " 'Cause I think I can corroborate a lot about the Taylor Mountain incidents, and you might be able to lead me to the evidence there. There are some things about Ott and Naslund, too, you could probably corroborate."

Confidently, Ted regained his composure after I temporarily had him on the ropes, no thanks to Bill Hagmaier. Mistaking my name for Bill's, Ted said, "Well, Bill, I could corroborate something on virtually every one of the—I mean, almost without a doubt on every one of these, in one way or another. I don't think anybody doubts that I've done some bad things. The question is what, of course, and how and maybe even most importantly why. And I—I'm not—"

More than slightly perturbed, I interrupted, "Well, most of the people that are coming here, you know, the law enforcement people, are wondering which cases you are talking about. What can you help us with in finding other bodies, and if there's any other physical evidence out there, like bicycles, clothes, and backpacks, what happened to the stuff that's missing—basic information that you're definitely the one."

"That's right," he reaffirmed. "And law enforcement is definitely one of the primary interested parties here, but not the only one. I think they represent many people, and rightly so, those who are the legitimate kind of interests here, but there are other interests."

With a scolding tone to my voice, I said, "At the beginning, I asked you, you know, where you wanted to start and you didn't know so I told you and then you started."

"Uh huh. Yeah?" Ted said, wondering what I was leading to.

"I can just move on to another one if that's what you want for me to do, but that's your order of things," I said to clarify.

Realizing that I was not going to stand for his stalling tactics, he decided to tell me what he was really thinking. He said, "Well, no, we got a little bit—see, I haven't been honest with you. This morning when I wrote down this itinerary—this outline of mine—I hadn't fully intended to talk any specifics today. What I wanted to do is sort of set out some ground rules and get you to understand where I'm coming from and what I'm looking for, okay? Now, earlier today, I received some information, and it became clear that it would be in my best interest to talk about specifics to show my good faith. And, at that time, we were talking about Colorado, to begin with. And maybe Utah. To let the authorities in each of those states know that this is not any kind of game, but that we have to have more, and I can't put myself in the corner of going through what I consider to be just the factual high points, and we're missing a lot of the stuff in between. You know, I make no bones about it; I am looking for an opportunity to tell the story as best I can in the way that makes sense to me and the way it will help not just you or the families—but that's very important—but also to help my own family. You see, I saw the look in my stepson's eyes yesterday, after he had been told for the first time that—you see, he's always believed in his heart—I mean, he's always wanted to believe that I had never done anything like this. As hard as it may be for you to believe that, there are people who do believe that. And there are people close to me who believe that. And to see the look in his eyes confirmed my worst fears. See, he said, he was just absolutely astounded. He couldn't understand. He was writing me questions, just furiously writing questions. I could see how really bewildered he was. And I need to give him a chance to know and others a chance to know what was really going on. What it was really like for me."

"Well, I think that a lot of that is going to come out with each stage we go through," I volunteered, faking understanding.

"Well, this is true," Ted responded.

"And if you want to start first with how you wanted to start and go with it, go ahead and do it," I offered, knowing time was wasting away for me.

Ted, at his best, was trying to gain sympathy for how hard it was for him to finally talk about his murders. He went into a long explanation. "What I wanted to show with you is something we haven't done before and which is talk about something very specific. This is something I've held, God forbid, but I've held for all these many years, fifteen years or so. And I think I'm glad we started with that particular individual—victim—case, because it was one of the unidentified ones, more or less, you know. I think you had your suspicions, obviously, and very strong suspicions. So we start with a case which I think kind of demonstrates or exemplifies what we're trying to do. What kind of information I have. I intend to talk to the Colorado authorities about one of their cases where they've found nothing. Absolutely nothing. And the same with Utah."

Quickly, I asked, "[Are] there any Washington cases that are like that? You mentioned Manson as a possibility—buried."

"Yeah. I think there may be only one, though," Ted replied.

"Only one that's actually buried?" I said.

"Yeah," said Ted.

"You want to talk about that one?" I asked, knowing that his answer was no.

"No," Ted said with a sigh of relief that time was running out with me.

"How about the location?" I continued, as though I didn't hear him.

"Well, all this—all this must come out and will come out. What I need is a chance to do it," Ted began to plead.

Confirming to Ted that if he told me where something was, I had the resources to search, I said, "We're a hell of a lot better at searching today than we were fourteen years ago. That's for sure. And we've got the auspices of the Green River task force to search in the most professional way possible, and that's about all I can offer, if we know a location where you think we can find something."

"Uh huh," Ted said, listening intently to me.

"But to my knowledge, you know, Hawkins and Manson were the only two that disappeared who we knew were possibly associated with you. We may have had the missing-person mistake, which is entirely possible, but those are the only two. The reason I asked you if you ever buried anybody—the chances of finding remains that have been left aboveground over a long period of time are slim to none," I said, referring to the 14-year time span since his murders.

"That's right. That's exactly true," Ted said. "Oh, nothing. Nothing. I mean, I could tell you exactly where some clothing was thrown, but you're not going to find anything. Not after all that time. Not along I-Ninety or anywhere else."

Aware that Ted would become incensed that I didn't really care about why he committed his murders, I ventured into dangerous territory with him by saying, "And from a factual standpoint—you know, the reasons why. To me, the why never caught anybody. So cops, with their mentality, think of what, where, when, and who. And so we're kind of stuck with you wanting to explain why and maybe the occasion with William [Hagmaier] here will help that out a lot more than the one with me. But I'm not interested in the why."

Ted took my statement calmly, because he felt the whole world wanted to know why. He continued as though he respected my opinion. Unshaken, he said, "Well, I'm not trying to convince you, Bob, that you should be interested in the why if you're not. I think there are a lot of people that are. I know I am. And I think a lot of people are interested in why. People constantly come up to me and they will ask me why. I mean, it baffles people. And they're not law enforcement folks. And I don't think you mean that the why never caught anybody, because understanding the people you're after is sometimes ninety percent of finding them, okay? That's what you're trying to do with the Green River guy. And more power to you, but I think why is important to a certain degree. I'm not saying we're going to make any tremendous breakthrough here that I'm some kind of different creature, but I think I have the ability to articulate what was going on inside me a lot better than a lot of other people in a way that maybe people can understand. But again, it may or may not benefit you to put it together into how this evolved, year by year, to the first incident, to the second, to the third, what happened before, during, after, in my own mind, what was inflaming me, what was inciting me, what was terrifying me. I mean, all those things. This is not by any means an attempt to gain sympathy. It's simply an attempt to understand. And it would help me. It would help, most importantly, my family. It's not worth it to me, really, to in the short run reawaken all these bad feelings and all this hurt and all this anger in a firestorm of publicity, which would hurt my family, without any kind of compensating ability to help them understand. And that's a major consideration for me. I mean, my feeling is we do it right—I do it right—or I don't do it, really, at all."

Since I had just received the Ted Bundy 101 lecture about the importance of why he did what he did, wasting more of my valuable time, I snapped back, "Okay, how is right for you, then? What do you want to do? I mean, we've got forty-five minutes."

"Well, we've got forty-five minutes left. We've got forty-five minutes left. And also, I haven't spoken to Bill at all," proclaimed Ted.

Not fully comprehending the rapport Bill Hagmaier had built up with Ted and what Ted was going to cover with Bill, I responded, "Well, Bill's got a time with you tomorrow, and I don't."

Ted explained, "Okay, all right. Well, I need the opportunity to go over all the cases with you and with others who are experts in the field of serial homicide and to piece it together. The hard data, the crime scenes, the psychological stuff, everything. And we can't do that in forty-five minutes and we can't do that in two days, 'cause there's more people involved than just you. There's more obviously than you. More states, more jurisdictions. And so, we don't have everybody scheduled right now, so for me to give them a demonstration of good faith, we only really have tomorrow and Sunday. Monday is basically just going to be for family. It could be the last day. So . . ."

Feeling that Ted should rewrite his agenda, I asked, "What do you want to do with the two days that we have here? 'Cause they're going to be asking the very same questions that I am, the other people coming in, wanting to know time and events."

Ted knew that the attorney general of Washington was not going to speak on his behalf to the governor of Florida. Now the real story about why Ted was stalling was about to come out. Ted explained,

"I know. Sure they are. Well, let me give you an example. I won't give you specifics right now. Well—I—a representative of the attorney general's office in one of the states got in touch with a friend of mine. And he said, 'Listen, we know that Bundy has a lot of things to talk about that happened in our state. We know we don't have enough time to really get into all that before Tuesday. Give us one thing, one tangible thing and our attorney general and our governor will do what they can to convince Florida to give us time to do it right, to develop this information, to find whatever needs to be found. And they're committed to that. And they're not asking for everything. We just want a demonstration of good faith. One hard thing to go on.' And that's basically my thinking at this point."

"So that state's not Washington. It's Colorado. And the hard thing is that you need to locate the bodies," I said.

"Well, that was the thinking, that was what came off the top there. It's not just Colorado. It's Utah and Idaho and other places," said Ted, not realizing that the locations of his victims in those states were under six feet of snow, and there wasn't time to dig for them before Tuesday. If Ted didn't understand this, I surely wasn't going to tell him.

"Well, how do you want to treat the time here with me now?" I asked. "We're not scheduled here. I've asked about nighttime visits. I don't know what the policy is here," I reminded Ted.

It was an appropriate time for the tape on the recorder to expire, so when Ted began again, his mood had changed to the wheeler-dealer, grandiose psychopath. He sarcastically asked, "What's the attorney general of Washington willing to do?"

"Willing to do?" I repeated.

"Anything? Who is the attorney general these days?" Ted asked in his swashbuckling tone.

"Ken Eikenberry," I responded, not knowing where Ted was going with this.

"Good old Ken Eikenberry," Ted said as if he were back on the committee of young Republicans being solicited for his support by one of the candidates.

"He's a Republican. You can imagine what he said already. He said we're not going to stop the execution, not for any reason. So, a lot of law enforcement agencies in our state are waiting to hear back from me," I said with a confident voice.

"Just a second," Ted said, looking at a guard approaching to remind Ted of the time.

I continued. "We've been discussing the fact that you've been focusing mainly, at least in your reactions—I mean, you went thoroughly through one particular case, fairly well."

"Yup," Ted said.

"And although there's some extra little things that are tough for you to talk about, the reality is that once we get to talking about another one, you're thinking more about the Colorado cases," I vehemently protested.

"No, I'm not," Ted said, defending himself.

"And what's behind your stalling rather than dealing with me?" I responded with force.

Protecting his backside by lying, Ted stammered, "No, I'm not. I'm telling you, I'm not, I'm not treating you—wouldn't treat you—any differently. And I'm not holding you hostage, Bob."

I responded tersely, as though Ted should have begun the day in a different fashion, "It sounds like, from what you've explained all through the past couple hours, is that maybe we should start with yourself—way back whenever you wanted to start off life, and start talking up through it. And maybe we might get to nineteen seventy-four and seventy-five, but your main interest is in making sure that people and humanity and those who deal with this know about the reasons for this activity and what goes on, the physical things that people can pick up on when somebody's life's going astray. And maybe that's probably the most important thing to society, more so than the cops."

"I know," Ted said.

"But if that sequence happens to lead through some cases as we go along through the history of your life, maybe that's the type of atmosphere that you'd rather be in," I offered.

Quickly, Ted replied, "That's the kind of atmosphere where I would be able to give it to you, at least in a verbal form like it was. Not bits and pieces. What we have been doing is taking stuff out of context. And I know you have narrow focuses. You have a narrow focus given your law enforcement perspective. And that's important for what you do. It's important that those questions be answered. But it's important for me that those questions be answered in context, for any number of reasons, but perhaps the most important reason is for my own family, so that they understand. But if they're only getting part of the story, they're only getting the worst stuff. You know what's going to happen if and when all this stuff goes public, if all we did was just hit the whos and the whens and the body count. It's going to be bad enough as it is."

I continued, "We're only here to represent one factor of the body count or whatever it is. You know, I personally, police, and law enforcement, we have an interest in knowing about the historical background."

Agreeing, Ted said, "Right."

I counseled Ted. "And you have talked on the other side of the wall to more cops than I have. My thinking is that the way things are confirmed with cops is just to tell the goddamn truth about the facts."

Moving his head back slightly, like I might come through the glass at him, he said, "That's right."

"Get it over with and you know when you got it. That's what they understand," I said.

"That's the way it is," Ted answered.

"The manner in which these interviews are organized, it's all cop-oriented." I was scolding Ted for not preparing himself better.

"Well, that's too bad," Ted said, bowing his head.

"One detective's turn, somebody else's turn, and then your time's up. Maybe you didn't organize this properly," I said, showing Ted that his strategy wasn't working as he'd hoped.

"Good point," Ted said.

I really pushed Ted to the limits by suggesting that he and his advisors planned poorly because they invited Idaho authorities, who had no idea to which murders Ted was referring. So I asked, "What are you going to tell the guy from Idaho that comes in? He wasn't even aware that there was a murder there."

Stuttering, Ted said, "Yeah. I don't think—do we have that set up yet?"

I explained, "When I called him first to tell him to come, I said, you know this might be a surprise to you, but he wants you down there. The guy from Idaho was totally unaware. You're going to have to tell him. He doesn't have a clue what you're talking about."

Ted said, "Yeah. All right, we've got twenty minutes. We've accomplished something here, but I don't feel like we've really joined heads on this thing. I don't know what you want to do. I know you've been on this case—so to speak, the Bundy case—for a long time. I know that you must have some deep-seated feelings about it. I don't want to make too many assumptions, but here's what it comes down to me. I want the truth, the truth that's going to be helpful to you, but the broader truth that has a wider application. That's my bottom line. There's just no way it can be done in these circumstances with this amount of time, and that's the way it is. I'm not holding you hostage. If you don't want to do anything with it, you're free to walk away. If you can put your heads together with these other law enforcement people and think of any way, I'm not asking for clemency, I'm not asking to get off. I'm not asking for sympathy, but I . . . I draw the line. We need a period of time, sixty, ninety days, a few months, systematically going over with everybody, bottom to top, everything I can think of. Get it all down. You can use it as you see fit. But—that's how it is. Now, if you can see a way . . . I know you're limited in what you can do. You've got your job and your political considerations and all that. Your boss apparently has taken a position against this, but all I can tell you is when you go out and talk to those other people, you can tell them this. Yes, I'm only going to give you part of it. I'll give you something substantial, right now, to show you that my head is in the right place. I will not put myself in a position of giving it all away and not getting the kind of result that I think is best for my people, and I think for society in general. But I don't want to sound like I'm too altruistic here—that is a consideration—but I am concerned about my own people. Bob, they're going to get me sooner or later. Ahhh, you don't need to worry about that, but you've been after this for fifteen years. A couple months is not going to make any difference. That's what I have to say," Ted said, his voice gradually becoming quieter and softer. His eyes teared up, and he began to weep. Comparing notes later with two detectives, I found out that this little episode was a staged event. He did the same thing to foster sympathy and as a stall tactic with the other detectives.

After waiting a few seconds for Ted to recover from his apparent sobbing spell, I lied. "I think essentially you're right. As a person, okay, knowing what I know today, I'd like to keep you alive forever so we could really go over the whole thing together. That's what I'd like to do as a person inside me."

"Yeah," Ted said, encouraged.

"The reality is that I'm a cop, a professional. I don't get upset because somebody didn't get the death penalty and should have," I obligingly told Ted.

"Yup," he said nervously.

I lectured him. "I want to just understand and learn about the process of investigation. We talked about this before. The fact that you're dead or alive makes no difference. If I got hung up on the fact that you were dead or alive, I may as well just go up in the mountains and just kill myself."

Struggling for the right thing to say, Ted said, "Okay, well, I'm not saying necessarily that you are, but you have got some interest in justice, I suppose, whatever your definition of that is. All I'm saying is if there is any worry on anybody's part, what I would like to help people understand is, if it's justice, whatever that means, they can get a lot more justice in a couple months than they can right now. And they can help a lot more people in a couple months than they're going to help right now. And they're not going to be doing a thing for me other than giving me a chance to tell the story. I'm repeating myself, but I've no one but myself to blame. I realize that."

"I was about ready to bring that up," I said, rubbing it in that he had run the show so far.

Unlike in the *Confessions of Job*, Bundy declared, "And I take full responsibility for it. I've procrastinated, I've waited too long, and I don't want to go into a long rationale or story about, you know, all the things that put me in a position of waiting this long. Believe me, on many occasions prior to today, I had seriously asked for people who represent me to take this approach, long before this warrant was signed, and they steadfastly opposed it and all but demanded that we stick with the conventional legal approach. And perhaps last February when I virtually begged them to go this way, maybe we wouldn't be in the position—we wouldn't be in the position we are today, I'm pretty sure. Yeah, I realize, Bob, I am whistling against the wind right now; the politics are pretty heavy-duty out there. And folks have made up their minds, the people in power, a lot of them. And I don't know if this is going to work. And if it doesn't, it's going to be too bad. Everybody loses."

Somewhat stunned, I just realized why, in February 1988, Bundy had talked to me about how to interview a serial killer. What I hadn't discerned then was that he really wanted to confess at that time. I felt he was hinky about something, but I didn't know what it was. I kept the conversation going by saying, "You are talking about a system oriented toward the chance to kill Ted Bundy. What sound politician wouldn't want the ax to fall right now? The governor doesn't care anything about you. All he's talking about is law and order. Here's this famous murderer that he has a chance to say, 'No, we're not going to support.' And, as a police investigator, I have to assume that you're going to die Tuesday."

Hanging his head in shame, Ted uttered quietly, "I know."

"I got to think about what you can give law enforcement between now and Tuesday," I reminded him.

Ted struggled to move his lips, saying very quietly, "Uh huh."

At this point, I decided to feed him a dose of the truth to reestablish my credibility. I said, "And if it's pieces, it's pieces—or nothing. I don't know which. But I'm not going to give you any advice. I'm sure not going to tell everybody you're a liar, that's for sure. And if they ask me, I'm just going to tell them the truth, that you did tell me some things and that I thought you were cooperating. Time is a problem."

Looking like a whipped puppy, Bundy repeated himself, saying, "I know."

Leaving no other route for him to pursue, I told him, "And there's no way I can leave here today, gather up these people, and come up with some plan of action about the interview with Ted Bundy. All I could ever expect when I heard I had two and a half hours . . . you know, out of fifteen years, two and a half hours is nothing."

"Sure," said Ted, realizing for the first time that he had made a huge mistake. He needed more time with me first to set up a strategy to establish his credibility, but it was too late.

Feeling that the interview was about to end, I said, "So one of the things that I wanted to do is at least find out the scope of your murders. You've helped me with that a little bit. I would like to know about the other three that we're talking about because I really don't have any clue about when, where, and how they occurred."

"Let me ask you this, again. I know the position you're in. But law enforcement in the past has been somewhat—they've not been shy. I remember years ago about holding conferences, getting together, and swapping ideas. The officers speculated about what is Ted Bundy really like, drawing diagrams on the wall, and coming out with statements to the press about what they think Bundy's about. You know, law enforcement has an interest here. Society has an interest, families have an interest, et cetera. Are the politics such that it's just not possible for you and others in a similar position to sit down this weekend—somehow sit down this weekend together with a cross section of interested parties, and try to get everybody in the same room? You know how this stuff goes. It's a Tower of Babel right now. Everybody talking it over, through the news media, and over the telephone. Nobody even getting together to find out, well, what do we really stand to gain, what do we lose—I mean, what's going on here. And see if a consensus of some kind can be hammered out without anybody having to stand out there alone, without Bob Keppel risking the wrath of his boss or anybody else. Or, everybody standing together and saying, 'You know, we're not for Ted Bundy, the son of a bitch, you know, or whatever, but we are for finding out. We think it's not unreasonable that this will come to pass because we have received some strong indications that he's opened up in a way he never has before.' Do you hear what I'm saying?" Ted pleaded in his most sincere fashion.

I muttered, "Uh huh," knowing he wasn't finished with his point.

"There's going to be a lot of police. Whether I call them in here or not, most of them would be here, don't you think? A lot of them would be here, waiting in the wings. I know they have before. If you can get everybody in a room and you say, 'This is what I know; I mean, I'm not Ted Bundy's advocate, I'm an advocate of Washington State's interest. I'm an advocate of Colorado's interest. I'm an advocate of the attorney general of Florida's interest. And this is what we think. What's at stake? What are we looking at? Is he trying to bullshit us? Is he, you know, trying to manipulate us? Or is he serious? Will he give us what we want? And can we justify this politically by saying we're getting this, and we're still going to be able to execute him anyway?' And coming up, again, with the kind of consensus that the public and the politicians respect. Because you say, 'Well, what do politicians have to gain?' I mean, in this law and order atmosphere. Well, part of the calling card of today's politicians, today's compassionate politicians, is their deep respect for families, okay? I would sound hypocritical if I were to say anything about the families of these individuals, even all the years I haven't said anything. But the fact of the matter is they still do count. They're still out there. They still deserve to find their people.

They can find their people. I can tell them how to find their people, and it's up to the politicians to give me a chance. And that's the bottom line. And if they don't give me the chance, which I will take advantage of if I am given it, they will be able to help those families they so righteously talk about all the time, and still get me. Well, it sounds to me like, you know, they have everything to gain and nothing to lose. Think about the predicament. Again, I know that it's going to occur to you, and I know the accusation's been made that I'm manipulating families, but the reality is they're out there. They're there. If we didn't talk about them, they'd still be there. There are a handful, several dozen, probably, mothers, you know, you've seen it firsthand, and I'm sure you probably don't like me talking about it, but I'm going to talk about it. I will tell you and your fellow law enforcement officers everything I can to locate the remains of a number of people in your state and elsewhere. And I can do that. And that can be done. There are some of these people who don't even know that I'm involved. That is, these family members. If I'm killed, they're doubly deprived. They don't even get the sense of satisfaction; they executed the guy who did it to their child," Ted said, with constant hand motions.

Ted, in a way, was preaching to the choir. But his effort to get me to hold a Ted Bundy summit was one more ploy to grandstand in his situation. Instead, he should have quietly and with humility started to tell his story. He chose instead to mess with us one more time, and I wasn't about to participate. I responded with the idea he was still going to push his cause. "Uh huh."

"This way they get both the knowledge, the remains of their loved ones, and that satisfaction of some justice being done," Ted restated as though he thought all the parents and relatives had compassion for his dilemma. "That's what it comes down to, really. I put myself in this position. Agh, but that's where we're at. That's one of the places we're at. We're also at a juncture where you as a law enforcement officer want something. You want facts, which you're entitled to, which you need, and I recognize that. But there's more involved, and you know that, too. And while I don't expect you to be a spokesman for me or for social science, let's get down to the practicalities of what can be done. I know that you as a law enforcement person, as a human being, are interested in families. You're interested in solving crimes, you're interested in preventing future crimes, and what I have to say goes to a lot of that. And I don't think I need to tell you that. But can't we get people in the same room and talk about the stuff, rationally, instead of taking rhetorical stands in [the] news media? They're going to be here. Think about it."

Ted tried to use the concerns of the family members to influence me to hold his summit conference. In his most clever psychopathic posturing, Ted attempted to convince me that he really was remorseful. It's typical of the conniving sociopath to have the resourcefulness to use remorse as a ploy to get sympathy, a feeling contrary to a psychopath's inner motivations, but he was still able to exploit the concept with other people. When Ted bargained for his life, he was really searching for whether he had any value.

The final Ted that I saw was Ted the victim, denigrated, confused, and powerless. This kind of personality sometimes appears in the final appellate stages of high-profile death-penalty cases where the issues surrounding the case become more important than the life of the convicted killer. The individual—in this case, Ted—becomes subordinated to the needs of lawyers, ministers, publicists, and even journalists, all of whom have their own causes to promote. So it was with Ted, who lost his sense of direction amid conflicting strategies and agendas and finally admitted to his own pathological fears, surrendered his bravado, and gave up control. Ted allowed himself to become a public display item for the anti–death penalty movement, the antipornography movement, and all the psychologists who wanted to use him to prove their theories. He'd listened to their advice and trusted in them. But when he discovered that they weren't interested in saving his life but in using him as an issue, he realized that his trust had been violated, and he broke.

On his own, Ted had survived by listening to his instincts. He knew when the coast was clear and he knew when to run. But in 1989, in part because he had allowed his own instincts to be influenced by others, he was without resources and without the precious time that he believed would run on forever. I saw how his strategy of playing information for time was doomed to fail because, as the U.S. Supreme Court said, "The world had had enough of Ted Bundy." And, in an oblique way, it pained me to watch it. Even his dramatic news-release strategy—dribbling out his confessions to tantalize judges, lawyers, and investigators and buy himself months or even years while he talked about his crimes one by one—was a failure. When his people in Florida broke the news to the press that Bundy was confessing to his murders, it was perceived as a very ill-timed and desperate announcement that was just another example of Ted's self-serving, last-minute strategies to save his life.

As a result of Ted's prolonged method of confession, the press commentators wrote that Bundy was simply holding the families of his murder victims hostage as he bargained for his life. If the U.S. Supreme Court justices and the governor of Florida hadn't made up their minds already about not granting Bundy a stay of execution, the withering press reaction to Bundy's slow confessions helped them do just that. The press announcement and the national reaction seemed to convince them that Ted Bundy's games were over.

At our final interview, Ted was a defeated man. It was then that Ted told me about his most bizarre murder. The fact that he chose to reveal the details of that murder two days before his execution convinced me that he could have told a lot more if it wasn't for bad timing and poor choices. Ted was a dead duck, and he and his attorneys refused to embrace this reality.

The essence of Ted's plea to be spared was his insincere attempt to benefit mankind, the altruism he never understood; he hopelessly tried to give his last four days a greater meaning for which he was desperately searching. The governor of Florida sustained his greatest fear: that he would die being ignored. No interference on my part could have saved Ted from his fate.

In Ted's last moments he ignored the black forces that festered in his head and dealt with the geographics of his crimes. He went to his grave after giving the warden one last location where the remains of a murdered woman might be found, a symbol of his effort to maintain his significance and keep his personality from imploding.

The fragmented personality of Theodore Robert Bundy was best expressed by his own closing: Peace, ted. Bundy used the lowercase "t" as a constant reminder to himself that he was a truly insignificant creature.

17

The Arrest of Gary Leon Ridgway

On November 30, 2001, at 3 P.M., the end of his shift as a truck painter at Kenworth Trucking in Renton, Washington, Gary Leon Ridgway was arrested by detectives from the King County police in connection with the murders of Opal Mills, Marcia Chapman, Cynthia Hinds, and Carol Christensen, the first victims discovered by police almost twenty years earlier in the Green River murders case. Ridgway, who had served in the navy from 1969 to 1971, had worked at Kenworth for more than thirty years and had been under scrutiny by the police since 1983, when he was contacted by Detective Fox of the Des Moines, Washington, police department in connection with the disappearance of a prostitute named Marie Malvar, whose murder he ultimately confessed to after he led police to her body and the bodies of his other victims. On November 5, 2003, Ridgway pled guilty to 48 murders in the Green River series.

Suspect Gary Leon Ridgway

On May 4, 1983, according to a King County Sheriff's Department November 2001 affidavit sworn out by Detective Sue Peters of the major crimes unit in support of a search warrant, Gary Ridgway first came to the attention of the Green River Murders Task Force because of Marie Malvar, who disappeared on April 30, 1983, from South 216th and Pacific Highway South in King County. Malvar's remains weren't recovered until October 2003. Her pimp, Robert Woods, saw her get into a dark colored pickup truck at a bus stop near a 7-Eleven. After Malvar got into the truck, it traveled northbound on Pacific Highway South for approximately five blocks before pulling into a motel parking lot. After stopping for a few moments, the driver turned the truck around and headed southbound on Pacific Highway South, turning left, eastbound, onto South 216th. Woods, who was following the truck in his own car, lost sight of the truck at the intersection. He described the truck as dark with a primer spot by the passenger side wheel well. The truck did not have a canopy over the bed, and Woods described the driver as a dark-haired male in his late thirties or forties.

Woods was quoted as saying that what made him suspicious about the pickup truck that stopped for Marie Malvar was the way the driver sped up to the bus stop; most johns slowly coast by to pick up a prostitute. And then when Malvar got in, the truck sped away. That was why Woods followed it. He said that when he managed to catch up to the truck, he thought he could see Malvar struggling with the driver, but he couldn't see much else. So when he lost the truck, he went searching the neighborhoods where he had last seen it and found it in the driveway at 21859 32nd Place South. He then contacted the Des Moines Police Department, and the police contacted Gary Ridgway because the address Woods had given them was Ridgway's.

Ridgway was interviewed by Detective Fox of the Des Moines police; He denied any contact with Marie Malvar, but readily admitted having been arrested during the previous year on charges of offering and agreeing to engage in a sexual act for money, a sexual solicitation of prostitutes offense. Fox turned Ridgway's name over to the Green River Task Force, and Ridgway was interviewed by task force detective Larry Gross on November 16, 1983.

Just over two months later—on February 3, 1984—Dawn White, identified as a prostitute, contacted the Green River Task Force and reported Gary Ridgway as the Green River suspect. Detective Randy Mullinax conducted a subsequent investigation as a result of the tip and discovered that Ridgway had been arrested for offering and agreeing to an act of sex in exchange for money with an undercover King County police officer on May 11, 1982. At the time of this arrest, Ridgway had been driving his 1975 maroon Dodge pickup with the canopy on and was wearing a dark plaid shirt and brown pants. Mullinax also discovered that Ridgway had been interviewed by Green River Murders Task Force detective Larry Gross in 1983 as a result of the Des Moines police contact by Detective Fox.

On April 12, 1984, Mullinax interviewed Gary Ridgway at King County Police Precinct #4, where he took a tape-recorded statement in which Ridgway admitted "dating"—a euphemism for sex in exchange for money—missing person Keli McGinness and seeing victim Kim Nelson at South 146th and Pacific Highway South by the Kentucky Fried Chicken restaurant. Ridgway had identified both McGinness and Nelson after viewing their photographs.

Ridgway said that he met Keli McGinness in July 1983 by the Spruce Motel on Pacific Highway South. McGinness, who was alone at the time, he said, was standing by the bus stop in front of a barbershop. After making a "date," they went to the area of Sunset Junior High School Field, at 1801 South 140th, where they began what Ridgway described as their date. However, they were interrupted by the Port of Seattle Police. After a short exchange with the police, during which McGinness provided them with an alias of Jennifer Kaufman, they returned to the Spruce Motel, where they completed the date in McGinness's room. Subsequently, according to Port of Seattle Police records, it was confirmed that the contact Ridgway described actually occurred on February 23, 1983, at South 140th and 22nd South and that Ridgway and McGinness were in Ridgway's 1975 Dodge pickup.

Ridgway also told Mullinax during the April 12, 1984, interview that he had seen Kim Nelson near the Kentucky Fried Chicken restaurant at South 144th and Pacific Highway South, but that he had not spoken to her. He said that later he had talked to Nelson's roommate, later identified by police as Paige Miley, who told him that Nelson was missing and that she thought the Green River Killer had gotten her. Miley told police that she had been with Nelson on the day Nelson disappeared and that that was the only time they had been on Pacific Highway South together. Miley also picked Ridgway out of a photomontage as the man who approached her on Pacific Highway South and made a reference to her roommate, Kim Nelson.

During the interview, Ridgway also told the police that he had dated five to ten women from Pacific Highway South and had caught venereal diseases at least three times. During this time he was driving his maroon Dodge pickup, which had a black canopy over the bed, but the truck was not operational during March, April, and May of 1983, he said, so he used his father's 1978 brown-and-tan pickup one or two times. Ridgway explained that he dated mostly during the day and that most of the dates were "car dates," although he said he used the Spruce, Airporter, and Ben Carol motels, and one other motel that was located at South 140th and Pacific Highway South.

Ridgway told his interviewer that he preferred dating white women and that he'd dated one girl from the Laundromat at 100th and Aurora Avenue North. That girl, who, he said, was white, took him to a motel during the day. He also mentioned having dated a hairdresser from Portland, whose first name was Kathy, and said that Kathy came to Seattle on weekends to make extra money. He only dated her one time. Ridgway did tell police that he had driven on Star Lake Road and that he was currently driving a 1977 brown Ford pickup with an eight-foot camper on it and owned a brown 1973 Plymouth Satellite four-door as well.

On May 7, 1984, Ridgway took a polygraph examination administered by Norm Matzke of the King County Police Department, who reported to Detective Mullinax that Ridgway had successfully passed the test. Based on both Detective Mullinax's follow-up investigation through May 1984 and the results of the polygraph, Ridgway was considered to be cleared as a possible Green River suspect.

Rebecca Garde Guay's Account

On November 29, 1984, Rebecca Garde Guay telephoned the Green River Murders Task Force to report that while she was working as a prostitute in November 1982, she had been the victim of a violent assault. Her report was investigated by Detective Ralf McAllister of the Green River Murders Task Force and resulted in the identification of Gary Ridgway as the perpetrator of the assault on Rebecca Guay. In 1986, Guay provided police with the following detailed account of the assault.

On November 9, 1982, she was approached by Gary Ridgway, driving his maroon-colored Dodge pickup with the black canopy over the bed, at South 200th and Pacific Highway South while she was hitch-hiking and standing at a bus stop. She said that Ridgway told her he had been arrested in a vice operation and that his son was being taken away by the court and he felt that everyone was out to get him that day. After agreeing to a twenty-dollar car date, Guay said she directed Ridgway to the area of South 240th off Pacific Highway South.

After stopping the truck, Ridgway, whom Guay described as wearing shorts, knee-high socks, and tennis shoes, told her that he wanted her to walk into the woods for the date and led the way into the woods and up a steep incline with Guay following several yards behind him. When she reached the area where Ridgway was standing, she noticed that he was partially undressed, his shorts down around his ankles, and naked from the waist down. There was very low light in the area, Guay said, because of the density of the trees and the time of day. She dropped to her knees in front of Ridgway, keeping her clothing on the whole time, and began the act of oral sex. However, at no time did she notice that Ridgway got an erection.

A short time later Ridgway began yelling at Guay, "You bitch, you bit my cock." She told police that at no time did she bite Ridgway. But as he pushed her back away from him, he turned her around, placed his arm around the front of her neck in a police-type choke hold, and forced her to the ground, facedown. He released the choke hold with his arm and immediately placed his hands around the back of her neck, choking her.

As the struggle continued, Guay managed to turn over onto her back, facing Ridgway, while he continued to choke her, his hands now placed around the front of her neck. She said at this time there was no doubt in her mind that he was going to kill her. Because he had a tight hold on her, she was unable to scream; however, she managed to plead for her life, asking him why he was trying to kill her. She said there were only her mother and her. It was at this time, she told police, that Ridgway loosened his hold and sat back slightly, which allowed her to seize the opportunity to break free and escape.

As she fled, she said to police, she believed that Ridgway's shorts were still around his ankles and that it seemed as if Ridgway was standing there in a "daze" as she ran away from him. She said she went to a nearby mobile home in a trailer park. She has never seen Ridgway again since this incident. Although she admitted she was involved in prostitution during the period when the alleged assault took place, police found no arrests for prostitution-related activities.

In Detective Ralf McAllister's investigation of this incident, he tape-recorded Ridgway's account of Guay's report. Ridgway had been advised of his constitutional rights, which he acknowledged and waived.

Ridgway's Account of Rebecca Guay's Report

Ridgway told Detective McAllister that he picked up Rebecca Guay, who was hitchhiking at about five P.M. at South 200th Street and Pacific Highway South, as he was driving his maroon-colored Dodge pickup with its black canopy in place. Guay asked him after he picked her up if he had "dated," to which Ridgway replied that he had, and they agreed to a twenty-dollar oral sex act. Ridgway and Guay performed their sexual act at 22nd South and South 204th, although he told police that he was not sure which of the two of them had chosen the location. He remembered wearing blue shorts at the time but seemed confused in the interview about the time of the year when the incident took place. He also said he couldn't remember whether Guay examined his identification in his wallet because there had been "so many of 'em." But Ridgway told police he and Guay walked seventy-five feet into the woods for privacy in case the police came by.

Ridgway admitted to police that he choked Guay after she had started to bite him. He kept choking her with his arm for ten to fifteen seconds, he said, after she bit him and he told her, "You bit me." However, he said to police that he did not remember slapping her at any time, and after watching Guay escape, he observed her run to a nearby trailer and go inside. Then he put his clothing back on and left the area in his truck.

Ridgway admitted to Detective McAllister that he dated on Aurora Avenue and in the city of Seattle and said that he was still dating, primarily during the day because he worked from 3:40 P.M. until 12:10 A.M. He had been on nights, he explained, since Halloween 1983, and the only vehicle he had driven for the previous three years was his Dodge pickup; he owned no other vehicles. During the times his truck was in the shop getting fixed, he explained, he usually took the bus or got a ride with someone. He had even hitched rides a few times.

Ridgway dated in motels by the airport, a motel in Auburn, and in a little field, as well as in other places the girls he dated had taken him. He admitted camping around the North Bend area and traveling through Enumclaw via Highway 410 to get to White Pass. He also admitted to dating missing person Keli McGinness, to having seen a lot of the victims and to probably dating some of them.

As a result of Detective McAllister's investigation of the Guay assault and his interview with Ridgway, McAllister recommended that the Ridgway case be reviewed. The inquiry into Ridgway's past was reopened and assigned to Detective Doyon, who was assigned out of state before he began his inquiry. The file on Ridgway was then turned over to FBI special agents O'Neill and Askeland.

On March 17, 1986, at the request of Special Agents O'Neill and Askeland, Gary Ridgway voluntarily came to the Green River Murders Task Force office for an interview. During it, he again admitted to the Guay incident, now saying that she had bit him hard enough to draw blood, but that it was the only time he had assaulted a prostitute. He also told the agents that he had not dated prostitutes during the previous one and a half years because of the Green River killings as well as his having caught venereal diseases at least fifteen times. He admitted to once having choked his ex-wife, Marcia, in 1972, saying also that he believed the incident had been reported to the police. He further told the agents that he had picked up prostitutes from the streets of Seattle and Tacoma using hotels, his vehicle, and prostitutes' apartments for paid sex. He also said that he had parked his car near the cemetery on Aurora Avenue North and in the parking lots of motels such as the Red Lion Inn on Pacific Highway South and South 188th Street, both of which are popular areas for prostitution.

Ridgway said to his interviewers that he had a fixation with prostitutes and that during the past one and half years he picked up prostitutes only to talk to them. He said that he was compulsive about prostitutes, explaining that they affect him as "strongly as alcohol does an alcoholic," and acknowledged that he had occasionally fished eastern Washington lakes as well as the Green River. At the conclusion of the interview, Ridgway was asked to take a polygraph test for the Federal Bureau of Investigation on March 20, 1986, which he agreed to do.

On the day set forth for the polygraph, attorney David Middaugh telephoned Special Agent O'Neill and advised that he was representing Gary Ridgway, who had contacted him after his interview with

O'Neill and Askeland. Middaugh advised that he did not want his client interviewed or talked to by any police officers or Federal Bureau of Investigation agents without Middaugh's approval. Ridgway's attorney said he had also advised his client not to take a second polygraph test. As a result of David Middaugh's contact with Agent O'Neill, the investigation of Gary Ridgway was inactivated by the FBI, even though in August 1986, based on a review of the Ridgway information, Green River Murders Task Force detectives decided that there were still a number of unresolved questions regarding Ridgway and that more follow-up work was necessary. The case was reopened.

Paige Miley

On August 12, 1986, the task force contacted Paige Miley in connection with victim Kim Nelson. Miley was a prostitute who knew and worked with Nelson in the Seattle area during 1983. Nelson's skeletal remains were found off I-90 on Garcia Road on June 13, 1986, the same area in which two other Green River victims were found.

Nelson, who was released from the King County jail on October 30, 1983, joined Miley the same day. Miley, Nelson, and their pimps all stayed at the Ben Carol Motel on South 144th Street and Pacific Highway South for two nights. Nelson and Miley then traveled to the Evergreen Truck Stop in Federal Way at South 348th Street and 16th Avenue South for two nights, where they performed acts of prostitution; during this period, they seldom ventured out of their motel room except to go to the truck stop. Miley said she did not recall ever going with Nelson to Larry's Market or the Kentucky Fried Chicken, which are located across from the Ben Carol Motel. Miley said she only worked with Nelson once on Pacific Highway South and had never known Nelson to work Pacific Highway South in the past.

After working the Evergreen Truck Stop for two nights, Miley got up on the morning of November 1, 1983, and decided to work Pacific Highway South to make rent money. At approximately eleven A.M., Miley and Nelson left their room together and went to the covered bus stop in front of the car wash at South 144th Street and Pacific Highway South. Shortly after arriving there, Miley got a car date and left Nelson sitting alone at the bus stop. Miley turned the quick car date nearby and returned to the bus stop fifteen to twenty minutes later to find Nelson gone. Nelson never returned and Miley never saw her again. This was, according to Miley, the one and only time she was on Pacific Highway South together with Kim Nelson. Nelson, police noted, was very distinctive in appearance because she was quite tall, 5 foot 11 inches, and had very short bleached-blond hair.

Several nights after Miley had left Nelson alone at the bus stop, Miley was working the same general area of Pacific Highway South in front of the Moonrise Motel when she was approached by a man driving a red pickup truck with a white cab-high canopy over the bed. She described the man as white with brown hair and a wispy mustache; in his late twenties to early thirties; wearing a plaid shirt, jeans, and a baseball cap with some writing on the front; and drinking a can of Budweiser beer that he held between his legs. After talking about a date, the man asked Miley where her blond friend was. Miley told police she immediately became concerned that the man was aware of her and Kim Nelson's presence on Pacific Highway South since the only time she had been seen with Nelson in that same area was during the brief period on the morning of November 1, 1983, immediately prior to Nelson's disappearance from the bus stop.

Subsequent to this interview, Miley assisted in an artist drawing of the man she had described to police, which drawing, police said, was later found to have closely resembled Gary Ridgway. Police recontacted Paige Miley and showed her a photomontage of six photographs, from which she picked Ridgway's picture as the person who had approached her on Pacific Highway South and asked about Kim Nelson.

After the task force reopened their investigation of Gary Ridgway, they conducted a number of interviews with individuals who said they had information about Ridgway. First among these was Dawn White, a prostitute who had tipped off Ridgway to the task force and was interviewed by Detective Randy Mullinax.

The Dawn White Interview

Dawn White told the police that in either December 1983 or January 1984, at about one or two P.M., she and another prostitute were walking northbound on Pacific Highway South at approximately

South 160th Street when Ridgway approached them, driving his maroon-colored pickup with a primer spot on the passenger door and a canopy over the truck bed.

As White and her friend walked north along the highway, Ridgway continued to circle them. He finally contacted them in the parking lot of Larry's Market at South 144th Street and Pacific Highway South, where White and her friend both got into the truck with him. Ridgway, White said, acted very paranoid, saying he had previously been arrested by two vice decoys. He made both of them show identification to prove they weren't police officers and then they talked about dating. But Ridgway didn't have enough money to date both of them, so he chose White, who was Caucasian, instead of her friend, who was African American. From this incident, Dawn White said, she got the impression that Ridgway did not like black people.

While she was sitting in Ridgway's truck, White noticed a roll of plastic in the truck bed. She was also shown some identification belonging to Ridgway, she said, from which she learned his name.

Dawn White said that Ridgway agreed to date her but told her that first he had to leave for a short time to buy something for his truck. White believed it was either wire or a fan belt because, she said, she remembered thinking that it was something with which he would be able to choke her. She had become uneasy about Ridgway's intentions, describing him to police as "weird and different." But she waited for him after he left.

Shortly after he had gone, ostensibly to buy the item he said he was looking for, White and her friend were contacted by the King County police in the Larry's Market parking lot. The police, she said, made them leave the area and the date she had agreed to have with Ridgway did not take place. She said she didn't see Ridgway again that day, but later in the afternoon she looked up his name in the phone book and called him at home to tell him what had happened with the police.

At a later date, White said she had arranged a meeting with Ridgway at Randy's Restaurant on East Marginal Way, to which she brought along her boyfriend and pimp. During the meeting, Ridgway talked about his history of both syphilis and herpes and said that he didn't want to date her and transmit these diseases to her. He also talked about a girlfriend whom he said disappeared but was later found in Portland. After the meeting, which White said took about an hour, they went their separate ways. Nevertheless, she told the police, Ridgway acted very strange during the meeting and behaved as though he had a guilty conscience.

Approximately a year and a half later, Dawn White and her husband she had since married saw Ridgway at a McDonald's in downtown Seattle at approximately 6th and Westlake around three in the afternoon. She observed him continually looking at her and asked if he knew her because he kept staring at her. It was at this time she finally recognized him from their prior contact on Pacific Highway South.

After a short conversation, Ridgway gave her and her husband a ride in his brown four-door car to a location that, White told police, she could not remember. And that was the last contact White ever had with Ridgway.

The Claudia Barrows Interview

Detective Randy Mullinax, along with FBI Special Agent John Gambersky, also interviewed Claudia Barrows (Ridgway), Gary Ridgway's first wife. Barrows married Ridgway on August 15, 1970, after they had courted each other in the Seattle area. Often, she said, the couple would visit Seward Park, where on a few occasions Ridgway would polish his car. They once had sex in the woods in a park near Alki and also had sex in Ridgway's car on a dead-end road off Military Road South, which overlooked the South center area.

Shortly after the couple married, they moved to San Diego, where Ridgway was stationed in the navy; soon after their arrival he was shipped out on a six-month western Pacific cruise. While her husband was gone, Claudia Ridgway became romantically involved with another man who was a mutual friend. They had all become friends prior to Gary's departure on his cruise. When Ridgway returned from the cruise, he found Claudia living with another woman, who was white and had a black boyfriend. Claudia told investigators that Ridgway knew their marriage was in trouble as soon as he got back from his sea cruise.

When he was discharged from the navy in July 1971, Ridgway returned to the Seattle area; his wife came back to Seattle a few weeks after him. The couple lived in Ridgway's parents' residence for a short time before getting their own apartment somewhere off of Pacific Highway South near the airport. Claudia said their attempts to reconcile their marriage failed and she then returned to San Diego to be with her boyfriend, whom she later married. Claudia, who said that Ridgway seemed to be normal sexually and a very social person, divorced her husband on January 14, 1972.

Ridgway himself subsequently told one of his girlfriends—"Girlfriend C," according to the King County Police Department affidavit—that when he returned from the western Pacific cruise he found Claudia living with several black men and that, in his opinion, she had turned into a "whore." He also said that Claudia had given him a case of genital warts before he left on the cruise. However, Ridgway's navy medical records show that he had warts on both hands and his forearm in December 1970 and that he was diagnosed as having had gonorrhea in December 1969. Claudia Barrows denied ever having had any type of venereal disease.

In their reopening of the Ridgway investigation, task force detectives Mullinax and Haney interviewed a series of Gary Ridgway's girlfriends who had relationships with him during the three-year period from 1981 through 1984. The detectives referred to them in the affidavit as Girlfriends A, B, and C.

Girlfriend A

Girlfriend A said she first met Ridgway in May 1981 through an organization known as Parents Without Partners. This girlfriend told police she had her first sexual encounter with Ridgway outdoors in an army bunker at Fort Casey on Whidbey Island, and a short time after this he moved in with her at her West Seattle house. They had sex, she told the police, as many as three times a day, also having sex outdoors at the South center area, Lincoln Park, Cle Elum, the Taylor River area near North Bend, and once at the north end of the Sea-Tac Airport. She said there were other areas, but she couldn't remember all of them, but she did tell police that it was not unusual for them to stop anywhere, at any time, and have sex both in and out of the truck.

On two occasions, Girlfriend A said that Ridgway had tied her up prior to having sex with her, an idea, she explained, that emerged after they both watched a pornographic movie in which a woman was tied up. Ridgway's second wife, Marcia, also told police that she had experienced being tied up by Ridgway on at least one occasion. Girlfriend A said that the first time Ridgway tied her up took place in the woods while they were camping outside of Cle Elum. Ridgway, without Girlfriend A's knowledge, brought wooden stakes along on their date; he drove them into the ground and used nylon rope to bind her wrists and ankles to the stakes, an act that she allowed. However, she said, Ridgway then inserted grapes and bananas into her vagina. She told police that although she didn't feel threatened by it, she realized she was tied tightly enough so that she couldn't get loose. However, Ridgway untied her at her request.

The second time she was tied down for sexual purposes, she said, took place at her residence while Ridgway lived with her. As happened the first time, she agreed with Ridgway's request. Thereupon Ridgway went outside to his truck and got some rubber-coated wire to tie her arms and legs to the bed. And, as before, when she requested to be let loose, Ridgway untied her.

Girlfriend A said that Ridgway was very withdrawn and seldom spoke of his personal life. Outside of his family, he had very few friends, and she felt that this was the contributing factor to their eventual separation. Ridgway had no friends, she said, and was basically dominated by women. He allowed her to make all of the decisions as to their life together and made no requests or demands of his own. She also said to police that ultimately she had to tell Ridgway to "back off" his constant lovemaking. She asked him to move out of her home prior to Christmas 1981, at which time he did so.

During their relationship, Girlfriend A said, the only vehicle she observed Ridgway driving was the maroon Dodge pickup with primer spots on it. The truck didn't have a canopy at first, but later Ridgway bought a black one, which he installed on the truck. It seemed to her that Ridgway did vehicle painting as a hobby.

Girlfriend B

Girlfriend B told Detectives Mullinax and Haney that she first met Ridgway in November or December 1981, just after he had broken off with Girlfriend A; again, they met through the organization Parents Without Partners. She began dating Ridgway and said they had sex at her apartment and at his residence located off Military Road South, but nowhere else. She told police she believed that while she was dating him, Ridgway was also having sexual relationships with other women. He had very low self-esteem, Girlfriend B believed, and she explained to police that she felt it was because of his relationship with his mother, a person Ridgway was never able to satisfy or please with his deeds.

Ridgway told her, according to her interview, that he had been adopted. He also talked about his ex-wife, Marcia, and even though he sounded angry when he talked about her, Girlfriend B believed he still cared for her and would have returned to her if given the opportunity. Girlfriend B also described Ridgway as sexually "well mannered" and said that he never asked her to engage in any unusual sexual activities. She felt that Gary Ridgway was very smooth around women and that he was usually in control of his emotions. She said that while they were dating, they usually went either to the White Shutters Inn or the Sandstone Restaurant on Pacific Highway South. She said that Ridgway usually wore jeans, Western-type shirts, and football jerseys.

On Christmas Eve 1981, Girlfriend B went to the White Shutters Restaurant at South 140th and Pacific Highway South with her sister to attend a Parents Without Partners social function. At approximately 11:00 or 11:30 P.M., Ridgway came into the lounge very upset, and while everyone else was on the dance floor, he sat down next to Girlfriend B and said that he had nearly killed a woman.

Girlfriend B, who was taken aback by this statement, asked him to repeat what he had just said. Ridgway said that he couldn't believe it himself, but that he'd almost killed a woman. Girlfriend B said he repeated this several times. Although he was visibly shaken, he had no apparent wounds and appeared as though his clothes were unruffled. Ridgway said he'd picked up the woman, or prostitute, Girlfriend B couldn't remember which, but it was her impression that Ridgway was talking about a prostitute. Before Ridgway could elaborate on his comments, Girlfriend B said, other people sat down at the table, causing the conversation to cease. Ridgway never mentioned the incident again.

In approximately June or July 1982, Girlfriend B was approached by Girlfriend C and told that Ridgway was at that time dating her.

Girlfriend B said that she already knew that Ridgway was dating Girlfriend C and that she had already begun to back off from the relationship. Girlfriend C told Girlfriend B that she believed Ridgway frequented prostitutes and that as a result he had contracted herpes and thus infected her.

Girlfriend B said that during the time she knew Ridgway, he drove a maroon Dodge pickup truck that had a canopy over the bed. He was always doing bodywork to the truck, and she believed he eventually painted it black. She said she thought he did this bodywork in a friend's garage or that he rented space to do the work.

Girlfriend C

Girlfriend C was also interviewed by Detectives Mullinax and Haney, and she told them that she met Gary Ridgway in January 1982, through Parents Without Partners, at a dance in Normandy Park. Ridgway was dating Girlfriend B at the time, and shortly after their meeting Girlfriend C began dating him. Shortly after they began dating, Girlfriend C contracted herpes and confronted Ridgway about it. Ridgway told her that he, too, had herpes, but that he believed she had given it to him. He would never admit that he had infected her. In May or June 1982, Girlfriend C told Girlfriend B at a Parents Without Partners dance that Ridgway had herpes and had given it to her. It was at this time, Girlfriend B said, that she broke off the relationship with Ridgway.

After they began dating, Girlfriend C saw Ridgway almost every weekend and occasionally during the week. Ridgway would usually come to her house in Renton for the weekend. Girlfriend C said she would seldom spend the weekends at Ridgway's house on Military Road South because she had two children and it was easier for them to stay at her house. They continued to attend Parents Without Partners' dances for about one and a half years while they were dating. They seldom attended any other social events. Ridgway had very few friends outside of work, she said. He occasionally went to the Annex Tavern on East Marginal Way after work, where he would have a beer with his coworkers.

Girlfriend C also said she saw other women on two separate occasions at Ridgway's house. She believed both of these women were associated with Parents Without Partners. She quickly realized, she said, that Ridgway was a less-than-faithful boyfriend.

Ridgway told Girlfriend C that he met his first wife sometime before, or while he was in the navy, and that he had contracted genital warts from his wife. He said that after returning from a cruise, he found that his wife was living with two black males and that she had turned into a prostitute. Girlfriend C believed this was the reason for Ridgway's strong reaction whenever he saw a black male in the company of a white female. Ridgway would make a comment that that type of woman must "like licorice." Ridgway said that he was very hurt by what his first wife had done to him but indicated that he still loved her after he found out what had happened.

Girlfriend C also said that Ridgway's second wife, Marcia, still lived somewhere in the area locally and that they had a son named Matthew. Ridgway told her that Marcia left him after she started singing in local bars. She also started hanging around with other men and began ignoring the welfare of their son. Girlfriend C said that although Ridgway was hurt by the divorce, she believed he still cared for Marcia at the time of the divorce. However, he now spoke of Marcia with contempt because he felt she was not a good mother.

Girlfriend C once overheard a conversation between Ridgway and her sister in which Ridgway was angrily complaining about Marcia. Girlfriend C's sister asked him if he could kill her, and he replied, "yes." Nevertheless, other than Ridgway's hostility toward Marcia, Girlfriend C told police she never saw Ridgway become violent or angry and described him as an even-tempered man who usually talked his way out of his problems.

Ridgway was a good lover, as she described him, who was always gentle and caring. They had sex on an average of twice a day while they were together. However, Girlfriend C believed Ridgway could have engaged in sex six or seven times a day. She said he never exhibited any abnormal tendencies while with her.

She believed that Ridgway saw prostitutes as "things" to be used. He once told her, "It's sure nice to make love to someone you like." Girlfriend C believed this comment was in reference to his contacts with prostitutes. She said Ridgway especially disliked Filipino prostitutes because of his contacts during his cruise in the navy. She knew that Ridgway had previously been arrested for offering and agreeing to an act of prostitution.

Ridgway did not smoke, Girlfriend C said, and she'd never seen him use any narcotics. He especially drank Bud Lite in cans, usually wore blue jeans, plaid-type shirts, and a jeans jacket. He either wore tennis shoes or boots, and occasionally a baseball cap or a watch cap. She described him as a physically strong man whose only hobby that she was aware of was going to swap meets and flea markets. Ridgway had once told her that he had applied to become a police officer somewhere in the area after getting out of the navy. However, she believed that he had failed the exam.

While she knew Ridgway, he drove a maroon Dodge pickup that had a silver-and-black canopy with smoked windows. After totaling the truck in an accident, he bought another pickup that was gold and had a white camper on it. During their relationship, she also knew that he used his dad's brown-and-white pickup and also borrowed his brother Eddie's older turquoise pickup.

Ridgway once took her to a cabin by Ravensdale, Girlfriend C said, that belonged to his brother Greg. The cabin was on the banks of a river. In 1983, he also once took her to a river outside of Cle Elum, where they camped in a tent. Ridgway said he knew this place from camping there on other occasions.

Ridgway and Girlfriend C were to be married in June 1984, but she called it off, she said, after she met someone else. She said Ridgway was not upset over this and quickly met another woman, who currently lived with him.

The Rose Hahn Interview

Detectives Mullinax and Haney interviewed Rose Hahn, who, with her husband, had moved into Gary Ridgway's house about April 1982, during a time in which Ridgway had implied he was having financial difficulties, needed money, and rented out the main portion of his residence. While Rose Hahn and her husband lived in the house, Ridgway lived in the garage, which had been converted to living quarters. Hahn said she remembered the carpet in the house was either gold or brown in the living room and green in the bedrooms. She said Ridgway rarely ate at home, if ever. She had firsthand knowledge of his use of the kitchen and bathroom because he shared these facilities with her family.

Hahn said Ridgway was usually not at home in the evenings, and that if he was, he stayed in his room or outside. She said Ridgway liked to wash his red truck, which had a white-and-silver canopy over the bed. He seemed to enjoy keeping it nice. She also said that Ridgway was very shy and kept to himself. He often wore blue jeans, cowboy boots, and red-and-blue plaid shirts and was usually not at home on weekends. Ridgway, she said, once spoke of his ex-wife, who, she felt, sounded like a "real witch." During the time she and her husband lived in Ridgway's house, Hahn remembered only one or two people calling at the house for Ridgway. The Hahns moved out about October 1982.

Marcia Winslow (Ridgway)

Detectives Doyon and Griffin interviewed Marcia Winslow, who married Gary Ridgway on December 14, 1973. They were separated from July 1980 until December 1980 and moved back together during the month of December 1980. At the end of that month, they separated permanently until their divorce May 27, 1981. During their marriage they lived in several residences, located in Renton, Federal Way, and West Seattle.

Marcia Winslow first met Ridgway on the Renton loop when she, with her girlfriend, was pulled over by Ridgway in what she described as a "police-like stop." Although Ridgway did not identify himself as a police officer, he had short hair at the time, and she believed he could have been a police officer. Shortly after they met, they lived together for a year prior to their marriage. Ridgway told her that because he had a venereal disease, he was afraid he would not be able to father children. During their sexual encounters, Ridgway used to call Marcia "Claudia," the name of his first wife. Ridgway told Marcia that Claudia was living with several black men when he returned from his western Pacific cruise.

During Ridgway and Marcia's marriage, they used to ride bikes on Frager Road along the Green River past P. D. & J. Meats and the Meeker Street Bridge in Kent. She said they would have sex in the tall grass of the Green River as well as inside a fenced area (the landfill off Frager Road). She also said that on occasion they would get off their bikes and splash in the water at the riverbank. They used to have sex in a wooded area by Ken's Truck Stop near North Bend and also while camping in the Greenwater area past Enumclaw. She described an incident while they were on their way to Spokane, when they pulled off onto the shoulder of the road prior to entering the city, climbed a fence, and had sex in a wooded area. They used to go to Swan Lake, where they swam and fished.

Ridgway, she said, used to frequent the Ravensdale Tavern and the Playmore Tavern east of Kent. He told her about a place near Sea-Tac Airport, where there were blue lights that he used to go to. However, she never went there with him. She also said they used to travel Highway 18 to Highway I-90 and they'd stop at the intersection of the two roads. She mentioned a road that went off to the east of Highway 18, where they'd driven. Marcia said they had also driven toward Echo Glen on Highway 18.

Marcia said she felt that Ridgway viewed her as a sex object and housekeeper, that he would often request anal sex, and that he had tied her up on one or two occasions. She said that he preferred sex either out in the woods or in the open. Also, she said that Ridgway would often ask her to perform oral sex while he drove down the road in their vehicle. Ridgway asked to use an ashtray that was shaped like a penis on her on several occasions, but she refused.

The Ridgways had a son, Matthew, who was born on September 5, 1975. She said Ridgway spent the majority of his weekends at his parents' residence. During their marriage they attended two churches, one Baptist and the other Pentecostal. Ridgway owned a motorcycle during this time, Marcia said, and he did all of his own auto-body work and owned a paint compressor, a tool frequently used to paint vehicles.

Ridgway told Marcia that the garage area was his private place and for her to stay away from it. He once told her that he had considered becoming a military policeman while in the service so he could become a police officer upon his discharge. He also told her he had applied locally to be a police officer but had been turned down.

Ridgway was often gone in the evenings for long periods of

time, Marcia said, often returning to the house dirty or wet. He explained his condition by saying that his vehicle broke down while he was out driving. Marcia said that during the latter years of their marriage Ridgway began coming home later and later without a logical explanation. She also said that Ridgway did not have any personal friends during their marriage.

Marcia related an incident in which she and Ridgway were returning home from a party where they'd been drinking. She got out of the van, stumbled, and then went to the front door. She started to reach for the door and the next thing she knew, Ridgway had his hands around her neck and was choking her from behind; his hands were getting tighter and tighter. She thought it was somebody else and started screaming. Then she realized it was Ridgway and started fighting him. He finally let go and kind of pushed her, and by the time she got her balance back, he had walked around to the other side of the van and tried to convince her that it was somebody else who had run off. She tried to get him to call the police, and he wouldn't do it. She knew then that it was Ridgway and thought maybe it was because they'd had too much to drink and that he was just playing around. She told the interviewers that it was a police-type hold, with his forearm and upper arm, and then he got his hands around her neck.

She said he always liked to sneak up behind her and scare her. He liked to hide in corners to scare her as she walked around them, or he'd push her into an arm-type choke hold. He liked to see how softly he could walk so that he'd be totally noiseless, which, she said, he was able to do.

It was Ridgway's mother, Marcia said, who "wore the pants in the family." Also, Ridgway's younger brother, Eddie, had been in prison for attempting to murder someone while he was in the army, an incident that has been verified by military records.

Key Locations Pointed Out by Marcia Winslow

On September 14, 1986, Detectives Doyon and Haney of the King County Police Green River Task Force took Ridgway's ex-wife, Marcia Winslow, to several locations she pointed out that she and Gary Ridgway had frequented during their relationship, the first of which was eastbound on Highway 18 from her residence.

The Arrest of Gary Leon Ridgway

Marcia had already told police that there was a small dirt road off Highway 18 just prior to the I-90 junction where they had gone several times to have sex. She was unsure of the exact time period but believed it was around 1974. As they neared Kerriston Road, Marcia asked them to slow down, which they did on Highway 18. She looked at the turnoff for Kerriston Road and decided that this was not the road because it now looked different to her. There was a guardrail on Highway 18 that she did not remember.

They continued on, eastbound on Highway 18 to the I-90 junction, but there were no other roads going off to the right. They drove Marcia back to the turnoff to Kerriston Road. However, they were only able to go a short distance up the road because there was a locked bar–type gate across the roadway. Marcia stated that the road, as she remembered it, did have a gate similar to this one, but again she did not recognize it as being the same one. Keeping in mind that there had been a time lapse of approximately twelve years, she did admit that the area could look much different now than it had then. Detectives Doyon and Haney did not advise Marcia that the skeletal remains of Green River victim Amina Agisheff had been recovered just beyond the locked gate on Kerriston Road.

Detectives Haney and Doyon and Marcia Winslow continued east on Highway 18 toward the I-90 junction; just prior to that location they turned into a large wooded area, where the remains of Green River victim Tina Thompson had been found. Marcia pointed out this area as being a place that she and Ridgway had stopped at several times and she recalled them once shooting shotguns there. She said Ridgway had stepped out into the woods one or two times at this location to urinate. Then they crossed Highway 18, westbound, to another turnoff, where the remains of Green River victim Maureen Feeney had been recovered. Marcia told the detectives that she did not recognize the area. They continued along Highway 18, under I-90, toward Echo Glen, but went no farther than the Highway 18 portion of the roadway.

Doyon, Haney, and Marcia then traveled eastbound on I-90 past North Bend toward Ken's Truck Town by taking the Edgewick Exit off I-90. Marcia stated that when she and Ridgway had been frequenting this area of Ken's Truck Town, the new I-90 had not been built, so the area no longer looked like it did back then. She directed the detectives to two paved roads that went toward the middle fork of the Snoqualme River. Marcia said she believed that this was the area to which she and her husband had gone several times to have sex together.

Next, the detectives and Marcia drove to Exit 38, where the remains of Green River victims Delise Plager, Lisa Yates, and Kim Nelson had been recovered. Marcia recognized Exit 38 as being one of the locations she and Ridgway had frequented, and she stated that there was an exit very close to there, she believed, where she and Ridgway had gone several times, and there were fire trucks behind a fence in this same area. They then drove to the next exit, which is Exit 42 for Tinkham Road, where the old fire-training center used to be. Marcia recognized this road as being the one she and Ridgway had used several times for inner tubing in the snow.

The task force detectives next drove Marcia to the Greenwater area east of Enumclaw on Highway 410. While en route to this location, Marcia related that Ridgway had always had plastic Visqueen and a blanket in their car and truck. Ridgway would often bring home rolled-up pieces of plastic in his lunch pail from his job at Kenworth. She also stated that Ridgway would mark on a standard Washington State map the areas where he preferred to go camping and the areas he liked.

Marcia said that after she and Ridgway were married, and not long after their son, Matthew, was born, they began attending a Southern Baptist church and Ridgway had become "fanatical" about religion. They later started going to a Pentecostal church; Ridgway easily made the transition to the new church, participating in going door-to-door but getting angry when people would close their doors on them. They had quit going to church by the time they separated. Marcia remembered that at night Ridgway would sit quietly watching TV with an open Bible on his lap and that he would frequently cry during or after the church service.

Marcia said that prior to her divorce from Ridgway and during their separation, he had accused her of going to motels on Pacific Highway South with other men. He told her that he wanted custody of Matthew and that he was going to use photographs he had taken of her dressed like a prostitute while going to these motels with other men. She said that her husband might have had photographs of her, but not of her going into any motels with other men. She also stated that when it came time for the divorce, Ridgway had not contested it and never did show any photos of her.

The Arrest of Gary Leon Ridgway

Marcia said that while they were married and she was working, an incident occurred involving her going to the Bear Cave Tavern/Topless Bar with a girlfriend who had asked her to stop by one afternoon after they got off work. Marcia had never been there before, but she agreed to go inside. However, after they went in, Marcia quickly became embarrassed, finished her drink, and then told her girlfriend that she was going to leave, which she did. After she got home, her husband came in, very upset, and accused her of dancing topless at the Bear Cave Tavern. He said that his foreman had seen her there dancing topless, and even though Marcia told him she had not done it and tried to explain, he never did believe her.

The detectives asked Marcia what type of relationship her husband had with his parents, and she said that Gary and his mother were very close but that he and his father were not. She said that Ridgway's mother ran the household and she was continually yelling at his father. As an example, Marcia related an incident that occurred while she and her husband were both at his parents' house: Mrs. Ridgway was upset with Mr. Ridgway and became angry. She broke a dinner plate over his head while he was seated at the table. Marcia said that her father-in-law did not retaliate in any manner, only got up and left. She also said that the first time she saw Mrs. Ridgway, she did not believe she was Gary's mother because Mrs. Ridgway was wearing a lot of makeup and tight clothes and, to Marcia, looked like a prostitute. Marcia later learned that Gary's mother always dressed that way, even at home.

The two task force investigators, Doyon and Haney, and Marcia Winslow continued their drive, and after arriving in the Greenwater area, she directed them to a fire service road that turned north from Highway 410, just prior to a railroad trestle approximately a half-mile east of Greenwater. Off this fire service road, Marcia said, she and Ridgway and Ridgway's family had camped. On the way back from this camping area toward Enumclaw, Marcia made the statement that Ridgway was very familiar with the entire area from Greenwater to Enumclaw. This is the area where the remains of Green River victims Bello, Authorlee, and Abernathy were recovered.

Marcia next directed Detectives Haney and Doyon to the Auburn–Federal Way area. At Highway 18 and West Valley Highway, Marcia said that when she and Ridgway lived in the Twin Lakes area of Federal Way, Ridgway would take the Peasley

Canyon Road and the Mountview Cemetery Road home. He preferred to use the back roads rather than the main highways. The Mountview Cemetery Road is where Green River victim Kimi-Kai Pitsor's remains were found as well as two sets of unidentified remains. Green River victim Brockmann was found in Jovita Canyon, which is the next canyon to the south, going from the West Valley Highway up toward the Federal Way area. Marcia said that her husband would take back roads traveling to and from work, looking for "dumping areas"—places where people would drop off their garbage on side and dead-end roads. He would then go through the garbage looking for anything he could salvage. He also enjoyed going to swap meets, including the one located at Angle Lake.

Haney and Doyon then took Marcia to Star Lake Road because she had stated that she and Gary Ridgway had swum and fished in Star Lake. While driving down Star Lake Road, Marcia stated that she still believed this was the lake where they had gone swimming and fishing but she no longer recognized it. Marcia was unable to locate an area where she thought there were picnic tables and a beach for swimming. She said that all this had taken place a number of years earlier. The remains of Green River victims Smith, Matthew, Rois, Gabbert, Williams, and Milligan were found and recovered on Star Lake Road. All of these victims were found close to where people dumped garbage.

Marcia was next driven to Frager Road and she pointed out areas where she and Ridgway had gone bicycling and then engaged in sex. These areas included the grassy banks by P. D. & J. Meats and also under a large tree next to a pond by the Peck Bridge, the location where Green River victims Cofield, Bonner, Mills, Chapman, and Hinds were found.

Farther north of Frager Road, Marcia pointed out an area across the street from Cottonwood Grove Park, where she and her husband had engaged in sex several times underneath a large tree. (Police recovered the skeletal remains of Tracy Winston on March 27, 1986, at Cottonwood Grove Park.) Just past the park to the north, Marcia pointed out a fenced road leading to a landfill, where she and Ridgway had engaged in sex, and also pointed across the street at the old boat launch on the Green River.

Marcia directed the detectives to an area south of the Sea-Tac Airport, South 200th and 20th Avenue South, where she said that she and Ridgway had picked blackberries and apples. This is now an abandoned area since the Port of Seattle purchased the land pursuant to a noise abatement program. The area is now fenced, and the detectives were unable to verify Marcia's directions. However, this is almost the exact location where Green River victim Lavvorn's remains were recovered. Also, just a few blocks away, Green River victims Naon, Meehan, and Ware were found.

Vehicles Associated with Gary Ridgway

1) 1975 Dodge pickup, Washington license PR-5996, maroon in color with a black hood and numerous rust-colored primer spots. This pickup was known to have two canopies associated with it, one white and the other black. The truck was purchased on 6/5/77 by Gary Ridgway and totaled in an accident on 2/21/84. This vehicle has since been destroyed.

2) 1973 Plymouth Satellite, 4-door, brown in color, Washington license FRD275. This vehicle was purchased by Girlfriend C on 12/2/83 and sold to Gary Ridgway on 2/22/84. Girlfriend C was Ridgway's girlfriend during 1982, 1983, and early 1984.

3) 1970 Dodge pickup, blue-green (aqua) in color, with a white cab-high canopy, Washington license A48731. This vehicle was later painted dark blue by Gary Ridgway. The vehicle was purchased on 7/9/81 by Gary Ridgway's brother, Thomas E. Ridgway.

4) 1977 Dodge pickup, brown and gold in color, Washington license XS5535. This vehicle was purchased on 10/18/78 by Gary Ridgway's father, Thomas N. Ridgway, and sold on 8/11/83.

5) 1983 Ford pickup, red and white in color, with cab-high canopy, Washington license HZ6684. This pickup was purchased on 8/11/83 by Gary Ridgway's father, Thomas N. Ridgway, and sold on 8/15/86.

6) 1970 Ford pickup, off-white or very faded light green in color, Washington license A01419. This pickup was previously owned by Girlfriend C and her ex-husband, who

signed off his interest in the pickup on 8/17/82 as part of a divorce settlement. Girlfriend C sold the pickup on 5/7/83.

7) 1977 Ford pickup, brown in color, Washington license PZ9609. This pickup was purchased by Gary Ridgway on 4/16/84 and occasionally had a gold-and-white 8-foot camper on it.

8) 1969 Dodge Dart, 2-door, beige/brown in color, Washington license OLF212. This vehicle was purchased by Gary Ridgway on 2/13/85 from his brother, Thomas E. Ridgway, who purchased this vehicle from his brother, Gregory L. Ridgway, on 3/24/75.

9) 1992 Ford Ranger pickup, red in color with red canopy, Washington license 75935Y. This vehicle is currently registered to Gary Ridgway.

10) 1992 Mercury Sable, 4-door, tan in color, Washington license 721EXO. This vehicle is currently registered to Gary and Judith Ridgway.

11) 1992 Flair Motorhome, beige in color, Washington license 131EKO. This vehicle is currently registered to Gary and Judith Ridgway.

It is also possible that Ridgway's employment allowed him unfettered temporary use of vehicles he was assigned to work on. Ridgway, in his statement to Detective Randy Mullinax, also said that he used his father's 1978 Dodge pickup, which was brown and tan and did not have a canopy associated with it. Dawn White, in her first interview, told Detectives Mullinax and Dave Reichert that she believed Ridgway had just sold a white pickup truck.

The Disappearance of Alma Smith

Alma Smith was last seen by a friend, Cynthia Basset-Ornelas, when they were working together as prostitutes on March 3, 1983, in front of the Red Lion Hotel on Pacific Highway South. At about nine P.M., Ornelas got a date, and when she returned about thirty minutes later, Smith was gone. Ornelas saw a white and blue pickup truck in the Red Lion parking lot and thought Smith might be on a date in it, so she went over and looked inside. Smith was not inside. The truck was occupied by a white male, 27 to 30 years old, approximately six feet tall, 160 pounds, with dark brown hair and blue eyes, and wearing jeans and a jeans jacket. The truck was described as white and blue in color, a standard-size pickup, of unknown 1970s make.

This male occupant asked Ornelas what she wanted, to which she replied, "Not you." She then began to walk away and the man exited the pickup and began following her. Ornelas told the man to leave her alone, and he then asked her where her blond friend was. (Alma Smith was blond. Ornelas had never previously worked with Smith on Pacific Highway South, and this contact is similar to Ridgway's contact with Paige Miley concerning Kim Nelson.) A short time later, Ornelas was told by a separate subject that Smith had left in that same pickup.

On December 30, 1986, Ornelas was shown a six-person photomontage, which included a photograph of Ridgway. Ornelas picked out Ridgway as "looking like the guy but having longer, thinner hair and thinner lips." She stated that she could not positively say that Ridgway was the driver of the pickup she had seen in the Red Lion parking lot.

The Disappearance of Gail Mathews

Gail Mathews was known to be involved in prostitution activities on Pacific Highway South from field interview reports and witness accounts. On April 10, 1983, Mathews was with her boyfriend, Curtis Weaver, at the VIP Tavern on South 208th and Pacific Highway South. Shortly before six P.M., Weaver left Mathews at the tavern and walked to South 216th and Pacific Highway South so that he could catch a bus to another tavern, where he planned to gamble. Neither Mathews nor Weaver had money to pay for a room that night at the New West Motel at South 216th and Pacific Highway South.

Approximately ten minutes after Weaver left Mathews at the tavern, he saw her sitting in a blue-green pickup truck that had a white canopy over the bed. The driver was described as a white male, 25 to 35 years of age, with curly brown hair and wearing a flannel shirt. Weaver described the truck as having numerous primer spots down the passenger's side. The truck was sitting in the left-hand turn lane of the Pacific Highway South, southbound, waiting to turn eastbound onto South 216th. Weaver said he attempted to get Mathews's attention but she appeared to be in a trance and never acknowledged his gestures. She continued to look straight ahead as if he weren't there. After watching the truck disappear eastbound on South 216th, he never saw the truck or Mathews again. Gail Mathews's remains were found on Star Lake Road on September 18, 1983, an area that yielded the remains of five additional Green River victims.

The Disappearance of Kimi-Kai Pitsor

Kimi-Kai Pitsor was last seen by her boyfriend of two years, Stephen Smith, on April 17, 1983, at about ten P.M. in downtown Seattle working as a prostitute. Smith said that a white male adult, in his mid-twenties, with dark hair, a two-inch tattoo on his right arm, and wearing a white T-shirt, drove past both Pitsor and him. Pitsor was approximately a half-block ahead of him and waved to the driver as he approached her, as if he were a known "date." The pickup slowed and Pitsor began to run toward it as it went past her. Both Pitsor and the pickup disappeared from Smith's view as it pulled into a parking lot and Pitsor followed it. Smith ran to see if Pitsor was going to make the date, only to discover both Pitsor and the pickup gone. Smith waited for seven hours for Pitsor to return, but she never did, and he never saw her again.

Pitsor's skull was discovered at Mountview Cemetery on December 18, 1983. On January 9, 1987, Smith was shown a six-person photomontage, which included the photograph of Gary Ridgway. Smith tentatively picked out Ridgway as the driver of the pickup truck. Smith requested to see a side view of Ridgway to attempt a more positive identification. On January 13, 1987, Smith was shown another montage including a side view of Ridgway. Smith again tentatively identified Ridgway but said that he "couldn't be a thousand percent sure."

Surveillance of Gary Ridgway

Gary Ridgway was surveilled between October 9, 1986, and October 24, 1986, when he was working the second shift (3:40 P.M. to 12:10 A.M. Monday through Friday) at Kenworth on East Marginal Way. He was surveilled from the time he left his residence in the morning hours until he arrived at work in the afternoon. Ridgway was driving his 1977 Ford truck. He was also periodically surveilled after leaving work.

During the time that Ridgway was surveilled, he displayed his familiarity with the area on and around Pacific Highway South near Sea-Tac Airport and was observed cruising Pacific Highway South and parking in areas known to be high areas of prostitution. Specifically, he was seen parked at Larry's Market, located at South 144th and Pacific Highway South, and at the 7-Eleven located at South 142nd and Pacific Highway South. Several Green River victims disappeared from these locations: Sandra Gabbert, Kim Nelson, Tina Thompson, Denise Bush, Terry Milligan, Shawnda Summers, Carol Christensen, and Yvonne Antosh. Ridgway was also observed on several occasions eating at fast-food restaurants in the immediate area. He also visited his parents' house, located at 4404 South 175th in Sea-Tac, several times.

On one occasion during this period of surveillance, Ridgway went to Rainier Avenue South between Seward Park Drive and Andover Street, where he drove back and forth two times. This section of Rainer Avenue South is also a very popular location for prostitution, and several Green River victims disappeared from it, specifically Lisa Yates, April Buttram, Pammy Avent, and Mary West.

During the surveillance, Ridgway usually drove well below the legal speed limit, and while driving he was very attentive to the activities of the area. On numerous occasions, while driving on Pacific Highway South, Ridgway would suddenly turn off the road, use a side street to turn around, and then begin driving in the opposite direction on Pacific Highway South for no apparent reason. It was obvious that he was also very familiar with the side roads in this area.

On October 17, 2001, detectives briefly surveilled Ridgway's travel from his job at Kenworth Trucking in downtown Renton to his home in Auburn. Instead of taking the most direct and quickest route, I-5, Ridgway drove on Pacific Highway South from Sea-Tac to Auburn. Again, he traveled below the speed limit and was distracted by a lone woman on the street, who appeared to officers to be working as a prostitute.

On October 23, 2001, detectives again briefly surveilled Ridgway on his way home after his workday ended at three P.M. and again observed him taking Pacific Highway South from Sea-Tac to Auburn. On both days, he first dropped by his mother's home in Sea-Tac for several minutes before continuing his trip. During his trip after he left his mother's house, Ridgway made two unexplainable U-turns in the middle of the highway. His speeds again varied from slow to fast, as if he were seeking something.

On November 28, 2001, detectives began another surveillance of Ridgway. Ridgway left his home at about 4:20 A.M. and once again went out of his way to take an indirect route to work that took him to Pacific Highway South. A commute that should have taken approximately twenty minutes, given the time of day, ended up taking almost an hour due to Ridgway's circuitous route.

Ridgway drove from Military Road to South 320th, then headed north on Pacific Highway South. Ridgway's driving was consistent until he passed an individual on the side of the road at about Pacific Highway South and South 150th. He then turned into a business parking lot and began making U-turns in parking lots and at intersections, which enabled him to look closer at the individual on the street. Ridgway then continued on Pacific Highway South and turned onto Martin Luther King Way and traveled to South Henderson, then Rainier Avenue to Airport Way. About a quarter-mile onto Airport Way, Ridgway took a hard right and went behind some businesses for no apparent reason, then reappeared and went to his job, where he arrived early and sat in the parking lot for forty-five minutes.

Police Contacts with Gary Ridgway

It has been documented that Gary Ridgway was contacted on at least two occasions by the Port of Seattle Police during 1982 and 1983. The first contact was at 1:14 A.M. on August 29, 1982, while

Ridgway was in his 1975 Dodge pickup, Washington license PR-5996, at South 192nd and the old Alaskan Airlines maintenance building. To illustrate the importance of this contact, it was made at the end of a dead-end street within a hundred feet of where victims Naon and Ware were later discovered, but prior to their disappearances. Victim Mary Meehan's remains were also recovered from this same street, but closer to Highway 99. The time and date of this contact is also significant because it occurred during the early Sunday morning hours following the Saturday noon (August 28, 1982) disappearance of Green River missing person Kase Lee. Also, victim Terry Milligan went missing from 144th and Pacific Highway South on August 29, 1982. Milligan's body was discovered on April 1, 1984, in the Star Lake area.

Ridgway's second contact involved his February 23, 1983, date with Green River missing person Keli McGinness. As documented, McGinness and Ridgway were contacted at South 140th and 22nd South in Ridgway's 1975 Dodge pickup, Washington license PR-5996.

On November 16, 2001, Ridgway was arrested by a King County Sheriff's Department undercover officer working as a prostitute decoy on Pacific Highway South at the 16500 block. The decoy was approached by Ridgway in front of Motel 6. Ridgway waved money at her through the window. He then pulled his red Ford Ranger pickup (Washington license 75935Y) into the parking lot and walked to the bed of his truck. Ridgway asked the decoy if she was dating. The decoy said she was interested and he told her he thought a cop was watching her from the cemetery lot up the street. Ridgway told the decoy he would meet her down the road at the bank. She said she would meet him and gave the arrest signal to the police. Ridgway was stopped en route to the bank at the 16200 block of Pacific Highway South in Sea-Tac and arrested. He was searched and found to have thirty dollars cash and latex gloves in his possession. Ridgway was booked into the King County jail for "loitering."

Police Summary of the Gary Ridgway Investigation

A. Green River Task Force detectives have conducted an intensive background investigation on Gary Leon Ridgway. This included Ridgway's daily work records for the years 1982, 1983, and 1984, and gas credit-card and bank records for this same period of time, as well as interviews of friends and associates. Ridgway was employed almost full-time during this time period and used his gas credit cards frequently. Even though the time of day and days of the week of most victim and missing disappearances have varied greatly, there are twenty-seven dates that have been pinpointed with relative certainty. Extensive review of documents obtained by subpoena of known accounts of Ridgway, including bank and charge records, work records, phone records, and interviews with former girlfriends contain information that shows he is available as a suspect on these known dates. It is also known that Ridgway lived at 21859 32nd Place, South Kent, Washington, from January 1982 to August 1989. This address is approximately six blocks from the corner of South 216th and Pacific Highway South, the location from where several Green River victims and missing have disappeared. Two victims (Bonner, Mathews) and one missing (Malvar) were last observed leaving or in the area of South 216th and Pacific Highway South.

B. From information gained in interviews with ex-wives Marcia Winslow and Claudia Barrows, and ex-girlfriend Girlfriend A, Ridgway liked to engage in sex in the outdoors. They also placed Ridgway at, or near, the following multiple-victim dump sites: Sea-Tac Airport, Highway 410, Star Lake Road, North Bend, the junction of Highway 18 and I-90, Seward Park, and the banks of the Green River. According to these witnesses, they engaged in sex with Ridgway at most of these locations and, of particular interest, Marcia Winslow states that she and Ridgway had sex numerous times in the tall grass on the banks of the Green River next to P. D. & J. Meats. This is the same location where the first five Green River victims were found.

C. In the interview of Gary Ridgway by Detective Randy Mullinax, Ridgway states his 1975 maroon Dodge pickup was broken down in the months of March, April, or May of 1983, while he put a V-8 engine in it. Ridgway stated he rode the bus and also borrowed his father's pickup during this time period. Task Force detectives have learned from interviewing Girlfriend C, who was Gary Ridgway's girl-friend during 1982, 1983, and the early part of 1984, that he also borrowed his brother's 1970 aqua colored Dodge pickup, Washington license A48731. The only sightings associating Green River victims with blue or green pickups occurred during March or April of 1983. The following victims were last seen in blue or green pickup trucks:

- Alma Smith, the first victim during this time period, was last seen on March 3, 1983, at about nine P.M. in front of the Red Lion Hotel on Pacific Highway South by Cynthia Ornelas. Ornelas picked Ridgway's photo-graph from a photomontage as looking like the suspi-cious man, wearing blue jeans and a jeans jacket, who she believes was involved in Smith's disappearance and who questioned her that same night about Smith imme-diately following her disappearance.

- Gail Mathews is the second victim during this time period, who was last seen on April 10, 1983, in an aqua or blue-green colored pickup that had a white canopy on it and nu-merous primer spots on the passenger side. The driver was described as a white male, 25–35 years of age, with curly light brown hair, wearing a flannel shirt. They were last seen going eastbound on South 216th and Pacific Highway South, which is a few blocks from Ridgway's residence.

- Kimi-Kai Pitsor is the third victim during this period, who was last seen by her boyfriend, Stephen Smith, on April 17, 1983, in downtown Seattle. Smith believes Pit-sor disappeared in a 1974 to 1976 dark pickup, possibly a Ford, with a primer spot on the passenger side. The pickup had a white canopy on it. The driver is described as a white male in his mid-20s, dark hair, with a 2″ tattoo on his right arm, and wearing a white T-shirt. Smith tenta-tively identified Ridgway from a photomontage as being the driver of this vehicle, though he could not be positive.

- David Ralph, a neighbor of Carol Ann Christensen, who disappeared on May 3, 1983, reported that he saw a blue pickup with a white canopy at her residence be-fore her disappearance.

- Information obtained by the Green River Murders Task Force detectives indicates that Gary Ridgway's brother, Thomas E. Ridgway, owned a 1970 Dodge pickup, which was aqua colored and had a white canopy. It should also be noted that the clothing, and basic physical descriptions of the three male subjects observed with the three above-named Green River victims, seen in the blue or green colored pickup trucks, are similar to the description of Gary Ridgway.

D. During the interview of Gary Ridgway by Federal Bureau of Investigation Special Agents O'Neill and Askeland, Ridgway stated that to him, "prostitutes are like alcohol is to an alcoholic." Ridgway went on to say that he no longer dates the prostitutes, only stops and talks to them.

E. During an interview with Girlfriend B, task force detectives learned on December 24, 1981, at approximately 11:30 P.M., Gary Ridgway entered the White Shutters Restaurant where Girlfriend B was and sat down next to her. He immediately blurted out to Girlfriend B he had almost killed someone. This shocked Girlfriend B and she asked Ridgway what he was talking about and he stated he had picked up a woman, or prostitute, and he couldn't believe he'd almost killed her. Girlfriend B was given the impression Ridgway was referring to a prostitute. This woman has never been identified.

F. On November 9, 1982, Ridgway contacted Rebecca Garde Guay on Pacific Highway South and arranged for oral sex for $20. Ridgway then took Guay to the location of South 204th and 22nd Avenue South and walked into the woods with Guay. While Guay proceeded to perform the sex act, Ridgway suddenly began choking her violently, claiming that she had bitten him. A very violent struggle ensued from which Guay was able to break free and run to a nearby trailer occupied by an older couple. She did not immediately report this incident to the police because she was fearful that her family would find out that she was working as a prostitute. When later interviewed, Ridgway admitted to this incident but could not give an explanation as to why he choked her for so long and continued to choke her until she was able to break free from him. There was no doubt in Guay's mind that Ridgway was attempting to kill her. This location is only a few blocks away from where several Green River victims were found.

G. On April 8, 1987, a judicially-authorized search warrant was served in King County on the following locations by Task Force members:

1. 21859 32nd Place, South Kent, Washington. (Residence of Gary Ridgway)

2. 1977 Ford pickup, Washington license PZ9609. (Registered to Gary Ridgway)

3. 1969 Dodge Dart, Washington license OLF212. (Registered to Gary Ridgway)

4. 1970 Dodge pickup, Washington license A48731. (Registered to Thomas E. Ridgway)

5. A personal locker at Kenworth Trucking Company, located at 8801 East Marginal Way South, Seattle, Washington. (Gary Ridgway's work locker)

6. Control samples of hair and saliva from Gary Ridgway.

7. Various evidence items were removed from Ridgway's residence and the above-listed vehicles such as carpet fibers, ropes, paint samples, and plastic tarps. These items and various other items were submitted to the Washington State Crime laboratory with negative results as far as linking Ridgway to a particular scene or victim. Pursuant to the warrant, a saliva sample and hair samples were obtained from Ridgway on April 8, 1987.

H. DNA evidence is as follows:

1) Opal Mills was found in the brush near the Green River on August 15, 1982. The King County Medical Examiner's office collected a "sexual assault kit" from her person during the autopsy.

   a. In March of 1988, vaginal swabbing and the vaginal wash from Opal Mills were sent to Lifecodes Corporation, a forensic laboratory in New York. Lifecodes reported that "an insufficient amount of high molecular weight human DNA" made DNA typing impossible with the technology available at that time.

b. In October 2001, the same samples collected from Opal Mills, which had been sent to Lifecodes thirteen years earlier, were subjected to a more sensitive DNA typing technique (PCR amplification of STR loci) by the Washington State Patrol Crime Laboratory (WSPCL). In preliminary findings, forensic scientists at the WSPCL reported that vaginal swabs from Mills contained a mixed DNA profile, and Ridgway cannot be eliminated as one of the sources of that DNA.

2) Marcia Chapman was also discovered in the Green River on August 15, 1982. During autopsy, a "sexual assault kit" was also collected from her and preserved. In October of 2001, these samples were subjected to a sensitive DNA typing technique (PCR amplification of STR loci) by the Washington State Patrol Crime Laboratory. In preliminary findings forensic scientists at the WSPCL report that Chapman's vaginal swab contains a partial male DNA profile. This partial profile is consistent with coming from Ridgway.

3) Carol Christensen was found on May 8, 1983, in the Maple Valley area. Samples were collected from her person as well as for future laboratory analysis.

a. In March of 1988, vaginal swabbing and the vaginal wash from Carol Christensen were sent to Lifecodes Corporation, a forensic laboratory in New York. Lifecodes reported that an "insufficient amount of high molecular weight human DNA" made DNA typing impossible with the technology available at that time.

b. In October 2001, a vaginal swabbing from Christensen was subjected to sensitive DNA typing (PCR amplification of STR loci) at the WSPCL. Forensic scientist Jean C. Johnston of the crime laboratory concluded that the DNA obtained from the sperm fraction of the vaginal swab sample is from a single male contributor. The profile was compared to Gary L. Ridgway and two other males of interest in the case. A match was declared at all 13 DNA loci between the sperm fraction sample and that of Ridgway. It can be estimated that not more than one individual, excluding identical twins, in the world's population would exhibit this DNA profile

I. Present Information on Gary Ridgway

1) On October 10, 2001, Quest security verified that Ridgway has a home telephone number, which phone number has been deleted for the purposes of this writing.

2) On October 10, 2001, it was verified that the following vehicles are currently registered to Ridgway: a 1992 Ford Ranger pickup, Washington license 75935Y; a 1992 Mercury Sable, Washington license 721EXO; and a 1992 Flair Motorhome, Washington license 131EKO.

3) In October 2001, through surveillance, Ridgway has been seen driving his 1992 Ford Ranger pickup with canopy. His truck has been seen at his home residence located at 4633 South 348th in Auburn and at his mother's residence located at 4404 South 175th in Sea-Tac. It is verified, also, that Ridgway is still employed at Kenworth Trucking Company, located at 745 Houser Way North in Renton. According to the company's Human Resources Department, his locker at the business is #1568 and has his name on the outside.

4) It is further verified through King County Assessor's records that Ridgway has owned three residences in King County from 1982 to the present.
   a. From August 1997 to the present: 4633 South 348th Street, Auburn, Washington.
   b. From September 1989 to November 1997: 2139 South 253rd Street, Des Moines, Washington.
   c. From January 1982 to August 1989: 21859 32nd Place South, Sea-Tac, Washington.

5) Ridgway is still active on Pacific Highway South. He was recently arrested on November 16, 2001, for Loitering for the Purposes of Prostitution.

6) It has been learned that Ridgway has had a safe deposit box (#0633305–0001–00110–89207) at Bank of America (formerly SeaFirst) at the branch located at 16640 International Boulevard, Sea-Tac, Washington, since 1985.

DNA evidence links Ridgway to the murders of Mills, Christensen, and Chapman. In addition, strong circumstantial evidence links him to the murder of Cynthia Hinds, whose body was discovered in the Green River on the same day and within feet of Chapman. Like Chapman, a rock was found in her vagina at autopsy.

Since the murders of Chapman, Hinds, Mills, and Christensen, the bodies or skeletal remains of approximately 44 murdered women have been discovered in King County. Virtually all of these victims had histories of prostitution or life on the streets. It appears that many of them were victims of strangulation, with a few of them displaying evidence of other causes of death, including blunt-force trauma. Despite extensive investigations, all of these cases remain unsolved.

Detective Sue Peters wrote:

In your affiant's opinion, it is highly likely that as this investigation continues and Washington State Patrol Crime Laboratory continues to employ extremely sensitive DNA typing techniques to these cases, Ridgway will be linked to other "Green River" victims and to more recent unsolved murders of women in King County and elsewhere. Many prostitute murders remain unsolved in Snohomish County, Pierce County, and Portland, Oregon. Prostitutes have disappeared in those jurisdictions as well as in Vancouver, B.C.

Your affiant believes Gary L. Ridgway is responsible for the murders of Marcia F. Chapman, Cynthia J. Hinds, Opal C. Mills, and Carol A. Christensen. Based on your affiant's training, experience, and research of serial killers, it is known that "serial killers" often remove evidence items from the scene. These items include souvenirs and trophies, such as jewelry or an article of clothing that the killer keeps and uses as a way to regain the thrill of the initial kill. Chapman, Hinds, and Mills were each missing articles of clothing. Hinds was also missing a gold chain with a heart shaped necklace, and Christensen was missing a white gold wedding band.

Your affiant knows through training and experience that trace evidence such as hairs, fibers, and stains were likely to be transferred from the victims to their killer and vice versa. Trace evidence in the form of fibers, hairs, blood stains, or body fluid evidence can remain at a site for many years, particularly if such evidence has seeped through carpet or is in an area inaccessible to routine cleaning. Trace evidence such as fibers, hairs, blood stains, and body fluid evidence may still be found in residences and vehicles formerly used by Ridgway. For example, in the Hinds case, a light blue paint chip was recovered from the scene blanket that was used to transport Hinds' body to the morgue. In the Christensen case, a few small fibers were recovered from her fingernail clippings, including a blue cotton fiber and a green acrylic fiber. It is possible that matching paint chips and/or fibers will be found in the residences and/or vehicles used by Ridgway. Your affiant also knows it is important to collect papers and documents associated to Ridgway to assist detectives in developing an accurate timeline on his whereabouts. Further, your affiant knows, through training and experience, that deliberate repeat "killers" have been known to record or photograph their victims for the same reasons such persons keep "trophies," to be able to relive the event. It is important for detectives to collect photographs and videotapes to review the possibility they contain this type of evidence. Detectives are also requesting permission to obtain blood, hair, and saliva samples from Ridgway for future crime laboratory analysis.

The Search Warrant

Subsequent to the filing of the affidavits by the King County Sheriff's Department, Gary Ridgway's various residences, his work locker at Kenworth Trucking, and his vehicles were all searched. As of this update, Gary Ridgway is currently awaiting trial in the state of Washington for the murders of Opal Mills, Cynthia Hinds, Marcia Chapman, and Carol Christensen.

18

Was Bundy Right?:
Ted Bundy's "Riverman"
and Ridgway's Confessions

Ted Bundy didn't know, when he wrote to me after I became the consultant to the Green River Murders Task Force, that police investigators had already made contact with an individual the task force would later scrutinize very carefully as the case progressed. Dave Reichert and I didn't tell Bundy about anybody the task force had spoken to with regard to the case. Naturally, that was to be kept secret until such time as the prosecuting attorney made it public. And with the public release of Sue Peters's affidavit of probable cause for a search warrant following the arrest of Gary Ridgway, a whole part of the case that was unfolding during the time we were speaking to Ted Bundy in Florida is now part of the public record, as are Bundy's confessions.

Accordingly, at this point, almost fourteen years after Bundy's execution and twenty years since our conversations with him began, it's instructive to ask one very basic question: Were Bundy's profile and observations about the Green River Killer correct? Was Bundy right? Given what Detective Peters wrote in her affidavit, we can compare what's in the public record about the investigation and Ridgway's admissions with what Bundy said to see just how accurate he was.

The King County affidavit describes the route the investigation took as police made contact with various witnesses including prostitutes, a pimp, friends of missing victims, at least one living witness, Gary Ridgway's girlfriends, and his first and second wives. Ridgway's admissions amplify and confirm the information in the King County affidavit. What we're concerned with as we compare Bundy's predictions with the record of the investigation as set forth in the public record is only whether Bundy's assessments about the nature of the investigation have any validity at all.

Bundy, as it became abundantly clear during the interviews, was projecting a lot about what he thought and did into the Green River case, which he was following in the newspapers. However, because he was being more subjective than objective, he was able to conjure up a prototypical suspect, whom he called the "Riverman," a name the suspect himself used in a letter to police, and impart to that creation what he thought such a suspect might think and do. He also made certain basic assumptions about what our investigation would find.

Knowledge of the Area

For example, Bundy assumed that anyone able to move in and out of the area with the bodies of his victims had to have an intimate knowledge of the area, particularly the areas from where victims had been recovered. Just the amount of victim recoveries, Bundy hypothesized, meant that his Riverman knew how to move around without attracting any attention, even if he were moving around in plain sight. Knowledge breeds confidence, exactly the kind of confidence Bundy didn't have when he frantically drove out of Vail, Colorado, with the semiconscious body of Julie Cunningham alongside him in his VW. Bundy's self-described panic led him more than 70 miles away from Vail to a wooded area off a dirt road, where, in complete isolation, he strangled Julie and left her body in the open. He returned weeks later to bury it.

Bundy's Riverman, he believed, did not exhibit this level of panic because he was completely familiar with the areas where bodies would be left. And as the Sue Peters affidavit shows, Detectives Haney and Doyon, on their September 14, 1986, driving tour with Marcia Winslow indicated that Marcia was taken to the Frager Road, and she pointed out areas where she and Gary had gone bicycling and had gotten off their bicycles to engage in sex. This area included the grassy banks by P. D. & J. Meats, and also under a large tree next to a pond by the Peck Bridge. (This is the location where Green River victims Coffield, Bonner, Mills, Chapman, and Hinds had been found.) There were other areas, the affidavit says, including Star Lake Road and Cottonwood Grove Park, where Marcia Winslow said she had visited with the subject of the King County affidavit and from where bodies had been recovered. If what Marcia Winslow told King County detectives, as reported in the affidavit, was accurate, then Bundy's assessment of his Riverman's knowledge of areas where bodies had been recovered was accurate.

Knowledge of the "Prostitute Scene"

Bundy said that for his Riverman to be able to pick up victims quickly and without attracting attention, he had to understand the entire prostitution scene. He had to know how to approach a prostitute, or a woman on the street who could be mistaken for a prostitute, make a date, and get out of the area quickly. The entire "date" itself, as we talked about it with Bundy, was a kind of mini-abduction for cash. He hypothesized that the Riverman would know where the prostitutes congregated, how to make a date so as not to set off an alarm, and where to dump the body in a place he knew so well that he believed it and he would be safe.

Again, the King County affidavit not only contained interviews with friends of the victims but actual witnesses to the contacts between the killer and women believed to have become victims. At least one witness, Paige Miley, reported to police how quickly her friend Kim Nelson had disappeared from a bus stop and how unnerved she was when a stranger casually asked her about her friend. The stranger seemed to be familiar with her friend, and who, evidently, knew the area.

Kim Nelson had disappeared from a covered bus stop in front of a car wash at South 144th and Pacific Highway South on November 1, 1983. Several nights later, while Miley was working as a prostitute in front of the Moonrise Motel, the affidavit says, "she was approached by a man driving a red pickup truck.... After talking about a date, the man asked Miley where her blonde friend was. Miley immediately became concerned with the fact that the man was aware of Kim Nelson's presence on Pacific High Way South." The man, whom Miley did not know but described as "a white male, late twenties to early thirties, with brown hair and a wispy moustache . . . drinking a can of Budweiser beer that he held between his legs," seemed familiar enough with the prostitution scene to talk about a "car date" and to have asked about her friend Kim Nelson. He also seemed familiar enough with Miley so as to be able to talk to her. Ridgway, in his confession, said he had already murdered Kim, and asked Paige about her on the spur of the moment to see if Paige suspected anything.

How the Riverman Manipulated Prostitutes

Bundy believed that his proto-Riverman used his familiarity with prostitutes on the Sea-Tac "scene" along Pacific Highway South so as to be able to manipulate them. He had to be able to get them into his car without arousing suspicion and to talk to them in their own language of dates and car dates. The King County affidavit, narrating the report of prostitute Dawn White, indicates how White, even though she thought the man who approached her was "weird and different," in her own words, still felt obligated to initiate contact with him after a car date they were trying to make was broken up by a police unit.

"White and her friend were contacted by the King County Police in Larry's Market parking lot," the affidavit says. "Because the police made them leave the area, the date did not occur. . . . However, later that day she looked up his name in the telephone book and called him at home telling what happened regarding the incident with the police." She arranged for a meeting with the stranger for a later date, but said they "went their separate ways," and she didn't see him until a year and a half later when they met by accident at a McDonald's in Seattle.

Even though Dawn White was not entirely comfortable with the stranger she said approached her and her friend in a parking lot, she nevertheless felt safe enough to initiate contact with him on her own and arrange for a later date. Perhaps this is the kind of behavior, the ability to get the people Ridgway contacted to trust him enough to do what he wanted, that Bundy was talking about when he described his Riverman as being able to manipulate the members of his victim pool. And, of course, Bundy was correct in that. Ridgway later bragged to investigators about how easy it was to manipulate his victims, especially the teenagers and runaways, with a photo of his own son.

Length of Time Between Disappearances and Body Discoveries

The amount of time between the discoveries of bodies and when the actual crimes might have taken place made it hard, Bundy said, for police to follow up. How can you reasonably follow up quickly on a missing person if you don't know the victim is missing? How can you prosecute a homicide investigation when the victim has been missing for so long you can't tell when she was actually abducted or killed? These were the questions Bundy admitted he had to appreciate when he talked to Dave Reichert and me about ways the police could identify his concept of the Riverman.

Indeed, the King County affidavit exemplified just such a problem when various witnesses reported to the task force that they believed they knew who the Green River Killer might be or reported that their friends might be missing and, perhaps, had become victims of a crime. For example, Paige Miley's report to the task force on August 12, 1986, presented police with just such a problem because her report of the missing Kim Nelson, whose remains were recovered off I-90 on Garcia Road on June 13, 1986, was made almost three years after Nelson disappeared from the bus stop.

Similarly, Rebecca Garde Guay's report of a November 1982 assault upon her when her assailant tried to choke her was made over two years later in 1984. The police contacted Ridgway, as the affidavit says, in February 1985, and in the ensuing conversation, according to the affidavit, "Ridgway said he picked up Guay, who was hitchhiking, at about 5 P.M. . . . Guay inquired of him if he 'dated,' at which time he replied yes. At that time they agreed to a $20 act of sex (blow job)." Later on, the affidavit states that Ridgway "admitted choking Guay after she bit him, saying he choked her with his arm for ten to fifteen seconds." The police report on this encounter was made two years after the encounter took place. The police interview with Ridgway took place three months later.

But the police investigator's acceptance of Ridgway's explanation only served to embolden Ridgway.

Bundy's point—that the length of time before reported assaults and reported missing victims was so great that the police were at a disadvantage in the investigation from the outset—is evidenced by the King County affidavit, which contains specific examples of how this was so and Ridgway's own admission of guilt, in which he explained his methodology of hiding victims' remains.

Lack of News Media and Police Follow-up

As the King County affidavit shows, missing persons reports and allegations of assaults against prostitutes were filed often months or years after the events took place. As a result, official police follow-up did not take place in a timely fashion, nor was there extensive media coverage of the allegations of missing persons until the bodies of missing women began to be recovered. It was only then that the media began focusing attention on the number of body recoveries and the identities of the victims. By then, even though some complaints of assaults had been made, it was difficult to pin down when victims who were reported missing actually went missing. Bundy suggested that part of the underlying reasons for this particular problem was the nature of the victim pool itself.

The Nature of the Victim Pool

Bundy reiterated that prostitutes and women who could be mistaken for prostitutes, such as hitchhikers and runaways, were a pool of ready-access women. These were "low-risk" victims, he explained, because they were already prepared to step into anyone's car for a date. They also tended to avoid the police because they, like the Riverman, were operating outside the law. Many of them were runaways, too, and cocaine abusers.

In the King County affidavit, prostitute Dawn White's account of her contact with a potential date who negotiated with both her and her friend for sex, chose Dawn White, asked her to wait while he went into a store to make a purchase, and then returned to find her gone is an example of the way members of this victim pool tend to avoid police. White explained that when the stranger who had made a date with her went into the store and asked her to wait in the parking lot, she was contacted by a police unit patroling the area. The police told her to move along. She did, not wanting to do anything that might get her arrested. However, she looked up the stranger's name in the phone book, called him, and scheduled a later date. By her own statement to the police, Dawn White was making herself available, and her story demonstrates the easy access any assailant might have had to members of this victim pool.

The Riverman's Confidence

Bundy believed that part of the Riverman's success in finding victims quickly and eluding police was the result of his confidence both in his dealing with members of the victim pool and his access to them. And Ridgway himself confirmed that Bundy was right. For example, Dawn White's account of her encounter with the stranger to the Green River Task Force also demonstrates how confident the stranger was. First, he encountered Dawn and her friend at the same time and negotiated with both about the costs of a double date. If the stranger was afraid, he certainly didn't show it. Moreover, he demonstrated a shared knowledge of the dating rules with Dawn White and her friend, chose the woman he wanted to have the date with, and simply asked her to wait for him until he returned. Dealing for him appeared easy and he seemed to be completely confident of his date's waiting for him. Even though she thought him "weird," if she was afraid of him, she didn't show it by her behavior.

The Police Officer Approach

Bundy believed that his Riverman might have used a "cop approach" to lure victims into his car. By showing them a badge, which could be purchased at any store selling police paraphernalia, he could have easily overcome his potential victim's reluctance to talk to a complete stranger on the street and even gained his victim's confidence to the point where she would get into his car. In

Bundy's attempted kidnapping of Carol DaRonch in Utah he used just such a cop ruse, which got the potential victim into his car long enough for him to try to apply the handcuffs.

The King County affidavit quotes Marcia Winslow, Gary Ridgway's second wife, describing how she first met Ridgway on the Renton loop. "Marcia, who was with a girlfriend at the time, was pulled over by Ridgway in what she described as a 'police-like stop.'" Also, Girlfriend C told King County Green River Murders Task Force detectives that "Ridgway once told her he had applied to become a police officer somewhere in this area after getting out of the Navy. However, Girlfriend C believed he failed the exam."

Normal "John" Approach

Bundy used a number of different approaches to lure his victims. He posed as a detective to Carol DaRonch, an injured guy with his arm in a sling in need of help at Lake Sammamish, and a guy on crutches in the Vail, Colorado, murder of Julie Cunningham. Bundy hypothesized that his Riverman might also use different methods of approach. He described the cop approach, which he believed would be effective in asserting control over prostitutes. But he said that prostitutes were most comfortable dealing with regular johns who did not come on like criminals but were potential customers simply looking for a quick date.

Both Rebecca Garde Guay and Dawn White described just such a typical john approach in their statements to task force detectives, according to the King County affidavit. Guay told police she was hitchhiking when the stranger who later assaulted her picked her up and negotiated with her for oral sex, and Dawn White described the encounter with the stranger driving the pickup truck along Pacific Highway South. Neither Rebecca Garde Guay nor Dawn White had any reason to believe, at first, that the man who picked her up was anything other than a potential customer looking for a date, and both women agreed to do business with him. And Ridgway himself told police that he would show a photo of his son to those potential victims who were suspicious of him so as to gain their confidence.

The Riverman Is Not an Oddball

Bundy tried to adopt the camouflage of normalcy in every aspect of his dealing with people, so he assumed that his Riverman would have done the same. Bundy practiced his approach to women and was confident enough of his ability to modify his demeanor that even when he was rebuffed at Lake Sammamish, he was able to bounce back and pick up Janice Ott after Mary Osmer had slipped out of his grasp. His approach was so confident that he didn't appear needy or strange at all. After Mary Osmer had declined to go with him because he hadn't told her that the sailboat he needed to load onto his car was at his parents' house, Bundy modified his approach to Janice Ott thirty minutes later, explaining that he needed help loading a sailboat that was at his parents' house. Ott agreed and became one of his victims. Osmer declined to go with him and lived to tell the police about it.

So it was with almost all of the witnesses who told their stories to the Green River Murders Task Force. Although Dawn White described the stranger she encountered as weird, he wasn't enough of an oddball to turn her off. In fact, she felt so guilty about having to break their date that she called the man to set up another date.

Marcia Winslow said that although she first met her future husband when he stopped her in a "police-like" way, she always thought of him as nice, even though she described an incident to police in which Ridgway had placed her in a police-type choke hold and applied pressure. But, she said, she attributed her husband's behavior in that particular incident, to their having had too much to drink at a party.

The Riverman Introduces Himself by Asking Victims About Their Friends

As a method of introduction, Bundy predicted, his Riverman might ask a potential victim about one of her friends, a person the Riverman knew, or even one of his own victims. It would be a way to start a conversation, to break the ice, particularly at a time when news might have been spreading within the victim pool about missing women.

In her statement to the task force, Paige Miley explained that one of the elements of her conversation with the stranger along Pacific Highway South was his mention of her friend Kim Nelson, who was a missing person. Miley was in the process, she said, of arranging a date with this stranger when his mention of Kim Nelson, with whom she had only turned tricks once, made her nervous. Nelson had disappeared on the one and only day she and Miley had been out together, and Miley became suspicious.

If, in fact, Bundy's prediction was accurate about his Riverman's using friends' names to further a conversation, in this one instance it turned out to be the factor that caused Paige Miley to report to the task force, even though she admitted that both she and Kim Nelson had been out soliciting dates.

The Riverman Lived Alone

Bundy believed that because of the time that had elapsed between the disappearance of the victims and the recovery of their bodies, his Riverman didn't need to dispose of his victims immediately. Accordingly, Bundy believed, his Riverman lived alone.

Rose Hahn, a tenant who rented Gary Ridgway's house, gave a statement to Green River Murders Task Force detectives in which she described how her landlord shared the kitchen and bathroom facilities in the main house with them, but lived alone in the garage. "While they lived in the house," the affidavit states, referring to Rose Hahn and her husband, "Ridgway lived in the garage that had been converted into living quarters. . . . She said Ridgway rarely ate at home, if ever. Ridgway shared the kitchen and bathroom with her family so she had first-hand knowledge of his use of these facilities. Hahn said Ridgway was usually not at home in the evenings, and that if he was, he stayed in his room or outside."

Marcia Winslow's statement contained in the Green River Murders Task Force affidavit says, "Ridgway informed Marcia that the garage area was his private place and for her to stay away from it. . . . Ridgway would often be gone during the evenings for long periods of time, often returning to the house dirty or wet. He explained his condition by saying his vehicle broke down while he was out driving. Marcia said that during the latter years of their marriage, Ridgway began coming home later and later without any logical explanation."

Ridgway told police that when he lived alone, he brought victims back to his house, where he killed them.

Riverman's Working Hours

Bundy believed that his Riverman had a stable job with a regular Monday-to-Friday work schedule. In fact, the affidavit states that for thirty years Gary Ridgway held a job as a painter at Kenworth Trucking, and that he had a Monday-to-Friday schedule, working a shift that began at 3:40 P.M. and lasted until 12:10 A.M. On those days when Green River victims disappeared, Ridgway was off work.

The Riverman's Religious Conversion

Something changed in the Riverman's life, Bundy said. He noted the patterns of body recovery and hypothesized that his Riverman might have gone through significant life changes that altered the way he seemed to operate. He hypothesized that the Riverman might have gotten "filled with the Holy Spirit."

In her interview with detectives that appears in the King County affidavit, Marcia Winslow says that after she married Ridgway and their son, Matthew, was born, "they began attending a Southern Baptist Church. She said Ridgway became 'fanatical' about religion. They later started going to a Pentecostal church, and Ridgway made the transition to his new church. Marcia said they had participated in going door to door, and that Ridgway would get angry when people would close their doors on them. . . . Marcia remembered that Ridgway would sit at night watching TV with an open Bible in his lap. Marcia also said that Ridgway would frequently cry during or after the church service." Perhaps he tried to refocus his anger or use religion to exorcise it, but Bundy was correct about Ridgway's religious conversion.

One of Bundy's most accurate observations was that his Riverman did not kill thirty-six-year-old Amina Agisheff. The Task Force had considered her one of the Green River Killer's victims for years, but Bundy told me that he was very skeptical about that. Ted believed that her age—she was twenty years older than some of Ridgway's younger victims—should have clued the Task Force that she did not fit the Riverman's typical victim profile. He was after teenagers and younger women. And during Ridgway's interviews with detectives after he was arrested, he not only refused to admit to having killed Agisheff, he most vociferously denied it. He wouldn't cop to it, he said, "Because I have pride in . . . what I do. I don't wanna take it from anybody else."

Given the requirements of Ridgway's plea bargain deal in which his full, complete, and honest confessions were the only way he could save himself from the death penalty, one would think that he would seek to err on the side of caution and plead out to every crime the prosecutors could possibly throw at him. And indeed, Ridgway mentioned crimes that the police didn't even know about. So why would he deny a crime that detectives put onto the Green River list? Again, Bundy seemed to have pointed to a reason without realizing that he was describing something about serial killers in general.

When Bundy asked me to believe, really believe, that some murders were okay, and to treat his statement in a nonjudgmental way, he was also telling me to look beyond the immediacy of the crime into what the victim might have meant to the killer. Thus, he was predicting something that Ridgway was hinting at in his denial of the Agisheff murder. Ridgway needed to have sex with his victims, and, as he told police, he sometimes returned to their burial sites to have sex with their corpses. He was graphic in his descriptions of his sexual murders, explaining why he liked younger victims, why they were easier to control and manipulate, why he liked to hear them beg for their lives, and why he liked to wrap his legs around them while he was choking them to death. These teenage victims were his unwilling sexual partners. Thus, it is my guess, and probably Bundy's experience, that Agisheff was not just outside of

Ridgway's victim pool, she was repellant to him because of her age. Why?

Marcia Winslow Ridgway's description of Gary Ridgway's mother to Task Force detectives, as described in the Sue Peters affidavit, as "wearing a lot of makeup and tight clothes" so that she would "look like a prostitute," and her asserting herself around the house and breaking a plate over Ridgway's father's head is very telling and may provide an answer. So is Ridgway's revelation to police that he had violent sexual fantasies about his mother as well as sexual feelings and fantasized about "sewing up her vagina." Were Ridgway's sexual conflicts about his mother somehow a fuel for his sexual fury? If so, it would make sense that Agisheff, because of her age, not only repelled Ridgway, she frightened him as well and, if we take him at his word, would not have been one of his victims.

Ridgway's overreaction to being asked about Agisheff might be only the tip of the iceberg of Ridgway's feelings of violence towards prostitutes in general. Was his attraction to young girls and teenagers his way of deflecting his real feelings of hatred toward his mother, his real target victim? Teenaged prostitutes were easy prey for the older Ridgway, he admitted to police. But they well might have been surrogate victims. Only time and further interviews with Ridgway might reveal his deeper feelings about his victims. But for the present, Bundy was not only clearly right about Agisheff, he seems to have given an example of how, in his mind, some murders could be okay.

Bundy wasn't psychic when it came to the Green River killings. He was simply creating a profile of the person he believed could commit these crimes based on his knowledge of himself, his knowledge of the area, and his knowledge of what it took to operate in the Green River Killer's areas, abducting prostitutes as his victims. But profiles are also wrong in many key areas and sometimes lead police astray. For example, there were things that Bundy believed about the Riverman that were dead wrong. His biggest mistake was that he suggested that the Riverman was from Tacoma. Bundy based his opinion on where some of the bodies had been dumped, at least one of which was in Pierce County. Since Bundy was from Tacoma and knew the body dump sites, he figured, pro-

jecting himself into the position of the Riverman, that the Riverman, too, had to be from Tacoma. Actually, that wasn't the case.
According to the King County affidavit, the individual they had
under surveillance, Gary Ridgway, had a residence in Renton and
was also from Auburn.

We can't be sure about whether Bundy was correct or not in his
assertion that the Riverman simply could not stop killing. Bundy
said that there had to be more killings after March 1984, but the affidavit submitted to the court does not account for any new crimes
after that date. Perhaps there were more crimes. But until there is
further investigation into what crimes might have been committed
after March 1984, we really won't know whether Bundy was correct or not.

I still believe that much of Ted Bundy's Riverman hypothesis
was a projection of himself. Certainly there was more to learn
about Bundy, about the emotional processes that drove him from
crime to crime, about the secrets he shared with the bodies of his
victims during his private moments at their gravesites. These were
the secrets that Bundy wouldn't allow himself to share with Detective Matt Linvall, even though he acknowledged that it was a secret
he had shared with Julie Cunningham. It was one of the things,
Bundy said about serial killers, that many of them would not talk
about, even though they would talk about their crimes.

As the clock on Bundy's life ticked down, the pressure to get
him to talk about a wide variety of crimes only increased. There
were scheduling arrangements to be made as each of the final minutes of his life increased in value to those who needed information
about open cases. Just how many secrets did Bundy retain as he
walked those final steps to the execution chamber amid the growing clamor outside the prison gates for the news that America's
most infamous serial killer was dead?

Only the prison warden would find out, and that would be on the
final night of Bundy's life.

19

Bundy's Last Night

The crowds had been gathering outside the prison for days once the news got out that Bundy's execution had finally been set, that a tiny piece of history was about to take place. They were an assortment of people milling outside the prison gates, setting up their soapboxes for the cameras and lights, and taking ownership of Bundy's execution for their own purposes. There were the anti–death penalty protesters with candles and signs, ready to stand their vigil; the pro–death penalty advocates, equally adamant, demanding an eye for an eye; perhaps friends or relatives of some of the victims across four states, wanting to be nearby when the switch was thrown; those people seeking both vengeance and the opportunity for a tailgate party, setting up outdoor grills and breaking open coolers to celebrate Bundy's execution.

Then there were the lookie-loos, the rubberneckers, the people wanting to be a part of the moment when the nation's most infamous serial killer walked the last few steps down death row to the electric chair. And there were the news vans, their satellite dishes reaching to the sky, recording the people outside the prison, waiting for the hearse to carry Ted Bundy's corpse to wherever he would be interred. It was an eerie twilight party atmosphere, anticlimactic really, and almost apocalyptic. It was as if these same people would be milling around outside dressed in their shorts and Hawaiian shirts on the evening before the midnight when the world came to an end.

For each group outside the prison, Bundy meant something different. For the anti–death penalty people, he was their poster boy. Why should he be executed when he held the key to so many cases that could be resolved with just a few words from him? The pro-death group saw Bundy as a monster incarnate, a description with which he, in his own words, had already concurred. He was a human predator whose career stretched across the four states we know about and maybe even more that he wouldn't talk about. Considering what he did to his victims and the terror that someone like Julie Cunningham must have endured during the ride from Vail, even Florida's electric chair was too quick and easy a punishment for the man. Those seeking vengeance and retribution were there to celebrate that final day.

For the others who were there to be a part of history, Bundy had become history. He realized it, tried to manipulate the moments even up to the end, but whether he ever understood what was happening, I may never know. As evil as Bundy's crimes were, he represented something at the very end of the human spectrum. His case made so many headlines that Bundy became transformed toward the end of his life into something he never was in real life. There were Bundy souvenirs, Bundy fan clubs, Bundy memorabilia, and a whole Bundy mystique. In fact, one of the souvenirs being passed around were bumper stickers that said: "I'll buckle up when Ted does." Yet for all the mythos surrounding Ted Bundy, he always remained a cowardly individual who could not even muster the courage at the end of his life to accept total responsibility for what he had done even though he tried to make himself as significant as possible by holding out the hope that he knew how to resolve even more unsolved cases. It was a pathetic attempt, but it was all he could do. Thus, Bundy probably didn't understand what his case had become to the nation, that he himself had become kind of an icon embodying a special kind of malevolence, even as he settled in before the tape recorder's microphone to contemplate his execution the following morning.

Bundy knew that people were gathering even before he sat down with the warden on his final night. It was his last chance to open up, to clear up cases that still lingered for hopeful investigators in different states. Had Bundy murdered women in New Jersey, Pennsylvania, and California? There were unsolveds from all over the country and cold case homicide detectives looking for a break. Maybe Bundy had stopped in one of their cities overnight, passed through on his way from Colorado to Michigan to Florida. Maybe one of their cases was his.

Again, fidgeting with a map of locations in different states where some his victims might have been buried and talking with the warden of Florida State Penitentiary, Bundy, as if he were an insurance claims processor working through a form, methodically began to go down the list of inquiries from investigators in different states that were fed to him by the warden.

"January 24, 1989," Bundy began. "For the Utah detective named 'Couch,' there's one more we didn't have time for. It's going to be hard. Between Price and Green River, about ten miles south of Price, a road going south out of Price, maybe five or ten miles, there is a side road to the left going toward the mountains, going east. A quarter mile in there's a dirt road to the left. This is not going to work too well," Bundy said, referring to the map he was looking at, "but I'll try to do something with it. A hundred to two hundred yards in on the dirt road, stop and to the left off the dirt road, maybe fifty yards in, there's the remains of a young woman who disappeared from Brigham Young University, June of 1975. That's as close as I can get it from the map that we have here."

"Do you know her name?" the warden asked.

"No, I don't," Bundy answered. She was a nameless victim.

"Is that it?" the warden asked again.

"To Mike Fisher and the Colorado detectives, the last woman they wanted to talk about, Denise Oliverson, I believe. Referring again to Denise Oliverson, or whoever it was out of Grand Junction that Mike Fisher wanted to discuss, I believe the date was in April 1975. The young woman's body would have been placed in the Colorado River about five miles west of Grand Junction. It was not buried. That's all the ones that I can help you with. That's all the ones that I know about. There are no missing ones outstanding that we haven't talked about."

"That's all of 'em, Ted?" the warden wanted to know.

"Yeah," Bundy said, then asked if he could "get a smoke off somebody."

"Ted, I had some inquiries from Illinois and New Jersey," the warden continued.

"Okay," Bundy answered. "Well, let's just deal with whatever is outstanding like that. I can say without any question that there is nothing that I was involved in in Illinois or New Jersey."

"How about Burlington, Vermont?" the warden asked. "Nothing there? Texas?"

"No," Bundy answered, his voice getting softer.

"Miami?" the warden continued.

"No."

"Okay," the warden said. "That's all we've got. Okay, Ted, thank you."

"You're welcome," Bundy said, and that was the end of the final interview he gave to law enforcement about his crimes on the last night of his life.

I don't know what secrets Bundy took to the grave with him, crimes that he was either too embarrassed to talk about or too close to the victim to reveal. He had indicated to me that there were crimes that serial killers would never reveal to authorities because they held a special meaning to them.

Very early the next morning, Ted Bundy walked the steps to the chamber where he would be strapped into the electric chair. Outside, the protesting, chanting, and celebrating crowds watched for the lights to dim, the indication that the execution was actually under way. At the moment the switch was thrown, even amid the chants from some of the spectators, there was still a pervasive silence from most of the people outside the gate. Bundy had officially gone into history and the cheering and jeering that followed the path of the hearse taking his body out of the prison was almost pro forma.

In the end it was the system that had trapped a frantic Bundy in its web and wouldn't let him crawl out. Bundy had tried everything—defending himself, using the appeals process, and finally employing a desperate gambit to trade names of victims and confessions for time. But the State of Florida gave him no wiggle room at all. And when the Supreme Court would not give him another stay of execution, it was the end of him.

Ridgway, starting his confession strategy, perhaps with Bundy in mind, at the beginning of the process rather than after a death sentence, will have a different end. He will live out his life in prison, but the outside world will come to him in the form of interviews and questions. Dave Reichert was right when he said he knew from the look in Ridgway's eyes that "he had fooled me. He had fooled the detectives."

For over twenty, perhaps even thirty years, Ridgway had killed and escaped to kill again. He was the consummate serial offender, venting his anger on victims who, because they lived outside the law, were the perfect targets for a perfect serial killer. "It was technology that caught me," Ridgway said after having slipped through two lie detector tests and a number of police interviews for homicides he knew he'd committed. So at the end, when he knew that there were crimes the police would never solve but for him, he played the card that Bundy should have played at the beginning. And in so doing, Ridgway now moves from invisible phantom, through the court system, and into prison, proud of his crimes and even prouder of his last-minute strategy that spared his life.

20

Gary Ridgway in Court

The Investigation and the Plea Bargain

According to the prosecutor's summary of evidence submitted by the King County District Attorney to the court, on December 5, 2001, the King County Prosecuting Attorney charged Ridgway with four counts of aggravated murder in the first degree for the murders of Carol Christensen, Cynthia Hinds, Marcia Chapman, and Opal Mills. In three of the four counts, DNA evidence linked Ridgway to the victims. The body of Cynthia Hinds was discovered within a few feet of two other victims, leaving no doubt that the same killer was responsible. On April 2, 2002, the prosecutor notified the court that the state would seek the death penalty against Ridgway.

After finding microtrace evidence of paint on the bodies of additional victims whose bodies had been discovered at sites near the bodies the women whom Ridgway was already charged with murdering, the prosecutor filed additional charges of murder in the first degree against the accused for the murders of Wendy Coffield, Debra Bonner, and Debra Estes.

Despite large numbers of additional victims, the prosecutor revealed, it was clear that the evidence developed by the police would allow the state to prosecute Ridgway only for those seven victims. The dearth of any other evidence pointing to any suspect meant in all likelihood that, absent a confession, the cases would remain unsolved. Gary Ridgway faced seven counts of aggravated first degree murder, but he could not be charged with more than a fraction of the Green River killings.

Shortly after his arraignment on the amended information, Ridgway's attorneys contacted the King County prosecuting attorney and asked whether the prosecutor would forgo seeking the death penalty against Ridgway in exchange for pleas of guilty to the charged counts and a number of additional cases. They subsequently prepared a proffer declaring that Ridgway was willing to plead guilty to the seven charged counts and to 40 to 47 additional counts of murder in exchange for the prosecutor's agreement to forgo the death penalty. Ridgway offered to provide a completely candid account of his criminal activity in King County, and to direct investigators to the undiscovered remains of a number of his victims.

Thus, in April 2003, the prosecutor faced a decision: He could reject Ridgway's proffer and proceed to trial on the seven charged counts alone. This would allow a jury to decide whether Ridgway was guilty of the charged crimes and, if so, whether he should be sentenced to death. A jury verdict of death would create the possibility that, after Ridgway had exhausted decades of appeals, he might be executed before he died of natural causes in prison. A fraction of the Green River killings would be avenged. Or, the prosecutor could deprive the jury of an opportunity to sentence Ridgway to death. If he did so, the truth about the Green River killings would be known, and the community's most enduring nightmare would be over, no longer a tragic enigma in the history of King County. The families of the dozens of victims of the uncharged killings would find a measure of justice and resolution at last. Ridgway would be held accountable for all the murders he committed, not just a select few. He would not be executed, but his convictions could not be appealed and he would die in prison.

On June 13, 2003, the King County prosecuting attorney and Ridgway entered into an agreement where, in exchange for avoiding the possibility of execution, Ridgway agreed to provide complete, truthful, and candid information concerning his crimes in King County and answer all questions during interviews conducted by the police or the prosecuting attorney. Ridgway agreed to disclose the existence and precise location of all undiscovered physical remains of his victims. Ridgway agreed to plead guilty to aggravated murder in the first degree for all the murders he'd committed in King County.

The terms of the contract specifically required Ridgway to address not only the "official" list of 49 victims, but any and all other crimes he may have committed before 1982 or after 1984. In addition to the finality this would provide the victims' families and the community at large, the contract served another purpose. By identifying unsolved murders for which Ridgway was not responsible, police could investigate these cases with an eye toward developing other viable suspects.

The Ridgway Interviews

In June 2003, and continuing over the next five months, the task force interviewed Ridgway extensively. Detectives confronted him with all of the Green River murders and similar unsolved homicides. In all, Ridgway claimed that he killed more than 60 women in King County. As part of the process of testing his claim to be the Green River Killer, Ridgway led the police to the places he left bodies and described what he did there. His memory for these locations surpassed all the information provided to his attorneys and the knowledge of detectives who had worked on the case for decades. In addition, he identified several dump sites on cases that were never considered Green River cases; information about these cases had not been provided to the defense.

Ridgway led the task force to numerous sites where he claimed to have left undiscovered bodies. To date, four sets of human remains have been discovered at those sites, including three of the "missing" victims on the original Green River list: Pammy Avent, April Buttram, and Marie Malvar. Even as the killer himself appeared in court to hear his confessions read into the record and acknowledge them before the families of the victims, detectives investigating the case were still trying to identify the fourth set of recovered remains.

In their attempt to come to grips with the nature of the individual whose murders had shocked the community and had dominated the national news during the 1980s, detectives spent more than four months interviewing Ridgway about specific homicides as well as delving into his general habits and thoughts related to the killings. Detectives quickly learned, as I had learned over the years of interviewing Ted Bundy and other serial killers, that the information came in bits and pieces.

Initially, despite his obvious incentive to be truthful in the interviews, Ridgway greatly minimized his behavior and acknowledged that he was a pathological liar. In candid moments, Ridgway acknowledged that it was difficult for him to be truthful after being so successfully deceptive about the killings for decades. Ridgway also suggested another reason why he would lie or minimize his conduct. He believed that a popular true-crime author would write a book about him and thus wanted to portray himself in the best possible light. However as the interviews progressed, Ridgway himself confessed to being a "pathological liar" and said that he had kept on killing well beyond 1985, only stopping in 2001 shortly before his arrest. There are still some murders Ridgway would not admit to, telling his interviewers, "Why, if it isn't mine? Because I have pride in . . . in . . . what I do, I don't wanna take it from anybody else."

In many respects, Ridgway was typical of serial killers for whom their victims have no meaning as individuals other than that they were victims of opportunity—they were in the wrong place at the wrong time. As Ridgway himself told police interviewers, he killed simply to satisfy his needs, For Ridgway, his victims existed only to satisfy his needs. "Like I said before, they don't mean anything to me. . . . Once I've killed 'em, I didn't kept it in memory. I just knew where they . . . I dumped 'em." When shown photographs of the victims, Ridgway almost invariably said he did not recognize them. "The women's faces don't . . . don't mean anything to me. . . . There were . . . the bodies, if they had a . . . had a pussy, I would screw and that was it."

Ridgway—like Bundy, who seemed to have an uncanny understanding of the Riverman's motivations—made killing his specialty, devoting hours of his day before and after work trolling, ("patrolling," he called it) those areas where prostitutes were known to congregate to pick up their "dates." One of his favorite locations was the Pacific Highway South, where he would back his pickup truck into the parking lot of the 7–Eleven and, in his words, "watch the traffic." Sometimes, he said, he even raised the hood on his truck so as to allow him to pretend to work on it while he watched the highway. And killing prostitutes consumed most of his waking hours. He only slept a few hours a night because the rest of his time, outside of work, was devoted to hunting for victims, killing them, and disposing of their bodies.

Ridgway told police he killed prostitutes because, he said, "prostitutes were the, the easiest. I went from, uh, havin' sex with 'em to just plain killing 'em." Ridgway claimed that he also picked these young women because he believed the police would not look as hard for a missing prostitute. Also, he claimed that because prostitutes were frequently on the move, it was more difficult for police to determine where and when they had been killed. Ridgway's assessment was correct. Police were often delayed in their investigation because no missing-persons report was filed; and, even when a disappearance was reported, it was difficult for investigators to pin down where the victim had last been seen. Complicating matters were numerous alleged sightings of the "missing" victims long after they had been killed. But Ridgway didn't kill men because, he told police and was quoted in the prosecutor's summary evidence as having said, " 'Cause they didn't give no sexual gratification to me."

Among the women he killed, he seemed to enjoy killing younger victims, those in their teens, more than women in their twenties or older because younger victims tended to plead for their lives more and were less hardened than older street prostitutes. "The young ones," he said, "stood out more when they were dying."

Ridgway made it clear to investigators and prosecutors that these were carefully planned, premeditated killings, not sudden impulses. "When I get in the truck," he said, "when I'm driving and, ah, might pick up a woman, ah, wanna be in the mood to kill. I . . . I don't have the mood, ah, like I don't get her in the truck and drive down the road and all of a sudden, you know, ah, jump on her and start chokin' her. No." However, he said, "I always had it in my mind to kill them."

Those killings he couldn't facilitate, especially after he had spent considerable energy on an intended victim, frustrated and enraged him to the point where he took it out on his next victim. He said, "I'm really mad at some of 'em because I . . . I didn't get a chance to pick 'em up, they want too much, they, ah, they were, ah, the pimp was followin' me or somethin' and so I'm . . . I just lost one, the next one I'm gonna do everything I can to sweet talk her . . . I'm gonna talk her into getting her out so I can . . . kill the bitch, kill the . . . first one I didn't get a chance to kill today, I'm gonna kill this one and I'm gonna strangle her head . . . strangle her neck so it . . . it breaks . . ."

During the mid-1980s, publicity about the Green River murders was at its height with television specials and news coverage profiling the Sea-Tac strip and other areas where prostitutes had disappeared. Yet, during the height of this publicity, Ridgway told police, he kept right on killing. When an intended victim asked straight out if he was the Green River Killer, he simply denied it, telling them, "Uh, do I look like the Green River Killer? And says 'no, you don't.' They always thought it was a big tall guy, about 6' . . . b-big guy. So, 6'3", 185 pounds or some'n like that." He had more trouble sometimes, he said, convincing prostitutes that he wasn't an undercover police officer, which was one of the reasons he liked to carry beer in his truck.

Ridgway developed a number of ruses to get the women to trust him. He offered to become a regular customer, to lend them his vehicles, to get them jobs, to feed them. He didn't have to worry about keeping these promises, because, as he said, "They were already dead. And I would . . . talk to her about that and get her mind off of the, uh, anything she was nervous about. And think, you know, she thinks, oh, this guy cares, and which I, I didn't. I just wanted to, uh, get her in the vehicle and eventually kill her."

Ridgway killed many of his victims in his own house. In fact, he said, one of his ruses to gain the trust of his victims was to take them into his son's room. He even carried a photograph of his son with him as a way to get intended victims, who might have been nervous about the murder spree in King County, to relax. After all, he told police, they'd see a photograph of a young kid next to Ridgway's own identification and they would lower their guard. Once at his house, they'd look around his son's bedroom, see the toys, and figure, "Hey, this guy has a son. He's not gonna hurt anybody. His name's written on the door and it's empty and it's got his bunk bed there, toys on the floor."

From the testimony that some of the informants gave to the Green River Murders Task Force and from Ridgway's own confession, he often negotiated with his intended victims for what he called a "half and half,"—oral intercourse followed by genital intercourse. He told police he wanted them as naked as possible. And when he took women to his house, he would encourage them to use the bathroom before they had sex. This was not for their benefit: He knew from experience that victims of strangulation frequently become incontinent. He told police, "I don't, I was in the idea of getting them in there and killing them. I didn't want them to shit in the bed. So that was the main reason."

During the sex act, the prosecutor wrote in his submission of evidence, Ridgway would tell the woman that he could only have an orgasm while entering her from behind. When the woman was on her knees—"doggie style"—he would get behind her. At the appropriate time, Ridgway claimed, he would wait for his victim to raise her head, and attack.

As Ridgway told a psychiatrist: "And after I got behind them, penis/vagina, I would climax and usually the woman would raise her head because, you know, the guy's through, I can get dressed. Usually when she raised her head up, I would wrap my arm around her or put something around her neck and choke her."

Other times, Ridgway said, he employed a variation on that ruse. "I'd tell 'em, 'Here's a car coming,' so guess what, she lifts up her head like that. . . . She's not thinking anything of it. Her hands are down normal and it's my time to wrap my arm around her neck and to choke her and not have . . . get in the way of her mouth. I got bit in the hand with a mouth one time . . . But it's my idea to get her head up so I could get a clear shot of her neck to kill her."

Ridgway described one technique he said was particularly effective. When he began to strangle the women, he told them that if they stopped struggling, he would let them go. He said that a number of women ceased to struggle when he said this, and were easier to kill.

"But I wasn't gonna let her go," he said. "It was just my way of lying to her to keep her from fighting. She stopped fighting and I just kept on chokin'."

Ridgway arrived at this solution to the "fighting" problem by trial and error. If they sensed that he was going to kill them, he said, his victims often would plead with him to spare their lives. Among the entreaties they used, he said, were: "Don't kill me"; "I'm too young to die"; "I've got family I'm taking care of"; "I've got a daughter at home"; "I don't want to die." These pleas did not persuade him, but, Ridgway said, he soon settled on telling the women that if they stopped struggling, he would release them. But he didn't release them. In fact, he told police, he choked his victims " 'cause that was more personal and more rewarding than to shoot her." He also said that he didn't experiment with other ways of killing women because choking worked so well. "Choking is what I did, and I was pretty good at it."

The only known living victim of an attack by Gary Ridgway reported her experiences to the Green River Murders Task Force in 1986. In this report, Rebecca Garde Guay said that although Ridgway took her into the woods for a "date," and removed all his clothing, he had no apparent sexual interest in her at all, and showed no signs of sexual arousal. Rebecca told investigators she could not even understand why he had removed his clothes. Then he attacked her. At that point, she said, his personality "clicked," she said. "His face looked white, clammy, cold. His arms and everything was cold. His hands. He was a totally different person and uh, he kind of made me think that if he did kill me, since he wasn't interested in me sexually before that, he probably would have tried to have intercourse if I was dead."

In 2003, Ridgway admitted to police that he had attempted to murder Rebecca Garde Guay.

Ridgway's Necrophilic Behavior

Was Gary Ridgway a necrophile? Ted Bundy seemed to pick up on this possibility when he suggested to me that one of the ways to catch the killer would have been to stake out his body dump sites. Of course, Bundy, as he admitted to Colorado state investigators, did return to the places where he buried his victims to have "private moments" with them. He clearly recognized that the Green River Killer had the same tendencies. Ridgway admitted to police that he was a necrophile only gradually. At first he denied it, but then said that he ejaculated immediately after choking them to death. Days later during the interview process he admitted he had post-mortem intercourse with some of his victims. Soon thereafter, he admitted that a few of these women had been decomposed enough that maggots had begun to appear on the bodies.

Ridgway described his feelings about having sex with one of his dead victims: "That would be a : . . uh, that would be a good day, an evening or after I got off work and go have sex with her. And that'd last for one or two days till couldn't . . . till the flies came. And I'd bury 'em and cover 'em up. Um, then I'd look for another. . . . Sometimes I killed one, one day, and I killed one the next day. There wouldn't be no reason to go back."

Ridgway's desire for sexual intercourse with a corpse was apparently so strong that he would engage in risky behavior to accomplish it. He described an occasion where he drove back to visit the body of a woman he had killed, with his son in his truck. While his son slept in the truck, Ridgway got out, had intercourse with the body some thirty feet away, and returned to the truck. Ridgway assured the detectives that his son was a "hard sleeper."

Ridgway talked to a psychiatrist after he was in custody about his having sexual intercourse with his dead victims, saying, at first, that it was "free sex." When he sought out victims for sex, he said, he had to pay for it. But after he killed them, he took his money back. However, the energy, gas, and time he spent on finding and killing a victim was an overhead he didn't have if he simply returned to a burial site and had sex with a victim he'd already killed. But he said it was difficult for him to achieve an erection over a dead body, and he eventually gave up having sex with the corpses of his victims.

Post-Mortem Sexual Fantasies

Ridgway's confessions to police about some of his more aberrant behaviors, such as inserting rocks into the vaginas of two of his victims, seem only to skim the surface of his darker visions. Perhaps there is more information that he divulged to detectives that has not yet seen the light of day. Perhaps, and this is more likely, Ridgway divulged only what he thought he had to divulge in order to satisfy the requirements of his plea agreement. As time goes on and Ridgway settles in to spend the rest of his life in prison, he may be more forthcoming in interviews about his darkest fantasies and explain them in greater detail.

During his interviews, Ridgway told detectives that he had inserted the rocks in order to "plug" up his victims. His second wife told police that Ridgway had threatened to "sew up" her vagina to prevent her from having an affair. Nevertheless, the description of Gary Ridgway's mother provided to police by one of his former wives, that the older woman walked around the house dressed like a prostitute and ordered Ridgway's father around as if he were a servant, and Ridgway's own descriptions of his conflicts with his mother, might, more than anything else, shed light on whatever visions he might have had about women with plugged or sewn vaginas that would keep them from being penetrated by other men. It might also shed light on the nature of his choice of prostitutes as victims. Perhaps they were more than convenient victims of opportunity and held out a special threat to him because of their availability.

Body Disposal

For any killer, but for serial killers especially, the disposal of the body is one of the most important components of the crime. As I learned from Bundy, not only is there the absolute necessity of getting rid of the most significant piece of evidence as quickly and efficiently as possible, but the culmination of the murder is also the immediate and initial disconnect between the killer and his victim. This is the moment when he feels most vulnerable to discovery because the evidence of his crime is right there in front of him. Therefore, he must get rid of the body. Gary Ridgway's admissions about his procedure for disposal of his victims was almost typical of what other serial killers have told police. Ridgway told detectives that after the kill, "I have a burden of having to find a place to put it." He usually dumped the body within a half hour of having killed his victim.

Ridgway explained a simple but effective method of dumping the bodies. He would drive, usually at night, to a secluded spot, park his truck, and quickly pull the body out of the vehicle and dump it just off the roadway. Then he would drive up the road and park just far enough from the body so that if the vehicle was approached by a police officer, the body would not be discovered. Then, making sure no motorists could see him, he would walk back through the woods to the body, and drag it farther from the road.

Ridgway was concerned that a victim might regain consciousness while he transported the body in the back of his pickup truck. To prevent his victim from escaping, he confessed to police, he tied ligatures around the necks of some of these victims before putting them in the truck, and he would watch his mirror for any signs of movement.

Ridgway's Possessiveness Over His Victims and Their Burial Sites

For long-term control-type serial killers, the body dump sites preserve the privacy of their kills from police discovery and serves to prolong the relationship of the killer over his victim, helping to define the nature of relationship the killer has entered into with his victim. After he killed her, he had to get rid of her. Her presence was the blood on his hands. Once she was dead and in a private location, she was his possession. Therefore, the prosecutor wrote in his summary of evidence, of all his secrets, the most precious to Ridgway were the as-yet undiscovered bodies of his victims.

When talking to a forensic psychologist, Ridgway explained what a victim's body meant to him. "She meant, she meant that uh, um, a beautiful person that was my property, my . . . uh, possession. Some'n only I knew and, I missed when they were found or where I lost 'em." And when the police discovered one of his dump sites, it was as if they'd invaded a sacrosanct location and breached the privacy he had established with his victims, he confessed.

Ridgway's sense of ownership and his need to retain possession of these bodies drove him to pin his third "river" victim beneath the surface of the Green River. It was an ordeal to hold the body at the bottom of the river and cover it with large rocks, but Ridgway did so because, he told his interviewers, "You had already found two of 'em by then. And she . . . I wasn't going to let this other one get away."

It was privacy, too, Ridgway told detectives, that explained why he had elected to take the drastic step of transporting victims' remains to Oregon. It was to "throw off" the task force. It had to do with his fear of discovery as well as his desire to maintain his privacy with his victims. " 'Cause the . . . bodies were already being found and I didn't want any more to be found," he said.

Prosecutors and detectives had speculated for years about the significance of the positions in which the Green River Killer had left the bodies of some of his victims. They appeared deliberately posed, on their backs, with their legs spread in unnatural positions. This mystery was resolved when Ridgway confessed that he had post-mortem intercourse with a number of his victims in the privacy of his secret dump sites, and often had to forcibly spread their legs apart to accomplish this. Then he simply left the victims in that position when he was done with them.

Ridgway confirmed what investigators and prosecutors had long suspected, that he often placed the bodies near physical objects visible from a distance—large trees, guardrails, hills, large fallen logs—which served as landmarks. It was useful for Ridgway to put the victims in dump sites for another reason. It made it easier for him to determine whether or not the bodies had been discovered, and, thereafter, to avoid those sites. He said he buried his victims in "[c]lusters so I won't forget where they . . . where they are. . . . So, I've done it before and, ah, just easy. When . . . if I drive by and think somebody's been . . . you know, found 'em then that way I would stay away from them."

The Face in the Crowd

Serial killers survive by being careful and private. Bundy was a master at leading a double life, hiding his criminal obsessions from even his fiancée and his closest friends, hiding it even while he worked at a rape crisis center. That care and deliberation extended, of necessity, to the commission of the actual crimes themselves and the disposal of his victims. Ridgway explained to police how careful he was not to be associated with any of the missing women. If another prostitute was present when he picked up his potential victim, he did not go through with the murder. Ridgway explained that he rarely picked up a woman at the curb where she was working. Rather, he would make eye contact with them and sometimes flash money at them as he drove by. Then he would pull off the road into the parking lot of an adjacent building, where there would be fewer witnesses, and wait for the woman to approach him.

If there was a witness to the pickup and conditions were not right for a kill, Ridgway might "date" the woman anyway. This practice had the added benefit of establishing that he was a good date with the prostitutes. He reasoned that, should he ever be caught, these women would serve as "references" to say that he had not hurt them. Ridgway also offered that another benefit to not killing every prostitute he dated was they served as a sort of "alibi" for him.

Ridgway took several steps to avoid picking up undercover police officers. He would usually watch women from a distance to see whether or not they were picked up by other "tricks." He often waited to agree to pay for a sex act until a woman got into his own vehicle. Ridgway would also request prostitutes to show him their breasts or vagina before he would agree to pay for sex, believing that undercover officers would refuse to do so.

Ridgway's chameleon-like behavior also extended to the crime scenes and his ability to recognize what forensic evidence was and how to leave as little of it as possible for crime scene investigators to find. He took precautions to leave no evidence at a scene. If one of his victims scratched him, he would cut her fingernails before disposing of the body so police would not find microtraces of his skin. In this way, he was able to elude detection precisely because he had left so little evidence behind. He told police, "Well, I was in a way a little bit proud of not being caught doing . . . like removing the clothes. Not leaving anything . . . any fingerprints on it, using gloves. . . . Not bragging about it. Not talking about it."

The same care he practiced at crime scenes extended to his avoidance at being identified as having picked up a victim or at having arranged an assignation with her. He explained that if he killed a woman after arranging a date with her pimp over the phone, he had a special technique. Using the same false name he employed to set up the date, he would telephone the pimp to arrange another date with her. In this way, he figured, if the police ever figured out that Ridgway had dated the victim, Ridgway's subsequent calls for the woman after her death would suggest he thought she was still alive and, therefore, could not be the killer.

In the case of Marie Malvar, the case that actually brought Ridgway to the attention of the local police and ultimately to the task force, his fear at being detected was so great that after Marie Malvar left deep scratches in Ridgway's forearms as he struggled with her, he later disguised the long scratches by burning his flesh with battery acid. The scars are visible today, reminders of how he fought with her in the cab of his pickup truck as her boyfriend and pimp looked on. This was one of the cases that brought him to the attention of the police in Desplaines and later to the task force.

From my perspective, the Green River case still shows how the myth or aura of serial killers, along with many misconceptions, still pervades popular thinking. Ridgway, like Bundy, who clearly empathized with him, was able to survive by doing many of the same things other long-term serial killers do. He was able to maintain his career not by dropping out of society but by keeping his physical presence in society and his killer psyche carefully compartmentalized so that no one would discover it. The most successful long-term serial killers, like John Gacy and Ted Bundy, aren't loners, as most people believe. They maintain jobs, maintain relationships, are a part of the communities in which they live. Serial killers have children and go to church. Some have violent pasts, as did Ridgway, but that's not the sine qua non of being a serial killer. Many self-described profilers still look for the wrong things about a serial killer and thus miss the obvious.

The case of Gary Ridgway is no different. The Green River Killer was not, of necessity, a loner, even though Ridgway himself was a loner only in his psyche. The part of him that he projected into society kept a job in Kentworth, married, had a child, and even became a Pentecostal Christian, just as Bundy predicted he would do. Police who had been investigating him since 1987 were not astonished to learn that even after his arrest in 2001, longtime coworkers, former girlfriends, and family members expressed sympathy for him and doubted that he could be a killer. This is a replay of what happened to Bundy after his arrest in Utah. Ridgway's wife claimed their relationship was excellent. Even learning that Ridgway had admitted killing dozens of women, his brother insisted that Ridgway had never displayed any abnormal behavior in his presence. Those who thought they knew Ridgway best did not know him at all. This is exactly what Ann Rule and others have written about Ted Bundy.

Ridgway killed for twenty years before he was charged with any of the Green River murders. He adopted the same unremarkable, non-threatening affect he used to lull his victims into complacency to avoid bringing himself to the attention of law enforcement. Remember, Ridgway was known to the task force and had been investigated by them, off and on, since 1987, all the time avoiding an arrest even though police knew he had been arrested for "offering and accepting" and had been tipped off by one of his victims. How was he able to maintain his innocence even in the face of police scrutiny?

The Mask of Normalcy

The prosecutor said that when interviewed by the task force, his apparent forthrightness and willingness to cooperate was disarming. Ridgway would admit everything he believed the task force already knew about him, and just a little bit more. For example, when he knew he had been observed by a witness, he usually admitted that he had dated some of the victims. By admitting that he was "addicted" to prostitutes, Ridgway explained away a huge body of otherwise suspicious evidence. By agreeing to be interviewed without an attorney, and to take a polygraph examination, Ridgway avoided suspicion all the more.

And during the polygraph examination, Ridgway said, he simply relaxed and felt no stress at the questioning. The results were inconclusive, a technical pass, which did not give investigators at that time the evidence to draw the net tighter around him.

He also appeared to defy the typical behavior of serial killers by apparently seeming immune to an ego-driven desire to keep trophies of his kills. Searches of his residence yielded no evidence of any criminal activity of any kind. But, from my own experience, Ridgway's behavior was more typical than not, because for Ridgway, his dump sites *were* his trophies. Just like Bundy, his sense of territoriality over the unknown presence of the bodies amounted to the killer's trophy. Sure he was ego-driven like other serial killers; only the police didn't know what he was ego-driven about.

Ridgway also took the jewelry from his victims after he killed them and placed pieces of that jewelry in the women's bathroom at Kentworth. This allowed the jewelry to be dispersed into a population, but it was a population where Ridgway himself could observe it. Thus the jewelry was a souvenir and not an actual trophy: Ridgway got to see at from time to time, without the fear of someone's associating him with evidence of his crime. It was almost the perfect way of taking a souvenir, keeping it in sight, and preserving its anonymity.

Throwing Investigators Off the Track

In fact, as Ridgway confessed to police, much of his behavior as he became more practiced amounted to an active methodology of throwing police off the trail. This is also typical of many long-term serial killers who know the habits of the police and know the evidence they're looking for. Their knowledge trips up police investigations. For example, Ridgway placed fake evidence at the dump sites to deliberately mislead police: cigarette butts and chewing gum, since he neither smoked nor chewed gum. At one scene, he scattered airport motel pamphlets and car rental papers to imply that the killer was a "traveling salesman." He tossed a hair pick at one scene, hoping that, if the body were discovered, investigators would suspect a "pimp." And in one particular case, he left one victim's driver's license at Sea-Tac airport, to suggest that she had left town.

In February 1984, Ridgway wrote a letter to a local newspaper that was designed to throw police off the track. The poorly typed letter was entitled "What you need to know about the Green River man" and contained many references to the killings, and a number of falsehoods about the killer's identity. The letter suggested that the killer was a traveling salesman or a long-distance trucker, and that the killings were motivated by profit or revenge. The letter mentioned that the victims' fingernails had been cut, a fact not known to investigators until Ridgway told them this in 2003. The task force sent the letter to the FBI for analysis, and an "expert" there proclaimed that the letter was not written by the killer. In 2003, Ridgway provided details about the crimes that he had included in the letter, providing additional confirmation that he was indeed the Green River Killer. Thus, the letter became evidence against him, but only after he had already confessed to the crimes.

Ridgway also returned to one of his dump sites, retrieved the remains of Denise Bush and Shirley Sherrill, and transported them to Tigard, outside Portland, where they were found in 1985. This was high-risk behavior, but he did this in order to convince police that the Green River Killer had moved south. The ruse worked. The prosecutor wrote in his summary of evidence that Green River investigators went to Tigard to investigate the discovery of the bodies. Ridgway further covered his tracks by paying for the trip in cash so that he would leave no paper trail.

Ridgway's History of Childhood Violence

It is now almost a matter of lore that most serial killers manifest problems early. They display a fascination with fire and engage in arson, they display abnormal cruelty to animals, and they may be dangerously violent toward other children. Ridgway displayed all this behavior. As a child, according to the prosecutor's summary, Ridgway was a "slow learner" and a poor reader. According to him, as an adolescent he also dabbled in arson, paid a child to let him fondle her genitals, committed a number of minor property offenses, and killed a cat by suffocating it.

Ridgway also admitted that he was sexually attracted to his mother. Ridgway's feelings toward his mother during this time in his life seem an admixture of lust and humiliation. Ridgway, who was a bed wetter until his early teens, seemed to have vivid memories of having his genitals washed by his mother. This imagery may have contributed to his sexual development, in that he fantasized about showering with prostitutes. But his attraction to his mother was accompanied by homicidal thoughts about her, such as entertaining thoughts of mutilating her, killing her, or burning down the house with her inside. As Ridgway described it to police: "I thought about stabbing her in the chest or in the heart maybe, uh . . . um . . . maybe, uh . . . cut her face and chest." Later, Ridgway tried to minimize the fantasy of cutting his mother. He said, "Just, you know, just a little whim of just, you know, cutting her just to, you know, take a knife and slicing her, not the whole defile."

Ridgway admitted to police that he had begun stalking his peers in elementary school, an early indicator of what he later would tell police was behavior he called "patrolling" and what investigators today describe as "trolling for victims." Ridgway described an incident in which he would surreptitiously follow girls home while in junior high school in a state of sexual arousal. "I'd have a . . . a hard-on and . . . think of the woman as a goal and be on the opposite side of the street. And find out where she lived." This history of acting out a childhood sexual-control fascination was another early manifestation of behavior that would become later violence.

Ridgway also described an incident which took place, he said, in the late 1960s, where he "tried forcing sex" on a young woman. In this early example of his failure to control his sexual impulses, he said he picked the girl up at the Seattle Center and offered to drive her home. He pulled off to the side of the road, asked her to have sex with him, and fondled her breasts. According to Ridgway, he allowed the girl to leave his car. But for Ridgway's backing off and letting his victim go, this was a prefiguration of the behavior that would become the methodology of his murders as the Green River Killer.

In one startling section of the prosecutor's summary, there is a confession and confirmation from the victim of Ridgway's first attempted murder when he was a teenager. For me, this story is an example of Ridgway's history of homicidally violent predilections, even when he was a kid; he had exhibited the exact same type of overly narcissistic, self-serving behavior most killers exhibit when they experiment with violence.

According to Ridgway's confession, when he was 15 or 16 years old, he approached a first-grade boy near some bushes on a street corner, and stabbed the boy in the side with a knife. According to Ridgway, he never learned what happened to the boy, who ran off clutching his side. Ridgway said to his interviewers, "Ah, he was playin' with a stick like, cowboys and Indians or somethin' like that. And, ah, he, ah, bent . . . bent down to pick up somethin' or somethin' and I just took the knife outta my pocket and stabbed him in the ah, side. He grabbed his side and ran away, and I ran up the hill."

Ridgway told police he simply "wanted to see how to stab somebody." Ridgway said the boy "cried and ran," but in his adult description of the event from his teens, he seemed remarkably unperturbed about the consequences to the boy or his own responsibility for the stabbing. Instead, he took a fatalistic view, and suggested that the incident was a coincidence: "Place at the right time I guess what you'd call it."

A task force detective managed to locate the person Ridgway stabbed some forty years later. Now living in California, the man confirmed Ridgway's account of the incident without any prompting from the detective. He said that he was six years old at the time, and in the first grade. He was playing near a wooded area close to his house and an adjacent school. He was wearing a cowboy hat, cowboy boots, two "six-guns," and a toy rifle—and he was playing with a stick. The victim said he was approached by a boy who, he estimated, was eight or ten years older than he was. This boy asked him if he wanted to build a fort, and the victim agreed. According to the victim, the boy who approached him said, "You know, there's uh, there's people around here that, that like to kill little boys like you." He led the little boy to the wooded area behind the school and stabbed him through the ribs and into his liver.

The victim reported, "And I asked him why he, why he killed me . . . I watched too many cowboy movies, you know! . . . And the, you know, and I saw all the blood pumpin' outta me. . . . It was, it was profusely. I mean, it was already runnin' down my leg into my boots. . . . And uh, with every heartbeat it was just pumpin' out. . . . It was the whole front a' my shirt was soaked. . . . And he, uh, started laughin', and he had a smile on his face and he stood there for a minute and he had his knife in his hand, and I didn't want him to stab me again, but he reached toward me and he just wiped the knife off—both sides of the blade, so he wiped it once across my shoulder and twice across my shoulder on the other side a' the blade. . . . Folded [the knife] back up, and he says, 'I always wanted to know what it felt like to kill somebody.' "

According to the victim, Ridgway seemed rather pleased with the experience. "Then he started walkin' down that knoll and he was laughin', you know, kinda puttin' his head in the air, you know, and laughin' real loud."

Ridgway's Persistent Return to Violence

Despite what the public believed about the Green River case, the killings did not stop in 1985 or 1986. In fact, they continued off and on for the next fifteen years. Ridgway confessed that although he slowed down, he never stopped killing until his arrest in 2001. Although he claimed he was "semi-retired" and an "amateur" compared to his earlier killing spree, he said that "[i]t was, like I said, like I was back starting all over again and I wasn't a well-greased machine. I was . . . I was rusty."

The Gary Ridgway Confession

Gary Ridgway finally stood up in court to admit to the crimes he'd committed. He had provided investigators with information about all 48 crimes in the state's charges against him and added details about his life and the nature of his crimes. That information corroborated what killers like Bundy had already said, but some of it was still startling.

In Ridgway's own words:

In most cases when I murdered these women, I did not know their names. Most of the time, I killed them the first time I met them and I do not have a good memory for their faces. I killed so many women I have a hard time keeping them straight.

I killed them all in King County. I killed most of them in my house near Military Road, and I killed a lot of them in my truck not far from where I picked them up. I killed some of them outside. I remember leaving each woman's body in the place where she was found. The plan was: I wanted to kill as many women I thought were prostitutes as I possibly could.

I picked prostitutes as my victims because I hate most prostitutes and did not want to pay them for sex. I also picked prostitutes as victims because they were easy to pick up without being noticed. I knew they would not be reported missing right away and might never be reported missing. I picked prostitutes because I thought I could kill as many of them as I wanted without getting caught.

Another part of my plan was where I put the bodies of these women. Most of the time I took the women's jewelry and their clothes to get rid of any evidence and make them harder to identify. I placed most of the bodies in groups which I call "clusters." I did this because I wanted to keep track of all the women I killed. I liked to drive by the "clusters" around the county and think about the women I placed there. I usually used a landmark to remember a "cluster" and the women I placed there. Sometimes I killed and dumped a woman, intending to start a new "cluster" and never returned because I thought I might get caught putting more women there.

Gary Ridgway, Serial Killer

Ridgway's confessions don't even come close to answering the basic questions of what drove him, what it was that motivated his compulsion to kill. And investigators probably won't get at that truth—if they ever do—for a while, because what Ridgway disclosed was only the tip of the iceberg. It was enough to satisfy the plea bargain and allow the police to close the cases. But there may be many more. As Ridgway himself admits, the 48 victims described above represent only a portion of the women he killed.

Why did he kill so many young women? Even the prosecutor in his summary of evidence concedes that the investigators cannot answer that question.

However, the prosecutor wrote, some of Ridgway's admissions reveal a deeply rooted psychopathy. It is readily apparent that Ridgway does not suffer from any mental disease or defect that would absolve him from responsibility for his crimes. While lawyers and psychiatrists can debate the nature of mental disease, this is primarily a legal question, depending upon the definition of insanity that appears in a state's criminal statute. In the Revised Criminal Code of the State of Washington, per RCW 9A.12.010, insanity, so as to be a defense to murder, is an an affirmative defense that requires that "at the time of the commission of the offense, as a result of mental disease or defect, the mind of the actor was affected to such an extent that he was unable to perceive the nature and quality of the act with which he is charged or he was unable to tell right from wrong with reference to the particular act charged." And because insanity is an affirmative defense, the burden is on the accused to establish that defense by a preponderance of the evidence. As Ridgway's own words in his confessions reveal, he knew that what he was doing was wrong, and he certainly understood and perceived the nature of the acts he was performing. Thus, he was not legally insane in the State of Washington.

The prosecutor's report also said that nothing in Ridgway's history, apart from the crimes recounted in his confessions, suggested serious mental illness. As a child, Ridgway said, he was never sexually molested or physically abused, and he denied contemplating suicide. When a forensic psychiatrist asked Ridgway if he thought he had a mental illness, Ridgway replied that he used to have a problem with "killing women."

Asked why he thought that this was an illness, Ridgway responded "I don't, I don't know if it was an illness, or just uh, I just wanted to kill." Asked if there was any additional evidence of mental illness, Ridgway cited his propensity to have sex with the women after they were dead. Asked if there was any evidence of mental illness apart from homicide and necrophilia, Ridgway replied: "No, I don't think so."

Ridgway told interviewers, including a psychologist, that he never gave a thought to how the victims felt while he was killing them. Asked by a forensic psychologist if he thought there was something missing in him that was present in other people, Ridgway replied: "Caring." This is a generally typical response by a sociopathic killer at the extreme end of the continuum of narcissistic behavior. His victims exist for him. Their dump sites are his private territory. His ownership extends over all of it and all of it exists to satisfy him. Also, whatever crimes he committed, as interviewers gleaned from talking to Ted Bundy, were crimes that glorified the killer. In Ridgway's case, his admissions frequently seemed motivated by a pride in his criminal accomplishments.

Ridgway told a forensic psychiatrist that he did not want to die, but that he thought he should be executed "for killing that many women." He expressed pride in being able to hide bodies that the task force never found and he was pleased that the detectives had to use ropes and ladders to recover the bodies he placed at Mountain View Cemetery. He felt that no investigator had caught him. Rather, he believed that he was a person police had talked about as far back as 1983, but that he was now the victim of new technology. He said, "What got me caught was technology got me caught." Inasmuch as the police had to wait until the PCR DNA analysis procedure was invented so as to utilize what DNA they had from the victims to see if they could get a match, Ridgway may not be far off in his assessment.

The prosecutor wrote that Ridgway once described his homicidal behavior as his "career." He said that he was "good in one thing, and that's killing prostitutes." His urge to kill, however, extended beyond just prostitutes. Ridgway acknowledged that he had to struggle with the temptation to kill his current wife and other family members. Ridgway reported that he rejected these thoughts because he recognized that he was likely to be caught if he did so, an awareness of the nature of homicide, which, under any legal statute, would probably exclude an insanity defense.

Ridgway adamantly insisted that he was not a rapist, claiming a near aversion to a sexual compulsion. He said, in a perversely logical disclaimer,

> I go with the, uh, a person that volunteers to have sex to, and then kill 'em. Where if I went and raped somebody and killed 'em, uh, that is uh, not what I would do . . . would be low on my uh, category of, of people. I am not a rapist, no. No, I'm not a rapist. I'm . . . I'm not a rapist I'm a . . . I'm a murderer I'm not a rapist.

Strictly following his logic, he was correct in his self-description. Ridgway was a serial murderer who used the easiest method of getting a victim under his control: he bought them. This is one of the reasons why Bundy looked down upon the Riverman, even though the presence of another serial killer in Bundy's territory was driving him into a frenzy. Bundy used what he would call his "charm" and "broken-wing act" to lull his victim into a false sense of security before he clubbed them with a tire iron. But he predicted that the Riverman—and Ridgway proved him to be correct—would make himself seem as nonthreatening as possible so as to convince his intended victim that he only wanted to buy sex for a few hours. Both of them used a ruse and both of them were murderers first, looking down with revulsion upon any hint that they were rapists, even though both were necrophiles and sexual offenders.

Periodically during the interviews, Ridgway would use the word "remorse." It appeared to investigators and prosecutors that Ridgway really meant something more like "regret." On one occasion, when Ridgway appeared to cry for his victims, a forensic psychologist challenged him.

DOCTOR: I mean if you killed these women before 1990 why are you crying about it now rather than . . .

GR: Well, because of how I screwed up. How I screwed up on killing them. Maybe leaving too much . . . mostly on . . .

DOCTOR: Did you say leaving too much?

GR: Too much . . .

DOCTOR: . . . evidence.

GR: Evidence at the time.

Another time, Ridgway said that he felt "a little bit of remorse" after killing a woman while his son was nearby in his truck.

GR: Killing her with Matthew by was not the right thing to do.

DOCTOR: Why was that wrong?

GR: Because Matthew mighta saw somethin'.

DOCTOR: Why would that be a problem?

GR: Well he'd have that . . . have that memory for his life.

DOCTOR: Maybe he would be a witness against you.

GR: And maybe he would be a witness against me too.

DOCTOR: If you had . . . if he had observed you kill one of the women, would you have killed him?

GR: No, probably not, I don't know.

DOCTOR: Possibly, though?

GR: It's possible.

DOCTOR: Did you think about that at the time?

GR: Yeah.

Occasional expressions of what appeared to be empathy for a victim usually transformed into something else when Ridgway was encouraged to elaborate. Ridgway told a forensic psychologist that he once departed from his usual method of killing his victims from behind, and faced a 16-year-old girl while he strangled her. He said that looking at her face while killing her was "painful to see."

GR: The . . . the way she was lookin' at me and . . . and beggin' for her life.

DOCTOR: Yeah.

GR: And that taught me a lesson not ever to choke 'em . . .

DOCTOR: I bet it did.

GR: . . . with my hands 'cause the 16-year-old or 17-year . . . it would be . . . I didn't want them to . . . I didn't want that part to be memorized in my mind, I wanted the . . . the back of the head 'cause I couldn't see their face.

DOCTOR: So she's looking at you look at her.

GR: She's looking at me and . . . and . . . tryin' to get me to stop, "Please, please don't." But I still kept on chokin' her, I couldn't let go. She was . . . she'd turn me in and I wouldn't be able to kill anymore. And that meant a lot to me . . . to kill.

What does this admission say about the type of killer Ridgway was? Was he driven by a sexual compulsion? Probably not. It's more the force of anger, an anger that's exciting him to the kill because he claims here that he cannot look into the eyes of his victim. Her accusatory stare threatens to dissipate his anger. Her immediate awareness that she is staring into the eyes of her killer freezes him and, if only for a moment, interferes with Ridway's desire to kill.

He wants to kill, not to have sex. Sex is a means to entice his victims into his control. Sex is what he exacts from his victims as a form of punishment for being prostitutes. And after he has sex, he wants to plug up his victim's vagina, just like he wanted to sew up his mother's vagina, so his victim can never be penetrated again, not even by her killer.

Ridgway also suggested that some of the responsibility for the murders should be attributed to his second wife, from whom he separated shortly before the first of the Green River victims was murdered. Frequently during the interviews, Ridgway attempted to blame his second wife for his current situation. According to Ridgway, if he had only killed his second wife when he had the chance, things might have turned out better for the community too. He said, "If I would have killed her then it's possible that it might have changed my life. I'd only have one instead of 50 plus."

Ridgway said he considered killing her. A divorce would be costly and, because he had already been divorced once, he "didn't want another one that's . . . label myself as, you know, a loser." Another problem Ridgway said, was that he would be an obvious suspect in her death because his wife's father knew that Ridgway had assaulted her in the past.

I couldn't even you know set the house [on] fire with her. I couldn't arrange any kind of accident or something like that. Because it had been obvious. Her sister or mother, dad knows I choked her.

Ridgway expressed similar sentiments about the woman he was dating after his second divorce, referring to her as his "girlfriend" during 1982 to 1984, when he killed dozens of women. Ridgway speculated that there might have been "a hell of a lot less people dying if I had a, a nice woman to go home, go home to." This is a stunning admission in light of Ted Bundy's prediction that a significant hiatus in the killing series might have resulted from the killer's getting into some extended relationship. But it wasn't the sexual component of a relationship that Bundy meant, it was the assuaging of the killer's anger that kept him from going out onto Pacific Highway South to find his victims. A "nice" woman, in Ridgway's terms, meant a woman under his control who, in turn, controlled his anger. A nice woman was someone other than his mother, someone whose sexual presence was not such a threat to Ridgway that he would have to kill and close her up just to remove that threat from his psyche. Bundy, talking more about himself than the Green River Killer, probably revealed more about his own motivations in making his predictions about a killer he had never met but who, in his own mind, was a projection of himself.

Psychologist Richard Walter has said that serial killers are pathologically selfish. They represent the absolute extension of self, of narcissism. Everything is an extension of them and a reflection of them. Accordingly, it makes perfect sense that Ridgway had little regard for his wife and his girlfriend, and no empathy at all for the women he killed. Moreover, he seemed to find this perfectly normal. In the midst of an interview about stealing money from the victims after killing them, Ridgway said

I thought I was doing you guys a favor, killing, killing prostitutes, here you guys can't control them, but I can. You can't hurt anybody. You can't, you can arrest them and put cuffs on them, might be a little bit rough on them a little bit. But you can't, uh, you can't stop the problem. I was doing, uh, like I said, doing you a favor that you couldn't, you guys couldn't do. You couldn't, uh, I mean if it's illegal aliens, you can take 'em to the border and fly 'em back outta there. But if it's a prostitute, you'd arrest 'em, they were back on the street as soon as they get bail and change their, uh, name, and you guys, you guys had the problem. I had, I had the answer.

The prosecutor's report suggested that Ridgway did not judge himself too harshly.

DETECTIVE: You're obviously a serial killer, obviously you've killed many, many people.
GR: Un-huh [yes].
DETECTIVE: And now we have the scale say one to five, and five being the worst possible evil person that could have done this kind of thing.
GR: Un-huh [yes].
DETECTIVE: Where do you wanna fall on the scale?
GR: I'd say a three.
DETECTIVE: Three?
GR: Un-huh [yes]. For one thing is, ah, I killed 'em, I didn't torture 'em. They went fast.

Even when Ridgway claimed to feel remorse, his expressions of this sentiment were patently false. He said, "I'm sorry for doing it but, um, it just, I wasn't killin' a person, I was killin' a . . . a . . . ah, I don't know how I . . . how I'm gonna say it but, ah, they were just in the wrong place at the wrong time."

This is a man devoid of human sentiment. He preyed upon a community's most vulnerable members, and still attributes their deaths to fate. As confounding as this seems, from the perspective of a Ted Bundy, as he explained it to me, it makes perfect sense because, in Bundy's own words, "Some murders are okay."

Why did Ridgway kill? He suffered from no mental illness that would absolve him of responsibility for these crimes. He murdered his victims deliberately, methodically, and systematically. He was uninhibited by any moral concerns. In five months of interviews with investigators and forensic psychologists, he displayed no empathy for his victims and expressed no genuine remorse. He killed because he wanted to. He killed because he could.

He killed to satisfy evil and unfathomable desires.

21

Gary Ridgway and His Victims

There are, of necessity, no conclusions drawn in the plain, deliberately colorless language of the prosecutor's summary admitted into evidence in the case against Ridgway, pursuant to his plea bargain. This is not argument, it is evidence, a summary of the admissions Ridgway made after his arrest in order to avoid the death penalty. We can learn a lot from the admissions Ridgway made, especially when they are lined up in the prosecutor's summary against what the police knew and discovered and the chronology of each victim's story as she crossed paths with her killer, was murdered, was deposited at one of his dump sites, and then, perhaps, transported elsewhere by her obsessed killer, who wanted to maintain his control over the victim.

What we do learn, in addition, is how the killer grew in confidence and how he applied his experience as police discovered bodies months or even years after he'd deposited them. In my own mind, and from my own personal experience as the task force consultant, I can compare aspects of this case to the Yorkshire Ripper murders in Leeds, England, approximately seven years earlier. Prostitute-killer Peter Sutcliffe, like Ridgway married and living an otherwise normal life, led task force investigators in Leeds on an equally wild goose chase.

Although these two cases have some key aspects in common, the one thing that stands out in my mind upon a review of the King County prosecutor's summary of evidence against Ridgway is that the killer usually understands not only the methods police use to investigate a case but also the thinking that supports those methods. This is why killers will change their modus operandi, transport the victims to different locations, and deliberately leave clues in one spot in order to get the police to use vital personnel resources in a vain effort to track down a false lead. In Green River, with the press and community demanding quick answers, police not only had to solve the case, they also had to appear successful as they were doing it. As anyone who has ever worked a serial murder case knows, until the offender is eventually caught, police can't look successful, because if the press reports that, the killer might leave the area to find new hunting grounds. This is one of the paradoxes of conducting a serial murder investigation. It is also the lure that brings in the amateur and wannabe profilers who spring up like dandelions on television screens in the wake of any announcement that a serial killer is on the loose in a community.

Sometimes the public and even the police are surprised at a serial killer's lack of remorse. This jumps out at anyone reading the prosecutor's summary of evidence. Time and again detectives will comment about their amazement that the physical location of a dump site and the tiniest details about that location at that time will be more important to a serial killer than details about the victim. There is a reason for this, which Bundy made very clear, and which the investigators in the Ridgway case focused on. For a serial killer, his dump sites are living places that permeate his memory. This is where his "possessions" are located. He "owns" these locations just as he "owns" his victims. The details of the victims themselves fade into memory, but the details of the dump sites come alive every time the killer drives by to see if anyone has disturbed his property. Ridgway made this very clear to his interviewers, just as Ted made it clear to me.

As one can see from the prosecutor's summary, whatever Ridgway believed about himself and his victims—and we still may be years away from learning the truth about that—he clearly believed in his own ability to stay ahead of the police. Moreover, because he believed he knew how the police would proceed in their investigation of the victim remains that were turning up all over King County, he actually placed parts of his victims in specific places, knowing that would create a false lead and trigger a blind-alley investigaton. Too many of these fruitless investigations tend to drain the resources of a task force, make them look inept in the eyes of their commanders, the politicians, and the public, and eventually can result in a level of frustration that cripples their ability to function. Thus, when one reads the prosecutor's summary, one has to appreciate the determination of my former ad hoc partner, Dave Reichert, now King County Sheriff Reichert, in seeing this case to the end.

From the Prosecutor's Summary of Evidence

The First Victim

Of vital interest to any serial killer investigation is the knowledge surrounding the killer's first victim. Police usually spend a considerable amount of time interviewing the killer about his first victim because what the killer did and who the killer chose say a lot about the offender and the nature of his later crimes. In Ridgway's case, he at first refused to admit to any victims before Wendy Coffield. Then in October 2003, he said that it was "very possible" that he killed a women in the 1970s, while living in Maple Valley with his second wife. He described one incident, claiming that he could recall no detail except that "some'n went wrong, uh, with the date and I, I killed her."

As it turned out, the very first victim was the 6-year-old boy whom Ridgway stabbed with a knife in the incident described in the previous chapter.

The Final Victim

Detectives also focus their attention on the last victim because what they learn about the first and last victims and the comparisons between these crimes often shed light not only on the killer, his motivations, and methods, but also upon the evolution of the offender as he moves along the continuum of violence. In Ridgway's case, he claimed at first not to be able to recall his last victim. He said that he only killed two women in 1985 and then stopped completely. But police confronted him with unequivocal evidence to the contrary.

Gary Ridgway and His Victims

He had informed detectives of a number of places on Highway 410 where, he said, he had dumped bodies that he was not sure had been recovered. At one of these sites—marked on a map drawn by Ridgway for the detectives—a body had been previously recovered. That victim (who was never part of the "official" list of Green River victims) was Marta Reeves, who disappeared in 1990. As soon as he was confronted with this evidence, Ridgway readily admitted killing the woman—and then admitted that he had continued to kill into the 1990s.

Later, when speaking to a psychiatrist, Ridgway suggested that this was an isolated incident. "In 1990, I . . . went off the wagon and killed." Ridgway admitted later that he killed another woman in 1998, but he said that she was an aberration. He admitted to a forensic psychologist that his urge to kill persisted into the 1990s, although he said he could resist it for months at a time.

He acknowledged that he continued to seek out prostitutes until his arrest in 2001, and agreed that this was "kinda like a hunt." He admitted that the sight of prostitutes was, for him, "like candy in a dish." Indeed, even after he was transferred in the late 1990s from the Seattle Kenworth plant near Pacific Highway South to the Renton plant, Ridgway continued to drive the Pacific Highway South and Rainier Avenue, before and after work, looking for prostitutes. The crack epidemic had arrived, and Ridgway found that sex with cocaine-addicted prostitutes was cheaper than ever. Ridgway finally admitted that, although he slowed down, he never stopped killing altogether until his arrest in 2001.

According to him, his last killings were, in comparison to those of his more prolific period, the work of an "amateur." In the 1990s, Ridgway said, he was "semi-retired."

Although he admitted that his last kill was relatively close in time to his arrest in 2001, Ridgway insisted in 2003 that he could recall absolutely nothing about it. He professed an inability to understand why he was withholding information from his interrogators. He alternatively suggested that he remembered the murder, but did not want to disclose the details, or that the facts were locked away in his head and he could not access them. Ultimately, Ridgway said that the last murder he could recall committing was in 1998.

The Victims Placed in the Green River

Wendy Coffield

Of the seven counts of aggravated first degree murder Ridgway was charged with, five of the seven charged victims were found at the first known dump site, the Green River. There, on July 15, 1982, two boys on bicycles on the Peck Bridge in Kent discovered the body of Wendy Coffield floating in the water below them. Sixteen-year-old Wendy Coffield, known to work as a street prostitute along Pacific Highway South in King County, left her foster home on July 8, 1982, and was never seen alive again.

When she was discovered, Wendy was naked, with the exception of her shoes and socks. The remainder of her clothing—jeans, underpants, and shirt—were knotted around her neck like a ligature. An autopsy confirmed that Wendy had been strangled. She suffered a fractured hyoid bone as well as significant hemorrhaging in her neck muscles. In addition, her left humerus (the upper arm bone) was broken. The condition of her body was consistent with death having occurred shortly after her disappearance on July 8, 1982.

In March 2003, a private forensic laboratory, Microtrace, reported that it had discovered tiny paint spheres on the jeans that formed the ligature around Wendy's neck. The paint composition of the spheres was identical to the DuPont Imron paint used at the Kenworth truck plant where Ridgway worked in 1982. In March 2003, the State charged Ridgway with the murder of Wendy Coffield. In subsequent interviews with the task force, he admitted to killing her and placing her body in the Green River.

Debra Bonner

Debra Bonner was last seen alive on the evening of July 25, 1982, when she left a motel on Pacific Highway South in King County to "catch some dates." Debra was 22 and had a history of prostitution; during the previous 30 days, she had been arrested twice for prostitution on Pacific Highway South. Two and a half weeks later, on

August 12, 1982, she was discovered in the Green River. Her body had apparently floated downriver until it was caught in a logjam. There was no clothing on the body. In March 2003, Ridgway was charged with the murder of Debra Bonner. In subsequent interviews with the Task Force, he admitted to killing her and placing her body in the Green River.

Marcia Chapman, Cynthia Hinds, and Opal Mills

In August 1982, 31-year-old Marcia Chapman was living with her three children in an apartment near Pacific Highway South. She was involved in prostitution. On August 1, 1982, Marcia left her apartment and was not seen again.

Ten days later, on the night of August 11, 1982, 17-year-old Cynthia Hinds was out on Pacific Highway South working as a prostitute. Her pimp last saw a man driving a black Jeep picking her up. She was never seen again.

One day later, on August 12, 1982, at approximately one P.M., 16-year-old Opal Mills placed a call to her parents from Angle Lake State Park, just off Pacific Highway South. After that call, she was never heard from again. Friends later reported Opal had been involved in prostitution.

On August 15, 1982, a man rafting down the Green River spotted two bodies in the water, approximately 600 yards from where Debra Bonner's body had been found a few days earlier. The police responded and discovered Marcia Chapman and Cynthia Hinds. They were a few feet apart in the river, pinned to the bottom by several boulders, and nude. Police found Opal Mills's body on the banks of the river a short distance away.

All three women had been strangled.

Debra Estes

On September 20, 1982, 15-year-old Debra Estes disappeared. At approximately three P.M. that day, Debra was seen near the Stevenson Motel on Pacific Highway South. She was known to engage in prostitution.

Nearly six years later, on May 30, 1988, construction workers, digging holes for a playground, discovered Debra's remains in a shallow grave in Federal Way. Buried with Estes were two items of clothing: a brassiere and fragments of a black knit sweater/shirt with metallic threads. An acquaintance of Debra's confirmed that she was wearing this sweater/shirt on the afternoon she disappeared.

In March 2003, Microtrace reported that it had recovered tiny paint spheres from the clothing found with Debra Estes' remains. The paint composition of the spheres was identical to the DuPont Imron paint that was used at the Kenworth truck plant where Ridgway worked in 1982.

In March 2003, the State charged Ridgway with the murder of Debra Estes. In subsequent interviews with the task force, he admitted to killing her and burying her body.

Carol Christensen

On May 3, 1983, at approximately 2:30 P.M., 21-year-old Carol Christensen left the Barn Door Tavern in Sea-Tac where she worked as a waitress. She was due to return later that day but never came back. Carol was known to hitchhike. Five days later, on May 8, 1983, her body was found in a wooded area in Maple Valley. She was still dressed, and her body had been posed. She was lying on her back, with two trout placed on her upper torso, an empty bottle of wine across her stomach, and a sausage on her hands. She had been strangled with a ligature.

In 2001, semen from Carol's body was matched to Ridgway. In December 2001, he was charged with her murder.

In interviews with task force detectives, Ridgway admitted that he killed Carol. He said that he posed her body to "throw off" the task force. Ridgway explained:

> And then they had these experts come in and say it was, uh, for the last supper. And it was just, it was, uh, basically, uh, just a, uh, you know, the woman I killed, put clothes back on her and, uh, posed her. It was, uh, it was basically a posing.

He claimed that the items he left with her had no deeper significance; they were items that he happened to have in his house when he killed her that were of no value to him.

Rebecca Garde Guay

Rebecca Garde Guay was Ridgway's living victim, who reported him to the task force in December 1984, telling them that she was the victim of someone she believed to be the prostitute killer the police were looking for.

According to Rebecca, the assault occurred in November 1982. She was hitchhiking on Pacific Highway South when a man in a truck offered her a ride. Rebecca asked him if he was dating and offered him a blow job for $20. The man agreed, and she directed him to a secluded area not far from the highway at approximately 204th Street. Rebecca questioned the man about whether he was the Green River Killer. He assured her that he was not and showed her several items from his wallet, including an ID card from the Kenworth Trucking Company.

When they arrived at the agreed-on spot, the man asked her to go into the woods for the sex act. Rebecca agreed, and the two went into the woods. The man pulled his shorts down, and Rebecca kneeled in front of him and began performing oral sex. However, the man's penis did not become erect. Suddenly, the man accused Rebecca of biting him. He knocked her to the ground, pushed her face into the dirt, and wrapped his arm around her neck in a police-type choke hold. Rebecca struggled and pleaded that all she had was her family and that she did not want to die. After ten or fifteen seconds, she broke free and ran to a nearby trailer for help.

After pulling up his pants, the man initially pursued her but then gave up. He redressed and drove out of the area. Hysterical, Rebecca told the trailer occupants how she had been attacked. Her blouse was torn, and there were abrasions on her neck. Rebecca was obviously terrified and was certain that the man had intended to kill her.

Rebecca was initially reluctant to report the assault, because she was engaging in prostitution when she was assaulted. Eventually, with the enormous publicity surrounding the Green River killings, Rebecca called the task force and reported what had happened. Rebecca gave a description of her attacker: a white male, 30 to 35 years old with light brown hair, possibly with a mustache. Although it was November, the man was wearing shorts, a T-shirt, and tennis shoes. She thought his vehicle was a 1980 burgundy or maroon pickup truck with a white canopy.

Rebecca told the police about the Kenworth identification the man had shown her, and this information led police to link the attack to Ridgway. Her description of her assailant and his vehicle generally matched Ridgway and his pickup truck. Rebecca was shown a photographic montage of six men and immediately identified Ridgway as the man who attacked her in November 1982.

In February 1985, a task force detective contacted Ridgway and confronted him about Rebecca's allegations. Ridgway admitted that he had dated Rebecca. He maintained, however, that he choked her as a reflexive reaction to her biting his penis. According to the detective, Rebecca told him that she did not wish to pursue the case, and Ridgway was not charged.

In 2003, Ridgway was questioned about strangling Rebecca. He admitted that he tried to kill her. He confirmed that Rebecca had selected the area for the date and that she wanted to do the date in the truck. Ridgway wanted the "date" to be outside. According to his account, it "just went bad because of the . . . she, ah, guaranteed sex but she would only give me, ah, oral sex." Ridgway likened the situation to the circumstances that, he claimed, lead him to kill Mary Meehan two months earlier.

Ridgway told his interviewers that he was unable to maintain a choke hold on Rebecca, who fought and scratched him. He recalled that his shorts, which were around his ankles, prevented him from wrapping his legs around her and subduing her. He accurately recalled that she said she did not want to die and that she had a family.

Ridgway was not charged with attempted murder in this case because the statute of limitations had run out by the time he was arrested and charged in the other killings.

Charges Filed in the Remaining 41 Cases

Ridgway pled guilty to the murders of these victims, whose cases were then closed. The prosecutor listed these cases in a rough chronological order based upon the areas from which the victims' bodies were recovered.

Gisele Lovvorn

In July of 1982, Gisele Lovvorn was 19 years old and working as a prostitute on Pacific Highway South. Around eleven A.M., Saturday, July 17, 1982, Gisele left her apartment, saying that she planned to turn several tricks on the highway and would return later in the day. She was never seen again.

Two months later, on September 25, 1982, Gisele's remains were found near an apple tree in a wooded area near South 200th Street and 18th Avenue South, King County, an area where Gisele was known to take her dates. She had been strangled with a pair of men's socks that were still wrapped around her neck. Apart from the ligature, there was no clothing on the body, even though her jewelry remained in place. Gisele's body lay on its back, with the legs flexed wide at the hip, and the knees bent at approximately 90 degrees.

In 2003, Ridgway admitted killing Gisele Lovvorn. He stated that he picked up Gisele on a Saturday night, while his 7-year-old son was asleep in his vehicle. Ridgway said Gisele directed him to the spot for the date. According to Ridgway, after he parked at the spot, he told his son to remain in the truck while he and the woman went for a walk. Ridgway then took Gisele out into the wooded area out of sight of his son. He and Gisele had sex "doggie style."

Once he climaxed, Ridgway said, he told Gisele that he thought he heard his son coming. As he had hoped, she raised her head to look, exposing her neck. Still behind her, Ridgway pinned her neck between his upper and lower arm, and choked her until she stopped moving. Ridgway then took off his socks, tied them together, and wrapped them around Gisele's neck. He used a stick to fashion a tourniquet from the socks. Then he twisted the stick, tightening the socks around her neck, until he was satisfied that Gisele would not regain consciousness.

Ridgway left the makeshift tourniquet on Gisele, put on his clothes, and returned to his truck. Ridgway's son asked his father where the young woman had gone. Ridgway replied that the woman lived nearby and had decided to walk home. Ridgway then drove his young son back to his home.

The next day, Ridgway returned and moved the body a short distance to a more secluded area. He collected Gisele's clothes and tried to take the socks off her neck. The socks were cinched so tightly around the young woman's neck that Ridgway could not get them over her head. He did not consider cutting the socks off because, he explained, he would not be able to wear them. Before he left, Ridgway engaged in sexual intercourse with the body.

Ridgway admitted that he visited Gisele's body at least one more time. He stated that he was uncertain whether he had intercourse with the body a third time, claiming that he may have been deterred by advanced decomposition.

During the interviews, Ridgway was shown photos from the crime scene area, without being told what the photos were depicting. Ridgway accurately identified the area and the location of the body. Later, Ridgway led investigators, without assistance, to the area where he left Gisele's body.

The Star Lake Victims

In the early 1980s, the task force recovered the remains of six women designated as victims of the Green River Killer along a short, approximately one-half mile, stretch of Star Lake Road, in King County. That portion of Star Lake Road runs steeply uphill from the main arterial South 272nd Street, heading south, then looping west, then north and west again. The remains were actually closer together than the serpentine road would suggest—no more than a quarter of a mile separated any of them. The area is approximately three miles southwest (less than a 15-minute drive) from the stretch of the Green River where five earlier victims were discovered and approximately the same distance southeast from Ridgway's residence at the time.

All six were working as prostitutes at the time they disappeared. Five of the six were last seen along Pacific Highway South where Ridgway was known to "hunt" for his victims. The circumstances of the sixth woman's disappearance are not known, but she had previously been arrested for prostitution along that stretch of Pacific Highway South.

With the exception of a blouse found on one victim's remains, all the victims were naked when they were left at the Star Lake dump site. No biological evidence had ever been developed linking any suspect to the Star Lake cases.

It appeared that all the Star Lake victims were killed by strangulation. All six women had been killed and left near Star Lake Road before the first remains were ever found. Obviously, the same person had killed and dumped them. The similarities among the women—such as their lifestyles, place of disappearance, and time of disappearance—as well as the concentration of the bodies at the dump site, the condition of body when dumped, and the apparent cause of death, all compelled this conclusion.

Ridgway has admitted killing the women found along Star Lake Road. The steep, secluded, wooded hillside falling away from Star Lake Road greatly appealed to Ridgway. It was, he said, "downhill where I could put a woman . . . a bunch of women. . . . It was, hey, fantastic. . . . It was, uh, woodsy, secluded, and, uh, it was a, a, site that I figured nobody would find her at, and uh, if they did, it would be a couple years later. Wouldn't be anything, you know, no, noth-nothing left of her. . . . I could go down there during the day and have sex with her. Nobody see me from, from the top. There was a road on the top and there's a road on the bottom. They couldn't see me. And even if it did, a car come by, I could lay down."

Not only was Star Lake secluded, it was remarkably convenient to Pacific Highway South and to his house. Ridgway said he managed to dump all the bodies there within an hour of when he killed them. Ridgway was familiar with the area; his second wife reported that they would go swimming in Star Lake.

Ridgway said he did not keep track of exactly how many bodies he placed at the Star Lake site. His estimates ranged from five to seven. Once he said that all the Star Lake victims had been discovered; another time he said that there was a seventh victim still along the road. He said, "Once I started dumping, I didn't care about the count."

Terry Milligan

Sixteen-year-old Terry Milligan disappeared on August 29, 1982. Terry was last seen at approximately six P.M. She—like victims Denise Bush, whom Ridgway murdered less than six weeks later, and Martina Authorlee—was living at the Moonrise Motel at Pacific Highway South and 144th Street, and working as a prostitute on the highway. Ridgway did not work that day, which was Sunday. He was two hours late to work the following morning.

On April 1, 1984, Terry's skeletal remains were discovered near the northern, downhill end of Star Lake Road, shortly after the discovery nearby of the remains of Delores Williams. A striped blouse, with buttons, was still around the neck and upper arms. This blouse matched a description of the one Terry was wearing when she was last seen. Both hips were flexed at nearly a 90 degree angle, and both knees were bent inward at approximately the same angle. This unusual position led investigators to conclude that her killer deliberately posed the body.

In 2003, Ridgway provided investigators with a detailed account of murdering Terry Milligan and dumping her body. Typically, he did not recall her by name or appearance. He knew he killed her in 1982, and thought it was in August or September of that year. Ridgway correctly recalled Terry's race and said that she was his first victim after Opal Mills. Moreover, he correctly recalled that when he killed Mary Meehan two weeks later he had already placed one body at Star Lake.

Ridgway said that he killed Terry where he had killed and left Giselle Lovvorn the previous month. Ridgway was in the area that night—a Port of Seattle police officer contacted him some eight blocks from where Lovvorn's body was discovered. He said that two boys had seen him in the area during his date with Terry, so he decided that he had to dump her body elsewhere.

Ridgway correctly recalled that, of all the victims he subsequently dumped there, her body was the closest to the bottom of the hill as the road ascends. Ridgway said that he recalled leaving a blouse with buttons on one of his early victims and guessed that she was the first woman he left at Star Lake.

When he was shown a photograph of the blouse found with Terry's remains, he said he recognized it. He said that he "didn't bother" to take the blouse off the body, and suggested that he did not because he was in a hurry to leave the area where he killed her because he had been seen there with her earlier. Ridgway said he returned the following day to the place where he dumped Terry and had sexual intercourse with her body. He said that the body had developed rigor mortis, and that he had to pry her legs apart. When he was shown a photograph of Terry's skeletal remains, with the hips spread wide and the knees completely bent, he said that he was sure that he left her in that position.

Alma Smith

On March 3, 1983, at approximately nine P.M., Alma Smith disappeared from the street outside the Red Lion Inn at 188th Street and Pacific Highway South. Two other victims, Delores Williams and Constance Naon had also disappeared from this location. Alma was working as a prostitute at that location with her roommate, who was her closest friend. Her roommate left the location with a john to turn a trick; by the time she returned some 40 minutes later, Alma had disappeared. A bystander told her roommate that Alma had left with a man meeting Ridgway's description, in a blue pickup truck.

While the roommate remained outside the Red Lion Inn, waiting for Alma to return, a man parked a blue pickup truck in the hotel parking lot. He got out, and tried to persuade her to date him. He asked about her "blonde girlfriend." Alma Smith was blonde. Her roommate was already anxious about Alma's disappearance, and the man so spooked her, she refused to date him. He drove off. On that day Ridgway got off work at 3:20 P.M. His home was less than three miles from where Alma was last seen.

In 1986, this roommate was shown a photographic lineup and picked a photo of Gary Ridgway as the person who "looked like," she told her interviewers, the man who tried to pick her up the night that Smith disappeared from Pacific Highway South. Her identification was tentative; she said she thought the man had "longer hair and thinner lips." In early 1987, she identified, but not positively, a photo of Ridgway's pickup truck as the one driven by the man she saw on the night of Alma's disappearance. Ridgway did not own a blue pickup truck at the time. However, his brother, who lived nearby, owned a 1969 one-half ton Dodge pickup that was painted turquoise. Gary's girlfriend during this time confirmed that Ridgway would use his brother's truck. In 2003, Ridgway admitted that he borrowed the truck and took at least one of his victims to Star Lake in that vehicle.

Another woman claimed that she knew one of Alma's regular tricks and said that she dated him at his residence with Alma. She said the "trick" lived east of Pacific Highway South—Ridgway lived east of the highway at 216th Street. and Military Road at the time—and drove a red pickup with a white canopy. Ridgway drove a maroon pickup with a white canopy. In 1986, this woman picked Ridgway's photograph out of a "trick book" shown to her by a detective. She said the photo resembled Smith's "regular trick."

Smith's remains—a scattered skeleton—were discovered on April 2, 1984, in the woods along Star Lake Road. The remains were approximately 50 yards off the road, 200 yards southwest of Gail Mathew's dump site, and 200 yards northeast of the site where the remains of Sandra Gabbert were discovered.

In 2003, Ridgway told detectives that he remembered the night he killed Alma Smith and dumped her at Star Lake. He recalled these events, he said, because that was the night when he tried to kill two consecutive women. Ridgway said he picked up a woman one night near the bus stop at the corner of 188th Street and Pacific Highway South. This is the location of the Red Lion Inn, where Alma was last seen. He said he took the woman to his house, killed her, and dumped her at Star Lake. Ridgway said that killing Alma went smoothly. He recalled that she did not become incontinent when he strangled her, which meant that he did not have to put his bedding in the washing machine before leaving to dump the body. He said it only took him an hour or so to pick Alma up, take her to his house, kill her, dump the body, and return. He correctly recalled that he had already dumped, in his own words, "at least" one woman at the Star Lake site before he left Alma there. But he incorrectly believed that he had dumped Alma just uphill from Milligan. He had placed Delores Williams, the third victim, there.

Ridgway said that things went so smoothly that he decided to kill another woman that same night. According to Ridgway, as soon as he dumped Alma's body, he returned to the same place where he had picked her up, and parked in the lot by the Red Lion Inn. He said he approached another woman and tried to date her. She refused, and, he told investigators, he was unable to find a second victim that night.

Were there times, like the night he killed Alma Smith, when Ridgway's urge to kill overcame his customary caution? a psychiatrist asked him. Ridgway answered that he tried to kill two women on another occasion. He told his interviewer that he picked up a woman, killed her, dumped her body, and then returned to the same spot and tried to date another woman. This was a mistake because, he said, a witness at that spot had seen the first woman get into his truck.

Delores Williams

Seventeen-year-old Delores Williams was the third victim that Ridgway dumped along Star Lake Road. Delores disappeared sometime between March 8 and March 17, 1983, within two weeks after Ridgway killed Alma Smith. The exact date of Delores's murder is not known, but roommates with whom she was sharing an apartment on Pacific Highway South at the time of her disappearance recalled the night she went missing. Just like Alma Smith, the woman who preceded her to the Star Lake dump site, Delores vanished while 'working as a prostitute near the bus stop outside the Red Lion Inn at 188th Street and Highway 99. There were no witnesses. Ridgway was in King County, working the day shift at Kenworth, during the week or so in which Williams disappeared.

On March 31, 1984, Delores's skeletal remains were discovered near the Star Lake Road. It appeared to investigators that Delores's body—like many of the Green River victims at the Star Lake dump site and elsewhere—had been covered with branches and debris. No clothing was found with the body. A rock was found in the area of the pelvis.

In the fall 2003, Microtrace, a nationally renowned private forensic laboratory, reported that, even after multiple analyses, paint fragments recovered with Delores's remains are indistinguishable from paint recovered with the remains of Cheryl Wims (disappeared May 1983, found at North Airport dump site) and Tina Thompson (disappeared July 1983, found at Highway 18).

Ridgway claimed he had no specific recollection of Delores Williams. He knew that her body was the second or third body he left at Star Lake. He "guessed" incorrectly that she was white. He knew that he had dumped her at Star Lake before he dumped "the lady by the log," Sandra Gabbert.

Gail Mathews

On April 10, 1983, one month after Ridgway murdered Delores Williams and dumped her body at Star Lake, Gail Mathews disappeared. Like the women whose bodies preceded and followed hers to the Star Lake dump site, Gail was working as a prostitute on Pacific Highway South. At 23, she was the oldest of the Star Lake victims. Gail's boyfriend last saw her at approximately six P.M. on April 10, 1983, a Sunday when Ridgway was not at work.

When her boyfriend saw Gail, he was walking along Pacific Highway South, and she was sitting in the passenger seat of a pickup truck on that street. The truck, in the southbound lanes of the highway, was stopped at the traffic light at the intersection of Pacific Highway South and South 216th Street. The driver of the pickup was a man. Gail's boyfriend watched as the light changed and the pickup truck turned left onto South 216th, heading east. He waved at Gail, trying to get her attention, but she did not appear to notice him. He never saw her again.

At the time, Ridgway lived one block south of South 216th, on Military Road. Military Road is east of Pacific Highway South, a little more than half a mile from the intersection where Gail was last seen in the pickup truck. South 216th Street is the most direct route to Ridgway's house from that section of the highway.

Gail's boyfriend said the driver of the pickup truck was a white man. He said the man had "blondish, curly-ish hair." This description, and the composite drawing he subsequently created, does not particularly resemble Ridgway. And Gail's boyfriend variously described the color of the pickup truck in which he last saw her as pastel green, greenish, and blue. He said it had a canopy. While Ridgway did not own a blue pickup truck at the time, his brother, who lived nearby, owned a turquoise pickup.

In 2003, Ridgway told investigators that he used his brother's truck to take at least one of his victims to Star Lake. Indeed, a color sample selected by Gail's boyfriend in 1984 closely matches the color of Ridgway's brother's pickup truck at the time of Gail's disappearance. After Gail disappeared, Ridgway painted his brother's truck a different color.

Gail's mostly skeletonized remains were discovered near Star Lake Road on September 19, 1983.

In 2003, Ridgway told detectives that he did not recognize Gail Mathews from a photograph. But he recalled a time when, contrary to his usual careful practice, he killed a prostitute even though a witness had seen him with her shortly before. He described picking a woman up on Pacific Highway South, taking her home, and killing her. He remembered that, en route to his house, as he waited to turn left onto South 216th, a man standing on the street saw the woman in his truck and waved at her. Ridgway said the woman did not notice, but it appeared to him that the man knew her. Ridgway said he took the woman to his house, murdered her, and took the body somewhere in the pickup truck and dumped it. He said he could not recall where he dumped the body. However, when he later discussed the Star Lake site with the detectives, Ridgway said that one of the women he dumped there might have been the one who had been seen in his truck at Pacific Highway South and South 216th.

Sandra Gabbert

Seventeen-year-old Sandra Gabbert disappeared on Sunday, April 17, 1983, one week after Gail Mathews. Like Gail, Sandra was working as a prostitute along Pacific Highway South. Like Alma Smith and Delores Williams, who were killed and dumped at Star Lake before her, Sandra regularly worked at the bus stop outside the Red Lion Inn at 188th and Pacific Highway South. At the time of her death, Sandra and her boyfriend/pimp were living in a motel on the highway. That day, she returned to the motel room in the early evening and gave him $70 she had earned. She said she was going back out to catch two more dates at the covered bus stop nearby. He last saw her at the 7–Eleven at 142nd and Pacific Highway South—the same place, according to both Ridgway and a witness, Ridgway met Denise Bush before killing her. Sandra's boyfriend never saw her again.

Sandra's body was discovered on April 1, 1984, in the woods just 100 feet below Star Lake Road. The body was lying on a steep hillside, in a small depression between a large log and the uphill side of the slope, covered with brush and branches.

Joel Hardin, an expert tracker, analyzed the scene. After carefully examining the area around Sandra's body, Hardin reported in 1984 that the body had been concealed by one man, who made repeated, calm, and organized trips from the body to a brush pile and back. According to Hardin, the man made no wasted movements, and showed no signs of panic.

A man who regularly jogged along Star Lake Road reported in 1984 that one morning in the spring of 1983 he ran past a pickup truck parked along the road just as a man stepped out from behind the truck into his path. His description of that man was generic, but his description of the pickup truck is remarkably consistent with Ridgway's brother's truck.

As with virtually all his victims, Ridgway said he did not recognize Sandra Gabbert from a photograph. However, when Ridgway was taken to the Star Lake site in 2003, he remembered dumping a woman where Sandra's remains were recovered. He recalled "rolling" the body down the hill and said that it came to rest against a large log. He said he camouflaged the body by covering it with brush—he called it "yard waste"—that someone had thrown down the slope. He said he made several trips from the brush pile to the body and back. He also said he did this during the daytime. All these facts are consistent with deductions Hardin made at the scene 20 years earlier.

Ridgway also correctly recalled that the woman he placed by the log was the "next to the last" woman he dumped at the Star Lake site. Moreover, he recalled that he placed her by the log before he killed Kimi-Kai Pitsor, whom he killed within a day of Sandra, and that during that same time he was also using the Mountainview Cemetery dumpsite.

Ridgway was asked if he recalled a jogger who might have encountered him returning to his truck along Star Lake Road. He said that there "might have been" such a man, but that it did not "faze" him because he had already dumped the body by that time.

Carrie Rois

The last known victim left near Star Lake Road, 15-year-old Carrie Rois, disappeared sometime between May 31 and June 15, 1983, although the circumstances of her disappearance are not known. She was the youngest of the Star Lake victims. Earlier that year, Carrie had been arrested for prostitution on Pacific Highway South, outside a motel at South 144th . According to a friend of hers, Carrie frequented the two-block area between South 144th and South 142nd on Pacific Highway South. This area includes the 7–Eleven where, according to both a witness and Ridgway, Ridgway met Denise Bush before he murdered her, and the sheltered bus stop where Sandra Gabbert was working when Ridgway killed her and dumped her at the Star Lake. Victims Tina Thompson, Martina Authorlee, Yvonne Antosh, and Kim Nelson were all staying in motels at this location when they disappeared. While under surveillance in 1987, Ridgway was observed cruising for prostitutes at this location.

Carrie's remains were found on March 10, 1985, in a relatively flat, swampy area approximately 50 yards downhill from Star Lake Road, and only about 25 yards downhill from Sandra Gabbert's remains.

Two acquaintances of Carrie's reported that she said she had an odd experience in the Spring of 1983 with a man who, she said, took her up to Snoqualmie Pass. Both of these individuals saw Carrie return from this trip in a pickup truck. One of these witnesses provided investigators with an extremely detailed description of the truck, which closely resembles the pickup truck owned at that time by Ridgway's father, who lived in south King County.

As was almost inevitably the case, Ridgway failed to recognize Carrie from a photograph. He did, however, describe placing one of his Star Lake victims at the bottom of a hill below Sandra Gabbert's remains. He did not recognize that scene in photographs, he said, because he placed her there at night.

The South Airport Victims

Like Ted Bundy, Ridgway alternated between using several dump sites. After placing his first victim at Star Lake, he began another dump site, an area that would be called South Airport or "Tyee," for a nearby golf course. This site would become the first discovered after the five women in the Green River, and with it, it became clear to law enforcement and to the community that a serial killer was operating in King County.

On October 27, 1983, on a stretch of land just south of the Seattle-Tacoma (Sea-Tac) International Airport, some citizens made a grisly discovery. Two people riding their bikes in the area of 25th South and South 192nd stumbled across a body buried in a shallow grave. Police responded and began processing the scene. It was decided, in light of the growing number of dead and missing prostitutes in the county, that an extensive search of the area was warranted. Using volunteer searchers and cadaver dogs, police began a methodical grid search of the vacant land surrounding the body. Two days into the search, one of those volunteers found another victim.

This second body was approximately one hundred feet from the first, again buried in a shallow grave. As police undertook the task of processing that scene, they continued their search. Approximately two weeks later, directly across the street from the two buried bodies, a search dog uncovered a third grave. The two previously discovered victims had been found in shallow graves, but this third set of remains was different. The killer had gone to a lot of effort to fully bury this victim. The only parts of her anatomy that protruded from the ground were her teeth. Six years later, in October 1989, investigators discovered that they had missed one victim during the 1983 searches. This fourth body was approximately 40 feet north of the spot where the bike riders had made the first discovery. Like the others at South Airport, this victim had been concealed from view. Her remains, remarkably intact, had been covered by a car fender and a wooden tabletop.

In all, the killer left four women at 25th South and South 192nd. Each was naked, each had been strangled, each had been hidden from view, and each had been engaged in prostitution at the time of her disappearance. They were, in the order in which they were found), Constance Naon, Kelly Ware, Mary Meehan, and Andrea Childers.

In 2003, Ridgway readily admitted responsibility for all four murders and recounted in detail what he recalled about killing and dumping each of those young women. Ridgway was taken to the area where the bodies were found and accurately pointed to the locations where these remains were found. He also correctly identified the position of each body in relation to the others.

Mary Meehan

Nineteen-year-old Mary Meehan disappeared some time after 8:30 P.M. on September 15, 1982. At the time of her disappearance she was living at the Western Six Motel at 165th and Pacific Highway South and, like the other victims, she was known to have engaged in prostitution along the highway. Mary was seven months' pregnant at the time of her disappearance, although, according to her boyfriend, her pregnancy was not so obvious as to deter her potential dates.

On November 13, 1983, Mary's remains were found, directly across the street from Constance Naon and Kelly Ware. Her grave was approximately 18 inches deep and long enough to accommodate her entire body. She was lying faceup, missing her clothes, jewelry, and the purse she was seen carrying the night of her disappearance.

During interviews in 2003, Ridgway had a distinct memory of picking Mary up and killing her. According to Ridgway, she was the first victim he killed at the South Airport location and the first victim he ever buried. Although he could not pinpoint exactly when he killed her, Ridgway said he began using the airport site after his first dump site, the Green River. He said it was a summer night some time after nine P.M. when he contacted Mary on Pacific Highway South. They agreed to date, and he drove to the Sandstone Motel. Ridgway parked his truck there and persuaded Mary to walk several blocks to the area of 25th South and South 192nd so the two could have sex outdoors. Ridgway claims Mary agreed to this arrangement. He said that when they arrived at the wooded area, Mary would only agree to engage in oral sex, not vaginal intercourse. This apparently angered him. Ridgway repeatedly told investigators in 2003 that he was "paying for the vagina," not for oral sex.

He described Mary performing the act. Ridgway said that he was "not getting hard," so he quickly jumped behind Mary and began choking her. After killing Mary, Ridgway said he was concerned that the body was too close to the road. He decided to bury her, and retrieved a shovel from his truck. He dug a shallow grave, undressed Mary, and laid her down. He then covered her with the soil, put the grassy sod back on top, and pressed down on it. Ridgway said he placed Mary somewhat on her side, with her face pointing up toward the sky, which is exactly how she was discovered. He then collected her clothes and jewelry and left.

Ridgway was vigorously questioned about Mary's pregnancy. Throughout interviews, Ridgway maintained that he did not know she was pregnant. He claimed she was not naked until after her death and that by that time he said it was dark and he could not see her body clearly. Ridgway did say, however, that even if he had known she was pregnant, he would still have killed her.

Andrea Childers

On April 14, 1983, 19-year-old Andrea Childers disappeared. She was last seen in Seattle at a bus stop located at 21st and Union and was reportedly headed to Southcenter Mall. Not much is known about her disappearance, although she was known to engage in prostitution and had been arrested for this offense by Seattle Police just one month earlier.

Six years after the discovery of the remains of Mary Meehan, Constance Naon, and Kelly Ware at the South Airport site, a Port of Seattle employee stumbled on the remains of Andrea Childers. Her body was found only 40 feet from the remains of Constance Naon. Like the others, she had been covered to conceal her from view. Her skeleton was remarkably intact because it was beneath a car fender and a large piece of wooden tabletop, which had protected her from the elements and animals. In the area of her body were numerous blackberry bushes and garbage. On the skeleton itself were pieces of rotted twigs and branches. She had been positioned facedown, with her legs spread wide.

In 2003, Ridgway admitted killing Andrea Childers. He correctly recounted that he killed her within months of Constance Naon and Kelly Ware. Ridgway could not recall where he met Andrea but said that he drove her to the South Airport location, where they walked to a place to have sex. Ridgway recounted that he later killed and buried Constance Naon at the spot where he had sex with Andrea.

According to Ridgway, he had sex with Andrea, then strangled her. Ridgway said he believes that Andrea may have defecated when he killed her, and that he "cleaned her up" and removed her clothes and jewelry. Once she was dead, Ridgway dragged Andrea's body about 50 feet, toward a fence, where he began digging a grave. While doing so, Ridgway realized he could be seen. He filled in the hole and dragged the body 50 yards or so to the east, near some blackberry bushes. Ridgway said he covered her body with dead brush, tree limbs, and other garbage he found there. Ridgway also recalled that he may have had sex with the corpse. Ridgway recalled correctly that Andrea's body was the one he dumped farthest to the east at the South Airport site.

Constance Naon

Less than two months after he killed Andrea Childers, Ridgway returned to South Airport with the woman who would become his third victim at that location. In June 1983, 20-year-old Constance "Connie" Naon was working at Obertos, a local sausage factory.

She had an expensive cocaine habit that she funded by engaging in prostitution. According to her friends, Connie would drive her prized Camaro to the Red Lion Inn at 188th and Pacific Highway South, park in the lot at the hotel, and then find customers by walking from car to car and soliciting the drivers. When she had earned enough to purchase her cocaine, Connie would quit for the day. Connie had been working as a prostitute for just a few months prior to her disappearance.

On June 8, 1983, Connie left work, returned to the apartment she shared with her boyfriend, changed her clothes, and told her boyfriend that she was going to a friend's house to buy cocaine. She left sometime around 4:30 or 5:00 P.M. She called about an hour later and said that she would be home in about 20 minutes. She never arrived. Several weeks later, her family and friends found Connie's Camaro, still locked, in the parking lot of the Red Lion Inn.

More than four months after her disappearance, on October 27, 1983, some bicycle riders discovered Connie's body at a vacant lot at 25th South and South 192nd, her remains partially buried in a shallow grave, beneath three to four inches of soil and leaves. In the pelvic area of the skeleton was a small triangular-shaped rock reminiscent of the rocks placed in the vaginas of Marcia Chapman and Cynthia Hinds, found in the Green River the previous year. Her clothing and jewelry were missing.

In 2003, Ridgway admitted that he killed Connie Naon. He recalled meeting her at the Red Lion Inn. They agreed on a date and Ridgway drove in his truck to the vacant lot south of the airport, where he parked. Ridgway said they had sex some 20 feet from the truck. Ridgway claimed that Connie would not allow him to touch her breasts. He said this angered him, and that immediately after he strangled Connie to death, he bit her on the breast.

After killing her, Ridgway used a shovel from his truck to dig a shallow grave. He estimated only three inches of dirt covered the body. When asked why he buried Connie, Ridgway claimed that he did so to suppress his "urge" to return and have sex with the body. Ridgway also admitted putting a rock in Connie's vagina after she was dead. Ridgway claimed to recall that she had a Camaro, although he could not remember whether he saw it, or she told him that she had one, or he saw a Camaro emblem on her key ring. He said he considered stealing the Camaro but rejected the idea.

Ridgway accurately described the location of Naon's remains, which were found between those of Kelly Ware and Andrea Childers.

Kelly Ware

In July 1983, a little over one month after Constance Naon was killed, 22-year-old Kelly Ware disappeared. Kelly had worked as a prostitute for several years. Her sister reported that Kelly was afraid to work downtown or the Sea-Tac area but was "very comfortable" working Chinatown and Aurora. On July 18, 1983, Kelly called her parents' home and was never heard from again. In December 1984, her sister reported her missing.

Kelly's remains were discovered in late October 1983, two days after those of Constance Naon. Like Connie, Kelly was covered with a thin layer of soil. Her remains were approximately 100 feet west of Connie's. Kelly's body was lying on its back with the arms outstretched and the legs extended straight down. Kelly's remains went unidentified for over a year.

In 2003, Ridgway correctly recalled that Kelly Ware was the last of the South Airport victims. He stated that he picked her up on a weekend, and dated and killed her near the other bodies at that site. Ridgway said that he returned to Kelly's body a few days after killing her. He recalled that it was night, and that his son was sleeping in the truck. Ridgway said that he believed that this occurred when he and his family were celebrating his son's birthday. Kelly disappeared on the weekend of Ridgway's brother's birthday. Ridgway said that he returned to have sex with the body. Just as he finished the sex act, Ridgway said, he heard and saw a police car. According to Ridgway, a Port of Seattle police officer pulled up and asked him what he was doing. Ridgway claims he calmly explained that he had stopped to urinate, and the officer did not investigate further. Ridgway said it was this police contact that caused him to stop using the South Airport dumpsite. This particular contact with Ridgway cannot be verified through police records or incidence reports. If true, the patrol officer most likely did not write it up. However, one year earlier, a Port of Seattle police officer contacted Ridgway one hundred feet from where Kelly's body was subsequently found.

Ridgway said that within a day or two after this police contact, he returned to the site. He moved Kelly's body, had sex with her yet again, and then dug a shallow grave and buried her.

Ridgway claimed he was most proud of killing Kelly Ware because of the "fine" way he hid the body. In his writings, Ridgway noted that he "would have" covered Kelly's grave with grass from the site because she was close to the road.

Linda Rule

Sixteen-year-old Linda Rule was last seen on Sunday, September 26, 1982, around 2:30 P.M. while she was on her way to the Kmart at Aurora and 130th Street, in north Seattle. She worked as a prostitute on the Aurora strip and was known to date at the parking lot of Northwest Hospital in Seattle. Four months later, on January 31, 1983, construction workers found Linda's skeletal remains in a wooded area at Northwest Hospital. All of her clothes and property were missing. The Sunday she disappeared, Ridgway was in the county and withdrew $50 from an ATM machine. In 1984, Ridgway admitted to a task force detective that he dated prostitutes he picked up on north Aurora Avenue.

Though Linda was never included as a victim of the Green River Killer, her murder had all the characteristics of a Green River case and occurred during the period of the Green River murders. Like most of the official Green River victims, she was involved in prostitution, and her body was both unclothed and outdoors when discovered.

In June 2003, Ridgway admitted killing Linda Rule. During the first day of interviews with task force detectives in 2003 and prior to any questioning about her case, Ridgway announced that he had killed a woman and dumped her body at Northwest Hospital. He recalled meeting Linda on Aurora Avenue during the day and driving to a field near Northwest Hospital. "We were just drivin' around," he said, "and found a vacant lot in front of the hospital and had a date and I killed her there, outside the . . . truck." He choked her from behind. After killing Linda, Ridgway claimed that he went through her pockets and found matches. Twice, he lit the back of her hair on fire. He was afraid that someone would see the smoke, and extinguished the fire.

When Ridgway was shown Linda's picture, he stated that she looked familiar. On July 10, 2003, Ridgway was taken to Northwest Hospital. He was unable to pick out the exact location where he left Linda's body; construction since 1982 had changed the campus.

There is now a parking lot where the body was found.

The Oregon Victims

Denise Bush and Shirley Sherrill, both known to work as prostitutes, disappeared within two weeks of each other in October 1982. Denise disappeared from Pacific Highway South on October 8; Shirley disappeared from the Chinatown area near downtown Seattle between October 20 and 22.

Nearly three years later, in June 1985, incomplete remains of both women were found off a rural road in Tigard, just south of Portland, Oregon. This discovery led to speculation that the Green River Killer had moved south. Ridgway would later admit that he killed these women and moved their remains in an effort to confuse the task force.

Denise Bush

On October 8, 1982, 23-year-old Denise Bush disappeared from Pacific Highway South. She and an acquaintance were staying at the Moonrise Motel, located across the street from Larry's Market and the 7–Eleven, at 144th and the highway. This was at the intersection of the sheltered bus stop where Sandra Gabbert and Kim Nelson were working as prostitutes when Ridgway picked them up and killed them. Tina Thompson, Martina Authorlee, and Yvonne Antosh were all staying in motels at this location when they disappeared. Denise left the Moonrise for a pack of cigarettes around midday and never returned. That day, Ridgway was off work for a claimed eye ailment and purchased $26 worth of gas from a station near the Moonrise Motel, where Denise was last seen.

On October 7, 1982, the night before Denise's disappearance, she met a girlfriend across the street from the Moonrise at the 7–Eleven. When her friend arrived, Denise was talking to a man who appeared to be working on his pickup truck. Denise's girlfriend described him as being 5 feet 10 inches, between 29 and 30 years old, wearing a blue plaid shirt and boots. The friend thought the man was driving a dirty or dull green GMC truck with oxidized paint. The hood of the truck was up and something about the man made Denise's friend suspicious. She later told police that when the man saw her looking at him, he jerked his head around and hid it under the hood as if he did not want her to see his face. She thought he looked like he had something to hide. The friend asked Denise who the man was; Denise dodged the question, but did say that she was going to meet him later. While the truck that Denise's friend saw did not match anything owned by Ridgway at the time, it was similar to his brother's turquoise truck.

In the 1980s, police interviewed Denise's friend about the man she saw at the 7–Eleven. She selected Ridgway's photo from a montage and said he was the man she had seen talking to Denise the night before she disappeared.

In June 1985, a construction crew discovered Denise's skull in Tigard, Oregon. Police secured the crime scene, but allowed construction to continue on the far side of the lot. Search crews also recovered Denise's femur and pelvis. A few days later, a worker discovered more remains at the site that turned out to be those of Shirley Sherrill, who Ridgway also admitted transporting to Tigard.

Five years later, in February 1990, a citizen discovered more of Denise's remains near Pacific Highway South in Tukwila, among them her mandible and a shunt that had been placed in her skull six months prior to her disappearance. Her skull without the shunt had been found in Oregon five years earlier. The presence of the shunt and mandible in Tukwila proved that Denise's body had decomposed in Tukwila and that the killer came later and took some of her bones to Oregon.

During interviews with task force detectives in 2003, Ridgway admitted killing Denise and transporting her remains to Tigard, Oregon. He correctly recalled that Denise was African American and correctly estimated her height. Ridgway told detectives he picked Denise up on Pacific Highway South and killed her where her remains were found in Tukwila. He thought that Denise had chosen the place for them to date. He said that the site was "an easy location" and that he probably had been there in the past. The Tukwila site is a minute or so drive from the intersection of Pacific Highway South and 144th Street where Ridgway picked up other victims.

Ridgway said he used his arm to strangle Denise and told her that if she did not scream, he would let her go. After he killed Denise, he covered her body with some type of plastic.

While Ridgway did not admit that he was the man talking to Denise at the 7–Eleven on the day before she disappeared, he acknowledged that at times he would park there, open the hood of his truck, check the oil, and look for a prostitute. He believed that the people at 7–Eleven knew him by sight—"a steady customer" was how he described himself—and knew that he was picking up prostitutes. He said he would meet the women there and make arrangements to meet them at another location, where he could pick them up without drawing attention to himself.

Ridgway acknowledged that, in an effort to throw off the task force, he moved Denise's remains and those of Shirley Sherrill to Oregon in the spring of 1984. One weekend, he took his son on what he described as a "camping" trip to Oregon. He transported the remains, with son's clothes and bicycle, in the trunk of a Plymouth Satellite. Ridgway paid cash for his food and gas on this trip and was careful not to leave any record linking him to Oregon. Based on Ridgway's statements and financial records, investigators determined that he most likely went to Oregon the first week of April 1984. In 2003, his son recalled taking a last-minute trip with his father to Oregon in the Satellite.

In June 2003, Ridgway led detectives to the site in Tukwila where he killed Denise Bush and left her body. According to a detective familiar with the crime scene, Ridgway led the task force right to the spot where Denise's remains were found. Ridgway did this despite changes to the area since 1982.

Shirley Sherrill

Eighteen-year-old Shirley Sherrill began working as a prostitute in Portland and Seattle in the summer of 1982, just a few months before she disappeared. Around this time, she also worked at the Goodwill store in Seattle on Dearborn Street. Shirley was last seen sometime between October 20 and 22, 1982.

Her pimp, who could not recall the precise date, reported that he last saw Shirley when he dropped her off in Seattle's International District in the morning. A fellow prostitute reported that she last saw Shirley at approximately four P.M. talking to two white men in a black pickup truck with a canopy. The pickup was "big, possibly a Ford" circa 1977 or 1978. The other prostitute left on a date and when she returned, Shirley was gone. In June 1985, construction crews found most of Shirley's remains, including her skull, along with Denise Bush's in Tigard, Oregon.

In 2003, Ridgway admitted killing Shirley. He claimed he could not remember any details about killing her other than transporting her remains to Oregon. Ridgway initially claimed that he had left Shirley at a site in King County and later returned and quickly picked up her skull and a few bones to take to Oregon. In 2003, the task force searched the site and did not find any remains. Most of Shirley's bones were found in Oregon, not simply the "few" that Ridgway initially claimed he picked up. When confronted with this, Ridgway equivocated on whether he just took Shirley's bones to Oregon or whether, after killing her, he transported her entire body there.

The North Airport Victims

In the 1980s, the task force discovered another dump site used by the Green River Killer: an area directly north of the Sea-Tac Airport. Three victims were found there: Shawnda Summers, Cheryl Wims, and an unidentified Caucasian female, designated Jane Doe "B10." Two of the women were found 200 yards apart and the third was a half-mile away. In the early 1980s, the road near where the women were found was largely undeveloped, aside from a few vacant lots, baseball fields and a tow yard.

Shawnda and Cheryl both worked as prostitutes and disappeared within eight months of each other. The background and circumstances surrounding the disappearance of the unidentified woman are, of course, unknown. The remains of all three were found unclothed. The cause of their deaths was unspecified homicidal violence.

In 2003, Ridgway admitted killing the three women. He referred to the North Airport site as one of his "clusters"—an area in which he grouped multiple victims—so he would not forget where he placed them. He was familiar with the area. A former girlfriend said that she and Ridgway had sex near the site and police had contacted him dating a prostitute nearby. He also stated that he took advantage of the frequent flights overhead, and acknowledged that

"I used that noise for advantage for one thing, you know, cut down any, ah, noise in case she screamed."

The North Airport site has undergone significant development since the early 1980s. A Boeing Company warehouse is now located where the police found Shawnda's remains. The water tower is still there, and the baseball fields where Cheryl and Jane Doe "B10" were found still exist. A fourth baseball diamond has been added. The vacant lots are all gone and much of the surrounding area has been either paved or developed.

Shawnda Summers

Seventeen-year-old Shawnda Summers was last seen alive sometime during the first week of October 1982. She was known to work as a prostitute along Pacific Highway South. There were no witnesses to her disappearance. Shawnda's stepfather filed a missing-persons report just weeks after she disappeared. Her mother traveled from California to search for her. They never saw her again.

At the time of Shawnda's disappearance, Ridgway was working at the Kenworth plant and had killed another woman he picked up on Pacific Highway South, Denise Bush.

On August 11, 1983, Shawnda's remains were found near the northwest corner of South 146th Street and 24th Avenue South. She had been placed in a shallow grave underneath an apple tree. Across the street and to the south of the dump site was a large, circular water tower. A vacant lot, where homes were frequently placed on blocks before they were moved elsewhere, was located to the south, between her body and South 146th Street.

In 2003, Ridgway admitted murdering Shawnda and placing her body by a water tower near Sea-Tac airport. Though he recalled that she was black, he was unable to recognize her photograph. Ridgway said that he took Shawnda to the North Airport site, had sex with her, and then choked her with his arm. While killing her, he wrapped his legs around her to keep her from moving. He then took off her clothes and jewelry and left. Ridgway could not recall whether he covered Shawnda's body. He believed he killed her at night and remembered that there was a house on blocks in a vacant lot near where he killed her, approximately four to five feet up off the ground.

In June 2003, Ridgway led task force detectives to the location where he killed Shawnda and left her body. According to a detective familiar with the crime scene and present with Ridgway during the visit to the North Airport site, Ridgway pointed out and described the specific area in which Shawnda's body was found.

Jane Doe "B10"

On March 21, 1984, a dog belonging to the Highline Baseball Field caretaker brought home a human femur. The caretaker called police, and a search began of a swampy, wooded area behind center field at the westernmost baseball diamond, just west of the intersection of 16th Avenue South and South 146th Street. This was a half-mile from where Ridgway killed Shawnda Summers and dumped her body in October 1982.

Over the next few days, police recovered the skeletal remains of Jane Doe "B10." As searching began on the second day, a bloodhound found the remains of yet a third victim, Cheryl Wims, 200 yards to the north of the crime scene. Repeated attempts by investigators to identify Jane Doe "B10" have been unsuccessful to this day. A forensic anthropologist concluded that the remains were those of a left-handed Caucasian female who stood about 5 feet 2 inches to 5 feet 7 inches and had a healed fracture in her skull. She was about 15 years old.

On the first day of interviews with task force detectives, Ridgway admitted killing a woman near the baseball fields off Des Moines Way. He thought she was Caucasian, in her early twenties, and had brown hair. He thought he picked her up in the Riverton (Tukwila) area. He said he killed her during the day and wanted to make certain she was dead, because he had attempted to kill another woman nearby, which person is still unidentified, but she had escaped.

Over the course of interviews, Ridgway made contradictory statements about whether he returned to have sex with the unidentified woman's corpse. Police took Ridgway to the North Airport site in June 2003. After some initial confusion, he pointed to the area where Jane Doe "B10" was found.

Cheryl Wims

Approximately seven months after Ridgway killed Shawnda Summers, on May 23, 1983, Cheryl Wims disappeared from the streets of central Seattle near Judkins Playground. According to her friends, she was involved with prostitution. She would also frequently hitchhike and was not particularly careful about the people from whom she accepted rides. Cheryl Wims was murdered on her eighteenth birthday.

Ridgway was on strike from Kenworth during May 1983 and was very active in his quest for victims. He killed a number of other women during that month, including Carol Christensen, Carrie Rois, Martina Authorlee, and Yvonne Antosh.

On March 22, 1984, police discovered Cheryl's remains a few hundred feet from Jane Doe "B10" and a half-mile from Shawnda Summers.

In 2003, Ridgway first claimed that he dumped only one victim near the baseball fields near Des Moines Way. This was Jane Doe "B10." After a task force detective informed Ridgway that there was a second body found at the ball fields, he admitted that he did not keep track of the number of victims he killed there.

Detectives took him to the dump site. Ridgway said the visit jogged his memory and admitted he had killed and left another woman near the baseball fields. Ridgway later recalled walking with a prostitute on the blacktop road just north of the ball field, stopping at a spot off the road, and killing her there. Aerial photos of the crime scene from March 1984 show a paved road slightly north of the baseball field running east to west. Cheryl was found underneath a large spruce tree just off this road. When shown these photos, Ridgway correctly identified where Cheryl's body had been found.

Ridgway said the woman he killed and left there was white even though Cheryl was a light-skinned African American, but he was unable to remember anything specific about her. As with virtually all the victims, Ridgway claimed not to recognize Cheryl's photograph. He explained that, after killing 60 women, he could not describe her. He had a better memory for garbage that he noticed strewn along the road while walking with his victim than for the woman he'd killed.

In the fall of 2003, Microtrace reported that paint fragments recovered with Cheryl's remains are indistinguishable, even after multiple analyses, from paint recovered with the remains of Delores Williams and Tina Thompson, who disappeared in July 1983 and was found at Highway 18.

Colleen Brockman

On December 24, 1982, 15-year-old Colleen Brockman, a frequent runaway involved in prostitution, made plans to meet an acquaintance near the Greyhound bus depot in downtown Seattle. Colleen and her friend had checked into a motel in downtown Seattle the night before. They had last spoken to each other around nine A.M. on Christmas Eve and had planned to meet around noon. She never showed.

A year and a half later, on May 26, 1984, three youths found Colleen's remains in north Pierce County about 10 yards north from Jovita Boulevard in thick undergrowth. The remains were between the boulevard and a creek that paralleled the road. Also near Colleen's body was a ditch that carried water from a culvert that passed underneath Jovita Boulevard. A piece of broken concrete culvert, approximately 24 inches in diameter and three feet long, was nearby. The King County Medical Examiner confirmed Colleen's identity through dental records. Her braces were still on her teeth.

In 2003, Ridgway admitted he killed a 16-year-old girl in Seattle around Christmas and dumped her body near Jovita Boulevard. He incorrectly identified the year, saying he believed he killed her in 1983 when it was actually Christmas Eve, 1982. Ridgway recalled that Colleen was white, and that she had about $20 on her. Detectives showed Ridgway a photo of Colleen, and he said he remembered the face and was 80 to 90 percent certain that it was the girl whom he killed and dumped near Jovita Boulevard. He said he could not recall whether she wore braces.

Ridgway said he picked up Colleen in downtown Seattle, north of Chinatown, and killed her in the back of his truck. He remembered that as he strangled her, she begged for her life. He told her, "Don't fight. I'm not gonna . . . I'll let you go." Then he put his foot into her neck and finished killing her.

Ridgway said he drove to Jovita Boulevard, parked, and pulled the body 20 feet off the road. He recalled the culvert passing under Jovita Boulevard and described it as 24-inch "tunnel."

In June 2003, Ridgway led detectives to the Jovita Boulevard site. According to detectives accompanying him on this trip, Ridgway was able to direct them to within 150 feet of where Colleen's remains were found.

The Mountainview Cemetery Victims

Kimi-Kai Pitsor

On December 14, 1983, a man walking along Mountainview Drive made a frightening find: a human skull lying along the shoulder of the road. Beneath the skull was a pile of leaves, yet none covered the top, suggesting that the skull had only recently come to be in that location. The man called police. An extensive investigation followed resulting in the identification of the victim as Kimi-Kai Pitsor.

Eight months earlier, in April 1983, 16-year-old Kimi-Kai disappeared. She was last known to have been in the downtown Seattle area with her boyfriend. According to the boyfriend's statement to police, he and Kimi-Kai had a disagreement over their relationship, and she ran off and jumped into an older green Ford pickup truck. The boyfriend hinted that Kimi-Kai was intending to engage in prostitution with the driver of the truck. He waited in the area for her to return but she was never seen again.

After her skull was found, task force detectives were dispatched to the scene, determined that the skull was found some two feet inside the King County line, and assumed responsibility for the case. By that time—December 1983—the local law enforcement agencies were fully aware that a serial killer was working in the area, targeting prostitutes and leaving their bodies in remote outdoor areas. Despite a further search of the area, no additional bones were found.

Two years later, in December 1985, the rest of Kimi-Kai's remains were discovered, along with the remains of two other victims, in a dump site down a steep slope across from Mountainview Cemetery. Kimi-Kai's case was added to a growing number of victims of the Green River Killer.

Her case was different, however, because there was a potential witness. Kimi-Kai's boyfriend might have seen the killer, and provided detectives with a description of the man last seen with her. In 1987, when task force detectives began focusing on Ridgway as a

suspect, the boyfriend was shown a photographic montage that
included Ridgway's photograph. With some uncertainty, the boyfriend identified Ridgway as the man driving the pickup truck.
However, he qualified his identification: he was not "one thousand
percent" sure. Moreover, none of Ridgway's trucks matched the
description of the truck seen by the boyfriend.

In June 2003, Ridgway admitted killing Kimi-Kai. He said that
he had picked her up in his girlfriend's truck. Ridgway's girlfriend
at the time owned a light green 1970s Ford pickup truck with a silver canopy. Ridgway had a fairly clear memory of the events surrounding the murder of Kimi-Kai. On the night he killed her,
Ridgway said, he was frustrated because he had a strong desire to
kill a woman and "couldn't find one." When he spotted Kimi-Kai,
he also saw her boyfriend. Ridgway said he was so desperate for a
kill that he broke his cardinal rule: never pick up a victim in the
presence of a witness. Ridgway said he drove around the corner,
and, as he hoped, Kimi-Kai came to his truck. He said she agreed
to date him at his house in south Seattle after he promised her he
would drive her back downtown after the date. This, of course, was
a hollow promise.

> There's no way I'm going to waste my time having sex
> with her, pay her $40, or $30 or $60 or whatever. And then
> drive her all the way back into Seattle. That's something I
> wouldn't do. I would get her there and kill her. I'm not
> going to waste my money driving all the way back.

True to his priorities, Ridgway said he had sex with Kimi-Kai,
killer her, put her body in the truck, drove to Mountainview Cemetery, and dumped her body.

Ridgway provided conflicting explanations for the discovery of
Kimi-Kai's skull by the side of the road in December 1983. First,
Ridgway suggested that he picked up her skull intending to take it
to Oregon with the remains of Denise Bush and Shirley Sherrill.
While retrieving Kimi-Kai's skull, Ridgway said he dropped it and
could not find it in the dark. However, in later interviews, Ridgway
acknowledged that he had not intended to take the skull to Oregon,
but that he had moved it simply to "throw off" the police. After retrieving the skull, he said, he accidentally dropped it while making

his way back up the steep hillside. When he tried to locate the skull, his flashlight batteries died. Although he felt around on the ground, he could not find the skull. Eventually, Ridgway said, he gave up the effort and left.

Questioned further about his motives for moving the skull, Ridgway explained that if the skull was found in a place like someone's yard, the task force would waste time and manpower searching the area for the remaining missing bones. "[T]hey'll waste all kind of man hours thinking the rest of the body's in there."

Jane Doe "B16" and Jane Doe "B17"

On December 30, 1985, two years after Kimi-Kai's skull was found, task force detectives returned to Mountainview Drive, where a car had gone off the road and down a steep embankment several hundred yards from the place where Kimi-Kai's skull had been found. Two men employed at the cemetery went down to look at the wrecked car and discovered what appeared to be human bones. When the task force detectives arrived, they immediately realized that this was another dump site. The bones found by the cemetery workers were obviously not those of Kimi-Kai Pitsor because they found another skull, indicating that they had located the remains of another person.

For the next week, detectives scoured the hillside in search of further evidence. When the search was over, they had found a total of three sets of skeletal remains. One of the remains proved by radiographic examination to be the rest of Kimi-Kai Pitsor. The other two bodies, despite extensive efforts, remain unidentified. They have been designated Jane Doe "B16" and Jane Doe "B17."

Although these skeletal remains have not been identified, both were young women. A forensic anthropologist's examination revealed that Jane Doe "B16" was an African American woman between the age of 20 and 25. She was approximately 5 foot 1 inch to 5 foot 4 inches tall. Her body had been placed along a large fallen log.

Some 40 to 50 feet uphill east from Jane Doe "B16" were the remains of Jane Doe "B17." She was lying at the foot of a very large rotten stump on the peak of a ridge. The forensic anthropologist concluded that she was a Caucasian, between 5 foot 4 inches and 5 foot 8 inches tall. She was between 14 and 17 years old.

Two hundred and fifty yards to the west of these two young women, detectives found the remains of Kimi-Kai Pitsor. She was located about 100 yards from Mountainview Drive and approximately 100 yards from where her skull was found.

Over the course of the next 15 years, numerous attempts were made to identify the two young women found along Mountainview Drive. Leads relating to Kimi-Kai's disappearance were likewise investigated but never led any further than the tentative identification of defendant Ridgway. The cases remained open, but "cold."

In 2003, Ridgway admitted murdering Kimi-Kai Pitsor and dumping her at the Mountainview site. When he was questioned about the other two unidentified remains, he claimed that he could not recall any specifics about them other than to say that he thought he killed one of the women before Kimi-Kai and one after her. Ridgway said that he staggered their bodies along the hillside, which was consistent with the way the remains were found.

Ridgway was asked why and how he chose the Mountainview site. He said that he drove up the road and thought, "There's a fantastic bank and trees. Just an excellent place to dump a woman and I can see ahead when I drop her off." According to his ex-wife, Ridgway knew the road well. During their marriage the couple lived in the Twin Lakes area, and Ridgway drove past the cemetery on his way to work at the Kenworth plant.

Investigators asked Ridgway to direct them to the location where he placed the bodies at Mountainview. Ridgway did so and identified the precise location where investigators had found the three sets of remains. Ridgway correctly recalled that he placed two of the bodies closer together and a third some distance away.

Marie Malvar

In April 1983, 18-year-old Marie Malvar lived in Des Moines, King County. On April 30, 1983, she went out to Pacific Highway South to work as a prostitute. Marie's boyfriend saw her get into a dark-colored pickup truck, occupied by a single adult male driver, at a bus stop near a 7-Eleven at South 216th and Pacific Highway South. After Marie got into the truck, the boyfriend got in his car and followed the truck as it traveled northbound on Pacific Highway South. The truck pulled over into a motel parking lot, turned around, and headed southbound on Pacific Highway South. The truck then turned left going eastbound onto South 216th. The boyfriend lost track of the truck at that intersection. Marie was never seen again.

The intersection at South 216th and Pacific Highway South where her boyfriend last saw Marie is exactly where, just a few weeks earlier, on April 8, Gail Mathews's boyfriend saw her for the last time. Exactly like Marie, Gail was in a pickup truck heading eastbound on South 216th.

At the time, Ridgway lived one block south of South 216th, off of Military Road. Military Road is east of Pacific Highway South. Ridgway lived a little more than half a mile from the intersection where Gail and Marie were last seen, and South 216th is the most direct route to Ridgway's house from that section of Pacific Highway South.

Three days later, on May 3, 1983, Marie's boyfriend reported to the Des Moines Police Department that she was missing. Initially, he lied to police, reporting that he had last seen Marie at their residence and that she was on her way to a phone booth on Pacific Highway South. The next day, on May 4, 1983, the boyfriend admitted that he knew Marie was working as a prostitute and that he last saw her being picked up by a trick. He described the trick as a 42-year-old Mexican or Indian male driving a black pickup truck. Later that day, the boyfriend returned to the police station and reported that he had searched the neighborhoods around South 216th and Pacific Highway South and thought he had found the truck that Marie had entered. The truck was Ridgway's maroon 1975 Dodge pickup. When Marie's boyfriend saw the truck, it was parked outside Ridgway's house at 21859 32nd Place South.

Two Des Moines detectives went to Ridgway's residence that day, noticed Ridgway's Dodge pickup in the driveway, and contacted him. He admitted that he had been arrested for picking up prostitutes in the past, but denied picking up Marie. He also claimed that he had been unemployed for the last year (he was actually on strike from Kenworth).

Several weeks later, on May 27, 1983, an airport worker discovered Marie's driver's license at the Sea-Tac Airport. In the years following Marie's disappearance, as in the cases of many of Ridgway's other victims, there were many reported sightings of her. Tips came in that Marie had moved to Hawaii and dyed her hair blonde or that she was working in Hollywood. In February 1985, her family reported that they had heard the rumors that she was in Hollywood, Long Beach, or Tacoma and expressed their belief that she was still alive. In 1986, one tipster claimed to have been with one of Marie's brothers when Marie had called from California.

Despite investigation, none of these tips were ever confirmed. Marie's boyfriend later provided several statements concerning Marie's last day, and even underwent hypnosis by a psychiatrist retained by the task force in an effort to recall additional details about the man in the truck. None of the later descriptions or details provided any further connection to Ridgway.

In 2003, Ridgway admitted killing Marie. He said he picked her up, drove her to his house, and killed her there. Ridgway said that Marie fought him, scratching him badly on his inner left arm. Ridgway recalled that he was worried about the scratches when the Des Moines detectives came to his house on May 4, 1983. He said he stood against the fence in his yard to conceal them from the police. Ridgway later attempted to disguise the scratches by burning his arm with battery acid; those scars are still visible today. Ridgway had first claimed that he received the scar from some pimps, but quickly retracted this lie. Ridgway admitted taking Marie's driver's license and putting it on the floor in the airport. He said he did so to make it look like she left the state.

Ridgway claimed he dumped Marie's body on the same day he killed her. He had planned to place her body near Mountainview Cemetery and was on his way there when he saw an area that looked like a good place to dump a body. He left Marie's body in a wooded ravine near 65th Avenue South in Auburn. Ridgway said he parked his truck, pulled Marie's body out, re-parked the truck a short distance away, and pulled her body 20 to 30 feet into the ravine.

After the Des Moines detectives' visit to his house on May 4, 1983, Ridgway said, he went back to the site to bury Marie's body. He spent about three hours unsuccessfully looking for her. He then planted leaflets from airport motels around the area, so that, Ridgway explained, if the body was found, the task force might think that someone like a traveling salesman was involved in the murder.

Ridgway never again returned to the site because soon thereafter he saw a co-worker driving in that area and learned that the co-worker resided nearby. He insisted that he did not put any more bodies in this area because he knew, after the Des Moines detectives' visit, that he was linked, however tenuously, to Marie Malvar's disappearance.

Task force detectives spent several days searching the area identified by Ridgway. On September 28 and 29, 2003, they recovered more than 60 human bones, including the skull and mandible. A ligature was found with the bones. Dental records confirmed the remains were those of Marie Malvar. The ligature appeared to be a woman's pantyhose; it was found near several neck vertebrae.

The Highway 410 Victims

In the early 1980s, the task force discovered the bodies of three women along a short, rural stretch of Highway 410. Investigators soon realized that they had discovered another dump site. Several years later, after the Green River Killer had purportedly stopped killing, the bodies of more women were found along the same stretch of roadway. Investigators now realize Ridgway did not stop in 1984, and he did not stop using Highway 410 as his dumping ground. In fact, he continued to use Highway 410 after that dump site was discovered. Ridgway has admitted killing two women, never attributed to the Green River Killer, one in 1987 and one in 1990, and placing their bodies along Highway 410.

In August 2003, Ridgway led the task force to an area along Highway 410 where they recovered the remains of an original Green River "missing" victim, Pammy Avent. She had disappeared in 1983.

Highway 410 generally runs in an east/west direction between the cities of Tacoma and Yakima, Washington. A 16-mile stretch of the highway runs through King County between the towns of Enumclaw and Greenwater, beginning at milepost 26, just east of the Enumclaw city limits, and ending at milepost 42, just west of Greenwater. The terrain along this stretch of highway is hilly and heavily wooded, alternating between thick underbrush and large evergreen and deciduous forests. A well-developed gravel road known as the Weyerhaeuser Mainline runs just south and parallel to this entire 16-mile stretch of 410. The White River runs south and parallel to the Weyerhaeuser Mainline and serves as the border between King and Pierce Counties up to the town of Greenwater.

Dozens of gravel and dirt logging roads spur off of the highway and the Weyerhaeuser Mainline.

Ridgway was extremely familiar with this 16-mile stretch of Highway 410. During interviews with the task force in 1987, Ridgway's second wife told detectives that Ridgway regularly traveled Highway 410 between Enumclaw and Greenwater. She and Ridgway camped in the Greenwater area many times. Ridgway later confirmed his familiarity with Highway 410. He told detectives that he could remember freely traveling the forest access roads, roads that were later blocked when he returned to the sites. Ridgway also stated that he and his third wife camped in the Greenwater area throughout the 1980s and 1990s.

In 2003, before the task force interviewed him, Ridgway prepared several documents that purported to detail the victims he left along Highway 410. Ridgway listed eight victims at different locations on this map. All but one of these victims was placed along the southern edge of Highway 410, between the highway and the Weyerhaeuser Mainline.

Once the task force began interviewing Ridgway, he provided additional details about killing and dumping as many as 11 victims along Highway 410. He was taken on many trips to point out the actual dump sites of the victims that had already been found and to locate missing remains. To date, the remains of six women murdered by Gary Ridgway have been recovered from Highway 410: Martina Authorlee, Debbie Abernathy, Mary Bello, Pammy Advent, Robert Hayes, and Marta Reeves.

Martina Authorlee

Eighteen-year-old Martina Authorlee, who had run away from home when she was 15 into a life of prostitution and who had a troubled childhood that included time in foster homes and several encounters with law enforcement, disappeared on the night of Sunday, May 22, 1983. Earlier that month, police arrested Martina for prostitution in downtown Seattle. After her arrest, Martina moved into the Moonrise Motel, on Pacific Highway South, in Tukwila. Like victims Terry Milligan and Denise Bush, Martina was living at the Moonrise at the time of her death.

On May 22, 1983, Martina and a fellow prostitute left the Moonrise Motel to work Pacific Highway South. After working the highway separately for a period of time, her companion last spoke with Martina in front of the "My Place" Tavern sometime between ten P.M. and one A.M. Martina told her companion that a date was picking her up in 20 minutes. The woman left Martina standing in front of the tavern. Martina was never seen again.

Ridgway did not work on the day of Martina's disappearance. According to financial records, he was in south King County, selling items at a swap meet.

On November 14, 1984, two elk hunters discovered Martina's remains just off Highway 410, near milepost 36 on the southern side of the highway just before a curve, near a fallen cedar log.

In 2003, Ridgway admitted killing Martina. Although he claimed that he could not identify her or recall any details of her murder, Ridgway accurately described her physical appearance. He remembered that she was African American, 5 foot 7 inches or 5 foot 8 inches and full-figured. He claimed that he picked her up one night between 1982 and 1984, and that he killed her in his house.

Ridgway correctly described the area where Martina was found, having drawn several maps that purported to depict where he dumped victims along Highway 410. On the maps, he described Martina as a "Black Lady" buried next to a log. He wrote that he placed her body at the eastern end of the stretch of highway, very close to a large southeasterly curve in the roadway. His map correctly showed the road, the location of the log in relation to the road, and the correct position of the log and Martina's body. Ridgway also said that he pulled Martina's body 60 to 100 feet off of the roadway, over a fallen redwood log that was approximately three feet in diameter. His description not only matched the geographic location of Martina's remains, he even knew the diameter of the log near her body.

Debbie May Abernathy

Twenty-six-year-old Debbie May Abernathy moved to Seattle from Texas with her boyfriend and their young son just four weeks prior to her disappearance. During that period of time, Debbie worked as a prostitute, mainly at the corner of 8th and Pike in downtown Seattle. On September 5, 1983, at approximately one P.M., Debbie left her residence near Rainier Avenue, south of Seattle, to work the downtown area as a prostitute. Her longtime boyfriend never saw her again. On the day of Debbie's disappearance, Ridgway was off work due to the Labor Day holiday. He gassed up his truck and withdrew cash from an ATM machine that day.

On March 31, 1984, an elk hunter discovered Debbie's skeletal remains approximately 0.2 miles east of milepost 37 on Highway 410, next to the Weyerhaeuser Mainline, near the White River.

During interviews in 2003, Ridgway admitted killing Debbie. Although Ridgway claimed that he could not identify her, he gave the task force specific details of her dump site. Ridgway told the task force that he carried a victim into the woods from Highway 410 and placed her very close to the Weyerhaeuser Mainline, so close that he could see it. He correctly recalled that Debbie was one of the first women dumped along 410. He said he hoped placing her next to the Weyerhaeuser Mainline would confuse the police into thinking she was a Weyerhaeuser employee.

Although Ridgway struggled to identify the exact location of the dump site when taken to Highway 410, he accurately described a gated entrance nearby that led to the location on Weyerhaeuser Mainline where Debbie was found. He also correctly recalled the terrain between the two roadways. He described the difficulty he had taking her body into the woods. Ridgway admitted that he threw the driver's license of one of his victims out of his truck window while traveling on Highway 18. Debbie's Texas driver's license was found along Highway 18 in 1983.

As with many of his victims, Ridgway claimed to remember little if anything about killing Debbie. When reminded that her disappearance fell on his son's eighth birthday, Ridgway told the task force that the date had no significance to him. Ridgway admitted that the times and circumstances of his killings were simply motivated by, as he described it, "opportunity."

Mary Sue Bello

Approximately one month after Ridgway killed Debbie Abernathy, he killed Mary Bello and placed her body along that same stretch of Highway 410.

Twenty-five-year-old Mary Bello had lived a troubled life, with an extensive history of prostitution and drug use. She was known to work as a prostitute along Pacific Highway South. In fact, she had contacted the task force on a number of occasions with information on possible Green River suspects. Thus it was ironic that she never recognized Ridgway as the actual killer until it was too late.

On October 11, 1983, at approximately five P.M., Mary left downtown Seattle to work as a prostitute. She was never heard from again. Ridgway was in south King County on the day of Mary's disappearance. On October 11, Ridgway worked until 6:35 P.M. On the day of Mary's disappearance, Ridgway filled up his truck at the Texaco Gas Station at South 172nd and Pacific Highway South, and withdrew $40 from a cash machine in Sea-Tac at 7:51 P.M.

A year later, on October 12, 1984, a mushroom picker discovered Mary's skeletal remains approximately 200 feet west of milepost 34 just off Highway 410. The area in which the remains were found was heavily wooded, with large evergreen trees and sparse surface vegetation. The only distinguishing landmark in the area was the milepost.

During interviews, Ridgway claimed that he could not identify Mary. However, he did provide an accurate description of where he left her body. After some initial confusion about the precise milepost, Ridgway told detectives that milepost 34 brought back memories. He described parking his truck in front of a milepost and pulling a victim into the woods without having to drag the body over a guardrail. He said he then got back into his truck, drove down the road, made a U-turn, and parked the truck on the opposite side of the road, facing west. Then, he said, he returned to the body and dragged it further into the woods. Ridgway's description matched the dump site where Mary's body was found.

When taken to the dump site, Ridgway first struggled to identify it. After he was informed that the area had recently been clear-cut, Ridgway suggested that he killed a woman in the early 1980s and pulled her body into the woods down the hill in this location. After reviewing historical photographs depicting the dump site, Ridgway confirmed this statement, telling detectives that after he dumped the woman's body, he threw her clothes out of his truck window, "as soon as he could." In the 1980s, the task force recovered a mixed print sundress with small straps, located approximately three miles west of Mary's dump site.

Mary's grandfather later told detectives that the dress was similar to the one Mary had worn on the day of her disappearance.

Pammy Avent

Approximately two weeks after killing Mary Bello and placing her body on Highway 410, Ridgway killed 16-year-old Pammy Avent, and left her body along the same stretch of road. Avent's remains were not discovered until August 2003, when Ridgway directed task force detectives to them.

Pammy Avent worked as a prostitute in the Rainier Valley area of Seattle. On October 26, 1983, at 7:30 P.M., she left her mother's Rainier Valley home in Seattle to work as a prostitute and was never seen again. Pammy's mother reported her missing four days later.

For several years after her disappearance, the task force received many tips suggesting that Pammy had run away from home and was living in Hollywood, that she had run away to Denver and given birth to a baby girl, and that she was working as a prostitute out of a local motel. The task force investigated the tips, but, despite their efforts, could not locate Pammy. For the ensuing 21 years her fate remained a mystery.

In 2003, task force detectives took Ridgway to Highway 410 in an effort to identify dump sites of undiscovered victims. On one trip, Ridgway asked to stop at a pullout on the south side of Highway 410 across the street from the Corliss Gravel Pit, just east of milepost 26. Ridgway told the task force that he'd placed a body across the street from the gravel pit in a gully. Six days later, the task force found Pammy Avent's remains in the location identified by Ridgway.

Her body had been placed up against a fallen cedar log that lay parallel to the highway, approximately 50 feet from the edge of the dirt road. The remains were largely intact, due to their position next to the log. A significant amount of the remains were found under three to six inches of dirt, bark, and other debris.

As with most of his victims, Ridgway claimed not to recognize Pammy's photograph. In fact, his description of the woman he thought he placed in this location was not Pammy, but rather a woman with a deformed leg. Pammy did not have a deformed leg.

No additional victims were found in the area.

Roberta Hayes

Twenty-one-year-old Roberta Hayes worked as a prostitute and traveled back and forth between Portland and Seattle on a fairly regularly basis. She disappeared sometime in early 1987. The last known sighting of her was on February 7, 1987, when she was released from the custody of the Portland, Oregon, Police Department after an arrest for prostitution. It was believed that she was headed back to Seattle.

On September 11, 1991, more than four years after she was last seen, a Washington State Parks employee discovered Roberta's skeletal remains at the end of a dead-end dirt road located north of Highway 410 between mileposts 36 and 37. The remains were to the east of the road, near piles of debris. A Weyerhaeuser security official later told detectives that the road had been blocked with boulders sometime between September 1986 and April 1987. Roberta Hayes is the only victim found on the north side of Highway 410.

During interviews in 2003, Ridgway provided a detailed description of Roberta's dump site. Ridgway described a white woman that he killed and placed on the north side of Highway 410. He repeatedly stated that he only placed one victim on the northern side of 410 and accurately described Roberta as having blond/brown hair, being 5 foot 7 inches and skinny. Ridgway's description of the dump site matched the location where Roberta's remains were found. He accurately described the end of a dirt road just past a large curve to the east in the highway: a dead end with both man-made and natural debris. He correctly recalled the slope of the terrain and the curvature of the road. He also knew that Roberta's dump site was just east and across the highway from the dump site of Martina Authorlee.

When taken to Highway 410, Ridgway identified the general vicinity of the roadway, but initially struggled to identify the precise road, which had changed significantly since the murder. But once the changes were described to Ridgway, he correctly identified the road upon which he dumped Roberta's body. Ridgway was later shown unmarked photos of the roadway, which he immediately identified as Roberta's dump site. Roberta was not originally listed as a Green River victim.

Marta Reeves

In the early spring of 1990, 36-year-old Marta Reeves lived apart from her estranged husband and four children. She had moved out in May 1989 due to her cocaine addiction and began prostituting herself. She spent most of her time in the Central District of Seattle and had twice been arrested for prostitution. Marta's husband last heard from her on the evening of either March 5 or 6, 1990, when she called him looking for money. When her request was rejected, she told him that she would have to work all night. He never heard from her again.

A month later, Marta's husband received an envelope in the mail from the U.S. Postal Service containing her driver's license. Her husband showed the license to numerous people while looking for his wife, and reported her missing on April 13, 1990. The driver's license was later tested for fingerprints with negative results, in part because it had been handled by so many people.

On September 20, 1990, a couple of mushroom pickers found Marta's skeletal remains approximately 600 feet east of milepost 33 on Highway 410. The remains were halfway down a looping dirt road that spurred off of the southern side of the highway. The police later recovered several pieces of clothing, which were examined for physical evidence with negative results. The remains were identified as Marta's in January 1991.

Ridgway's drew a looped road on the south side of Highway 410 and indicated he'd left a body there. He accurately described the location of Marta's body some 20 to 30 feet into the woods. During the course of task force interviews, Ridgway provided more detailed descriptions of Marta's dump site, describing the road dropping down below Highway 410 with heavy foliage on either side. He remembered the foliage rubbing up against the side of his truck as he drove down the road. He told the detectives that he drove about halfway down the road and then pulled the body into the woods about 30 feet.

When Ridgway was shown unmarked photos of the dump site as it appeared in 1990, he immediately identified it as the "lower loop road" off of Highway 410. Photographs confirmed Ridgway's descriptions of the scene, including the fact that the loop road was so narrow that foliage struck the sides of vehicles traveling upon it.

When taken to Marta's dump site on Highway 410, Ridgway was unable to locate the roadway, but he did point out the correct stretch of highway where the original road, now blocked off and completely overgrown, had been.

Ridgway claimed that he could not recall any details about Marta or her murder. He first told detectives that the victim was black and that he killed her in the early 1980s. When told that Marta went missing in 1990 and that she was white, not black, Ridgway acknowledged, "I killed the one on the loop road. And I just, you know, I killed so many of them, so I had to kind of guess if she was white or black." He later added, "I get screwed up on time frames." Finally, Ridgway admitted placing a woman's driver's license in a mailbox on one or two occasions. When asked to explain why he did this, Ridgway could only respond, "I don't know, get back at the family or somethin', I don't know."

Marta was not initially listed as an "official" Green River victim, but was added to the list of Ridgway's victims after he confessed to the crime.

Yvonne Antosh

Nineteen-year-old Yvonne "Shelly" Antosh was last seen on May 31, 1983, at about eleven P.M., when she left the Ben Carol Motel on Pacific Highway South. She and a childhood friend had come to Seattle from Vancouver, British Columbia, and the two were staying together. Shelly had been involved in prostitution for just a few weeks when she crossed Ridgway's path. The night Shelly disappeared, Ridgway made a cash withdrawal for $20 on Pacific Highway South at 11:44 P.M. This was an especially active period for Ridgway, who was on strike for most of May 1983, and he devoted this time to what he called his "career." During that month, he killed Shelly, Carol Christensen, Carrie Rois, Martina Authorlee, and Cheryl Wims.

In October 1983, two boys discovered Shelly's remains about 25 to 30 yards downhill from the Auburn–Black Diamond Road, south of Big Soos Creek, in King County. She had been placed between two large alder trees. The area was heavily overgrown with swamp grass and other thick vegetation.

On the first day of interviews in 2003, Ridgway informed detectives that he had killed a woman and dumped her body along the

Auburn–Black Diamond Road. He believed the task force had found the body. Ridgway indicated there were two bodies on the Auburn–Black Diamond Road, one of which he had placed "down a hill." In 2003, police took Ridgway to the Auburn–Black Diamond Road area. According to detectives who were with him on this trip, Ridgway directed them to almost the exact location where Shelly's remains were found. Ridgway could not provide any specific details concerning Shelly. He recalled that she was "just a white woman . . . picked her up on Highway 99 . . . or uh, maybe uh, the Central District."

Ridgway also said he picked her up and killed her at night. He said he killed her in the bedroom of his house. Ridgway was vague on exactly how he killed her and vacillated between claiming that he killed her with his arm and that he used a ligature.

The Interstate 90 and Highway 18 Victims

Ridgway admitted that he dumped three victims, Tina Thompson, April Buttram, and Maureen Feeney, near the intersection of Interstate 90 and Highway 18. All three women worked as prostitutes and were killed within a span of approximately two months. In the 1980s, the task force recovered the remains of two of the women, Tina Thompson and Maureen Feeney. Their bodies were found across the street from each other. In 2003, based upon information provided by Ridgway, the police recovered remains of the third woman, April Buttram, who had been missing for twenty years.

Tina Thompson

Twenty-two-year-old Tina Thompson disappeared on or around Monday morning, July 25, 1983. She was staying at the Spruce Motel on Pacific Highway South and working as a prostitute. A fellow prostitute reported that their pimp had talked to Tina in the early hours of July 25, 1983, but was unsuccessful in reaching her again later that day. Tina was never reported missing to the police. Ridgway did not work Sunday, July 24, 1983, and arrived at work on July 25, 1983, at approximately 6:45 A.M.

On April 20, 1984, Tina's remains were discovered near the intersection of Highway 18 and Interstate 90. Her clothing was missing and her body was wrapped in sheets of plastic. She remained unidentified until June 1986.

During interviews with the task force in 1986, Ridgway's second wife reported that she and Ridgway had been to the area where Thompson's body was later recovered. She recalled Ridgway's stopping his vehicle and urinating there.

In 2003, Ridgway admitted killing Tina Thompson at night and leaving her body near Interstate 90 and Highway 18. He recalled killing her. He initially stated that he could not recognize her photo or remember exactly where he killed her.

Ridgway later recalled a victim who almost escaped him and suggested she was Tina. He said he was trying to strangle her in his bedroom, as was his practice, when she slipped away from him. He said he caught her just inside the front door, and killed her there. Ridgway recalled dumping a body at night at the location where Tina's remains were found.

In June 2003, Ridgway directed the police to the "Leisure Time" dump site where the remains of another victim, April Buttram, were subsequently discovered. While at that scene, Ridgway offered to lead the detectives to a nearby location where, he said, he'd dumped two other bodies. Ridgway accurately directed the police to the area where Tina's body had been discovered. He recalled correctly that he put her under some plastic that he found at the site.

Microtrace laboratory reported in Fall 2003 that paint fragments recovered with Tina's remains are indistinguishable, even after multiple analyses, from paint recovered with the remains of Cheryl Wims, whose body was found at the North Airport dump site, and Delores Williams, whose body was found at Star Lake.

April Buttram

In July 1983, 17-year-old April Buttram left her home in Spokane and headed to Seattle. She shortly became involved in prostitution. Approximately one month later, she became a victim of the Green River Killer. In late August 1983, she disappeared and was never seen again. A significant obstacle to the investigation of April's case, as it was with the cases of many other victims, was the inability to determine the exact date of her disappearance. She was arrested for prostitution on August 4, 1983, and released from juvenile detention on August 10, 1983. The police contacted her on Rainier Avenue South on August 18, 1983. Her pimp stated that he last saw her on Rainier Avenue South and believed that it was some time before September 1, 1983. He never reported her missing, claiming that he thought that she had run away. April's mother reported her missing in March 1984.

Though her body had not been found, due to the circumstances and timing of her disappearance, she was added to the list of Green River victims.

As with other "missing" victims, numerous tips trickled in to the task force claiming that April was still alive. In July 1984, after a news release that April had been added to the list of victims, several individuals claimed that she was working as a prostitute in Tacoma and California. All these tips were investigated. None were ever confirmed.

In 2003, Ridgway admitted killing April. He claimed he recognized her picture and thought he'd picked her up on Rainier Avenue. Ridgway was not completely certain where he placed April's body but suggested that he buried her under a fern near Lake Fenwick. However, he also stated that she might be the victim he placed at a site north of the intersection of Interstate 90 and Highway 18, referred to as the "Leisure Time" site because Leisure Time Resorts had a camp nearby. He also suggested that the woman he dumped at Leisure Time was someone other than April.

Ridgway said he recalled dumping a woman at the Leisure Time site after picking her up on Rainier Avenue. Ridgway claimed that he returned to the Leisure Time site in the spring of 1984, some eight months after dumping a body there. He said there were only a few bones left at the site, and he picked up the skull, which he transported along with bones from Denise Bush and Shirley Sherrill to Oregon on a weekend trip with his son in 1984. Ridgway reported that he left the skull near an exit off Interstate 5. He said he moved the bones because he thought they would be found and this discovery would confuse the task force. This skull has never been recovered.

Ridgway later joined Leisure Time Resorts specifically because he knew he had placed a body nearby. "I, um, talked my parents into buying a membership, uh, of the campground there because I could always go up and walk that road and, uh, knowing that there's a woman there," he told interviewers.

He said that he and his current wife would camp in the area several times a year and walk their dogs on the road near the dump site. His son also recalled family walks along that road.

In June 2003, Ridgway was taken to the Leisure Time site, and he identified an area where he was "one hundred percent" certain that he had left a body. He claimed that the area was "grown up" and that the trees had been "baby trees" at the time he dumped a body. Historical aerial photographs from the early 1980s confirm that the area had been clear-cut before Ridgway dumped the body in 1983.

In late August and early September 2003, task force detectives conducted an extensive search of the area identified by Ridgway and recovered two human bones. A mtDNA profile was developed from the bones and the results proved it to be April Buttram's.

Maureen Feeney

In August 1983, 19-year-old Maureen Feeney moved from Bellevue to an apartment in Seattle, and her lifestyle began to change dramatically. Maureen was working at a day-care facility, and around the time of her move, her co-workers had noticed a change in her attitude and behavior. While in Seattle, Maureen became involved with a new boyfriend. The boyfriend eventually admitted that Maureen became involved in prostitution though he denied knowing any details of her activities.

On September 26, 1983, two infractions were written to "Kris Ponds," a probable alias for Maureen. "Ponds" had the same physical description, birth date, telephone number, address, and employer as Maureen. "Ponds" had been cited in Seattle for jaywalking, a common citation written to suspected prostitutes. The next day, Maureen quit her job at the day-care center. The following day, on September 28, Maureen's boyfriend reported that she left her apartment sometime in the afternoon and never returned. Ridgway's work records reveal that he left work around 3:20 P.M. that day and returned to work the next day. Maureen's family learned of her disappearance from her boyfriend and, on September 30, 1983, reported her missing to the Seattle police. Her family went to considerable efforts to find her.

Nearly three years later, on May 2, 1986, an employee at the Echo Glen juvenile detention center was looking for an escapee when he came across some of Maureen's remains on the west side of Highway 18 at 105th, a short distance south of the intersection of Highway 18 and Interstate 90. A pull-out and utility shed were near the area. Tina Thompson's remains had been found two years earlier on the other side of Highway 18. The task force subsequently recovered Maureen's remains, which were spread out over some distance. Some bones were found near a barbed-wire fence.

During interviews with the task force in 2003, Ridgway admitted killing Maureen. He recalled that he picked her up in Seattle. He claimed that he killed her at night in the back of his truck. He recalled that Maureen was a white woman and had brown hair, and thought she was between 18 to 22 years old.

In June of 2003, while directing task force detectives to the as-yet undiscovered Leisure Time dump site, Ridgway suggested that he show detectives where he dumped two other bodies nearby. He pointed out the area where he left Tina Thompson's body and also said he had dumped a body across Highway 18 next to a fence and near the shed where Maureen was found. Ridgway recalled that he dropped her off around midnight, and, while he was there, a work crew came by and some lights came on. He also admitted that he had sex with the body after he placed her near the fence.

Tracy Winston

In September 1983, 19-year-old Tracy Winston was staying with her boyfriend at the 99 Motel on Aurora Avenue in the north end of Seattle. She had just finished serving a jail sentence for prostitution on September 12, 1983; later that day she called a man whom she had previously dated and asked him to meet her and give her money to pay her rent. The man drove to the 99 Motel and gave Tracy some money. After paying rent, Tracy asked for and received a ride to the Northgate Mall. The man dropped her off around six P.M. Although another acquaintance reports seeing Tracy three days later on September 15, 1983, it is believed that Tracy disappeared on the night of September 12. She never returned to the 99 Motel and her family had no further contact with her.

In March 1986, two park employees discovered human remains at the base of a large tree in Cottonwood Park in Kent, a relatively small piece of land along the banks of the Green River. The remains were approximately one-quarter mile from the Peck Bridge, where Wendy Coffield's body was found in July 1982. The remains essentially consisted of a human torso. Despite an extensive search, detectives were unable to find either the skull or any other portion of the skeleton. Without the skull or mandible, an identification of the remains could not be made. However, thirteen years later, in 1999, advances in DNA analysis made identification of these bones possible. The mtDNA profile of the bones revealed that they were the remains of Tracy Winston.

In June 2003, Ridgway admitted he killed the woman found at Cottonwood Park. Ridgway has little memory of killing Tracy. Despite his lack of specific memory, he has convincingly maintained that he was responsible for her death and included her on a list of his victims that he provided to investigators shortly after interviews began in June 2003. Ridgway recalled that he killed Tracy at night and that he dumped her body in or near the park. He previously visited the park multiple times and had sex with one of his wives and a girlfriend, not far from where he left Tracy. He explained why he chose the park as a dump site: "Like Cottonwood Park was a good place, along the river, and it was a while after the other ones were found, so that's why I chose it."

Cottonwood Park is within a quarter-mile of where Ridgway dumped the bodies of six other women he murdered: the five women left in the Green River and the unidentified woman, referred to as Jane Doe "B20," found just off the Kent–Des Moines Road. Ridgway equivocated on the exact location of where he placed the body, eventually deciding that it was not far from the road and likely in the park itself. He was unable to account for those parts of Tracy's skeleton that have not been found.

The Interstate 90, Exit 38, Victims

Ridgway has admitted that he killed three women—Delise Plager, Kim Nelson, and Lisa Yates—whose bodies he dumped near Exit 38, off Interstate 90. All three women were prostitutes, and they disappeared from Seattle or Pacific Highway South within approximately three months of one another. The bodies of Delise Plager and Lisa Yates were left on different sides of the Exit 38 road, not far from each other. Ridgway placed the body of Kim Nelson a few miles up a dirt road.

Delise Plager

Delise Plager, 22 years old and working as a prostitute in downtown Seattle, was living with a friend in the city at the time of her disappearance, Sunday, October 30, 1983, at approximately three P.M., when she was dropped off at a bus stop in Seattle's Beacon Hill neighborhood. She promised to return with a Halloween costume for her friend's child. She was never seen again. Ridgway was off work the Sunday that Delise disappeared.

Almost five months later, on February 14, 1984, Delise's remains were discovered at Exit 38 off Interstate 90, underneath a pile of logs. At the time the bones were not identified, possibly because Delise had not yet been reported missing. In April 1984, a friend reported her missing because she thought Delise matched the Green River victim profile. A year later, the King County Medical Examiner identified Delise's remains through a comparison of medical records.

During interviews, Ridgway stated that he killed and placed three women near Exit 38. He correctly recalled that he placed two women on opposite sides of the Exit 38 road (the old Interstate 90). Delise Plager and Lisa Yates were on opposite sides of the road from each other.

Ridgway recalled that he placed Delise on the south side of the road between two logs. He further recalled that it was raining and that he was in a hurry to dump her. He has suggested that he went back and had sex with the body. Ridgway claimed to remember virtually nothing about killing Delise other than where he dumped her body. He mistakenly said she was black; Delise was white. Ridgway said he was angry during this period of time because he was forced to work the night shift at Kenworth beginning on November 1, 1983.

In 2003, the task force took Ridgway to Exit 38. He had difficulty pointing out precisely where he'd placed his victims. He accurately recalled that Delise was on the other side of the street from Lisa Yates. He also accurately recalled that the women were left on different sides of a bridge. The Exit 38 road also bridges a stream near the dump sites.

Kim Nelson

Less than two days after Delise was killed, Ridgway picked up and killed another woman, 21-year-old Kim Nelson, who worked as a prostitute in several cities on the West Coast. She was distinctive in appearance, nearly six feet tall with very short, bleached blond hair. Kim came to Seattle in August 1983, and was arrested numerous times.

On October 30, 1983, she was released from the King County Jail and began staying at the Ben Carol Motel at South 144th and Pacific Highway South with fellow prostitute Paige Miley. Two days after Kim's release from jail, on the morning of November 1, 1983, at approximately eleven A.M., Kim and Paige went to the bus stop in front of the car wash at South 144th and Pacific Highway South. Shortly after arriving at the bus stop, Paige got a car date and left Kim alone at that location. Paige turned her quick car date nearby and returned to the bus stop to find Kim gone. Kim never returned. This was the only time the two had been on Pacific Highway South together.

Several nights later, while Paige was working on Pacific Highway South, a man driving a red pickup truck approached her and asked for a car date. Paige later described him as a white man, late 20s to early 30s, with brown hair and a wispy mustache. The truck had a white, cab-high canopy over the bed. This description matches the truck Ridgway was driving at the time. The man asked Paige where her tall blond friend was, an obvious reference to Kim Nelson. Knowing that she and Kim had only been together on Pacific Highway South for a very short time on the day that Kim disappeared, Paige suspected that this man was involved in Kim's disappearance, and she refused to go with him. A few days later, Kim was reported missing and Paige told police about the man who had asked her about Kim.

In April 1984, Ridgway was interviewed about his contacts with prostitutes on Pacific Highway South and admitted that he had seen Kim and had contact with her roommate shortly after her disappearance. Ridgway claimed that the roommate had told him she believed the Green River Killer had gotten Kim. In June 1986, almost three years after she disappeared, Kim's skull and a few bones were recovered in a deeply wooded area off I-90 and Exit 38. Two other murdered women, Delise Plager and Kim Yates, had been found near this location a couple miles away.

In 1987, as the investigation into Ridgway progressed, Paige was re-contacted and shown a montage containing Ridgway's photo. Paige quickly identified Ridgway as the person who had approached her on Pacific Highway South and inquired about Kim Nelson.

In 2003, Ridgway admitted that he murdered Kim and provided a fairly detailed description of killing Kim and disposing of her body. Ridgway recalled that he had just gone on the night shift and that he picked up Kim during the morning hours. He stated that he picked her up near a car wash on Pacific Highway South on the day after Halloween. He recalled that she was tall and blonde.

Ridgway admitted he approached Paige Miley and asked her for a date. When asked why he mentioned Kim Nelson to her, Ridgway claimed that he had not given it much thought and was simply trying to date Paige Miley.

Ridgway claimed that he took Kim to his house and killed her in his bedroom. He thought that she fought with him and noted that she was taller than he was. After he killed her, he took her clothing and jewelry. He wrapped her body in a rug, pulled his truck up to his front door, and swung her over into the truck bed. He covered the body with his green rug and drove out to Exit 38. He recalled driving up a long dirt road because it was in the middle of the day and he wanted to take her where no one could see him. He pulled her out and placed her on the left side of the road, which sloped downhill. He said the dirt road ran parallel to Interstate 90. Ridgway's description of where Nelson's body was found was accurate. Although he had difficulty recognizing the area in 2003, Ridgway claimed it was due to the fact that trees had grown significantly since he'd deposited Kim's body.

Lisa Yates

Nineteen-year-old Lisa Yates worked as a prostitute on Rainier Avenue in Seattle and on Pacific Highway South. According to her pimp/boyfriend, he last saw Lisa sometime in December 1983. She left at approximately eleven A.M. to work on Rainier Avenue. She was never reported missing. Three months later, on March 13, 1984, a soldier in a convoy that stopped at Exit 38 discovered Lisa's remains. The body was north of the road, lying between two large logs, part of an old logging skidder. She was not far from the stream that ran next to the road.

Ridgway admitted killing a woman and leaving her in the area where Lisa's remains were found. He recalled that he killed her at night in the winter and that it was cold and wet. He recalled that he was in a hurry when he dumped her body at Exit 38. He thought there was a bridge near the dump site, and he was correct; there is a bridge nearby. He also correctly recalled that he killed this victim after he killed Kim Nelson. He claimed not to recall any details about killing Lisa and could not remember where he picked her up.

Ridgway had a new roof placed on his house on or around December 17, 1983, the same period of time Lisa Yates disappeared. He distinctly recalled picking up and killing a woman on the day the roof was being worked on. After picking up the woman, he drove her to the house, but the workers were still there. He then took her to the Levitz parking lot near the Southcenter Mall and strangled her in the back of his truck. Though this murder would have occurred close in time to when Lisa disappeared, Ridgway equivocated on whether Lisa Yates could be this victim.

Ridgway was taken to Exit 38 while being interviewed by the task force in 2003. Initially, he had difficulty pointing out the precise locations where he placed his victims. He accurately recalled that Delise Plager was on the other side of the street from Lisa Yates. The Exit 38 road bridges a stream near the dump sites, and he also accurately recalled that the women were left on different sides of the bridge.

Mary West

Sixteen-year-old Mary West worked as a prostitute in Seattle's Rainier Valley, along Aurora Avenue North and in downtown Seattle. On February 6, 1984, around 11:30 A.M., Mary left her aunt's house, located several blocks west of Rainier Avenue. She was last seen a few hours later on Rainier Avenue. Mary had been punctual in her comings and goings, and her aunt reported her missing to the police two days later on February 8, 1984. Over a year and a half later, on September 8, 1985, a teacher on a field trip found Mary's skull in Seward Park. A later search recovered her entire skeleton, which was lying near the base of a large fir tree. No clothing or other items were found with the body.

During interviews in 2003, Ridgway admitted killing Mary West. He remembered that she was black and under 20 years old. When shown her photograph, he acknowledged that she looked "familiar." Ridgway said he believed he killed Mary on a weekday in the morning. He claimed not to remember where he picked Mary up but speculated it would have been in the Rainier Valley area.

Ridgway had been to Seward Park before. He told investigators in 2003 that he "figured [it was] a good place to have a date and kill a woman." According to Ridgway, he and Mary walked up a trail and put down a blanket. Ridgway claimed that he killed Mary after having sex with her. He said he distracted her by suggesting that a car was coming and, when she raised her head, he grabbed her neck and strangled her. When she fought him, he told her that if she would stop fighting he would let her go. Ridgway said she continued to struggle and that he had scratches on his back after killing her. When she was dead, he said, he pulled her farther into the park and covered her body with debris. He took her clothes and jewelry and later disposed of them.

In 2003, Ridgway was able to direct the task force to Seward Park and, while in a van, correctly pointed out the area where Mary West's body had been found.

The Highway 18 Victims

Cindy Smith

In March 1984, 17-year-old Cindy Smith called her mother from California and told her she wanted to come home to Seattle. Cindy grew up in Seattle but had recently moved to California with a boyfriend. For the past couple of years, Cindy had been involved in topless dancing and prostitution. When she called her mother, she told her that she was ready to get away from the boyfriend and the life they had been leading. Her mother immediately arranged for an airline ticket, and Cindy flew home a few days later.

Cindy spent her first few hours in Seattle, with her family. Around eleven A.M. on March 13, 1984, Cindy left her parents' home in Des Moines and headed toward Pacific Highway South. According to her family, Cindy intended to go to Seattle and visit her sister or apply for a job at one of the topless dance establishments located along Pacific Highway South. She disappeared that day and was never seen again. Ridgway did not begin work until four P.M. on March 13, 1984.

On June 27, 1987, two children were playing in a ditch alongside SE 312th Way. This roadway is a turn-off from Highway 18 leading to the Green River Community College campus. They began exploring a pile of garbage and debris. Using a stick, they poked at the garbage pile and out rolled a human skull.

Task force detectives quickly located the remainder of the skeleton under the pile of garbage. A piece of old wood, likely from a door, had been placed over the body, shielding it both from the elements and scavenging animals. The investigation revealed that the victim was naked with the exception of a piece of material later determined to have been a tube top that was wrapped around the clavicle area. The medical examiner quickly identified the remains as those of missing person Cindy Ann Smith.

Like most of his murders, Cindy's case remained unsolved until June 2003 when Ridgway began talking to detectives about his crimes. Although Ridgway claimed not to recall the specifics surrounding Cindy Smith's murder, he was insistent that he had killed her and described the dump site. Ridgway stated that he placed her off a small road that exited to the left from Highway 18, near the community college. Ridgway also recalled that he placed the body very close to the road and that he covered it with some debris he found at the site. Ridgway correctly recalled that one piece of debris was "a piece of wood." He expressed surprise that it took three years to find Smith; he expected since she was close to the road she would be found quickly. In fact, Ridgway considered his placement of this body a "mistake": he should have put her farther out so she would not have been found at all.

During one of the many trips taken with Ridgway, detectives asked him to show them where he left Cindy's body. Ridgway was unable to direct detectives to the correct location, and was unable to find the exit he used the night he dumped the body. In fact, the exit that Ridgway took to gain access to SE 312th no longer exists, and the area has changed significantly. When shown aerial photos from 1984 depicting Highway 18, Ridgway quickly pointed to the exit he had taken to access SE 312th.

Ridgway was also shown photos of the scene where Cindy was

found. He was not told the location, but rather asked if he recognized what was depicted in the photographs. Ridgway correctly identified the photographs as the location where he'd placed her body.

Patricia Barczak

In 2003, while discussing Cindy Smith, Ridgway also disclosed that he'd placed another victim nearby. He referred to this victim as "SIR [Seattle International Raceway] Lady." Ridgway considered this body and Cindy Smith's a sort of "cluster," which was his word for a dump site with numerous bodies, because the two were less than a half-mile apart. Ridgway believed that this woman's body had not been found. Ridgway claimed that he placed her body in the area "where people take shortcuts into 'SIR' " and that he expected she would be found. Ridgway was shown a historical aerial photograph that depicts the Seattle International Raceway. He pointed to a spot where he left the woman he killed. The area identified by Ridgway was the location where the remains of Patricia Barczak had been found in 1993.

Nineteen-year-old Patricia Barczak had disappeared on October 17, 1986, several years after the Green River Killer had purportedly stopped killing. She had been staying at the Airporter Motel on Pacific Highway South, went out to engage in prostitution, and never returned. She had dark brown hair and was slightly overweight. Ridgway began working the swing shift at Kenworth in October 1986 and did not report to work until late afternoon on October 17, 1986.

Six and a half years after Patricia's disappearance, in February 1993, a road worker found her skull just off Highway 18 between milepost 8 and 9. This area was commonly used by people sneaking into the Seattle International Raceway. Ridgway incorrectly thought that he killed Patricia prior to 1985 and that she was either black or "black-haired." He correctly recalled that she was approximately 20 years old and a little bit overweight. Ridgway further remembered that he killed Cindy Smith prior to killing Patricia.

Patrica Yellowrobe

On Tuesday, August 4, 1998, at approximately 1:30 P.M., the owner of a South Park, King County, business, "All City Wrecking," located at 9328 Des Moines Way South, closed his office and locked the fence surrounding the wrecking yard. He returned on the morning of Thursday, August 6, 1998, and discovered the body of Patricia Yellowrobe lying just outside the fence on the east side of the tow yard, in a gravel parking lot west of an entrance ramp to the southbound lanes of Highway 99. Patricia had a history of prostitution and chronic alcohol abuse. Her body lay at the edge of the parking lot, near some tall bushes. It was fully clothed, in a bra, T-shirt, underpants, jeans, socks, and boots.

An autopsy was performed at the Office of the King County Medical Examiner. No evidence of significant injury was found. No spermatozoa were seen on vaginal, anal, or oral swabs. High levels of alcohol and controlled substances were found in the blood. Patricia's vaginal swab and pubic hair were subjected to DNA typing at the Washington State Police Crime Lab. The vaginal swab showed a low amount of semen that was insufficient to obtain a profile. A partial male profile was developed from the pubic hair; Ridgway can be excluded as a source of this DNA profile.

The autopsy report concluded: "The cause of death is acute combined opiate and ethanol intoxication. The circumstances scene investigation and postmortem examination, which did not reveal evidence of significant injury, indicates that the manner of death is probable accident."

Because Patricia was believed dead from an accidental drug overdose, and because she died in 1998, she was never considered a Green River victim. No documents, photographs, or other material on her death were ever provided to Ridgway or his attorneys before he began discussing his victims with investigators.

However, during interviews in 2003, Ridgway confessed to killing Patricia and leaving her body at that location. His admissions came slowly, but, in the end, he provided details to investigators that only the killer would have known.

His statements concerning this homicide unfolded as follows:

On June 26, 2003, Ridgway said he never killed anyone in South Park, the neighborhood where Patricia's body was discovered.

On July 3, 2003, Ridgway said that he had not killed or even hurt any of the prostitutes he dated in the 1990s.

On July 7, 2003, Ridgway said "I don't think I killed anybody in South Park."

Gary Ridgway and His Victims

On July 9, 2003, detectives took Ridgway to various sites in King County where they had found bodies associated with the Green River Killer, and others, like South Park, where they had not. Their motive was, in part, to determine whether Ridgway could recall sites where he had dumped bodies some 20 years before. Some of the sites visited were considered "false sites," where no homicide victim had been found, to test Ridgway's veracity. Investigators chose a South Park site as one of the "false sites," even though the victim of an apparent drug overdose had been found at that location in 1998.

The scene had changed dramatically because new buildings had been erected. While at that location, Ridgway told detectives that he had dated nearby, but only once, and that he had never assaulted anyone at that location. At the other "false" locations, Ridgway maintained that he had not left any bodies there.

Then, on July 22, 2003, toward the end of a lengthy interview session that ranged over a number of topics having nothing to do with South Park, the following exchange took place between Ridgway and a detective:

DETECTIVE: What else? There anything else I should talk to you about?

GR: I, ah, promised I wouldn't lie but . . . and I . . . it . . .

DETECTIVE: You know, if you told me a lie, I don't care.

GR: I . . . I know.

DETECTIVE: I just wanna know the truth.

GR: I thought and thought about that site at South Park, and I told you I'd never been there before and everything, you know, you got it on tape.

Ridgway recounted a vague memory of killing a woman in South Park. He said he was not certain that he had murdered someone there, but he had been thinking about the murder, and it had been "bugging" him for days. The memory, he said, involved killing a black woman after struggling with her on the ground at "a site next to the freeway that was, ah, surrounded by blackberry bushes, and a road going in and it was like a U-turn." This describes the site where Patricia's body was found. Highway 99 is a divided freeway at that location.

Ridgway said he could not recall whether she was naked or

clothed, which was unusual since most of his victims were unclothed when he dumped them. He said he could not recall what vehicle he had driven to the spot, or the decade in which the murder took place. He said he believed that she "seemed to be pretty easy" to kill.

Ridgway told detectives that he thought he remembered "a lot of glass on the ground" where he struggled with the woman. Crime scene photographs taken of the parking lot where the body was found depict numerous glass fragments. Detectives did not ask Ridgway any questions about this incident during the following week. On July 30, 2003, a forensic psychologist interviewing Ridgway was addressing the issue of Ridgway's last victim when the following exchange took place:

DOCTOR: So who . . . all right. Who was next after her?
GR: Uh, I vaguely remember uh, killing a woman over in South Park.
DOCTOR: Where . . . and tell me again. In South Park? That doesn't mean anything to me.
GR: Uh. South . . . is a South Park and uh, right next to the freeway I . . . first thought I'd . . . I killed her and she was naked. But I've been thinking about it. And I think I was havin' sex with her in the back of the truck and um, was ready to . . . Uh, walked out to the passenger side to, to um, open the door for her. And I didn't wanna pay for the sex. And uh, I choked her. And she was fully clothed, I think. And I don't remember if she uh . . . one of the women uh, when I choked her, she wet her pants. But I don't know if that one was the one or not.

It cannot be determined whether or not Patricia urinated at the time of her death. However, according to Ridgway, the vast majority of his victims were naked when he murdered them, and therefore could not have "wet their pants."

During the rest of the psychologist's interview, Ridgway occasionally protested that his memory about the incident was vague. However, he provided considerable detail about the murder. He said he had sex with her in a parking lot "right next to the freeway on a, um, dead-end driveway." This, he said, was also where he left the body. He explained: "I left her in the . . . in the park . . . in the, ah, dead-end circle you drive around. I think I just left her on the

588

ground." The parking lot where Patricia's body was found was, indeed, a dead end.

Ridgway also told the psychologist that he had sex with the woman in the back of his truck at that location, but did not kill her then. He said he killed her after she'd re-dressed and was standing at the passenger door of the truck, preparing to get in the passenger compartment. Asked to describe her, Ridgway said that she was "a little skinny and, um, um, hundred and a . . . maybe a hundred and thirty-five pounds, hundred and forty."

According to the autopsy report, Patricia was 5 foot 10 inches in height and weighed 132 pounds. Ridgway told the psychologist that the murder at South Park was somewhat abnormal for him. This killing was not as well planned as the others. He said he became enraged when Patricia's sexual performance failed to meet his expectations: "I just didn't wanna pay for somebody just layin' around."

On the following day, July 31, 2003, detectives showed Ridgway an aerial photograph depicting the wrecking yard, the parking lot, and Highway 99 as they appeared in 1998. He pointed to the location where Patricia's body was discovered. When the detectives showed him a photo of her body lying at the scene, he said, "Yeah, that looks, looks like her, yeah." Ridgway could not identify Patricia from a photograph taken of her while alive. Ridgway also told detectives that he recalled that the business nearby was not open and the gate was closed. Detectives later interviewed the owner of the fenced business (the wrecking yard) adjacent to the parking lot where Patricia's body was found. The body was left in the parking lot on a Wednesday, when the fenced gate to that business had indeed been locked.

On August 8, 2003, Ridgway's memory of killing Patricia Yellowrobe seemed to have improved. "I remember that one," he told interviewers. "Uh, uh, the one at South Park, yeah. . . . she wouldn't, uh, she wouldn't, uh, let me get behind her and, uh, and screw her. And so, uh, I got madder and madder. And when we got out, uh, the back of the truck, I opened the door for her and I started choking her."

Later, he contended that Patricia was responsible for her own death:

> She didn't want to spend an extra three or four minutes to, to, uh, have me climax and be, have a customer. She just

uh, said, "You're over with," you know, some'n like that, and, uh, got dressed and when we got out I was still angry at her, and ch-choked her and I, after that I panicked. I didn't, I didn't put her in the back 'a the truck and, and take her some place. I just left it there.

Later still, Ridgway told detectives again that he did not "climax" during intercourse with Patricia. Ridgway's admissions were brought to the attention of the King County Medical Examiner. According to the medical examiner, manual strangulation can be accompanied without any physical findings whatsoever. It is possible that Patricia Yellowrobe's level of intoxication compromised her ability to withstand even a few seconds of asphyxia.

Jane Doe "B20"

On June 13, 2003, the first day of interviews with the task force, Ridgway described a site off the Kent–Des Moines Road and stated that he was "100 percent certain" that the victim's remains were still there. He stated that he drove by frequently and always remembered it as a dump site. He stated that this victim was not on the list of missing Green River Killer victims and described her as white, 16 to 20 years old, skinny, approximately 135 pounds with brown or blond shoulder-length hair. When Ridgway made this disclosure, no remains had been found at that location. Ridgway gave inconsistent accounts of when he'd killed the girl or young woman he said he'd dumped at that location. He stated that the murder occurred during 1982 or 1983, but he also acknowledged that it could have occurred in the 1970s.

In August 2003, Ridgway visited the site and pointed to a specific area. The task force then recovered approximately 23 human bones. No skull was found. To date, the victim has not been identified. A mtDNA profile confirmed that the victim is female, but the profile does not match that of any of the official missing Green River Killer victims. A forensic anthropologist with the King County Medical Examiner's Office has suggested that the bones are consistent with a 13- to 24-year-old female. The age of the bones is estimated to be at least ten years old but likely as much as twenty plus years.

Task force detectives are continuing to attempt to identify this victim.

Three Missing Victims

Based upon Ridgway's statements, investigators believe or strongly suspect that he is responsible for the disappearance of at least three women on the "Green River" list who remain missing: Keli McGinness, Kase Lee, and Patricia Osborn.

Keli McGinness was a prostitute who worked in Seattle, Portland, and California. She disappeared on June 28, 1983, after checking into a motel on Pacific Highway South. Ridgway was known to have dated Keli several months before she disappeared. During interviews in 2003, he claimed that he killed her. He has suggested multiple sites where he may have left Keli's body but has been inconsistent about the circumstances of her murder.

Ridgway also suggested that he killed Kase Lee. Kase, who also worked as a prostitute, disappeared on August 28, 1982, after leaving her apartment near Pacific Highway South. Ridgway has suggested that Kase Lee may be a woman that he killed and left in south King County. However, he was unable to recognize a photograph of her, and it is impossible to search the site because of development.

Ridgway also thought that he may have killed Patricia Osborn. Patricia worked as a prostitute and disappeared from Aurora Avenue in October 1983. Ridgway could not, however, provide any details about her or where he placed her body.

Investigators continue to work on these cases.

In addition to these three missing women, Ridgway has claimed that he left victims at a number of locations. In some cases, he has provided a general description of the victim. In others, he claims to remember virtually nothing other than the act of placing a victim in that location. The task force has searched all of the areas where subsequent development has not made it impossible.

To date, no remains or other evidence has been found there.

Conclusion

The Politics of Serial Murder

As the prosecutor's plea agreement contract made clear, Gary Ridgway was to be honest, forthright, and truthful in his admissions to his crimes. If he deliberately held back or if the State found another crime he committed to which he did not plead, he could be prosecuted for that crime. Thus, it was in Ridgway's best interest to confess to whatever he could remember, lest a prosecutor somewhere find a crime with which he could charge Ridgway and so open up the door to another prosecution, this one resulting in the death penalty. The result was the revelation of the official list of Green River victims and other victims whose deaths fit the Green River profile, but for one reason or another did not make the list. The other result was the revelation that Ridgway continued to kill after the official Green River murders seemed to have stopped in 1985, killings that went on almost up to Ridgway's arrest. As in the case of Patricia Yellowrobe, the killing might not have been a planned event, but it was nevertheless a killing that fit the same pattern as Ridgway's Green River murders.

The Ridgway Surprise

When a serial killer, especially one who has terrorized a community for decades, is finally identified in public, arrested, and confesses the secrets of his crimes, the community is usually shocked. For example, in Ridgway's case, how could he have remained at large for so long? He was tipped off to the police on at least three to four occasions, interviewed, and left on the street. At least one living victim came forward to report that she believed he was the Green River Killer and that she was his victim who escaped. Yet Ridgway talked his way out of it, even though other evidence already in possession of the police should have corroborated Rebecca Guay's accusation.

Ridgway's intuitive methodology when it came to understanding police procedures were surprisingly accurate, just as Bundy had predicted. Ridgway sent police on fruitless searches and proved to be as invisible to authorities as other serial killers have been even while he was in plain sight and sometimes even visible to his victims. But all the while, even as far back as 1983, Gary Ridgway's name was in a database, not only because he had been tipped off to local Des Moines police by Marie Malvar's boyfriend, but also because he had been arrested by an undercover anticrime officer on a solicitation of prostitution charge.

The other surprise was that it continued to be easy for Ridgway to find victims at the height of the Green River murders scare. With television specials, local news coverage, large headlines announcing every body discovery, and rampant rumors about the identity of the killer, Gary Ridgway did what he told his interviewers he did best: He approached his victims, made himself as nonthreatening as possible, took them back to the privacy of his own house or his favorite locations in the woods, and, when they were at their most vulnerable, applied a stranglehold that was his favorite method of murder. Why weren't his victims supicious?

The same question can be asked of Jeffrey Dahmer's victims in Milwaukee during the height of the missing-young-men scares in the late 1980s and early 1990s. And the same answer is that a serial killer lives and navigates amid his victim pool. He is indistinguishable from anyone else in that community. Dahmer was a young gay man on the streets of Milwaukee soliciting for models and paying for their time. Bundy was a young college-type guy hobbling about with an injured limb, looking for help. Gary Ridgway was a typical john looking for a date. He was like the other johns driving by in a car or a truck along Pacific Highway South, catching a prostitute's eye, flashing money, and speaking their language. "How much for a car date or a half and half?" Bundy accurately predicted this as well. He knew because he was there.

Gary Ridgway wasn't about to fight pitched battles with his victims. He picked the most vulnerable of a vulnerable lot, the teenagers and runaways, 15-, 16-, and 17-year-olds. He picked victims who were so desperate for a hit from a crack pipe that they would do anything for a five- or ten-dollar bill. This is what serial killers do, and police still have to reconcile themselves with the relative ease with which serial killers do it.

The Serial Killer's–Eye View

The Green River case has spanned decades, remaining constant even as the scenes changed around it. Dave Reichert cut his teeth on the Green River case. As a young detective wielding a difficult press camera, he fell ass-backward over a victim's floating body in the tall weeds along the banks of the Green River as he was trying to compose a shot. He went on, as the case progressed, to rise through the police department until he entered politics and won election as sheriff. Reichert prevailed and caught his man. Maybe he will be a future governor of Washington.

I began as a street cop with the King County Sheriff, cut my teeth on the Bundy case, went on to consult on the Green River case, and wound up an associate professor of criminology and author of the textbooks criminal investigators will read as they move through their careers.

Gary Ridgway left the navy, got a job as a truck painter, and kept that job for the two-plus decades he made a career out of murder. He got better and better at it until, in his own words, he was caught by technology.

When I went to Florida to visit Ted Bundy on death row, Ridgway was one of five key suspects the task force was interviewing. We'd had a cab driver, we'd had a law student flashing police badges around, and we had a truck painter who'd been tipped off by one of his unhappy victims. We had no DNA we could use. It took the development of technology invented by Kary Mullis at Berkeley called Polymerase Chain Reaction—it's similar to taking a photocopy of DNA so as to get it to reproduce—that allowed task force detectives to harvest just enough of the DNA left on a victim to match it with a Ridgway specimen that had been taken in 1987 during the midst of my conversations with Bundy. And in 2001, when Detective Tom Jenson, the lone detective on the Green River Murders Task Force, told Dave Reichert that Gary Ridgway's DNA had tested positive against the DNA found on victims Opal Mills, Cynthia Hinds, Carol Christensen, and Marcia Chapman, Reichert knew he had enough probable cause to go to the King County Prosecutor.

It was technology that brought Ridgway down in the end, a surprise to him but not to the investigators who had waited for the piece of technology to allow them to harvest what they prudently had saved over all those years.

Someday, a criminologist thinking out of the box will take the high-risk step of looking at the world from the serial killer's point of view. In other words, since a serial killer sees the world in terms of victims upon whom he preys and police from whom he hides, what does the world look like? Were we to do that with Ridgway we'd get a view very different from that which Ted Bundy might have had.

When Bundy went prowling, no one even knew what a serial killer was, and his broken-wing ruse played on the honest trust of his victims. When Ridgway went prowling as early as 1982, most people knew what a serial killer was, especially in Seattle after Bundy, but didn't know how to recognize one. More than 20 years later, that's still the case. However, when one serial killer looks at another serial killer, it's like looking at a subject through infrared goggles. It turned out that Bundy saw what investigators did not see, and his predictions about what we would find when we caught the Green River Killer were stunningly accurate.

Ridgway was right about his ability to elude police and keep on killing even while he was being interviewed by detectives until technology made the match that allowed the prosecutors to get a case against him into court. And Bundy was right about Ridgway.

Sheriff Dave Reichert himself, who had waited for more than 20 years to confront the man who so influenced his career and whom he'd vowed to bring to justice, noted that Ridgway believed he had won after all. But Reichert still had to be friendly with the smirking